# EARLY WARNING INDICATORS OF CORPORATE FAILURE

# Early Warning Indicators of Corporate Failure

A critical review of previous research and further empirical evidence

RICHARD MORRIS
*Professor of Accounting*
*University of Liverpool*

# Ashgate

Aldershot • Brookfield USA • Singapore • Sydney

Published by
Ashgate Publishing Ltd
Gower House
Croft Road
Aldershot
Hants GU11 3HR
England

Ashgate Publishing Company
Old Post Road
Brookfield
Vermont 05036
USA

**British Library Cataloguing in Publication Data**

Morris, Richard, 1941-
    Early warning indicators of corporate failure : a critical
    review of previous research and further empirical evidence
    1. Business failures  2. Business failures - Mathematical
    models
    I. Title  2. Institute of Chartered Accountants in England
    and Wales
    338.7'1

**Library of Congress Catalog Card Number:** 97-73608

ISBN 1 85972 565 1

Printed in Great Britain by The Ipswich Book Company, Suffolk.

# Contents

*Acknowledgements*     *x*
*Preface*     *xi*

**Executive summary**     1

**1 The background**     20

     Introduction     20
     The meaning of 'failure'     24
     The meaning of 'prediction'     24
     Methodological issues     26
     Informational market efficiency     30
     User needs     31
     Assessing whether or not a business is a going concern     34
     Summary     41
     Notes     43
     Appendix 1.1: Sampling bias error     48

**PART I: Previous research**     51

**2 Normative theories of corporate failure**     53

     Introduction     53
     Disequilibrium models of corporate failure     54
     Financial models of corporate failure     64
     Valuation theories     69
     Agency models of corporate failure     79
     Management theories of corporate failure     82
     Summary     82
     Notes     84
     Appendix 2.1: Informational decomposition measures     85
     Appendix 2.2: The gambler's ruin model     88

**3  Positive theories of corporate failure: I – Univariate models**          90

    Introduction                                                    90
    The interpretation of financial statements                      91
    Traditional ratio analysis                                      95
    Systematic ratio analysis                                       108
    Summary                                                         110
    Notes                                                           110

**4  Positive theories of corporate failure:  II – Multivariate models**      113

    Introduction                                                    113
    Control and validation procedures                               114
    Regression analysis                                             116
    The discriminant model                                          133
    Survival models                                                 141
    Summary                                                         150
    Notes                                                           151

**5  Positive theories of corporate failure:  III – Iterative models**        153

    Introduction                                                    153
    Subjectively weighted variables                                 154
    Recursive partitioning                                          156
    Artificial intelligence                                         158
    Neural networking                                               159
    Summary                                                         164
    Notes                                                           165

**6  Positive theories of corporate failure: IV – Early warning studies**     166

    Introduction                                                    166
    Share price behaviour                                           168
    Laboratory experiments                                          185
    Summary                                                         191
    Notes                                                           192

**7 Positive theories of corporate failure: V – Case study research**     195

    Introduction     195
    Turnaround studies     196
    Case study research     199
    Summary     202
    Notes     202

**8 The explanatory variables: I – Financial ratios**     204

    Introduction     204
    Common characteristics in ratios     205
    Statistical distributions     207
    Industry specific ratios     211
    The effects of applying different accounting policies     212
    Summary     216
    Notes     217

**9 The explanatory variables: II – Non-financial ratio indicators**     219

    Introduction     219
    Measures used in economics and finance studies     220
    Measures used in management and corporate strategy studies     235
    The acquisition/failure alternative     237
    Summary     239
    Notes     239
    Appendix 9.1: Company liquidations 1972-1996     242

**PART II: The empirical studies**     243

**10 The data**     245

    Introduction     245
    The sample companies     245
    The variable sets     247
    Summary     249
    Notes     250

**11 Univariate analysis**    251

Introduction    251
Univariate financial ratio models    251
Univariate qualitative variable models    254
Share price variables    257
Entropy models    259
Gambler's ruin models    261
Summary    267
Notes    268

**12 Multivariate analysis: Logit and survival models**    270

Introduction    270
Logit models – qualitative variables    272
Logit models – financial ratios    274
'Rolling' logit models    282
The impact of misclassification costs    285
Taffler variable models    286
The use of matched pairing as a control technique    288
Survival analysis    289
Summary    290
Notes    292

**13 Multivariate analysis: Iterative models**    294

Introduction    294
Neural network models    294
Comparison with logit models' predictions    300
Summary    301
Notes    302

**14 Share price behaviour models**    303

Introduction    303
Share price returns and event identification    304
Market identification of failing status    308
The information content of failure identification models    309
Summary    317
Notes    318
Appendix 14.1: The El Hennawy and Morris failure
         identification models    319

**15 Case study analysis**                                              321

    Introduction                                      321
    The causes of failure                             323
    The causes of failure, 1973-1983                  323
    The causes of failure, 1988-1991                  332
    Summary                                           340
    Notes                                             341
    Appendix 15.1: Short case histories of 25 failed companies    341

**16 Summary and conclusions**                                          373

    Introduction                                      373
    The background                                    373
    The empirical findings                            375
    Summary                                           378

*Appendix: Sample and control companies*                                379
*Bibliography*                                                          383
*Glossary*                                                             406
*Subject index*                                                        422

# Acknowledgements

The data on which the empirical studies reported in Part Two of this book were based proved far more difficult to collect than was originally envisaged. The assurances given by various parties that comprehensive files and records were readily available regrettably proved well wide of the mark. Unfortunately this was not immediately evident, and a great deal of effort was therefore required to construct the necessary data files. In the circumstances, thanks are due to all those former students who helped to collect the necessary material, but especially to Ian Finney. The assistance of Donna McDougall of Strathclyde University is also gratefully acknowledged.

The empirical studies reported in Part Two of the book were the result of extensive collaboration, and consequently joint authorship of chapters 11-15 should be acknowledged as follows:

11   S. Blackman, S. Kaletzis, R. Morris and N. Samios
12   S. Blackman, S. Kaletzis, R. Morris and N. Samios
13   E. Edmond and R. Morris
14   D. Brookfield and R. Morris
15   E. Almond, K. Cleaver and R. Morris.

The helpful comments of two anonymous referees (one a practitioner, the other an academic) are also acknowledged. As a result, the text has been altered to try to accommodate their suggestions (e.g. a section now deals with the assessment of whether or not a business is a 'going concern'; and a glossary is provided). The opportunity has also been taken to explain various issues in more detail (e.g. why the studies focus on the experience of listed rather than private companies; and why it is inappropriate to try to control for size when calculating share price residuals, since the former is a potential explanatory factor in the failure identification models being studied.).

Finally, thanks should be expressed to the Research Board of the Institute of Chartered Accountants in England and Wales, which made a grant available to meet the cost of collecting the data.

# Preface

Over the past thirty years businessmen have become increasingly aware that there are procedures which claim to be able to distinguish failing from non-failing firms. However, this poses some awkward questions, namely:

If indeed there is a relatively straightforward way of discriminating between financially sound and financially distressed companies, why is it – given the large potential payoffs – that analysts are not already using or mimicking the procedures?

If there is a widespread belief that the discriminatory procedures *forecast* accurately, then they should be self-fulfilling. This should mean that once they enter the public domain they will no longer have any predictive power: i.e. they should no longer be able to distinguish between failing and non-failing firms, except immediately before the distressed companies go bankrupt.

To what extent are the models merely capturing information that can be inferred by using relatively crude methods of analysis: i.e. how much of the news they appear to contain is incremental?

To be fair, academics do usually enter caveats about the use of their models, although the qualifications are often buried in the small print. Instead, the impression is generally given that their procedures are extremely good at the discriminating between failing and non-failing businesses.

In fact, what the models really seem to be indicating is (rather unsurprisingly) that companies which go bankrupt overwhelmingly report low profits and high borrowings immediately before their demise. But what is generally not pointed out is that the reverse is *not* the case: i.e. not all companies reporting low profits and high borrowings collapse. Indeed, it is only a minority of companies exhibiting these signs of financial distress which eventually go bankrupt. Thus out-of-sample even the best performing models – derived using the latest statistical and computer based procedures – report unacceptable misclassification rates for non-failing companies of around 20 per cent.

However, the search for a model which will give its author an advantage (albeit a short-lived one) is likely to continue. Moreover, no analyst can afford to ignore a supposedly predictive device which is referred to by his/her rivals.

In order to shed more light on the subject, and to provide answers to the three questions posed above, it is necessary to survey the extensive literature on corporate bankruptcy, to which academics in a variety of disciplines have made contributions. In this way it should be possible to adopt a critical stance and review both the arguments put forward and the empirical evidence gathered from a number of different sources.

Given that this book is aimed at both practitioners and academics, its written style is deliberately not that which would be appropriate for an academic treatise. Rather, wherever possible an attempt has been made to try to explain the issues and procedures – even straightforward bivariate regression, for instance – in terms which hopefully an interested practitioner might understand. Equally it is intended that the reader should be able to 'pick-and-mix': i.e. select topics which are of special interest and skim through the rest.

For the record, the results of the empirical studies reported in Part Two suggest that, when allowance is made for potential sampling bias and overfitting, the ability of the models to discriminate between bankrupt and surviving companies is considerably less than is generally claimed, and much more like that reported for well tried models out-of-sample. Nevertheless, a careful study of the evidence yielded by various models and by case study research is likely to improve understanding of the phenomena which lead to bankruptcy. Moreover, society in general should benefit if researchers are able to extract some incremental information from data in the public domain but which has previously not been fully exploited.

# Executive summary

## Chapter 1: The background

Finding ways of trying to identify failing companies as early as possible is clearly a matter of considerable interest to investors, creditors and auditors, especially as upwards of a third of newly established private companies collapse within five years of incorporation. The rate of failure amongst listed companies is much lower – around 2 per cent per annum – but for a variety of reasons (e.g. the availability of accounting and share price data) most studies of corporate bankruptcy relate to quoted companies. Yet given that many, well publicised models purport to 'predict' potential bankruptcies, it is puzzling that their forecasts do not appear to be reflected in the behaviour of share prices. If they were, one might reasonably expect the latter to fall sharply in reasonably efficient capital markets as soon as potential bankruptcy is identified, and the companies to be forced into receivership. In fact, this is generally not what seems to happen. Consequently, unless one believes that securities markets are grossly inefficient – which seems unlikely given their highly competitive nature – it would appear more plausible that there are defects in the models themselves.

In fact, close scrutiny of the models, derived using a variety of techniques, indicates that they frequently exhibit high misclassification rates outside the sample period. Thus, while immediately before their demise they often correctly identify over 90 per cent of companies which collapse, they typically also diagnose an unacceptable 20 per cent of surviving companies as prima facie failures. This in turn appears in large part to be because the procedures used frequently do not adequately allow for the true incidence of failures in a population; and because heterogeneous data are pooled from a broad cross section of companies over periods of time when underlying economic circumstances are changing. As a result, the models tend to identify the lowest common denominator of failing businesses, such as low profits, high levels of borrowing, and the relatively small size of financially distressed companies: i.e. they focus on the *symptoms* rather than the underlying *causes* of bankruptcy. Moreover, they tend to perform best when a company is beyond redemption and the news content of the 'predictions' is minimal. In the circumstances, the models are probably best used as a shorthand procedure for summarising data about a business.

In any bankruptcy study it is necessary to consider the meaning of the terms 'failure' and 'prediction'. The former can embrace various types of financial distress, ranging from bankruptcy at one extreme to a decline in profitability at the other. 'Prediction' for its part can refer to an ability to identify an event before it occurs; or instead an ability to discriminate correctly afterwards. The models are inevitably derived using historical data, although they are generally tested on 'hold out' samples to see how well they might forecast future failures.

A general weakness of failure identification models is that there is usually little or no economic theory underpinning them which could indicate *why* certain companies might be expected to fail and others survive and prosper. Rather, they tend to be derived on an ad hoc basis. Further problems which give rise to unjustified inferences are inadequate allowance for the fact that only 2 per cent of listed companies in a population are likely to fail in any one year; and various other 'sample selection biases' (e.g. data is less easily available for defunct businesses, giving rise to 'survivorship bias'; and there is inadequate allowance for industry and general economic factors because of the use of a 'matched pairing' technique).

Even in highly competitive financial markets, investors and creditors have strong incentives to identify financially distressed companies, and in particular to be the first to get the news. However, any advantage gained is likely to be short lived. Nevertheless, the search for early warnings of financial distress is reflected in the pressure placed on auditors to flag up impending difficulties in their reports on the annual accounts of client companies. In the circumstances, how to assess whether or not a business is a going concern is a matter of considerable concern to accountants in public practice, especially as the risk of litigation has increased. This has given rise to considerable discussion of the issue, and there is a growing amount of guidance in law (affecting both directors and auditors), the code on corporate governance, the Accounting Standards Committee's SSAP 2, the Accounting Standards Board's recommendations on preparing the Operating and Financial Review, and the Auditing Standards Board's SAS 130. Nevertheless, the incidence of going concern qualifications in audit reports is still extremely low, and the accounts of most companies which eventually go bankrupt are not so qualified. Furthermore, such warnings, when given, are not generally issued until the companies concerned are effectively beyond redemption. On the other hand, many companies whose accounts receive a going concern qualification in fact survive. Nevertheless, despite this evidence there have recently been suggestions that the signals given by failure identification models could be used as the pretext for entering such qualifications. This would seem dangerous, given the weaknesses in such models, which it seems are often not fully appreciated by practitioners.

**Part I: Previous research**

## Chapter 2: Normative theories of corporate failure

As mentioned previously, most bankruptcy prediction models are derived on an ad hoc basis with little theoretical underpinning. However, there are a number of theories which inform a general understanding of corporate failure.

The first group of such theories views financial distress as the result of disequilibrating shocks. Some (such as chaos and catastrophe theories) can equally well be applied to the natural sciences, the idea being that an unexpected event disturbs an equilibrium and has 'knock on' effects. Obvious examples are the way the body reacts after an accident or with the onset of a disease; or how the countryside recovers its equilibrium after a storm or a fire. In the same way, economic systems are frequently knocked out of kilter by unanticipated shocks: e.g. a hike in oil prices; the outbreak of a war; a sudden change in exchange parities or interest rates; a prolonged strike by employees; or the collapse of a bank or a major company in an industry.

Chaos and catastrophe theories provide a general framework for studying the ways in which systems adjust to an unanticipated event, but they offer relatively little in the way of statistical procedures for analysing the position, certainly with respect to bankruptcy. However, the entropy (or informational decomposition) approach has been used in a number of studies, the idea in terms of its application to financial distress being to examine changes in balance sheet structures over time. The suggestion is usually that one might reasonably expect the proportions of current/non-current assets and claims to alter more for failing companies than for their surviving counterparts, reflecting the disequilibrating shock to which they are subject.

In industrial economics, academics have developed theories to explain why there are changes in market structure (i.e. why a few companies come to dominate in some industries). This in turn has led them to examine possible causes (e.g. the existence of so-called 'barriers to entry'; and the 'exit characteristics' in an industry: i.e. through mergers or bankruptcies). Another factor identified is the financial structure of a business. While in a 'perfect market' setting the level of gearing should be of little consequence, in practice firms and individuals are unable to borrow at will, and bankruptcy risk is a factor which has to be considered, even where there are sizeable 'clienteles' of investors who might be prepared to develop investment portfolios to offset the risks inherent in holding any one security.

Another aspect examined by industrial economists is the growth characteristics of an industry, the implication being that there is a (probably changing) optimal size for a firm operating in a particular industry. If a firm is too small, it is unlikely to survive. Similarly, economic geographers have argued that in some (if not all)

3

industries, location is a critical factor in determining a company's costs, and hence its ability to compete with rival firms.

Various financial models of corporate failure have been developed. The simplest is to view the firm as an option in the hands of the shareholders, giving them the right to buy the business back from its creditors at a future specified time (e.g. when loan stock can be redeemed) if there is then a positive equity value. Clearly, as with all options, the value will be greater the higher the variability of expected cash flows. Another way of explaining the bankruptcy phenomenon is to consider the compound probability of a company running out of cash (i.e. of a net cash outflow in one period being followed by net cash outflows in successive periods). Where a company is subject to 'capital rationing' (i.e. it cannot raise new capital or borrow easily), such a path (the 'gambler's ruin' scenario) will lead to a firm's failure. However, where there is no capital rationing, a company should be able to raise new capital regardless of its operating cash flow position so long as investors believe that the value of the business is positive. In practice, even listed companies are likely to be subject to some degree of capital rationing, and the incidence of inflation is another factor which is likely to make it more difficult for firms to survive when faced with a succession of negative cash outflows over time. In the circumstances, one might therefore expect firms with highly variable operating cash flows (or, as a proxy, profits) to be more likely to fail than those with more-or-less constant cash flows or profits. Models have been developed with some success to test this argument, relating the variability of cash flows to an opening 'cash reservoir'. Moreover, the more conventional failure identification models, developed on a more ad hoc basis, can be rationalised and justified in terms of the gambler's ruin hypothesis.

Essentially the option pricing and gambler's ruin models argue that a firm will not go bankrupt until such time as the going concern value only equals the break up value of its net assets. It is therefore necessary to consider how firms are valued in the market place. The appropriate setting, however, is to view a company's securities in a portfolio context, and it is relatively easy to show that combining assets together will reduce risk to an investor, except for that element of risk which is 'market related'. This can be done within the framework of the 'capital asset pricing model' (CAPM) and/or 'arbitrage pricing theory' (APT), the principles of which are relatively easy to understand.

More recently, academics have begun to explore so-called 'agency' models of corporate failure. These attempt to analyse the nature of the contractual relationships between various parties (such as shareholders, creditors and managers). This of special interest, given that financial distress is often resolved by various interests being redefined (e.g. bankers accepting equity shares in exchange for cancelling debts outstanding).

Finally, the management and business strategy literature has attempted to popularise basic concepts in industrial economics. Writers have in fact tried to identify the key causes of financial distress and then undertake case study analysis to see what evidence there is of their existence in practice. The main variables discussed are shortcomings in management (a portmanteau label which, with the advantage of hindsight, can be used to cover most eventualities); inadequate financial controls; slow reaction to changes in the economic environment; the incidence of mistakes by management; and the fact that the symptoms of distress (e.g. declining profits, increasing indebtedness) become more evident as failure approaches.

## Chapter 3: Positive theories of corporate failure: I – Univariate models

The most widely applied models used to identify companies at risk of failure are so-called 'univariate' models. These involve the analyst examining a series of variables (usually financial ratios) one-by-one. However, the 'traditional' basis for interpreting financial statements is full of potential flaws which are rarely identified in standard text books. In particular, it is essential to identify an appropriate bench mark against which to compare a ratio; and it is also important to remember that the figures relate to a legal rather than an economic entity. Moreover, while it is widely acknowledged that economic events can be accounted for in a variety of equally acceptable ways, the reverse is far less commonly recognised, although anyone with practical experience will be aware of the fact: namely, that various combinations of economic circumstances can give rise to similar accounting numbers. It follows that unless an analyst is careful, it is extremely easy to draw incorrect inferences from figures reported in a company's financial statements.

Traditional textbooks do not generally examine the nature of accounting ratios: e.g. there are commonalities and interrelationships between them; there is an implicit assumption of linear proportionality; the statistical distributions tend not to be symmetric (i.e. they are not 'normal'); and – perhaps most important of all, and well understood by practitioners and professional analysts – the means and distributions of particular ratios tend to vary between industries and even between different types of firm  operating  within  the same sector. (These matters are further discussed in chapter 8.)

Traditional ratio analysis usually focuses on three matters: a company's long term financial position (i.e. primarily its financial structure); its short term financial position (i.e. its liquidity); and its profitability and efficiency. With respect to long term financial position, financial statement indicators only paint part of the picture. It is probably best to focus on a company's cost structure (i.e. its mix of fixed and variable costs), the variability of its net revenues, and the redemption terms and security available to support additional borrowing. As for the short term position, the main aim should be to try so far as possible to construct a crude cash (or working capital) budget, much as internal management will do. In such circumstances, financial ratios should only be used for screening purposes – and particular care should be exercised when referring to ratios where both numerator and denominator have been drawn from a balance sheet as the coefficients are

5

particularly susceptible to distortion. 'Mixed' ratios (i.e. where one of the figures represents a flow through time) may be more helpful, but there are still potential problems (e.g. the 'position' figure taken from a balance sheet is unrepresentative; lack of linear proportionality; etc). Overall, it is probably safer to concentrate on the picture revealed by a flow of funds statement and try to use this as the basis for projecting future likely cash flow outcomes.

As for assessing profitability and efficiency, it is important to examine both proportional and absolute changes. Moreover, care is needed when examining margin ratios, as it is necessary to allow both for the impact of the economic factors which help to determine outcomes; and for the incidence of particular accounting conventions, either over time within a single firm or as between different companies. At first sight it may appear best to refer exclusively to 'rate of return on capital employed' (ROCE) ratios. However, regardless of which of several versions of this statistic are used, it is important to remember that the numbers can be quite seriously affected by the accounting conventions used. In particular, other things being equal the so-called 'concept' of prudence (i.e. conservatism) employed by accountants can increase reported returns for firms which are declining or only growing slowly; whereas those which are expanding will tend to be penalised. This results from overdepreciation (in economic terms) of relatively new wasting fixed assets and underdepreciation of relatively old ones, and the phenomenon will be accentuated when price levels are increasing. Similarly, firms which invest heavily in (say) R&D will tend to be penalised; and the basis of valuing stocks and work in progress is another potentially distorting factor. Certainly, as anyone with practical experience knows, such factors (the incidence of which differs from industry-to-industry and even from firm-to-firm) makes it very difficult to make meaningful cross sectional comparisons on the basis of figures alone; and it also indicates the potential dangers of trying to construct models based on ratios, especially where data have to be aggregated across industry sectors.

In fact, the first bankruptcy identification models devised were based on univariate ratios, the earliest matched pairing experiment dating from 1932. The best known model developed along these lines was that of Beaver in 1966, and its prima facie discriminatory power was impressive, being not all that inferior to the more complex models devised subsequently. Other univariate ratio models have since been developed, but they have tended to focus on specific explanatory variables, notably operating cash flows. However, insufficient allowance seems to have been made for sampling bias (especially for the fact that the incidence of failures in the population is nearer 2 per cent rather than the 50 per cent assumed). Moreover, in a follow up study, Beaver seemed to find that share prices reflected impending problems if anything a little earlier than the accounting indicators (and probably quite a lot earlier if allowance is made for the lag between year end and the publication of the financial statements).

# Chapter 4: Positive theories of corporate failure: II – Multivariate models

Most failure identification models that have been developed are not univariate in nature but multivariate: i.e. the status of potential bankrupt/non-bankrupt firms is determined in terms of a series of variables, thus allowing for simultaneous interactions between them. The variables are usually in the form of financial ratios (the properties of which are examined in chapter 8), but are also sometimes qualitative in nature (see chapter 9). As for the multivariate models themselves, they can be derived in two main ways: using statistical procedures or iterative (i.e. search) techniques. The former are discussed in this chapter, the latter in chapter 5.

One of the weaknesses of bankruptcy identification studies is the potential inadequacy of the control and validation procedures used. In particular, the matched pairing technique used and pooling of data over time tend to make models 'sample specific'; and as mentioned previously there is the difficulty of sampling bias, the true incidence of bankruptcy in the populations being studied usually being around 2 per cent rather than 50 per cent. Even where attempts are made to adjust for such bias, it is commonplace to allow simultaneously for differential costs of misclassifying failing and non-failing businesses. This latter adjustment generally offsets the impact of the sampling bias and has the effect of making it appear that the models perform well on the sample from which they are derived. However, when tested on hold out samples, and especially subsequently when they are applied in a practical context, the models seem to perform far less well.

The simplest type of multivariate model that can be derived is to apply regression analysis, with the dependent variable being a dichotomous fail/non-fail classification. However, it appears that some of basic requirements of the regression model (e.g. linearity) are violated. A more realistic procedure in the circumstances is logit regression, which potentially has the advantage that it should enable meaningful probabilities of failure/non-failure to be calculated. Yet the computational requirements are such that for the model to work properly it is necessary to work with large samples with the distinguishing characteristics. This is rarely possible with bankruptcy studies, which greatly reduces the advantage of using the logit model. On the other hand, it is relatively easy to adjust for sampling bias and make the model valid where the prior probability of failure is around 2 per cent rather than the 50 per cent usually assumed in order to use the matched pairing technique.

The logit model has been increasingly applied in recent years in bankruptcy studies, and various refinements have been introduced (e.g. to formulate models at various intervals before failure; to explore the incremental information generated year-by-year as bankruptcy approaches; and to develop multilogit models using data over a number of years to derive the discriminatory function). Other refinements include attempts to identify a number of states of financial distress and not just the two extremes, fail and non-fail. However, to be valid this would once again appear to require large samples of companies with the different distinguishing characteristics, a requirement which cannot generally be met. Another variation is to develop a 'rolling logit' model, which includes the dependent variable score of the preceding year's model as an explanatory variable for the current period.

Although regression would seem to be the most obvious statistical model to use for bankruptcy identification purposes, before the comparatively recent popularity of logit it was another but essentially equivalent statistical technique that was generally applied, discriminant analysis (DA). In fact, the technical requirements for using this approach frequently seem to have been violated, but this has not prevented its widespread use for deriving bankruptcy prediction models from different sets of explanatory variables (e.g. based on cash flows and inflation adjusted accounting numbers). The best known models are Altman's ZETA in the US and Taffler's Z-score models in the UK, and they have now been in commercial use for around 20 years. The former is applied by over 80 commercial clients and the latter by more than 40. But while they are known to identify correctly almost all failing listed companies, they also crucially misclassify around one fifth of surviving companies as being potentially bankrupt.

In recent years there have been attempts to develop 'survival models' in a failure prediction context. Whereas other models attempt to predict *which* companies in a population will go bankrupt within a given period of time (effectively a few months), duration models estimate the length of time for *all* companies up until their 'deaths'. There are various versions of the model, the simplest being that which assumes the probabilities of survival are strictly proportional. However, a more severe problem in practice is 'censoring' (i.e. inevitably the deaths of most companies in a population will not be known, but frequently, and more importantly, for all except cohorts of newly formed private companies it will usually be impractical to obtain and include all data since each individual firm's birth). Despite these difficulties, the approach has been used in a small number of studies, assuming explicitly or implicitly for long established businesses a common birth date. Despite its unsuitability for listed company studies, the models appear to perform about as well (or as badly) as their regression, logit, or discriminant counterparts. However, the most interesting application of the technique, given the high attrition rate amongst private companies, is its recent use by industrial economists, who have studied the survival patterns of newly created small businesses in various countries.

## Chapter 5: Positive theories of corporate failure: III – Iterative models

Various iterative (or search) procedures have been employed to develop multivariate models, and in general they have performed as well (or as badly, when sampling bias is allowed for!) as those derived using statistical techniques. The best known are probably those which have been developed to produce credit scores, with the variables included generally being those most frequently referred to by analysts. The weightings applied to each explanatory factor are then found by a process of trial and error until the ability to discriminate between failing and surviving firms is maximised.

A development of the above approach is 'recursive partitioning', whereby there is a sequential search for the combination of weighted explanatory variables which best separates failing from non-failing businesses. Experiments along these lines have worked as well as the statistical procedures in correctly classifying bankrupt and non-bankrupt firms; and the technique has also been used to determine bond ratings.

A natural evolution of recursive partitioning is to develop 'artificial intelligence' models on a computer, using IF...THEN...ELSE statements. This has been done with as much success as other models, and a further step has been to employ 'neural networking' procedures. These non-linear models, which are supposed to mimic thought processes, are becoming increasingly popular in a variety of applications, including a number in the field of finance. The algorithms are expensive in terms of computer time, the number of iterations needed to adjust the model until it minimises forecasting errors often exceeding a thousand cycles. Moreover, it is not possible for outsiders to identify precisely how the initial weights attached to the half a dozen or so explanatory factors alter as the models are continuously refined. This is because there are complex interactions with so-called 'hidden' variables. The process works with the model being derived from a 'training set' sample and then being tested on a hold out sample. A number of such models have been developed in recent years to try to discriminate between failing and non-failing companies, including some in the UK. Generally they perform at least as well as, and often slightly better than, more conventional statistically derived multivariate bankruptcy identification models. However, there is a hint of 'overfitting', and the error rates out-of-sample would still appear to be of such magnitude as to make them of limited practical value to investors, creditors and auditors.

## Chapter 6: Positive theories of corporate failure: IV – Early warning studies

As indicated previously, if failure prediction models have the strong discriminatory power that is usually claimed for them, it is puzzling that share prices and credit ratings do not immediately reflect the forecasts, forcing the companies into bankruptcy straight away. The implication is either that financial markets are seriously inefficient in absorbing information; or, alternatively, that claims with respect to failure identification models are somewhat overstated. The purpose of this chapter is therefore to examine the evidence which indicates how decision makers react to the signals conveyed by the models. This can be done by studying, on the one hand, share price behaviour; and on the other how analysts react to such signals in tightly controlled laboratory experiments.

The methodology for studying share price reactions to specific news is well developed. The dependent variable is essentially security returns, which can be explained in terms of a number of independent variables – generally market- and industry-wide factors and the firm-specific event or news release that is the real focus of interest. However, there are many technical problems which have to be overcome when undertaking such studies if the possibility of drawing inappropriate inferences is to be avoided. Certainly there are a number of stock market anomalies which have been brought to light in recent years which have yet to be satisfactorily explained, but despite this the overall picture is that the markets are generally efficient in almost immediately impounding information perceived as having predictive power.

With respect to bankruptcy prediction models there are some additional problems (e.g. it is especially difficult to allow for market- and industry-wide factors). However, studies of share price behaviour are really rather different from most other 'event studies' inasmuch as the focus of interest is less on share price movements around the specific date of a news announcement, but rather the trend of relative share prices over a much longer period leading up to failure. Consequently it is far less important in such studies to try to allow for each of the many factors which must be taken into account when undertaking a more conventional event study.

The evidence from previous studies, even allowing for the inevitable imperfections in the research methodologies applied, is fairly conclusive. It appears that the market gradually marks down the relative share prices of companies which eventually go bankrupt, beginning on average some 2-3 years before their eventual demise. This is slightly ahead of the signals transmitted by most failure prediction models. Moreover, it also appears that the share prices of surviving companies which are signalled as prima facie failures react in a not dissimilar way. Overall, the evidence does not seem to support the argument that bankruptcy prediction models are imparting a significant element of news to the market, but rather that they appear to be capturing information that has for the most part already been impounded in share prices.

Behavioural research involving laboratory experiments has been extensively used in financial reporting and auditing contexts to study the reactions of analysts and decision makers to specific situations and news announcements. In practice, the major problems with such experiments are on the one hand to ensure that the scenarios are sufficiently realistic; and on the other that the controls are adequate. In terms of bankruptcy prediction, subjects have tended to perform well in distinguishing between failing and non-failing firms, although it is noticeable that their discriminatory ability declines if they are unaware of the proportions of failed and non-failed businesses in the population that is the subject of the study. Moreover, in most experiments the subjects perform slightly less well than mechanistic bankruptcy prediction models; and there is evidence of 'hindsight bias'.

Finally, there have been several behavioural research studies focusing on the way in which information can be presented. In this context it appears that a useful shorthand way of summarising key accounting ratios in a bankruptcy setting is to represent them in terms of human faces, with a smile suggesting a healthy financial outlook and a frown impending problems.

## Chapter 7: Positive theories of corporate failure: V – Case study research

An alternative approach to the study of corporate failure is to engage in case study analysis. This has the advantage that it should be possible to examine not just the symptoms of failure but also the causes. Equally, the interaction between different variables can be identified.

Most studies of this type are 'turnaround' or 'sharpbender' studies, which with the advantage of hindsight identify how some companies have recovered from financial distress while others have not. The framework for such analysis is usually the somewhat eclectic theory of corporate strategy, with writers such as Argenti and Slatter identifying a series of factors which can often contribute to corporate failure.

The case studies themselves tend to be largely descriptive in nature, and the general conclusion unsurprisingly is that financial distress cannot usually be explained in terms of one or two variables. Rather, it is the result of a conjunction of events, some of them controllable by management, others not, and to some extent each potential failure can be viewed as 'situation specific'.

## Chapter 8: The explanatory variables: I – Financial ratios

There are significant commonalities amongst accounting ratios, indicating that generally they do not exclusively measure just one financial characteristic of a company. Consequently it is necessary to screen the potential variables to try to ensure that overlaps between them are minimal; and that they are stable over time in capturing specific economic characteristics. This can be done in a variety of ways, including factor analysis and multidimensional scaling.

Conventional interpretation procedures seem to assume that the relationships between accounting numbers are strictly linear. In fact, this is the exception rather than the rule, and it helps to explain why observed ratio values are not usually normally distributed. This can be a problem when developing ratio based models. However, more important in terms of discriminant analysis is multivariate normality, a requirement that is rarely met.

A particular problem is the fact that the average values for individual ratios tend to vary substantially between quite narrow industry categories. One way of trying to handle this would be to measure variations from such an industry average, but this has rarely been attempted. 'Creative accounting' is another factor which can undermine the validity of specific ratios, and there is certainly evidence of manipulation when companies are in financial distress – although whether it fools analysts is highly dubious.

**Chapter 9: The explanatory variables: II – Non-financial ratio indicators**

Financial ratios are not the only variables which might explain corporate failure. It is clear, in fact, that failures increase when an economy goes into recession; and, moreover, certain industries seem to suffer more than others. Various procedures can be used to try to allow for these factors, although their use is the exception rather than the rule in most studies. However, special models have been developed for private as opposed to listed companies; and there have also been attempts to explain financial distress by geographical location.

A variety of non-accounting firm specific variables have been, or could be, used in bankruptcy identification studies. Examples are the firm's age since incorporation; the degree of diversification in its activities; changes in lines of business; changes in company name; rates of organic growth; records of acquisitions and disposals; the existence of closure and redundancy costs; dividend policy; years since a dividend was last declared; years since a profit was last reported; years since sales last increased; share price returns; bond yields; and published risk indicators. Other non-accounting measures can relate to directors (e.g. the proportions of shares they hold; changes in their holdings; changes in the board; and changes in directors' remuneration); to the accounting year end date (e.g. changes in year end; and the lag between year end date and publication of the accounts); to changes in accounting policy; to the auditors (e.g. changes in the auditors; qualifications in their reports; changes in the lag between the year end and the date of the auditors' report; and changes in auditors' remuneration); and to indebtedness (e.g. with respect to changes in debt covenants or the register of charges; and bond and credit ratings). Various studies have been undertaken using one or more of these qualitative variables in bankruptcy identification models, and frequently they have been found to have explanatory power.

Another variable that has been studied in this context is the characteristics of the chairman's report. Various techniques exist for textual analysis, the aim being either to assess readability or the extent to which a report will be understood. As one might intuitively expect, the reports of failing companies are more complex than for non-failing counterparts as the chairmen attempt to explain the position. However, it is unclear if, when sampling bias is allowed for, the existence of a complex report necessarily means that a company is financially distressed. It seems unlikely.

As has been mentioned previously, writers on management theory have often identified key factors which can lead to corporate failure (e.g. weaknesses in accounting and control systems, a slow response rate to changes in the environment, and poor overall management, leading to too many mistakes when decisions are made). Various proxy variables have been used to measure the incidence of these factors, usually by undertaking questionnaire surveys.

Another area where non-financial indicators are relevant concerns studies of the acquisition/failure alternative, a number of which have been undertaken in the UK context. They suggest it may be possible to identify financially distressed firms which will be rescued by a take-over rather than go into receivership, although as usual the picture is not entirely clear because of the need to adjust for sampling bias.

## Part II: The empirical studies

## Chapter 10: The data

The data used for the empirical research studies reported in chapters 11-14 comprised three sets of 111, 75 and 61 matched pairs of listed companies. The first two were determined by the ability to obtain detailed accounting and qualitative data for periods of five and ten years respectively before the bankruptcy of the failing company. In the end, 19 accounting and 16 qualitative variables were used as the primary basis for developing the models. The third sample represented those pairs of companies for which five years share price return data were available. The periods covered were all within the time frame 1973-1983.

In addition, the circumstances of 25 of the failed companies were examined in some depth so that the case studies reported in chapter 15 could be undertaken. For control purposes, a further 21 listed companies which failed between 1988 and 1991 were selected, and these were used both as an inter-temporal hold out sample to test the various models previously derived; and for comparative purposes with respect to the case study analysis.

## Chapter 11: Univariate analysis

Logit models were used to assess the discriminatory power of a number of individual financial ratios. These measured various company attributes – namely profitability, liquidity, gearing, size and asset turnover. When the intercept term was suppressed, only profitability seemed to have much explanatory power in distinguishing between failing and non-failing firms. However, the introduction of a constant term greatly improved the performance of the models, although (as might have been expected) profit ratios were still the main indicators of likely bankruptcy, discriminatory power in the last two years of a failing company's life being relatively good with between 70 per cent and 80 per cent of companies correctly classified. The discriminatory power of individual liquidity and gearing indicators was rather less good, but it was still reasonably strong.

Comparing the incidence of qualitative indicators over successive five year event windows for the ten year data sample of companies showed clearly that audit qualifications and changes in lines of business, in registered charges, in auditors, in company name, and in financial year end were all more likely to occur with bankrupt firms. Moreover, failed firms were significantly smaller than their non-failed counterparts. By contrast, there was no evidence that the failed companies were more likely to change their accounting policies than their non-failed counterparts.

Rather surprisingly there was little difference in *annual* residual share price returns between bankrupt and non-failed returns. However, *cumulative* residual returns on shares in companies which failed or were 'signalled' as failures are significantly worse than on those in companies which survived or were 'signalled' as non-failures (see chapter 14).

Informational decomposition models performed reasonably well on matched pair data, and not much worse than many multivariate models tested on hold out samples. However, in overall terms their discriminatory power seems to be no better than that of the univariate logit models using a single profit ratio. By contrast, the gambler's ruin models (also derived using a matched pairing procedure) did rather better, classifying correctly with an almost 90 per cent accuracy rate in the final year before failure and a success rate generally over 75 per cent two years before bankruptcy.

But the major problem with all the univariate models is that if allowance is made both for the overrepresentation of failed firms in the sample and for the costs to decision makers of misclassifying surviving companies as bankrupt, the operational usefulness of the models is greatly reduced. On the other hand, this is a defect which equally afflicts multivariate models and undermines their practical usefulness.

## Chapter 12: Multivariate analysis: Logit and survival models

Logit models were first derived for qualitative variables for the 74 paired companies ten year data sample employed in the single variable study, using the same five year windows (see chapter 11). The models fitted well, and the results reinforced the conclusions of the single variable study. Moreover, misclassification rates before allowing for sampling bias were very similar to those recorded in other bankruptcy identification studies, and were clearly lowest immediately before failure.

The next step was to develop logit models from the 111 matched pairs of companies using a number of different financial ratios. These proxied for five independent variables which might capture the following characteristics: profitability, liquidity, gearing, size, asset turnover, and asset proportions. The various models were then tested to see which performed best. The final version fitted well, with several of the individual ratios having strong explanatory power. Misclassification rates in the years leading up to bankruptcy were impressively low and comparable to those reported in similar studies undertaken previously.

However, when the prior probability of failure was altered to be more realistic the models did not work as well, and the misclassification rates, especially for non-failed companies, were much higher.

Similar results were obtained when the models were reworked from a reduced sample of 70 matched pairs of companies, using the remaining 41 as a hold out set. However, misclassification errors were substantially reduced for the 2 per cent failure probability model when misclassification costs were allowed for. The models were then tested on three other hold out samples, taken some years after the original study period: one of 21 companies which failed between 1988 and 1991, and two of 100 non-failed companies, in 1983-84 and 1993-94 respectively. As expected, the models' ability to classify companies correctly declined quite sharply – for bankrupt companies for the 50 per cent failure probability model; and for surviving companies for the 2 per cent failure probability model.

Further tests were undertaken to see how well models derived on one year's data classified failed and non-failed companies in other years; and how 'rolling' logit models performed. The results were again much as expected, with inclusion of the previous year's dependent variable scores in the 'rolling' logit models improving classificational accuracy. Comparisons were also made with logit models developed using the variables included in Taffler's discriminant models, and classificational accuracy was found to be similar to that achieved with the corresponding models described previously.

The validity of applying the matched pairing procedure was also briefly examined. Surviving companies were randomly assigned to two groups and then matched to each other by year and industry. Logit models were then developed, the expectation being that discriminatory power would be negligible. Surprisingly it was not. Moreover, further replications of the experiment produced similar results. This would seem to imply that the matched pairing technique itself introduces a degree of misclassification error into failure prediction studies. Clearly further research is required on this.

Finally, although survival models are not really appropriate for studies of listed companies which have very different birth dates (see chapter 4), out of curiosity the data were run through the appropriate statistical packages to see what happened. This was done first assuming equal numbers of bankrupt to surviving companies in a population and then a more realistic ratio of 2:98.

## Chapter 13: Multivariate analysis: Iterative models

Two experiments involving the use of neural networking (NN) procedures were undertaken. Each was derived from a 'training set' of 41 matched pairs of companies and validated on a hold out sample of 20 pairs.

In the first study, without allowing for sampling bias the misclassification rates for non-failed companies were much lower than for bankrupt companies. By contrast, those for the financially distressed companies showed a gradual worsening as bankruptcy approached, reflecting the fact that the five independent variables used became increasingly unstable. Moreover, misclassification rates on the hold out set tended to rise when the number of processing elements (or 'neurons') exceeded two, suggesting a degree of 'overfitting'. However, the errors were reduced when the forecasts of the models were averaged over time. Overall, it was found that the models were not insensitive to the starting values chosen to initiate the simulations, but despite this the results were not dissimilar to those reported for other NN studies.

A different variable set was used to develop the second group of NN models, with share price returns being included this time as an explanatory factor. Although the models produced slightly more accurate classifications on the hold out data, this was at the expense of increasing errors on the training set.

To assess the relative forecasting accuracy of the NN models, corresponding logit models were derived. On the whole, the NN models seemed to produce slightly fewer misclassification errors, but their superiority over the logit models in this respect was by no means clear cut.

**Chapter 14: Share price behaviour models**

For this part of the study, monthly share price residuals were calculated as the net returns for each matched pair in the 61 twinned company sample. This should provide an adequate measure of market response, given the difficulties of estimating systematic risk in a bankruptcy context and the fact that all that is required in such a setting is a profile of average residual returns over a long window of time. Moreover, it would be inappropriate to try to allow for the impact of firm size on the calculation of residual returns as this factor is already allowed for in the bankruptcy identification models.

Various potential event dates can be identified, but none is entirely satisfactory because of heterogeneity in the sample. However, given that the focus of attention is merely average residual share price behaviour over a period of several years before failure, the choice should not be that critical. All that is really required is consistency in definition.

The behaviour patterns of the net returns for the whole sample were first examined, and on average they showed a clear downward spiral from 2-3 years before the failing company's last financial year end, the cumulative negative returns being very large during the final twelve months. This is consistent with findings in previous studies, where it has been interpreted as suggesting that the market marks down relative share prices slightly before bankruptcy identification models suggest financially distressed companies are potentially bankrupt.

The next step was to try to see whether the market marked down share prices of companies in line with the *signals* transmitted by bankruptcy identification models, rather than just in terms of their ultimate fate. This was initially done using the 50:50 and 20:80 failure probability logit models derived using financial ratio data and referred to in chapter 12. In fact, the results suggest that generally market behaviour is consistent with the signals transmitted rather than a company's ultimate fate, with analysts probably identifying the prima facie risk of failure slightly before it is reflected in bankruptcy identification models.

One difficulty with this approach is that the failure identification models employed were derived historically using data for the same period over which share price returns were studied. Not only can this lead to overfitting in terms of the classification of companies as prima facie failures and non-failures, but also analysts would not at the time be able to apply such well-specified models for diagnostic purposes. Consequently it was decided to repeat the experiment using two other bankruptcy identification models. These were devised some years earlier, and their discriminatory power seemed to be comparable with that of other rival models. The number of misclassifications was, as expected, considerably higher because the models were being applied out-of-sample. Interestingly, however, average share price reaction was again consistent with the signals of a company's prima facie status as a potential failure or survivor, except towards the very end of the life of a company which ultimately went bankrupt. Moreover, this result was generally robust when the procedure was replicated on randomly selected subsamples of matched pairs of companies.

Overall, the results are not inconsistent with the view that failure prediction models are of limited practical usefulness, since all they may really be doing is capturing information that analysts are already using to revise the probabilities they attach to likely bankruptcy.

## Chapter 15: Case study analysis

The evidence reviewed above suggests that at best failure identification models for listed companies probably contain only a limited amount of new information for analysts. This is in part because they seem not only to measure a lowest common denominator, but also they tend to identify symptoms rather than causes.

In order to throw further light on these matters, the characteristics of a number of companies which failed in the sample period, 1973-1983, and in a later period, 1988-1991, were analysed. The main focus was 25 companies which went bankrupt during the first period, and the key factors which characterised their declines were identified. These could then be compared against a similar analysis of the main contributory causes of the collapse of 21 companies which failed in the second period.

For both samples, the years when bankruptcy occurred were for the most part in periods of deep and prolonged economic recession. It was not surprising, therefore, that there were certain common characteristics between the two groups: e.g. the extent of the downturns took all companies – and not just those which failed – by surprise; some industries were hit harder than others; firms most vulnerable were those where demand fell sharply, which had significant borrowings, and which faced high levels of unavoidable fixed operating costs. These factors were inevitably reflected in the key accounting indicators (namely, sharply declining profits and high gearing ratios). But it was also clear that in most industries there is a constant jockeying for competitive position. As a result, it was those companies which had become the weakest players at the onset of the recession which found it most difficult to survive. In particular, their plight was often brought about by a specific (but not especially unusual) misjudgement by management, which in better times would probably not have been so catastrophic.

But what was particularly interesting was that the combinations of factors which characterised failing companies in the two samples differed quite markedly. Thus in the first period, most of the bankruptcies arose as a result of an extensive shake-out in British manufacturing industry, when overcapacity in a number of key sectors had to be shed. This painful process was sometimes accelerated by the prolonged high foreign exchange value of sterling in the early 1980s. By contrast, in the second period many of the victims were firms which had grown rapidly in the boom years in the mid 1980s. In particular, companies most severely hit were those whose growth was on the back of the property boom, the collapse of which took the banks as much by surprise as anyone else and left them trying to decide if and when to call in their debts and precipitate the failure of their clients.

Overall, the implication is that bankruptcy tends to be very much 'situation specific' and is usually the result of a particular conjunction of events, most of which could not be accurately forecast either by management or by outside analysts.

## Chapter 16: Summary and conclusions

A priori reasoning suggests that it ought to be very difficult to devise failure identification models for listed companies which will consistently be able before the event to signal probable bankruptcy. Yet despite this, the impression is often given that the models perform extremely well.

In fact, a close examination of previous empirical work suggests that academics have spent much of the past 60 years applying a number of statistical and iterative procedures to various different sets of independent explanatory variables, but for the most part without greatly improving discriminatory power. In part this is probably because the models tend to identify a 'lowest common denominator' distinction between failing and surviving firms – an inevitable consequence, really, of having to pool data over time for companies operating in different industries. This probably helps to explain why out-of-sample most models seem to generate rather high misclassification rates, often identifying around 20 per cent of surviving firms as prima facie failures. This error rate is such as to explain why analysts do not seem to react as one might expect if the models' predictions could be relied on. Moreover, the evidence from share price reaction studies is not inconsistent with such an interpretation, implying that the models are probably doing no more than summarising data already in the public domain.

The empirical studies on British data reported in this book tend to reinforce the above arguments.[1] Thus the classificatory power of balance sheet decomposition measures and of gambler's ruin and multivariate models does not appear to be all that different, even in the latter case when the independent variable set is altered to comprise qualitative variables reported over a five year window. Far more important is the effect of making allowance for an appropriate prior probability of failure, which greatly weakens a model's ability to discriminate accurately. Further, it is clear that misclassification rates rise quite sharply when models are applied out-of-sample – hardly surprising, in fact, as economic conditions will have changed and firms from different industries will be under threat.

Further insight into the failure process is offered by case study analysis, and this confirms what seems to be intuitively obvious – namely, that listed companies which collapse tend to be victims of an unfortunate conjunction of a variety of events which, for the most part, are largely unanticipated.

That said, it seems likely that analysts will continue to refer to failure identification models, not because they believe their use will give them a momentary advantage over their rivals, but rather because failure to do so could possibly put them at a short term disadvantage.

**Note**

[1] The results are summarised in Table 16.1 on p. 376.

# 1 The background

## Introduction

### The argument

Finding ways of trying to identify failing companies as early as possible is clearly a matter of considerable significance to businessmen and other interested parties. For instance, if an investor or creditor is able to predict a company on the path to bankruptcy before anyone else, he or she will be able to liquidate the investment or obtain settlement of a debt and so minimise losses. Similarly, it is vitally important for an auditor in preparing his or her report to be able to assess whether or not a company is a going concern.

In fact, the rate of failure amongst new small businesses has always been high, upwards of a third of newly established companies collapsing within five years of incorporation.[1] By contrast, the rate of failure amongst listed companies is much lower, the attrition rate being rather less than 2 per cent per annum. Nevertheless, it is a matter of some concern that the number of bankruptcies, both of listed and unlisted companies, has increased in recent years as the British economy has suffered a series of destabilising shocks (see Figure 1.1). Moreover, it is noticeable that over time financial distress appears to be experienced in different industry sectors.[2]

Against this background there has inevitably been a growing urgency on the part of investors, bankers, trade creditors, company directors and auditors to try to find better ways of trying to identify firms likely to go bankrupt,[3] a demand which researchers have sought to satisfy by developing a number of different procedures which aim to give early warning of financial distress. But for a variety of reasons (see p. 27) this research has overwhelmingly concentrated on predicting the fate of *listed* companies rather than their far more numerous unquoted counterparts, where however the risk of failure is far greater.

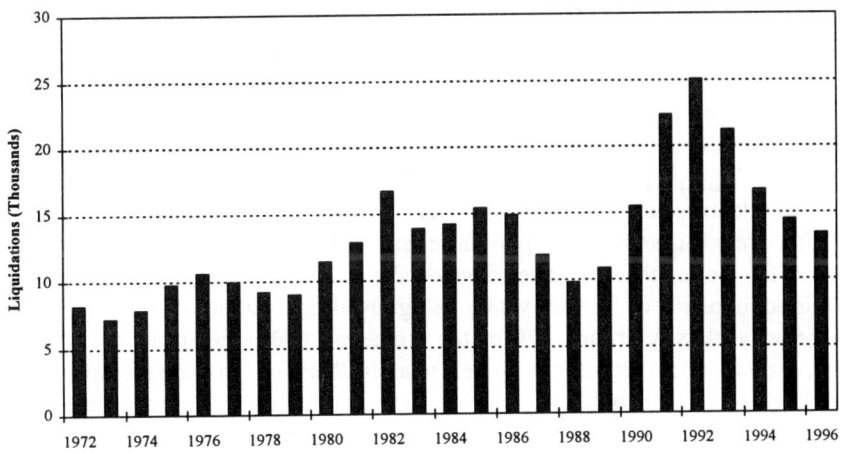

**Figure 1.1 Company liquidations[5]**

*Source: Annual Abstracts of Statistics*

What is puzzling is that if there is a well established method of identifying failing listed companies in advance of their final collapse, one might reasonably expect investors and creditors to use the procedure and immediately act upon its predictions. Consequently, as soon as a new and accurate forecasting approach has been established, one would expect it to be universally adopted. The result should be that listed companies forecast as very likely to go bankrupt ought to fail immediately.

In the circumstances it is therefore a little perplexing that many experts in the field seem to claim that they can successfully predict with remarkable accuracy which listed companies are very likely to fail and which are not.[6] Indeed, it is not unusual to find that success rates of over 90 per cent are claimed, not just immediately a new prediction model has been derived, but consistently thereafter when the diagnostic procedure has been well publicised, which stretches credulity to the limit.

Of course, investors and creditors, and the agents who work on their behalf, will search endlessly for a novel procedure that might give them a narrow (and presumably short-lived) advantage. If successful, analysts and their clients stand to make a lot of money – or, at least, in the case of the latter, not to lose heavily! It is therefore quite easy to believe that each innovation which improves the accuracy of predictions will be well worthwhile. But what is more difficult to accept is that a new approach will continue to be successful in terms of earning abnormal risk-adjusted returns after its existence becomes known and analysts

21

are able to mimic its forecasts. Its prophecies should then become self-fulfilling. In fact, the argument and evidence presented in this book appear to provide an answer to the conundrum. Basically the 'prediction' models, however derived, seem to come up with a very similar (and unsurprising) answer: namely, that immediately prior to bankruptcy, the accounts of failing listed companies show high levels of borrowing and low profitability. The problem is that, outside the sample period and/or when allowance is made for sample selection bias, a relatively high proportion of *non*-failing listed companies – some 20 per cent – are also identified as prima facie failures.

Effectively this seems to imply that in any one year a UK analyst referring to one of the models that have been developed would correctly identify the dozen or so listed industrial companies which will go bankrupt within 12 months, but will incorrectly classify around 120 of the remaining 600 as likely to fail. Clearly analysts who might refer to the models to assist them in managing their portfolios are likely to try them out before relying on them blindly and thus make them self-fulfilling. It seems improbable, in fact, that a misclassification error rate of 20 per cent for non-failing listed companies would be regarded as acceptable, even allowing for the significantly higher costs of incorrectly identifying a failing company as sound when compared to those of misclassifying a non-failing company as prima facie bankrupt.[7]

Consequently it would seem that, where analysts refer to the models, they do so primarily as a shorthand procedure for summarising data about a company. Given the diversity of the businesses from which the underlying financial ratio data are derived, it appears that the classifications really just reflect the fact that listed companies reporting losses or low profits and which are burdened with debt are more at risk than otherwise similar companies which are recording reasonable profit figures and which have lower gearing ratios. But the plight of a financially distressed company should be fairly obvious anyway, and it would not be unreasonable to expect relative share prices to reflect the outward condition of a business, regardless of whether it eventually fails or not. Interestingly, the evidence reported later in this book seems to support this argument.

The implication therefore seems to be that there are few, if any, unambiguous early warning signals of impending bankruptcy. On the other hand, there is a significant proportion of listed companies – around a fifth, perhaps – which in any one year might be regarded as 'at risk', but the vast majority of which are turned round and/or do not fail.

*Some basic issues*

It is against this background that various basic issues will be reviewed in this chapter. This will set the scene for the argument and review of the evidence which follows.

In particular, it is first necessary to identify what exactly is meant by the term 'failure'. At one extreme it can obviously mean liquidation; but at the other it could just mean reporting a profit figure below that expected. In between are various possible definitions of what precisely is meant by the term.

It is also appropriate to consider what is meant by 'prediction'. In fact, it can mean being able to discriminate *after* an event or *before* an event – although it is only the latter which is really of interest to a decision maker.

In addition, there are a number of other fundamental methodological issues which need to be considered. For instance, before engaging in empirical research it is highly desirable to try to establish by deductive reasoning what factors might reasonably be expected to bring about the failure of a business. Such theories are known as 'normative theories'. By contrast, it is possible to develop 'positive theories' (explaining *what is* rather than *what ought to be*) through empirical observation.

In fact, most of the research into corporate bankruptcy seems to be driven by empirical evidence, and it is therefore appropriate to try to identify potential difficulties in developing research designs which might bias the results in a particular direction. One obvious distorting factor is the matched pairing technique generally adopted, when the annual incidence of failure is far less than 50 per cent of a population of companies in a given year. Interestingly there are ways this can be allowed for, and when suitable adjustments are made it appears that the discriminatory power of so called prediction models is substantially reduced. Another problem concerns the way in which the accuracy of predictions is calculated, either pairwise or across complete samples of failed and non-failed companies.

It is also necessary at the outset to say something briefly about informational market efficiency and various 'user needs'. In the case of the former, the argument presented above suggesting that a successful prediction procedure should immediately be applied by analysts implies informational market efficiency. Brief reference will therefore be made to the very substantial body of empirical evidence which suggests that, after allowance is made for search costs and rewarding special skills, financial markets do appear to be very close to being informationally efficient.[8]

As for user needs, it is also appropriate to focus more closely on what might be of interest to investors, creditors, company directors, auditors and other third parties. In particular, it may well be that some investors or creditors will be prepared to put their money into specific high risk companies, knowing that some will fail but that overall the rewards will more than offset the losses they will make on some of the investments or loans in their portfolios.

As for directors and auditors, they have always had to decide whether or not a company is a 'going concern', since that will determine whether a company's accounts will be approved by the board and the nature of the audit certificate attached to them. However, recent changes in legislation affecting the rights and duties of directors, as well as to rules concerning the audit of company accounts, have focused attention more closely on the matter. It is therefore necessary to consider the significance for both directors and auditors of being able to assess the likelihood of a company failing in the foreseeable future.

## The meaning of 'failure'

'Corporate failure' fairly obviously encompasses 'bankruptcy', which for a company effectively means a creditors' liquidation or the appointment of a receiver. However, the net can be drawn more widely to embrace situations where there is evidence of 'financial distress'. It may therefore be useful to list a spectrum of potential indicators of such distress, beginning with situations where there is general agreement on what constitutes failure and working down to other circumstances which are more indicative of a company's possible financial difficulties, e.g.

(1)  creditors' or voluntary liquidation, appointment of a receiver;
(2)  suspension of Stock Exchange listing;
(3)  going concern qualification by the auditors;[9]
(4)  composition with the creditors;
(5)  protection sought from creditors (e.g. under Chapter 11 of the US Bankruptcy Code);
(6)  breach of debt covenants, fall in bond or credit rating, new charges taken over the assets of the company or its directors;
(7)  company reconstruction;
(8)  resignation of directors, appointment of a company doctor, etc;
(9)  take-over (although not all take-overs are witness to financial distress, of course);
(10) closure or sale of part of the business;
(11) a cut in dividends or the reporting of losses; or
(12) the reporting of profits below a forecast or acceptable level; and/or the fall in a company's relative share price.

Generally corporate failure studies concentrate on the first few items in the above list, although some of the others may be taken as indicators of impending difficulties. There is also an extensive literature on changes in corporate bond and credit ratings[10] and on corporate turnarounds.[11]

## The meaning of 'prediction'

Many studies on corporate failure specifically refer to *predicting* bankruptcy. It is therefore necessary to deal with another semantic issue which is all too rarely addressed in the literature – namely, what exactly is meant by 'prediction'.

In fact, 'prediction' has two distinct meanings, and it is important to distinguish between them.

(1) Prediction can mean 'identification' – i.e. in a narrow statistical sense it should be possible historically (or 'ex post') for a given population of companies to predict (identify) which businesses went bankrupt and which did not. Such an *autopsy* can be useful as a way of enhancing understanding of the phenomena which characterise corporate failure.

(2) Prediction can mean 'forecast' – i.e. it implies that it should somehow be possible to distinguish in advance (or 'ex ante') those firms which, within a given time span, will fail and those which will not.

For decision makers it is essentially the second of these which is of interest, especially if there is a procedure which would enable them to increase returns (reduce losses) on their investment portfolios. However, in a highly competitive market analysts would be expected to use *any* procedure which would enable them to distinguish between 'winners' and 'losers'. In other words, just as in betting markets, it is difficult to conceive of an 'unfair game' situation existing for any length of time. Consequently, although it is possible that a new innovatory form of analysis might give its creator a momentary advantage, this would quickly be eroded as other 'players' mimic the procedure.

But, just as the alchemists of old sought to find the mystical substance, phlogiston, that would turn base metals into gold, so investors seek to find ways of 'beating the market'. Clearly there are situations where such opportunities exist: e.g. the whole notion of project appraisal, where positive net present values (NPVs) are identified, implies that there are situations where there is short term disequilibrium in markets. However, these are likely to arise where peculiar factors exist which limit competition: e.g. where the nexus of skills and resources which exist within a company gives it a competitive advantage over its rivals; or where there are other 'barriers to entry'. Where there are no such impediments, any risk-adjusted 'excess returns' can normally be viewed as a reward for 'search activity', and if individuals act rationally in a competitive economic environment such excess returns should be eliminated after search costs have been taken into account.

Essentially what is being argued is that, in a competitive market environment, it would be surprising to discover a way of successfully discriminating between failed and non-failed firms. If there were a means of identifying companies which are likely to collapse, the diagnosis should immediately be reflected in market judgements. As a result, as soon as a business is forecast as being highly likely to fail, presumably bankers and suppliers would starve it of credit,[12] auditors would enter going concern qualifications, and equity holders themselves would attempt to bale out to minimise their losses. Consequently if a failure 'prediction' model is successful, not only would it become self-fulfilling, but it would lose its ability to forecast as its predictions would immediately be impounded by the market. Further, there are incentives which would help to ensure such an eventuality. Thus an analyst who concludes that a listed company's shares are overvalued will benefit most by selling short and then disclosing his privileged information. This should push down prices so that he can close his speculative position and take his profit.[13]

Of course, in practice there may be institutional barriers which prevent analysts making such easy money – e.g. it is not always possible to implement a short selling strategy even with a listed company, and virtually impossible with a private business.[14] In the circumstances, the analyst has to pursue an alternative policy: for example, sell his innovatory diagnostic model to bankers or brokers who hope – for a moment at least – to steal a march on the market.[15]

In short, one might well expect that – for listed companies, at any rate – so called 'failure prediction models' will not enable investors to outperform the market significantly. Instead they will merely tend to mimic analysts' diagnoses, which will already (or simultaneously) be reflected in relative share prices.

## Methodological issues

### Normative and positive theories[16]

A basic distinction is drawn in the social sciences between 'normative' and 'positive' statements. The former are assertions of 'what ought to be', and consequently they require the application not only of value judgements, but also of deductive reasoning. By contrast, positive statements assert 'what is', and they can therefore be tested using inductive reasoning against empirical evidence.

Theories are essentially constructed to try to identify and explain cause-and-effect relationships. All are to a greater or lesser extent abstractions from reality, and they are therefore based on a number of simplifying assumptions. (Indeed, if they were not stylised 'models' of the world, but merely duplicated it, they would add very little to our understanding.) Consequently the fact that the assumptions underlying a theory at first sight appear to be unrealistic should not necessarily be a matter of great concern, particularly if the effects of relaxing them are later examined closely. Further, there are 'instrumentalists' who argue that the realism of a model is relatively unimportant so long as operationally it seems to explain observed phenomena.

From the point of view of studying company failure, it is first of all desirable to try to develop well defined normative theories which might explain corporate collapse. Yet, as will be argued in the first part of this book, this has usually not been the case. Rather, researchers have chosen to gather empirical evidence and rationalise inductively what phenomena may have led to bankruptcy. But it is also necessary to devise appropriate methodologies for testing hypotheses relating to positive statements. Regrettably there are various problems in undertaking research studies into the subject which seem likely to have led to 'inference errors'.

*Research methodologies*

In the pure sciences (such as chemistry, physics and medicine) it is usually possible to conduct tightly controlled experiments in laboratories. Thus, for instance, when testing a new drug it is common practice to treat a representative cross section of patients with a pharmaceutical compound; while another similar control group of patients is given a placebo. The results can then be compared to see whether there is any evidence that the new drug has healing properties. Of course, when undertaking such experiments it is vital to try to ensure that the two populations of patients are to all intents and purposes identical, otherwise it is quite possible to draw incorrect inferences. Equally, it is necessary to try to identify all relevant outcomes. Sadly, from time to time methodological errors come to light (e.g. with thalidomide).

In the social sciences it is often impossible to construct realistic experiments within a tightly controlled laboratory environment (although there are some examples in economics and accounting: see below, p. 185 et seq.). More commonly researchers have to collect statistical evidence from real world events and use the data to test various hypotheses.

It is this latter approach which is usually employed in bankruptcy studies. Moreover, there are various reasons why the vast majority of failure prediction studies relate to listed rather than private companies. One obvious factor is that it is easier to access data for the former. However, there are other reasons why researchers prefer to use data for quoted companies: e.g. fewer than half the small companies registered in the UK publish their profit figures,[17] and even when they do such figures are unreliable because of the somewhat arbitrary nature of directors' emoluments; the picture of small companies' indebtedness is often incomplete because of the widespread use of guarantees by directors and others; as indicated previously, some 30-40 per cent of small companies fail within five years of incorporation, so it is not only difficult to build up a track record of performance, but the data are effectively censored, giving rise to a 'survivorship bias'; and the accounts of small companies are often filed 8 or 9 months after the financial year end, which – given the high attrition rate – frequently makes reference to the figures irrelevant.

Another consideration is the fact that the use of data relating to listed companies makes it possible to compare the results of discriminatory models against those previously devised for such companies in the US and UK. But perhaps the most important factor is that, by examining share price behaviour, it is possible to assess how analysts in a 'multi-person' decision setting appear to use failure prediction information. Clearly this is less feasible for a sample of small companies, where – for equity investors, at least – there is effectively a 'single person' decision environment. This means that it is necessary somehow to identify an individual decision maker's attitude to risk, rather than let the market mechanism take account of the differences in attitude through trading.[18] More generally, however, it would not seem unreasonable to infer that bankers and creditors might use failure prediction information in a broadly similar way to investment analysts operating in a stock market environment.

At a wider level, as with all research experiments, it is especially important that the methodologies used should be carefully worked out to try to ensure that no unjustified inferences are drawn. In fact, researchers into the possibility of successfully discriminating between failing and non-failing businesses have spent a great deal of time and effort in critically examining their models. Frequently their concerns have been about the technical statistical requirements of the various models they have used to study corporate bankruptcy. Unfortunately, however, the research methodology generally used seems to be seriously flawed in two key respects, and while these are usually now acknowledged, the full implications are rarely spelt out in detail.

The first difficulty is that for studies involving listed companies – the vast majority, it will be recalled – the number of failures is relatively low (e.g. between 0.5 per cent and 2 per cent per annum across all such businesses). This means that it has been necessary to 'pool' the data over time to produce reasonably sized experimental samples, the implicit (and unwarranted) assumption being that the underlying economic circumstances are the same each year. This procedure also produces a discriminator that applies to all companies in a sample. This means, for instance, that a critical value for (say) the gearing ratio, return on capital employed or a combination of the two should apply regardless of industry membership. The implication must therefore be that where there is a degree of heterogeneity in the sample – as there usually will be, since (as already indicated) to make the sample large enough observations have not only to be taken from different industry categories but at different points in time – the ratios which represent a 'lowest common denominator' will be the best discriminators. These are likely to be indicators of profitability and indebtedness, since companies in crisis are almost certainly going to find themselves with low or negative profits and with increased borrowings. In other words, the best discriminator ratios are likely to be *symptoms* of financial distress rather than the *causes*. In the circumstances, it seems intuitively likely that in most cases a failure identification model is probably not telling analysts much they don't already know.

A second problem relates to the difficulty of collecting data, even for listed companies. This can be particularly awkward in the case of defunct businesses, since by their very circumstances it will often be well nigh impossible to obtain their records. This introduces another example of a 'survivorship bias'.[19]

A further difficulty is that in constructing a control sample of businesses it has been commonplace to use a 'matched pairing technique'. This approach is understandable, if only because it is desirable to try to isolate key factors which distinguish otherwise similar firms. On the other hand, the procedure does have a number of drawbacks. Thus if the pairing criteria are years, industry membership and size, these three possible explanations of failure are automatically excluded from consideration. This may be regarded as unfortunate, since size and industry membership certainly seem to be key factors in determining a firm's vulnerability to collapse.

But far more important is the problem already referred to, namely that there is a *sampling bias* in that the matched pairing procedure produces an experimental sample of companies which is totally different from that in the real world. Thus it is not uncommon for bankruptcy studies to be based on populations of (say) 60 failed and 60 paired non-failed companies. This *state* (or *choice*) *based sampling* approach assumes that there is an equal 50:50 per cent probability of any firm selected from the wider population of companies being a potential failure. Clearly this is untrue: as indicated previously, the prior probability of a randomly selected listed company failing in any one year is really between 0.5 per cent and 2 per cent. As has been demonstrated by Zmijewski (1984) and Palepu (1986), the effect of this has been greatly to exaggerate the discriminating power of failure identification models (see below, pp. 114, 126, 138 and 140-1).

Despite these problems, a number of writers have been all too ready to point out with the 20:20 vision of hindsight that companies which have failed were correctly identified as being at risk by one or other of the previously devised bankruptcy prediction models. But just as it would be a logical fallacy to say that because all failing companies earn low profits, therefore all companies which earn low profits must fail, it is equally unjustifiable to infer that because a failed company would have been correctly identified by a model, therefore the model accurately discriminates between failed and non-failed companies.

Further, as previously argued, it is evident that the market can hardly believe the models, since if it did it would automatically and immediately bankrupt all companies strongly signalled as likely to fail. Consequently just what the models are telling the reader is unclear.

Finally, there is another problem that arises with the matched pairing procedure which is rarely referred to. This relates to the basis of comparison between pairs. The usual procedure is to apply the discriminatory function to *all* companies in a sample. However, an alternative approach is to rank each pair. This can give rather different results and makes some allowance for differences in the industry membership, size and time of failure which are captured in the pairing process.

In fact, it is easy to demonstrate the impact this may have if, for instance, a single ratio (such as return on capital employed) is the discriminator and is applied to a population of matched pairs of failed and non-failed companies.

*Example:*

Suppose that there are four pairs of companies with the following ratios (failed first, non-failed second): *Pair I* .02, .03; *Pair II* .03, .04; *Pair III* .09, .10; *Pair IV* .10, .11. In terms of a pairwise comparison of basically similar companies, the failed companies always have lower ratios: i.e. there is a 100 per cent correct discrimination. However, if the data are pooled and an average of the ratios is calculated, a cut-off point of .065 results.[20] According to this, for the first two pairs of observations both failed and non-failed companies are classified as failures; and the last two pairs as non-failures. Consequently at best there is only a 50 per cent success rate in categorising the companies.

The main problem which arises when a strict matched pairing criterion is adopted is that it is difficult to devise suitable hold out tests to assess the predictive ability of a model. All that can be done is to see whether a procedure correctly ranks *pairs* of companies out-of-sample (e.g. in terms of the greater risk of their going bankrupt). Consequently the best that can be achieved is to see whether a model derived in this way still correctly discriminates between pairs of bankrupt and surviving firms in subsequent periods. It will not generally be feasible to apply the procedure to the general population of companies and so identify those which appear to be prima facie failures.

## Informational market efficiency

In a competitive environment investors, creditors and other interested parties would be expected to search actively for any clue which gives them an inkling of which companies are going to be winners and which losers. But one result of such activity ought to be that it will become increasingly difficult to steal a march on rival investors and creditors. Any informational advantage, though real enough and valuable, will be slender and short-lived.

This concept of informational market efficiency has been the subject of intense study by financial economists, and a substantial body of empirical evidence indeed suggests that in active markets there are few opportunities to make easy money. The only obvious occasions where investors can earn profits are where they have particular skills or advantages – or they are the result of pure chance, just as there will always be a punter who wins the national lottery or the football pools.

As an entrepreneur, an investor's advantage can be the result of a particular skill or combination of skills; or, alternatively, of having a degree of monopoly power. As explained earlier, such advantages give rise to the net present values which are the focus of attention in investment project analysis. By contrast, in highly competitive securities markets the opportunities to secure such a superiority might be expected to be much more limited. Certainly there should be many potential investors engaging in search activity in the hope of securing the equivalent of 'inside information' and thus gaining a momentary advantage. Moreover, it is true that someone has to be first with the news. But if any method of obtaining superior information is discovered, it is only to be expected that the technique will be copied.

It follows from this that, after extracting trends (e.g. for inflation or other systematic factors), prices of actively traded assets, such as securities, might be expected to follow a random walk. In fact, there is an impressive amount of empirical evidence which suggests that this is indeed the case, the phenomenon being referred to as 'weak form' market efficiency.

The reason why prices move, of course, is that unanticipated news items impact the market in a random fashion. It is therefore appropriate to see whether prices move in response to the release of news items (such as profit announcements, some of the content of which will not have been correctly anticipated by the market). Again, a substantial body of empirical research has been undertaken to test so called 'semi-strong' form market efficiency. In undertaking such studies, great care has to be taken to avoid the risk of making unjustified inferences. Thus it is necessary to allow for the market's expectations prior to a news announcement so that the incremental piece of news can be isolated. But it is equally necessary to eliminate systematic factors which are driving asset prices so that only the *residual element* responding to a specific news announcement is identified. Again, a substantial body of empirical research gathered over the years is impressive in suggesting that financial markets are 'semi-strong' informationally efficient.[21]

At the extreme it has been suggested that at any moment in time *all* analysts might be able correctly to perceive future outcomes and hence the true value of assets. This is the equivalent of suggesting that somehow they possess inside information. In practice it does not seem likely that this 'strong form' of informational market efficiency holds, and indeed empirical evidence suggests that it does not.

## User needs

Information relevant to failure identification can be viewed from a number of angles, but it is probably most appropriate to concentrate on the user demand perspective.

The most obvious *decision makers* who might use accounting information would seem to be equity investors, creditors and employees. Yet typically they will hold portfolios of assets, and it follows that they will have to adjust their holdings to maintain the desired risk/return balance if one of the assets suffers a sharp fall in value. This is especially important to those users whose asset holdings are not widely diversified as their exposure to risk will be that much greater. This is likely to be a particular problem for employees, for some types of creditor, and for private equity investors. The result is that such users will have an especially strong incentive to search for early warnings of potential bankruptcy, and the procedure which provides most information in relation to search costs ought to be preferred. However, users with well diversified portfolios will also be anxious to get prior warning of an impending fall in the value of one of their assets, since this would enable them to sell out before others learn the news.

In practice, users may deliberately invest in some securities which have a high potential risk of failure, so long as in budgeted terms they help to provide the desired risk/return mix. Consider, for instance, a person who invests in two companies, one totally reliant on oil, the other on coal. If there is an unforeseen hike in world oil prices, the former may have to go into liquidation, whereas the latter would increase its prospective profitability and value to compensate. Likewise the reverse might be true if there were an unexpected fall in the price of crude. Other things being equal, it is not obvious how the investor is any worse off under such an arrangement than from, say, investing in a conglomerate whose activities are comparable and use both oil and coal. What an investor, creditor or employee really requires is *prior* knowledge of an event, here the occurrence and direction of the oil price shock.[22]

In an informationally efficient market setting, it therefore seems intuitively unlikely that a model derived from variables (such as financial ratios) reflecting *historic* data will be of very much use. What instead would seem to be helpful is a means of identifying as early as possible a firm's vulnerability to financial collapse, and as Argenti (1976) has argued, this may best be inferred from the behaviour of management or from other pieces of information available to the market. Thus, to the extent that investment analysts refer to failure prediction models when examining the accounts of listed companies, one might reasonably expect share prices to reflect or anticipate the information captured in the models.

Where failure prediction models would appear likely to be of more value to analysts is where an attempt is being made to assess the creditworthiness of a business, especially where it is relatively small and privately owned. However, as mentioned previously, it is frequently difficult to obtain the necessary accounting data to use in such a model. Moreover, although UK credit analysts have been well aware of the existence of failure identification models for the last 25 years, only limited use appears to have been made of them. Thus a survey by Morris and Ormrod (1990) of a sample of credit managers and credit assessment agencies showed that in the mid 1980s only 12 per cent of the former and none of the latter referred to such models.[23] Furthermore, the corresponding percentages for applying other credit scoring routines were only 18 per cent and 6 per cent respectively. It was therefore hardly surprising that out of a list of 14 sources of information on which credit ratings were based, the two procedures (failure prediction models and credit scoring routines) were ranked as 14 and 13 respectively by both groups of respondents. On the other hand, this survey did not extend to the clearing banks, some of which it is known have experimented with failure prediction models. Moreover, the largest credit assessment agency, Dun and Bradstreet, certainly uses an algorithm based on some 30 variables to determine a risk rating. Although its basis is a closely guarded secret, much of the raw data is known to come from sales ledger details supplied by a large panel of creditors.[24]

But in the context of user needs, there is another point (already alluded to) that needs to be made, namely, the failure rate for small businesses is extremely high. Indeed, over the past one hundred years a third or more of small firms in the UK have failed within five years of their creation, compared to only about 2 per cent of listed companies.[25] This immediately suggests that size and diversification are critical factors – points that will be picked up in later chapters. But there is further interesting – and rather puzzling – feature, and that is that most small businesses rely very heavily on banks for their finance. It is therefore worth asking whether bankers in deciding to lend to small businesses know in advance which 3-4 of any portfolio of ten are most likely to fail. And, if so, are they merely being cynical in providing finance while protecting their own positions by taking security and/or charging high interest rates? Or, alternatively, are they (like the owners, presumably, if they are risk averse) unable to discriminate in advance?[26]

In fact, such questions can be directed at other interested parties besides lending bankers who have diversified portfolios of 'investments'. Thus, for instance, in the past the auditors of many small companies have not qualified the accounts – presumably because they have not considered the probability of failure sufficient to warrant a going concern reservation. Similarly, major trade creditors have often continued to deal with a small company even when it has gradually become clear that all is not well. Usually in such circumstances they take steps to protect themselves (e.g. by imposing reservation of title clauses).

Overall it seems likely that bankers, auditors and creditors find it far from easy to identify firms which have a high probability of failure, although casual empiricism suggests that some small businesses are set up which have very little chance of long term survival. Moreover, another aspect which has to be taken into account within the underlying portfolio framework is the individual decision maker's attitude with respect to trading off risk against expected return.

Finally, another matter already referred to which concerns user needs is the relative cost of misclassifying a failed company as non-failed; and a non-failed company as failed. Some researchers have quite rightly pointed out that the cost of the latter should be far less than the cost of the former (e.g. Altman, 1977).[27] Accordingly in many studies the weighting of the discriminant function has been adjusted to allow for this. Clearly this will to some extent neutralise the sampling bias referred to above. However, the adjustment really only relates to the analysis sample of companies. It will not eliminate misclassification errors, and when a model is used out-of-sample for prediction purposes it will still be necessary to allow for the differential costs of classifying a failed company as non-failed and vice versa. Moreover, if analysts accept the predictions of a model, presumably all companies classified as failures should in fact fail, regardless of whether or not they would have done had they not been so classified. Consequently the validity must be questioned of introducing such weights into the discriminant function for ex ante forecasting purposes.

**Assessing whether or not a business is a going concern**

Directors and auditors have long had to consider if a company is 'a going concern' when deciding whether or not its accounts represent 'a true and fair view' of its financial affairs. However, 'going concern' is not a term defined in law, although its meaning is explained as follows in Statement of Standard Accounting Practice 2, *Disclosure of Accounting Policies*:

> The enterprise will continue in operational existence for the foreseeable future. This means in particular that the profit and loss account and balance sheet assume no intention or necessity to liquidate or curtail significantly the scale of operation (SSAP 2, para. 14).

Recently the issue has been highlighted by the publication of a Statement of Auditing Standards, SAS 130, *The Going Concern Basis in Financial Statements*. This statement, issued in December 1994, was released two years after the *Code of Best Practice* was published by the Committee on the Financial Aspects of Corporate Governance ('the Cadbury Committee'), which in turn indicated that directors of listed companies 'should report that the business is a going concern, with supporting assumptions and qualifications as necessary' (para. 4.6). This suggestion has since been endorsed in *The Listing Rules of the London Stock Exchange* (para. 12.43 (v)); and in the Accounting Standards Board's recommendation that directors of a listed company should publish in its annual report an *Operating and Financial Review* (para. 36).

*The directors' responsibility*

Prior to the Insolvency Act 1986 the only remedy available to a liquidator against a director who had permitted his company to incur debts when it was prima facie insolvent (and hence not a 'going concern') was to institute proceedings for 'fraudulent trading'. This remedy still exists and can give rise to both criminal and civil consequences (Companies Act 1985, s. 458; Insolvency Act 1986, s. 213). However, it is often difficult to prove that a director has intended to defraud creditors rather than has merely acted recklessly, a necessary condition since it is necessary to show that the company carried on business and incurred debts when, to the knowledge of the director, there was no reasonable prospect of the company being able to pay off its creditors (i.e. it was not a going concern).

The Insolvency Act 1986 introduced a new concept, that of 'wrongful trading' (s. 214). This does not constitute a criminal offence, but it can lead to action under s. 10 of the Company Directors Disqualification Act 1986. To establish 'wrongful trading' the liquidator must show, first, that a company has gone into insolvent liquidation (i.e. that its assets are insufficient to discharge its debts and other liabilities and meet the expenses of winding up). But, second, it has to be established that the director, prior to the liquidation, knew or ought to have concluded that there was no reasonable prospect that the company could avoid going into insolvent liquidation, and that he took insufficient steps to minimise the potential loss to creditors. Consequently dishonesty on the part of a director is not a necessary condition to establish 'wrongful trading', merely that his behaviour has been unreasonable or negligent.[28] If wrongful trading is established, the court may require a director to make a contribution to the company's assets to help make good the creditors' loss, and then disqualify the offending party from being a director for a period of between 2 and 15 years.

The Company Directors Disqualification Act 1986 also empowers the court under s. 6 to disqualify directors of insolvent companies if their conduct makes them 'unfit to be concerned in the management of a company'. In fact, since the Act came into force there have been very few disqualifications for wrongful trading (i.e. where the question of going concern status is at issue), the most in any one year being 10 in 1990/91, the average being less than 3 per annum. By contrast, the number of disqualifications under s. 6 has been much higher, averaging just under 350 a year over the period 1988/89 to 1994/95, and doubling to more than 700 in 1995/96. The vast majority of these orders relate to directors of small private companies.

Just how effective this legislation is is a matter for debate. According to an enquiry undertaken in 1996 by the credit assessment agency CCN, nearly one million company directors (i.e. about one in eight) had been involved in a series of corporate bankruptcies. The study also showed that more than 300,000 directors were classed as 'serial failures', with a string of disasters behind them; while there were over 3,500 who were associated with 10 or more failures.[29]

*The Code on Corporate Governance*

The implicit legal requirement that directors should consider the going concern status of a business when approving a company's accounts, referred to above, has been specifically recognised by the Cadbury Committee, and although it was charged to consider the financial aspects of corporate governance with respect to listed companies, its conclusions have more general application.

In its general report the Committee recognised that although a company's accounts are prepared on the general assumption that it is a going concern, there

35

is no explicit requirement for directors to satisfy themselves that this is a reasonable assumption (e.g. by preparing a cash flow forecast) (para. 5.18). It proceeded to argue that in view of 'the understandable public criticism of the audit process when companies collapse without apparent warning, there are strong arguments for amending company law to place an explicit requirement on directors to satisfy themselves that the going concern basis is appropriate' (para. 5.19).

The Committee went on to argue 'that going concern problems are more likely to be addressed successfully if they are identified early'. However, it was concerned that there 'must be a risk that any qualification about a company's financial viability, however it is expressed, will precipitate the company's collapse'. It was also concerned that directors probably did not fully appreciate that 'going concern' was interpreted in the then *Auditing Guidelines* 'as meaning that the company will still be operating six months following the date of the audit report or one year after the date of the balance sheet, whichever is the later', which might well be further ahead than many companies could see (e.g. in a recession) (para. 5.20).

The Committee concluded that new auditing guidelines should be developed, applying the going concern principle enshrined in the Companies Act 1985 (Sched. 4, para. 10) and SSAP 2 (paras. 2 and 14). However, the new guidelines should 'strike a careful balance between drawing proper attention to the conditions on which the continuation of the business depends, and not requiring directors to express unnecessarily cautious reservations that could of themselves jeopardise the business'. Directors should therefore be required to satisfy themselves 'that the business is a going concern on the basis that they have a *reasonable expectation* that it will continue in operation for the time period which the guidelines define' [emphasis in original]. However, 'directors should not be expected to give a firm guarantee about their company's prospects because there can never be complete certainty about future trading' (para. 5.21).

*The Operating and Financial Review*

The ASB's recommendations for preparing the Operating and Financial Review (OFR) for a company include a number of suggestions which might help an outsider to assess its future prospects and the likelihood of it failing. Indeed, one of the main aims is to identify 'the principal risks and uncertainties in the main lines of business' and to explain how such risks will be managed (para. 12).

The recommendation believes that this aim will in part be achieved by discussing the significant features of a company's trading performance, if necessary at segment or divisional level, with particular attention being paid to trends and factors that have affected results in the past and are likely to affect them in the future; changes in market conditions (e.g. affecting raw material supplies, the workforce and the competitive environment); the impact of

36

acquisitions, disposals, undertaking new activities and introducing new products; changes in market share and margins; the impact on the company of changes in inflation and interest and exchange rates; and the likely effects of engaging in capital investment projects (including those involving marketing campaigns, training programmes and expenditure on research and development).

The section of the OFR which should deal with the financial review is expected to explain the capital structure of the business, its treasury policy and the dynamics of its financial position (i.e. the sources of liquidity and the application of funds). The capital structure should be explained 'in terms of maturity profile of debt, type of capital instruments used, currency, and interest rate structure ... [with] comments on relevant ratios such as interest cover and debt/equity ratios' (para. 25). The management of interest rate and exchange rate risks should be discussed, giving a broad indication of the currencies in which borrowings are made and cash is held, the extent to which borrowings are at fixed interest rates, and the extent to which risks have been offset by hedging operations (para. 26). In addition, the liquidity position should be discussed, with a comment on the level of borrowings, the seasonality of borrowing requirements, and a maturity profile of both borrowings and committed borrowing facilities (para. 32). There should also be an indication of the extent to which the resources and value of the business are not reflected in the assets recognised in the balance sheet (para. 37).

Overall, the picture painted should confirm that the company can indeed be regarded as a going concern, and this fact may therefore be formally recognised in the OFR (para. 36).

*SAS 130: The going concern basis in financial statements*

SAS 130 indicates that in 'forming an opinion as to whether financial statements give a true and fair view, the auditors should consider the entity's ability to continue as a going concern' (SAS 130.1, para. 2). In order to do this, account should be taken 'of all relevant information of which [the directors and the auditors] are aware at the time' (para. 13).

Critical to this concept is the extent of the 'foreseeable future'. This 'depends on the specific circumstances at a point in time, including the nature of the entity's business, its associated risks and external influences' (para. 11). It is therefore impossible to prescribe a minimum length for the period that should be reviewed, but where 'the period considered by the directors has been limited, for example to a period of less than one year from the date of approval of the financial statements, [they] will have determined whether ... any additional disclosure [is required] to explain adequately the assumptions that underlie the adoption of the going concern basis' (para. 13).

The auditors will base their procedures on 'the information upon which the directors have based their assessment and the directors' reasoning' (para. 14). Such information in turn will be determined by the nature of the entity (e.g. in terms of its size and complexity) and whether the information relates to future events; and, if so, how far into the future those events lie (e.g. forecasts relating to periods more than one year ahead are likely to be far less detailed than those for more immediate periods) (para. 15).

In examining the audit evidence, the auditors should assess both the adequacy of the means by which the directors have satisfied themselves that it is appropriate for them to adopt the going concern basis; and that the financial statements include sufficient disclosures with respect to going concern to ensure that they reflect a true and fair view. For this purpose it is not only necessary to examine the information on which the directors have based their assessment of whether or not the going concern basis is justified, but also to apply procedures over the future period under review which are designed to identify material matters which could indicate concern about the entity's ability to continue as a going concern (SAS 130.2, para. 21).

It is further suggested that auditors may need to consider the length of the future period reviewed by the directors; the means which ensure that there is 'timely identification of warnings of future risks and uncertainties that the entity might face'; budget and/or forecast information (especially cash flow information); whether the assumptions underlying the budgets are appropriate and the sensitivity of those budgets to factors within and outside the directors' control; the adequacy of borrowing facilities; and the directors' plans for resolving matters which might call into doubt whether the going concern assumption is appropriate (para. 23).

The auditors are also required to determine and document their anxiety, if any, about an entity's ability to continue as a going concern (SAS 130.3, para. 29). This is likely to be supported by various pieces of evidence, including (for instance) an excess of liabilities over assets; a working capital deficit; default on loan agreements and/or insufficient borrowing facilities; liquidity and/or cash flow problems; post balance sheet events involving losses; forced sales of fixed assets; major restructuring of debt; tightening of credit terms by suppliers; delays in paying creditors; inability to adapt to changes in the market or in technology; loss of key staff and/or labour disputes; loss of key suppliers or customers; products becoming obsolete; and projects or litigation where the downside risk is so great that the company's future will be imperilled if there is an adverse outcome (para. 31).

On the basis of the evidence the auditors may conclude 'that there is a significant level of concern about the entity's ability to continue as a going concern, or they could disagree with the preparation of the financial statements on the going concern basis' (para. 32). In the former case 'they should include an explanatory paragraph when setting out the basis of their opinion, [but] they should not qualify their opinion on these grounds alone, provided the disclosures ... are adequate for the financial statements to give a true and fair view' (SAS 130.6, para. 42).

Moreover, 'if the period to which the directors have paid particular attention in assessing going concern is less than one year from the date of approval of the financial statements, and the directors have not disclosed that fact, the auditors should do so within ... their report, [although] they should not qualify their opinion ... on these grounds alone' (SAS 130.7, para. 45).

In assessing the evidence on which the directors have based their assessment of going concern for a period one year ahead, the most persuasive material is likely to be cash flow forecasts and budgets, but less formal evidence may suffice. However, if the auditors feel that the directors have not taken adequate steps to satisfy themselves that it is appropriate to adopt the going concern basis, this amounts to a limitation on the scope of the auditor's work and should be acknowledged as such (paras. 46-48).

'Where the auditors disagree with the preparation of the financial statements on the going concern basis, they should issue an adverse audit opinion' (SAS 130.8, para. 49). Moreover, they should not agree to 'a preliminary announcement if they have concluded that there is a significant level of concern ... [and this is not] disclosed ... in the announcement' (para. 53).

*The incidence of going concern qualifications*

The implications of the above pronouncements are fairly clear: namely, that on the basis of their privileged information, a company's directors and auditors should generally assure themselves that the business's going concern value exceeds its break up value. Moreover, in evaluating the former, special emphasis should be given to likely events over the next twelve months, attention being paid to downside risk (i.e. the 'worst case' possible outcomes).

But when issuing a going concern qualification, auditors have to be fairly sure such an indicator of high bankruptcy risk is justified. An auditing firm which is more ready than its rivals to so qualify the accounts of non-failing companies will almost certainly lose clients, so there has to be a careful comparison of the potential costs and benefits. Moreover, there is the possibility of degenerative competition between rival auditors, so there is a strong case for trying to prevent failure in the market for audit services by having clear rules specifying the circumstances when going concern qualifications ought to be made.

More generally, it should be recognised that in assessing whether or not a business can be regarded as a going concern, directors and auditors are not directly assessing whether or not it can be categorised as a 'failure' or 'non-failure'. Rather, they have to take into account a variety of considerations of which they are aware at the time they are approving or reporting on the accounts. In other words, they are trying to assess the *risk* of a company failing, and a going concern qualification or its absence in the auditors' report should be viewed in that light. Consequently a going concern qualification should be regarded as just one amongst a number of possible signals of potential problems facing a business.

It is this which appears to explain the fact that in the UK only a relatively small proportion of the audit reports attached to the last accounts published by failing companies include going concern qualifications. Thus with respect to private companies, a survey by Barnes and Hooi (1987) found that in 1985 only 5 per cent appeared to attract going concern qualifications, despite the fact that some 20 per cent of companies then on the register were in course of liquidation.[30] Moreover, only a third of the accounts of a sample of failed companies received going concern qualifications, whereas 94 per cent of another sample of companies, whose accounts had attracted such qualifications, were still trading two years later.

With respect to listed companies, there is evidence that relative share prices are marked down when published accounts fail to receive a clean certificate, with the size of the adjustment being related to the type of qualification.[31] Moreover, a number of surveys have shown that, of those listed companies which go bankrupt in the UK, only some 20-27 per cent have their last published accounts accompanied by a going concern qualification.[32] It also appears that in most cases these companies have been in fairly advanced states of financial distress.[33] On the other hand, it seems that there are many more surviving companies which receive going concern qualifications, Taffler and Tseung (1984) identifying 40 companies in their sample whose accounts were so qualified, of which only 10 failed.[34] Consequently, if a going concern qualification is interpreted as a strong indicator of likely bankruptcy, there is a misclassification error problem of a similar order to that previously identified where failure prediction models are used to classify failed and non-failed companies. This presumably is one reason why there is little evidence of such qualifications precipitating the automatic collapse of the companies concerned.

The evidence from a series of North American studies is similar, although for failing listed companies there appears to be a considerably higher rate of going concern qualifications in the US.[35] Why this should be so is unclear, although the greater risk there until recently of the auditor being sued for negligence and having to pay larger sums in damages might help to explain the difference.[36]

A matter of some interest in the US is whether going concern qualifications attracted by failing companies have increased following the introduction in 1988 of a new auditing standard similar to SAS 130. So far, the evidence gathered is not entirely clear. Thus a study by Carcello, Hermanson and Huss (1995) found little evidence of a significant change in the practice of Big Six firms in the US over a 20 year period, once industry membership, client size and audit lag had been controlled for. However, their sample related to 446 client companies, all of which went bankrupt. By contrast, another study by Raghunandan and Rama (1995) focused on the incidence of going concern qualifications, regardless of whether the financially distressed companies ultimately went bankrupt, before and after the 'change in regime' in 1988. After controlling for changes in the economic environment, client size, and bankruptcy and audit report lags, they found that the likelihood of auditors issuing going concern qualifications for failed companies increased from 39 per cent prior to 1988 to 62 per cent afterwards. Moreover, the likelihood of such qualifications being made appeared to be linked to some of the criteria which the standard suggests should be referred to by auditors when considering whether to make a going concern qualification, namely, negative working capital, negative operating cash flow, and negative net income. But it was equally clear from the study that the incidence of going concern qualifications for prima facie financially distressed companies which did *not* subsequently go bankrupt also increased, from 22 per cent to 35 per cent.[37]

*Policy implications*

Given the importance of discriminating correctly when making a going concern qualification, it is hardly surprising that auditors – like investors and creditors – should examine all procedures that might give them early warnings of impending failure. As a result, practitioners have been amongst the first to study the reported performance of bankruptcy prediction models, since, if they are successful, their signals could be used either to trigger a going concern qualification (which, of course, is then likely to become a self fulfilling prophecy); or to enable a quantified risk indicator to be published with the accounts.

The latter has in fact recently been canvassed by a research partner in one of the Big Six firms in the UK,[38] but of course to justify this step such indicators have to be regarded as being reliable and capable of communicating information which is not already available to interested parties. Yet the argument presented in this book is basically that such failure prediction models are relatively poor at indicating bankruptcy risk, generally identifying around a fifth of listed industrial companies as potential failures, when only some 2 per cent at most will collapse in any one year. Consequently accountants in public practice, as well as investment and credit analysts, should be very careful before they place uncritical reliance on such indicators.

**Summary**

It is often suggested that there are ways of distinguishing between those companies which are going to fail and those which will survive and prosper. But if this is true, one would expect analysts to learn how to draw such distinctions in a relatively short space of time and develop trading rules in order to try to exploit such information. The predictions should then become self fulfilling, thus extinguishing opportunities to profit from the information.

In the circumstances, it is necessary to consider carefully what exactly is meant by the words 'failure' and 'prediction'. But it is also important to reflect on the nature of the research methodologies that can be applied when studying corporate bankruptcy. In particular, it is appropriate to distinguish between normative theories, which are the result of deductive reasoning; and positive theories, which for the most part are descriptive and are derived from empirical research.

With respect to failure identification studies, there are various problems inherent in the research designs normally used, in particular resulting from the pooling of heterogeneous data and the commonly used matched pairing technique. The most important of these is potential sampling bias, which if fully allowed for will greatly reduce the discriminatory power claimed for the models.

In fact, the forecasts of any model with apparently strong predictive power should soon be incorporated in market assessments of a company's prospects, and this makes it necessary to consider the implications of informational market efficiency. But it is also appropriate to identify users' presumed needs. For instance, there will be some occasions when investors and creditors will expect to have within their portfolios investments and loans which eventually turn out to be worthless. This is the price that has to be paid for portfolio diversification. But the fact that banks provide finance for small businesses, a high proportion of which fail within five years of incorporation, suggests that this is a strategy they feel they have to pursue in order to maximise their profits.

Company directors and auditors have a special interest in being able to identify businesses heading for bankruptcy as they are required to assess and report whether or not a firm is a going concern. Recent changes in regulations and recommendations relating to corporate governance, the directors' operating and financial review and forming an audit opinion are directly concerned with the matter, which is of special interest given the fact that empirical evidence shows that the incidence of going concern audit qualifications is a poor indicator of a company's ultimate fate.

Given this background, it would seem inherently unlikely that bankruptcy identification models will perform well in practice. However, the impression is usually given that they do in fact possess considerable predictive power. Possible explanations of this would seem to be:

(1) The studies reflect the wisdom of hindsight. In fact, the models would seem to be self-fulfilling and do not have much 'ex ante' prediction value for decision makers.
(2) The reported results suggesting that the models perform well are misleading (e.g. because of inadequate allowance for sampling bias and/or unjustified weighting for misclassification errors; or because of some more fundamental artefact in the experimental research designs, such as the widely used procedures of matched pairing and pooling heterogeneous data across industries and over time).
(3) The models do indeed have considerable predictive power and analysts have irrationally ignored their existence.

(4)  The models are innovatory and possess discriminatory power which has yet
     to be acted on by decision makers.

The remainder of this book is divided into two parts, as described in the
Executive Summary. The first provides a critical review of previous research;
while the second provides additional evidence from a series of empirical studies
relating to relatively large samples of British listed companies which failed over
the period 1973-1983.

## Notes

[1] Indeed, this was the experience as far back as the second half of the nineteenth
century (Shannon, 1954). Recent studies in the UK suggest that between 30 per
cent and 40 per cent of small firms fail within five years of their creation, and a
considerably higher percentage if allowance is made for voluntary closures: see
p. 236. However, estimates of attrition rates vary depending on the size
definitions used: generally the smaller the size criterion used, the higher the
casualty rate.

[2] See below, p. 221 et seq., for further discussion of this point.

[3] The search by auditors to find better measures of identifying bankruptcy risk
is examined later in this chapter (pp. 34-41).

[4] A leading US academic, Abdel-khalik (1993, pp. 702-703), has recently
expressed a degree of scepticism about the readiness of researchers to adopt
new statistical procedures to produce indicators of bankruptcy risk. As he puts
it, the ability to discriminate between bankrupt and non-failing firms has 'been
known in the literature for some time, perhaps since the Winakor and Smith
study [of 1935] or even earlier. Historically, it appears that when accountants
are challenged to improve upon the predictive ability of simple ratios, they look
to new techniques ... In brief, a stronger case still needs to be made for
adopting methodological refinement in predicting financial distress.' In fact, it
is widely acknowledged that there are just a few key indicators which enable
analysts to distinguish bankrupt from non-failing companies. Thus, as another
leading US academic, Ohlson (1980, p. 123) has argued, 'four factors derived
from  financial statements ... are significant for purposes of assessing the
probability of bankruptcy ... (i) size ... (ii) ... leverage [i.e. financial structure]
(iii) some performance measure ... [and] (iv) some measure(s) of current
liquidity.'

[5] The underlying data are shown in Appendix 9.1, p. 242.

[6] One of the most recent commentators to suggest that he has an ability to
predict which listed companies will fail is Terry Smith. In the second edition of
his best-seller, *Accounting for Growth* (1996, pp. 189-193), he claims to be
able to recognise them in advance – and not only those which go into
administration, but also those whose share prices collapse.

Such second sight matches that of other seers of the future (e.g. Nostradamus and Old Moore; and, more recently, Mystic Meg, who prefers to tell others how to win the National Lottery rather than doing so herself!) But more to the point, if it is possible to forecast when the price of a particular share is going to fall, one might reasonably expect analysts to use this privileged information to sell short in order to make money. See below, p. 166, and note 14.

[7] Altman (1977) estimated relative error costs for commercial bank loans of misclassifying failed companies as 'non-failing' and non-failing as 'failed' at 7:1.

[8] Economists refer to rewards for possessing special skills as 'rents of ability'.

[9] Guidance on the types of indicator which should be referred to by auditors when assessing going concern status is given in the auditing standard dealing with the subject, SAS 130, para. 31: see below, pp. 37-39.

[10] Kaplan and Urwitz (1979), for instance, examine the main determinants of US corporate bond ratings. For a review of more recent developments in relation to corporate debt, see Altman (1993). Similar research has been undertaken in order to try to establish the main determinants of sovereign risk ratings (i.e. the ratings accorded to bonds issued by governments). Wynn (1993), in fact, reviews ten such studies, which together identify 28 potential independent variables, suggesting a degree of data mining (i.e. analysing data with little or no underlying theory in the hope of finding statistically significant relationships).

[11] This literature is briefly reviewed in chapter 7.

[12] Trading in the market will normally 'adjust' for different attitudes to risk. However, there may well be circumstances when there is limited competition (e.g. between suppliers) where such attitudes may have a significant bearing on a company's ability to survive.

[13] The 'self-fulfilling' argument is in fact recognised in relation to auditors making going concern qualifications by the Cadbury Committee in para. 5.20 of its Code (see below, p. 36). However, there is little evidence of such a 'self-fulfilling' effect in this context (see p. 39 et seq.).

[14] Institutional restrictions prevent certain types of investor (e.g. pension funds) closing short positions. Short trading has also become more difficult in UK conditions now that the fortnightly account system has been abolished. However, there are still opportunities to short trade (e.g. over the five day settlement period, or by 'borrowing' stock), and the workings of the market should not be substantially affected so long as there are enough investors who are free from these constraints.

Evidence on the impact of short selling restrictions on market behaviour is unclear, although they may help to explain why good news tends to be disclosed earlier than bad news (Diamond and Verrecchia, 1987).

More generally, there is empirical evidence in the US that corporate insiders exploit privileged information concerning impending bankruptcy to make profits/reduce losses (e.g. Eyssell, 1991). Clearly their selling activities constitute a 'bad news' signal, and are interpreted as such by the market.

[15] Indeed, this is what has happened in practice, with the forecasts of the Altman ZETA model being sold commercially in the US; and likewise the predictions of the Taffler and Marais models being marketed commercially in the UK. (These models are briefly described in chapter 4.)

[16] For further discussion of normative and positive theories, as well as the role of 'instrumentalism', see Boland (1979).

[17] Recent statistics show that the number of companies filing full accounts fell sharply in 1993-94 and 1994-95 to a mere 34 per cent. This reflects the fact that the proportion of small companies filing abbreviated accounts increased from just over 30 per cent (a ratio which scarcely changed during the ten years which followed the introduction of the concession in 1981) to just under 50 per cent in 1994-95 (*Companies in 1994-95*, HMSO, London, 1995: p. 47). However, there was a reversal of this trend in 1995-96, with the proportion of companies filing full accounts recovering to 38.6 per cent, with only 43.2 per cent of small companies lodging abbreviated accounts (*Companies in 1995-96*, HMSO, London, 1996: p. 43).

[18] The individual's attitude to risk will be represented in his/her 'utility function', measuring subjective preferences. This is sometimes described as a 'loss function' in the context of investment decisions, and it will not be linear if an individual is risk averse.

Individuals' different attitudes to risk are handled in terms of the Capital Asset Pricing Model (CAPM) by applying Tobin's separation theorem: see, for example, Brealey and Myers (1996), ch. 8, and especially p. 179. This permits the market to determine an equilibrium price for a security, leaving the individual to choose the portfolio mix in terms of a risk free asset and the market portfolio of risky assets which suits his/her risk/return preferences. See p. 69 et seq.

[19] A further bias noted by Zmijewski (1984) is that relatively new companies will be censored out of a population if, for instance, five years data are the criterion for inclusion and the company has been in existence or listed for fewer than five years.

[20] The sum of the returns of the four failed companies is .24 and of the four non-failed companies .28. Consequently the average return for the former is .06 and the latter .07, the boundary between the two being .065.

[21] A considerable amount of research over the past decade has been concerned to identify and explain various anomalies, which at first sight appear to suggest that securities markets are informationally inefficient. This is further discussed on p. 180 et seq.

[22] There are losses associated with bankruptcy, of course, which are not only borne by shareholders but also by creditors, management and employees. Such parties will demand compensation for the increased risk that they bear. This in turn will raise a company's credit and salary costs, and other things being equal this should lower its equity value. The theoretical argument is briefly explained on p. 59 et seq.; and an indication of empirical research findings on bankruptcy costs is given in note 7 on p. 84.

[23] Similarly, Doukas (1986) found in a survey of Canadian banks that around half were aware of the existence of bankruptcy prediction models, although very few were using them. This compared with a survey undertaken by Makeever (1984) in the US which showed that 19 out of the largest banks were using bankruptcy prediction or other credit scoring models in commercial loan evaluation. Of these, 11 used their own, internally generated models, 7 Altman's Zeta model (Altman, Haldeman and Narayanan, 1977) (see p. 137), and one a gambler's ruin model (see p. 65 et seq.). Nevertheless, it remains puzzling why, more than 15 years after the apparently impressive performance of the original Altman model was publicised, such a small number of banks were using it or one of its derivatives. After all, if it did offer its users a clear competitive advantage, it might be expected that its use would be near universal amongst the (surviving) population of banks.

[24] See Carty (1996). Credit scoring software packages are now readily available, so the use of such routines is probably greater than in the mid 1980s.

[25] See note 1, above. In the circumstances, it might be regarded as rather strange that the government has sought to reduce mandatory disclosure and auditing requirements for small companies, where the risks to creditors and other third parties are greater than when they deal with larger businesses. Certainly there would potentially seem to be a greater failure in the market for financial information concerning small firms than for large companies.

[26] It could be argued, of course, that for many small businesses the natural expected life is only about five years and failure/liquidation is the normal exit route for creditors and entrepreneurs. Frequently there are no significant 'barriers to entry', so if a firm is successful in the short term it is likely to face fierce competition and will find it difficult to survive unless the owner-managers can adapt and innovate. Generally they lack the expertise or access to financial resources to make the necessary changes, and this is reflected in declining profits and increasing indebtedness.

[27] See note 7, above.

[28] For instance, the fact that directors have addressed the reality of the situation by preparing revised business plans and forecasts may be taken as evidence of a reasonable belief that a company will survive: *Re Sherborne Associates Ltd* [1995] BCC 40.

[29] See *The Times*, Monday, 28 October 1996, p. 47.

[30] The proportion of companies in liquidation or being removed from the register has since fallen steadily, to around 11 per cent in 1996 (*Companies in 1995-96*, HMSO, London, 1996).

[31] e.g. Firth (1978) for the UK; and a number of similar studies for the US, the most recent being that of Choi and Jeter (1992).

Chen and Church (1996) have found that there is less surprise in the market when a company whose accounts have received a going concern qualification subsequently files for bankruptcy. From this they infer that such opinions have information value (although, of course, it could well be that it is just easier for both auditors and analysts to identify the problems which face such companies).

[32] e.g. those of Taffler and Tisshaw (1977) 22 per cent, Taffler and Tseung (1984) 25 per cent, Peel (1989) 27 per cent and Citron and Taffler (1992) 26 per cent. The proportion of the 111 failed companies that formed the basis of the study reported in Part II of this book was 20 per cent.

[33] Taffler and Tseung (1984), Peel (1989) and Citron and Taffler (1992) all found that the qualified companies had very poor risk index scores. Moreover, Taffler & Tseung and Citron & Taffler reported that the financial distress of the great majority of qualified companies was already widely recognised in the financial community.

[34] Citron and Taffler (1992) found that with matched pairs of 'at risk' companies, 21 of the 86 receiving going concern qualifications subsequently failed, compared to 22 from those companies whose accounts were not so qualified.

For the 111 matched pairs used in the study reported in Part II of this book, there were 90 qualifications on the accounts of 59 of the bankrupt group over a five year period prior to failure. This compared to only 25 qualifications on the accounts of 15 of the non-failed companies. Of the 90 qualifications affecting failed firms, 32 were in relation to going concern, affecting 27 different companies, and 22 were attached to the last published accounts. There were no going concern qualifications on the accounts of the companies in the non-failed group.

[35] See Altman and McGough (1974); Altman (1982); Menon and Schwartz (1987); Hopwood, McKeown and Mutchler (1989); McKeown, Mutchler and Hopwood (1991); and Chen and Church (1992). The respective proportions of going concern qualifications observed in the last published accounts of failed companies in these studies are 45 per cent, 48 per cent, 42 per cent, 39 per cent, 40 per cent, 42 per cent and 42 per cent. For further description of this research, see p. 233 et seq.

[36] There is certainly evidence that as risk associated with a client increases, so does the audit fee: e.g. Pratt and Stice (1994).

[37] Likewise Nogler (1995) found that one third of his sample of relatively large US companies whose accounts received going concern qualifications

47

subsequently filed for bankruptcy. But another third changed their status for other reasons, usually surviving as the result of a merger, although this still left around 35 per cent misclassified as prima facie failures.

[38] See *Accountancy*, July 1995, p. 16.


## Appendix 1.1

*Sampling bias error*

As Palepu (1986, pp. 6-11) explains, the misclassification error induced by state (or choice) based sampling can fairly easily be calculated. Thus the sample forecast error rate, $e'$, is

$$e' = (m_1 + m_2)/(n_1 + n_2) \qquad (1.1)$$

> where $m_1$ is the number of failed firms in a sample $n_1$ that are misclassified; and
> $m_2$ is the number of non-failed firms in a sample $n_2$ that are misclassified.

Hence it will be claimed from the sample that a model has a success rate in classifying companies of

$$1 - e' \qquad (1.2)$$

Where the population proportions are not as reflected in the sample, the expected error rate in the population, $e$, will be

$$e = [N_1(m_1/n_1)+N_2(m_2/n_2)]/(N_1+N_2) \qquad (1.3)$$

> where $N_1$ and $N_2$ are respectively the true numbers of failed and non-failed companies in the population.

The true classification success rate is therefore

$$1 - e \qquad (1.4)$$

To illustrate the problem, suppose the following is the result of a matched pair experiment, involving 50 failed and 50 non-failed companies: a model's classification error rates are 2 per cent for failed companies and 10 per cent for non-failed companies. However, the entire population of companies is 2,000, and although all failures are represented in the sample, only 50 out of 1,950 non-failed companies are.

The values to be inserted into expressions (1.1) and (1.3) are:

$$m_1 = 1; m_2 = 5; n_1 = 50; n_2 = 50; N_1 = 50; N_2 = 1,950$$

So expression (1.1) is

$e' = (1+5)/(50+50)$
$\quad = 6$ per cent.

(i.e. the model will claim a classification success rate of 94 per cent).

However, expression (1.3) shows the true rate is

$e = [50(1/50)+1,950(5/50)]/(50+1,950)$
$\quad = [1+195]/2,000$
$\quad = 9.8$ per cent.

(i.e. the model's classification success rate is really 90.2 per cent).

Closer examination will show that the critical factor is the misclassification rate of non-failed companies. The greater this is, the less successful will be a model. Here the implication is that, while all 50 failing companies are correctly identified, another 195 businesses which would otherwise survive are classified as prima facie 'failures'. If the model is to be believed, presumably these 195 concerns will be forced into bankruptcy.

If the cost of such a misclassification is regarded as too great, the model will not be used.

# Part One
## PREVIOUS RESEARCH

# 2 Normative theories of corporate failure

## Introduction

In most studies on corporate bankruptcy there is generally little or no reference to a specific 'normative theory' which might explain why a certain number of businesses might be expected to fail, nor even a clear identification of a 'positive theory' which could attempt to explain why they do. Yet there are in fact several normative theories which are relevant to such studies. One group can be described as 'disequilibrium theories'. These include those which focus on extraneous shocks, such as is envisaged in chaos and catastrophe theories. A similar approach is based on the notion of 'homeostasis', a phenomenon more usually associated with the natural sciences. Other theories are related to specific economic causes (e.g. related to market structure, capital structure, and the location of firms).

But as Scott (1981) has noted, there are also four normative finance theories which help to explain corporate bankruptcy: a single period option pricing model; the gambler's ruin model, where there is no access to outside capital markets; a similar model, where however there is perfect access to outside funding; and a hybrid of the last two, when there is imperfect access to outside capital.

In dealing with the last two models it is necessary to consider how the market prices shares in a company. It is therefore appropriate to examine (albeit briefly) various theories of share valuation.

More recently the bankruptcy phenomenon has been analysed within a contracting (or agency) framework. This attempts to take account of the potential conflicts of interest between creditors and shareholders, and it therefore offers new insights into the corporate failure process.

Finally there are what might appear at first sight to be normative theories developed by writers on management and business strategy. However, on closer inspection it seems that they are more positive in nature, having generally been derived from a close study of companies that have failed. Essentially what they identify are various weaknesses in the strategic management of companies.

The primary aim of this chapter is to summarise competing normative theories and to indicate how models can be – and have been – developed to test various underlying propositions. However, an understanding of the basic normative concepts also provides a benchmark against which positive theories (and the empirical models from which they are derived) can be assessed.

Much of the empirical evidence which indicates whether or not the normative theories seem to hold in practice will be reviewed in chapter 4.

## Disequilibrium models of corporate failure

*Chaos and catastrophe theories*

In recent years chaos and catastrophe theories have attracted a good deal of comment from outside the academic world. In fact, each in its own way is concerned with the impact of disequilibrating shocks on a system, but they are essentially descriptive models. In other words, they identify the symptoms of a problem but not its causes. Consequently they provide no easy remedies. All that they succeed in doing is further understanding of the nature of the problem.

Chaos theory is often described in terms of the potential impact of a relatively minor disturbance on a system which has major disequilibrating consequences through a series of knock on effects. Thus the beat of the wings of a butterfly in the Brazilian jungle could conceivably trigger off a series of other disturbances to ecological and climatological systems, culminating perhaps in a hurricane that could wreak havoc in, say, the southern United States.

The point about such a theory is that the original minor disequilibrating event and its conjunction with a series of subsequent events, culminating in a major disturbance to a system, can be regarded as extraneous to it and largely uncontrollable. The theory lends itself to mathematical analysis, much of it based on the notion of unpredictable shocks and stochastic processes (i.e. random walks), statistical concepts which are already well recognised in economic and financial research.[1]

Catastrophe theory can also be useful in explaining a variety of observed phenomena, including the nature of social systems, but it too does not offer an easy remedy to a problem. It merely helps to identify it.

Basically the theory is concerned with different points of potential equilibrium in a system and analyses the effects of sudden, discontinuous changes following a period of more gradual and smoother change. This is illustrated diagrammatically in Figure 2.1. However, it is probably easiest to understand the argument if the plane shown there is thought of as a length of cloth. It can then be seen that in the middle of the cloth there is a fold, so that half the length of the cloth is horizontal at one level, while the other half is horizontal at a lower level. The fold (or kink) occurs half way across the full length of the cloth, and at a given point there is a sudden drop from one level to the lower level.

It can be seen from the diagram that there are three lines, representing two 'control' variables and one 'state' variable. In terms of corporate bankruptcy the latter can be regarded as representing one of two states: 'fail' and 'non-fail'. The control variables can be regarded as reflecting two attributes of a company – say profitability (e.g. rate of return on capital employed, ROCE); and a measure of risk (e.g. a gearing ratio). The 'control variables' are the independent (or explanatory) variables which determine the state (or dependent) variable.

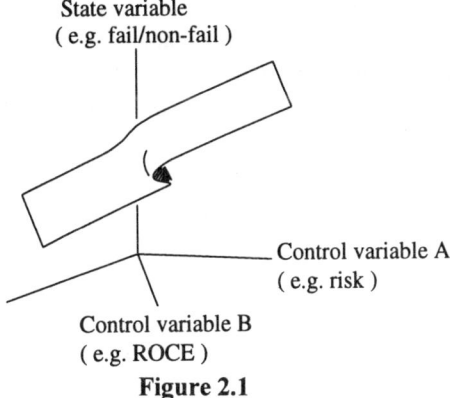

State variable
( e.g. fail/non-fail )

Control variable A
( e.g. risk )

Control variable B
( e.g. ROCE )

**Figure 2.1**

The elements shown in Figure 2.1 can be projected onto another plane, as illustrated in Figure 2.2. There a 'normal' variable (e.g. ROCE) is distinguished from a 'splitting' variable (e.g. risk).

In terms of the parallel drawn with a length of cloth, the splitting variable indicates where across its width the fold commences. In fact, Figure 2.2 illustrates a cusp, so this version of the model is known as the 'cusp catastrophe model'.

'Normal' variable b

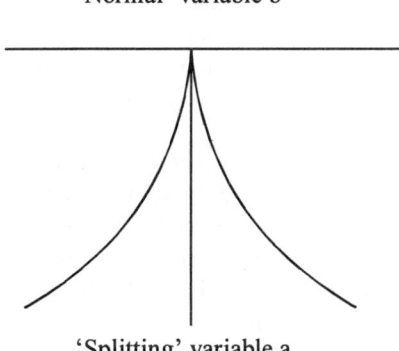

'Splitting' variable a

**Figure 2.2**

Clearly in practice it might well be that, over a given range, there is no clear cu distinction in terms of the ROCE and risk variables between firms which are failures and those which are non-failures. In other words, although it might be fairly easy to distinguish those firms which are obviously insolvent from those which are financially very strong, there may well be a 'grey area' in the middle where it is difficult to discriminate successfully between the two categories.

One way of trying to sharpen the discriminatory power is to introduce a third or fourth explanatory variable into the process. This allows for a more complex fold in the cloth. Essentially what happens is that an area is created where combinations of high (low) values of the independent variables to some extent offset each other, producing a 'pocket of compromise'. This is illustrated in Figure 2.3.

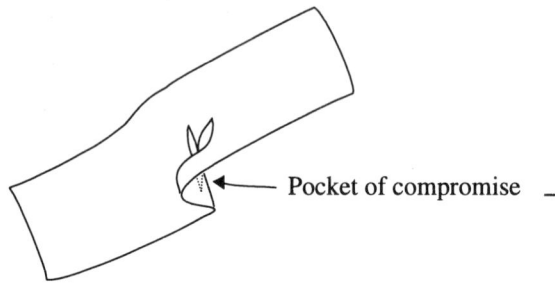

**Figure 2.3**

When this is projected onto another plane, in the same way that Figure 2.2 was derived from Figure 2.1, the diagram becomes relatively complex. Because the result looks something like a butterfly, this version of the model is known as the 'butterfly catastrophe model'.

The potential relevance of the catastrophe model in the context of corporate bankruptcy was first identified by Ho and Saunders (1980). They applied it in the context of bank regulation in the US, arguing that failure was unlikely to be the result of a gradual process of decline, but rather a sudden collapse initiated by the actions of the regulator.[2]

Subsequently Scapens, Ryan and Fletcher (1981) also argued that catastrophe theory provides useful insights into the way in which corporate failure occurs. However, although it can be formulated mathematically, the catastrophe model is not strictly operational in an economic context, since – as Dodgson (1982) has pointed out – it is really only applicable where there are multiple disequilibria. Nevertheless, the approach offers an alternative perspective of how the statistically derived models described in later chapters may be viewed.

Another disequilibrium framework is provided by Shannon's entropy theory, as developed by Theil and, in particular, Lev (1969a). The basic argument is that systems tend to move towards equilibrium in response to extraneous 'shocks'. The parallel drawn is with the 'homeostasis' phenomenon, well known in the biological sciences, whereby systems naturally seem to revert towards a new equilibrium following an external 'disturbance' (e.g. the way the body heals after an injury).

The entropy measures described by Theil and Lev are based on probability theory and are concerned to identify the size of adjustments over time. In an accounting context this can be done, for instance, in terms of the significance of the *structural change* in assets and claims over a year or a period of years. In terms of corporate bankruptcy, according to Lev (1969a, 1971), it might reasonably be expected that companies facing financial problems would experience large changes in the composition of the assets and claims categories in their balance sheets, reflecting disequilibrating shocks. These changes would be difficult to control, and it would therefore seem likely that such changes would be symptomatic of companies which subsequently went bankrupt.

Rather than measure change merely in terms of shifts in the proportions of assets and claims in successive balance sheets, Theil and Lev suggest that an entropy measure should be used to identify the size of movements in assets and claims. The informational decomposition measure they propose is derived from probability theory, and in many respects it is not dissimilar from the standard statistical procedure of analysis of variance (ANOVA), except that it can be applied to data which are not normally distributed and to ordinal scale variables (such as rankings).

In fact, the informational decomposition measure is not difficult to calculate and can be applied as a screening device to assess the magnitude of changes in the fractional structure of balance sheet categories. The basis of the calculation and various methodological issues are outlined in Appendix 2.1 at the end of this chapter.

The procedure has been applied on a number of occasions in empirical studies, the first such study being that of Lev (1971). He examined changes in the financial structure of businesses as they approached bankruptcy using entropy measures to see whether failing companies were subject to greater destabilising shocks than non-failing businesses. His results for a sample of 37 companies and their matched pairs were encouraging. For this purpose he used five balance sheet categories as the basis for calculating his informational decomposition measures. The combined balance sheet measure was a better identifier of failed firms than 12 of 13 ratios used separately as alternative indicators of bankruptcy status, the one ratio to perform better being cash flow/debt.[3]

Despite these encouraging results, researchers preferred to use other models which appeared to have stronger discriminatory power between failed and non-failed businesses. Thus Moyer (1977) used the balance sheet decomposition measure and the cash flow/debt ratio as independent variables in a discriminant model to see how they performed against the (relatively crude) discriminant model developed by Altman (1968).[4] He concluded that while his model performed reasonably well, it was inferior to Altman's; and that the cash flow/debt variable was a better single variable discriminator than the balance sheet informational decomposition measure.

Subsequent research did not alter this perception. Thus few of the many multivariate studies undertaken to try to identify failing companies have incorporated an entropy measure in the variable sets examined, and even fewer have found that such a variable has explanatory power.[5] Other studies directly applying entropy theory, while confirming that balance sheet decomposition measures were greater for failed than non-failed firms, have found that financial ratio models discriminate better between the two groups.

This was the result determined by Walker, Stowe and Moriarty (1979) on a very small sample of 8 failed and 8 non-failed Australian companies over a nine year period. They found that both the decomposition measures and the most relevant of 20 ratios discriminated quite well in the last three years prior to failure.

Booth (1983) tested the procedure on data covering the period 1964-1979 for 35 matched pairs of companies. He used four decomposition measures, and he found that both the size and the coefficient of variation of the claims decomposition measures were significantly greater for failed companies than for non-failed businesses. However, when the decomposition measures were included in a discriminant model derived from the data of 22 failed and 22 non-failed companies between 1964 and 1968, the results were less encouraging. Although misclassification errors were only 18 per cent for failed companies and 12 per cent for non-failed, these rose to 25 per cent and 50 per cent respectively on a hold out sample for the years 1973-1979. A further test on another hold out sample produced no greater accuracy, and when allowance is made for the sampling bias problem it can be seen that there was little if any potentially useful discriminatory power in the model.

More recently Booth and Hutchinson (1989) compared five years data within the period 1964-1979 for a sample of 33 failed Australian groups against those of 33 newly listed companies. They tested hypotheses to see whether balance sheet decomposition measures, both in terms of their size and coefficients of variation, were different as between the failing and newly launched (and hence probably rapidly growing) companies. In fact, they could not identify any significant differences between the two types of company. This was perhaps not all that surprising, since while failing firms typically exhibit lower profitability, lower liquidity and higher gearing than non-failing firms, businesses which are growing rapidly similarly experience increases in profitability, reduced liquidity and higher leverage. As a result, one might a priori have expected balance sheet decomposition measures – which focus on change, regardless of direction – to be not dissimilar between failing and rapidly growing concerns.

*Economic theories*

Economics, in the form of the theory of the firm and theories of managerial and industrial economics, has relatively little to say directly about corporate bankruptcy, although in global terms it identifies a number of phenomena which can lead to a weakening in a company's market position and which, if not addressed, can lead to its demise.

*(i) Microeconomic theory.* The basis of much microeconomic analysis is the study of disequilibrium and the ways in which the economic system, working through the market mechanism, reacts to destabilising events. The effects of disturbance to the economic system at the firm level are seen to be a possible erosion of a company's competitive advantage because of a variety of factors, including shifts in its demand curve as consumers' tastes and incomes alter; changes in the price elasticity of its products; changes in its production function (i.e. the combination of inputs required to produce a given output); and a lack of ability to match innovation by its rivals which can make its products inferior.

*(ii) Theories of industrial and managerial economics.* An issue which has long concerned industrial economists is *market structure*: i.e. why a few companies dominate some industries, while in others there is far less concentration of power. In fact, it is possible to identify three underlying factors which help to explain these differences: the entry characteristics of an industry; its exit characteristics; and its growth characteristics. All three have been the subject of a substantial amount of empirical research, giving rise to positive theories which seem to explain some of the observed phenomena.[6]

*(iii) Entry characteristics of an industry.* In many industries there are likely to be significant 'barriers to entry', especially where market demand is more-or-less fixed. Some barriers will be absolute: for example, where a company owns key assets for which there are no close substitutes (e.g. land or mineral resources); or where there is a legally enforceable monopoly. Others arise because of the nature of the cost function in an industry, so that small companies are unable to benefit from economies of scale and compete with larger rivals. This may mean that large and diversified companies have a potential advantage over smaller competitors if individual investors cannot achieve the same levels of diversification for themselves, a point referred to below. Incidentally, it should be noted that in this

context diversification does not merely refer to a situation where a company has interests in a portfolio of different industry sectors. Companies can also diversify geographically, within national boundaries and internationally.

Where possible, existing companies might be expected to erect their own barriers to entry, most obviously by engaging in predatory pricing and by differentiating their products through branding and then promoting them through advertising. Other barriers can be created by engaging in research and development (R&D) activity and seeking patents which give firms exclusive rights to market innovatory products. Clearly it is only feasible to do this where an industry is subject to technical change. However, the direction of causality is not always easy to determine. Is it the expense of investing in R&D and advertising which creates a cost advantage and thus helps to determine the level of concentration in an industry? Or instead is it the level of concentration that encourages companies to erect such barriers to entry? Moreover, the dynamics of technical change are such that sometimes the very basis of a company's competitive advantage is changed. Thus, for example, the development of the microchip radically altered the cost characteristics in the computer mainframe industry, and IBM rapidly found its market dominance across the world was undermined.

*(iv) Exit characteristics of an industry.* The 'exit characteristics' of an industry relate to *mergers* and *bankruptcies*. Economists generally try to explain the former in terms of companies taking advantage of potential economies of scale and so reducing their costs. Alternatively it is seen as one way of trying to circumvent a barrier to entry, or of providing an opportunity for managers to pursue their own objectives within the constraints set by market forces.

By contrast, there is little in the industrial economics literature itself concerning bankruptcy, except in relation to the risk associated with raising finance,[7] and the growth characteristics of firms in a particular industry (see below, p. 63).

*(v) Finance theory: the firm viewpoint.* Basically, a firm's *economic risk* can be regarded as being related to the industry in which it operates and to general economic conditions. The latter cannot be diversified away by an investor, and essentially it is only this element of *systematic* economic risk that should be priced in the market place.

Economic risk will be reflected in the variability of a company's earnings over time, which in turn will be the result both of fluctuations in its gross revenues and the extent to which its costs are fixed rather than variable. However, where a company chooses to finance its operations by borrowing it adds a further layer of *financial risk* to its risk structure, and the (substantially fixed) interest payments will further accentuate the variability of net earnings.

It is fairly easy to demonstrate that if

(1) there are no transactions costs or barriers to the free flow of information in securities markets;
(2) there are no corporate income taxes;
(3) individual investors can borrow or lend at the same market rate as companies; and
(4) there is no possibility of bankruptcy

the value of a firm is independent of its debt/equity mix. This is because investors can adjust for a company's financial gearing by varying the levels of debt and equity that they hold in their portfolios: i.e. homemade gearing is a perfect substitute for corporate gearing. The fact that under these conditions the value of the firm is unaffected by the debt/equity mix chosen by a firm is shown in Figure 2.4 as the horizontal line AA'.

However, when the second of the conditions listed above is relaxed, and debt interest attracts relief from corporate income taxes, the value of the firm will increase the greater the debt/equity ratio. This is illustrated as line BB' in Figure 2.4, and the logic is that a company should gear up as much as possible to take advantage of the tax shield, so $X_B$ is optimal.

A moment's reflection will show that if the third of the above conditions holds – investors can borrow or lend at the same market rate of interest as firms – individuals will prefer the company to raise debt rather than borrow themselves as it will be able to shift some of the risk of bankruptcy onto creditors because of its limited liability status. However, it is unrealistic to assume that creditors will not demand full compensation for taking on this risk.

In fact, it is easiest to analyse the situation by assuming that a company can insure itself against bankruptcy risk. If, unrealistically, the present value of the expected pay-outs by the insurer exactly equals the present value of the insurance premiums, the effect will be entirely neutral, and the optimal capital structure in terms of the debt/equity mix will again be $X_B$ in Figure 2.4. But in the more likely event that the risk averse insurer sets premium rates to cover its costs and to earn a profit, the expected net present value of the insurance transaction is negative from the policy holder's viewpoint. This means that the size of the negative expected net present value will after all depend on a company's debt/equity mix. Yet, as shown in Figure 2.4, the optimal level of gearing will vary between firms operating in different industries depending on the economic risks to which they are subject, reflected in the volatility of their pre-interest earnings or net cash inflows. Thus $X_C$ is the optimal debt/equity mix for a company exposed to relatively high economic risk, and $X_D$ the optimum for a company exposed to a rather lower level of economic risk. Essentially the probability of investors facing a gambler's ruin situation will be greater where the volatility of earnings or net cash flows after charging interest is high, a point examined below (p. 65 et seq.)

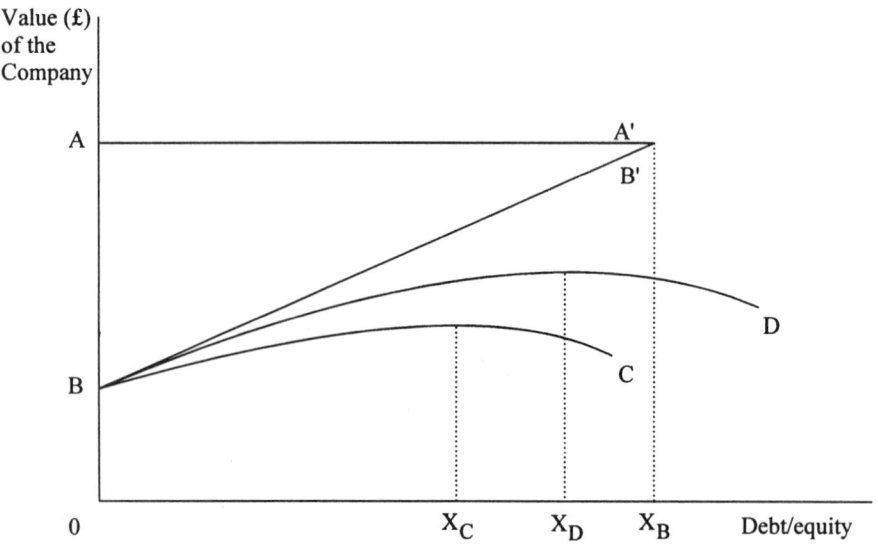

**Figure 2.4**

In practice, the first of the above conditions – no transactions costs or barriers to the free flow of information in securities markets – does not hold. Thus, for instance, companies attempt to pursue stable dividend policies, partly to meet the requirements of various 'clienteles' of shareholders (e.g. pension schemes can recover some of the tax imputed to be borne on dividends, and they also concentrate investment in 'trustee' securities which must have unbroken records of dividend payments). Dividend policy is equally used to signal management's expectations about a company's future prospects, although it is possible to offer the option of 'scrip' dividends to help offset the impact of capital rationing. The latter is generally present for all companies, however large, if only because it is far from costless to raise funds, and in particular it is infeasible to issue equity on a continuous basis as and when new capital is required. These imperfections in the market further accentuate the importance of the level of gearing in determining a company's value.

*(vi) Finance theory: the investor viewpoint.* It is also instructive to try to view bankruptcy risk from the viewpoint of equity shareholders, creditors or employees, who typically hold portfolios of assets. They will normally have to adjust their holdings to maintain the desired risk/return balance if one of the assets suffers a sharp fall in value, and this is particularly important for parties whose asset holdings are not well diversified: e.g. most employees and some types of creditor, as well as private equity investors who typically hold only 4-8 securities in their portfolios. The result is that these individuals will search for early warnings of

potential bankruptcy, and the procedure which provides most information in relation to search costs ought to be preferred.

But the point ought to be made that interested parties may deliberately invest in some securities which have a high risk of failure so long as they are expected to provide the desired risk/return mix. Thus, to repeat the example given in chapter 1, it is possible to consider an individual who invests in two companies, one totally reliant on oil for its manufacturing process, the other on coal. If there is an unforeseen hike in oil prices expressed in $, either because of the activities of a cartel or because of a sudden shift in exchange rate parities, the former may have to go into liquidation, whereas to compensate the latter would increase its prospective profitability and value. Likewise the reverse might be true if there were an unexpected fall in the price of crude. Other things being equal, it is not obvious how the investor is worse off under such an arrangement than from, say, investing in a conglomerate whose activities are comparable and which embrace manufacturing using both oil and coal. What an investor really requires is *prior knowledge* of an event that will occur, here the occurrence and the direction of the oil price/exchange rate shock. In an informationally efficient market setting it seems intuitively unlikely that a failure identification model derived from variables (such as financial ratios) reflecting hindsight data will necessarily be of much help.

*(vii) The growth characteristics of an industry.* As indicated previously, the incidence of bankruptcy has also been discussed in the industrial economics literature in another context, namely the growth characteristics of an industry. The focus of interest is then the survival of firms and, for a given technological environment, their optimal size within an industry.

In fact, industrial economists have approached the problem in two distinct ways, effectively developing positive rather than normative theories which explain firms' growth characteristics. The 'traditional' approach is to examine statistical growth and survival patterns over time. More recently, however, it has become commonplace to apply other procedures within a given period in order to examine firms' entry and exit behaviour. One such approach is to analyse the problem in terms of mixed strategy game theory. In this context it has been found helpful not just to identify a unique equilibrium, but rather a space (or configuration) in which businesses can survive at different equilibrium points.[8]

In terms of the traditional time series approach, it is evident in most studies of market concentration that in many sectors a relatively small number of companies dominate an industry, but there is a large 'tail' of small firms which, in the short term at any rate, survive. When the logarithm of size is taken the distribution appears to be normally distributed (i.e. it follows the classic bell shape), hence its description as a *lognormal* distribution. What has interested economists is that this pattern seems to persist over a period of years, suggesting that the size distributions of firms observed at different points in time are the result of random shocks.

The process of random growth leading to a lognormal distribution is often referred to as Gibrat's *Law of Proportionate Effect*. According to this there should be three components of growth producing the lognormal pattern: first, a systematic growth rate related to the market in general; second, a growth path related to the initial size of a firm; and third, a random error term. Gibrat's Law relates to the second component and suggests that size should have no effect on growth.

A number of studies, both in the UK and the US, have shown that there is indeed some evidence that the rate of growth is independent of firm size, but this finding is by no means universal. As a result, interest has also focused on the impact of the birth and death rates of firms, in particular examining the survival of firms over time.

*(viii) The location of firms.* One particular variable that is sometimes felt to have a critical bearing on the likelihood of a firm surviving or failing is its location, since this may significantly determine its competitive advantage over its rivals. In particular, it is likely to determine its cost function.

As might be expected, such an argument appeals to economic geographers, who have undertaken empirical investigations using spatial analysis to try to identify key differences in firm behaviour in different locations (e.g. concerning the incidence of firm births and deaths in specific industry categories, as well as their growth rates over time).[9]

## Financial models of corporate failure

As indicated previously, Scott (1981) identifies four normative financial models which explain bankruptcy.

### The single period option pricing model

The first of these is a single period option pricing model, similar to that derived by Black and Scholes (1973). A *call option* gives its owner the right to buy a security at a specified exercise price, and the critical dates are the beginning and end of a period, the former being the time when the option is valued and the latter the time when the option can be exercised.

One can view a company which has issued debt as being acquired by the debt holders. The equity shareholders have a call option to buy it back by paying off the debt. However, they will not exercise this option if the company is worthless, and the creditors will have to bear the loss.

For the purpose in hand, the value of a company's equity can be viewed as a call option which will be valuable to shareholders at the maturity date of any debt (D) outstanding only if the total market value of the company (i.e. debt plus equity, MV) is greater than the debt obligation: i.e. if MV>D.

The value of such a call option is determined by a number of factors, notably the rate of interest, the length of time to the option's expiry date, and the probability of the value of the company increasing. In fact, it is the last of these which is crucial, since the greater the variability of the company's total market value, the greater will be the value of the call option.

This can be appreciated by considering a call option which allows the holder to purchase shares for £100 in a week's time. Clearly if the value of the share rises above £100 (say to £120), the option has a value at the expiry date of £120 - £100 = £20. However, if the value is below £100 at the expiry date the option will be worthless – i.e. it will not be exercised. But it should be noted that the value will only be £20 at the option expiry date. If that is still some way off, even if it were certain that the share price would remain at £120, the £20 would have to be discounted to a present value. In practice, the price may well *not* be £120, so the possibility of the price being above or below the exercise price has to be considered as well. Fairly obviously, the greater the variability of the share price, the greater the chance that the value will be above £120 at the option expiry date.

In the circumstances, the value of an option relating to a company as a whole is basically determined as

$$\frac{[E(MV) - E(D)]}{var\ MV} \tag{2.1}$$

where var MV is the variance of MV;
MV is the market value of a firm (i.e. debt plus equity);
D is the redemption value (i.e. loan stock or debts in general);
and E(.) is an expectations operator (i.e. the expression within the brackets is expected rather than observed).

*The gambler's ruin model with no access to capital*

The second way of explaining bankruptcy is to refer to the gambler's ruin model but assuming that there is no access to security markets to raise capital. Under this approach it is assumed that in any given period a company will experience either a positive or negative cash flow. The probability of a positive cash flow is p, that of a negative cash flow is q. It follows that over a sequence of periods there is one possible compound probability that cash flows will always be negative. In such an eventuality the company will ultimately run out of cash, at which point it will have reached the 'absorbing state', bankruptcy. This is illustrated in Figure 2.5, in which the hatched downward path from N shows the route to failure.

Clearly there is a probability for every company that it may ultimately fail, although for most blue chip concerns this will be extremely remote.

The basic determinant of failure under this model is

$$\frac{[\text{mean CF} + \text{NA}]}{\text{var CF}} \qquad (2.2)$$

where CF is cash flow;

NA is net assets (here at liquidation value);

and var represents the variance

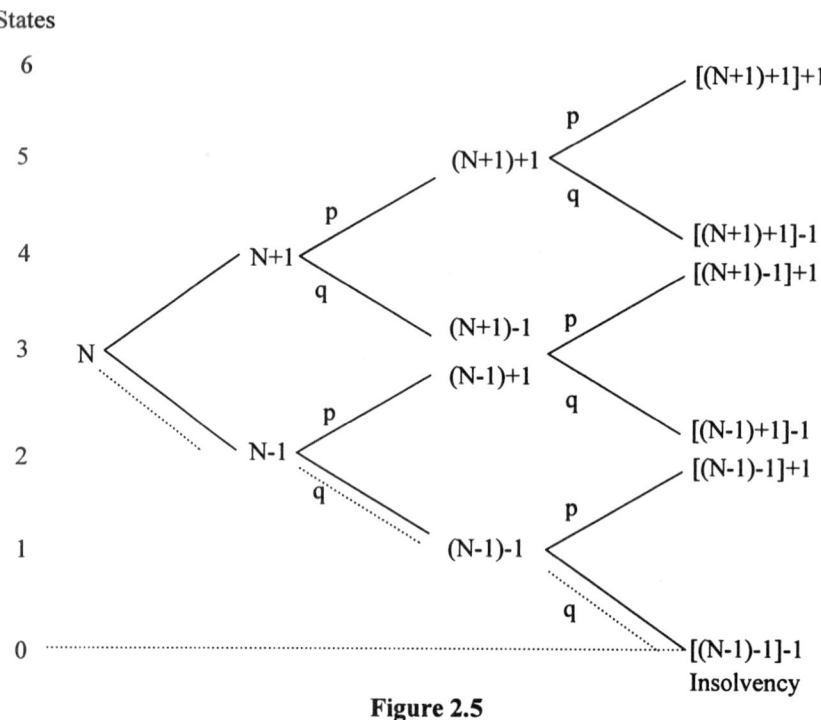

**Figure 2.5**

*The gambler's ruin model with perfect access to capital*

The third normative model drops the restriction that there is no possibility of raising further capital. In such circumstances not all losses have to be met by selling assets. Instead new shares can be issued or loans raised. Under this scenario a company will be solvent so long as the equity market value is greater than zero.

66

Thus so long as the equity value is expected to be greater after new finance has been raised than previously, the company will not be liquidated.

The basic determinant of failure under this model is therefore

$$\frac{[\text{mean CF} + \text{MV}]}{\text{var CF}} \tag{2.3}$$

where CF  is cash flow;
MV is the market value of equity;
and var  represents the variance.

### The gambler's ruin model with imperfect access to capital

In practice companies do not have perfect access to capital markets but face some form of capital rationing. The above model therefore has to be modified to allow for the costs of raising finance; the impact of the tax system, which may favour the use of retained profits for investment; and other market imperfections.

In such circumstances, the increasing size of a company will tend to reduce risk where the expense of raising capital involves fixed costs. Likewise, imperfect markets for a company's assets suggest there are significant differences between a company's going concern value and the liquidation value of its net assets – in which case, a liquidity indicator potentially becomes a significant measure of the risk of bankruptcy. In particular, a company's ability to survive will depend on the time over which it can carry on when all its other sources of finance are cut off. This can be measured in terms of funds flow indicators or the so-called 'no-credit-interval', discussed below on p. 102.

A further problem is that when a company begins to experience financial distress it may have to sell off its most liquid assets. This may well leave it with an unbalanced portfolio of assets which will impair its ability to operate as efficiently as before.

### The impact of inflation

Scott (1981) does not specifically deal with the likely impact of inflation, but this issue has been discussed by Wadhwani (1984a). He argues that in the absence of formal indexation of loans, inflation is likely to accentuate the problems of companies with imperfect access to capital, since if costs tend to rise faster than revenues it will lower their net cash inflows as well as squeeze their profits. This in turn will reduce interest cover ratios and raise the default premium on debt. This would also tend to depress share prices, which (according to Modigliani and Cohn, 1979) may be systematically undervalued during periods of inflation.[10]

67

*Inferences from gambler's ruin models*

It should be noted that in developing the above models a measure of profit – such as earnings before interest and tax (EBIT) – could be substituted as a proxy for cash flows (CF). It can also be seen that all the models except the second involve reference to the market value of a company or its shareholders' equity interest. This creates a problem since from a 'prediction' perspective it really puts the cart before the horse, as presumably such market values will already reflect analysts' best perceptions of the probability of a company failing. Consequently, if markets are reasonably informationally efficient, market prices should substantially reflect the likelihood of a company failing. It therefore follows that it should be sufficient merely to study the behaviour of share prices rather than test the models posited.

In the circumstances, perhaps the best way to try to test the normative models empirically would seem to be to apply the restricted gambler's ruin model (i.e. equation (2.2) above), which exclusively employs published accounting indicators. Its 'predictive' power can then be assessed against the behaviour of share prices.

However, because of market imperfections it may well be that a relatively naive version of the gambler's ruin model will be less 'efficient' in identifying potentially failing companies than other models which capture alternative attributes, such as size, indebtedness and liquidity. Consequently it is desirable to compare the classificational accuracy of gambler's ruin models against such empirically derived models as well as against share price behaviour.

*Applications of the gambler's ruin model*

Various approximations to the gambler's ruin model can be used to test the theory. Wilcox (1971, 1973) developed a relatively naive version with two key indicators: cash flow; and cash position (i.e. liquidation value). Statistics can then be calculated showing the likelihood of insolvency and the expected life of a company.[11] Wilcox (1973) tested the model on 41 pairs of outwardly similar US companies, one of which in each pair had failed during the period 1949-1971. A minimum of five years data were required for each company so that cumulative means and variances could be calculated, and for many firms in the population up to nine years data were available. However, it is fairly clear that if a company suffers a decline in its annual operating cash flow – which is likely if it gets into financial difficulties – this will not only lower the mean cash flow, but it will also almost certainly increase the variance. Nevertheless, without adjusting for sample selection bias, the percentages of correct pairwise classifications for the five years prior to failure were impressive: year -1 94 per cent, -2 90 per cent, -3 88 per cent, -4 90 per cent, and -5 76 per cent.

One problem with the Wilcox model is that it only allows the cash position to worsen or improve each period, when perhaps the most likely outcome is no significant change (Benishay, 1973). In the circumstances it is useful to refer to the rather more complex versions of the gambler's ruin model that were developed by Santomero and Vinso (1977) and Vinso (1979). The former focused on the banking industry, the latter on another group of US regulated companies, electricity utilities.

In their study, Santomero and Vinso re-emphasised Benishay's point that the Wilcox model assumes a zero or negative drift in cash flows, which is unrealistic in most industries. They therefore developed a more complex measure of risk exposure and applied this to 224 banks which filed weekly returns with the Federal Reserve over a nine year period, 1965-1973. Of these, 37 could be classified as being at risk. Further analysis showed that more conventional measures of banking risk (such as the capital/asset ratio) substantially agreed with the risk index produced by the gambler's ruin model.

Vinso later developed indices of safety and the risk of ruin, and he compared these against bond ratings for 20 electricity companies and, as a control group, another 20 but vulnerable concerns. The safety index correlated well with bond ratings,[12] and the indicators were more accurate discriminators than either Altman's Z-score index and Wilcox's version of the gambler's ruin model.[13]

Wilcox's model remains the best known version of the gambler's ruin model, and it has been used in one study as a means of determining likely failures so that their share price behaviour could be examined (Katz, Lilien and Nelson, 1985).[14]

**Valuation theories**

Of the four models described in the previous section, three required that a company and/or its shares should be valued. It is therefore appropriate at this stage in the argument to consider briefly a number of valuation models that might be applied.[15]

The basic form of an 'intrinsic' share valuation model is

$$V_0 = \frac{1}{1+k} (D_1 + V_1) \tag{2.4}$$

where $V$ = the capitalised market value of a company;
$D$ = dividends
$k$ = the rate of return required by shareholders;
and the subscripts relate to time.

Assuming constant prices, if a company were to pay out all its earnings as dividends, its stock of assets would presumably remain constant. In other words, it would merely replace its wasting fixed assets from funds retained within the business as a result of making provision for depreciation.

In such circumstances it would not be unreasonable to expect sustainable earnings (E) to equal dividends (D) over the long run and be a constant, as shown in the following diagram:

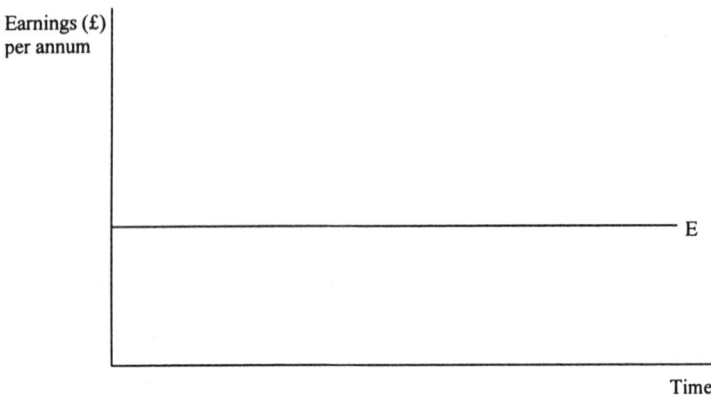

**Figure 2.6**

The intrinsic value of the company would then simply be the present value of a perpetuity of constant cash flows or their transform, earnings (E), namely

$$V_0 = \frac{E_1}{k} \qquad (2.5)$$

In practice companies typically do *not* pay out all their profits as dividends but instead use part of them to add to their stock of net assets. As a result profits will not be expected to be a constant, but instead can be expected to follow a growth path. The finance literature has explored the possibilities at some length, but the most obvious assumption to make is that a company's asset base, and hence its profits, will expand at a constant rate, g, giving rise to a projected cash flow/earnings stream of the form shown in Figure 2.7.

The valuation model then becomes

$$V_0 = \frac{E_1}{k - g} \qquad (2.6)$$

Other models (such as the well known Gordon growth model) are described in finance texts, but the basic argument is the same. Moreover, they usually include a term which is the present value of a perpetuity of earnings, which indicates that

70

what investors *collectively* want is, firstly, a signal of sustainable future earnings; and, secondly, a signal of the growth strategy being pursued by a business.

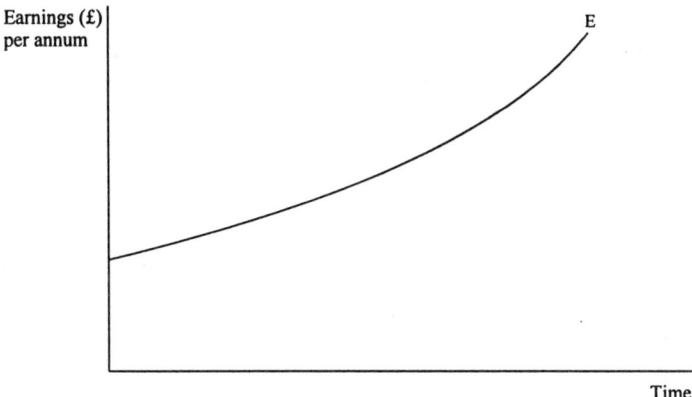

**Figure 2.7**

The well known Price/Earnings (or P/E) model is probably the most widely used intrinsic value model. The P/E ratio is of course just the reciprocal of (k - g) in the perpetuity growth model described above.

The interest rate, k, requires further explanation as it comprises two elements: a risk free rate of return and a premium to compensate for risk. To understand the nature of the latter it is necessary to look briefly at portfolio theory.

Typically investors invest in a range of securities, not just one asset. The reason for this can be better understood by referring to a series of simple examples.

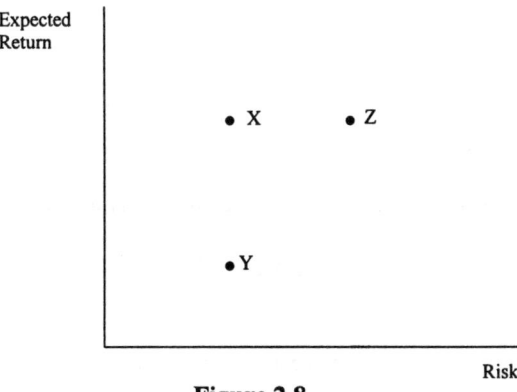

**Figure 2.8**

*Example 1*

Suppose first that an investor has a choice of investing in any one or a combination of three securities: X, Y and Z. Their expected returns and risk are shown in Figure 2.8.

A risk averse investor will prefer X to Y; and X to Z. (In other words, a higher return will be demanded for taking greater risk; and lower risk will be preferred for a given return). However, if X did not exist it would be impossible to say whether an individual will prefer Y or Z – it depends on the risk/return trade off acceptable to him/her.

Portfolio theory was originally developed by Markowitz in 1952 to analyse the above situation. The underlying principle is that an individual can construct a portfolio which helps him/her minimise risk for a given return. This is simply explained where risk is taken to be the variability of returns.

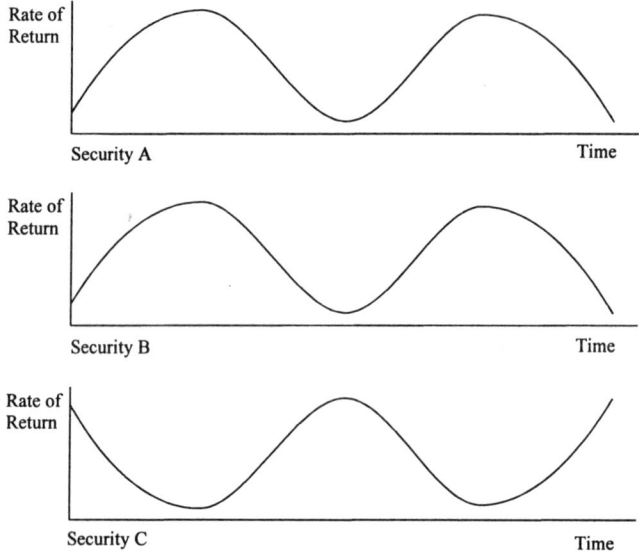

Correlation of A to B, r = +1; correlation of A to C and B to C, r = -1.

**Figure 2.9**

*Example 2*

Three securities A, B and C have the same mean expected return, and the patterns of their anticipated price changes (and hence returns) are shown in Figure 2.9.

It can be seen that a combination of A and B will *not* diversify risk (where this is measured as variance of returns) as the expected returns move in

72

perfect lock-step. But a combination of 0.5:0.5 between either A and C; or B and C will, producing the pattern of portfolio returns shown in Figure 2.10. (The straight line results, of course, because C is a mirror image of A and B, i.e. its returns are perfectly negatively correlated (r = -l) with theirs.)

**Figure 2.10**

In fact, it is not necessary for returns to be negatively correlated either perfectly as r = -l or even (say) as r = -0.2 to get the benefits of variance reduction. All that is necessary is that there is not perfect positive correlation between returns of securities. In other words, r must *not* be +1. But if r is <+1 (say r = +0.8), there will be opportunities for reducing risk by dampening the variance of returns.

Again this can be readily illustrated with the help of a simple example.

*Example 3*

Suppose two securities, E and F, have the same expected mean return but have different expected patterns of price changes across time, as shown in Figure 2.11. A combination of E and F (say 0.5 E and 0.5 F) will then produce a lower variance (and hence represent lower risk) for the same expected mean return, indicating that it will be advantageous to construct a portfolio comprising E and F (see Figure 2.12).

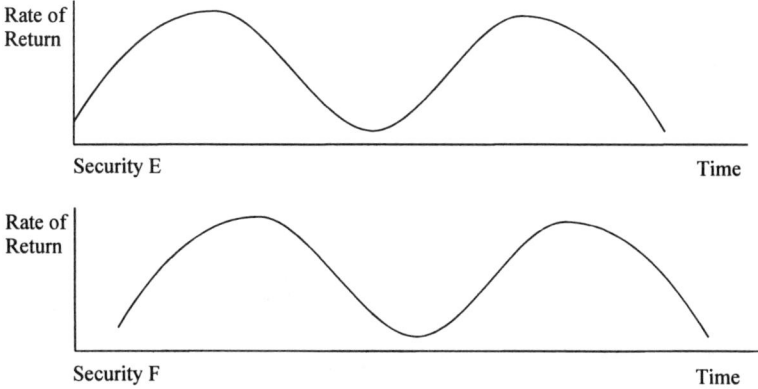

**Figure 2.11**

73

The logic of the Markowitz model is that risk averse individuals should normally buy into a portfolio of securities. But there is also an implication that where returns are uncorrelated, it should be possible to eliminate risk completely by broadening the portfolio.

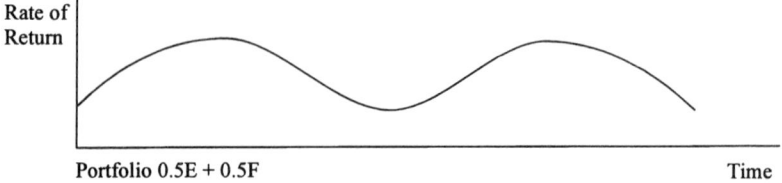

**Figure 2.12**

In fact, this is not possible because in practice the expected returns on most securities are strongly correlated. This is because there are *systematic factors* which – to a greater or lesser extent – are reflected in the expected returns of virtually all securities. Thus in a boom period, when all share prices are rising, there will inevitably be a strong degree of correlation between expected share price changes.

The risk associated with market-wide factors which for the most part cannot be diversified away is referred to as 'systematic risk'. However, the relationship between share price returns (i.e. dividends plus capital gains divided by the share price at the beginning of a period) and returns on a market portfolio (proxied by a market index, such as the FT-Actuaries All Share Index) does not appear to be a

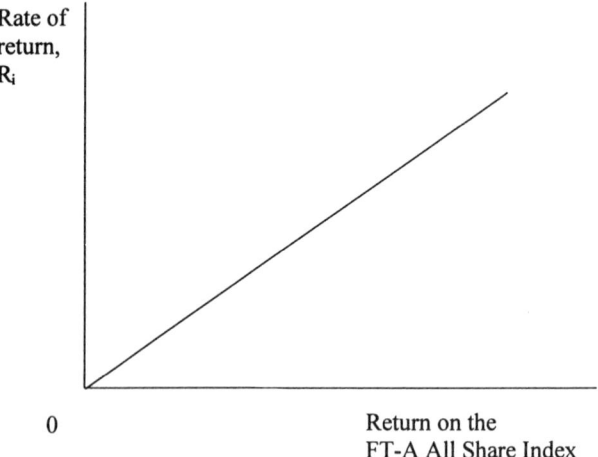

**Figure 2.13**

strictly proportional linear function as illustrated in Figure 2.13. Rather, the observed relationship appears to be more appropriately approximated as linear with a constant term, as shown in Figure 2.14.

Such functional relationships are not uncommon in business. For instance, cost functions usually comprise a fixed as well as a variable element – a fact well known to accountants because of their familiarity with the break even diagram.

The best way of identifying a relationship such as that illustrated in Figure 2.14 is to undertake a regression analysis of changes in individual share prices and the corresponding changes in a market index of security price changes.[16]

Symbolically the relationship can be expressed as

$$R_i = \alpha_i + \beta_i R_M \qquad (2.7)$$

where $R_i$ is the expected return on security i;
$R_M$ is the expected return on the market portfolio, M;
$\alpha_i$ is a constant;
and $\beta_i$ is a measure of the co-movement of the returns on security i with the returns on the market portfolio, M

$\beta_i$ is a measure of 'systematic risk'.

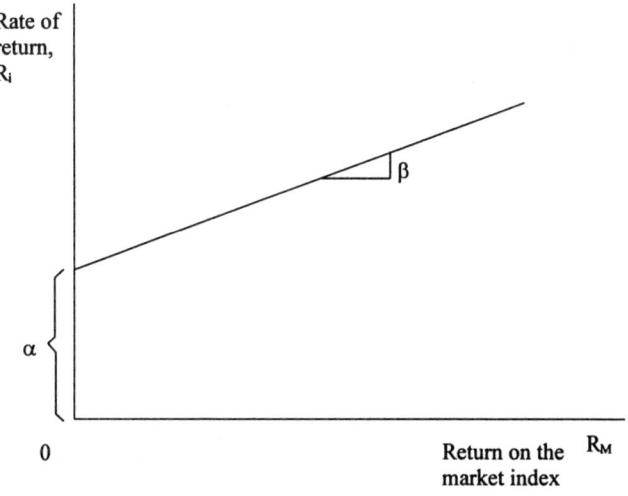

**Figure 2.14**

In fact, studies have shown that it is possible to eliminate 90 per cent or more of 'unsystematic' (i.e. firm-related) risk from a portfolio by selecting *at random* as few as 16-20 company securities. Moreover, it does seem to be the case that for the most part it is only 'systematic' (i.e. market-related) risk that commands a premium in investors' expected rates of return, i.e. k in the intrinsic share valuation model described previously in equations (2.4), (2.5) and (2.6).

Other empirical studies have shown that on average about 60 per cent of share price movements can be explained by market-wide factors, another 10 per cent by industry-related factors, and only the remaining 30 per cent by firm-specific factors.

It is also possible to arrive at the 'market model' illustrated in Figure 2.14 and identified in equation (2.7) using deductive reasoning and extending portfolio theory. Thus Sharpe, Lintner, and Mossin long ago demonstrated what would happen if there were just two assets in which funds could be invested, one which was risk free, F, and the other risky, M. Individuals could then find what for them is best level of diversification by buying a mixture of these two assets. In terms of Figure 2.15 this means that they could move up or down the diagonal line FM. (Indeed, they could move up to the right beyond point M by borrowing at the risk free rate and investing in M.)

In fact, M is not just a single asset but a portfolio of risky assets. However, the useful conceit in the argument is that in a highly competitive environment most investors are effectively 'price takers'. Consequently at any *momentary equilibrium*

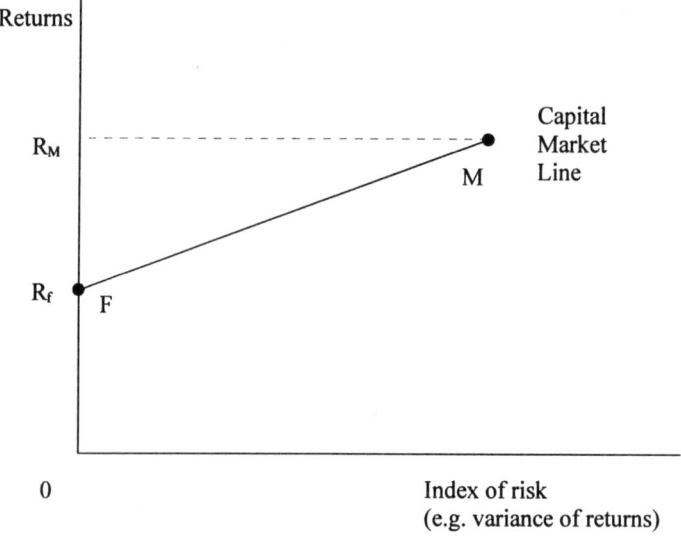

**Figure 2.15**

there will be *one* portfolio of risky securities (the 'market portfolio') which dominates, so the situation illustrated in Figure 2.15 is probably not far from being a reasonable description of how the capital market works.

The model illustrated has in fact become known as the *capital asset pricing model* (CAPM). The 'market portfolio' can be approximated as all equities listed on the stock market and the returns measured as the change in a representative market index (e.g. the FTSE 100). The 'risk free asset' is one whose expected returns are completely uncorrelated with those on the market portfolio of risky securities. The slope coefficient (or 'market beta') in equation (2.7) is therefore zero; and the risk free return, $R_f$, is the equivalent of the intercept, $\alpha$, in the market model as previously described and illustrated in Figure 2.14. The most obvious example of such an asset is likely to be an index linked gilt edged security.

The above diagram can be re-expressed to make it analogous to Figure 2.14 by redefining the X axis as 'beta', the covariance of returns with those on the market portfolio (see Figure 2.16). Clearly the covariance of market returns with itself must be one, hence $ß_M = 1$. Likewise, the ß of the risk free asset must be zero, $ß_F = 0$. Further, since the model is an equilibrium model, it should be possible to read off from the diagram the beta of a security or portfolio, i (measuring the covariance of its returns with those on the market portfolio).

One of the problems with the CAPM is the technical assumptions that underpin it, namely, investors are risk averse; they have homogeneous (i.e. similar) expectations; capital markets are 'perfect' (i.e. there are no transactions costs or

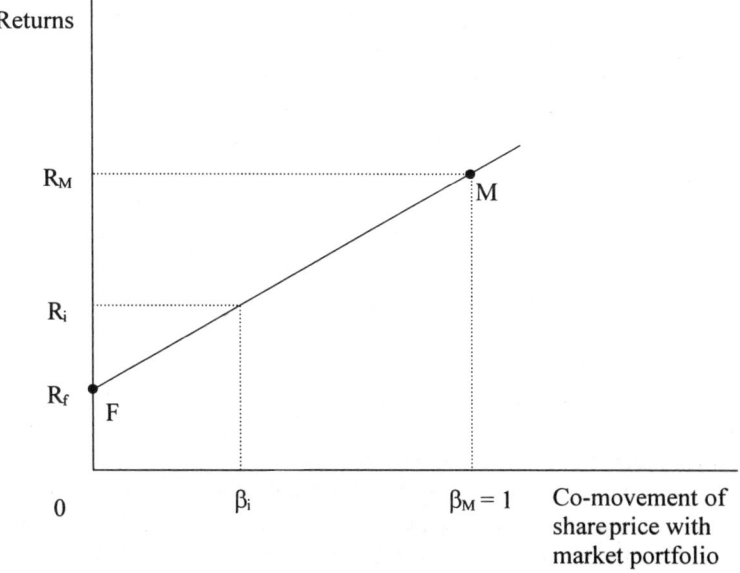

**Figure 2.16**

taxes); investors can borrow and lend at the risk free rate; and investors behave rationally. In fact, these assumptions are not as unrealistic as might at first sight seem to be the case, but the real difficulty is that the CAPM is a single period equilibrium model (i.e. it relates to an instant in time).

A way of avoiding this – and an alternative way of interpreting the 'market model' illustrated in Figure 2.14 – is to develop an explanation of share price determination based on arbitrage pricing theory (APT). This disequilibrium approach, developed by Ross, is based on the argument that an investor will balance a speculative portfolio against a hedge portfolio. However, in order to minimise risk he/she should manufacture the hedge portfolio in such a way that it has similar characteristics with regard to systematic movements as the speculative portfolio. If there were just one such systematic factor it is possible to reinterpret the market model of equation (2.7) as a special case of the APT, but without the restrictive assumptions of the CAPM. Thus $R_i$ becomes the speculative portfolio, while the terms on right hand side of equation (2.7) represent the hedge portfolio. In practice, however, there are likely to be several systematic factors affecting both the speculative and hedge portfolios.

To illustrate the argument, suppose an investor has superior knowledge and believes that in a week's time Sainsbury's will report profits 20 per cent higher than market analysts have been predicting. The obvious strategy is then for him/her to buy Sainsbury's shares in the confident expectation that they will move up in 7 days' time when a preliminary earnings announcement is made. However, there is a risk that there will be systematic factors which will force supermarket companies' security prices down between the purchase date of Sainsbury's shares and the news release (e.g. because of an unexpected sharp fall in the market index; and because of unanticipated announcements of planning restrictions on superstore developments, food scares, etc). The investor can fairly obviously best immunise himself/herself from these 'systematic factors' by selling short[17] equivalent holdings in a portfolio of rival companies' shares (e.g. in Tesco, Asda, Safeway, Kwik Save, Morrisons, etc). Thus if there is a systematic fall in the prices of shares in supermarket companies, the gains on the hedge portfolio in Tesco, Asda, Safeway, Kwik Save, Morrisons, etc, should offset the losses on the investment in Sainsbury's – except that there should be an extra element of profit on the latter if the superior knowledge about Sainsbury's reported profits proves to be correct.

In fact, the number of individuals with superior knowledge and who are able to trade on it is likely to be relatively small. Indeed, in highly competitive markets for information (such as the City of London and Wall Street) only a few expert analysts (the 'price makers') are likely to be able consistently to come up with better-than-average estimates. The abnormal profits which they will earn will either be a reward for their search activity or for their superior analytical skills. The vast majority of investors (including the institutional investors who seek advice from the few expert analysts) are 'price takers'. In the circumstances, it is probably not unreasonable to accept the market model as a reasonable and practical way of trying to identify the way in which share prices are determined for 'price takers'. It is only for the small minority of expert analysts that the APT is a better description of their activities.

## Agency models of corporate failure

The bankruptcy process has more recently been analysed within a 'contracting' (or 'agency') framework, which takes into account the conflicting interests of various parties (namely shareholders, creditors and management).

Essentially financial distress arises when a company's internal resources are insufficient to meet its contractual obligations. This problem can only be dealt with by

(1) restructuring asset holdings (i.e. prematurely liquidating assets, which to a greater or lesser extent will involve destruction of going concern value and incurring liquidation costs);
(2) restructuring financial contracts; and/or
(3) raising additional finance by issuing new claims against future cash flows.

Such arrangements can be secured as part of a private contracting process, but a major difficulty which may impede progress towards a resolution of the problem is 'information asymmetry'. In practice, therefore, an alternative is offered by a court adjudication system.

In recent years there has been extensive empirical work examining the bankruptcy process within an agency context. As a result studies have been carried out investigating inter alia the effect on share prices of asset sales, leveraged buyouts and compositions with creditors. Similarly there have been numerous comparisons of the experience of US companies which have chosen to restructure privately against those which have resorted to the courts.[18]

The basic agency model of the bankruptcy process has been formulated by Chen, Weston and Altman (1995). Essentially their argument relates to a two state world, where a firm faces either a good or a bad cash flow outcome and where there are three parties (shareholders, banks, and a collection of trade creditors with whom shareholders cannot directly negotiate). Assuming the parties are risk neutral and that managers act to maximise shareholders' wealth, there are three basic criteria which need to be considered in order to assess the efficiency of investment decisions:

(1) the expected net present value (NPV) of an investment project;
(2) the expected market value of equity if the investment is made, determining the anticipated return to shareholders (RSH); and
(3) the anticipated return to debtholders (RDH) if the investment is made, which will be determined as the expected market value of debt (D) less the liquidation value (L) of the company's assets (which is also the value of debt if the investment is *not* made).

Initially the analysis does not distinguish between large and small, unco-ordinated creditors, although typically there will be differences in terms of bargaining power and the restrictions attached to the debts outstanding. This simplification enables attention to be initially concentrated on just two groups: shareholders and creditors.

The analysis proceeds by identifying the various combinations of positive and negative changes in NPV, RSH and RDH. These define four types of investment actions: efficient investment, underinvestment, overinvestment and no investment. The position is illustrated in Figure 2.17.

Investment occurs where RSH>0, even when RDH<L (i.e. segment U). Overinvestment (S) can occur where the expected RSH is positive but both the NPV of the project and the RDH are negative. This result can be more easily appreciated where the equity interest is viewed as a call option, since if the uncertain cash flow is large the shareholders gain and the creditors bear the loss. Q is a segment of the 'no investment' area in which RDH is positive (i.e. the bank might be prepared to provide finance or creditors to continue to supply a company, notwithstanding the fact that the NPV=0).

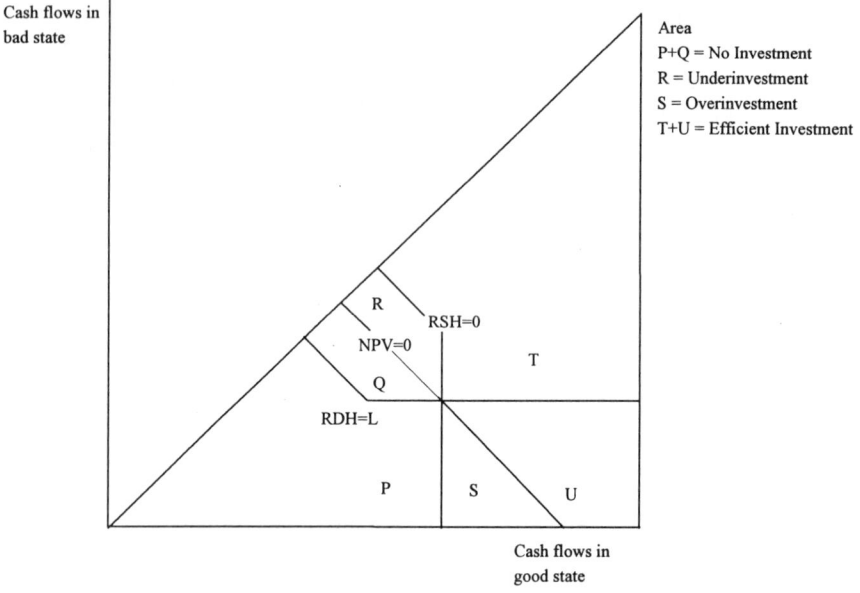

**Figure 2.17**

Chen et al. analyse the position in more detail allowing for relationships between liquidation value (L) and the face value of debt (D); and for the variability of projected cash flows. In fact, there will be a greater likelihood of overinvestment the higher the D/L ratio, as with an out-of-the-money call option the shareholders

80

cannot lose more. On the other hand, when the D/L ratio is extremely high, shareholders may feel that it is not worthwhile even making the effort to invest, leading to underinvestment. As regards risk, because equity can be regarded as a call option, the greater the cash flow risk associated with a project the larger is the value of the option. The result is that as the level of risk increases, the greater is RSH and the lower RDH. The implication underlying the RSH=0 line is therefore that with increasing risk the NPV required to induce equity investors to undertake the new investment is lower.

Chen et al. go on to examine other aspects of the relationship between equity and debt holders. Thus the maturity structure of debt is another factor which influences investment efficiency. With long term debt there may be overinvestment as shareholders effectively gamble using creditors' funds. On the other hand, the shorter the maturity dates the more likely is a firm to have an underinvestment problem as the equity call option is less valuable to shareholders. This explains why an underinvestment problem is frequently resolved by restructuring debt, with junk bonds or equity being offered in order to defer repayment obligations. It is also possible to resolve overinvestment caused by a high degree of cash flow uncertainty by increasing short term borrowings. This should create a tendency to underinvest, which will offset the overinvestment problem resulting from having substantial amounts of long-term debt. Overall this should lead to a more efficient level of investment. Conversely, if cash flow uncertainty is relatively low, an optimal strategy will be to substitute long term for short term debt. It follows that firms will attempt to resolve over- and under-investment situations by trying to manipulate the priority of claims amongst creditors (e.g. through the use of restrictive covenants or by exchanging debt for new securities).

It is also possible to analyse the position of banks and the impact of insolvency regulations (e.g. where financially distressed companies are afforded protection by legislation, such as a breathing space or a moratorium on interest payments). With respect to banks, typically they are better informed than other creditors; their debts tend to be short term to facilitate monitoring and recontracting; they are generally in a more powerful bargaining position than other creditors; and they usually seek a priority ranking amongst creditors. It follows from the previous arguments that when all forms of debt enjoy the same seniority, the higher the ratio of short term bank debt to total debt, the more efficient is the investment decision as the bank will seek to maximise the joint welfare of itself and the shareholders.

The implication of the contracting framework analysis is that bankruptcy is a rather more complex process than is implied by the more general finance and valuation theories referred to earlier. Nevertheless, it is clear that once again the critical factors are the variability of expected cash flows and the liquidation value of a company's assets. Consequently a realistic model of corporate failure should capture proxies of these firm characteristics.

**Management theories of corporate failure**

The management and business strategy literature attempts to popularise basic concepts in industrial economics. Thus Porter's Five Forces Model concentrates on competitive rivalry, threats of entry and of substitutes, and the bargaining power of buyers and suppliers. A careful study of these matters enables an analyst to identify a business's competitive advantage in terms of its having lower costs or differentiated products. As a result, the position of a firm in an industry can be appraised and the strategic options available can be identified.

A number of writers in the management area have used this framework to develop theories of the causes and symptoms of corporate failure. Hardly surprisingly, most suggest that mis-management is a key factor leading to corporate collapse. Beyond this, though, there is a considerable degree of agreement on what are believed to be the main reasons for financial failure. These will be described in more detail in chapter 7. All that will be attempted here is to summarise the main causes that have been identified.

(1) There are shortcomings in management (e.g. too much power is concentrated in the hands of one person, and the control mechanisms are ineffective).
(2) There are weaknesses in the accounting system and inadequate financial controls.
(3) The company is slow to react to changes in its environment (e.g. in responding to competition by developing new products, cutting costs, etc).
(4) Mistakes frequently lead to failure (e.g. overtrading, overborrowing, lack of diversification, bad acquisitions policy).
(5) Symptoms of failure become evident as a company faces collapse (e.g. key ratios worsen).

Although on the face of it these may seem to comprise a normative model of corporate failure, a closer examination shows that the ideas have for the most part been derived as a result of a study of a series of case histories. In other words, the reasoning is positive rather than normative in nature. For this reason, the arguments and the evidence will be further elaborated in chapter 7.

**Summary**

It is a necessary precondition of any empirical research to develop, however sketchily, a normative theory which indicates the likely relationships that might be observed. Rather surprisingly, most studies of corporate bankruptcy do not clearly specify such normative theories. In fact, there are many such theories which offer insight into the possible causes of financial failure.

In the first instance there are disequilibrium theories. Some of these, such as chaos and catastrophe theories, are hardly operational, although they do provide a useful framework within which to consider the possible cause-and-effect relationships. At a more practical level entropy theory concentrates on changes in the structure of a business. There are also various economic theories which examine the possible causes of disequilibrium at different levels of aggregation – e.g. for the economy as a whole, for an industry, and for individual firms. Finance theory in particular identifies the potential reasons for failure in terms of gearing (both financial and operational) and the impact on risk. By contrast, industrial economics focuses on other aspects, such as size, as major determining factors.

There are four basic financial models which help to explain corporate failure. The first is a single period option pricing model, and the second a gambler's ruin model where there is no access to outside capital. The third and fourth models are variations of the latter, in the first instance allowing for perfect access to outside capital, and then modifying this by restricting access. In fact, the critical variable in all four models except the second is the value of the company: i.e. rather unsurprisingly, a company will fail when its break up value exceeds its going concern value. Only with the gambler's ruin model when there is no access to outside capital are accounting variables directly of interest – and then the critical factor is the variability of cash flows.

Given the importance of valuation in financial models of corporate failure, it is necessary to consider the main determinants in some detail. So called intrinsic value models (such as the price/earnings formula) discount back an earnings stream to a present value. Earnings are, of course, a transform of cash flows, but the projected stream that is the subject of forecasting normally represents a 'permanent earnings' element and a growth factor. As for the interest rate used for discounting, this generally includes a premium for market related (or 'systematic') risk. This can be justified in terms of the observed relationship between, on the one hand, a company's dividends and share price movements; and, on the other, changes in an overall market index. Moreover, this can be done without necessarily trying to explain the phenomenon in terms of the capital asset or arbitrage pricing theories.

Further insight into the bankruptcy process is given by referring to 'contracting' (or 'agency') theories. The analysis shows in fact that because of conflicts of interest between creditors and equity holders the phenomenon is rather more complex than the relatively simple finance and valuation theories seem to imply. Nevertheless, it is clear that critical factors are once again cash flows, their variability and the break up value of the assets.

The management and business strategy literature has also identified a series of critical variables which appear to help explain which companies are likely to fail and which are not. However, on closer inspection it appears that this hardly represents a coherent normative theory of why some companies in financial distress collapse and others do not. On the other hand, it does emphasise that there is no single factor which explains corporate bankruptcy. Rather, it seems in practice that there are many causes of financial collapse, and frequently it is an unhappy conjunction of a number of these factors that brings a company down.

**Notes**

[1] Gleick (1988) and Stewart (1989) provide succinct introductions to chaos theory, the latter being particularly readable on the subject.

[2] Ho and Saunders' model was based on the variability of cash flows, and consequently the arguments they develop are not dissimilar to those implicit in the gambler's ruin model discussed below.

[3] This was the best discriminator found by Beaver (1966): see p. 108.

It should be noted that Lev was in fact testing a joint hypothesis in his study, namely that the structural changes in the balance sheets were greater for failed than non-failed firms, regardless of direction (which could well be the opposite as between slow and rapidly growing firms); and that the distinction between short- and long-term assets and claims in the balance sheets was economically significant in discriminating between bankrupt and non-bankrupt businesses.

[4] Altman's model is described on p. 135.

[5] These multivariate models are described below in chapter 4. Examples in a British context where entropy measures were included in the variable set are the studies of Betts and Belhoul (1983, 1987).

[6] See note 8, below; and pp. 146-7 and 237-9.

[7] This is generally discussed in terms of the arguments originally put forward by Modigliani and Miller (1958) on gearing and dividend policies. These ideas have since been reinterpreted within the framework of general equilibrium theory by Stiglitz (1969, 1972, 1974); and by Hamada (1969) and Haugen and Pappas (1971) in terms of the *capital asset pricing model* (CAPM). (The CAPM is outlined later in this chapter, p. 74 et seq.)

A number of studies have attempted to estimate the direct and indirect costs of bankruptcy so as to evaluate the likely impact on individual companies' costs of capital and, more generally, the economic and social costs of corporate failure. The direct costs (i.e. involving legal and other administrative costs) have generally been estimated as being relatively low. Weiss (1990), for example, concluded that in the US they are on average around 3 per cent of a company's capitalised equity value when it is in a non-distressed state, although there are other non-quantifiable costs because of frequent violations of the priority rights of interested parties. The indirect costs (in terms of lost sales, higher operating costs and a reduction in competition) are considerably greater than the direct costs. Using earnings estimates generated by a regression model and alternatively as forecast by analysts, Altman (1984b) calculated the indirect opportunity costs in terms of lost profits to be nearer 20 per cent of the capitalised equity market values of non-distressed companies. However, there was a significant variation between industry sectors. As for the more general economic and social costs of corporate failure, Easterbrook (1990) concluded that allowing the courts to decide how a bankrupt company's assets should be distributed might well be more efficient than leaving the allocation to be determined by market forces.

[8] For a brief survey of the evidence relating to the traditional approach, see Hay and Morris (1991), pp. 537-541. For an early example of a theory to explain entry and exit behaviour taking into account other factors, see Jovanovic (1982), who argues that only firms which are able to adapt and grow will survive, while others will be forced to exit from an industry. Audretsch and Mata (1995) and Geroski (1995) offer more recent reviews of research exploring different explanations of optimal size, the degree of concentration in particular industries, and rates of entry and exit.

[9] See below, p. 226.

[10] Modigliani and Cohn's argument, of course, suggests that the market is inefficient in valuing securities, and it should therefore be possible for investors to make profits on the assumption that the true intrinsic value will ultimately be recognised. However, this assumes that the market will cease to value securities in what appears to be an irrational way, and there are a number of institutional reasons which suggest that analysts may indeed systematically undervalue securities when price levels are rising.

For the record, Wadhwani's (1984a) empirical study suggests that a 1 per cent fall in the rate of inflation over the period 1964-1981 would have reduced liquidations by 5.8 per cent of their mean value, the default premium by 0.15 per cent, and relative share prices by 8.04 per cent. In addition, the incidence of inflation also causes a fall in employment (Wadhwani, 1984b).

[11] See Appendix 2.2 for further explanation.

[12] Somewhat surprisingly it also correlated with 'market betas', which measure 'systematic risk'. (Market betas and systematic risk are explained below, p. 74 et seq.)

[13] Altman's model is briefly described on p. 135.

[14] See below, p. 184.

[15] For a fuller discussion of valuation theory, see Brealey and Myers (1996). In order to simplify the discussion, constant price levels are assumed in the argument which follows.

[16] Regression is briefly discussed on p. 116 et seq.

[17] Assuming that short selling is possible, of course! (See p. 44, above, note 14.)

[18] A recent review of the literature is given by John (1993).

## Appendix 2.1

*Informational decomposition measures*

Entropy is defined as the degree of uncertainty over the occurrence of a given event. The measure of surprise is the logarithm of the probabilities $p_1 \ldots p_n$:

$$H_n = H_n (p_1,...,p_n) \tag{2.8}$$

$$= -\sum_{k=1}^{n} p_k \ln p_k \tag{2.8a}$$

where $\Sigma$ means the sum of a series;<br>
and $\ln$ indicates a natural logarithm.

Entropy can then be represented as

$$h(p) = \ln (1/p) \tag{2.9}$$

The greater the entropy score, the greater the 'surprise' and hence the larger the informational value conveyed by a model.

It has been argued by Lev (1969a) and others that this can be captured in an informational decomposition measure, which is probably best explained in terms of an example.

A balance sheet can be represented schematically, where the asset and claim proportions are represented as p at time t=0; and q at t=1. The fractions in each cell can therefore be designated by subscripts in standard co-ordinate matrix notation, ij, as: claims i1; assets i2. Likewise, current items are designated as 1j; and long term as 2j. The fractions of components of claims or assets at one moment in time must also clearly sum to unity.

*Balance sheets (in proportions)*

| | Claims | | Assets | |
|---|---|---|---|---|
| | $t_0$ | $t_1$ | $t_0$ | $t_1$ |
| Current | $p_{11}$ 0.4 | $q_{11}$ 0.6 | $p_{12}$ 0.7 | $q_{12}$ 0.4 |
| Long-term | $p_{21}$ 0.6 | $q_{21}$ 0.4 | $p_{22}$ 0.3 | $q_{22}$ 0.6 |
| | 1.0 | 1.0 | 1.0 | 1.0 |

An *asset decomposition* measure, $I_A$, can be defined as

$$I_A = \sum_{i=1}^{n} q_i \log_e (q_i / p_i) \tag{2.10}$$

where $p_i$ is the fraction for each of the n categories at $t_0$;<br>
and $q_i$ is the fraction for each of the n categories at $t_1$.

So

$I_A$ = 0.4 $\log_e$(0.4/0.7) + 0.6 $\log_e$(0.6/0.3)
    = 0.19198 nits

(The index is expressed in 'nits' because natural (Naperian) logarithms are being used.)

A *claims decomposition* measure, $I_C$, can be similarly defined and calculated:

$I_C$ = 0.6 $\log_e$(0.6/0.4) + 0.4 $\log_e$(0.4/0.6)
    = 0.0811 nits.

If there is no change in asset structure, $I_A$ = 0; and similarly $I_C$ will equal zero if there is no change in the structure of claims. By contrast, when $I_A$ and/or $I_C \neq 0$, the higher the nit values, the greater the structural changes that have taken place.

A *balance sheet decomposition* measure, $I_{BS}$, can be calculated as

$I_{BS}$ = $(I_A + I_C)/2$
     = (0.19198 + 0.0811)/2
     = 0.13154 nits.

Alternatively it can be calculated from first principles as

$$I_{BS} = \sum_{i=1}^{2} \sum_{j=1}^{2} q_{ij} \log_e (q_{ij}/p_{ij}) \tag{2.11}$$

where the symbols are as previously defined;
i=2 (asset/claim categories, i.e. current and long-term)
and j=2 (assets; and claims)

It should be noted that in order to calculate $I_{BS}$ it is necessary to halve the fractions so that the sum of assets and claims fractions for a year totals to unity.

Of course, in practice neither $I_A$ nor $I_C$ would be calculated on their own. Rather, $I_{BS}$ would be calculated first, and if the value were reasonably high, $I_A$ and $I_C$ would then be examined to see where the main changes have occurred.

Three points should be noted about applying informational decomposition measures in order to try to discriminate between failing and non-failing companies.

(1) The user has to decide which financial statement categories have potential economic significance – e.g. the current/long term dichotomy may do; but the distinction between debtors/cash is unlikely to be important because the two categories are close substitutes.

In practice researchers have tended to use two or three categories on each side of the balance sheet: namely, on the assets side – current and fixed assets; quick assets, inventories and fixed assets; quick assets and other assets; and on the claims side: current liabilities and other claims; liabilities and equity; and current liabilities, long term liabilities and equity.

(2) The user should be sure that change is connected to the phenomenon being studied – e.g. a substantial change in the structure of a balance sheet may be the result of rapid growth rather than impending bankruptcy.

(3) A decision has to be made about the interval over which structural changes should be measured. Thus there is no reason why it should just be 12 months. Indeed, one might expect balance sheet proportions of non-failed firms to alter to some extent over a year, but this might just be noise: i.e. a small random-like increase in one period is quite likely to be reversed the next. What is being sought is a significantly different proportionate movement in one group of companies (here failed versus non-failed), and this might be most apparent over a two or three year interval.

In practice, most researchers seem to have focused on a 12 months interval, although Lev (1971) found that the discriminatory power increased when the period was lengthened.


**Appendix 2.2**

*The gambler's ruin model*

Briefly, the procedure developed by Wilcox (1971, 1973) requires that two accounting based measures should be employed

(1) adjusted cash flow per period; and
(2) adjusted cash position at the end of each period.

Various proxies can be used to measure the first, although Wilcox just took the period-by-period change in the end-of-period 'adjusted cash position' (i.e. an estimated liquidation value of the business). The 'mean cash flow' (Mean CF) figure is simply the average of cash flow observations; while the variance of the cash flows (Var CF) is precisely that: the variance of the cash flows.

The procedure used by Wilcox was to calculate the probability of a company moving from a 'state' N, the probability of moving to N+1 being p; and to N-1 q (see Figure 2.5 on p. 66). Where N=0 (the 'absorbing state') the firm has run out of cash and is prima facie insolvent. The aim is to calculate the probability that a firm will end up insolvent, which is given by

$$p(N = 0) = \begin{cases} 1 \text{ if } p \le q \\ (q/p)^N \text{ otherwise} \end{cases} \qquad (2.12)$$

N can be estimated as the 'adjusted cash position' divided by $\sigma$, the estimated size of the interval between adjacent states in cash terms. The expression $(p-q)\sigma$ is the average drift rate per period along the sequence of states in cash terms, and $(p-q)\sigma$ is the 'mean adjusted cash flow'. Since $q=(1-p)$, $q/p = [1-(p-q)/1+(p-q)]$. Thus if x represents the 'mean adjusted cash flow' divided by $\sigma$, $q/p = (1-x/1+x)$. For this purpose

$$\sigma = \sqrt{(\text{Mean CF})^2 + (\text{Var CF})} \qquad (2.13)$$

In this way the (Mean CF) and (Var CF) figures can be used to calculate the two statistics, N and x.

It will be evident that the lower N is, the closer is the company to insolvency (i.e. it shares some of the properties of the hazard function in survival models, discussed on pp. 141 et seq.)

The two statistics, N and x, can then be compared for any pair of companies in the following way:

*Domain I:* x>0 and N>0. The probability of ultimate failure is $[(1-x)/(1+x)]^N$.

*Domain II:* x<0 and N>0. The firm is losing cash but has reserves. The mean time time to failure is -N/x.

*Domain III:* x>0 and N<0. The company is already prima facie insolvent, even though it is recovering liquidity.

*Domain IV:* x<0 and N<0. Again, the company is prima facie insolvent.

# 3 Positive theories of corporate failure: I – Univariate models

**Introduction**

The previous chapter examined a number of theories which could loosely be described as being normative in nature: i.e. they attempt to explain by deductive reasoning why a certain proportion of businesses might be expected to fail. The alternative approach is to develop positive theories, which attempt to explain by inductive reasoning why in practice they do fail. Such theories (when formally identified) are usually supported by analysis of empirical evidence.

The primary purpose of this and the four chapters which follow is to describe the procedures used to examine the characteristics of financially distressed companies and to review the empirical evidence. Although there is often only a tenuous link to an underlying positive theory which might explain why such companies fail, it will nevertheless be convenient to regard them within that context.

In fact, there is along tradition in business of trying to assess a company's performance and financial position by referring to numbers taken from its financial statements. However, the nature of the analysis is essentially 'univariate': i.e. the variables are usually examined seriatim one-by-one. As a result, no formal attempt is made to allow for interactions between the variables, except judgementally. Potentially more powerful 'multivariate' analytical procedures can be applied which allow for the simultaneous interactions between variables.

The aim of this chapter is to consider univariate methods of analysis. In the first instance this means reviewing the 'traditional' methods of interpreting financial statements, and in particular ratio analysis, which have been described in financial accounting and banking textbooks for over one hundred years. However, in many respects the conventional mechanistic approach (with which most readers will be thoroughly familiar) is flawed. For instance, there are generally few explanations of the piecemeal nature of traditional accounting measures, which only capture some of the economic factors that affect a company's operations and determine its financial position. Equally, the underlying nature of ratios and the weaknesses inherent in their calculation – for instance, with respect to the current ratio, stock turnover, and the rate of return on capital employed – are rarely discussed. Nor is much usually said about the implicit assumption that specific ratios are of equal relevance for companies, regardless of the industries in which they operate. Similarly, little guidance is normally given to indicate how ratios should be used, not as an end in themselves, but as a means of trying to identify specific features of a company's performance and financial position; and how an analyst might try to identify interactions between different indicators in terms of the general economic environment facing a business.

But the conventional approach is only one way in which financial ratios can be analysed on a univariate basis. It is also possible to apply more systematic procedures to analyse such data and thus try to obtain a picture of a company's performance, position and future prospects. It is therefore necessary to examine briefly the evidence from studies where such an approach has been adopted.

## The interpretation of financial statements

### Standards of performance

In the context of financial statement interpretation it is important to recognise that there is little informational content in a number itself. Rather, it is necessary to relate it to a benchmark, such as a budgeted standard; a rival's performance or position ('cross sectional analysis'); or a comparable figure achieved in the past ('time series analysis').

In practice it is often also useful to scale a figure by relating it to another drawn from the financial statements. This can sometimes additionally reflect a cause-and-effect relationship.

Financial ratios were certainly used by bankers to try to assess performance and creditworthiness in the nineteenth century,[1] and accounting and banking textbooks from then on have frequently described them as the principal tool in financial statement interpretation.[2] But it is often argued in the management accounting literature that ratios can equally be used as a control mechanism, the DuPont pyramid system being particularly well known. Ratios are also widely used to make inter-firm comparisons, and in addition have been used in this role by price regulatory agencies (such as the Monopolies Commission, the Restrictive Practices Court, the Prices and Incomes Board and the Price Commission).

In the circumstances, it is rather surprising that there is very little discussion in standard accounting texts of the nature of financial ratios, or indeed of the logic behind their use. In particular, little is said about their basic statistical properties, or whether it is sensible to try to refer to them one-by-one on a univariate basis rather

91

than together simultaneously as part of a more ambitious multivariate analytical process.

In fact, in most bankruptcy identification studies it is financial ratios that are the key independent variables which are used to explain differences between failed and non-failed businesses. It is therefore appropriate to consider in more depth their underlying properties, and this will be done in chapter 8.

*The context of financial statement interpretation*

Textbook discussions of financial statement analysis often overlook two basic points:

(1) Decision making relates to an economic entity (such as a colluding group of companies, or a segment or division of a business), and this may well not coincide with the legal entity to which the published accounts relate – typically a limited company.
(2) Accounting statements are merely *one* source of information, and the details they contain are usually defective from the point of view of the user – e.g.
    (a) they are often out of date, the lag between year end date and publication typically being 3 months for listed companies and over 6 months for private companies;[3]
    (b) they are often incomplete (i.e. certain assets and claims are omitted from the balance sheet); and
    (c) they are often ambiguous and capable of being manipulated.

Moreover, accounting indicators are essentially imperfect representations (or 'surrogates') of economic events, and can only capture some of their key characteristics.[4] Thus, for instance, if an income statement shows turnover has increased by 10 per cent from £10m to £11m over a year, it is not evident what has given rise to this change. Has the volume of goods sold risen by 10 per cent while prices have remained constant? Or has the volume sold remained the same while prices have increased? Or has the sales mix altered? And if prices have increased, how much of that is due to erosion in the general purchasing power of the currency?

The list of potential explanations is endless, and this emphasises the fact that the analyst is really interested in the *substance* (i.e. the underlying economic events and what has caused them), *not* in the figures themselves. In other words, accounting indicators are a means to an end, not an end in themselves.

But it should also be acknowledged that cause-and-effect relationships are often extremely difficult to identify without access to supplementary information, partly because there are numerous interdependencies between economic variables, but also because accounting labels may not clearly indicate the nature of causal relationships. Thus, to take a simple example, an increase in selling expenses could be associated with an increase in turnover in various ways. For instance, such expenditures could be sales commission or distribution costs, in which case the expense would appear to be a function of the level of sales. Alternatively, they might be promotional outlays, in which case the causation is in the reverse direction, sales being a function of selling expenses. But even if additional evidence makes the direction of causation clear, the figures will only reflect *average* rather than *marginal* relationships, when presumably it will be the latter which will be of most interest to the analyst. Moreover, there is also the question of whether the selling expense has been appropriately matched against sales revenue: if it has not, the whole basis of interpretation may be undermined.

The implications of the above argument are that the analyst should approach an interpretation exercise with an open mind. Usually accounting texts emphasise that the choice of an accounting convention (such as a depreciation method) means that a given economic event can be measured in a whole variety of different ways. This is of course true, and it gives rise to the situation illustrated in Figure 3.1.

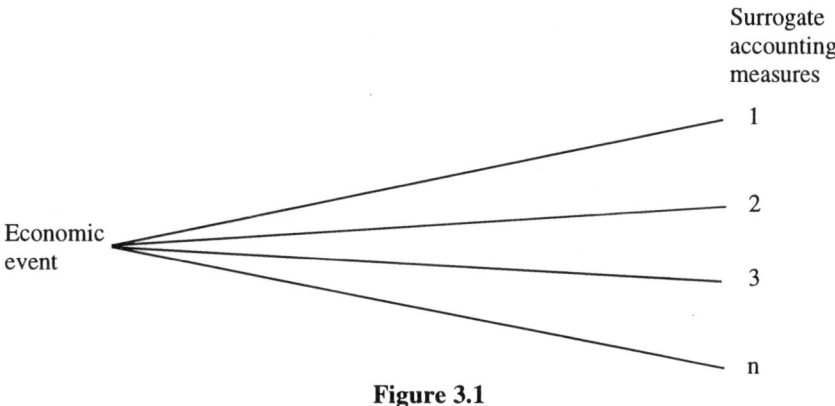

**Figure 3.1**

What is less widely acknowledged is that the reverse is equally true, namely that different economic events could give rise to the same observed accounting measure. This is illustrated in Figure 3.2.

In such circumstances it is the task of the analyst to try to identify the events which could have generated the figures which appear in financial statements (i.e. to establish cause-and-effect relationships). In practice, it will straightaway be possible to eliminate some of the more remote possibilities by referring to easily obtainable supplementary information. But it will sometimes be necessary to search out additional details to clarify events, and the analyst will then need to investigate carefully the underlying causes of the phenomena identified.

What is needed really is a *structure* for analysing changes and their possible causes, and in this context a diagram along the lines of the well known break even chart may be useful. However, it will be necessary to draw various versions which

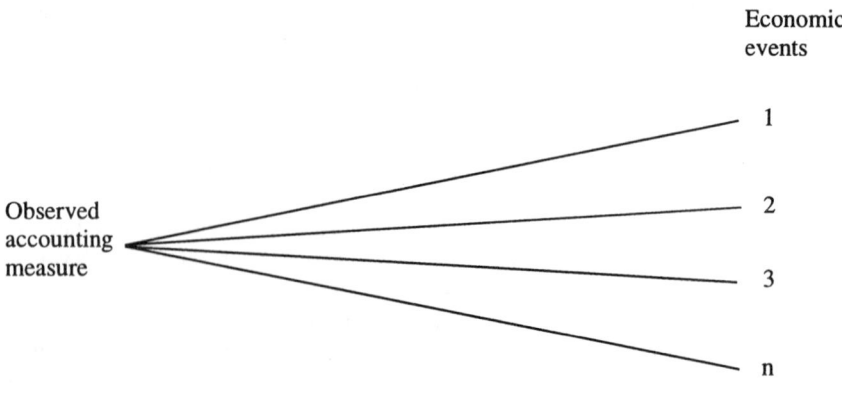

**Figure 3.2**

may equally well explain the reported figures. Clearly this will generally be easier to do where a company is a small business. The task is much more daunting when a company manufactures and/or sells a number of different products or services at various locations.

In the circumstances, too much should not be expected from traditional financial statement interpretation techniques. Nevertheless, procedures such as ratio analysis do provide a ready means of summarising data, and to the extent that they highlight abnormal and unexpected relationships or changes, they can act as a useful starting point for an investigation.

*Financial ratios*

For most interpretation purposes it is usually assumed that the only source of information to which analysts have access is the financial statements, and this is certainly the assumption adopted in most failure identification studies. Relatively few try to incorporate qualitative variables.[5]

As already indicated, there are a number of features about financial ratios which should be identified, and these will be examined in more detail in chapter 8. For present purposes it is sufficient just to note a few of the key issues that need to be considered:

(1) There are usually a number of ratios which measure similar attributes of a business. It is therefore convenient merely to use the most appropriate one from each group which captures a different aspect of a company's financial characteristics.

(2) Generally there will be interrelationships between ratios, implying that multivariate rather than univariate analysis would probably be more appropriate. Care should therefore be exercised when univariate analysis is attempted to ensure that unjustified inferences are not made.

(3) An implicit assumption seems to be made in conventional financial statement analysis that the relationship between the numerator and denominator of a fraction is strictly proportionate. Clearly this is unrealistic.[6]

Thus, for instance, with respect to stocks of goods there is usually a fixed (or base) level of inventory which must be held to meet unanticipated demands. Equally it is generally assumed that there will be economies of scale, which means that quantities held in stock will not increase pro rata to demand. Such indeed is the justification for the 'economic order quantity' (EOQ) model, which assumes that stocks will only increase at a rate equivalent to the square root of the increase in demand. By contrast, the stock turnover ratio (cost of sales/inventories) implicitly assumes proportionality.

But proportionality is not only an invalid assumption at a moment in time because of the existence of economies of scale. It is also invalid in a time series context where there are learning effects. However, in practice most companies carry a number of lines of inventory, so in overall terms the fact that proportionality is assumed when it cannot technically be justified is unlikely to lead to a significant misinterpretation of a company's position.

(4) Misspecification of the underlying relationship may help to explain the widely observed lack of statistical normality in distributions of particular ratios. This means that special care needs to be taken when trying to draw inferences when interpreting financial statements or when attempting to make interfirm comparisons. Certainly it seems in practice that there is a tendency to assume that averages are pitched in the middle of a distribution and that the dispersion is even around the mean.

(5) Another factor to bear in mind is that there are systematic differences in the distributions of ratios between industries (e.g. especially in terms of industry averages). These partly reflect differences in trading, but may also to some extent be the result of the incidence of particular accounting conventions (e.g. with respect to R&D).

## Traditional ratio analysis

Accounting textbooks dealing with the interpretation of financial statements generally focus on three major aspects of a business's activities: namely, how to appraise

(1) a company's long term financial position;
(2) its short term financial position; and
(3) its profitability and efficiency.

Usually the process is described on the assumption that no other information than that contained in the annual accounts is available to the analyst.[7]

*Long run financial position*

In this context analysts will want to know

(1) whether the company is going to be able to meet its debts in the long run;
(2) the volatility of its earnings; and
(3) its ability to raise new capital through borrowing.

For (1) they will really need information to help them estimate a firm's ability to generate long term net cash flows. This can only be done by identifying permanent earnings potential and the expected growth path of earnings – exactly the same information that is required by equity investors to value a business on a going concern basis.

As for (2), it will be relevant to identify both the company's fixed costs and the nature of its revenues (e.g. whether they are highly cyclical or not).

With respect to (3), the best that can be done is to try to establish

(a) the redemption terms of any loan outstanding;
(b) the firm's long term capital budgeting plans; and
(c) the security that can be offered.

Information in the financial statements only provides some of the pieces in the jigsaw puzzle, and it is up to the analyst to fill in the gaps as best he or she can. What can be inferred from the accounts is summarised below.

*(1) Cost structure analysis.* As a first step in identifying the potential volatility of a company's earnings the analyst will have to examine various ratios, both in a time series and a cross sectional context.

In the finance literature it has been argued that the systematic risk of a company can to some extent be explained in terms of its debt/equity ratio and its operating risk, as measured by its ratio of fixed to variable costs.

In practice financial and operating risks are difficult to distinguish, and analysts will probably therefore look at the overall position. Typically they will approach the problem by first calculating various ratios taken from a balance sheet, from the profit and loss account, or from both these financial statements.

The main ratios that are generally used for this purpose are debt/equity; and debt/(equity+debt), both taken from the balance sheet; and operating profit/debt interest or funds flow/debt interest, both derived from the profit and loss account.

Problems arise in the case of the former – or have done prior to the implementation of SSAP 21 and FRS 5 – with off balance sheet financing (including leases and hiring arrangements) and the inclusion of intangibles (such as brands); and the use of unreliable values for assets and – especially before the implementation of FRS 4 – claims (e.g. deep discount bonds). With respect to the profit and loss account ratios, problems can arise where leasing and rent costs are disguised interest payments. Moreover, when appraising the ratios special care should be taken to allow for whether the year is a 'good' or 'bad' one, i.e. whether the profits are relatively high or low.

Another technique sometimes recommended is to calculate the rate of return before interest on equity plus debt and compare that to the return after interest on equity, the difference showing the gain to the equity holders from borrowing.

The main difficulty with this type of analysis is that none of the measures really gets to the heart of the matter as each one concentrates on financial leverage rather than overall leverage (i.e. the ratio of fixed to variable costs). Fortunately the analyst should be able to deduce the approximate fixed cost/variable cost relationship by identifying:

(a) financial fixed costs (interest, lease payments, hire charges, etc);
(b) depreciation – a fixed cost assuming it to be the result of the decline in value of the asset that results from the passage of time rather than from use alone. (This is likely with obsolescence being a major determinant of declines in wasting asset values); and
(c) wages (assuming that this item is to some extent a variable cost).

The analyst will then be left to estimate raw material costs[8] and fixed and variable overheads. Knowledge of industry characteristics and the firm itself should be especially useful in this context.

*(2) The pattern of revenue receipts.* For this purpose the analyst will need to refer to past experience of the business and the industry in which it operates so as to be able to forecast the likely pattern of future sales and profits or working capital funds flow. Important guideposts are whether the industry is in the primary, secondary or tertiary sectors; the size of the company; and the degree to which the company's activities are diversified.

*(3) Redemption terms and available security.* The analyst can of course discover redemption dates for loans from a company's Register of Charges, if not from its annual accounts. It should similarly be possible to find out which assets are the subject of security. A company's borrowing powers are also specified in its Memorandum and Articles, which can be inspected at its registered office or at Companies House.

But in assessing security it would ideally be necessary for an analyst to refer to the net realisable (rather than going concern) values of assets. In the circumstances it will be necessary to estimate these having some regard to the nature of the assets themselves and to the industry in which the particular company operates.

*Short term financial position*

Typically analysts will also study a company's accounts in order to try to find out something about its short term financial position. In this context they will need to establish

(1)  its solvency; and
(2)  its potential to generate working capital funds.

Management within companies can, of course, use a variety of techniques to control a company's short term financial position: e.g. referring to inventory control and cash budgeting models. (Management accounting texts usually describe optimising models in this context – e.g. the economic order quantity inventory model; and linear and dynamic programming models – but in practice managers tend to use more flexible spreadsheet based simulation models to determine the best strategy.)

At a lower level of sophistication more basic methods of stock control can be employed, debtors can be monitored by referring to an age break-down, and overall the position can be appraised by projecting a cash budget.

The main point to appreciate is that basically the external user of company financial statements needs the same information as internal managers, but has access to inferior data.

Against this background, the analyst will need to try to prepare his/her own crude cash budget, for example by projecting a working capital or cash flow of funds statement. However, as a first step he/she will probably refer to a series of ratios, which are likely to give much the same picture. Those most frequently described are referred to below.

*(1) Balance sheet ratios*

(a)  Current assets/current liabilities (generally known as the 'current' or 'working capital' ratio).

To make much sense of this ratio it is really necessary to compare it against an industry average or focus on the trend over time. Consequently the frequently quoted rule of thumb that the minimum value should be 2 is particularly misleading. What is a reasonable minimum will vary from industry to industry. Thus companies with short trading cycles will probably carry relatively low levels of stocks; and if they predominantly sell goods and services for cash, they are likely to show *negative* working capital positions in their balance sheets, especially if they operate with bank overdrafts. By contrast, civil engineering contractors, for whom the trading cycle may be in years rather than months or weeks, are likely to carry substantial amounts of stocks and work in progress in their balance sheets. Certainly most British companies survive very well with ratios some way below a coefficient of 2.

(b)  Stock/current assets.

This ratio shows the relative liquidity of current assets. However, it is a crude indicator: the liquidity of raw material lines, finished goods stocks and work in progress will vary considerably.

(c)  Liquid assets/current liabilities (generally known as the 'liquidity', the 'quick' or the 'acid test' ratio).

Again, it is necessary to compare this ratio against the industry average or to examine its trend over time. (The frequently quoted textbook rule of thumb that the minimum value should be 1 is as misleading as the corresponding argument that the current ratio should never be below 2.)

There are a number of problems which arise with these ratios which are all too often not pointed out in standard texts.

First, the figures used in the ratios are taken from balance sheets, which merely show the position at a moment in time. Not only do such figures rapidly get out of date, but it is also quite likely that a company's financial position will have changed completely when the analyst examines the figures some months after the financial year end.

A second point is that the ratios are inherently unstable. For instance, the current ratio can be improved by deducting a common amount from numerator and denominator. Thus, for instance, if debtors are liquidated the cash can be used to pay off creditors. This can be achieved either as a result of a deliberate manipulative policy on the part of management; or it can happen fortuitously if the two ratios being compared reflect different positions in an operating cycle. However, it should be noted that if the current ratio exceeds one and the liquidity ratio is less than unity – which will usually be the case – the liquidity ratio will deteriorate as the current ratio improves.

*Example*

The existing current assets/current liabilities ratio is £200/£100 = 2. If £50 of current assets are converted into cash, which is then used to pay off current liabilities, the ratio will alter as follows:

$$\frac{£200 - £50}{£100 - £50} = \frac{£150}{£50} = 3$$

A third problem is that the accounting figures representing current assets or current liabilities are often incomplete (e.g. unused overdraft facilities or planned capital expenditure are excluded). As a result, the ratios can give a misleading picture of the short term financial position. Likewise, bank overdrafts included as current liabilities may be 'hard core' (i.e. long term) liabilities; while some mortgages (or parts of them) and tax provisions may really be relatively short term debts.

A fourth point is that distortions can occur as a result of seasonal trading (e.g. with arable farms, which appear to be illiquid before the harvest but have unusually large cash balances afterwards; and likewise with toy retailers before and after the Christmas period). Since financial year ends are normally chosen when stocks will be seasonally low (e.g. stores groups often used to have a 31 January balance sheet date), the annual accounts will frequently suggest that the underlying liquidity of a company is better than is in fact really the case.

A fifth point to note is that a misleading impression of liquidity can be given because of stock valuation errors or because of the inventory valuation procedure adopted. Thus, for instance, the use of average cost rather than FIFO and/or the amount of fixed overheads carried forward may have a significant impact on the current ratio.

*(2) Mixed balance sheet/profit and loss account ratios*

The inherent instability in the ratios noted above will to some extent be ameliorated where 'mixed' ratios are used. However, the underlying problem will not be completely removed.

Widely used mixed ratios include the following:

(a)  Sales/working capital
     An increase in this ratio could either mean that working capital is being used more efficiently; or, alternatively, that overtrading is present (i.e. where sales are expanded without the business having adequate financial support, usually because of capital rationing).
(b)  Stock turnover (i.e. cost of sales/ stocks)
     To be valid, the numerator and denominator of this ratio should be expressed in similar terms – e.g. if stocks are valued at cost, the numerator should be cost of goods sold; and if the former is at prime cost, so too should be the latter.
     Stock valuation can also give rise to problems if there are significant price changes. Thus, in the extreme, the use of LIFO would render the ratio meaningless, and the application of average cost will likewise potentially cause difficulties. Moreover, seasonal trading will again be a problem.
     It should also be noted that stock turnover ratios would not necessarily be expected to remain constant. For instance, as has been pointed out previously, the economic order quantity (EOQ) model implies economies of scale,

whereas the need to create minimum buffer stock levels on launching a new product will work in the opposite direction.

(c) Debtors turnover (i.e. credit sales/ trade debtors)

With this ratio it is really necessary to match *trade* debtors against *credit* sales, but the latter is not usually separated out from *cash* sales in the published turnover figure. Allowance should also be made for seasonal trading if a reasonable assessment of the average period of credit allowed to customers is to be made. Generally, use of this ratio is no real substitute for an age analysis of debtors.

(d) Creditors turnover (i.e. purchases/ trade creditors).

With this ratio it is again really necessary to match *trade* creditors to purchases, but this may often not be possible where only published accounts are available.

One way of assessing whether the current or liquidity ratios are strictly comparable with the bench mark (such as the previous year's ratios) is to look carefully at the stock, debtors and creditors turnover ratios. Thus if debtors are liquidated and the cash used to pay off creditors, other things being equal the debtors and creditors turnover ratios should increase quite sharply.

*(3) Flow of funds analysis*

Flow of funds statements are usually prepared and presented by accountants on a 'bottom up' basis, i.e. beginning with profit and then adding back charges which do not involve outflows of funds (such as depreciation). But arguably the best way for an external user of financial information to try to develop a proxy cash budget is to examine a 'top down' flow of funds statement, i.e. starting with sales and then deducting expenses which involve the outflow of working capital funds so as to derive the 'funds from operations' figure.[9] This can then be used as a budgeting framework – e.g. to project future sales and variable expenses in order to examine the likely future level of working capital funds that will be generated from operations.

The importance of studying movements in a company's working capital position is that it focuses attention on the underlying causes of changes in liquidity rather than on the ratios themselves. In fact, short term financial difficulties generally occur because

(a) sales revenue falls – when either production is maintained and goods are stockpiled; or production is cut back, with a lower contribution towards fixed costs (i.e. there is 'undertrading'); or

(b) sales increase too rapidly for the business's working capital resources (i.e. there is 'overtrading').[10]

*(4) Interval ratios*

Interval ratios are frequently referred to in American textbooks. Their aim is to show how long it will take to pay off a liability.

*Example*

If a company has a bank overdraft of £9,000 and is generating £6,000 of working capital funds a year, the length of time it will take to pay off the debt can be calculated as

$$\frac{\text{Overdraft at year end}}{\text{Expected net inflow of funds}} \times 365$$

$$\frac{£9,000}{£6,000} = 1 \text{ year } 183 \text{ days}$$

This, so it is argued, shows the 'defensive position' of a firm. Another example of such a ratio referred to later is the 'no-credit-interval': i.e. the length of time it will take to pay off debts.

*Assessing performance*

The third matter of concern to analysts is how they might try to assess a business's performance.

First, as mentioned previously, it is necessary to have a standard of performance (i.e. a bench mark) against which to assess outcomes. There are basically three possibilities: a forecast standard; a level based on past performance; and a rival's performance.

Second, differences between actual outcomes and the bench mark standard can be expressed either in absolute terms or in percentage terms. In practice, it will generally be helpful to examine both as reference to one alone may be misleading. This is illustrated in the following example.

*Example*

|  | Year 1(£) | Year 2(£) | Change Absolute | Change Percentage |
|---|---|---|---|---|
| Wages | 3,000 | 2,700 | -300 | -10 |
| Rent | 300 | 330 | + 30 | +10 |

Clearly here the 10 per cent decline in wage costs is more important in absolute terms than the 10 per cent increase in rent, indicating the often overlooked danger of referring only to proportionate differences. Referring to absolute differences alone may be reasonable, however, when comparing outcomes to forecasts (e.g. in budget variance analysis); or for time series analysis. But for cross sectional analysis it will generally be more appropriate to try to identify *functional relationships* by 'decomposing' the statement categories, as illustrated below.

*Example*
Setting the index 'standard' as sales, proportions might be calculated as follows:

|               | X     | Y     |
|---------------|-------|-------|
| Sales         | 100.0 | 100.0 |
| Cost of sales | 66.7  | 50.0  |
| Gross profit  | 33.3  | 50.0  |
| Expenses      | 11.0  | 22.5  |
| Net profit    | 22.3  | 27.5  |

Such a procedure can also be used for budgetary and time series comparisons. Other things being equal, a constant percentage over time should indicate a variable cost. However, the use of particular accounting conventions may undermine comparability over time or between companies.

Two of the above ratios are often regarded as being of special significance:

(1)  gross profit margin (i.e. gross profit/sales); and
(2)  net profit margin (i.e. net profit/sales).

A number of problems arise with time series comparisons:

(a)  The accounting numbers will be affected by the accounting conventions used (e.g. with regard to depreciation and stock valuation).
(b)  In a competitive environment a firm has no control over the selling price of its product, so the sales index is inherently unstable.
(c)  Most firms are multi-product in nature, with the result that the overall gross profit margin is a weighted average of the contribution margin of each product. Consequently, as the sales mix changes over time, so will the overall margin.

Similar difficulties arise with cross sectional comparisons and thus undermine the validity of studies by agencies such as the Centre for Interfirm Comparisons.

(a)  Different accounting practices. This problem is made worse because outwardly similar firms adopt different organisational structures. This is then reflected in the nature of their costing systems and how costs are allocated.
(b)  Different competitive environments – e.g. to repeat a point made previously, Harrods sells high margin products, often on credit, whereas Littlewoods sells low margin products for cash, although both companies are classified as

103

multiple stores. Similarly, as between manufacturers, products will tend to be at different stages of maturity, illustrated in Figure 3.3.

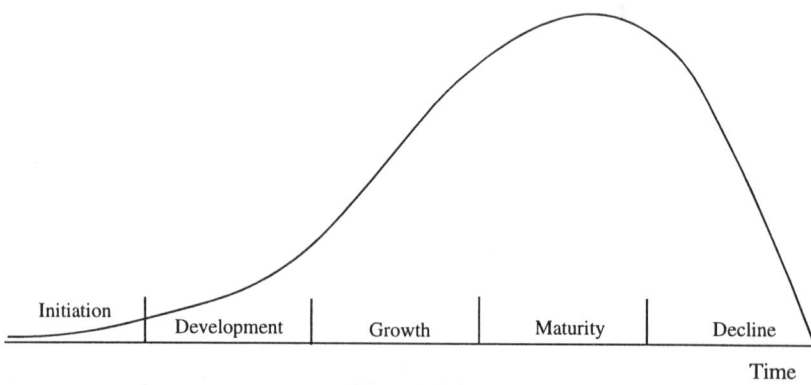

Initiation | Development | Growth | Maturity | Decline

Time

**Figure 3.3**

Large businesses should of course have extensive portfolios of products at various stages in their life cycles, so the 'errors' will tend to cancel each other out. However, for smaller businesses, or even those large concerns which have relatively small product portfolios – e.g. in the manufacture of aircraft – the distortions are potentially a major problem.

(c) Sales mix will differ as between firms (e.g. one supermarket may sell more wines and spirits than another because of lack of local competition). This will mean that the results of one business when compared to those of another may just reflect a different market environment rather than any fundamental difference in performance. In such circumstances, examining ratios would seem to be a rather long-winded way of finding out that the environments in which two businesses operate are different.

In practice analysts will refer to other measures of profitability and efficiency, such as 'earnings per share' (EPS). However, as is well known, because the numbers of shares in issue differ as between companies, it is not possible to make cross sectional comparisons using EPS, only time series comparisons. Further, adjustments are needed for dilution when there are bonus issues, rights issues, convertible stock, and share options, a matter which of course is dealt with in SSAP 3 (as amended by FRS 3). Allowance also has to be made for inbuilt growth of the EPS as the investment base is expanded as a result of profit retentions.

Reference to price/earnings (P/E) ratios will enable analysts to make cross sectional EPS comparisons as the share prices act as a deflator. However, differences in P/E ratios between companies will also reflect investors' varying perceptions of risk and their differing expectations of future earnings growth.

But perhaps the most widely used profit index used for cross sectional comparisons of performance between companies is the 'return on investment'

(ROI) or 'return on capital employed' (ROCE) ratio, which uses the asset base of a company as the deflator.

There are various versions of this ratio – e.g.

(1) profit/equity
(2) profit before interest/(equity + debt)
(3) profit before interest/total assets
(4) profit before interest and depreciation/gross cost of assets.

Other adjustments are sometimes made – e.g.

(a) adding back tax charges (to avoid the problems of different tax rates and allowances and different deferred tax accounting policies);
(b) adjusting for unrealistic proprietors' or directors' remuneration; and
(c) adjusting asset bases (e.g. excluding goodwill and intangibles; capitalising leases, etc; revaluing assets).

As a number of academics have pointed out, another major problem with the return on investment ratio is that there will be an error to the extent that the depreciation method does not reflect economic reality.[11] However, it is probably just as easy to illustrate the point with the help of the following simple example.

*Example*
Assume an asset costing £1,736 is expected to generate net cash flows of £1,000 over two years, after which it will have a scrap value of zero. The company uses straight line depreciation and has a cost of capital of 10 per cent per annum.

| Year | 1 | 2 |
|---|---|---|
| Revenues | 1,000 | 1,000 |
| *Less* Depreciation | 868 | 868 |
| Profit | 132 | 132 |

Defining the ROI as *profit/beginning of year asset value*, the annual returns are:

| Year | 1 | 2 |
|---|---|---|
| | 132/1736 | 132/(1736-868) |
| | = 7.6 per cent | = 15.2 per cent |

Clearly the depreciation procedure produces an error because it is *too conservative*, i.e. the capital consumption charges do not reflect the annual net benefits of using the asset. In fact, the internal rate of return (IRR) – which is presumably the meaningful economic rate of return that is the aim of the

105

calculation – is 10 per cent per annum, i.e. $1000/1.10 + 1000/(1.10)^2 = 1,736$. Applying sinking fund (annuity) depreciation, the depreciation charge for the first year, $D_1$, is

$$1,736/[1 + (1.10)] = 827.$$

The charge for the second year, $D_2$, will then be $D_1(1.10)$, giving rise to the following profit figures:

| Year | 1 | 2 |
|------|------|------|
| Revenues | 1,000 | 1,000 |
| *Less* Depreciation | 827 | 910 [=827(1.1)] |
| Profit | 173 | 90 |

The annual ROI as previously defined will then be equal to the internal rate of return expressed as a yearly average, namely, 10 per cent per annum:

| Year | 1 | 2 |
|------|------|------|
| | 173/1736 | 90/(1736-827) |
| | $\cong$ 10 per cent | $\cong$ 10 per cent |

This illustrates the distortion which results from the conservatism practised in conventional accounting as a result of applying the prudence doctrine in relation to depreciation policy. This biases returns downwards in the first half of an asset's life, but then biases them upwards in the second half. (The annual return is approximately 'right' mid-way through the life of a wasting fixed asset, here approximated by averaging the reported return as $(.076+.152)/2 = 11.4$ per cent.)

In the example no allowance has been made for retentions offsetting the depreciation provisions, which in practice will be invested in other assets. If these are taken into account it means that the ROI for a firm becomes a *weighted average* of individual asset returns. Moreover, the weighted average will depend on the proportion of assets that are relatively new and the dividend/growth policy being pursued by a business.

A moment's thought will show that the 'error' affecting the ROI/ROCE ratio will manifest itself in a number of ways, e.g.:

(1) The ROI will tend to fluctuate around a mean for a particular firm or industry.
(2) There will be a narrower dispersion of rates around a mean for larger firms holding sizeable stocks of wasting assets with a more-or-less even age distribution.

(3) There will be different mean returns for particular industries and firms because
  (a) they will use different accounting valuation conventions;
  (b) the proportions of assets subject to these conventions will differ;
  (c) the incidence of price changes will vary as between industries and businesses; and
  (d) growth rates will vary as between industries and firms.
(4) ROI will tend to be relatively lower for rapidly growing firms because
  (a) there will be a downwards bias from overstating depreciation in the early years of asset lives – and rapidly growing firms will have relatively more of such assets;
  (b) firms with high growth goals and/or which are not subject to severe capital rationing are likely to operate with lower 'hurdle' interest rates for project appraisal;[12] and
  (c) inflation is likely to accentuate the bias from overstating depreciation in the early years of asset lives.

Whether analysts are fully aware of the above matters is a moot point, but the incidence of such 'errors' will probably in most circumstances be ameliorated by other factors. However, there have been instances where such 'measurement error' appears to have misled those trying to interpret accounts: e.g. the Restrictive Trade Practices Court in the celebrated Cement reference in the late 1950s (Sutherland, 1965).

In practice, analysts will not refer to return on capital employed alone when trying to assess performance. Rather, they will look at other indicators as well. These will include:

(1) Dividend cover (i.e. profit/dividend)
  This ratio may be taken to reflect management's perceptions regarding the uncertainty associated with future earnings.
(2) Turnover ratios
  An examination of trends over time in ratios such as sales/stocks of finished goods may reflect on the operating efficiency of management.
(3) Productivity ratios
  It is frequently suggested that reference should be made to productivity ratios, which relate an index of output to an index of input (e.g. profit/capital employed; profit/employees; profit/man-hours; capacity utilisation). However, what analysts should really concentrate on are *marginal* rather than *average* returns. And, of course, if there is more than one limiting factor, technically it is necessary to look at the overall position via linear programming (a possibility not available to external analysts, of course, although the principle is still valid).

### Systematic ratio analysis

Empirical univariate ratio studies have been developed by academics on a rather different basis to the traditional form of financial statement analysis described in standard textbooks.

Essentially what is done in the context of bankruptcy studies is that populations of failed and non-failed companies are selected and then each of a number of ratios is tested to see which one best classifies the two groups of firms over a number of years prior to failure.

The first paired sample study of this type was undertaken by Fitzpatrick (1932) in the US. For his sample of 19 matched pairs of companies the best discriminators were net profit/net worth; and net worth/debt.

However, despite the apparent success of this experiment, it was not until some 30 years later that a comprehensive study along similar lines was undertaken by Beaver (1966). The basis of his argument was not dissimilar to that adopted in order to develop the gambler's ruin model, namely, a firm is regarded as comprising 'a reservoir of liquid assets, which is supplied by inflows and drained by outflows. [Its] solvency ... can be defined in terms of the probability that the reservoir will be exhausted.' In order to test this concept of ratio analysis he initially identified 30 ratios for a population of 79 pairs of companies, and the ratios were allocated to six groups reflecting different financial characteristics. The best discriminators were working capital funds flow/debt (which identified the firms correctly in 90 per cent of cases one year prior to failure); and net income/total assets (which had a success rate of 88 per cent at a similar stage). The proportion of misclassifications increased as the years prior to bankruptcy were increased, but the discriminatory power was still on the face of it impressive and not greatly inferior to that of the first multivariate studies published around the same time by Tamari (1965) and Altman (1968).[13]

There have been relatively few specifically univariate ratio studies undertaken since Beaver's pioneering work in 1966, most researchers preferring to use multivariate models. However, one exception is Casey and Bartczak (1984), who assessed the discriminatory power of 'operating cash flow' (OCF) and other cash flow ratios. Their reason for examining this was that a survey showed that funds flow indicators were regarded as a key indicator of bankruptcy risk by US financial executives, and a study by Largay and Stickney (1980) had found that OCF was more accurate and timely in indicating impending failure than traditional financial ratios or movements in share prices. Comparing 60 failed companies against a control sample of 230 businesses, Casey and Bartczak found that they could correctly classify 90 per cent of bankrupt firms one year prior to collapse and 92 per cent two years before. However, the discriminatory power was far worse for non-failing firms, namely, only 53 per cent and 44 per cent for the corresponding two years prior to bankruptcy of the matched companies.[14]

Casey and Bartczak compared the performance of their univariate model against a multivariate descriminant model based on six accrual based ratios. This was far superior in classifying failing and non-failing firms, and Casey and Bartczak concluded that cash flow variables were probably not useful in classifying non-failing firms because some of the latter were growing rapidly, which left them short of cash.

Four key issues need to be noted at this stage, and they equally apply to the multivariate studies.

(1) First, as mentioned in chapter 1, the sample selection procedure using matched pairs is biased, inasmuch as the chances of a company failing even in the 'window' studied is probably not 50 per cent but more nearly between 2 and 10 per cent, with 20 per cent the upper boundary.[15]

(2) The second problem also concerns sample selection. It has been pointed out previously that 'average' ratios will differ from industry to industry (e.g. the current ratio and the rate of return on capital employed: see pp. 99 and 106 respectively). Consequently it is necessary to ensure that like is compared to like, and this is normally achieved (as was explained in chapter 1, pp. 30-31) by pairing companies. However, the wider implications of adopting such a procedure are rarely discussed. In fact, not only will it eliminate certain potential explanatory variables, such as size and industry membership, but it also assumes a degree of homogeneity in the data (i.e. that each of the ratios considered will be of equal importance for the companies in the sample). If instead there is a degree of heterogeneity – as seems likely – ratios which represent a 'lowest common denominator' will be the best discriminators. These are likely to be general indicators (e.g. of profitability and indebtedness), and as they will reflect symptoms rather than causes, they will probably not tell analysts much they don't already know.

One way of trying to check on this is to study share price behaviour of failing companies – although it is difficult to allow for the impact of systematic market movements in share prices. This was attempted by Beaver (1968a), and (as will be described in chapter 6) his results suggested that the market was picking up the distress signals at least as early as his best performing ratios were indicating the problems afoot.

(3) The third issue relates to the basis of comparison between pairs and follows on from the previous point. Beaver (1966) in fact applied his critical ratios to *all* companies in his sample. An alternative, as indicated in chapter 1, is to rank each pair, which can give rather different results and makes a more direct allowance for variations in industry membership, size and time of failure captured in the pairing process.

(4) The original univariate studies suppressed the constant: i.e. they assumed changes should be strictly proportionate. While this may not be an

unreasonable simplification for single industry studies, it seems likely to create problems when data for companies operating in different sectors are pooled.[16]

Academics undertaking studies in more recent years have overwhelmingly chosen to employ multivariate methods of analysis. As part of this process they have generally undertaken univariate analysis as a preliminary step, employing the same technique (such as regression, logit or discriminant analysis), which involves estimation of a constant. Unfortunately they have rarely reported the classificational accuracy of univariate models, which – given the relatively good performance of Beaver's ratios – is disappointing.

## Summary

The conventional approach to financial statement analysis is univariate and variables (usually purporting to indicate a company's gearing, liquidity and profitability) are examined one-by-one. Not only does this approach ignore interactions between variables, but it concentrates narrowly on numbers drawn from the accounts. They in turn can be generated by completely different combinations of economic events, and the task of the analyst is further complicated by having to identify suitable benchmarks and by various problems which are encountered when calculating particular financial ratios. In the circumstances, it is usually necessary to refer to information outside the framework of the accounts to build up a picture of a firm's financial performance and its current position.

Despite these problems, a number of studies have been undertaken by academics referring systematically to a series of individual ratios. Using a matched pair research design, these have been quite successful in discriminating between failed and non-failed companies. However, they appear to rely heavily on general financial indicators, which seem to reflect symptoms rather than causes. Moreover, they have been outperformed by *multivariate* models, and it is for this reason that the latter are most generally discussed in the literature.

## Notes

[1] See Foulke (1968).

[2] Dev (1974) provides a useful short history of the development of ratio analysis.

[3] Bird (1965) and subsequent annual surveys of accounts by the Institute of Chartered Accountants in England and Wales have shown the lags for listed companies are fairly stable: namely, 25 per cent publish their accounts within three months of the year end, 75 per cent within four months, and 100 per cent within five months. This means they meet the Stock Exchange rules, which also require them to publish half yearly interim accounts, for which the lags before publication are similar.

The time lag before publication is obviously longer for private companies (partly because s. 244 of the Companies Act 1985 permits them 10 months to file their accounts – or 13 months if they trade overseas – compared to only 7 (or 10) months for public companies). The survey of bankers by Egginton (1977) showed the average lag to be five months (assuming that the date on the audit report was the publication date of the financial statements) – and the bankers were looking at the accounts about seven months after the year ends. (And it is important to remember this is probably biased on the short side as companies seeking bank loans have an incentive to produce their accounts relatively early.)

[4] The measurement attributes of accounting numbers are, rather surprisingly, rarely discussed in accounting texts. Yet it is especially important to understand their properties in terms of different measurement scales. This matter is well described by Mattessich (1964). Thus, for instance, accounting representations are generally combinations of *nominal scale* representations (i.e. where the use of descriptive labels, such as 'labour', 'raw materials', etc, conveys not inconsiderable discriminatory power) and a *ratio scale* measurement, employing a particular number system. But the use of accounting measurements as *surrogates* for the economic events that are really the focus of a reader's interest is equally important. This is a matter dealt with by Ijiri (1967), who points out that the focus of interest is on the underlying reality (e.g. the layout of streets in a town) rather than their scaled representations (e.g. on a map).

[5] These are the subject of discussion in chapter 9.

[6] In practice *rankings* are commonly used in everyday life where relationships are not proportional. Thus, for instance, in a 100 metres race the runners are ranked first second and third, applying an *ordering* measurement scale. This is because the times recorded (applying a *ratio* scale – say 9.7, 9.8 and 9.9 seconds) have, of themselves, relatively little absolute significance (except in relation to a record). It is irrelevant whether the winner is twice as fast as the second placed runner or only 1 per cent faster.

Few economic relationships are proportional in a strictly linear sense, and in practice analysts allow for this. Thus, to take a widely used financial ratio, the rate of return on capital employed (ROCE) might be expected for most companies in a particular industry to be above a certain threshold (say 10 per cent per annum). The majority might report returns between 12 per cent and 15 per cent, and the best performer 24 per cent. Experienced analysts will use such statistics as general indicators, not as precise measurements: e.g. they will not infer that the best performer is doing twice as well as a company reporting 12 per cent. Prima facie it is just doing better – much better – that's all.

[7] In what follows it is assumed (where relevant) that the analyst has access to a company's full statutory accounts as laid before the shareholders in general meeting, but to no other information about the business.

[8] Formats 2 and 4 for the Profit and Loss Account in the Fourth Schedule to the Companies Act 1985 require that raw material and staff costs should be itemised,

whereas Formats 1 and 3 do not. However, particulars of employees and their remuneration have to be disclosed under para. 56 of the Fourth Schedule, so it is possible to make estimates on the basis of the information included in the accounts.

[9] For most interpretation purposes it will probably be preferable to analyse flows of working capital funds. This is because current assets are usually fairly close substitutes for cash, and what is generally needed is an overall picture of changes in liquidity. However, the two fund concepts ('cash' and 'working capital') are not mutually exclusive, and analysts should use the approach most relevant for their needs.

(Working capital funds were, of course, the focus of interest in statements prepared under the now withdrawn accounting standard, SSAP 10. The current standard, FRS 1, prescribes a statement tracing pure cash flows.)

[10] Overtrading generally arises where there is capital rationing. It therefore is a problem more associated with private than listed companies, since the latter should be able to raise additional finance to support expansion if they are engaged in a profitable business.

A rather different problem (which is often confused with overtrading) sometimes afflicts listed companies, and that is over-rapid growth. This arises where a company expands its asset base, usually via acquisition as well as through organic growth. This increases its fixed costs, and an unanticipated shortfall in demand (e.g. as a result of recession, unexpectedly fierce competition, or changes in consumer tastes, exchange rates, or technology) can leave it operating below its breakeven point. Such a crisis is therefore really one of under- rather than over-trading.

[11] For example, Harcourt (1965), Solomon (1966) and Kay (1976).

[12] Essentially this means that the objective of such companies is not shareholder wealth maximisation. Instead it is left to investors to construct portfolios which are optimal from their perspective. So long as there are *some* companies prepared to take on projects with positive net present values at the market (opportunity) cost of capital, there should be no misallocation of resources within an economy and hence no loss of welfare to society.

[13] These studies are described respectively on pp. 154-5 and 135.

[14] The ratio of failed to non-failed firms in this study is roughly 1:4 compared to the true ratio for listed companies of around 2:98. In the circumstances the inability of the model to identify non-failed firms correctly more than half the time is a very disappointing result, implying the procedure will not be very helpful as a practical means of discriminating between failing and non-failing firms.

[15] It is difficult to be precise as companies in some industries are most unlikely to collapse, whereas others are much more vulnerable, especially in certain economic circumstances.

[16] See chapter 8.

# 4 Positive theories of corporate failure: II – Multivariate models

## Introduction

The previous chapter was the first of five whose purpose is to describe procedures used to examine the characteristics of financially distressed companies and to review the empirical evidence relating to their application. As was explained then, there is often only a tenuous link to an underlying positive theory which might explain why such companies fail. However, it is nonetheless convenient to regard them within that context.

Chapter 3 was concerned with the use of univariate models to try to discriminate between bankrupt and non-failing companies. This chapter and the two which follow will examine the application of multivariate models (i.e. where two or more independent variables are analysed to assess how together they appear to be able to distinguish between companies which go bankrupt and those which survive). In particular, the focus of this chapter is statistically derived models.

In fact, over the past thirty years various statistical techniques have been used to develop failure identification models. Probably the most obvious procedure to use would be the well known *regression model*. However, this has certain drawbacks for the type of study usually undertaken, and the potentially more robust *logit model* has been applied in recent years. But rather surprisingly, perhaps, it was not the regression model that was generally used in the original multivariate failure studies but another procedure, *discriminant analysis*. In fact, as has been shown subsequently, this approach will produce very similar results to the straightforward regression model as it is computationally equivalent (Dhrymes, 1974, pp. 74-76; Hamer, 1983). Moreover, it has also been pointed out that although logit is potentially more powerful than conventional linear regression, many of its advantages are lost when the samples being examined are relatively small – which is usually the case with bankruptcy studies. More recently attempts have been made to use a different type of regression model, the duration model, where the focus of interest is not so much a dependent 'state variable', fail/non-fail (as it is with dichotomous regression and discriminant analysis), or even the probability of failure (as it is with logit), but rather the likely length of time before a company fails. However, such an approach is only really operational when examining the experience of a cohort of firms with a common 'birth date'.

Against this background, the purpose of this chapter is, first, to examine the control and validation methods employed in multivariate studies, since these are common to all procedures; and, second, to describe briefly each of the procedures used and the results of key studies undertaken applying them: regression, logit, discriminant analysis, and duration (survival) models.

## Control and validation procedures

The usual approach followed in developing multivariate – and, indeed, univariate – failure identification models is to pair bankrupt and surviving companies, matching by criteria such as year, industry membership and size. Clearly this will control for these common factors, but it also has the effect of excluding them as possible explanatory variables.

A problem, referred to in chapter 1, is that the matched pairing procedure introduces a potential sampling bias as the number of non-failing listed companies in a population in any year is not 50 per cent but more like 98 per cent or 99.5 per cent. If there is no adjustment for this the results can overstate the discriminatory power of a model. Although in early multivariate bankruptcy studies no such adjustment was made, more recently the effect of the bias has been recognised. However, it has to a considerable extent been offset by allowing for the cost of misclassifying failed companies as non-failed and vice versa, the argument being that it is far more expensive not to spot a bankrupt firm than to misclassify a healthy company as a failure. Yet whether such an adjustment resolves the problem must be questioned, as it is generally made with the advantage of hindsight and relates to the specific sample on which the model is estimated. When the amended model is used, either on hold out samples or in practice, it will still misclassify companies, and the resulting costs cannot be ignored.

Another difficulty is 'overfitting', which results from basing claims for a model on its performance on the sample data from which it is derived. This can also lead to discriminatory power being overstated. One way of dealing with the problem is to apply a 'jackknife' procedure: i.e. estimate a model on n-1 companies' data. The model should then classify the missing company. Such a procedure can be repeated n times for all companies in the sample to derive a misclassification rate.

However, a more obvious solution is to test the model on a hold out sample of companies, either selected at random covering the same period as the data from which the model was derived; or, better still, over a different period to see how robust discriminatory power is over time. Such tests can be time consuming, and alternative procedures are available (Stone and Rasp, 1993).

A further issue is the extent to which a model is 'sample specific'. Thus in practice models are estimated on a specific set of data which are pooled over time and across a number of industries. This is largely inevitable if a sufficiently large population of listed companies is to be obtained. However, there are variations in the ratio characteristics of companies operating in different industries (see p. 211 et seq.), and equally general economic conditions change over time. As a result, the models to some extent represent the lowest common denominator of factors which characterise failing businesses. But the attributes captured are also specific to the circumstances represented in the estimation sample. This helps to explain why researchers have generated a variety of different discriminatory models which (ignoring the sampling bias problem referred to above) seem to work well in classifying failed and non-failing companies in terms of the estimation sample. Interestingly, they generally seem to perform less effectively on hold out samples, especially where they are drawn from a different time period.

The significance of these matters has rarely been examined in any depth, although Mensah (1984) specifically addressed the issue on a sample of 110 matched pairs of US listed companies covering failures over the period 1972-1980. He identified four distinct economic phases during that period and split his sample into two broad industry categories (mining and manufacturing; and retailing). As expected, he found that there were significant differences in the factors which distinguished bankrupt from non-bankrupt companies, depending on the time period covered and the industry membership of companies.

But there is another general control issue which rarely, if ever, appears to have been considered. This is the fact that there will almost certainly be a degree of random error in the classification procedure. Thus, for instance, if the aim is to classify bankrupt and non-bankrupt companies correctly, the objective is presumably to obtain a 100 per cent identification success rate. Yet in practice this is unlikely to be achieved, just as if a coin is tossed 100 times it will almost certainly not result in exactly 50 heads and 50 tails being observed. Of course, in practice it is possible to check on the significance of this by referring to statistical tests, conventionally applying a 95 per cent confidence level. However, it equally means that if a model classifies (say) 85 per cent of companies correctly, there is a degree of error implicit in this figure. But beyond that, it is also conceivable that, as a result of overfitting, a model will discriminate between *non-failed* companies because of the nature of the statistical procedures, the data and the matched pairing research design being used. If this is so, it is yet another reason for interpreting the results of any failure identification experiment with some caution.

### Regression analysis

*Bivariate regression analysis*

The basic bivariate regression procedure is well known, its aim being to express an observed cause-and-effect relationship. The latter is generally expressed as

$$Y = bX \qquad\qquad (4.1)$$

> where Y is the dependent variable explained in terms of X, an independent variable.

Thus in terms of Figure 4.1, Y (representing total costs, for instance) might be explained in terms of X (volume of output). The 'parameter' value, b, would represent the variable cost per unit.

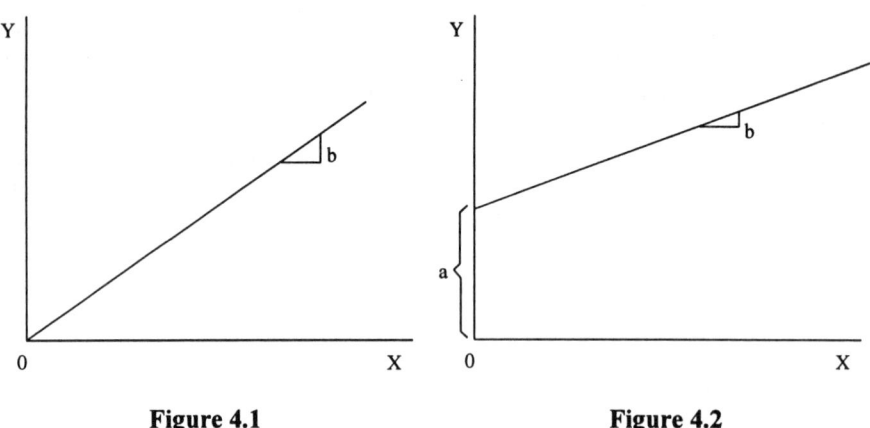

**Figure 4.1**                    **Figure 4.2**

In practice it is most unusual for linear functions to run through the origin, as drawn in Figure 4.1 (although the conventional sales function is one example where this does happen). Far more common is a function where there is a 'constant' (or 'intercept') where the value of X = 0. Thus with a cost function, it is usual to incur fixed costs even if no goods are produced. This gives rise to the function illustrated in Figure 4.2,

$$Y = a + bX \qquad\qquad (4.2)$$
where a is the constant.

The problem in practice is how to estimate the equation that explains an observed functional relationship. The easiest way, described in some management accounting texts, is to take the highest and lowest observations and draw a line between them. This procedure is extremely crude, however, and ignores most of the data points that could be plotted. A far better approach which takes account of these other observations is to fit a line statistically, as suggested in Figure 4.3, the generally favoured procedure being the 'least squares' method, which minimises the sum of the squared deviations between the plots and the fitted line.

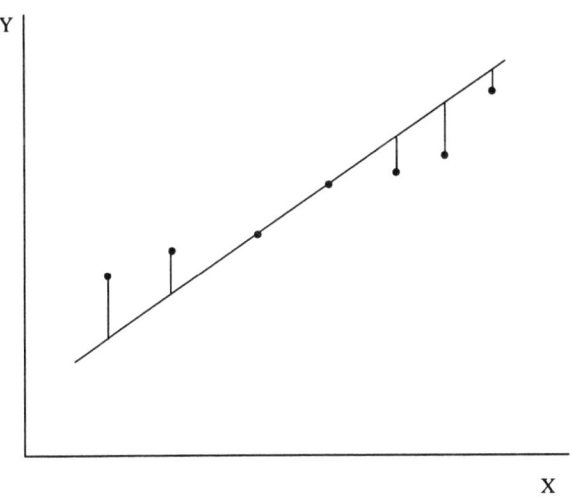

**Figure 4.3**

One of the key assumptions that underlies the regression procedure is that the relationship being observed is linear. Of course, this condition may well be violated. For instance, in terms of a cost function there may be economies of scale: i.e. the coefficient b is not a constant gradient but gradually declines as X (the number of units produced) increases. Alternatively, if the data underlying a relationship cannot all be collected at the same moment in time, it may be necessary to 'pool' observations over a number of periods. This can cause problems if the relationship is unstable: e.g. it is commonly anticipated that over time average unit costs will decline because of 'learning effects'.

One way of trying to handle these problems is to *transform* a curvilinear function until it becomes linear before applying regression: e.g. where there is a logarithmic learning curve, taking the antilogs of the observed costs should achieve the desired result when the objective is to estimate a company's cost function.

The other key assumption is that the residual 'error term' (i.e. the difference between actual observations and the corresponding plots on the fitted regression line) should be randomly distributed with a constant variance. The variance (or standard deviation) can then be viewed as a measure of the scatter of the observed plots around the regression line. The standard deviation (or 'standard error') can then be used to assess the probability of a given observation falling either side of the fitted regression line. This is illustrated in Figure 4.4, where the probability distributions of plots straddling the estimated line are shown.

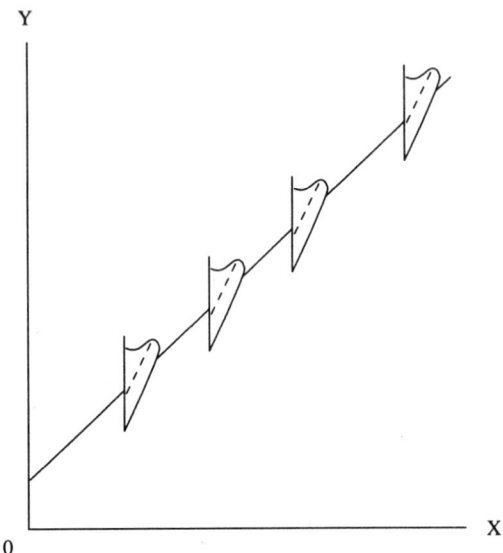

**Figure 4.4**

If the residual error term is not randomly distributed with a constant variance, it implies that there is a 'systematic factor' which has not been captured in the model. This would happen, for instance, if there are economies of scale (i.e. marginal costs decrease as output volume increases) and a linear function were fitted to data which had not been transformed. The picture would then be as shown in Figure 4.5, where Y represents costs and X output volume. (Similar problems would arise if there was a learning process and data were pooled over time.)

It can be seen that in Figure 4.5 there is a systematic pattern in the error terms, measured as the difference between the broken fitted line and the 'true' unbroken curve. What is wanted is error terms that are randomly distributed with constant variance (in other words, without systematic bias).[1]

With bivariate regression there are two key statistics which indicate how well the model fits. The first is the t statistic, which indicates whether the explanatory power of the independent variable is significantly different from zero. (Generally if the t value is greater than 1.7 the variable is regarded as being statistically significant, i.e. there is no more than a 5 per cent possibility that the relationship could have occurred by chance.) The second key statistic is the 'coefficient of variation', or $R^2$, which indicates the percentage of the movement in the dependent variable that can be explained by the independent variable.

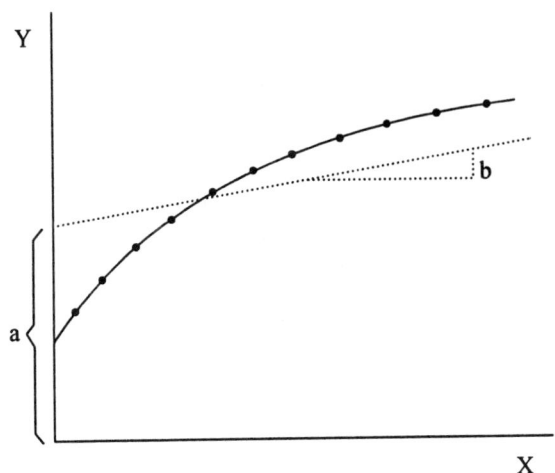

**Figure 4.5**

The importance of the two statistics is that the t statistic could, for instance, be (say) 6.7, but the $R^2$ only 0.30. This would indicate that the dependent variable Y certainly appears to be driven by the independent variable X, but overall the equation only explains 30 per cent of movements in the dependent variable. In other words, there must be other factors not captured in the equation which explain movements in the dependent variable.

Finally it should be noted that sometimes there are 'outliers' in a population of observations which may have an undue influence in determining the regression equation. In the circumstances, it may be necessary to exclude them to see what difference it makes to the 'goodness of fit' of the regression line. However, there is always the danger that such censorship will introduce a new bias into the exercise, so it is necessary to be parsimonious in excluding observations on these grounds.

*Multivariate regression analysis*

This leads naturally to a discussion of *multiple regression*, where there is no longer a single independent variable X on the right hand of the equation. Rather it takes the form

$$Y = a + b_1X_1 + b_2X_2 + b_3X_3 + .... + b_nX_n \qquad (4.3)$$

where $X_1$. .. $X_n$ represent a series of independent variables;
and $b_1$ ... $b_n$ are the corresponding parameter values.

119

Diagrammatically, where there are two independent variables rather than one the regression line can no longer be represented in two dimensional terms. Rather, a three dimensional plane has to be fitted (see Figure 4.6).

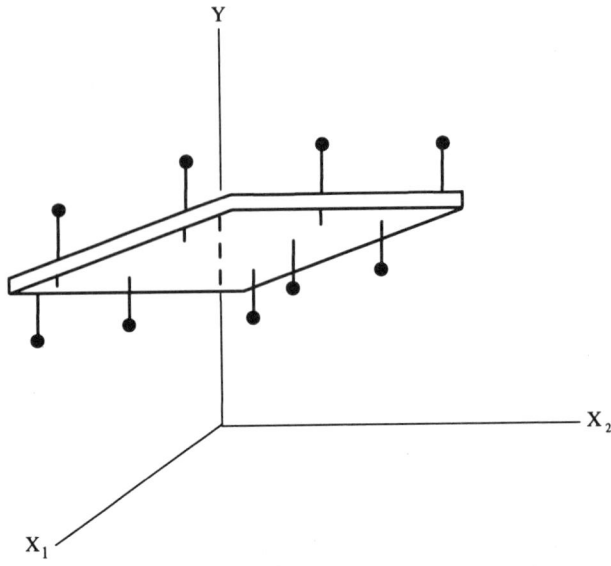

**Figure 4.6**

The explanatory power of each independent variable can again be assessed in terms of its t value; and the explanatory value of the equation overall is measured by its F statistic. Normally any value above 6 in the latter indicates significance at the 5 per cent confidence level. As for the coefficient of variation, this is calculated in a slightly different way as $\bar{R}^2$ (R bar squared).

Multiple regression computer programs are widely available these days (e.g. in spreadsheet packages), and the diagnostic statistics are printed out automatically. However, there are problems in using multiple regression models: namely, some variables are highly correlated with others already included in a model; and other key variables may be omitted. In the first case, this will show up in a low t value for one or more independent variables and relatively low F and $R^2$ values. Higher F and $R^2$ statistics can be achieved by dropping a variable which otherwise seems plausibly to be driving the dependent variable. This should also increase the t values of the remaining variables. (A check can be run on the relationships between variables by producing a correlation matrix.)

As for the omitted variable problem, this can sometimes be identified if there is evidence of 'heteroscedasticity', i.e. the error terms are not randomly distributed with constant variance.[2] This implies that there is an unidentified systematic factor driving the dependent variable. (As indicated above, with most packages diagnostic statistics indicating whether this is a problem will usually be printed out with the regression equation.)

An example of where heteroscedasticity would occur would be the situation described above where there is a learning curve which has not been taken into account when a cost function is being estimated from data pooled over time. Rather than by transforming the data, this could just as well be estimated as

$$Y = a + b_1X_1 + b_2X_2 \qquad (4.4)$$

where $X_1$ refers to observed cost data; and
$X_2$ refers to the appropriate scaling factor.

The error term residuals should be normally distributed, since if this condition is not met the F and t statistics will not be strictly applicable. However, it is usually assumed that this condition is met if the other requirements are fulfilled and if the number of observations is reasonably large.

Where a qualitative factor (such as an industry category) needs to be included in a model, this can be done by inserting a so-called 'dummy variable'. This takes a value of zero or one, and a model with such a variable (in addition to a ratio scale variable, such as return on capital employed) might appear thus

$$Y = a + b_1X_1 + b_2X_2 \qquad (4.5)$$

where (say) if $Y<0$ a company is prima facie a failure; and
if $Y>0$ a company is prima facie a non-failure;
$X_1$ is profit/capital employed; and
$X_2$ takes a value of 0 for a company in manufacturing and a value of 1 if it is in the
in the services sector.

The parameter values are found using least squares regression applied to a set of data. Let it be assumed that they are found to be $a = -1.0$; $b_1 = 6.0$; and $b_2 = 0.2$. If company M has a profit/capital employed ratio of 0.20 and is in the manufacturing sector, while company N has a profit/capital employed ratio of 0.10 and is in the services sector, M will score +0.2 and N will score -0.2. Consequently, M should prima facie be a non-failure, while N should be a failure.

One of the problems with dummy variables is that effectively they partition the data. Consequently their introduction will rapidly reduce the size of the subsamples on which the regression equations are estimated, and as this is done so called 'degrees of freedom' are reduced indicating that less confidence can be attached to the estimated parameter values.

A further difficulty which arises is that many economic variables are interdependent and consequently causal relationships are two way (e.g.

management sets prices according to a projected level of sales, but price also determines the level of sales). To solve this problem, 'endogeneous' variables (i.e. those determined within the system) have to be described in terms of 'exogeneous' variables (i.e. those determined externally). The resulting 'structural equations' have to be solved simultaneously using what is known as the 'indirect least squares' method.

*Dichotomous regression analysis*

*(i) The methodology.* Generally the regression model is described in terms of the dependent variable, Y, being expressed in terms of a 'ratio scale' measure (e.g. units of output or values expressed in £). However, it is also possible to define Y in terms of an 'nominal scale' variable, where Y takes a classificatory value 1, 2, 3, 4, etc. Often, in fact, a 'binary choice' or 'dichotomous' classification is envisaged, as it is if there are just two possibilities: a firm is either a 'failure' or a 'non-failure', the former being designated as (say) 0 and the latter as 1.

When this is done a boundary value has to be found which will distinguish between those firms in a population which are failures and those which are non-failures. This is done by minimising classification errors. Thus it could be that after fitting the regression line firms which score below 0.4 are prima facie failures, while those which score above that figure are prima facie non-failures. (Usually for convenience the models are rescaled so that the 'cut-off point' is either 0.5 or zero: the latter is implied in equation (4.5) above.)

*(ii) Empirical applications in failure studies.* Dichotomous regression was first used to identify financially distressed firms by Meyer and Pifer (1970), who were concerned to assess the risk of failure amongst US banks. Their study concerned 30 matched pairs of banks, the failures occurring between 1948 and 1965. The results were checked on a hold out sample of a further 9 matched pairs, and a set of 32 variables for each of six years prior to bankruptcy was screened. They found that with a lead time of two years they could correctly identify around 80 per cent of the failing banks, but at three years prior to failure it was impossible to discriminate effectively.

Subsequently the multiple regression analysis (MRA) technique was applied by Edmister (1972) in a study of small firm bankruptcies in the US. He expressed some explanatory variables as dummies, depending on trends identified or differences between a firm's ratios and industry averages.[3]

In the UK the MRA approach was used by Marais (1979) to develop a failure identification model for the Bank of England. The failed sample comprised 38 listed companies which went bankrupt between 1974 and 1977, and the control sample was 53 listed companies. The model was derived from a set of 59 financial variables, and the final version comprised four indicators, representing profitability, size, liquidity and funds flow. The main problem with the model was the relatively high proportion of 'Type II' errors (i.e. misclassifying non-failed firms as failed), which were anyway probably understated because of the potential sampling bias problem. Subsequently Marais developed the model for use by Datastream, with four different financial variables being included in the final discriminant function. However, no fewer than 40 per cent of the 1350 or so companies on the Datastream files were subsequently flagged as possessing a failure profile.[4]

## The logit model

*(i) The methodology.*[5] The usual regression model is in fact a 'linear probability model' of the form when estimated

$$Y = a + bX + e \qquad (4.7)$$

where the symbols are as previously defined, and
e is a random error term.

This permits the interpretation of values of Y not merely as indicating membership of one of two groups, fail and non-fail, but it also enables probabilities of membership of one or other of the groups to be calculated.

However, such a simple interpretation is flawed, since the score values are bounded at 0 and 1. The expected probability distribution, P, of Y can be described as

$$E(Y) = 1(P) + 0(1\text{-}P) \qquad (4.8)$$

where E(.) is the so-called expectations operator (i.e.
where the expression within the brackets
is expected rather than observed).

Unfortunately this means that the error term will be heteroscedastic, since there will be higher variances in the error term e when Y = 0.5 than where Y = 0 or 1. Equally a problem arises when the predicted value lies outside the 0-1 range. This is illustrated in Figure 4.7, where it can be seen the broken *estimated regression* line is different from the *true* regression line. (As drawn the slope is underestimated; it could equally well have been overestimated, in which case the cross over points would be reversed.)

The problems with the linear probability model can be avoided if the probability functions are transformed using a 'cumulative probability function'. Three of a number of possibilities which can achieve this are

(1) cumulative uniform probability function (which is a constrained form of the linear probability model);
(2) cumulative normal probability model ('probit'); and
(3) cumulative logistic probability model ('logit').

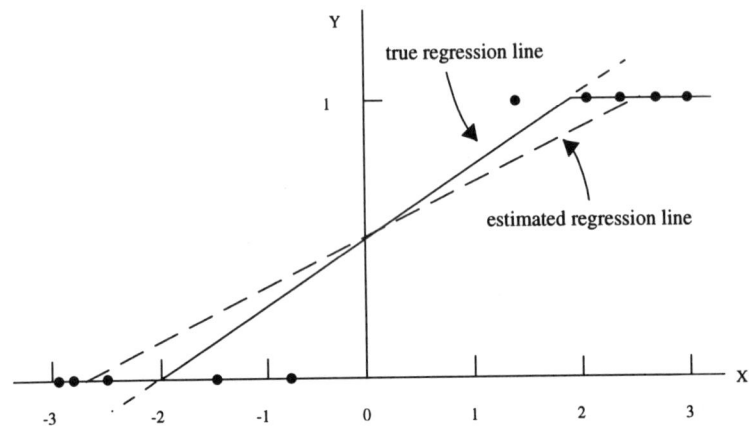

**Figure 4.7**

Here only logit will be dealt with. Under logit the dependent variable is simply the logarithm of the odds that a particular classification (fail/non-fail) will be made. Because the slope of the cumulative logistic distribution is at its greatest at $P = 0.5$, changes in the independent variable X will have the greatest impact at the mid-point of the distribution. But at $P = 0$ or $P = 1$ the logarithm of the odds will be undefined. This is illustrated in Figure 4.8.

The effect is that for logit the model should be estimated for *each point* in the distribution across X with a minimum of 5 observations per value of X. This is unlikely to be possible where

(1) the sample population is small;
(2) the variables are continuous; or
(3) where X represents several independent variables.

Thus Figure 4.8 merely shows the situation in two dimensions. Clearly many observations are needed to plot the non-linear function with any degree of accuracy. A moment's thought will show that in three dimensions, when another independent variable is introduced into the equation, the function will be like a snake or a sausage. It will then be necessary to have more observations for each datum point to locate the function.

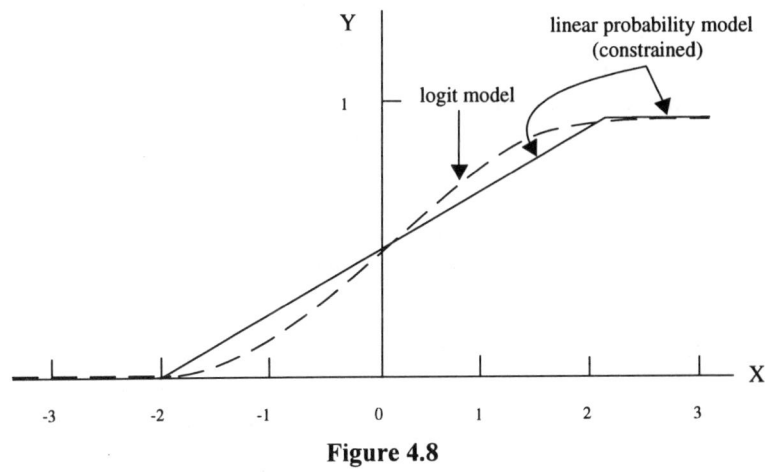

**Figure 4.8**

The solution is to apply what are called 'maximum likelihood estimates' using non-linear techniques (i.e. estimate where the function is most likely to plot). However, where samples are small, the parameter values are likely to be the same as for the 'linear probability model' given by conventional regression. Since samples in most failure studies are typically small – i.e. less than 100 failed companies – and several independent variables are used, it seems unlikely that logit will produce results that are very different from those generated by simple regression models. This was indeed argued by Lo (1986), who showed there was little difference between his logit results and those generated by discriminant analysis, which has many of the same properties as the straightforward regression model.

But even if the logit model might not be expected to discriminate much better than the regression model, its statistical requirements are less onerous (e.g. it can easily accommodate dichotomous independent variables). Moreover, when it is applied, a 'log-likelihood' (LL) coefficient is calculated. This is derived using non-linear techniques to estimate where the function is most likely to plot. Unlike the $R^2$ statistic, this ratio is not bounded by values 0 and 1, although (like the $R^2$ coefficient) the higher the value the greater the explanatory power of the model. Because there is no standard upper limit to the LL statistic, it has to be assessed against the estimated maximum in order to generate a test (the 'likelihood ratio' (LR) test), which is analogous to the F test in the linear regression model. This is done by comparing the unrestricted LL estimate for a model against the LL value of the function where all the coefficients are restricted to zero. The LR coefficient can then be tested as a chi square statistic with degrees of freedom equal to the number of independent variables (excluding a constant).[6]

The problem of using logit when the sample size is small has since been examined by Noreen (1988) and Stone and Rasp (1991). Noreen, in fact, accessed data comprising three accounting ratios for a population of 1,299 firms. He then randomly generated a dummy variable for each company and used simulation to create a large number of samples of 50 and 100 companies. After exhaustive testing he concluded that ordinary least squares regression performed as well as probit (the procedure similar to logit that he applied). The Stone and Rasp study also used simulation and reached similar conclusions. Their results suggest that where there are 4-6 predictors and skewed data, sample sizes of 200 or more will be needed to ensure that logit test statistics will be properly calibrated. However, much of the miscalibration when samples are smaller will be the result of skewness rather than the smallness of the sample size. On the other hand, they argued that the results of most accounting based studies which have applied logit are unlikely to have been misleading because the chi square test for overall significance is not usually the focus of interest. Rather, more attention is generally paid to the individual parameter estimates. But in addition, the reported chi square statistics have normally been so large relative to the critical value that they would still have been statistically significant even if they had been halved.

Before they can be interpreted as probability estimates, the dependent variable score, Y, in a logit model needs to be transformed. Effectively this is done by applying the following formula

$$e^Y / (1 + e^Y) \tag{4.9}$$

Assuming that 0 indicates bankruptcy, the greater the resulting decimal fraction is above 0.5 (which implies an equal chance of a company being a failure or non-failure), the less chance there is of the subject firm going bankrupt.

As indicated previously, it is in fact unrealistic to assess an equal prior probability of failure. However, the problem of adjusting logit and probit models to avoid sampling bias is not easily resolved. Zmijewski (1984) identified various procedures that can be adopted to reduce the bias, the easiest being the 'weighted exogenous sample maximum likelihood' (WESML) method. His study compared various probit models on six different sets of data where the proportions of failed to non-failed companies varied considerably, ranging from 40:40 to 40:800. Half of the 1,681 firms used in the study were in the derivation sample, the other half in the hold out sample. When sampling bias was not allowed for and it was assumed that there was an equal likelihood of a firm failing or surviving, 97.2 per cent of bankrupt firms were correctly identified and 92.5 per cent of non-bankrupt firms. However, when the 40:800 ratio was applied the respective correct classifications were 71 per cent and 99.5 per cent. Applying the WESML adjustment substantially eliminated the bias.

The adjustment to allow for differential misclassification costs is more straightforward. Thus if the cost of a 'Type I' error (i.e. incorrectly identifying a failed company as non-failed) is estimated to be seven times greater than that of a 'Type II' error (i.e. incorrectly identifying a non-failed company as failed), misclassification costs will be minimised by using a cutoff point of 0.125 rather than 0.5. Effectively this means that a firm with a probability of failure greater than 0.125 would be presumed bankrupt, at which the relative expected cost of a Type I error $(0.125 \times 7)$ would be equal to the expected cost of a Type II error ($[1 - 0.125] \times 1$).[7] However, as argued previously, while this procedure will be appropriate for assessing the classificatory effectiveness of the model on the sample of data from which it is derived, it will be of little help in ensuring its effectiveness as a predictive device. Misclassification errors will still arise even where an adjusted cutoff point is used, and consequently Type I and Type II errors will not be eliminated, giving rise to misclassification costs which will still have to be taken into account when the model is applied out-of-sample. Ultimately the only true test of its potential usefulness must be how well it performs in practice (i.e. the proof of the pudding will be in its eating).

*(ii) Empirical applications in failure studies.* The first researcher into corporate failure to use the logit model appears to have been Martin (1977), who employed it to examine failures in the US banking sector. Subsequently Ohlson (1980) applied it more generally to a sample of 105 bankrupt firms and some 2,000 surviving US companies over the period 1970-76. The ratios used were the log of a price-level deflated measure of total assets; total liabilities/total assets; working capital/total assets; current liabilities/current assets; net income/total assets; flow of funds/total liabilities; and a dummy where total assets were greater than total liabilities. The model did not discriminate between failed and non-failed firms as well as the MDA/MRA models reported in previous studies, but this might have been because the methodology differed in several important aspects, most obviously because of the relatively unbiased sampling procedure used by Ohlson, which suggests that previous researchers may have overstated the discriminatory power of their models. Many other studies have since been undertaken applying the logit/probit technique, both in the US and elsewhere. Thus Zavgren (1983), despite using a matched pairing technique, found misclassification errors for a 45 failed company sample similar to those reported by Ohlson, and somewhat surprisingly she also found the profit/(equity+debt) ratio was not significantly different between the two groups of companies, although liquidity and gearing measures were.

*Expanded logit models*

A model based on a single year's data is potentially helpful, but it only conveys a limited amount of information to an analyst. It would be useful to see if there is *incremental information* in signals of impending doom over a number of years.

Various attempts have been made to try to capture information over a period of time prior to failure. One procedure is to develop a score based upon dependent variable characteristics over a number of years. Taffler (1983), for instance, describes a 'performance analysis score' (PAS) procedure developed from applying his multiple discriminant analysis (MDA) model, discussed below (p. 140). This measure has been evolved on an adaptive basis, but according to Taffler it seems to work quite well. Basically it uses as its three inputs the MDA value of a company, its trend over time, and the number of years the firm has had a prima facie 'failure' score.

Another approach is to try to develop failure identification models on data other than those relating to years immediately before failure. Although these are relatively uncommon, there are some examples, for the most part being derived using discriminant models (e.g. Deakin, 1972; and El Hennawy and Morris, 1983a: see below, pp. 139, 310-1 and 319).

As indicated above, logit models have the advantage that the dependent variable score can be interpreted as indicating the probability of a company failing. It is therefore not only feasible to use the procedure to derive models at different points in time before failure to estimate the chances of a company going bankrupt, but it is also possible to see to what extent (if any) the models show the chances of bankruptcy increasing as failure approaches. This can be done in four main ways: using entropy indicators; by developing multilogit models; by developing a multiple-state distress model (i.e. at the lowest level of distress merely recognising a cut in dividend, say, and then defining other states which progressively recognise increasing distress, culminating in bankruptcy); and by developing a 'rolling' logit model, whereby the dependent variable score for a model estimated for t-1 is included as an independent variable for a model estimated at time t.

(1) Entropy measures

*(i) The methodology.* It will be recalled from the brief discussion of entropy measures above (pp. 57-58 and 85-88) that entropy is defined as the degree of uncertainty over the occurrence of a given event. The measure of surprise is measured as a logarithm of the probabilities, $p_1 \ldots p_n$

$$H_n = H_n\,(p_1\,,\,\ldots\,,p_n) \tag{4.10}$$

$$= -\sum_{k=1}^{n} p_k \ln p_k \tag{4.10a}$$

Entropy can then be represented as

$$h(p) = \ln\,(1/p) \tag{4.11}$$

As with the balance sheet decomposition measures discussed earlier, the greater the entropy score the greater the 'surprise' and hence the larger the informational value conveyed by a model.

The above is essentially an ex post (or hindsight) measure of information content. In order to obtain an ex ante (or forward looking) estimate of the uncertainty remaining over the occurrence of a two state event (e.g. fail versus non-fail), the entropy measure has to be weighted by its probability of occurrence:

$$H = p \ln(1/p) + (1-p) \ln[1/(1-p)] \qquad (4.12)$$

*(ii) Empirical applications in failure studies.* Zavgren (1985) developed a series of individual logit models for up to five years prior to bankruptcy on a sample of 45 matched pairs of US companies, failure occurring between 1972 and 1978. She then used ex post entropy measures to assess the extent to which incremental information was added by the models as failure approached. The nit scores decreased over the period from the fifth year to the first year prior to failure by an average of 0.10 for bankrupt companies and by 0.08 for non-failed concerns. She therefore concluded that the amount of information increases by an average of 18 per cent for the failed companies as against 16 per cent for the non-failed matched pairs.

However, as Keasey and McGuinness (1990) subsequently pointed out, the Zavgren ex post approach assumes that it is already known by the researcher *when* the firms of interest are going to fail/not fail. In practice an analyst will not know if a company is four years prior to failure and therefore whether it is appropriate to use the 'four year' logit model rather than (say) the 'five year', 'three year', 'two year' or 'one year' logit models. What is really needed therefore is an ex ante entropy measure. This can only be achieved if it is assumed that any of the five models might equally be applicable to the data.

Keasey and McGuinness therefore applied both ex ante and ex post entropy measures to the results of the logit models that they developed on a sample of 43 pairs of UK failed and non-failed companies. To proxy an ex ante measure they applied the 'first year' model to all five years to see what the impact would be. Their findings were that while the ex post entropy measure (like Zavgren's) showed increasing information content on the experimental sample as failure approached, this could not be repeated on a hold out sample. There the value of information for failing companies tended to decrease, while it increased for the non-failing businesses.

The relatively clear cut pattern evident from the ex post measure could not be repeated with its ex ante counterpart. On both the experimental and hold out samples the entropy scores indicated that the fate of the failed firms became more certain as bankruptcy approached, but the pattern was less clear for the non-failed companies. They therefore concluded that Zavgren's analysis was basically flawed.

## (2) Multilogit models

*(i) The methodology.* Another way of trying to identify whether or not it is possible to extract incremental information by studying successive year models is to use 'multilogit models'. Essentially this requires that a set of data covering (say) five years should *simultaneously* be analysed, rather than just developing separate models for each year prior to failure one-by-one. This was first done by Peel and Peel (1988) and subsequently further examined by Keasey, McGuinness and Short (1990).

The basic procedure is to pool the data and stack. Thus if there is a sample of 50 companies and their matched pairs for which data are available for five years prior to the failure of the former, the data set will be 500 observations (i.e. 100 for each year for five years). If the non-failed company data are regarded as being homogeneous, the stacked data can be represented as follows:

| Data year (before failure) | Dependent variable outcomes[*] | Independent variable | No. of observations |
|---|---|---|---|
| 1 | NF (A) | $X_{-1}$ | 50 |
| 1 | F (B) | $X_{-1}$ | 50 |
| 2 | NF (C) | $X_{-2}$ | 50 |
| 2 | F (D) | $X_{-2}$ | 50 |
| 3 | NF (E) | $X_{-3}$ | 50 |
| 3 | F (F) | $X_{-3}$ | 50 |
| 4 | NF (G) | $X_{-4}$ | 50 |
| 4 | F (H) | $X_{-4}$ | 50 |
| 5 | NF (I) | $X_{-5}$ | 50 |
| 5 | F (J) | $X_{-5}$ | 50 |

F = failures; NF = non-failures; [*] panels in parenthesis.

The stacking of the data then facilitates the generation of a number of models, e.g.

(1) A conventional final year logit model, using data in panels A (50 non-failed observations) and B (50 failed observations).
(2) A final year logit model, using data in panel B (50 observations) but matching it against data in panels A, C, E, G and I (250 observations) on the grounds that for non-failed companies the data ought to be homogeneous regardless of year.[8]
(3) A second year before failure model, using data in panel D (50 observations) and in panel C (50 observations).

130

(4) A mixed model: e.g. using data from panel D (50 observations of failed companies two years before failure) against data from panels A, C, E, G and I, alone or in combination.

(5) Another mixed model, but (say) comparing the final year's data of the failing companies (panel B) against their data two or three years before bankruptcy (panels D or F), i.e. treating the latter as if they related to non-failing firms (which after all is what they were 2-3 years out).

Other combinations are also possible, of course; and where there is more than one independent variable (e.g. return on capital employed and gearing), it would be possible for the failed group to take (say) the return on capital employed ratio from one panel (e.g. B) and the gearing ratio from another (e.g. D).

However, a major problem with this approach would seem to be that generally it must rely on hindsight. Thus, for instance, when companies have failed, it is fairly easy to select variables from stacked data. By contrast, it is a rather different matter to develop models for continuing firms using stacked data which might discriminate successfully between those which, within a given period, will fail and those which will survive.

*(ii) Empirical applications in failure studies.* Peel and Peel's (1988) study involved 35 bankrupt and 44 healthy British listed companies, the former predominantly failing over the period 1978-1982. The data, relating to size, flow of funds and lag in publishing annual accounts, were stacked for three years, and various multilogit models were generated. This enabled the researchers to generate probabilities for a company failing one year ahead, two years ahead, three years ahead or remaining healthy. No real adjustments were made for sample selection bias, but misclassification rates on a hold out sample of 12 failed and 15 healthy companies were high except for the last year before failure.

The Keasey, McGuinness and Short (1990) study adopted a similar approach for a sample of 40 UK listed companies which failed in the period 1976-1984. These were pair matched by size, years and industry category, and a 12 company validation sample was also used. The independent variable set used for stepwise selection comprised 16 ratios. Misclassification rates for the individual year-by-year logit models were again relatively high except for the last year before failure: namely, experimental sample, 14 per cent (year -1 model), 18.5 per cent (-2), 23.5 per cent (-3), 30 per cent (-4) and 24.5 per cent (-5); and on the hold out sample 37 per cent (-1), 25.5 per cent (-2), 35.5 per cent (-3), 35 per cent (-4) and 59 per cent (-5). Certainly it seems that the models would have had very modest predictive power if allowance had been made for a more realistic prior probability of observing failures.

The multilogit model fitted relatively well, and misclassifications for the non-failed firms for the final year before bankruptcy were only 4.5 per cent on the experimental sample and 10 per cent for the hold out sample. For failing firms misclassification rates were much higher one year prior to failure (32.5 per cent on the experimental sample and 41.7 per cent for the hold out companies), and the error rates rose steeply for previous years, both on the experimental and hold out samples, reaching 100 per cent for the third year prior to failure. Once again, if allowance had been made for sampling bias, the predictive power of the model would have been even weaker. Moreover, the fact that performance was best in the last year before failure is of little comfort as frequently the publication of the final set of a failing company's accounts is the trigger for its collapse.

Keasey McGuinness and Short then analysed the consistency of the signals being transmitted by the model in the years before failure – namely, for the failing firms, did they indicate failure at (say) year -3, then non-failure at years -2 and -1? Or were they consistent in showing increasing probabilities of failure as bankruptcy approached? In fact, as Keasey et al. point out, it is not always easy to interpret the results where the dependent variable is expressed as a probability score. Nevertheless, the overwhelming impression is that for the failing companies there was little consistency in the pattern of the signals reported. Moreover, sometimes when there was consistency the 'predictions' were unjustified by the eventual outcomes.

(3) Multiple state financial distress models

*(i) The methodology.* Another way of using the multilogit approach is where the objective is to allocate a company to one of a number of states according to the value of the dependent variable, rather than to just one of two states (fail and non-fail). However, for the models to work satisfactorily, it would seem to be necessary to have large samples of companies in each state (see above, pp. 125-6).

*(ii) Empirical applications in failure studies.* Lau (1987) was the first to use this approach in the context of corporate financial distress. She defined five states (no distress, passing the dividend, default on a loan, Chapter X and XI protection, and bankruptcy). Two samples were used: one for analysis on 1976 data, the other for hold out purposes on 1977 data. Each comprised 350 financially healthy firms, 20 which passed the dividend, 15 which defaulted, 10 which sought protection and 5 which went bankrupt. Models were developed using 10 explanatory variables from data for one, two and three year horizons, and companies were assigned to each of the five states according to the values of the dependent variable. Generally the models performed quite well, especially in classifying the financially healthy firms as non-failures. Subsequent studies that have adopted a similar approach (e.g. Bahnson and Bartley, 1992; Ward, 1994; and Ward and Foster, 1996, examining the explanatory power of cash flow variables) have reported similar results.

## (4) The 'rolling' logit model

*The methodology.* The dependent variable of the logit model, it will be recalled, measures the logarithm of the odds of a company failing. It should therefore be possible to incorporate as an independent variable for a model derived at time t the dependent variable of a model derived at t-1. This should then enable the modelling process to capture the incremental value in other independent variables published at time t. This has the advantage that it is relatively easy to apply.

The main problem would appear to be that ex ante an analyst would not know how many years a company was prior to failure, and consequently he/she would not be able to choose the appropriate year's model. However, in practice it might not be unreasonable to apply the last year's model to any year's data.

The 'rolling logit' procedure was employed in this study, though with the benefit of hindsight, and the results are reported in chapter 12.

## The discriminant model

*The methodology*

Although regression might have seemed to be the obvious multivariate technique to use in bankruptcy studies, it was in fact another analytical method that was usually employed in the early studies: *discriminant analysis* (DA).

In many respects to the outsider the procedure looks similar to regression, as the model takes the form

$$Z = a + b_1 X_1 + b_2 X_2 + e \tag{4.13}$$

> where the terms on the right hand side are as previously defined, and Z is the dichotomous dependent variable.

The difference is in the techniques used to separate the two groups. With DA the data are divided into two categories, failed (F) and non-failed (NF). The technique then derives two 'centroid points' for F and NF by maximizing the ratio of between-groups to within-groups variances. The best combination for a sample of data is usually expressed as a linear function. This is illustrated in Figure 4.9, where there are two independent variables, $X_1$ and $X_2$ (e.g. representing profitability and liquidity), and a dependent variable, Z (hence the frequent description of DA functions as 'Z-score models'). The dependent variable is not shown as the conventional vertical axis but instead at the bottom of the diagram with a 0.5 cutoff point. This makes it possible to illustrate how in three dimensional space the two 'balloons', F and NF, overlap, but a discriminating function plots onto the Z-axis. This is at right angles to each of the two independent variable axes, $X_1$ and $X_2$, and the distributions of F' and NF' can be plotted. The model once derived is used in exactly the same way as the regression model described in equation (4.5) above.

In fact, the discriminant model is in some ways less easy to use than regression, and certainly than logit. Thus it is a requirement that the group dispersion (variance-covariance) matrices should be equal for failed and non-failed samples; and that there should be multivariate normality in the distributions. As has been demonstrated (e.g. by Karels and Prakash, 1987) these conditions are frequently

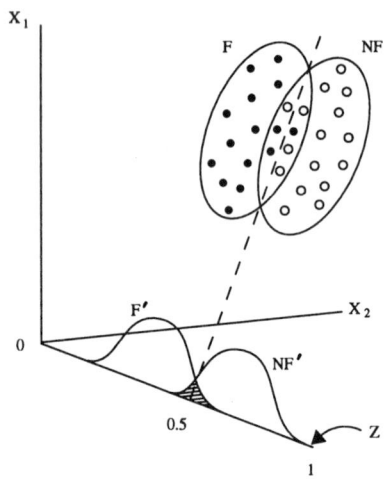

**Figure 4.9**

violated. Moreover, the diagnostic statistics are slightly different from those used in regression. Thus although the F test is still valid, the overall significance of the discriminant model can be assessed in terms of Wilk's lambda statistic, which is distributed as a chi square. There are also a number of ways of determining the explanatory power of the individual independent variables, although basically these parallel the t statistic (e.g. standardised coefficients, the Mosteller-Wallace test, conditional deletion, and Mahanalobis's $D^2$). However, there is some doubt as to the reliability of these tests where the basic requirements of MDA are not met.

Faced with these difficulties, researchers have proposed various ways in which the problems might be mitigated. Gupta, Rao and Bagchi (1990), for instance, used the distribution free linear goal programming (LGP) procedure to avoid the usual MDA requirements that the independent variables should be multivariate normally distributed and the dispersion matrices across groups should be equal. In a similar vein, Barniv and Raveh (1989) developed a nonparametric version of the discriminant model with continuous scoring.

With discriminant analysis the problem of sampling bias can be dealt with by adjusting the cutoff score by

$$X = \ln (p_1/p_2) \qquad\qquad (4.14)$$

where $p_1$ and $p_2$ represent the prior probabilities<br>of failure and non-failure.

The adjustment will move the cutoff point away from between the group means and closer to the mean of the failing group. Adjustments for error misclassification costs – if indeed they are appropriate – can be made in the same way, although they will move the cutoff point in the opposite direction.[9]

*Empirical research in the US*

Altman (1968) was the first researcher to develop a multivariate statistically derived model to try to discriminate between failed and non-failing firms. He used multiple discriminant analysis (MDA), and his sample was 33 US manufacturing companies which went bankrupt over the 20 years 1946-1965. Against these he paired an equal number of surviving companies, matching by industry, size and year. Five ratios were included in the model out of an original set of 22, and the equation was estimated on the last year's data before failure (year -1). The ratios included in the final model were working capital/total assets; retained earnings/total assets; earnings before interest and tax/total assets; market value of equity/book value of total liabilities; and sales/total assets. Classification errors were low for the year of estimation, but misclassifications of failed firms increased sharply for earlier years (e.g. 28 per cent at -2 years, 52 per cent at -3, 71 per cent at -4, and 64 per cent at -5). However, the model performed well on a hold out sample of 25 bankrupt companies, although no allowance was made for sampling bias and the estimation period covered a 20 year interval when there were significant changes in the US economy.

Deakin (1972) modified the Altman model to include the 14 best ratios identified by Beaver (1966) in his univariate study.[10] His sample of distressed firms comprised 32 companies which failed between 1964-1970, and the control group of firms was selected on a random basis, but matched by size, industry and year. The final model included all 14 variables, and equations were calculated on data for each of the five years before failure. Deakin also used a version of MDA which assigns a probability of membership to the failed and non-failed groups on the basis of its Z scores in previous years. This lowered error levels to 3 per cent, 4.5 per cent, 21 per cent and 17 per cent respectively for the five years prior to bankruptcy. However, the model performed less well against a random sample of 11 bankrupt and 23 non-bankrupt firms, misclassifying 22 per cent companies at year -1, 6 per cent at -2, 12 per cent at -3, 23 per cent at -4, and 15 per cent at -5. Again, no adjustment was made for sampling bias.

Blum (1974) constructed an MDA model to assess the probability of failure, his sample comprising 115 firms which failed between 1954 and 1968 and 115 non-failed concerns matched by industry, size and year. Twelve ratio and twelve non-ratio variables were used as the basis for the model, with 6 of the former measuring the variability of ratios. The data were divided into 21 ranges of at least three years, and a discriminant function was fitted to half the data in each range. The model fitted to the middle ranges (which once more did not allow for sampling bias) correctly classified over 90 per cent of the companies in the hold out sample, but the error rates increased rapidly in years -2, -3, -4 and -5.

Other MDA models were developed in the US in subsequent years.[11] Diamond (1976), for instance, used a sample of 75 failed and 75 non-failed companies, and as well as applying a stepwise selection procedure, he screened ratios employing a number of pattern recognition techniques, including principal components analysis.[12] Adjustments were made for potential sampling bias and for misclassification error costs. The overall predictive accuracy was initially assessed at around 90 per cent for 2-3 years before failure, although this fell to 80 per cent when allowance was made for sampling bias and an offsetting adjustment for misclassification error costs.

Casey and Bartczak (1985) added cash flow variables to six accrual based variables in a discriminant model to see whether their inclusion improved the model's explanatory power. The study, based on accounting data for 60 failed and 230 non-failed companies, did not show any incremental information, which was attributed to the high degree of variability in the cash flow variables within the failing group. Other researchers to focus on cash flow variables have been Castagna and Matolcsy (1985), Gombola, Haskins, Ketz and Williams (1987), Aziz, Emanuel and Lawson (1988), Aziz and Lawson (1989), Gentry, Newbold and Whitford (1985, 1987), Bahnson and Bartley (1992), Laitinen (1994), Ward (1994) and Ward and Foster (1996), although (apart from the first four) these studies employed logit rather than MDA models.[13]

Other MDA studies have examined the effect of broadening the basic accounting data set. Thus Ketz (1978) and Norton and Smith (1979) included general inflation adjusted data; Mensah (1983) specific price level indicators; and Dambolena and Khoury (1980) a number of measures of ratio variability. While Norton and Smith were unable to detect any incremental information in the price level adjusted information, both Ketz and Mensah concluded that the additional data might have been useful if allowance had been made for the relative costs of misclassification. For their part, Dambolena and Khoury developed MDA models, albeit on a small sample of 23 failed and 23 non-failed companies, first of all from 19 variables, and then on the same variables plus their standard deviations calculated over a period of four years. The model based on the broader variable set performed far better, although intuitively it seems that variability measures used in this and similar studies (e.g. relating to operating cash flows or profits) are doing little more than reflect a steady decline in ratio values over the period under review, rather than their inherent instability before the failing companies experienced financial distress (see p. 68).[14]

The MDA methodology originally employed was criticised on various grounds by Joy and Tollefson (1975), Eisenbeis (1977), Scott (1978), Altman and Eisenbeis (1978) and Karson and Martell (1980). As a result, the analytical procedures were modified in later studies (e.g. it became standard to test the models on hold out samples). However, as mentioned previously, it has been shown that the requirements of multivariate normality and the equivalence of the covariance matrices of the failed/non-failed groups have usually been violated (e.g. Hamer 1983; Karels and Prakash, 1987). It is therefore interesting to note the performance of the nonparametric models developed to avoid these rather onerous statistical requirements. Gupta, Rao and Bagchi (1990) tested their LGP version of MDA in models estimated for each of five years before failure for a sample of 60 bankrupt and non-bankrupt firms. They found that it outperformed the original Altman model in terms of classificational accuracy. Similarly, Barniv and Raveh (1989) tested their nonparametric version of MDA on two samples, one comprising 58 failing companies and 142 non-bankrupt concerns, the other 69 matched pairs of general insurance companies. Using both MDA and probit/logit models as benchmarks, and allowing for sampling bias and the cost of misclassification errors, their results showed the nonparametric procedure performed better than its rivals on models estimated for up to 3 years before failure.

Nevertheless, the most widely used MDA model in the US is that of Altman, Haldeman and Narayanan (1977). They developed a revised version of Altman's original discriminant function, which they refer to as the ZETA model. This was done to base the estimation on larger companies and update the sample period to 1969-1975 when new accounting practices were being adopted (e.g. the capitalisation of leases). According to Altman (1993, p. 209), the model is still performing well.

The ZETA model was derived from a population of 53 bankrupt and 58 non-bankrupt manufacturing and retailing firms. A linear discriminant function proved to be more effective as a discriminator than its quadratic counterpart, and classificational accuracy was 90 per cent one year prior to failure and still around 70 per cent four years before that. The seven variables included in the final version were earnings before interest and tax/total assets, stability of earnings, interest cover, retained earnings/total assets, current assets/current liabilities, five year average of the market value of equity/total capital, and total assets (proxying for size). Validation checks were thorough, the model being tested successfully on a hold out sample and applying the Lachenbruch jackknife procedure. (As mentioned on p. 114, the latter involves taking each company out of the sample one-by-one, re-estimating the model on the remaining population and seeing whether the excluded observation is correctly classified.) However, classificational accuracy weakened as the period before failure was extended (e.g. correct classifications declined from 96.2 per cent for failed companies and 89.7 per cent for non-failed in the final year before bankruptcy to 69.8 per cent and 82.1 per cent respectively four years before that).

Altman, Haldeman and Narayanan (1977, p. 43) were 'acutely aware ... of the potential [sampling] bias' but initially assumed that this was neutralised by the error costs. Later, like Diamond, they analysed the position more thoroughly, and their estimates of sampling bias and misclassification costs were indeed such as to substantially cancel each other out. However, as has been suggested previously, the latter adjustment will not prevent misclassification errors being made, so it seems likely that the discriminatory power of the model is being overstated.

In fact, Altman (1993, pp. 219-220) reports that the ZETA model has correctly classified 94 per cent of 150 US companies which failed over the 17 year period 1975-1991, although 20 per cent of the total population of companies has been identified as being 'at risk'. This is a little puzzling, since he argues that its widespread use by analysts is testimony to its perceived value. Yet if the model were regarded as an extremely good predictor, one might reasonably expect the consensus market view to bankrupt all companies signalled as being 'at risk'. The fact that this has not happened presumably means that the 'predictions' are regarded as being largely confirmatory in nature. Part of the reason may well be that the model's forecasting accuracy, particularly with respect to non-failing companies, is nowhere near as good as implied by the original specification checks. Presumably this to some extent is because of the sampling bias problem – which indeed would suggest an error rate of this magnitude – and the relative inaccuracy probably explains why the market does not place complete reliance on the procedure.[15]

*Empirical research in the UK*

The best known applications of MDA techniques in the UK are the models developed by Taffler. His first model was developed in 1974 and based on a sample of 23 companies which failed over the period 1968-1973, together with a control sample of 45 companies. Principal components analysis[16] and stepwise selection were used to reduce a set of 50 ratios, normalised where necessary, to derive a model with five variables: earnings before interest and tax/total assets, total liabilities/net capital employed, quick assets/total assets, working capital/net worth, and stock turnover. Incorporating prior probability odds of 1:10 (failed:solvent) in the model, the procedure – which was adopted by a firm of City stockbrokers – discriminated extremely well in the last year before failure, but far less well for previous years.

Subsequently the model was refined (Taffler, 1982, 1983). The bankrupt sample was expanded to 46 listed manufacturing firms which failed over the period 1969-1976, the companies being matched by industry and size against another 46 firms. After screening 80 ratios applying principal components analysis, the variables in the final model were profit before tax/average current liabilities, current assets/total liabilities, current liabilities/total assets, and the no-credit-interval. The respective Mosteller-Wallace contributions to the power of the model were 53 per cent, 13 per cent, 18 per cent and 16 per cent. The constant term was adjusted for the prior probability of failures being observed and for misclassification costs, and the model fitted the data extremely well in the last year before failure. Of the 14 per cent of companies on the EXSTAT database which were classified as being 'at risk', by the end of 1976 25 per cent had gone into receivership or been baled out by the government. Another 11 per cent had been rescued in take-overs, and 7 per cent had disposed of or closed parts of their businesses. This left 57 per cent still at risk or turned around. Almost all failed companies were classified as at risk in the last year before failure and 67 per cent, 41 per cent and 29 per cent respectively two, three and four years before their collapse.

Taffler (1984) subsequently developed separate models for companies in the distribution sector and for private companies. The sample for deriving the former was 22 failed and 49 healthy listed companies, and the key ratios were cash flow/total liabilities, debt/quick assets, current liabilities/total assets, and the no-credit-interval. Allowance was made for both the prior probability of failure and costs of misclassification, and the fit was again extremely good in the year immediately before bankruptcy. The private company model was developed from a sample of 39 companies failing in 1978-1979 and 56 non-failed companies, the critical ratios being earnings before interest and tax/sales, debt/net worth, average creditors/cost of sales, and liabilities/total assets.

Other MDA models have been developed in the UK: e.g. by Lis, Tisshaw, Mason and Harris, Betts and Belhoul, and El Hennawy and Morris (see Taffler, 1984). The last of these is unusual in that it attempts to develop an MDA failure identification models on data other than those relating to company years immediately before failure. Previously only Deakin (1972, 1977) in the US had really attempted this (see pp. 128 and 135).

The El Hennawy and Morris (1983a) study developed two MDA models on a sample of 22 failed and 22 non-failed British companies. The bankruptcies occurred between 1960 and 1968, and the models were based on data the year immediately prior to failure and five years before the event. The models were tested on a hold out sample of another 22 failed companies and their matched pairs, together with a second intertemporal validation sample of 18 companies (9 failed and their matched pairs, the bankruptcies occurring between 1969 and 1971). Both were able to classify firms with more than 80 per cent accuracy, and although profitability was a key factor in each of the models, there were differences in the variables included and in the parameter weights.[17]

More recently Piesse and Wood (1992) have proxied Datastream's and Taffler's models and applied them, together with Altman's original 1968 US model, to the UK motor components industry. The purpose of the exercise was to see how effective the models might be in distinguishing between failed and non-failed companies over the period 1974-1986. For this purpose, the experiment

139

distinguished between ex ante and ex post 'predictions'. The former applies models to data for a population of companies where the outcome (fail/non-fail) is assumed not to be known, whereas ex post it is. (In other words, the argument is essentially about sampling bias.) Although the results indeed suggested that there is an ex post bias, the rather crude procedures used to proxy the Datastream and Taffler models undermined the validity of the exercise.[18]

Since his first Z-score model was developed, Taffler has regularly reviewed the performance of later versions (e.g. Taffler 1983, 1994). In terms of the scores calculated from figures in their last published accounts, the 1977 manufacturing company model has correctly identified all but 2 of the 152 listed industrial groups which failed in the 18 years between 1977 and 1994. The bankruptcy rate averages between 2 per cent and 3 per cent a year, but it is clear that a large number of non-failing companies have also been identified as being 'at risk', the annual proportion of the total population varying between 11 per cent in 1978 and 1988 to 23 per cent in 1982 and 27 per cent in 1992. Of course, although most of the 'at risk' companies have not gone into receivership or been voluntarily liquidated, some have been 'failures' in a broader sense, undergoing financial reconstructions or being the subject of rescue attempts (e.g. by being taken over). Moreover, the pragmatically derived PAS tracking signal (see p. 127) suggests that many of the companies which eventually collapse show signs of distress for some time before they go under. Nevertheless, the Type II misclassification error rates (i.e. mistakenly identifying a surviving company as failed) are high, and the associated opportunity costs if the model's 'predictions' were to be followed regardless would be substantial.[19] Only in the best performing year, 1991, was this not true, when 6.5 per cent of listed industrials failed, i.e. over a third of the 17.5 per cent of the number of companies signalled as being 'at risk'.

Although his models are 'widely used by practitioners', Taffler is in fact very careful not to claim too much for them. Thus it is noticeable that the reported Z-score results relate to a failing company's last published accounts, the release of which in many instances probably precipitates the final downward spiral. Moreover, as Taffler (1983, p. 303) emphasises 'the appraisal is principally descriptive in nature' and 'the model is doing little more than reflecting and condensing the information conveyed by the set of accounts itself'. However, it is clear that many analysts are actively seeking a predictive device, even if they do not in practice appear to accept Z-scores uncritically at their face value. Moreover, Taffler himself, despite his caveats, often seems to interpret the results as though they have ex ante predictive power (e.g. Taffler 1983, p. 300; 1994, pp. 9-10),[20] and the very fact that the models' power is usually assessed in terms of their ability to discriminate correctly between failures and non-failures can only be justified if they are perceived as being a potentially useful forecasting device.

More generally, as with Altman's model, the misclassification rates for non-failed companies are far higher than was the case when the model was being derived, which once more would primarily seem to reflect the impact of the sampling bias. Certainly the opportunity costs of such misclassifications might be regarded by analysts as sufficient for them not to follow its signals blindly and help to explain why its predictions are not immediately impounded in share prices.

## Survival models

### Duration models

'Duration' models have long been used in engineering and medicine, when the focus of interest has been, for instance, how long a structure, engine or patient is going to *survive*. Similarly such models have been central to the calculations of actuaries trying to estimate how long life policy holders or pensioners are likely to live.

More recently economists have shown interest in these models as they can be applied to business problems, concerning such matters as product durability (and hence what is an appropriate warranty period); the interval between investment and payback (both generally and more specifically in terms of research and the subsequent development of a product); the duration of unemployment; the length of industrial disputes; the time interval between trades in financial markets; the period before loans are redeemed; and the expected lives of firms (in particular, small businesses).

In the present context, the life expectancy of a business can be viewed analogously to the life expectancy of a policy holder with a life assurance company. In the case of the latter, it is certain that the policy holder will die sometime. What is of interest to an actuary is *when*. And in making their calculations the actuaries will allow for various observable characteristics (e.g. whether the insured is overweight, is a smoker, and so on).

Duration models are derived by applying probability theory, and in particular in terms of compound (or 'conditional') probabilities. In this respect they can be regarded as a natural extension of the reasoning behind the gambler's ruin model discussed previously (p. 65 et seq.)

With a logit model it is the probability of failure in the next period that is being estimated. But clearly in such circumstances it should be possible to estimate the probabilities of failure in a sequence of periods from the present time t: namely, t+1, t+2, t+3, ... t+n. It is then a fairly simple task to calculate the period by which failure is most likely to occur by cumulating the probabilities, and the dependent variable can then be switched so that it becomes the survival period.

To appreciate the argument, consider 8 tennis players at the quarter final stage in a tournament. If every time they play there is a 50 per cent chance of them progressing to the next round, it is not difficult to map out their chances of survival. The independent and conditional probabilities are shown in Figure 4.10.

Fairly obviously, at the quarter final stage player A has a chance of $0.5^3 = 12.5$ per cent of surviving until the end of the tournament and becoming champion. If he/she progresses to the semi final stage the chances of surviving and becoming

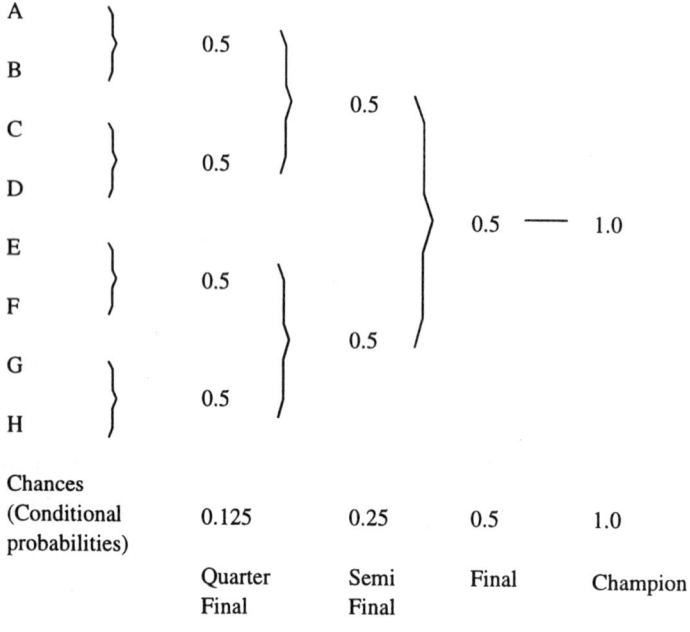

**Figure 4.10**

champion are $0.5^2 = 25$ per cent; and so on. The situation is illustrated in Figure 4.11.

The function, Y, drawn in Figure 4.11 is an exponential curve and can be expressed as

$$Y = Pe^n \qquad (4.15)$$

where P is the independent probability, 0.5, and from the quarter final to the champion stage is n rounds, i.e. n = 3.

Thus

$$Y = 0.5e^3$$
$$\ln Y = (-0.693)3$$
$$= -2.079$$

antilogging

$$Y = 0.125$$

A procedure for estimating a model along these lines was developed by Cox (1972) and is known as 'the proportional hazard model'. This has the advantage that in statistical terms it is distribution free (i.e. it does not assume that variables are normally distributed around the average). But in practice it would be unlikely

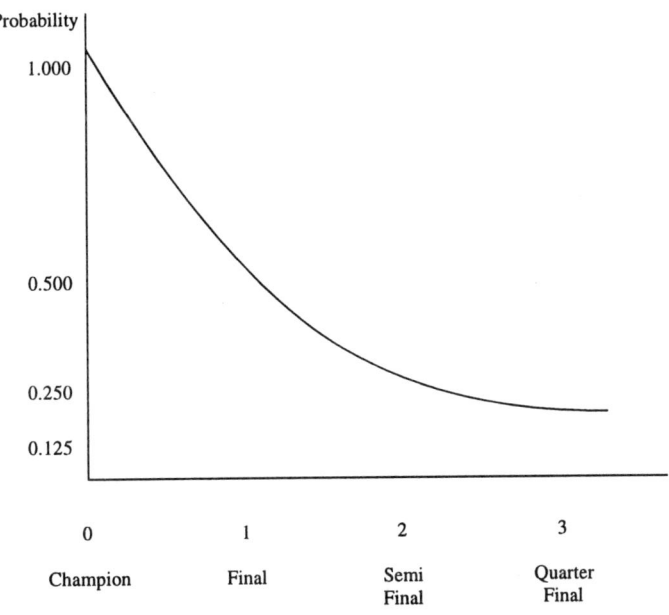

**Figure 4.11**

that the chance of progressing from one round to the next would remain constant (e.g. at 50 per cent). Rather it might be expected that the odds would change. For instance, for a low seeded player the chances of becoming champion might be expected to increase if the quarter final is unexpectedly won but not pro rata. If this is the case, the probability function as drawn in Figure 4.11 is inappropriate. Rather a curve like that marked with a broken line in Figure 4.12 might be a better representation of the likely outcomes. This curve can no longer be expressed in terms of a simple function with one parameter, P. Instead it has to be expressed in terms of two parameters: e.g. showing the independent probabilities declining period by period. Such a behaviour pattern can be approximated applying a number of functions (e.g. lognormal and logistic), but the best known is the Weibull distribution.

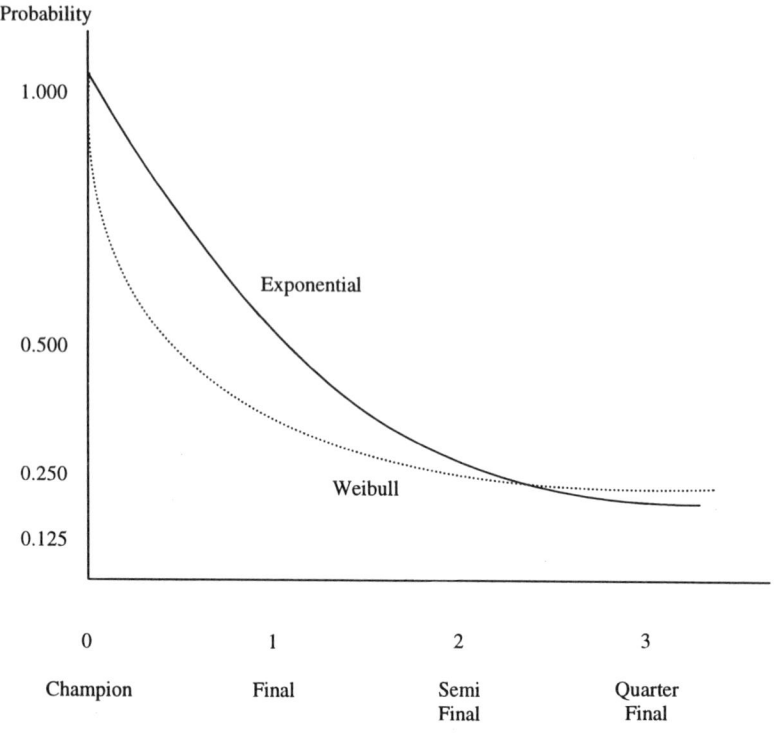

**Figure 4.12**

It ought to be evident that for a given group of firms it should be possible to estimate an observed probability distribution indicating how long they are likely to survive. In estimating such a 'duration' (or 'survival') period it will be necessary to take into account certain characteristics. Thus with a tennis player the critical independent variable might be the world rankings; and, with a life policy holder, his/her lifestyle and health record. Likewise for a company, the chances of it failing will be measured by its economic characteristics (e.g. as reflected in a set of financial ratios).

Whereas the 'survivor' function measures the probability that a firm will survive longer than n months or years, the 'hazard' function measures the probability of failure in the next instant, given that the firm was 'alive' at a given time, t.[21]

In estimating the hazard and survivor functions, it is important (just as it is with straightforward regression) to try to ensure that the data from which the characteristics of a population are estimated are homogeneous. Unfortunately they are unlikely to be so because of censoring. This can happen in a number of ways. Thus, for instance, in examining a population of companies, some of which have gone bankrupt, there is firstly a problem with the non-failures. This is that some of them will almost certainly fail in the years immediately following the period that is the subject of study, but others (the majority) will not. Obviously this is a potentially important bias when the focus of interest is survival. This is illustrated on the right hand side of Figure 4.13 and is sometimes referred to as 'right censoring'.

But there is equally another problem, namely that the history of some companies will be incomplete: e.g. if a period of five years up to bankruptcy is being studied, some of the companies in the sample will have been 'born' just five years before their financial collapse, but others will have been in existence for far longer. This is illustrated on the left hand side of Figure 4.12 and is sometimes referred to as 'left censoring'.

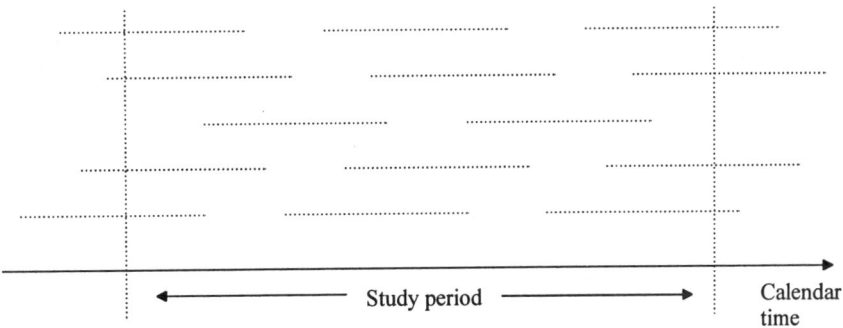

Figure 4.13

Clearly a procedure is needed to try to eliminate (or at least reduce) the potential bias that will be present in the data set as a result of this censoring. Basically this is done, where possible, by assuming that censored data not recorded generally 'behave' in a similar way to that for companies where the entire set of data is available. Thus, for example, if on average 2 per cent of companies in a population fail in any one year, it can be assumed that 2 per cent of the non-failures will go bankrupt a year after the period under review, another 2 per cent the year after, and so on. Adjustments can then be made to try to eliminate the bias.

It should be evident that for the censoring bias to be successfully countered it is necessary to have a large number of observations within the window of time being studied. This should include a representative number of firms which have both been born and died. Usually these conditions will be met where a 'birth' date can be clearly established (e.g. for a product, for life policy holders, for a building, etc).

There is however another type of censoring, and this arises where the sample of a full population is unrepresentative. Thus, for instance, if a sample of failed and non-failed companies is derived on a matched pairing basis, whereas in practice the incidence of failures in a period is between 2 per cent and 10 per cent of the population, the vast majority of non-failed companies will have been censored out.

It should immediately be evident that there are potentially severe problems in trying to use duration models as a means of analysing corporate failure. However, it may be possible to overcome them or ameliorate them. Thus, for instance, if the focus of study is small firms, it should be possible to examine the experience of a complete cohort of firms born in a particular year, and – as explained below – this has indeed been done by industrial economists. Equally, it is possible to concentrate attention on a particular industry. First, this should enable data for an entire population of businesses to be analysed; and, second, it may be possible to deem a 'proxy birth date' if all companies in the industry have been subjected to a major destabilising shock at a given point in time.

More generally, it might be possible to handle the problem of an unrepresentative sample of companies by repeating the data for the matched (but otherwise randomly selected) control sample the requisite number of times so that the non-failed businesses more closely reflect their true proportion in a population. Similarly, a datum point equivalent to a birth date could be deemed to take place at a given point in time – e.g. at the onset of a recession. However, the fact that it is necessary to resort to such manipulations does not inspire confidence in the use of duration models in this particular context. Moreover, if they are to be applied, it seems likely that the Weibull version will be more appropriate than the Cox proportional hazard model (CPHM).

*Empirical evidence on the survival of businesses*

*(i) Industrial economics studies.* In the industrial economics literature there have been a number of studies which have examined the survival records of new businesses. These relate to experience in different countries and different industries, but until recently they have focused more of the probability of a firm exiting an industry rather than the length of time it is expected to survive.[22]

With respect to the UK, a recent study by Dunne and Hughes (1994) has examined growth and survival amongst more than 2,000 listed and large unlisted companies over the period 1975-1985. Of the 2,149 companies in their population in 1980, 79.5 per cent survived in 1985, with the very smallest being the most likely to have disappeared. But the smallest companies were also those which grew most rapidly, and over half of company deaths were because of take-overs. To assess whether slow growing small firms were more likely to die than slow growing large firms, probit analysis was undertaken. The key relationship examined was firm survival in the period 1980-1985 as a function of net asset growth in the period 1975-1980. The results showed that slow growth between 1975 and 1980 increased the probability that a company would not survive until 1985. However, while this result held for small and medium sized companies, it was not true for the largest groups. Moreover, this seemed to be true for most of 19 industry groupings identified. Overall, the findings were in line with the findings of nine other studies of firm growth in post-war Britain, specifically in terms of behaviour since the early 1960s. Moreover, tests for bias resulting from the censoring of data in terms of age of firms and attrition rates proved negative.

As a sequel to a logit regression study by Audretsch (1991), Audretsch and Mahmood (1994) used the Cox regression model to examine the performance of a cohort of some 12,000 US firms set up in 1976. The analysis shows that over 75 per cent survived for more than two years, but after 6 years this figure had fallen to below 50 per cent and after 10 to around 30 per cent. Further, the evidence suggests that the survival of new businesses depends significantly on the existence of scale economies, the technological environment and the initial start-up size. However, these factors are of little significance in determining the survival rate for new branches or subsidiaries established by existing concerns.

In another study, Wagner (1994) examined the experience of over 10,000 small firms which entered German manufacturing industry (specifically in Lower Saxony) between 1979 and 1982. On average, only half survived up until 1990, but surviving firms grew at rather faster rates than average. The hazard rates, reflecting the probability for active firms of disappearing within the next year, tended to increase over the first three years, but declined thereafter. The survival models used were essentially dichotomous using a form of logit model which accommodates censoring of data, tobit, to assess the probabilities of firms set up in each of four years, 1979-1982, remaining in business in 1990. Although the pattern of results was similar for each cohort, there were differences. However, these could not be related to industry membership.

Mata and Portugal (1994) investigated the experience of 3,169 Portuguese manufacturing firms which commenced business in 1983 in 20 different industries. One fifth of these did not survive their first year of operations, and only a half of them survived four years. Size and ownership structure were found to be important determinants of firms' lives, as well as growth and turbulence within an industry. Cox proportional hazard and Weibull duration models were used to analyse the data with size, ownership, growth rate, entry and industry characteristics, and minimum efficient scale used as the main independent variables. The conditions for using duration models seem to have been appropriate, and the researchers found that survival rates differed significantly according to size and to industry membership. The results were confirmed with logit analysis.

*(ii) Finance studies.* In the finance literature there have been relatively few survival studies. This is presumably partly because researchers have not been familiar with duration models, but also probably because the data have not really lent themselves to such analysis. The best documented are in fact US industry studies, relating to banking and the oil and gas sector.

Lane, Looney and Wansley (1986) examined the behaviour of 130 US banks which failed between 1978 and 1984, matching against them 334 non-failed banks.

This control sample comprised all similar institutions to those that failed which filed reports with the US federal authorities. Consequently, although this procedure excluded the largest banks, Lane, Looney and Wansley nevertheless used a comprehensive subsample of the institutions that seemed to be particularly susceptible to failure.

A Cox proportional hazard survival model was applied to the data, which comprised four ratios chosen stepwise from an original set of 21. Models based on data one and two years prior to failure fitted well; and the same data were also used to construct multiple discriminant analysis (MDA) models. The MDA models performed as well as others previously developed for the banking industry (see above, pp. 122 and 127), but the survival models matched them. Moreover, on a hold out sample of 38 banks, although only two failed by the predicted date, another 28 failed within the following six months.

It is not entirely clear from the study how a common birth date was determined, nor whether the control sample represented the true population of non-failed banks. Nevertheless, according to Lane, Looney and Wansley, the survival models could be especially useful for regulators. Thus while the latter should be able to assess the probabilities of failure (e.g. by using a logit model), a survival model would additionally tell them *when* banks are most likely to fail. This should enable appropriate remedial action to be taken before the predicted date of failure is reached.

Chen and Lee (1993) applied survival analysis in a slightly different context. They largely dealt with the data censoring problem by arguing that particular industries could be subject to destabilising extraneous shocks at specific points in time. This would be likely to manifest itself afterwards in an affected industry with a number of firms going bankrupt. The main focus of interest would therefore not only be the likelihood of their failure, but *when* this was likely to occur. Further, the inclusion of merged firms in the sample meant that they could be used as a means of estimating the impact of censoring as they represented an alternative way to bankruptcy for companies to exit from the industry.

To examine the situation the researchers began with a potential 'full' population of 300 US oil and gas companies. However, they eliminated very large and diversified groups, as well as pipeline and service companies, to arrive at their final sample of 175 businesses. They studied their experience between 1981 and 1988, choosing this period because oil prices fell from $35/barrel in 1981 to just $10/barrel in 1986. Of the 175 companies, 67 experienced financial distress in some form or other; 44 merged; and only 64 remained independent and survived. Using a Cox proportional hazard survival model, they identified 10 possible independent variables. These measured working capital margin, gearing, cash flow, investment in prospecting, success in finding new oil and gas reserves, the extent of product diversification, ownership, firm size and age. Using stepwise selection procedures these were reduced to six. The results were compared to the output of a logit model. While both fitted well, Chen and Lee pointed out that the survival model gives additional information – for instance, by indicating the remaining life of a firm, management would have time to set up a rescue package and devise a survival strategy.

In a perceptive critique of the Chen and Lee study, Abdel-khalik (1993) argued that care should be taken in adjusting for censored data (e.g. using merged companies as examples of surviving concerns voluntarily withdrawn from a population: some of them may have merged because they were in distress). He also pointed out that the impact of a change in macroeconomic conditions on an industry (e.g. a steep fall in oil prices) would typically be accompanied by other changes (e.g. lower pump prices might well increase motorists' demand for petrol). Consequently it would be better to compare survival experience over various periods – e.g. when the industry was subject to an oil price shock and when it was not.

More important, Abdel-khalik made the point that using the Cox proportional hazard model assumes a proportional increase in financial distress for a given change in ratio values. He therefore queried, for instance, whether it would be true that the risk of failure for a company doubles when its gearing ratio increases from 5 per cent to 10 per cent. On the other hand, its chance of going bankrupt might more than double if the ratio increases from 150 per cent to 300 per cent. Tests showed that the proportionality assumption could not in fact be justified. In the circumstances Abdel-khalik reworked the data using not only a Weibull model, but also lognormal and logistic regressions. The three models produced similar results to each other, but overall they were rather different from those generated by the Cox proportional hazard model. Abdel-khalik concluded that the proportional hazard model might well overstate the probability of survival.

Abdel-khalik went on to compare the survival model results against those generated by a simple ordinary least squares regression model. He concluded that the latter produced much the same underlying information. Moreover, Chen and Lee's conclusion that gearing, liquidity and size are important characteristics in distinguishing failing from non-failing firms was in line with most previous research on corporate bankruptcy, including univariate studies dating back to the 1930s. It therefore appeared that, although the survival model adds a new dimension, it really says very little that is new.

The survival model approach has also been applied in relation to Australian and British failing company data.[23] Thus Crapp and Stevenson (1987) used a 'life table' approach, applying the Cox proportional hazard model to examine financial distress experienced by all 288 Australian consumer depository financial institutions (i.e. broadly the equivalent of building societies). The years covered were 1978-1985, and 76 of the institutions had failed in that period. The independent variable set comprised 18 indicators reflecting the quality of assets, financial risk, managerial efficiency, growth and macroeconomic factors. (Some of the variables were qualitative indicators rather than financial ratios: e.g. staff/members; and membership growth.) A stepwise selection procedure was used to estimate the model, and total income/total assets was the critical discriminatory variable. It is not clear how Crapp and Stevenson dealt with the left censoring problem, but they did identify a major structural change in the industry around 1981-1983. Full results on the probabilities of failure were not reported, but apparently the managers of relatively immature institutions were less able to cope with change, and size was a critical factor.

Kassab, McLeay and Shani (1991) applied survival models to British listed company data between 1974 and 1983. Working with a five year window, the maximum number of failed companies in their sample was 21 one year prior to failure, when there were 337 non-failed concerns. This fell to 14 failed and 206 non-failed five years before bankruptcy. Censoring was partly allowed for by using merged companies as a proxy for firms which had been eliminated from the sample. However, the proportions of failed to non-failed companies in their sample seem to be out of line with actual experience; and it is unclear how the left censoring problem was dealt with. The Cox proportional hazard and Weibull versions of the survival model were fitted, using a set of 21 ratios as independent variables, and they compared satisfactorily with discriminant and logit models. The preliminary results reported in the paper suggested that high funds flow/current liabilities and quick assets/current liabilities ratios were most consistent with survival.

## Summary

Over the past 25 years a considerable number of multivariate studies of corporate bankruptcy have been undertaken. The original studies were undertaken applying multiple discriminant analysis (MDA) rather than multiple regression analysis (MRA), although the two procedures effectively produce equivalent results.

Recently the more robust and flexible logit procedure has been used. The dependent variable in such models measures the logarithm of the odds, and this property has made it possible to develop the technique to derive models which incorporate prior probabilities of failure or which allocate firms to different categories of financial distress. However, a major problem is still the fact that usually the samples of failed companies are relatively small, and to be viable they have to be pooled across time. Even so, the number of observations is normally such as to prevent the logit models from demonstrating their potential superiority over MRA and MDA models. Moreover, although the models appear to be able to distinguish impressively between failed and non-failed companies, their discriminatory power seems to be greatly reduced when the true incidence of bankruptcy in a population of companies is allowed for.

In recent times interest has been shown in another technique, which instead of using failure/non-failure as the dependent variable focuses on the life expectancy of a business. However, the data requirements to use such models are onerous, inasmuch as there needs to be a good run of data from the 'birth dates' of a large number of companies. Usually – except possibly for small companies – such data are not available. Rather, the common event time is the *date of death*, not the *date of birth*. Nevertheless, there have been one or two studies employing the duration model technique, and the results are of some interest.

**Notes**

[1] The characteristic of equal standard deviations around the fitted regression line is known as 'homocedasticity'. Its opposite, 'heteroscedasticity', exists when standard deviations are not equal. A particular situation where standard deviations around the fitted regression line are not equal arises when the residual error terms are serially correlated (i.e. there is 'autocorrelation'). This is illustrated in Figure 4.5.

[2] See note 1.

[3] The Edmister study is briefly summarised below, p. 225.

[4] See Taffler (1984). For a brief description of Marais's original model and the Bank of England's experience in using it, see *The Bank of England Quarterly Bulletin*, June 1982, pp. 221-223.

[5] For a fuller explanation, see Pindyk and Rubinfeld (1976), ch. 8.

[6] See Kennedy (1992).

[7] See Jones (1987, p. 154). Altman (1977) estimated relative error costs for commercial bank loans at 7:1 for Type I and Type II misclassifications.

[8] Whether it is entirely reasonable to assume this is debatable, since there tends to be a clustering of failures in particular years (e.g. when there is a recession, or when there is a sharp movement in exchange rates).

[9] The cutoff becomes equal to $\ln [p_1 c_1 / p_2 c_2]$, where $c_1$ and $c_2$ represent the costs of misclassifying failed and non-failed companies: see Jones (1987, p. 154).

[10] Beaver's study is briefly described on p. 108.

[11] For surveys, see Zavgren (1983), Dambolena (1983), Altman (1984b), Jones (1987) and Keasey and Watson (1991). However, the most detailed analysis, both of the procedures used and of the extant research to 1980, is in the book by Altman, Avery, Eisenbeis and Sinkey (1981).

[12] See below, p. 205 et seq., for a description of the use of principal components and factor analysis to identify common elements in ratios.

[13] Earlier Gombola and Ketz (1983) used factor analysis on a set of 40 variables for 119 companies over a 19 year period and found that cash flow indicators were a separate and significant variable.

[14] Similar results to Dambolena and Khoury's have been obtained by Betts and Belhoul (1987) for a sample of British companies.

[15] The relatively poor performance of the ZETA model out-of-sample is consistent with results derived by Gilbert, Menon and Schwartz (1990). Their study demonstrated that ratio based bankruptcy identification models were unable to distinguish failing companies from distressed firms, leading them to conclude

that there are overlapping financial characteristics, implying that distress is resolved by non-financial factors.

[16] See below, p. 205 et seq., for a description of the use of principal components and factor analysis to identify common elements in ratios.

[17] Other studies which have examined the effects of developing models using different base years and/or including trend variables are Falbo (1991) and Laitinen (1991, 1993).

[18] Letza (1994) adopted a similar approach to Piesse and Wood. He applied proxied Altman and Datastream models to a sample of UK listed companies and reached similar conclusions.

[19] Technically, of course, one should allow for the size of the companies misclassified and not just their number.

[20] Taffler's somewhat ambiguous view on the predictive power of his Z-score models is also reflected in other research undertaken by him. Thus in a paper on stock market reaction to divestments by financially distressed and healthy firms (Lasfer, Sudarsarnam and Taffler, 1994), it is specifically recognised that 'the market anticipates bankruptcy ... well before the actual bankruptcy event occurs' (p. 4). Nevertheless, the Z-score model is used in a predictive role to identify potentially failing firms.

[21] Kiefer (1988) provides a succinct summary of the principles behind the analysis of duration data.

[22] For recent reviews of research on the post-entry performance of firms, see the papers by Audretsch and Mata (1995) and Geroski (1995), which appear in a special issue of *The International Journal of Industrial Organisation* (vol. 13, no. 4) reporting a number of other studies applying logit and duration models to analyse the survival record of businesses.

[23] Another study recently reported is that by Luoma and Laitinen (1991), relating to 36 failed Finnish companies and their matched pairs. The Cox model was applied with a set of 12 potential explanatory variables. However, although an arbitrary birth date was chosen working backwards from the death date (thus introducing a hindsight bias), the model was outperformed by MDA and logit models.

# 5 Positive theories of corporate failure: III – Iterative models

## Introduction

The previous two chapters have described procedures used to examine the characteristics of financially distressed companies and reviewed the empirical evidence relating to their application. In particular, chapter 4 was concerned with the use of multivariate, statistically based models, such as regression, logit and discriminant analysis. But as was explained then, there is often only a tenuous link to an underlying positive theory which might explain why such financially distressed companies fail. However, it was nonetheless convenient to regard them within that context.

In fact, although academics have generally sought to develop bankruptcy identification models using statistical techniques, it is possible to adopt a completely different approach, experimenting until a suitably robust discriminatory model evolves. There are four main ways in which this can be done:

(1) applying subjective weights to variables;
(2) using the 'recursive partitioning' approach;
(3) developing 'artificial intelligence' models; and
(4) applying 'neural network' analysis.

With respect to the first of these, a number of 'off-the-peg' computer based credit scoring routines are on the market, and they are probably now the most widely used corporate risk assessment models. Of the others, increasing attention is being paid to neural networking analysis for a variety of purposes as increased computer power has made it feasible to develop such routines, a major application being in finance (especially with respect to failure identification and the assessment of debt risk).

Once again, there is often only a weak link between what are essentially data analysis routines and an underlying positive theory which might explain why financially distressed companies fail. But as previously, it will be convenient to regard them within a broad positive theoretical framework.

Against this background, the purpose of this chapter is to describe briefly the four types of iterative models identified above and to summarise the empirical evidence on their success in discriminating between bankrupt and non-failing firms.

**Subjectively weighted variables**

Probably the best known models using subjectively determined variables and parameter values are those of Tamari (1965, 1978). The original version was developed for the Bank of Israel on a sample of 28 companies over the period 1956-1960. Of these, 16 failed and 12 were classified as non-failing. The initial choice of variables and the parameter weights accorded to them was driven by the results of a survey of lending bankers.

Essentially the models take the following form:

$$Y = a_1X_1 + a_2X_2 + a_3X_3 \qquad (5.1)$$

where Y, the dependent variable, is a percentage score;
$X_1 \ldots X_n$ are the independent variables (usually financial ratios); and
$a_1 \ldots a_n$ are weights initially determined from surveys and subsequently adjusted in the light of experience.

Thus, to give a hypothetical example, it might be that an initial survey of lending bankers suggests that they place most weight on the equity/total assets ratio, followed by the current assets/current liabilities ratio, and then the debtors turnover ratio (sales/trade debtors). A given number of percentage points will therefore be given to a firm which meets certain 'threshold' requirements for a particular ratio. It might therefore be that in the above model the following points will be earned:

|  | maximum points |
|---|---|
| $X_1$ = equity/total assets | 50 |
| $X_2$ = current assets/current liabilities | 30 |
| $X_3$ = sales/trade debtors | 20 |
|  | 100 |

154

The weights (or scores) for each variable will then be determined according to the rules of the system. Thus, for example, it might be that the score (effectively $a_1X_1$) with respect to the first variable, equity/total assets, might be the full 50 points if $X_1 > 0.5$; 40 points if $X_1$ is between 0.4 and 0.5; 20 points if $X_1$ is between 0.2 and 0.4; and zero points if $X_1 < 0.2$. Points would then be awarded in a similar way for the other two variables, $X_2$ and $X_3$, and the total score be added up for the company. The nearer to 100 per cent the total score, the more financially sound a company would appear to be.

Such a credit scoring model is relatively crude, but it has the merit of being easily adjustable to allow for changing conditions. On the other hand, it is naive (e.g. it excludes many aspects of a business's operations and it also ignores the statistical problems associated with ratio distributions). Intuitively one might expect such a model to work quite well in practice, since it is basically seeking to mimic the heuristic (i.e. search) procedures employed by lending bankers. But there is a danger that if it is used mechanistically it will merely reinforce the criteria already applied by lending officers. It will thus become self-fulfilling and might encourage bank staff not to look too closely behind the figures. Equally it could encourage loan applicants – once they learn how such a model is being used – to manipulate the accounting numbers they report to achieve a higher score.[1]

Tamari's original model included six ratios, and after fine tuning it performed reasonably well. Only 26 companies in a sample of 130 Israeli businesses used to test the model went bankrupt. In this sample, 52 per cent of companies with scores below 30 per cent went bankrupt, but only 6 per cent of those scoring between 30 per cent and 60 per cent; and just 3 per cent of those scoring over 60 per cent.

This record does not appear at first sight as good as those reported for many of the statistically determined models developed in the US, UK and elsewhere, but care needs to be taken in assessing relative performance as the discriminating power of many of the latter is probably overstated because of the incidence of sampling bias (see above, p. 29).

Models along similar lines have been developed in a number of other countries, including the UK, when Tamari did work for the Bolton Committee which investigated the activities of small firms.[2] In a similar vein, Barthory (1984) developed a 'synoptic' model, equally weighting five ratios, and he found it performed well.

Tamari's approach is very like that developed by credit analysts over the years to calculate credit scores when assessing clients. Moreover, in the last decade computer spreadsheet packages have become widely available in the US and UK which enable analysts to calculate scores for companies which are the subject of scrutiny. All the credit manager has to do is to enter the values of ratios of the companies in question and run the program.

## Recursive partitioning

'Recursive partitioning' is an iterative technique which classifies sequentially in terms of a series of independent variables. This is done by a computer program which separates cases according to the lowest misclassification cost. This enables a suitable cut off point to be established.

This can perhaps best be illustrated by referring to a simple example. Suppose that there is a sample of 100 companies, of which 50 failed and 50 survived. Let it be assumed that the best discriminator is profit/capital employed (ROCE), and that when the cut off point is set at 10 per cent there are two groups of companies formed, A (above) and B (below). The initial screening in terms of this ratio shows that 60 companies fall into the $A_1$ group and 40 into the $B_1$ group. Of the $A_1$ group, 12 companies have failed and 48 have not; whereas in the $B_1$ group 38 have failed and only 2 have not.

Overall, as the following classification matrix makes clear, only 76 per cent of the failed companies are correctly forecast as such.

| Prediction | Actual outcome | | |
|---|---|---|---|
| | Fail | Non-fail | Total |
| Fail [F]        ($B_1$) | 38 | 2 | 40 |
| Non-fail [NF] ($A_1$) | 12 | 48 | 60 |
| | 50 | 50 | 100 |

If this error rate is considered to be unacceptably high, a further screening of the $A_1$ group is required using a second variable. This may use equity/total assets (EQ/TA) as the discriminator with the cut off point set at 40 per cent. On this criterion the $A_2$ and $B_2$ groupings at this stage may show: $A_2$ – 4 failed, 36 non-failed; $B_2$ – 8 failed, 12 non-failed. The situation is shown in the tree diagram in Figure 5.1.

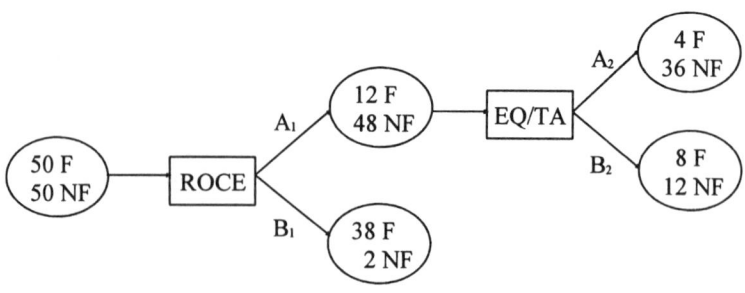

**Figure 5.1**

156

In terms of Figure 5.1 there are three 'terminal nodes': $B_1$, $A_2$ and $B_2$. From this it is possible to construct a second classification matrix as follows:

| Prediction | | Actual outcome | | |
|---|---|---|---|---|
| | | Fail | Non-fail | Total |
| Fail [F] | $(B_1+B_2)$ | 38+8=46 | 2+12=14 | 60 |
| Non-fail [NF] | $(A_2)$ | 4 | 36 | 40 |
| | | 50 | 50 | 100 |

Now 92 per cent of failed companies are correctly classified (although the forecast accuracy of the non-failing firms has actually declined). However, screening can continue indefinitely for all A and B groups by sub-classifying in terms of new variables. Moreover, a ratio used earlier as a discriminator can be used again but with a different cut off point. In practice, it would be usual to end the process when misclassification costs reach an acceptable level.

It is clear from studies using the technique that it is difficult to assess the relative importance of the variables. This is partly because the procedure employs a forward selection process and does not review previous classifications in the light of the most recent ones; and partly because the same variable can be used two or more times as a discriminator. But perhaps the greatest problem is that of overfitting, since the iterative procedure can continue until there is 100 per cent correct classification on the basis of the analysis sample. This makes it vital to test the model, once derived, on one or more hold out samples.

The procedure has the advantage that it can easily accommodate qualitative variables, but against that it provides much less information on probabilities and variable coefficients than other techniques such as logit.

The two pioneering studies where the technique has been used are those of Frydman, Altman and Kao (1985), who used it to distinguish failed from non-failed firms; and Marais, Patell and Wolfson (1984), who employed it to assess loan classifications.[3]

The Frydman, Altman and Kao study used a sample of 58 companies which failed during 1971-1981, and against these the researchers randomly selected another 142 nonbankrupt companies. However, there was no matching by year. They began with 20 ratios which had been found relevant in identifying failure in three previous studies, and they specified a prior probability of failure of 2 per cent, as well as a number of different costs of misclassification. Beginning with cash flow/debt, they developed two models. The first had a tree with one branch having two screenings, the other just one, the result being that there were five terminal nodes. The second model had a tree with one branch having three screenings, the other two. The end result for this model was that there were seven terminal nodes. Both models were tested on hold out samples and compared against the classificatory power of two discriminant models. Overall the recursive partitioning models were found to perform best.

The Marais, Patell and Wolfson study compared their recursive partitioning results against those of a probit model where there were a number of dependent variable categories. Interestingly, they concluded that in estimating loan classifications with minimum error cost there was very little to choose between the two procedures.

## Artificial intelligence

A natural evolution of the recursive partitioning technique is to develop 'artificial intelligence' models on a computer which discriminate between failed and non-failed concerns (Messier and Hansen, 1988). These work at three levels:

(1) 'structural validity', whereby the model aims to mimic accurately an expert's decision making processes;
(2) 'diagnostic validity', whereby the model must be able to infer correctly the importance of the different variables in influencing the final decision; and
(3) 'predictive validity', whereby the model must be able to perform satisfactorily out-of-sample (i.e. in the context of a hold out sample).

Essentially the models are developed using algorithms which can be either 'data driven' or 'model driven'. The processes used employ a series of programming iterations of the form of IF...THEN...ELSE statements: e.g.

IF      profit/capital employed <10 per cent
THEN   company will fail
ELSE   company will survive

Messier and Hansen applied this approach to data used in two laboratory studies of subjects' interpretation of data on loan defaults (Abdel-khalik and El-Sheshai, 1980) and bankruptcy (Libby, Trotman and Zimmer, 1987).[4] In the original studies, the results of the experiments were compared against 'predictions' given by statistical models. Messier and Hansen then developed 'data driven' artificial intelligence models. By contrast with the Frydman, Altman and Kao study, where the objective was to minimise the expected cost of misclassification, their goal was to minimise the number of misclassifications.

The set of rules derived by Messier and Hansen correctly classified the loans and failing/non-failing companies with 100 per cent accuracy, even on the hold out samples. This was not of itself too surprising, given the derivation of the models, but what was potentially interesting was the relatively simple set of rules they employed. However, Messier and Hansen warned that the experiments were conducted on relatively simple problems: the models might not perform as well if the problems were more complex. Moreover, potential error could arise from omitting important instances or diagnostic attributes.

**Neural networking**

'Neural networking' (NN) models take the iterative approach one step further. But as they are non-linear 'black box' models derived by search procedures, it is impossible to describe them in terms of equations with parameter values.[5] All that can be done is to identify the variable inputs and outputs of a particular routine which outperforms its rivals. Nevertheless, because of their increasing popularity, it is worthwhile describing the general nature of the technique.[6]

Essentially there are five features of such models:

(1) The model comprises a number of 'processing elements' (or 'neurons') and 'connections' (or 'links'). The former are organised in layers and can be constructed heirarchically. The first layer is called the 'input layer' and the last the 'output layer'. The intermediate layers are referred to as 'hidden layers'.

(2) The models are generally constructed as a 'feed-forward network'. Each processing element (neuron) receives and combines 'input signals' from neurons in the preceding layer and transforms them into a single 'output signal'.

(3) Each output signal is in turn sent from its processing element as an input signal to other processing elements (and even possibly back to itself).

(4) Signals are passed around the network via 'weighted interconnections' (or 'synapses') between the processing elements. Each connection between neurons has a numerical weight associated with it. This shows the influence of an input neuron on an output neuron, with positive weights indicating the reinforcement of a relationship and negative weights a weakening.

(5) Network knowledge is stored not only on the way in which processing elements connect with each other in order to transfer signals, but also on the nature and strength of the connections.

Computer algorithms establish a 'training network' to detect relationships between 'input data' and 'output data' in order to 'classify' situations correctly.

The topology of a feed-forward neural network comprising six processing elements (characterised as 'nodes' in a 'tree') is illustrated in Figure 5.2.

In the example there are three 'input nodes' at the 'input layer'. Taken together these represent one 'pattern' to be studied by the NN model. As there is no linearity requirement in NN models, these input signals can either be quantitative (e.g. company financial ratios) or qualitative (e.g. whether or not a company's accounts are subject to an audit qualification).

The 'output layer' of the NN comprises a single 'response' (or 'condition') node. This can classify either in terms of a nominal scale (e.g. by a number of different geographical locations) or on an ordered scale (e.g. where classifications are ranked). For the purpose in hand the classification is a simple fail/non-fail dichotomy.

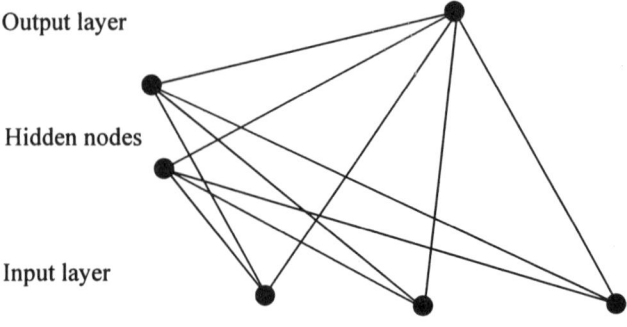

**Figure 5.2**

The feature that distinguishes NN models from other models (such as regression, discriminant or logit models) is that it has a middle layer of 'hidden nodes' (of which there are two in Figure 5.2). NN models begin with none of these hidden nodes, but incrementally these are created and added sequentially to improve the network's classificatory accuracy. As more of these hidden nodes are added, the network becomes completely general and can separate the 'decision space' into an arbitrary number of 'regions'.

The numerical weight assigned to the connection of any two nodes reflects the direction (positive or negative) and the relative strength of the relationship between the nodes. Determining these weights is essentially the focus of the NN model's computational process.

The 'training' process is a learning procedure in which the model identifies the relationship between the output and patterns in the inputs. This knowledge is incrementally captured in a unique structure of hidden nodes and connection weights which produce the correct classifications. The NN model develops by minimising the average residual forecast error for the set of training patterns. Once the network has examined all the patterns in the training sample, the process begins again and cycles through the entire set of training examples. (Each pass through the set is known as an 'epoch'.) When further adjustment of the weights reduces the error to the preset acceptable level, the training of the connection weights ceases.

Once the training process is complete, the NN model has to be tested rigorously on one or more hold out samples to ensure that it can be generally applied.

An important feature of NN models, which makes them potentially attractive, is their adaptive nature. This enables them to be fine tuned to accommodate changes in economic and industry conditions over time. Against that is the criticism that they encourage 'data mining',[7] and there may well be a tendency to 'overfit' them on the sample data.[8] Moreover, it seems that the computation processes are such

160

that they can normally only handle satisfactorily data relating to a relatively small number of independent variables.

The relevance of NN procedures for financial analysis has been recognised for some time (e.g. by Hawley, Johnson and Raina, 1990). However, so far there have been relatively few NN studies specifically relating to bankruptcy identification, although one or two have been undertaken on related matters (e.g. corporate bond ratings).[9]

One of the first NN failure studies was that of Odom and Sharda (1990). They used the same five ratios employed by Altman (1968) in his original multiple discriminant analysis (MDA) study,[10] applying them to a sample of 65 failed and 64 non-failed US companies, where the former went bankrupt between 1975 and 1982. The training set comprised 38 failed and 36 non-failed companies, the remainder being used as a validation sample. A three layered network was created with five hidden nodes. Convergence was reached after 24 hours and 191,400 iterations. The NN model correctly identified all failed and non-failed companies in the training sample, compared to a successful classification rate of only 86.8 per cent for a benchmark discriminant model. Both models were then tested on the hold out sample using prior probability of failure estimates of 50:50, 20:80 and 10:90. The neural network model correctly classified bankrupt firms in 77.7 per cent or more occasions under all three probability priors – a far better record than the discriminant model, which could only manage between 59 per cent and 70 per cent. However, for the non-failed businesses there was little to choose between the models, the correct classification rates being between 79 per cent and 89 per cent.

The study by Fletcher and Goss (1993) used backpropagation NN models to identify US corporate bankruptcies from a sample of 18 matched pairs of companies. Using three accounting ratios as the explanatory variables (the current ratio, the quick ratio, and net profit/working capital), they investigated the impact on the performance of their NN models of the number of neurons in the hidden layer. The results showed that NN models with between 3 and 7 hidden nodes were better able to discriminate than comparable logit models, though only marginally so, with the 4 hidden node model performing best. However, the 82 per cent correct prediction rate (compared with only 71 per cent for the logit model) was achieved without adjusting for sampling bias, which suggests that none of the models would be very helpful in practice.

Another NN bankruptcy study is that of Coats and Fant (1993). They used going concern audit qualifications as their criterion of failure, identifying 94 listed US manufacturing companies over the period 1970-1989 which met this requirement. Against these they used 188 non-failed listed companies, almost half of which however were not in the manufacturing sector. Eight sets of company data were created, two for each of the four years prior to failure, one being used to derive the NN model, the other as a hold out sample to assess its predictive power. Each year's training and test sets comprised 47 failed and 94 non-failed companies, membership of the training set in each of the four years being determined by random selection. As in Odom and Sharda's study, the variables in the training set data were the five accounting ratios used in Altman's 1968 MDA study, and the latter's ability to identify failing companies correctly was used as the benchmark against which to assess the NN model's performance.

Working to a 100 per cent correct classification objective, some of the networks developed required up to 1,400 training cycles and installed as many as 8 hidden nodes. The MDA models correctly identified over 90 per cent of the non-failed companies over the four years, but did far less well in classifying the failed companies, only achieving success rates of between 64 per cent and 70 per cent over the four years. By contrast, the NN models did far better in identifying failed companies, achieving a success rate of over 80 per cent and almost matching the MDA models' ability to identify non-failures. Coats and Fant concluded that, after allowance was made for misclassification costs, the NN model appeared to be making a useful contribution to the task of identifying firms that might be the subject of going concern qualifications, especially when the time interval before this type of 'failure' was extended.

A further NN model developed in a bankruptcy context is that of Tam (1991). This was constructed on a sample of 59 Texas banks which failed between 1985 and 1987, and another group of 59 matched Texas banks which survived over that period. Each bank was described over a two year period in terms of 19 financial ratios, reflecting capital adequacy, asset quality, earnings and liquidity. These were normalised by transformation and reduced to a set of 6 for constructing a one year prior to failure MDA model; and to 7 for a two years prior to failure MDA model. Other models were developed to provide bench marks for assessing the NN models, including logit and artificial intelligence models.

Two and three layer NN models were developed for each period, the latter having 10 hidden nodes. Different prior probability rates of failure and different misclassification costs were used. Both the one and two year NN models dominated the other models in their ability to discriminate, with the three layer NN models doing best. However, the superiority was less obvious in the second year before failure, possibly suggesting that the failing and non-failing banks comprised a more homogeneous population at that stage than in the last year of a failing bank's life. The results were checked out on hold out samples, comprising 22 failed and 22 non-failed banks in the last year before failure; and 20 failed and 20 non-failed banks in the previous year. The two layer NN model was less effective in some respects than the MDA and logit models, but the three layer NN model again dominated all others. However, the misclassification errors were much higher than on the original sample, especially for the Type I errors one year prior to failure (i.e. classifying a failed company as non-failed), which even for the three layer NN model were around 20 per cent.

In a subsequent study, Salchenberger, Cinar and Lash (1992) applied the NN procedure to discriminate between 100 US savings-and-loan (S&L) institutions (i.e. equivalent to building societies in the UK) which failed in 1986-1987 and a similar number of non-failed matched pairs. Applying five ratios, the NN model consistently outperformed a logit model, although both on the face of it were impressive in their forecasting accuracy. However, the performance of both models fell away slightly with respect to failing S&Ls as the time interval before collapse was lengthened, although only marginally in the case of the NN model. Moreover, when the model was applied to a sample where the proportion of non-failed to failed S&Ls was more realistic, the NN model still performed tolerably well, although the misclassification errors for failing thrifts were much larger.

A more recent – and in some ways the most detailed – examination of the NN technique as a means of identifying failing businesses has been undertaken by Altman, Marco and Varetto (1994). They tested a number of NN models against the existing MDA predictions provided by a consortium of Italian banks. These are derived annually for a population of nearly 40,000 medium and small sized businesses. The MDA diagnostic procedures are in fact applied in two phases: first, to distinguish healthy from vulnerable firms; and then with respect to the latter to separate those which are prima facie failures from those which are not. Using a 404 matched pair analysis sample and a 150 matched pair hold out group, the first phase model was very successful in discriminating both over the estimation period and over a control period. However, the classificatory accuracy of the second phase model was somewhat weaker. It was also based on a 404 matched pair analysis sample and a 150 matched pair hold out group, but only around 80 per cent of failing firms were correctly identified.

Various NN models were then developed to see how they performed in relation to the MDA models. One, two and three layer NN models were devised with different numbers of hidden nodes and with different learning times. The best results in distinguishing between healthy and vulnerable firms were initially achieved with a three layer network, the second layer having four hidden neurons. The inputs comprised 10 financial ratios, and training was interrupted after 1,000 cycles. When the number of layers in the network were varied, the most satisfactory results were achieved after 2,000 cycles for a three layer model, with 15 neurons in the first layer and six in the second. The model was able to discriminate with 97 per cent accuracy compared to between 86 per cent and 90 per cent for the corresponding MDA model.

The next step was to use the MDA ratio set as the basis for deriving the NN model. When this restriction was introduced the best result was achieved after 4,030 epochs with a three layer model which had 5 hidden nodes in the second layer. However, its classificatory power was slightly inferior to that of the corresponding MDA model. Separate NN models were then developed to capture each of eight different financial characteristics (e.g. gearing, liquidity, profitability, etc), and these were then linked together to generate a second level NN model. This discriminated well with a success rate of 89 per cent or more, despite some peculiar behaviour patterns with the second level network. Discriminatory power was further improved to over 99 per cent when NN models were derived from three

163

years data rather than restricting the inputs to ratios calculated from figures in firms' last sets of published accounts.

Overall, Altman, Marco and Varetto concluded that the MDA approach performs rather well when compared to NN models. Moreover, it is helpful to be able to follow the economic logic implicit in the equations. Nevertheless, they regarded the approaches as complementary, and they suggested that there is a strong case for trying to integrate the results from the two types of model in order to develop a more powerful diagnostic procedure for discriminating between failing and non-failing businesses.

A number of NN models have been developed in the UK to see how well they discriminate between failing and non-failing companies, and their performance has been reported in a number of papers. One of the few to be formally published is that by Wilson, Chong and Peel (1995), whose sample period covered the years 1972-1979. They applied a backpropagation algorithm to see whether NN models could outperform their logit and multilogit counterparts in distinguishing between 40 failed, 32 distressed-but-acquired and 40 non-failed listed companies. A total of 79 potential explanatory variables (including 8 qualitative indicators) was reduced to 18 for the experiment, and two and three group discriminatory models were derived. The topology of the models comprised an input layer, a hidden layer, and an output layer. There was rapid convergence in the early stages of training, with classification errors being significantly reduced after the first 30-40 epochs, and in terms of the analysis sample both the two category and the three category NN models were extremely efficient in discriminating between the different types of company, even marginally outperforming the impressive accuracy of corresponding logit models. However, the NN models performed far less well on hold out samples (as indeed did their logit counterparts), and especially so in discriminating between failed and distressed-but-acquired companies. This once more suggests that there is a degree of overfitting inherent in the models. Moreover, no allowance was made for sample selection bias, which (although the classification errors were greater with respect to failed rather than non-failed companies) further suggests that discriminatory power is probably significantly overstated when it is just based on results relating to the analysis sample.

**Summary**

Iterative models have long been used to try to identify failing businesses, and they have the great advantage that they are relatively easy to understand and apply. The big question, however, is whether they capture as much information as statistically derived models.

Subjectively weighted variable models were greatly refined by Tamari, but simple versions of these models are now readily available for use on computers (e.g. to calculate credit scores). The recursive partitioning procedure is a more elaborate procedure which has a certain appeal, but taken to its logical conclusion such an approach leads to artificial intelligence and neural networking models. Advances in computer technology have now made it possible to apply the latter to a variety of business problems to see whether it is possible to squeeze extra information out of a database. Thus far the technique has rarely been applied to the problem of bankruptcy identification, but doubtless this will change in the near future. However, those studies so far undertaken seem if anything to overfit the data, and their performance in discriminating between failing and non-failing firms in hold out samples (especially where no adjustment has been made for sample selection bias) does not seem to be very different from that of other, statistically derived models.

## Notes

[1] It should not take too long in a competitive environment for potential lenders or agencies seeking their business to learn how such models are being applied.

[2] Cmnd. 4811 (1972), *Small Firms* (The Bolton Committee Report), HMSO. For further details of Tamari's work, see Tamari (1978).

[3] The Marais, Patell and Wolfson study used a number of qualitative variables. It is briefly described below on p. 232.

[4] Laboratory studies of analysts' ability to predict failing companies are discussed below, pp. 185 et seq.

[5] A black box model is where it is only possible to identify the inputs and outputs. What goes on inside the 'black box' cannot readily be seen.

[6] Most papers reporting the results of financial applications of the NN technique do no more than this. See Trippi and Turban (1993) for a general discussion of applications of neural networking models to issues in finance.

[7] Data mining refers to the practice of analysing data with little or no underlying theory in the hope of finding statistically significant relationships.

[8] Overfitting refers to the situation where a model fits exceptionally well on to the data from which it is derived, but far less well on to other data from a hold out sample.

[9] An application with respect to credit scoring is reported by Jensen (1991). More generally, the book by Trippi and Turban (1993) includes 5 papers on failure identification, 4 on debt risk assessment, and 7 on the prediction of share and commodity prices. Several other NN studies have been undertaken relating to bankruptcy prediction, but the results have yet to be formally published.

Wilson, Chong and Peel (1995, p. 33) refer to an application of the technique by Barclaycard, which has used an NN model to recognise fraudulent transactions. This enabled the company to reduce losses from such activities by 20 per cent during a period of six months.

[10] See above, p. 135.

# 6 Positive theories of corporate failure: IV – Early warning studies

## Introduction

The evidence presented in previous chapters suggests that on the face of it bankruptcy prediction models, whatever the methodolgy used to derive them, have considerable discriminatory power. Moreover, the impression is given by researchers that the best known models are still able to discriminate long after the market has been made aware of their existence and their underlying nature. This continuing success is rather puzzling, since a sustained ability to distinguish between failing and non-failing listed companies suggests irrationality on the part of investors and a significant degree of informational market inefficiency. Rather, in a reasonably efficient market, such as that for securities, one would expect that a model which has all the attributes of a 'money making machine' would soon cease to be so, if only because the best way to use the information it generates is to publicise it so that those using it can close their speculative positions. But, even if details of the model are not made public, rational investors and their advisors have a major incentive to discover and mimic its information content.

The alternative explanation is not that the market is seriously inefficient, but rather that there are flaws in the procedures used by researchers who develop bankruptcy prediction models. Thus Johnson (1970) and Wood and Piesse (1985, 1987, 1988) have argued that even if the evidence suggests that such models perform well ex post, this does not indicate whether they impart incremental information to analysts or merely mimic their conclusions reached in less formal ways. It is therefore important to note that the best known and most widely applied models do not in fact appear to perform well outside the sample period over which they were derived, misclassifying an unacceptable 20 per cent or so of surviving companies as prima facie failures.

In the circumstances, it is important to try to assess whether failure prediction models do in fact contain incremental information for analysts. There are two research avenues which can cast light on this: first, share price reaction studies[1]; and, second, behavioural (or 'cognitive') experiments. Thus in the case of the former, one might reasonably expect that if a forecasting model is perceived as working well, it should become self-fulfilling: i.e. the share prices of companies identified as prima facie failures should collapse suddenly rather than decline gradually as bankruptcy approaches. As for behavioural experiments, if the models are capturing new information, it should be possible to demonstrate under laboratory conditions that groups of analysts significantly underperform the models in discriminating between failing and surviving companies.

'Market based research' in accounting has become well established over the past 25 years. The main focus of study has been how share prices react to various 'events' or 'signals'. The latter most obviously include reported earnings, although many other financial reporting procedures have been the subject of scrutiny. The overall picture is that analysts absorb news from a wide variety of sources and continuously revise their forecasts of future company earnings in the light of news releases. Nevertheless, there is residual information in earnings announcements, confirming and confounding analysts' collective projections of profits and causing them to revise their forecasts for future years. Generally the evidence suggests that financial markets are 'semi-strong efficient': i.e. as a result of competition between analysts, financial markets absorb information virtually instantaneously once it enters the public domain.

This has important implications for failure identification models. Firstly, it makes it very difficult to believe that procedures which are well known or can relatively easily be replicated have much information for the market. And, secondly, it makes it especially interesting to see whether there is any evidence that the market is identifying problem cases as early as the so-called failure prediction models.

In fact, the 'event study' methodology which is at the heart of market based accounting research is well developed. However, for various technical reasons it is not easy to apply it to bankruptcy studies (e.g. it is difficult to control for systematic (or market related) risk; and the focus of interest is not share price behaviour around a specific event date, but rather over a much longer period). Nevertheless, such evidence as there is seems to suggest, first, that share prices of prima facie failing companies do not collapse suddenly, but rather decline gradually; and, second, that the market reaches the same conclusions implied by failure identification models, and even possibly anticipates their predictions.

The behavioural research studies have essentially focused on the interpretation by analysts of certain accounting messages, the aim being to see which of them are regarded as signalling likely failure. But there is another aspect of the problem that has been examined – namely, how best to convey information to analysts concerning the financial health of a company.

In this context, it is first necessary to describe briefly the nature of behavioural research in accounting, before reviewing a number of empirically based studies. Specifically, laboratory experiments have examined how analysts react to accounting data which might indicate the likelihood of corporate failure. However, there is evidence of 'hindsight bias'. Finally, there is a brief discussion of research which has explored how multidimensional graphics might be used to convey in a succinct manner the relevant information that is included in a company's accounts and which reflects its financial position.

## Share price behaviour

### Introduction

Research into the share price behaviour of failing companies has addressed two main issues. The first is to identify when relative share prices of financially distressed companies move down and whether in doing so they anticipate the signals generated by statistical failure prediction models. The purpose of the second is to establish the extent to which the signals contained in specific models applied outside the original sample period appear to be impounded in share prices.

### Event study methodology

*Modelling share price returns.* The approach adopted in order to study share price behaviour prior to impending bankruptcy is a variation of the standard procedures developed in so-called 'event studies'. The aim of the latter is to see how share prices react to particular items of 'news'. With bankruptcy studies the object is rather different, namely to examine share price behaviour over a much longer period as failure approaches.

The basic focus of interest in event studies is

$$R_i = f(S_1) \tag{6.1}$$

> where $R_i$ is the observed return on security i (the dependent variable) in a given period;
> $f(.)$ indicates a functional relationship (i.e. $R_i$ is driven by the independent variable within the brackets); and
> $S_1$ is an event (e.g. a *signal* or *news item*).

In conducting event studies, the key point is to focus clearly on the appropriate events and the appropriate returns. Thus in the case of the former, it is necessary to isolate the 'incremental news' (i.e. it is necessary to factor out what the market has been anticipating); while in the case of the latter, it is necessary to focus on share price movements which are *alone* driven by the event and not, for instance, by market- or industry-wide factors. In fact, researchers have developed relatively sophisticated ways of trying to achieve these two objectives, and it will be helpful to review these briefly.

Beginning with $R_i$, returns are usually modelled to isolate 'abnormal returns', $e_i$, which can formally be defined as

$$e_i = R_i - E(R_i) \qquad (6.2)$$

where i is a security, R is the return, and E(.) is the
expectations operator.

In practice, researchers generally use logged returns as this helps to ensure normality in the distribution of returns.

Expected returns, $E(R_i)$, can in fact be modelled in various ways, e.g.

(1) using a matched pairing technique to control for systematic economy- and industry-wide factors;
(2) applying the capital asset pricing model (CAPM) in one of its several forms to identify expected market (and sometimes industry) related share price movements;
(3) applying the arbitrage pricing theory of asset valuation to identify expected share price movements; or
(4) applying option pricing theory to model expected share price movements.

Where (1) is applied, so-called 'raw returns' are used as the dependent variable (i.e. the data are the returns as reported for each security without adjustment). By contrast, with (2) and (3) so-called 'residual returns' are the focus of interest (i.e. the returns are calculated after deducting expected market-wide movements from the raw return).[2]

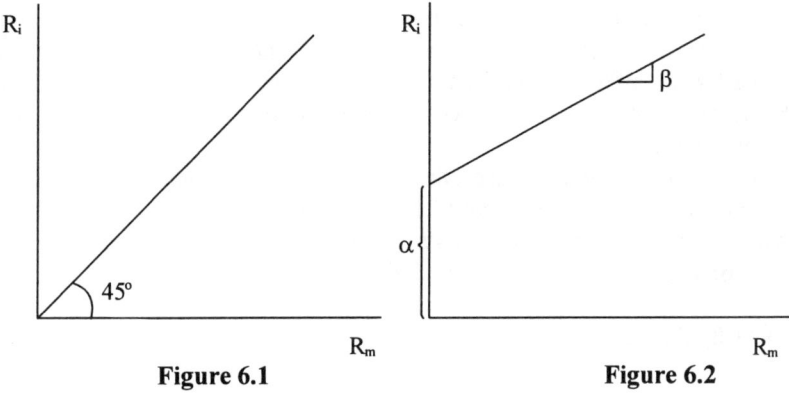

| Figure 6.1 | Figure 6.2 |

169

The expected market-wide returns, insofar as they will impact individual security returns, are modelled by examining the usual relationship between individual security returns, $R_i$, and returns on a market index, $R_m$. At its simplest, this might assume that share prices go up and down in a fixed proportion with the market index (e.g. 90 per cent). This is illustrated in Figure 6.1. Such a relationship would have to be established by examining historical price movements.

In practice, however, as was pointed out in chapter 2 (p. 74 et seq.), the relationship does not appear to be linear running through the origin. Rather it seems to be far better represented as linear with an intercept.

The model illustrated in Figure 6.1 is known as the 'zero-one' model, since the intercept is zero and the slope coefficient must be one. It is represented thus:

$$R_{it} = R_{mt} + e_{it} \tag{6.3}$$

> where  e represents an error term with a zero expected value,
> t refers to a period in time,
> $R_t$ indicates the return for period t,  and
> i and m respectively refer to security i and the market portfolio (the latter proxied by a market index).

The relationship illustrated in Figure 6.2 is represented by the 'simple market model' (SMM) (see pp. 74-5).

$$R_{it} = \alpha_i + \beta_i R_{mt} + e_{it} \tag{6.4}$$

> where $\alpha_i$ is the intercept; and
> $\beta_i$ is the slope coefficient (or 'beta') found by least squares regression for data pooled over time.

It might be noted in passing that it is implicitly assumed that there is no serial dependence through time: i.e. $R_i$ for period t is not in a fixed relationship to $R_i$ for period t-1. If it were, it would imply irrationality on the part of the market, since if it were possible to infer a given pattern of prices through time, it would be reasonable to expect that all analysts would appreciate this and react accordingly, so neutralising the relationship.

Sometimes researchers prefer to use a theoretical model to explain expected share price movements rather than the 'theory free' SMM. The most widely used version is the Sharpe-Lintner version of the CAPM, which explains the intercept in terms of the return on a 'risk free asset', $R_f$ (see chapter 2, p. 76 et seq.):

$$R_{it} = R_f + \beta_i (R_{mt} - R_f) + e_{it} \tag{6.5}$$

$R_f$ is usually measured as the return on a gilt edged security, or, if the risk of inflation is to be taken out, an index linked gilt.

In practice it has sometimes been found that a single gilt edged security is not a good proxy for a risk free asset whose returns are uncorrelated with returns on a market index. In the circumstances it may therefore be preferable to develop a portfolio of securities whose returns collectively are uncorrelated with the market. This is known as a 'zero beta portfolio', $R_z$. The Black model rewrites the Sharpe-Lintner equation (6.5) as

$$R_{it} = R_{zt} + \beta_i(R_{mt} - R_{zt}) + e_{it} \qquad (6.6)$$

Despite its naivety, the 'zero-one' model (equation (6.3)) is not infrequently used to calculate residual returns, when the model being applied is generally referred to as the 'market average residual' (MAR) model. The reason for this is that there are frequently problems in estimating betas using the SMM or CAPM (e.g. they may be unstable across time). The MAR procedure may then provide a useful check, the argument being that if the population of companies in a sample is large enough, the errors in calculating residual returns should cancel each other out. Consequently if the outcomes are similar to those generated using SMM and/or CAPM residual returns, it tends to confirm that the results of a study are not an artefact of the research design adopted.

Essentially the MAR approach assumes that the average beta for a cross section of securities equals 1 and consequently the alpha will equal zero. This is fairly easy to check. Of course, it means that the $R_i - E(R_i)$ errors will be greater than they ought to be if the SMM or CAPM were appropriate, but so long as they are not biased in a particular direction this does not matter as they should cancel each other out.

The question obviously arises as to whether it is likely to make much difference which share price generating model is used in a particular study. In fact, research by Brenner (1977, 1979) and Brown and Warner (1980) suggests that generally it will not. However, there have been one or two studies where the choice has had a major impact: i.e. sufficient to change the overall result in terms of accepting or rejecting the null hypothesis that the event under study is not driving share price movements. Interestingly, one of those concerns a bankruptcy study (Altman and Brenner, 1981).

A major problem with empirical studies using the CAPM to model share price returns is 'beta stability' (i.e. the relationship between price movements for a specific share and movements on a market index such as the FTSE 100 is unstable through time). In fact, evidence shows that individual company betas (and even portfolio betas) are indeed unstable. This means the residual returns could be incorrectly calculated, which might corrupt the experiment. The problem can be dealt with in several ways:

(1) analysing data for small portfolios geared to produce a beta of one (e.g. of around 5 securities each);

(2) using WLS (weighted least squares) rather than OLS (ordinary least squares) regression as this can give greater emphasis to more recent observations;

(3) using 'moving' betas (i.e. the betas are re-estimated over successive sub-periods, a procedure used in a bankruptcy share price study by Theobald and Thomas, 1982); and

(4) using so-called 'Bayesian adjusted' betas. (These allow for the observed phenomenon that betas revert towards unity over time using conditional probability theory.)

'Thin trading' also gives rise to a difficulty (the 'intervalling problem') when shares in a company are traded at irregular intervals. To illustrate the point, consider the following data which show imaginary share prices recorded for a security over a period of 10 days; and the corresponding daily market index observations. Trading in the company's shares only occurs on days 1, 5 and 10 (i.e. the underlined figures represent the prices actually recorded for trades). The problem is that share price returns will be regressed day-by-day against proxy market portfolio returns, yet on days 2-4 and 6-9 the relationships being observed are spurious: the share prices recorded for those days relate to the last notified trade on earlier days.

| Day | 1 | 2 | 3 | 4 | 5 | 6 | 7 | 8 | 9 | 10 |
|---|---|---|---|---|---|---|---|---|---|---|
| Quoted share price | $\underline{50}$ | 50 | 50 | 50 | $\underline{55}$ | 55 | 55 | 55 | 55 | $\underline{60}$ |
| Market index | $\underline{100}$ | 102 | 104 | 105 | $\underline{103}$ | 104 | 108 | 112 | 114 | $\underline{109}$ |

It should be noted that thin trading is sometimes regarded as primarily a problem with small companies, whose shares are traded at relatively infrequent intervals. However, it is a more pervasive difficulty. For instance, the last recorded trade for a particular company – even a large one – might have taken place at (say) 2 p.m. on a particular day. The market index might, however, have moved up or down by (say) 1 or 2 per cent between then and the close of trading. In other words, there is a problem even *within* days.

In fact, this difficulty – like all potential sources of bias – is not of great significance unless the bias is systematic: i.e. the errors are not randomly distributed and will therefore not tend to cancel each other out. Fortunately studies suggest that the thin trading problem is unlikely to cause major inference problems, although procedures have been developed for handling it.

Other factors which might affect beta estimation are

172

(1) The length of the event window (i.e. the period during which the event, such as an earnings announcement, will occur). (Usually this is extended around the actual announcement date to allow for leakages of information, etc.)

(2) Should the sample observations which provide the basis for estimating the beta precede or straddle the event window?

(3) Should returns for the company and the index be calculated on a daily, weekly or monthly basis?

(4) What index should be used as the market proxy? (It has been found, for instance, that *general* market indices can be inappropriate for medium-to-small sized companies).

(5) Betas appear to change immediately around earnings announcement dates (Ball and Kothari, 1990).

*Identifying news events.* As indicated previously, there are two variables which are the subject of scrutiny: *rates of return*; and the *news event* itself. It is now necessary to consider the latter.

News, of course, is *only* information that has not been correctly predicted, so there is a need to model expectations of an event (e.g. an earnings announcement). However, it is again important to recognise that, where the objective is merely to study the *direction* of share price reactions, it is unnecessary to use the best forecast, only an 'unbiased' prediction. This is because the errors in a reasonable sized sample of companies should tend to cancel each other out.

The procedures used for modelling earnings expectations are

(1) time series of earnings (i.e. establish whether there is a pattern over time in earnings);

(2) cross sections of earnings, where the co-movement between a company's earnings and aggregate corporate earnings is estimated using regression and then applied ex post to aggregate corporate earnings for a particular year (Ball and Brown, 1968);

(3) the average of analysts' forecasts of earnings.

In recent years considerable efforts have been made by researchers to improve the quality of earnings forecasts used in empirical studies, and as a result there has been renewed interest in share valuation models of the type discussed in chapter 2. This has become necessary as researchers have become more ambitious and have not merely sought to identify the *direction* of market reaction to a particular news announcement but also the *size* of the reaction. A problem also arises where signals are simultaneously released (e.g. dividends and profits; or current cost accounting (CCA) profits and conventional historical cost accounting (HCA) profits).

There are two possible solutions to this latter problem of 'contemporaneous news announcements':

(1) Partition the data and only study those sample companies where the signals $(S_1,S_2)$ (for instance, CCA and HCA profits respectively) point in the *opposite* directions (+ or -) (see Figure 6.3).

(2) Use multiple regression as follows:

$$R_{it} = \alpha_i + \beta_i R_{mt} + \lambda_1 S_1 + \lambda_2 S_2 + e_{it} \tag{6.7}$$

where $S_1$ and $S_2$ are signals, and
$\lambda_1,\lambda_2$ are parameter coefficients found by least squares regression, sometimes referred to as 'response coefficients'.[3]

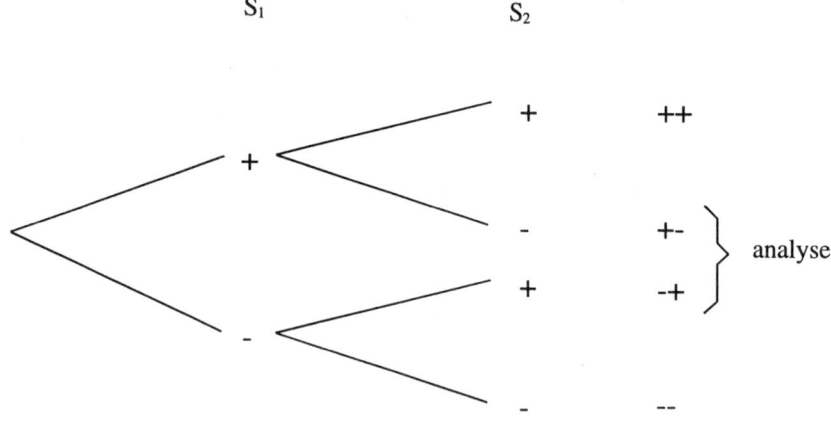

**Figure 6.3**

Some researchers have attempted to 'orthogonalise' the data (i.e. eliminate commonalities – for instance, by regressing $S_2$ onto $S_1$ to remove the common element, and then using the residuals in place of $S_2$), but this will not improve the fit of the model.

It should be noted that it is possible to avoid having to model expectations by just examining the size of share price *movements* – which is useful when there is uncertainty whether a signal is good or bad news.

The simplest approach is to use the 'first moment' (or mean) of the distribution and just study the 'unsigned' average abnormal returns for a population of companies. However, it is also possible to employ a 'second moment' (or variance) procedure and examine a *measure of abnormal variance* of security returns. In its simplest terms, such a measure was first used by Beaver (1968b) on normalised returns, and it can be expressed as follows:

$$\frac{P_i{}^2}{\sigma_i{}^2} \hspace{5cm} (6.8)$$

where $P_i{}^2$ is the squared return for security i; and
$\sigma_i{}^2$ is the empirically determined variance in the
non-event period.

However, Patell (1976) made the point that the original Beaver test was improperly specified. The appropriate test is a *conditional* test: before one can legitimately examine variance or standard deviation, it is necessary to be sure that distributions of the analysis and control samples have similar means. If they do not, the distributions must be different and it would be invalid to proceed to test for differences in their variances.[4]

A similar 'second moment' test procedure can be applied to data on share trading volumes to assess whether activity around an event is greater than in the non-event period.

It is now common practice in event studies for researchers to study the impact of a news announcement on both first and second moments of the returns distributions.

*Studying the behaviour of share price returns.* Once an unanticipated event has been isolated, it is then necessary to aggregate residual share price returns in some way so that their behaviour can be studied over time (the 'window' that is the subject of interest). The analysis can then basically be carried out in one of two ways: using regression; or partitioning the data in some way.

(i) Regression

With regression, the basic form of the model will be:

$$R_i = \alpha_i + \beta_i R_{mt} + \lambda S + e \hspace{4cm} (6.9)$$

where the symbols are as previously defined (although R could be
the variance of returns or even the underlying value of a share).

In practice this model is too sensitive for many types of study as it identifies a proportionate relationship between the dependent and independent variables.[5]

(ii) Partitioning the data

Although equation (6.9) can be used even when a proportionate relationship is not expected between S and R, until recently (when it has become commonplace to focus on the behaviour of 'response coefficients'), it was usual to rearrange the equation as follows:

$$R_i - [\alpha_i + \beta_i R_{mt}] = \lambda S + e \tag{6.9a}$$

The right hand side of the equation can then be dropped and the data be partitioned in terms of the 'dichotomous variable' S (i.e. where only one of two states is possible, such as 'good news' and 'bad news'). The expectation is that the left hand side of the equation will be greater than zero if S is 'good news' and less than zero if S is 'bad news'. However, returns conditional on the latter can be added to returns conditional on the former if the signs are changed.

When the partitioning approach is adopted – and until recently it has easily been the most frequently used procedure – the abnormal returns can be analysed in various ways, the two most common being

(1) Cumulative Average Residual (CAR) returns; and
(2) an Abnormal Performance Index (API) of residual returns.

Generally the two procedures will produce very similar patterns of portfolio returns over time, although the API approach is less likely to be biased (Brown and Warner, 1980).[6]

The CAR approach was pioneered by Fama, Fisher, Jensen and Roll (1969). The average (abnormal) return (AR) at time t for a cross section of companies is defined as

$$AR_t = \sum_{i=1}^{n} e_i \tag{6.10}$$

where $e_i$ is the residual return for company i in period t;
and there are n companies.

The ARs can then be cumulated through time:

$$CAR_m = \sum_{m=-k}^{1} AR_m \tag{6.11}$$

However, as Conrad and Kaul (1993) have pointed out, cumulating single period monthly returns over long intervals implicitly amounts to rebalancing the loser and winner portfolios to equal weights every four weeks. A more appropriate measure of investment performance would be to calculate buy-and-hold returns over long intervals.

176

Some of these difficulties are avoided with the API approach, which was first used by Ball and Brown (1968). The API is an index which can be defined at month m for a period commencing k months previously and covering the returns for n companies as

$$API_m = \frac{1}{n} \sum_{i=1}^{1} \prod_{m=-k}^{m} (1 + e_{im}) - 1 \qquad (6.12)$$

[**NB**: $\sum$ means 'sum of' – i.e. a series is additive; $\prod$ means 'product of' – i.e. a series is multiplicative].

Equation (6.12) can be interpreted as identifying the return that can be earned by investing £1 equally between securities in a portfolio.

The two approaches can probably best be understood with the aid of a simple numerical example.

## (1) CAR

In the table immediately below the residual returns on a share in company 1 are shown across the page for each of the four weeks prior to the week of the event; for the week of the event itself; and for one week afterwards: namely, +1 per cent, 0 per cent, +1 per cent, 0 per cent, 0 per cent and +4 per cent. Similar data are given on the lines below for companies 2, 3 and 4.

|  | Week | -4 | -3 | -2 | -1 | Event date 0 | +1 |
|---|---|---|---|---|---|---|---|
| Company |  |  | Weekly returns |  |  |  |  |
| 1 |  | .01 | .00 | .01 | .00 | .00 | .04 |
| 2 |  | .00 | .01 | .00 | .00 | .00 | .03 |
| 3 |  | .00 | .00 | .00 | .00 | .01 | .04 |
| 4 |  | .00 | .01 | .00 | .01 | .00 | .02 |
|  |  | .01 | .02.... |  |  |  |  |

The 'average residual returns' (AR) for the weeks 4 and 3 before the event date are

| $AR_t$ | $AR_t$ |
|---|---|
| t=-4 | t=-3 |
| $\dfrac{.01}{4}$ | $\dfrac{.02}{4}$ |
| = .0025 | = .005 |

177

The 'cumulative average residual return' (CAR) for the two week period (-4 and -3 before the event date) is

$$.0025 + .005 = \underline{.0075}$$

(2) API

Below are shown the residual returns on an investment of £1 in each of the shares in companies 1, 2, 3 and 4 for the four week period commencing four weeks prior to the event under study.

| Company | Week -4 | -3 | -2 | -1 | | |
|---|---|---|---|---|---|---|
| 1 | (1.01) | (1.00) | (1.01) | (1.00) | -1 = 1.0201-1 = | .0201 |
| 2 | (1.00) | (1.01) | (1.00) | (1.00) | -1 = 1.0100-1 = | .0100 |
| 3 | (1.00) | (1.00) | (1.00) | (1.00) | -1 = 1.0000-1 = | .0000 |
| 4 | (1.00) | (1.01) | (1.00) | (1.01) | -1 = 1.0201-1 = | .0201 |

$$.0502 \div 4$$

$$= \underline{.01255}$$

Hence the API for the period t = -4 to t = -1 is .01255 (i.e. the abnormal return on investing £1 evenly divided between securities in the portfolio over the 4 week period is 1.255 per cent).

The CARs and API can be cumulated over successive periods (such as -4 to -3; -4 to -2; -4 to -1, etc.), and they or the ARs can be examined on a graph. Typically the 'average abnormal returns' (ARs) might appear as in Figure 6.4.

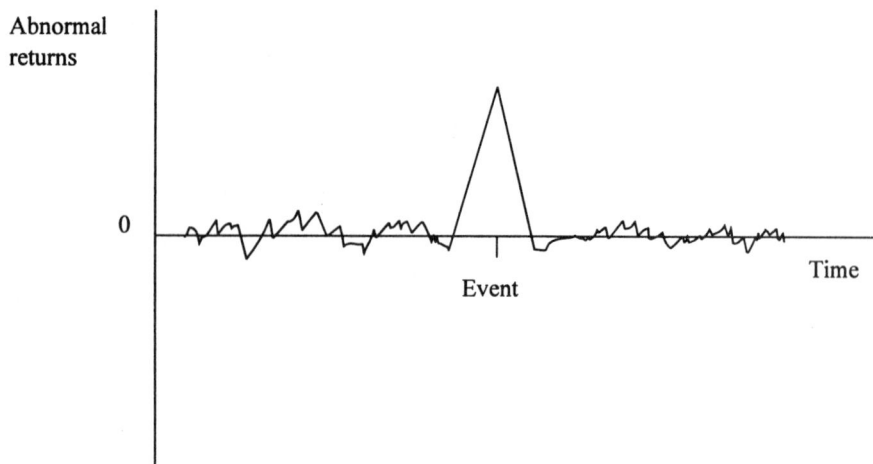

**Figure 6.4**

Similarly, the CARs and APIs would typically 'map' as shown in Figure 6.5.

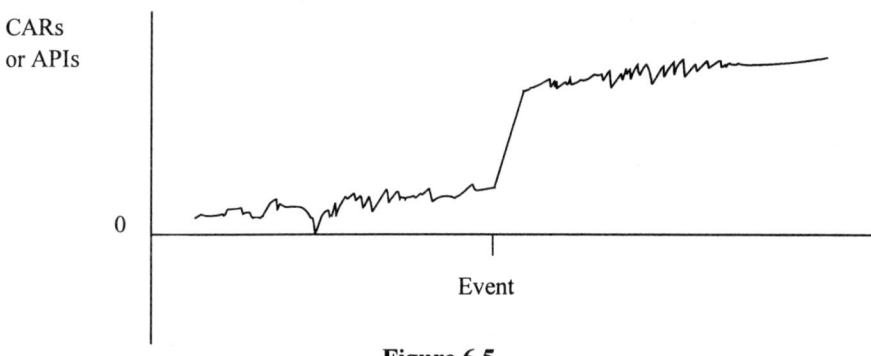

**Figure 6.5**

*Hypothesis testing.* The next step is to test a 'null hypothesis' to see whether the result could have occurred by chance – e.g.

$H_0$: event X has no impact on the market

The statistical tests will be either

(1) 'parametric' (e.g. t or Hotelling's T) if the returns are normally distributed; or
(2) 'non-parametric' (i.e. assessing the probabilities of a certain *ordering*, using tests such as the Mann Whitney U or chi square) if they are not.

The logging of returns should of course help to produce normal distributions, thus helping to justify the use of so-called 'parametric' statistical tests. 'Non-parametric' tests (such as the Mann Whitney U) might require abnormal returns to be ranked. The U then tests to see whether the observed rank ordering could have occurred by chance (e.g. most of the positive abnormal returns at the top of the ranking would be expected to come from companies for which the news is good, while those ranked with the lowest or negative returns would be those for which the news is bad).

It should be noted that using the conventional 95 per cent confidence level is not always necessarily appropriate. Thus if in only 2 per cent of cases current cost accounting (CCA) had an impact on market expectations, it might still be important in social welfare terms if the benefit to society of having resources properly allocated as a result of the incremental information more than outweighs the costs to all companies of having to prepare and publish supplementary CCA financial statements.

A major problem with empirically based research studies is the possibility of Type I and Type II inference errors. (A Type I error is rejecting a hypothesis which is true: e.g. identifying a failed company as non-failed; and a Type II error is accepting a hypothesis which is false: e.g. classifying a non-failed company as failed.) These errors could occur because

(1) various joint hypotheses are being tested (e.g. concerning the return generating process; market efficiency; the information content of signals; the validity of the expectations model; etc.); and/or
(2) key variables have been omitted from the equation.

Particular problems are

(a) The Sharpe-Lintner CAPM is not always satisfactory because of difficulties identifying the risk free asset and the appropriate proxy market index. Its shortcomings are most obvious when the share prices of small firms are the subject of study. (The solution would be to use a more appropriate 'small company' index).
(b) With the SMM the $\alpha$ can impound abnormal price behaviour around the event date.
(c) Quoted prices are 'middle' prices: if the spreads between buying and selling prices are large, this can be a seriously distorting factor.

Of course, it is difficult to 'control' for all these potential sources of error and for the other technical factors referred to previously. Typically, therefore, the researcher has ultimately to rely on the fact that any errors which are present will be randomly distributed. To the extent that they are not, there will be a very real risk that the empirical results may be misleading or – at the very least – may be misinterpreted, despite the care taken by researchers to avoid these problems.

*Anomalies and market inefficiency*. Although the evidence strongly suggests that securities markets are for the most part 'semi-strong efficient' (i.e. they react to and almost immediately absorb published information), there are some features in the behaviour of share prices which have long puzzled researchers. Thus, for instance, numerous studies on the behaviour of share prices around preliminary announcements of earnings have identified both an anticipation effect and, more worryingly, 'post announcement drift'. Clearly the latter is to some extent a violation of true market efficiency, since it implies that analysts do not react instantaneously to news when it is announced, thus leaving open opportunities for traders to make easy profits. However, the very fact that the adjustment process is slow suggests that traders for some perverse reason do *not* take advantage of the opportunity which presents itself.

This and various other systematic 'anomalies' which have been detected (e.g. relating to the size of companies, and abnormal share price behaviour in January and on certain days of the week) have been the subject of close scrutiny by researchers for many years, but especially since the mid 1980s (see reviews by Bernard 1989, 1992; Fama, 1991; and Ball, 1992). (Indeed, there is a sharp contrast in the way in which academics have sought to explain these anomalies in relation to earnings announcements, but not with regard to the use of bankruptcy prediction models!)

With respect to 'weak form efficiency', there is evidence of both negative and positive serial correlation in prices over time (e.g. Fama and French, 1988), implying over- and under-reaction by the market. Certainly overreaction would suggest that it should be possible to trade profitably applying a 'contrarian' investment strategy (i.e. buy shares which have underperformed in the past and sell those which have overperformed: see DeBondt and Thaler, 1985, 1987; Chan, 1988; Jegadeesh and Titman, 1993).[7] There is also evidence of seasonal anomalies (see the review by Cochrane, 1991), of which the best known are the January and weekend effects referred to above. (However, the January effect appears to be the result of investors having to pay tax bills in the New Year, while weekend effects might to some extent be explained by a tendency on the part of companies to hold back bad news).

Other factors that need to be considered in this context are the existence of 'noise' (Black, 1986) and 'herding behaviour' (Bikchandani, Hirshleifer and Welch, 1993; Lev and Thiagarajan, 1993; Trueman, 1990, 1994). 'Noise' in fact arises as a result of errors in analysis and interpretation, and because of the need of investors to trade for liquidity reasons. However, it is possible for individuals to increase noise and as a result trade profitably (De Long, Schliefer, Summers and Waldmann, 1990). 'Herding' arises where traders pursue speculative bubbles in the short term – not entirely irrational if the best estimate of the next price change is in a specific direction, although everyone knows the bubble must sooner or later burst, if not exactly when.[8]

With respect to 'semi-strong form efficiency', a variety of factors could help to explain apparently irrational behaviour, evident in the behaviour of share prices (e.g. as reflected in the distributional characteristics of security returns before and after news releases, and in particular the anticipation of news and the existence of 'post announcement drift'). These, as explained above, include misspecification of risk in the research designs used (e.g. the use of biased estimates of systematic risk and inadequate controls for gearing, bankruptcy risk, and firm size). In fact, small firm size has been identified as an important explanatory factor in a number of studies, not only proxying for risk, but also for greater search and information processing costs, higher gearing ratios, increased risk of bankruptcy, and higher transactions costs.[9] Other potentially distorting factors are biases in analysts' forecasts (see, for instance, Mendenhall, 1991; Arbarbanell, 1991; Arbarbanell and Bernard, 1992; Trueman, 1994); fixation on reported accounting numbers (e.g. Hand, 1990); transactions costs (e.g. Bhushan, 1994); short selling restrictions (which may be particularly important with respect to the shares of small companies) (e.g. Diamond and Verrecchia, 1987); the extent of institutional share ownership (e.g. O'Brien and Bhushan, 1990); analyst following (e.g. Bhushan, 1989); the precision of public and private information (e.g. Kim and Verrecchia, 1991a,b, 1994; McNichols and Trueman, 1994; Atiase and Bamber, 1994); the costs of obtaining and interpreting information may exceed the expected benefit (e.g. Grossman and Stiglitz, 1980; Kim and Verrecchia, 1991a,b, 1994; Demski and Feltham, 1994; McNichols and Trueman, 1994); there is less news coverage for smaller firms, which leads to greater volatility in their share prices (e.g. Dow and Gorton, 1994); managers tend to advance the reporting of good news and delay announcing bad news (e.g. Skinner, 1994; Kasznik and Lev, 1995); and the market reacts differently to good and bad news (e.g. McNichols, 1988; Engle and Ng, 1993; Skinner, 1994).[10]

*Applying the methodology in bankruptcy studies*

Studies into the share price behaviour of failing companies have addressed two main issues. The first is to identify when relative share prices of financially distressed companies move down and whether in doing so they anticipate the signals generated by statistical failure prediction models. The purpose of the second is to establish the extent to which the signals contained in specific models outside the original sample period appear to be impounded in share prices.

Corporate failure, however, does not easily lend itself to event study analysis for a number of reasons. Most obviously, there is no unique event which is common to all failing companies except their ultimate financial collapse. For some, the market will not have been aware of impending problems until very near the end. For others, the warning signs may have been there earlier, although the market presumably felt that there was a good chance of recovery.[11] But exactly when the market appreciated the difficulties will almost certainly have varied from company to company. As a result, there will not only be a substantial degree of heterogeneity in the data, but the focus of interest will be a relatively long period leading up to failure rather than the narrow window of time covered in most event studies. It follows from this that the most suitable way of examining share price behaviour will often be 'profile analysis' (i.e. mapping relative share price movements for a cross sectional sample of financially distressed companies over a period of years rather than weeks or even months).

But there is a second major problem with bankruptcy studies of this type, and this concerns the calculation of the *relative* share price movements. As mentioned above, the share prices of some (though certainly not all) failing companies may have been declining for some time prior to eventual bankruptcy, regardless of general directional movements in the market index. Clearly this means that the co-movement between the returns on these companies' shares and the return on a market index is not constant: i.e. their betas are unstable.[12] But moreover, in order to produce reasonably sized samples of failed companies, data typically have to be pooled across time. This means that some companies will experience distress during bull markets (Figure 6.6), whereas others will suffer when share prices generally are in decline (Figure 6.7). In the case of the former betas will be declining; in the case of the latter increasing.

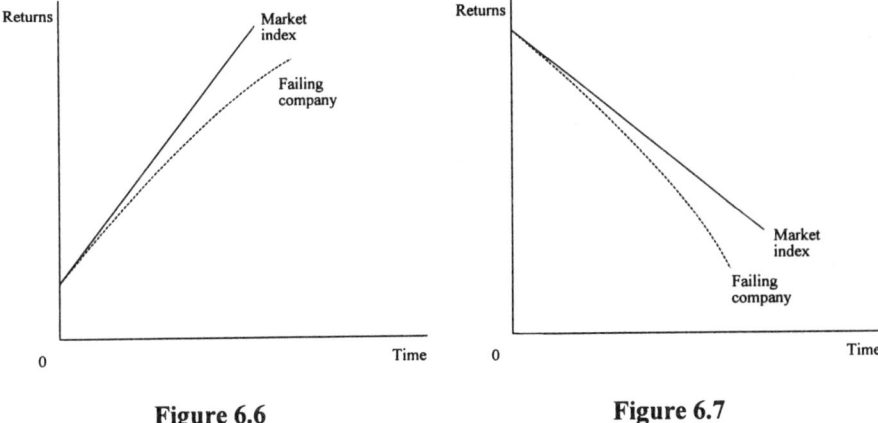

**Figure 6.6**              **Figure 6.7**

There are various ways of trying to combat the problem of beta instability. One approach, for instance, is to use 'moving beta' estimates, constantly updating the data so that (say) only the most recent 24 observations are used to estimate the relationship between share price and market index returns. Such, indeed, was the procedure used by Theobald and Thomas (1981). Another, possibly sounder, approach is that adopted by Beaver (1968a), who matched companies, failed against non-failed. Such a procedure should control for industry- and economy-wide factors over the event periods being studied.

Because of the heterogeneous nature of the data, there seems little to be said in favour of making relatively sophisticated adjustments in order to try to isolate residual returns. Rather it would seem sensible just to try to control for industry- and economy-wide factors which can probably best be done by applying Beaver's matched pairing technique. However, it may also be helpful to use the 'market average residual' (MAR) metric as there may be additional problems when companies change their reporting periods. Overall, so long as there is a greater proportion of companies in the bankrupt group whose prospects are causing concern to the market, the average return of failing companies should be lower than for non-failing companies – and this should be evident some years before the final collapse of the former.

*Empirical studies on failing companies*

The usual approach in undertaking these studies has been either to split a sample of matched pairs of companies into failed and non-failed groups and then examine when the market appears to mark down the share prices of the former relative to

183

the latter; or, alternatively, just to deal with a sample of failed companies, and after controlling for market- and/or industry-wide effects, examine the time series of security returns relative to the date of ultimate financial collapse. As argued above, the former approach is preferable, if only because the latter gives rise to considerable problems in trying to control for systematic risk when betas are non-stationary.[13]

The study by Beaver (1968a) appears to have been the first to examine the share price behaviour of failing firms, and he found that the market seemed to anticipate by a short interval the information contained in his best single ratio predictor of impending bankruptcy. Subsequently Westerfield (1970), Pettway (1980), Aharony, Jones and Swary (1980) and Clark and Weinstein (1983) also found that the market seemed to anticipate insolvency relatively early (e.g. as much as 4.5 years before final collapse). Research in Australia (e.g. by Castagna and Matolcsy, 1981) and in the UK (e.g. by Gooi, 1974; Theobald and Thomas, 1982; and El Hennawy and Morris, 1983b) seemed to find the same, although there were problems in these studies in controlling for systematic risk.[14]

The first study to examine whether the market seems to be processing similar information to a particular model was undertaken by Altman and Brenner (1981). It showed that the market appeared to react to information captured in a bankruptcy identification model for both failing and non-failing firms, although the results depended to some extent on whether a one or two factor model (i.e. the SMM or CAPM) was employed to calculate betas. Subsequently Katz, Lilien and Nelson (1985) examined share price reactions for both deteriorating and recovering firms, and they too found directional movements consistent with signals given by Wilcox's (1971, 1973) gambler's ruin model and Altman's (1968) original discriminant model.[15] Moreover, the size of the reaction seemed to indicate a greater element of surprise for the recovery group.

Later Zavgren, Dugan and Reeve (1988) examined market reaction over a twelve month period for companies which went bankrupt but which were not forecast to do so; and for companies which were forecast to fail but which did not. The market reaction was assessed both in terms of share price movements and trading volume; and the forecasts were generated by a logit model based on financial ratios. Analysing the data in terms of probabilities, there appeared to be considerable anticipation by the market, suggesting analysts were using a broader information set than the logit model itself. However, surprise was still reflected in market reaction for companies predicted to fail but which did not in the period under review.

But perhaps the most comprehensive study in this area is that of Burgstahler, Jiambalvo and Noreen (1989). They calculated unexpected changes in the probability of bankruptcy for a sample of 218 firms and examined residual security returns over a 10 year period. To calculate unexpected changes in the probability of bankruptcy, they used Ohlson's (1980) logit failure identification model,[16] which (it will be recalled) had the advantage that to some extent it dealt with the sampling bias problem. This was then applied in conjunction with other accounting information. Their results were consistent with unanticipated changes in the probability of bankruptcy helping to explain the behaviour of security returns, even after controlling for unexpected earnings.

Other bankruptcy related research examining share price movements in the US include studies by Bonnier and Bruner (1989) and Eyssell (1991). Bonnier and Bruner found that share prices of financially distressed companies reacted significantly to management changes; while Eyssell not only confirmed that for his sample of 27 failed companies cumulative average residuals were negative from 2.5 years before the filing date for bankruptcy, but also that corporate insiders were heavy net sellers of shares over the final 300 days.

Overall, the evidence does not seem to support the argument that failure identification models are imparting a significant element of news to the market but rather that they appear to be capturing information that has for the most part already been impounded in share prices.

## Laboratory experiments

*Behavioural research methodologies*

In constructing positive theories of accounting there are basically two types of approach which employ inductive reasoning:

(1) those which are derived from readily observable data (such as accounting numbers, share prices, credit ratings, audit qualifications, bankruptcies, etc); and
(2) those which involve behavioural experiments where subjects express their own judgements and thus create the data which can then be the focus of analysis.

Whereas the former approach is that overwhelmingly employed by economists, it is the latter which is favoured in experimental psychology. In fact, both methodologies have been extensively applied in accounting research, but in terms of failure identification studies it is the first that has been described in previous chapters.

It is convenient to consider the experimental psychology approach in terms of what is described as the 'lens' framework. This was originally developed by Brunswik in 1952, and essentially it focuses on the reactions of a 'judge' (e.g. an analyst) in respect of a given event. The reaction may be in the form of an *assessment* or a *prediction.*[17]

A simplified diagram of the lens model is given in Figure 6.8. In an accounting context the *event* could be a set of financial statements containing a particular set of messages; the judge could be an analyst; and the assessment/prediction could be the judge's estimate of a company's share value or a future likely outcome.

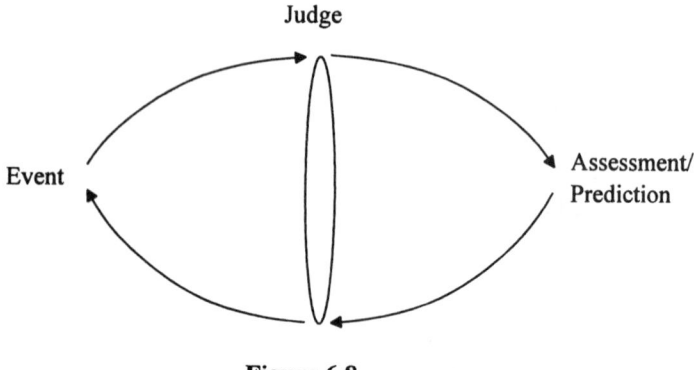

**Figure 6.8**

Once the data have been originated a variety of relationships can be studied: e.g. that between the event and the assessment/prediction itself; or the outcome and the event; or the outcome and the prediction; and so on. The procedures used to analyse the results can either be based on regression or conditional probability theory (e.g. if the analyst observes X, what is the probability of the prediction being Y?)

Ideally the experiment will be closely controlled in a laboratory environment. Thus, for instance, the researcher will develop an appropriate 'research instrument' (e.g. two summarised financial statements) and expose them separately to two groups of judges. The two financial statements will be different in one key respect, which is the focus of interest to the researcher, who can then study the reactions of the two groups of judges (assuming they are drawn in an unbiased manner from a common population).

Examples where such experiments have been carried out by accounting researchers have included the reaction of analysts to current purchasing power (CPP) and current cost accounting (CCA) information; and to the use of different accounting policies (e.g. acquisition versus merger accounting in consolidations; the use of LIFO rather than FIFO in inventory valuation; the use of deferred tax accounting; and the inclusion of capitalised leases in financial statements rather than treating them as off balance sheet financing). Such experiments have also commonly been used to explore a variety of auditing issues.

The great advantage of the laboratory type approach is that the researcher can closely control the experiment. Thus sometimes it will be decided not to split the sample of judges into two groups (one as the experimental sample, the other as the control set), but instead to have just one population of judges. The research instrument can then be designed so that there is a sequence of information: e.g. with respect to the impact of inflation accounting, the conventional accounting data will be given first, with reactions recorded against that; then incremental CPP information, with a second set of reactions recorded. If necessary, further controls can be built into such an experiment – e.g. by putting the CPP information before the conventional data for some subjects, but second for others.

Of course it is often difficult in practice to organise an experiment in closely controlled laboratory conditions. This problem is overcome either by using surrogate analysts (typically postgraduate students); or by undertaking field study research (i.e. sending the research instrument by mail to a number of potential respondents). Naturally the latter considerably weakens the controls, most importantly inasmuch as usually only a fairly small proportion of subjects respond (typically between 20 per cent and 30 per cent). This introduces the problem of 'non-response bias' (i.e. are those who reply representative of the whole population?)

Potentially the weakest form of experiment along these lines is just to issue a questionnaire to elicit opinions, since there is no detailed research instrument to ensure that subjects are all focusing on the same issues. Equally there is no way of studying the cause-and-effect thought processes of subjects.

The main problem with these behavioural studies is one of 'external validity': i.e. being sure that what is observed is a true representation of what goes on in the real world. This can occur for a variety of reasons: e.g. the analysts do not have access to the full amount of data that would be available to them in real world situations; the research instrument (case study) is unrealistic or leads the subjects to a particular conclusion; the subjects are only playing a game, so the payoffs/penalties for incorrect decisions are not as they would be in the real world; the controls, however well constructed, are inadequate; and so on.

Interestingly, many of the findings from behavioural experiments are in conflict with the inferences that can be drawn from statistically based studies using observed accounting and market variables.

*Laboratory based bankruptcy studies*

A number of experiments have been undertaken to ascertain to what extent credit managers and bankers can accurately identify potentially bankrupt firms from sets of financial ratios.[18]

The pioneering work in this area was undertaken by Libby (1975). He provided 43 experienced US loan officers with financial profiles of 60 real but disguised companies, half of which had failed (a fact that was made clear to the subjects). The profiles comprised five ratios: profit/total assets; current assets/current liabilities; cash/total assets; current assets/total assets; and sales/total assets. The task set was for the subjects to discriminate between failed and non-failed concerns. The loan officers' mean prediction accuracy was 74 per cent, which compared to 72 per cent for a discriminant model estimated on a different set of data.

187

Kida (1980) carried out a study along much the same lines as Libby but used auditors as the subjects rather than loan officers. He selected 20 US companies which failed in 1974/75 and then obtained matched pairs. A discriminant model was developed which had a misclassification rate of less than 10 per cent, and this was compared against the audit qualification assessments of 27 practitioners. They correctly identified 83 per cent of the companies, but going concern qualifications would only have been made for 75 per cent of the problem cases.

In another experiment, Casey (1980) asked 48 experienced bankers to assess the financial viability of 30 firms, half of which had failed within 3-5 years of the financial statement date. Subjects were given six ratios for each company for three years (Libby's five, plus total liabilities/equity). However, subjects were not told that the sample unrealistically included a 50 per cent proportion of failures. Although there was a high degree of agreement between the bankers, average forecasting accuracy was only 56.7 per cent. This was because although on average 86.7 per cent of the 'sound' firms were correctly classified, only 26.7 per cent of those which eventually went bankrupt were identified as being 'failures'.

At much the same time, Zimmer (1980) used a similar research design to examine the discriminating ability of 30 Australian lending bankers on 42 companies, 50 per cent of which had failed. However, on this occasion subjects were told that half the firms in the sample had failed. The results were much closer to Libby's than to Casey's, the mean predictive accuracy of the forecasts being 77 per cent, which compared to 83 per cent for a discriminant model. The implication is clearly that knowledge of the likely failure rate in a sample of companies is a critical piece of information.

Some time later Doukas (1986) conducted a similar experiment with 22 loan officers from a Canadian bank. They were asked to distinguish between satisfactory and unsatisfactory accounts on the basis of 15 ratios for 30 lending accounts. Subjects were warned that the proportion of satisfactory to unsatisfactory accounts was possibly unrepresentative, but they were not told the exact proportions in the portfolio. Interestingly on this occasion the bankers discriminated reasonably well between the satisfactory and unsatisfactory accounts – and they were not outperformed by two well known statistical failure prediction models.

In order to explore further the importance of prior knowledge of the incidence of failures in a population, Casey (1983) conducted another experiment using as subjects 109 loan officers in US banks. The data to which they were exposed related to a sample of 49 companies, of which only 15 had failed. When informed of the expected failure rate, the mean predictive accuracy of the loan officers was 82 per cent – rather less than the 96 per cent achieved by the discriminant model on the original estimation sample, but similar to that achieved in the Libby and Zimmer experiments. However, the success rate of the analysts was far less when they were not told beforehand of the proportion of failed companies in the population, confirming the findings in Casey's original 1980 study. Nevertheless, they were able to extract enough information from the accounts between one and three years before failure to identify potentially bankrupt firms at a rate significantly better than chance.[19]

Another factor which might help to explain the difference between Casey's results and those of previous studies is the age of the data. To test this, Houghton (1984) used 32 bank loan officers to assess the likelihood of companies failing, the sample comprising 12 failed and 12 non-failed companies. He controlled for both the subjects' expectations of the number of failures and non-failures in the population and for the extent to which they were using data immediately before failure or some time previously. He found that both failure expectation rates and the age of the data helped to explain predictive accuracy.

A matter of some interest is whether subjects merely estimate different parameter values from those derived using a discriminant model; or, whether left to their own devices, subjects would choose a different set of variables. This was tested by Abdel-khalik and El-Sheshai (1980), who used a sample of 16 pairs of companies. Their discriminant model achieved a successful classification rate of over 90 per cent. When the 28 subjects were allowed to choose from a limited set of ratios, they selected a different subset to those used in the statistically derived model. The items they most frequently 'purchased' were earnings trend, current ratio, cash flow/debt, and the trend of this last ratio. On the basis of the information they selected, their success rate in classifying companies was only 62.5 per cent – not all that much greater than the 50 per cent that would be expected from random selection.

It is sometimes suggested that it is inappropriate to use statistically derived discriminant models as a benchmark because of their possible misspecification (e.g. as a result of overfitting, sample selection bias, etc). Rather it might be better to try to determine a 'judgemental' model by observing subjects' behaviour in terms of a lens framework (e.g. by constructing a regression model of their decisions conditional on their exposure to a series of signals). In a financing context this has been done by Dietrich and Kaplan (1982) in relation to a corporate lending decision. They found that the model they derived had a tendency to mimic and even lead the judgements of credit managers. Similar results have been reported for other judgemental models dealing with loan classifications, but a critical attribute is that the dependent variable in such models is continuous (or nearly so), not dichotomous as with discriminant analysis bankruptcy models into fail/non-fail categories. For this reason it has been argued that they might usefully be employed in a failure identification context to establish the perceived probability of a company failing (Whittred and Zimmer, 1985).

*Hindsight bias*

There have been many experiments by psychologists in a variety of situations which suggest that subjects who are familiar with particular outcomes cannot objectively try to assess the perception of likely outcomes before the event. This can be important. Thus lenders, auditors or managers can be accused after the event of not having the foresight to see that a company was going to fail.

Buchman (1985) conducted an experiment to see to what extent the 'wisdom of hindsight' might be exercised in the context of bankruptcy. Subjects were divided, firstly, into those who knew beforehand that a particular company might go bankrupt, be taken over, or merely continue as previously; and, secondly, those who knew with hindsight that the company had in fact filed for bankruptcy. Further, subjects in the two groups were either given a qualified or unqualified set of summarised financial statements. They were then asked to assign probabilities summing to 100 per cent that the company would, in the following year (a) go bankrupt, (b) be taken over, and (c) would continue as previously. (For this purpose, the hindsight group were asked to discount their knowledge that the company had in fact gone bankrupt.) Subjects were also asked to rate 10 elements of data. Overall, there was evidence of hindsight bias, but not all the results were as clear cut as was originally anticipated.[20]

*Multidimensional graphics*

Another aspect of behavioural research has nothing directly to do with assessing the ability of analysts to discriminate between bankrupt and non-failing businesses. Rather it is concerned with trying to identify the best means of communicating information concerning the financial health of a company.

In this context a particular graphical technique has been suggested by Moriarty (1979) as being relevant with respect to failure identification: namely, the use of 'Chernoff faces'. These are graphs in the form of cartoon faces which capture the salient features of a company's position.

The argument for using faces is that people are immediately familiar with them; they are rich in detail, offering up to a dozen distinct features (variables); and they are easy to draw.

Basically the argument is that a smiling face suggests 'good news' (e.g. a low likelihood of failure); whereas when the mouth is turned down it suggests unhappiness or anxiety. Likewise, the position of the eyes (e.g. furtively looking to the left or right) suggests concern, as does an elongated nose which lengthens the face in a sombre attitude. The shape of the eyebrows and the size of the ears similarly helps to convey part of the overall picture.

The two faces shown in Figure 6.9 show on the left hand side an optimistic picture, and on the right a pessimistic impression.

In Moriarty's experiment the features in the faces represented certain key characteristics: e.g. the size and shape of the face were determined by current assets/current liabilities; the mouth by profit/capital employed; the eyes by the debt/total assets ratio; the nose by inventory/total assets; and the size of the ears by fixed assets/equity.

Cartoons were drawn on the basis of 6 years' data from 1969-1974 for a group of 7 failed US department stores and a group of 15 non-bankrupt firms in the same industry. The faces were sketched relative to industry standard ratios. The cartoons were then shown to students to see how they rated the groups of firms, as between each other and over time. As a control, similar assessments were required from another group of subjects who only had access to the ratios themselves.

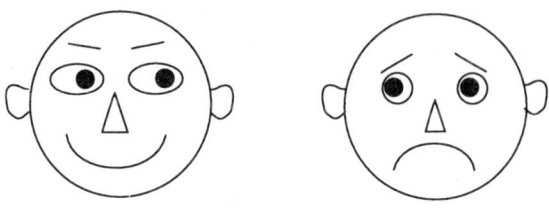

**Figure 6.9**

The results showed that responses were far quicker for the group which had access to the faces, especially when there was not even any explanation of what they represented. The error rates were quite high (possibly because of the naivety of the subjects), but the groups exposed to the faces made fewer misclassificational errors. To check this out, a second experiment was carried out with practising accountants. The errors were systematically lower, but the groups exposed to the faces once again performed best.

Smith and Taffler (1984) applied the technique to key variables reported by a number of British companies, including several included in the failed company sample which is the focus of study in later chapters (namely, Airfix, Dunbee-Combex-Marx, and Fodens). Profit before tax/current liabilities controlled the mouth and the pupils in the eyes; current assets/total liabilities the nose and the size of the head; current liabilities/total assets the eyebrows; and the no-credit-interval the position of the eyes. Certainly the failing company faces managed to look miserable, while their healthy counterparts appeared happy.

**Summary**

Two types of empirical research, based on separate methodologies, can help to indicate whether statistically derived failure prediction models impart incremental information to analysts: market based and behavioural studies.

The event study methodology is extremely well developed, enabling researchers to identify the apparent market reaction to specific news releases. Nevertheless, there are a number of anomalies (e.g. post announcement drift) which on the face of it might suggest that securities markets are not entirely semi-strong efficient (i.e.

there is a failure to act upon published information). However, closer inspection suggests that there are various reasons which can help to explain the observed behaviour of share prices.

The problem with market based bankruptcy research is that the data are heterogeneous, the period under study is relatively long (covering years rather than weeks or months), and there are severe difficulties in measuring relative share price returns. In the circumstances, the more complex techniques developed as part of the event study methodology are probably too sophisticated for the type of research envisaged. Rather, relatively simple procedures should give an indication as to whether market analysts appear to be independently impounding data captured by failure identification models in share prices. Interestingly, the empirical evidence appears to suggest that they are.

Behavioural research is ambiguous. In laboratory conditions analysts do not perform substantially worse in identifying failing companies, so long as they know the proportion of failed to non-failed companies in the samples they are studying. However, their ability to discriminate correctly declines sharply when they lack this information. On the other hand, the conditions under which such experiments are conducted are artificial, and it must be wondered whether they truly replicate the real world, where the rewards and penalties for identifying or not identifying problem companies are substantial. Certainly there is evidence which suggests that lending bankers generally do not use mechanistic failure prediction models, even when they are aware of their existence – which is puzzling if such procedures are so clearly superior in diagnosing problem cases. Moreover, some survey evidence seems to indicate that in practice lending bankers are able to distinguish between satisfactory and unsatisfactory accounts as well as any statistical model.

## Notes

[1] This is a major justification for studying bankruptcy in relation to listed rather than small, privately owned companies.

[2] Other approaches are possible. For instance, the 'mean return' approach calculates residual returns in relation to the average return on a security. However, this is unlikely to be a satisfactory approach as it fails to control for market-wide movements in share prices. See Strong (1992) and Bernard (1989, 1992) for recent discussions of the issues raised in applying the events study methodology.

[3] Indeed, this approach has become common in recent years when the focus of researchers has tended to switch from 'returns' (i.e. changes in the values of securities) to 'levels' (i.e. the underlying values of shares): see Bernard (1989).

[4] It is necessary, in fact, to exercise special care when interpreting the abnormal variance of returns (see Cready, 1992).

[5] Additional problems can arise where the independent variable is not expressed in corresponding terms to the dependent variable (e.g. where one is a ratio and the other is not: see Kothari, 1992; Donnelly and Walker, 1995).

[6] Particular sources of error which can lead to an upwards bias in portfolio returns are the use of 'middle' prices, when there is actually a bid-ask spread; thin trading; and/or price discreteness. As Conrad and Kaul (1993) have demonstrated, such factors help to explain why some researchers (e.g DeBondt and Thaler, 1985, 1987) have found evidence that 'contrarian' investment strategies would appear to be profitable.

[7] But see note 6 above.

[8] Keynes described such behaviour in terms of a 'pure expectations economy'. In fact, 'herding' behaviour may be encouraged by the dominance of institutional shareholdings in the stockmarket, as the four main investment intermediaries in the UK (insurance funds, pension schemes, and investment- and unit-trusts) together now own well over 75 per cent of the equities of British companies listed on the London Stock Exchange. In a highly competitive market the performance of fund managers is assessed in terms of league tables, and there is little evidence of persistent superiority/inferiority on the part of individual fund managers. This is only to be expected, of course, as inferior fund managers would soon be forced out of business; while if one group of investment managers were persistently to outperform their rivals, they would presumably attract every potential client and end up in a monopoly position! It follows that there is a strong disincentive for any group of analysts to step too far out of line with the consensus view – except for the very short term – since to do so carries substantial risks if their opinion of future likely outcomes turns out to be wrong.

[9] Fama and French (1993, 1996) have found that a three factor model is able to control for anomalies associated with price/earnings and cash flow/price differentials, book value/market capitalisation, past sales growth, and historically high rates of return.

For evidence of stock market anomalies in the UK context, see Levis (1989).

[10] Relatively little research has so far been undertaken to see to what extent firm specific bankruptcy risk might explain anomalous returns, although Fama and French (1994, 1995) have suggested it could be a significant factor, quite apart from systematic risk, size and gearing. One reason might be the methodological difficulties that would have to be overcome in order to engage in such studies: e.g. unstable betas (see pp. 182-3 and note 12, below); and the fact that Z-scores themselves are typically derived using size and gearing ratios.

Preliminary work on UK data by Kothari and Taffler (1996), trying to assess whether Z-score indicators contain incremental information over beta, book value/market capitalisation and short term trends in returns appears to be inconclusive.

[11] This could be analysed with respect to individual matched pairs of companies, rather than in terms of cross sectional averages (see the analogous point made on

pp. 29-30). However, this is unlikely to be helpful for two reasons. First, there are considerable difficulties in isolating residual returns for individual financially distressed companies (see below). Second, a trading strategy which requires securities in companies which actually failed to be sold short will ultimately appear to be profitable because of the way in which the sample will have been constructed (i.e. with the advantage of hindsight).

[12] See Aharony and Swary (1988) and Ro, Zavgren and Hsieh (1992) for empirical evidence of the behaviour of betas of failing companies.

[13] Rather surprisingly the study by Beaver (1968a) appears to be the only one in this context to have adopted the matched pairing technique.

[14] Share price behaviour in these studies has usually been examined in terms of cumulative average residuals (CARs). While these will be subject to upwards biasing, and there are difficulties in interpreting the implicit trading strategy (see Conrad and Kaul, 1993), this would appear to be a relatively minor factor. Certainly Clark and Weinstein (1983) found little difference in their results when they applied both the API and CAR metrics; and besides, the general *average* pattern of share price behaviour, based on a heterogeneous set of observations, seems unlikely to differ greatly if other analytical procedures are applied.

[15] See pp. 68-9 and 135 respectively.

[16] See p. 127.

[17] See Libby (1981) for a description of the lens framework and the use of the experimental psychology approach in accounting research.

[18] Tennyson, Ingram and Dugan (1990) and Smith and Taffler (1992) have taken a wider remit and compared the relative importance of narrative disclosures to quantitative indicators of financial distress: see p. 234 et seq. for a summary of research involving textual analysis.

[19] Casey and Selling (1986) subsequently undertook a further study to assess whether forecast accuracy was improved when subjects had access to 'better' data. They concluded that the differences in the results of Casey's previous studies and those of Libby and others might well be the result of variations in 'task predictability' rather than just disclosure of the prior probability of bankruptcy.

[20] Another issue examined in the context of bankruptcy identification is whether individuals in a group follow the lead of the most expert member or are collectively better able to process complex information. Iselin (1991) found little evidence to support either proposition, but it appeared that subjects learned fairly rapidly how to interpret data for the task in hand.

# 7 Positive theories of corporate failure: V – Case study research

## Introduction

One of the problems with statistically based studies is that they tend to concentrate on the *symptoms* of failure rather than the *causes*. As explained in chapter 3, a number of different combinations of economic events can give rise to a given set of accounting numbers. In the circumstances, what is perhaps required is a more detailed examination of the causes of failure, and this can really only be done by undertaking a series of case studies.

In fact, such research has been carried out by academics specialising in management and business strategy formulation, the focus of their attention being so-called 'turnaround' situations.

Briefly, the general thrust of this work suggests that there are various combinations of economic events which lead to the decline of a business, and – hardly surprisingly – no one case is exactly like another. In many instances the companies under study have been turned round, either by a radical change in strategy, but also sometimes as a result of being taken over by another company.[1] However, some financially distressed businesses are less fortunate and are forced into bankruptcy. Efforts have therefore been made by closely examining the circumstances of these companies to try to find out what peculiar defects have characterised them and helped to bring about their downfall.

Unfortunately, as might have been anticipated, there is no easy answer which might help the owners or managers of a business to identify a standard way of turning a financially distressed company round. After all, if there were, it is not unreasonable to expect that company doctors would have been installed and would have been successful. It is only with the 20:20 vision of hindsight that it is possible to diagnose the problems and suggest what ought to have been done.

## Turnaround studies

One of the criticisms frequently levelled at the industrial economics literature is that it too often deals in generalities. By contrast, the management and business strategy literature attempts to apply the arguments at the individual firm level, often by popularising basic economic nostrums. In so doing, it also seeks to provide practical procedures for analysing a firm's position at a particular point in time. Thus Porter's well known Five Forces Model focuses on competitive rivalry, ranging from collusion to competition; the threat of entry, which requires consideration of a number of barriers which may protect a company from new competition; the threat of substitutes; the bargaining power of buyers; and the bargaining power of suppliers. Attention is also focused on industry and product life cycles.

*Planning strategies*

In terms of planning, managers are encouraged to study the social, technological, economic and political environments before identifying a firm's strengths, weaknesses, opportunities and threats. This is a prelude to a more in-depth study of a company's competitive advantage. This requires a study of the possibilities both in terms of cost leadership and product differentiation. The former necessitates an examination, first, of the resources possessed by a business; and, second, of its 'value chain', which breaks down the activities of a firm into its strategically relevant operations, such as its support activities (e.g. the management of its labour force, the potential for technical development, and the procurement of supplies) and the sequence of its operations. The latter concerns the supply of raw materials, the series of operations during which value is added, the distribution of finished goods, and marketing and after sales service activities. Careful study of the cost characteristics of each component activity should make it possible for managers to identify the critical 'cost drivers'. A study of the sub-markets being served by the firm should also enable managers to identify the possibilities for differentiating products and marketing them in a way to defeat rival businesses in the short term. This in turn requires a careful analysis of a firm's main competitors so that its 'value drivers' can be identified. It is then possible to draw the analysis together to determine the appropriate 'positioning' of a firm within its industry and determine the relevant generic 'strategies'.

Such an approach to analysing the position of a firm also requires a careful study of how a generic strategy might be achieved. This may necessitate the development of new products by engaging in R&D activity, increasing penetration of existing markets (e.g. by increasing marketing effort), or entering new markets, especially overseas. In so doing it is necessary to examine all possibilities, including weighing up the advantages and disadvantages of internal expansion as against growth achieved via merger. The latter often offers a rapid way of securing entry into new markets, and in particular avoiding barriers to entry. It also provides an opportunity to obtain synergistic gains, either by vertically integrating forwards or backwards, or by integrating horizontally. Another possibility is to try to spread risks by diversifying as a conglomerate.

## The causes and symptoms of decline

It is against this background that a number of writers in the management area have put forward their somewhat eclectic and subjective theories of the causes and symptoms of corporate failure.[2] These include Smith (1966), Ross and Kami (1973), Schendel, Patton and Riggs (1976), Biebeault (1982), and Kharbanda and Stallworthy (1985) in the US; and Argenti (1976, 1983, 1984), Slatter (1984), and Grinyer, Mayes and McKiernan (1988) in the UK.

All in fact – somewhat tautologically – argue that mismanagement is a key factor leading to corporate collapse, and there is a general consensus as to what are believed to be the main causes of financial failure. As a result, attention will mainly be focused here on the theories put forward by Argenti and Slatter.

Argenti developed his 'A-score' approach by identifying several different types of problem which may face a company. These can be summarised as follows:

(1) There are five possible management defects: the style of the chief executive is too autocratic, the posts of chairman and chief executive are not separated, the board is passive, the board lacks all-round skills, the finance director has little authority, and there is a lack of management depth below board level.
(2) There are three potential weaknesses in the accounting system: budgetary control is inadequate, the cash flow projection (if it exists) is out of date, and managers have little idea of the costs of the activities they supervise.
(3) The company may be slow to appreciate the changes in the environment in which it operates and even slower to react to it.
(4) There can be mistakes which frequently lead to failure: too high a level of borrowing, overtrading, and a lack of diversification (often characterised by overreliance on one customer or on a major project).
(5) There are various symptoms as a company approaches failure: key financial ratios decline (though probably only in the last two years before collapse), the company engages in creative accounting to try to hide unpalatable facts, there are non-financial signs of weakness (e.g. basic expenditures are cut, investments are delayed, staff turnover rises, etc), and ultimately there are terminal signs of collapse immediately before the receiver is called in.

In a similar vein, Slatter (1984) identifies a number of factors which seem to be the principal causes of corporate decline.

(1) Four are associated with poor management: an autocratic chief executive, an ineffective board of directors, neglect of the core business, and a lack of general management skills.

(2) There is inadequate financial control, characterised by: poorly designed management accounting systems, poor use of management accounting information, overcentralisation which impedes effective control, and costs are distorted by inappropriate methods of allocating overheads.

(3) There is an inability to respond to competition, with a reluctance to develop and/or introduce new products; or a failure to respond to price competition by focusing on market demands, by differentiating the product, or by trimming costs to match those of rivals.

(4) Costs are too high: in relative terms because of an inability to take advantage of scale economies or to benefit from learning effects; in absolute terms because of lack of access to raw materials, know-how, appropriate location, or skilled labour at a competitive price; high overheads because of a particular diversification strategy or organisation structure; inefficient operations (e.g. because of poor maintenance, production planning, plant layout, etc); and unfavourable government policies.

(5) Adverse changes in market demand can seriously affect a firm: e.g. because of secular or cyclical declines in demand, or because of a change in tastes.

(6) Adverse movements in commodity prices can severely damage a firm's viability, often as a result of changes in exchange rate parities.

(7) Marketing may be ineffective: e.g. because of a poorly motivated workforce, ineffective advertising, lack of market research, an outdated product, or poor after sales service.

(8) Overreliance on a major project, for which capital requirements may have been underestimated, on which there may have been start up difficulties, for which capacity was inadequate, for which the costs of penetrating a new market were underestimated, or where the contract price was set too low.

(9) Acquisition strategies sometimes go sour: this can arise for a variety of reasons (e.g. 'losers' are acquired, too high a price has been paid for a company, or post-acquisition management is poor).

(10) Financial policy is flawed (e.g. because gearing is too high, not enough resources are invested to meet demand, or there is a failure to raise suitable finance).

(11) Finally overtrading, where a company's sales grow at a faster rate than it is able to sustain from internally generated cash flow and it faces capital rationing conditions.

Like Argenti, Slatter identifies a number of symptoms of decline that can be picked up from a company's financial statements: declining profitability, decreasing sales at constant prices, increased borrowing, a decline in liquidity, a cut in dividends to conserve cash, the use of creative accounting, changes in auditor, increasing delays before accounts are published, rapid management turnover, declining market share, lack of planning, and a paralysis of management decision making.

More recently Pratten (1991) has identified a number of factors which lead to corporate failure: namely, changes in the business environment (e.g. with respect to competition, technological developments, etc, which may often be industry related); changes in the economic environment (e.g. which may be reflected by shifts in the relative prices of factor inputs, such as labour, oil, and other raw materials; movements in exchange and/or interest rates; and increasing rates of inflation); overtrading, when a company cannot raise finance to support growth (i.e. it faces capital rationing); and management failure (i.e. where managers have miscalculated when pursuing a particular strategy). To a large extent these factors reflect disequilibrating shocks to the economy. However, Pratten argues that a number of new factors arose in the late 1980s and early 1990s which led to a series of spectacular corporate collapses, namely globalisation (i.e. the increasing intensity of international competition); macroeconomic instability (i.e. increasing instability in the national and world economies); deregulation (which has led to greater instability as a result of fiercer competition); creative accounting (possibly the result of profit-related-pay contracts, as well as a perceived need to report high profits to satisfy – presumably myopic – institutional shareholders), which could lead managers to take greater risks and/or engage in economically suboptimal policies; the threat of takeovers; a more rapid rate of technological change; and changes in legislation (e.g. with respect to insolvency, which initially might have triggered a number of bankruptcies which might otherwise have been deferred).

## Case study research

### The evidence

In his study of turnaround situations, Slatter (1984, p. 53) has listed the number of instances in which his identified causal variables have been observed. The single most important factor which distinguished failed from turned round companies in his sample was an inability to combat price competition. But almost as significant was having a relatively high cost structure, usually because the company was too small to benefit from economies of scale. By contrast, many companies were able to survive situations either where a major project went wrong, or where a fall in demand for their products was merely the effect of a cyclical downturn.

In identifying potential turnaround situations, Slatter spread the net wide: e.g. in the early 1980s such blue chip companies as ICI, Courtaulds and Tube Investments had each had to devise a new long term strategy to reverse their flagging fortunes. On the other hand, the 20 case studies described in detail in the fourth part of his book relate to companies which came close to, or indeed experienced, financial collapse. Included as successful turnarounds are Stavely, Burton, MFI, Queensway, Pentos, Mount Charlotte, and Keyser Ullman, while Burmah Oil and Ferranti were rescued by government intervention. Amongst the failures are Barker & Dobson and Inveresk, as well as three companies included in the failed sample used in the empirical studies reported in the second part of this book: Bamford, Foden, and Dimplex.

Grinyer, Mayes and McKiernan (1988) concentrated on what they term 'sharpbenders': i.e. companies which have dramatically turned round a relative decline in performance to become industry leaders. (The term 'sharpbender' was coined to describe a graph of relative performance over time.) Nine financial measures of performance were employed in the study, three relating profitability to capital and the number of employees; another two measuring value added against employee numbers and capital employed; and two measuring size, in terms of sales and employee numbers. The analysis sample comprised 26 companies, including such household names as Fisons, Glaxo, McCarthy & Stone, Ferranti, Arthur Bell & Sons, Macallan-Glenlivet, Collins Publishers, Associated Book Publishers, Ellis & Goldstein, Dawson International, Pringle, Sirdar, Low & Bonar, Sidlaw, Ward White, and Tube Investments.[3]

Like Argenti, Slatter and others, Grinyer et al. diagnose the causes of the sharpbenders' relative decline: shrinking total market demand, competitive pressure, poor marketing or quality of product, poor management, inadequate financial controls, inappropriate organisational structure, high costs, unsuitable acquisitions, and major projects that failed. However, they also identify the trigger mechanisms which turned the companies around – e.g. outside intervention, change of ownership, a new chief executive, a recognition by management of the problems, or a perception by management of new opportunities. They also give evidence on the 12 steps most frequently taken by sharpbenders in transforming their positions (e.g. management changes, stricter financial controls, new products, diversification, entering new markets, improving marketing, cutting costs, reducing debt, acquiring new subsidiaries, and windfalls).

The final third of the Grinyer et al.'s book comprises short case histories (or 'vignettes') of the 26 companies studied. However, this is preceded by a statistical analysis of the cause-and-effect relationships that could be identified, based on a matched pair sample. The purpose is to identify the linkage between the causes of decline and the remedial steps taken; and the continuing characteristics of firms and those remedial steps. Given the nature of the data, the regression results are much as might have been anticipated. For instance, the types of sharpbending observed were found to depend very much on the nature of the industry in which a subject company operated. But equally it is evident that companies which turned round successfully directly addressed the causes of their decline, although generally one remedial step on its own was insufficient to explain the 'sharpbend' in a company's fortunes.

In another book on turnarounds, published at much the same time as the Grinyer et al. study, Nelson and Clutterbuck (1988) edited a compendium of 20 case studies. Many of these vignettes were written by senior executives of the subject companies, amongst which are British Airways, Waterford Glass, Low & Bonar, Vickers, Kwik-Fit, the Enka Group, ICI, IRI, Acorn Computers, SAS, UDT, Tesco, Fiat, Woolworth, Grattan, and Lucas.

The Nelson and Clutterbuck book is notable in that it offers no formal analysis of the reasons why companies got into a position where they needed to turn themselves around; or, indeed, what remedial steps they took to achieve recovery. In a sequel to Nelson and Clutterbuck, however, Clutterbuck and Kernaghan (1990) attempted to remedy the situation, first of all surveying accountants, receivers, management consultants, trade unionists, bankers and venture capitalists to identify the main reasons for decline and recovery. They then circulated a questionnaire to 300 receivers and lending institutions (the latter including venture capitalists). The response rate was poor, only 46 completed questionnaires being returned. The most highly scored reasons for business failure by the respondents were poor financial information, lack of control, insufficient working capital, inexperienced management, lack of strategy, poor understanding of the market, low margins, overreliance on one product or customer, and obsolete technology. The book then contains 13 case studies to illustrate the various points made in the authors' analysis of the questionnaire responses, the subject companies including Dunlop, Raleigh Industries, Alfred Herbert, Sinclair Research, Rolls-Royce, Stone-Platt, and Wardle Storey.[4]

The circumstances leading to more recent failures of listed companies are well documented. Thus, for instance, Pratten (1991) reviews the circumstances which led up to the failure of a number of companies during 1988 and 1989, including Coloroll, British & Commonwealth, Polly Peck, Lowndes Queensway, Parkfield, Charterhall, Rush & Tomkins, and Sock Shop. However, no detailed in-depth analysis is given of each company's experience. By contrast, Smith (1992, 1996) summarises the circumstances which led to the debacles at Coloroll, British & Commonwealth, and Polly Peck. There have also been reports by DTI inspectors and parliamentary select committees concerning some of the more celebrated collapses in recent years (e.g. Maxwell Communications, Brent Walker, BCCI, Ferranti), as well as reports of court actions. In addition, there are more general sources providing case histories of large companies,[5] although the best descriptions of the circumstances leading up to bankruptcy are probably now to be found in the reports which have to be filed by receivers with the Registrar of Companies in order to comply with s. 67 of the Insolvency Act 1986.

The studies referred to above generally conclude that financial distress is not simply explained in terms of one or two variables. Rather, it is the result of a conjunction of events, some of them controllable by management, others not. Indeed, to some extent one is forced to conclude that the events leading up to a potential failure situation are 'situation specific'. Moreover, it is much easier to see what went wrong with the advantage of hindsight than it probably was when the companies concerned were faced with a deteriorating financial position.

The question remains as to whether it is possible to identify which companies may successfully be rescued and which not. In fact, the studies fail to shed much light on this matter, although they seem to suggest that it should be possible to identify turnaround candidates. But if it were possible to discriminate in this way, a failing company ought to collapse immediately the market identifies the fact that it is beyond rescue.

Nevertheless, it is undoubtedly a worthwhile exercise trying to analyse the strengths and weaknesses of a company's position, even if it seems intuitively unlikely that there will be many occasions when it will be possible right up until the very end of its life to identify with any clear certainty that it will fail or survive. All that will be possible, presumably, will be to monitor its weakening position and see the odds against its surviving steadily lengthening.

## Summary

Case study research provides a useful and complementary perspective on the complex reasons which lie behind corporate bankruptcy. Certainly it offers greater insight into the underlying causes of failure, although it is difficult to believe that there is any easy way to discriminate between those distressed companies that are capable of being turned round and those which are not.

What is generally missing in most studies is a systematic attempt to identify patterns of events which characterise companies that go into financial decline. Moreover, even if that could be done, it would generally only be achievable *after* the event, when what is really needed is an ability to diagnose problems *before* they occur.

## Notes

[1] See below, pp. 237-239, where the acquisition/failure alternative is examined in more detail.

[2] A more formal structure is provided by 'downward spiralling' theory. Thus Hambrick and d'Aveni (1988) argue that bankruptcies can be seen as 'downward spirals' triggered by changes in four independent variables: domain initiative (i.e. an ability to change products and move into new markets); environmental

carrying capacity (i.e. the ability of the environment (market) to support a given number of firms); slack (i.e. the extent of surplus capacity which enables firms to weather a storm and adapt to new circumstances); and performance. Hambrick and d'Aveni proxied these variables for 57 matched pairs of companies and found there was some evidence of decline in failing firms as early as 10 years prior to bankruptcy. (See p. 240, note 9.)

[3] Ellis & Goldstein is one of the control companies included in the sample which provides the basis for the empirical studies reported in the second part of this monograph.

[4] Stone-Platt is one of the failed companies in the sample used as the basis for the empirical studies reported in the second part of this book. The circumstances leading up to the flotation in 1980 of another, Hesketh Motorcycles, are described in Dimson and Marsh (1988) – although the subsequent collapse of the company in 1981 is not discussed.

[5] *The International Directory of Company Histories*, published by the St James Press in five lengthy volumes, is a valuable encyclopaedia indicating the background of many companies listed on the world's stock exchanges. While the circumstances leading up to the failure of a particular company – assuming that it is the subject of an entry – will not necessarily pinpoint the reasons behind its financial distress, the background can be invaluable as a starting point in a case study investigation.

# 8 The explanatory variables: I – Financial ratios

## Introduction

It is evident from the discussion in previous chapters that the main independent variables used in corporate failure studies are financial indicators, and these are generally expressed in the form of ratios. Indeed, as was pointed out in chapter 3, accounting ratios have long been used by analysts in a univariate context as one way of trying to assess a company's position and appraise its future prospects. Moreover, recent studies have suggested that, notwithstanding the extensive evidence of informational market efficiency, it may be possible to develop profitable portfolio strategies by referring to such ratios (Ou and Penman, 1989).[1]

It has also been argued, however, that accounting numbers by themselves merely reflect the *effects* of economic events, not their *causes*. This is evident from case study research (briefly reviewed in chapter 7), which confirms that financial distress is the result of a conjunction of a number of disparate factors. Nevertheless, although every failure is to some extent 'situation specific', there are certain broad patterns of events which frequently underlie a downward spiralling in a company's fortunes, even though it is almost certainly not as clear at the time as it is with hindsight that its position is beyond redemption.

But it is not only the fact that accounting indicators reflect symptoms rather than causes that is a matter of concern. The point was also made in chapter 3 that the numbers themselves only capture some of the characteristics of an economic event (i.e. they are imperfect surrogate representations), a matter rarely acknowledged in traditional accounting textbooks. Even more surprising, however, is the fact that they say very little about the properties of financial ratios, nor do they generally refer to alternative 'qualitative' indicators that might be referred to by analysts. Of course, to some extent it may be true that the shortcomings inherent in individual ratios may be overcome when multivariate analysis is applied, but this cannot be guaranteed. It is therefore the purpose of this chapter to examine the nature of accounting ratios, while the next will deal with other explanatory variables which may help to explain a company's position and future prospects.

A brief review of the literature indicates at once that there are well over a hundred ratios that can be calculated from accounting numbers included in published financial statements. Many of these, however, will reflect similar attributes (e.g. profitability, liquidity, gearing, size, growth, etc). Some means has to be found to reduce the number of ratios to manageable proportions and avoid duplication, and indeed procedures have been developed to achieve this.

A second aspect relates to the statistical properties of ratios. The traditional textbook approach implicitly assumes that ratios are strictly proportional, yet intuitively – as was argued in chapter 3 – this seems unlikely. Empirical research in fact suggests that most ratios are not normally distributed. It is therefore desirable either to transform them in some way or to adopt a method of analysis where normality is not a basic requirement.

A further point is that most empirically based failure studies inevitably have to pool data across industries as well as over time to produce reasonably sized samples for analysis. It is therefore necessary to establish the extent to which the mean values of specific ratios are likely to vary between industry categories, and equally how the application of different accounting policies may affect the results of a study.

**Common characteristics in ratios**

As indicated above, the first matter to note about ratios is that several of them appear to measure similar attributes of a business. It is therefore useful to identify those which possess such commonalities as this should enable analysts to focus on a more parsimonious group of indicators than would otherwise be the case.

A number of research studies have specifically addressed this problem, and generally 'factor analysis' has been used to reduce the number of ratios to manageable proportions. This technique applies regression to identify the extent of correlation between variables and enables their number to be reduced while still capturing the same characteristics. Briefly, the procedure operates so that j observed variables (here ratios) are linearly described in terms of n common factors and a unique factor. Formally, if $x_{ij}$ is the original value of variable j for case i, then

$$x_{ij} = a_{j1} F_{i1} + a_{j2} F_{i2} + \ldots + a_{jn} F_{in} + e_{ij} \tag{8.1}$$

where the $a_{jk}$ terms are called 'factor loadings', and each indicates
the importance of the k[th] factor in measuring variable j;
$F_{ik}$ are the new coordinates of case i with respect to factor k;
and e refers to an error term.

The k factors or groupings may be either uncorrelated (or 'orthogonal') or correlated (or 'oblique').

Basically factor analysis searches for commonalities to produce a parsimonious set of *heirarchical relationships*. Typically researchers have found that, with populations of about 50 ratios drawn from financial statements of cross sectional samples of manufacturing companies, around 90 per cent of variation can be accounted for by six or seven characteristics. These are usually labelled in descending order in terms of their overall significance. Table 8.1 lists the categories for a sample of 44 non-failing British companies identified in a study by El Hennawy (1981).

### Table 8.1: Characteristics Explaining
### the Variance of Ratios

|  | % of variance explained |
|---|---|
| Liquidity | 35.6 |
| Profitability | 22.1 |
| Asset composition | 10.4 |
| Size | 8.6 |
| Gearing | 6.3 |
| Retentions ratio | 4.2 |
| Growth | 3.1 |
|  | 90.3 |

Other studies in the UK have produced slightly different broad categories and different rankings of explanatory power (e.g. Taffler, 1977; Taffler and Sudarsanam, 1979; and Ezzamel, Brodie and Mar-Molinero, 1987). Likewise in the US Pinches, Mingo and Caruthers (1973) identified as key components return on investment, capital turnover, inventory turnover, financial gearing, debtors turnover, short term liquidity and cash position. Other studies have since been undertaken in the US (e.g. Johnson 1978, 1979; Zavgren, 1985) and elsewhere. However, the differences in their findings partly reflect the nature of the capital markets in the various countries, the samples of companies chosen, the basic ratios selected for reduction, and the years to which the data relate. Moreover, it is evident that there are differences in the explained variances and the representative ratios for non-failed and failing groups of companies, a result which makes it clear that it should be possible to develop multivariate discriminatory rules merely by referring to financial ratio data.

An alternative data reduction technique to factor analysis is 'multidemensional scaling' (MDS). This involves mapping observations for variables (such as ratios), and algorithms are available to apply the technique to financial data (Mar-

Molinero and Ezzamel, 1991). However, the results produced are very similar to those generated by factor analysis.

The important point to note is that generally it seems to be possible to identify half a dozen or so key characteristics of companies which are captured by different ratios.

Overall, most of these data reduction studies seem to suggest that profitability is the most important single influence on ratios. This is especially the case for failing companies, presumably because when a company makes low profits it is likely to become less liquid and more highly geared.

One important issue identified by the factor analysis and MDS studies is that the loadings of some ratios are unstable through time. Thus Pinches, Eubank, Mingo and Caruthers (1975) found that cash flow/debt may be strongly related to profitability in some years (i.e. be strongly correlated with return on net assets); but in others it may be strongly associated with liquidity (i.e. move in line with (say) the current assets/current liabilities ratio). Clearly for analytical purposes there are advantages in concentrating attention on ratios whose characteristics are stable across time or between companies.

An important implication of the factor analysis and MDS studies is to confirm that there are important interactions between ratios, not only within groups but between groups. This would seem to support the view that multivariate methods of analysis are more suitable than the commonly applied univariate techniques described in textbooks and outlined in chapter 3.

## Statistical distributions

As indicated previously, it often seems to be assumed in conventional financial statement analysis that ratio observations are normally distributed. However, such an assumption seems to be unjustified for a number of reasons.

The first problem is that univariate analysis generally focuses on a bivariate relationship between the numerator and denominator of a fraction. However, as was pointed out in chapter 4, few relationships of this kind are strictly proportionate. Certainly it seems unlikely to be the case with financial ratios, nor is it so in practice (Deakin, 1976; Whittington, 1980; Ezzamel and Mar-Molinero, 1990). Thus, for example, costs (C) in relation to output volumes (V) are not usually of the form

$$C = \beta V \tag{8.2}$$

where $\beta$ is a slope coefficient.

If the equation did hold it would imply a relationship as shown in Figure 8.1, where the function runs through the origin.

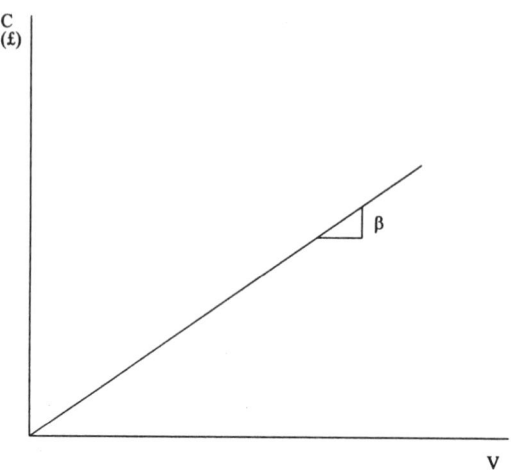

**Figure 8.1**

Clearly a misspecification of the underlying relationship is likely to cause problems. In fact, a more typical cost function would involve a constant, and it would therefore be more appropriately modelled as

$$C = \alpha + ßV \tag{8.3}$$

where $\alpha$ is an intercept; and
ß is a slope coefficient.

Diagramatically the position would appear as in Figure 8.2:
But it is not only cost functions as drawn in the well known break-even diagram that might be expected to follow such a pattern. Thus, for instance, a stock turnover ratio is equally likely to be best modelled with a constant because for precautionary reasons firms generally have to carry a minimum level of inventories. Similarly, most businesses would not expect to earn rates of return on capital employed below a return on a risk free investment, such as gilt edged securities, so again the expected pattern of observed returns is likely to involve a constant.
But a second problem, again identified by Whittington, is that functional relationships may not be strictly proportional (i.e. linear). Thus, in the above example, ß may not be constant gradient because of scale economies. Rather, if empirical observations were to be plotted, the function would probably appear as in Figure 8.3.[2]

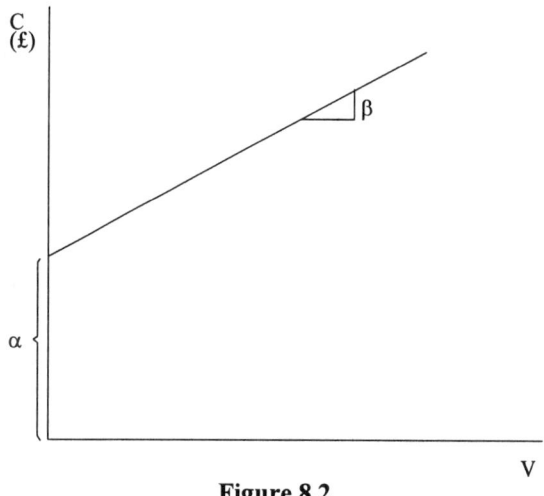

**Figure 8.2**

The fact that the function is no longer linear implies a second explanatory factor will need to be introduced on the right hand side of the equation if linearity is to be restored; or, alternatively, that the function should be transformed in some way until it becomes linear (e.g. by taking the logarithms of observations).

Of course, the fact that a cost or other relationship is not strictly proportional may not be associated with volume, as implied above. Instead, where observations are pooled over several periods it may be the result of instability in the underlying relationship across time. Thus in terms of cost functions, typically there will be a learning process. Consequently, if this takes a logarithmic form (which is what is normally assumed with learning curves in management accounting), it will be necessary with observations that are pooled over time to log the data and thus transform them so that they are homogeneous (i.e. strictly comparable).[3]

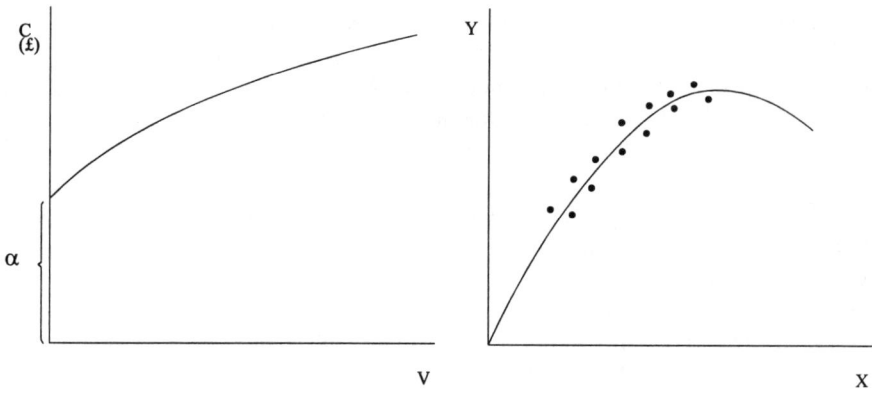

**Figure 8.3**                                              **Figure 8.4**

The fact that functions may not be linear highlights another problem identified by Whittington, namely that a series of observations may be better explained by a quadratic relationship rather than that implied by bivariate regression. This possibility is illustrated in Figure 8.4, and indeed Whittington found some evidence to support this.

In fact, studies by McDonald and Morris (1984, 1985) and Fieldsend, Longford and McLeay (1987) have found that *within* industries it may well be reasonable to use conventional ratios, but not *between* industries. However, it seems that a major factor which affects the validity of applying conventional ratio analysis is the size of companies (McLeay and Fieldsend, 1987).

Misspecification of an underlying relationship may contribute to an observed lack of statistical normality in distributions of particular ratios. But whatever the reasons, it is evident from empirical evidence that the distributions of many bivariate ratios are not normal, so efforts should be made to try to allow for this when the data are being analysed. In practical 'one-off' analyses of an individual company's position there is relatively little that can be done, except to make allowance when trying to interpret specific ratio calculations, especially where the distortion is well known. However, adjustment should be made where cross sectional studies are undertaken and where the distribution will be subjected to statistical significance tests. This is easier to achieve when the samples are relatively large, but it is far more difficult to transform successfully when samples are small (Ezzamel, Mar-Molinero and Beecher, 1987).

One factor which can induce non-normality in ratio distributions in the incidence of outliers (So, 1987; Ezzamel, Mar-Molinero and Beecher, 1987). Many researchers choose to exclude such observations, but even where this is done distributions may still be non-normal. This means either that the ratio distributions must be subjected to non-parametric or similar statistical tests (McLeay, 1986); or they must be transformed until they become approximately normal (e.g. by taking logarithms or square roots of the ratios).

The above arguments about the normality of ratio distributions relate to univariate analyses of data. A more difficult problem arises where multivariate analysis is attempted as it is a requirement of some procedures (e.g. discriminant analysis) that there is 'multivariate normality'. Many researchers have ignored this condition or tried to ensure that the individual ratios used in the model are normally distributed, although this will not of itself guarantee that the problem is resolved.

In fact, Karels and Prakash (1987) tested the assumption of multivariate normality on the sets of ratios used in a number of corporate failure studies. They found the condition was generally violated, and that discriminatory power was considerably improved when the requirement was more nearly met.

As it happens, normality is not a requirement with logit regression, which is a good reason for using the model. However, it is worth noting the point made by

Whittington (1979) with respect to the 'error' in the accounting rate of return (ARR or ROI/ROCE) when compared against the internal rate of return (IRR) (see pp. 104-7): namely, that for the purpose of empirical studies using regression analysis, what is important is not that the ARR is correct or incorrect but that the 'errors' are unbiased. The problem in that particular instance is that the errors may well be biased: e.g. the ARRs of rapidly growing firms are likely to be systematically biased downwards.

## Industry specific ratios

It has long been recognised that there are systematic differences between many ratios for companies operating in different industries. Thus, for example, the proportion of stocks to total assets held by a civil engineering contractor is totally dissimilar to that held by a food manufacturer or a retailer.

This arises in part because of differences in the trading cycle. For companies in the food processing industry, for instance, the cycle is at most a few weeks. By contrast, major building contracts often take several years to complete. In other words, the calendar year used as the basis for preparing annual accounts does not necessarily coincide with an economic trading cycle. As a result, for those companies where the trading cycle is much longer than twelve months the profit figures are far more sensitive to 'errors' in stock valuation. Thus it is widely acknowledged that a 5 per cent 'error' in stock valuation for a contractor – and this would be on the low side – will translate itself into something like a 15 per cent 'error' in the profit figure.

But it is not just a question of the relative reliability of some of the figures taken from the annual accounts. The incidence of accounting conventions will also systematically affect ratios. Thus consider again a contracting business. Typically much of the stocks and work in progress will be undervalued in terms of their economic value to the business (or opportunity cost), even though it is now customary to carry forward some of the fixed costs to the next period under the requirements of SSAP 9. The effect in general will be to lower the denominator in one of the key ratios, the rate of return on capital employed.

Of course, initially profits will be sharply reduced for a company which expenses debits rather than carrying them forward in its balance sheet and treating them as an asset. However, after the initial period, so long as trading activity is relatively stable the impact on annual profits will be very small. It will be the denominator in the rate of return ratio that will be systematically low, leading (other things being equal) to a higher index of profitability.

The same argument can equally well be applied, of course, to companies which write off assets such as R&D or follow conservative depreciation policies. A moment's reflection will indicate that net profit margins and debtors turnover ratios are also likely to vary from firm-to-firm.

211

In the circumstances, as Lev (1974) has pointed out, it may be sensible to calculate what are in effect 'industry averages' and then subtract these from individual company ratios to isolate 'residuals'.[4] These will then give some indication of relative performance, although it must be recognised that such a procedure focuses entirely on the first moment of the ratio distribution, the mean, completely ignoring the other attributes captured by the second and third moments (i.e. the variance and the degree of skewness). For this reason it may be helpful to be able to refer to quartile or even decile points in the distribution. However, care must be taken to ensure that like is being compared to like, since some ratios (such as profit margins) are likely to vary within the same industry categories (e.g. for stores like Harrods compared to Littlewoods; or supermarkets such as Sainsbury's compared to Kwik Save).

Nevertheless, despite this, various studies have shown there is a tendency for company ratios to be 'mean reverting' and move towards their industry averages over time (e.g. Lev, 1969b). This may in part reflect the underlying economic realities, but it could also to some extent be the result of measurement 'errors' working themselves out over a period of years.

### The effects of applying different accounting policies

A great deal has been written in recent years about so-called 'creative accounting', which draws attention to the fact that there is still a considerable amount of choice in the accounting treatment of specific transactions, despite the efforts of successive standard making bodies, such as the Accounting Principles Board and the Financial Accounting Standards Board in the US and the Accounting Standards Committee and the Accounting Standards Board in the UK.

One point which often goes unremarked is that, over a finite period, the *total* profit that will be reported by a company should be the same, whatever conventions are applied, so long as they are consistently adhered to.[5] What is really at issue is the *timing of recognition* of profit over the subperiods into which a business's life is broken up.

The effect is shown in Figure 8.5, where the area under the two curves AA' and BB' is the same (i.e. the total profits reported are identical). AA' represents the application of a conservative valuation convention, so that subperiod profits are lower in the earlier subperiods (years) than in later subperiods. BB' represents the application of a less conservative valuation convention.

It can be seen that the only way total reported profits can be inflated over the long run is to switch from one convention to another (e.g. from BB' to AA' in later subperiods). This will have the effect of reporting the same element of profit twice. However, usually such a change in accounting practice has to be disclosed, together with an indication of its impact on reported profits, so an analyst should be able to monitor the impact of such switches in accounting treatment.

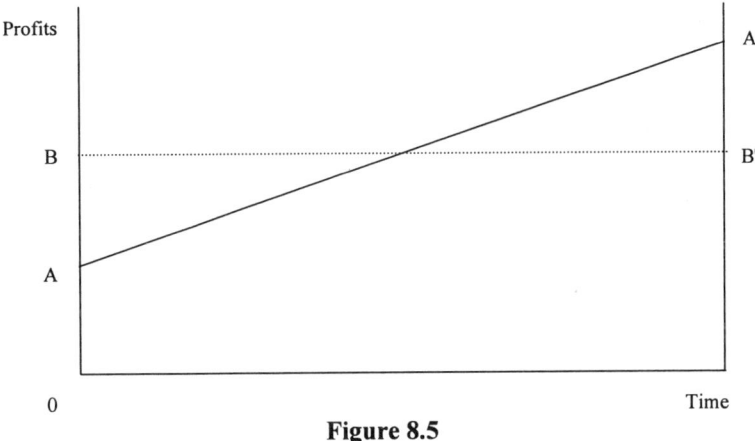

**Figure 8.5**

The impact of applying specific conventions on particular ratios has already been indicated above, namely that it can systematically affect their values from year to year. However, it is not only the mean values that may be affected, but also their dispersion over time. Yet if a company has a broad portfolio of wasting fixed assets, the 'errors' in the depreciation charges will tend to cancel each other out, providing a smoother pattern of profits over time (a point referred to below with respect to the return on capital employed ratio). Clearly this suggests that larger businesses may appear to have less volatile profits, regardless of the underlying economic realities (which may themselves be pushing in the same direction, of course).

With respect to the deliberate manipulation of accounting numbers – which is what seems to be the focus of attention of most writers – it is worthwhile summarising the various ways in which this can take place.

Manipulation can refer to a number of accounting indicators – e.g. gearing or liquidity ratios, as well as profitability measures. Moreover, it is really necessary to try to distinguish the motives. Thus one objective is to reduce or increase contractual payments that are determined by reported accounting figures: e.g. income tax payments, profit related pay, and debt covenant restrictions. Another goal, however, is to try to 'signal' expected likely outcomes to interested third parties, such as analysts, who will want to learn about the profit and growth prospects of a company

In a signalling context 'profit improvement' is essentially a short term strategy which may be employed when a business is in financial trouble.[6] A longer term manipulative strategy is 'profit smoothing', of which there are two basic types. First there is 'classificatory smoothing': i.e. where, for instance, certain items are classed as extraordinary. However, for this to affect analysts' perceptions, the manipulator has to be fairly sure which profit figure they study most closely – and how uncritically they do so. Second there is 'intertemporal smoothing': i.e. where reporting profit in one period will automatically mean it cannot be reported in a subsequent period. One way this can be achieved is by manipulating discretionary expenditures (e.g. by advancing or delaying R&D and welfare programmes; altering the frequency of work certification and stage payments on long term contracts; or varying the speed at which invoices are issued to customers). Another is by choice of accounting conventions – which can even be altered for successive investments in wasting fixed assets by classifying them differently from their predecessors.

The empirical evidence certainly suggests that manipulation takes place, both to affect contractual payments and to signal likely future outcomes to analysts. The studies which suggest this are of four types:

(1) those reporting anecdotal evidence;
(2) statistically based studies that demonstrate the properties of earnings time series;
(3) studies directly concerned with trying to identify evidence of manipulation and smoothing; and
(4) research aimed at identifying analysts' reactions to overt manipulation.

With respect to anecdotal evidence, many examples of manipulation have been observed both in the US (e.g. Briloff, 1972) and in the UK (e.g. Stamp and Marley, 1970; Griffiths 1986; and Smith, 1992, 1996). However, the very fact that such instances have been noted suggests they are not a problem – at least, not in a signalling context.[7] The real problem is manipulation which is not disclosed – and which even the auditor cannot identify.

A large number of studies have shown that the first differences (i.e. rates of change) in company earnings overwhelmingly follow a random walk (e.g. Ball and Watts, 1972). Only for a small minority of companies is there any evidence of serial correlation over time, and then only for short periods (e.g. Brooks and Buckmaster, 1976, 1980).

By contrast, there is clear evidence that ratios (notably the return on capital employed) oscillate around a mean (e.g. Beaver, 1970; Lev, 1969b).

With respect to direct evidence of smoothing, a number of the early studies were flawed because they failed to identify an appropriate earnings trend, and they also only dealt with one or two of the possible instruments that might be used to smooth profits. In a study which attempted to take these matters into account, Ronen and Sadan (1981) interestingly found some evidence of smoothing in regulated industries, where there is clearly an incentive to try to manipulate reported profits in order to avoid criticism.[8]

As for the responses to overt manipulation by users of financial statement information, a series of laboratory and field test experiments suggest that analysts react quite strongly to the type of accounting messages transmitted (i.e. to the *form*

214

of accounts rather than their *substance*). This is true when current purchasing power (CPP) and current cost accounting (CCA) indicators are transmitted rather than conventional accounting data; when LIFO is used rather than FIFO for inventory valuation; or where merger rather than acquisition accounting is applied. However this may well be the result of the unreal nature of the experiments (the so-called 'external validity' problem).[9] Certainly research on these same matters based on share price movements and other market indicators suggests that in practice analysts for the most part *do* identify the economic substance underlying reported accounting numbers, whatever their form.

In terms of accounting manipulation, a laboratory experiment by Koch (1981) interestingly found that profit smoothing was a favoured strategy amongst managers working for companies whose shares were widely held – i.e. where there is a clear need to signal future intentions. He also found that manipulation of accounting conventions was preferred to changes in the patterns of discretionary expenditures, presumably because the latter would have economic consequences in terms of changes in cash flow patterns: i.e. substance would be changed, not just form.

As for market reaction studies, where changes in share prices conditional on the method of reporting are examined, a large number of studies have shown that analysts appear to adjust for disclosed differences in accounting treatment. The issues examined include depreciation, deferred tax, FIFO/LIFO, merger/acquisition accounting, the treatment of leases, and reporting in terms of CPP and CCA adjusted statements.

Rather fewer studies have examined the impact on the prices of securities where accounting conventions have been *changed* by individual companies. However, one such study was that of Kaplan and Roll (1972). They found the market did adjust, but only after a short time lag, which implied that profits could be earned by trading on this publicly available information. Subsequently Ball (1972) eliminated this anomaly by adjusting the research methodology.

More recently, researchers have been studying the correspondence between share price returns and earnings over long periods of time, the argument being that both are ultimately based on a company's net cash flows (e.g. Easton, Harris and Ohlson, 1992). As the length of the time interval is extended, the difference between the opening/closing book values of a company's net assets and the corresponding market capitalisations will be of diminished importance. Of course, it is then but a short step to compare over different intervals the correspondence between share price returns and alternative reported earnings series, the most obvious being those which are all-inclusive (i.e. where even asset revaluations are put through the income statement) and those where certain items are excluded (e.g. where adjustments are made directly on reserves). The former series (known as 'clean surplus' accounting) has been shown in the UK context to be less closely correlated with security returns than the latter ('dirty surplus' accounting) over both short and long term intervals, the implication seeming to be that the exclusion of certain items from the income calculation to focus on 'permanent' (i.e. sustainable) earnings has not misled the market.[10]

In conclusion, the implications are that one might well expect there to be differences in the accounting conventions adopted as between firms and between industries. These can systematically affect ratios, both in terms of their average values and the dispersion around the means over time, yet not necessarily reflect any differences in the underlying economic substance of their operations. It is therefore interesting to note that a number of bankruptcy studies have been undertaken where independent variables have been adjusted to allow for these differences: e.g. capitalising leases (Elam, 1975; Altman, Haldeman and Narayanan, 1977; Lawrence and Bear, 1986); and using CPP (Ketz, 1978; Norton and Smith, 1979) and CCA indicators (Mensah, 1983; Keasey and Watson, 1986; Skogsvik, 1990).

However, a priori there are good grounds for suspecting that companies in financial distress may be tempted to try to change accounting practice as part of a strategy of 'profit improvement'. This may well show up in the 'qualitative indicators' where these identify changes in accounting treatment; and/or in an audit qualification, where the matter is referred to in the audit report. On the other hand, where new assets are classified differently from their predecessors this may be very difficult – if not impossible – to identify.

Finally, it is worth noting that there are even more severe problems with data when dealing with small companies since the figures are not generally prepared with signalling in mind. In particular, since 1981 some 40 per cent of such businesses have taken advantage of the concessions which enable them to file abbreviated accounts.[11] However, even when full accounts are available, the precise profit figure reported depends largely on how much is charged as directors' salaries and how much is withdrawn via so-called expense preferencing. How this has been allowed for (if at all) by researchers who have undertaken empirical studies involving small firms (such as Edmister, 1972; and Keasey and Watson, 1986, 1987) is not always clear.

**Summary**

Accounting ratios are the most widely used independent variables in bankruptcy studies, but because there are so many relationships that can be identified it is necessary to reduce the number of variables to manageable proportions. The usual way of doing this is to apply factor analysis, and it is now fairly well established that there are 4-5 financial attributes that need to be measured: i.e. profitability, liquidity, gearing, size and growth. Once the data set has been reduced, it is possible to choose the best ratios for inclusion in a model by following an iterative routine (e.g. stepwise selection).

However, before this is done it is necessary to ensure, firstly, that a ratio is stable across time in capturing a particular characteristic; and, secondly, that its statistical characteristics (e.g. with respect to normality and the absence of outliers) are such that its inclusion will not distort the results. This is especially important where data are being pooled both across time and across industries as this substantially reduces homogeneity in the variable set. Fortunately, logit regression is fairly robust in this respect as its statistical requirements for independent variables are less demanding than (say) discriminant analysis.

Another potential problem is the impact of particular accounting conventions on the accounting numbers reported by companies. This is likely to produce different ratio distributions for different industry categories, and it may introduce systematic bias into the data. This might not matter too much if the data are drawn from a fairly narrow population of companies which are subject to similar influences. However, it is likely to be a problem where data have to be pooled across time and between industry categories, which (as has already been indicated) is usually the case in bankruptcy studies. Of course, this will to some extent be controlled for by the matched pairing of companies, but it nevertheless means that there is a strong likelihood that a discriminatory model will reflect the 'lowest common denominator' features which distinguish failing from non-failing firms.

## Notes

[1] The Ou and Penman study is interesting as the research methodology applied is rigorous. Its results are consistent with those of a number of studies which suggest that abnormal returns can be earned by pursuing so-called 'contrarian' investment strategies, although it has not always proved possible to repeat them profitably. Ou and Penman in fact began with a set of 68 accounting variables, a number which was later reduced to 18. As they acknowledge, the results could possibly reflect the fact that risk was inadequately controlled for, and in practice it would be necessary to allow for transactions costs, etc.

[2] Such indeed is the logic behind the well known economic order quantity (EOQ) model, which assumes a completely different behaviour pattern to the stock turnover ratio that is usually given prominence in many accounting textbooks in chapters on the interpretation of financial statements.

[3] See p. 117.

[4] Lev (1974, ch. 3) in fact suggests that regression should be used to calculate an expected industry value for a particular ratio. The residual would then be calculated by deducting this from the observed value. By contrast, Edmister (1972), who used residual ratios in his failure study of small firms in the US, apparently deducted industry averages (i.e. with the constants suppressed).

[5] Indeed, this is equally true regardless of the value system used, be it current (opportunity) or historical costs.

[6] The distinction between 'profit improvement' and 'profit smoothing' strategies is drawn by Breakwell and Morris (1975), who found some evidence of the former in the UK. Similar evidence on profit improvement is reported for the US

by DeAngelo, DeAngelo and Skinner (1994), who found that distressed companies appeared to manipulate earnings regardless of the impact on cash flows, both when they were subject to debt covenant restrictions and when they were not. The reasons for such manipulation appear to be a combination of pressures from auditors and creditors; and the result of manager-shareholder conflicts over cash retentions, shifts in policy because of changes in management (including attempts to 'clear the decks'), negotiations with trade unions, and efforts to secure preferential treatment from government agencies.

[7] It may well be worthwhile manipulating profit figures if the effect is to alter property rights and/or the incidence of cash flows (e.g. tax payments, profit related pay, the impact of debt covenants, price regulation, etc), and there is abundant empirical evidence suggesting that this a primary motive for creative accounting.

[8] Ronen and Sadan (1981) provide a thorough survey of the empirical evidence of creative accounting up until the beginning of the 1980s.

[9] See p. 187.

[10] Of course, the fact that such results hold for a cross section of companies does not necessarily mean that clean surplus accounting might not have a closer correspondence to share price returns for individual concerns.

[11] See p. 45, note 17.

# 9 The explanatory variables: II – Non-financial ratio indicators

## Introduction

Apart from financial ratios drawn from a company's financial statements, there are other variables that can be examined in the context of corporate bankruptcy studies to see whether they help to distinguish failing from non-failing businesses. These are really of two types. The first are those which can be measured on a *ratio scale* – i.e. using money values (such as GDP) or other proportionate measures (for instance, the size of directors' shareholdings; or a change in an index, concerning such items as share prices or the cost of living). The second are those that involve a dichotomous *ordinal scale* – i.e. where 0 might indicate the absence of an audit qualification, 1 a going concern qualification, and 2 another type of audit qualification. However, it is not always easy to measure in terms of an ordinal scale, and not all statistical models can easily accommodate such indicators.

Quite apart from their measurement properties, non-financial indicators can be grouped into two other categories: those which have been used in studies that have appeared in the finance and economics literature; and those which have been discussed by researchers in management and business strategy. In the former case, the criterion for their use seems to be that they can be measured with a reasonable degree of objectivity; in the latter, measurement is usually on the basis of the observation of a researcher or someone who has to assess the likelihood of a firm going bankrupt (e.g. a lending banker, a credit rating agency, or an auditor).

This chapter first of all describes measures used in economics and finance studies (namely, macroeconomic and industry indicators; and variables used in private company and locational models). Firm specific variables are also identified: company characteristics, the board of directors, the accounting year end date, changes in accounting policy, changes in auditor, audit qualifications, and company indebtedness and changes in the register of charges. In addition, procedures for analysing the text of chairmen's reports are described.

Proxy variables for weaknesses in management and corporate strategy are then outlined, together with a brief discussion of research into the acquisition/failure alternative.

**Measures used in economics and finance studies**

*Macroeconomic indicators*

As might be expected, the incidence of corporate bankruptcies appears to vary with the business cycle, the number of failures being greater during periods of recession. On a priori grounds it would therefore not be unreasonable to consider including one or more macroeconomic variables in a failure identification model, as these might be expected to improve its explanatory power.

The leading study in this area is that of Rose, Andrews and Giroux (1982), who examined the contribution of 28 business cycle indicators in explaining quarterly failure rates of US companies over the period 1970-1980. The independent variables they studied were selected for two reasons: they were generally accepted leading or coincident indicators (such as share indices, GNP indicators, and the unemployment rate); or they were suggested by economic theories of the business cycle (e.g. supply/cost-push theories; monetary theories; or savings-investment theories). The variables examined under the latter heading included cost, price and profit indicators; interest rates and money supply statistics; and measures of savings, consumption, investment, output, productivity, capacity utilisation, retail sales, and new orders for durable goods.

As might be expected, there was a high degree of correlation between many of the variables, and this enabled the number dealt with to be reduced from 28 to 10. The resulting regression model fitted extremely well, explaining over 90 per cent of changes in the rate of business failures over the business cycle. However, even this was improved upon when lagging was introduced (e.g. when the failure rate in quarter t was associated with the interest rate at quarter t-4), the final equation including the following independent variables:

(1) change in a stock exchange index;
(2) private investment/GNP;
(3) post tax company profits/value added by companies (e.g. wages, profits, etc);
(4) two measures of interest rates; and
(5) retail sales/GNP.

In fact, the Rose, Andrews and Giroux study was not the first to try to relate the incidence of corporate failure to macroeconomic indicators. Altman (1971) tried to explain changes in the number of US quarterly bankruptcies over the period 1947-1970 in terms of changes in GNP, a stock exchange index and money supply aggregates. However, these three variables only accounted for 19 per cent of movements in the corporate failure rate.

In terms of the UK, Goudie and Meeks (1982) examined the effects of macroeconomic changes on the working capital funds flows of failing companies. Subsequently Goudie (1987) integrated the Cambridge Growth Project (CGP) multi-sectoral dynamic model of the UK economy – which forecasts activity levels in 39 different industries – with a model incorporating company financial ratios (reflecting profitability, liquidity, cash flow, and income and capital gearing). This was done retrospectively for the Top 100 companies over the period 1976-1980. Of these companies, 9 were correctly classified as being in difficulty, 9 were incorrectly so classified, and 3 were wrongly classified as not being in distress. These results are not all that impressive, but in part they are dependent on the accuracy of the CGP model in being able to forecast correctly changes in the UK economy.

In another UK study, but one primarily concerned to distinguish bankrupt from non-failed companies, El Hennawy and Morris (1983a) attempted to capture economy wide factors by including changes in a share price index as an independent variable. However, this did not add to the explanatory power of their model, and consequently it was dropped.

In practice, it is not easy to include macroeconomic indicators in a corporate failure model with any great expectation of success. This is because the samples are often relatively small, the data are generally pooled over a short period of time, and there is a selection bias towards including failures at low points in the business cycle. A further difficulty is that matching procedures are normally employed which will substantially neutralise systematic economic factors that affect all companies.

In the circumstances, it is probably best to consider using macroeconomic variables as a means of screening data and determining when corporate bankruptcies are likely to arise. Only subsequently will it be appropriate for analysts to examine industry and firm specific variables to try to determine which companies are most at risk.

*Industry indicators*

Attempts to develop industry based models have been made on a number of occasions. These have the advantage that they capture industry specific economic and accounting characteristics, which should mean the models are more effective in discriminating between failed and non-failed businesses as it will no longer be necessary to pool non-homogeneous data.[1] Consequently, the models will be less likely just to reflect general 'least common denominator' financial characteristics, which in broad terms will (not unexpectedly) distinguish bankrupt from surviving firms (e.g. profitability and indebtedness). Moreover, they might also be expected to identify failing businesses rather earlier.

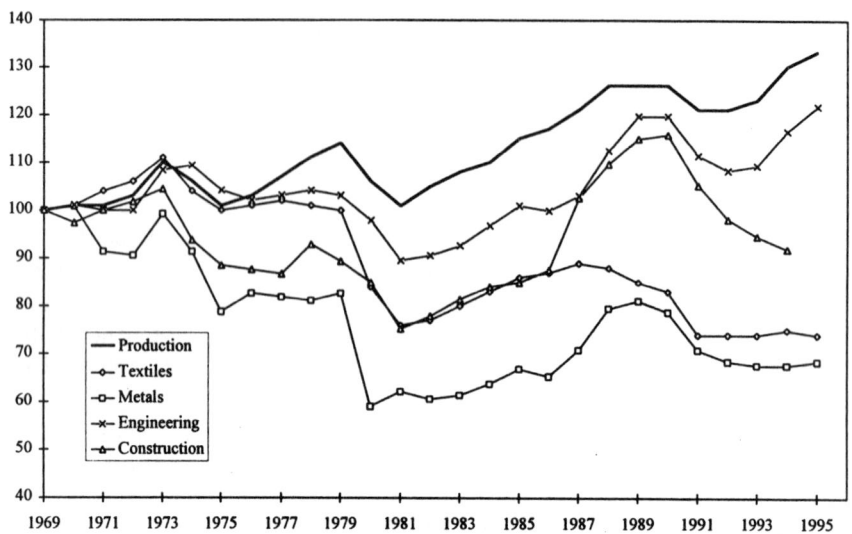

**Figure 9.1**

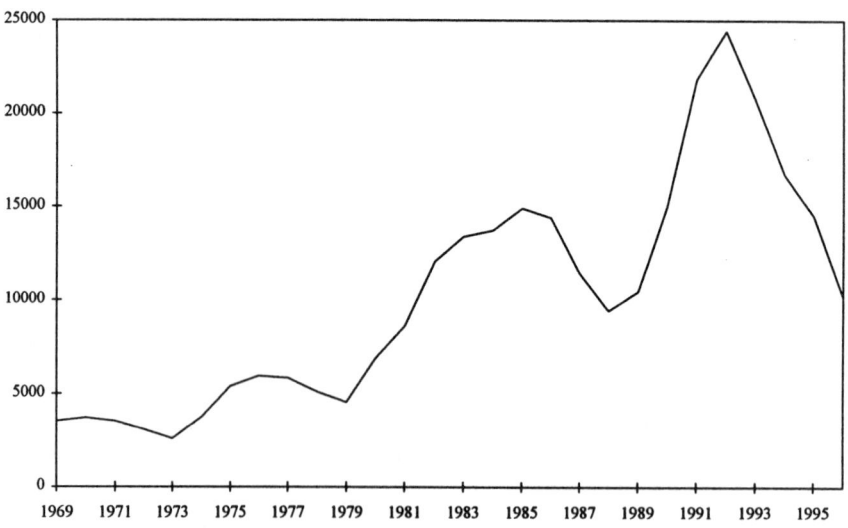

**Figure 9.2**

222

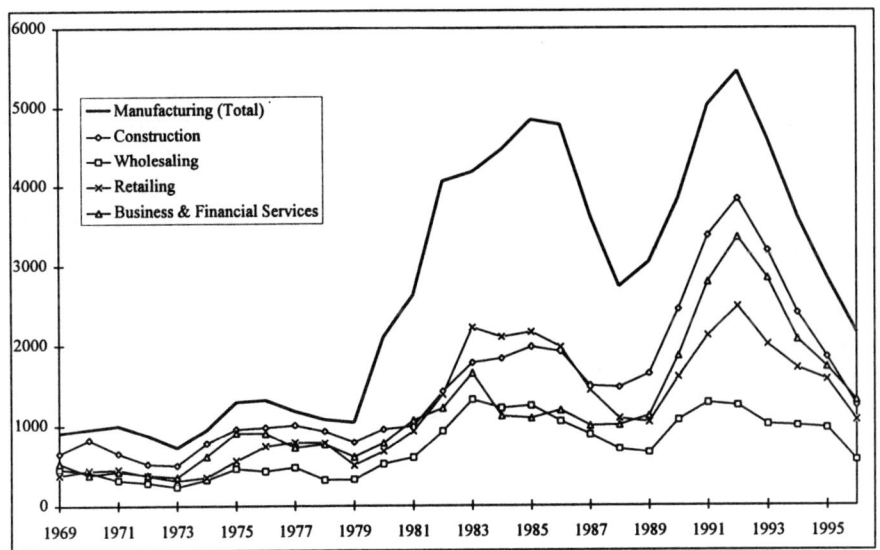

**Figure 9.3**

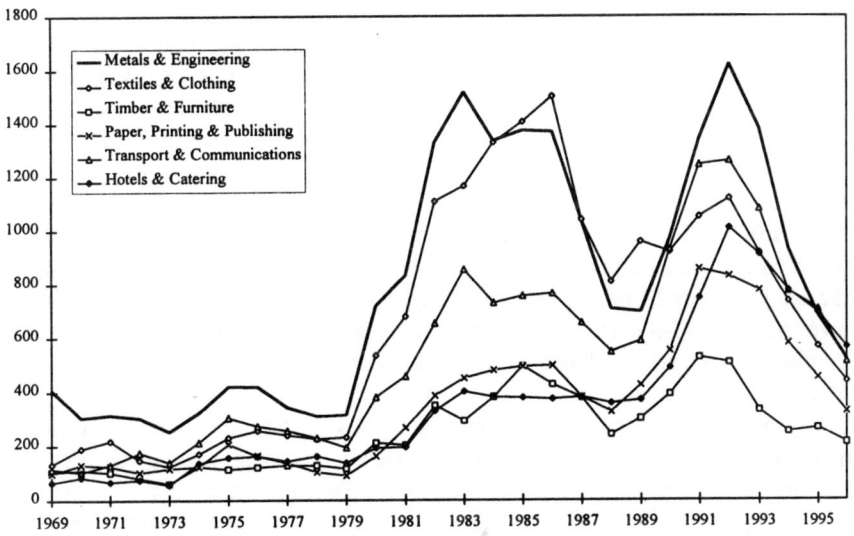

**Figure 9.4**

The fact that particular industries are vulnerable at different stages in the economic cycle is easily appreciated. Thus in 1974 property companies in the UK suffered when there was a sharp decline in the value of their assets, which in turn precipitated a crisis in the secondary banking sector. Similarly, in the late 1970s companies which were overdependent on oil were hit when OPEC raised the price of crude; and likewise competition from abroad virtually wiped out the British toy industry. Other sectors have also suffered for a variety of reasons largely outside their control (e.g. movements in exchange rates which affect the prices of their raw materials or their competitive edge in export markets; or technical innovations by overseas competitors).

The experience in industries in which there were significant numbers of bankruptcies in England and Wales over the period 1969-1996 is shown in Figures 9.1-9.4. Figure 9.1 plots industrial production index data for the period, using 1969 as the base year. It can immediately be seen that there is a systematic pattern, with all industries tending to suffer in periods of recession. However, it is also evident that some sectors have fared worse than others over the 27 year period. From 1976 onwards all four broad industry sectors whose output data are plotted (textiles, metals, engineering and construction) fared worse than manufacturing industry in general; and in particular the steady decline in metals and textiles can be seen, with a very sharp fall in output in these sectors in 1980. By contrast, the construction industry experienced much stronger recoveries when the economy came out of recession. Behaviour in other sectors whose data are not plotted (e.g. chemicals) was very different: sustained growth was achieved over the 27 year period, with at worst a temporary slow down during recessionary periods.

Figure 9.2 plots total corporate bankruptcies in England and Wales (see also the series reported in Appendix 9.1), and it can be seen that these rose sharply from 1980 onwards, reaching peaks in 1985 and 1992. However, it is necessary to remember that these data merely record absolute numbers: they do not allow for the size of the businesses forced into receivership, the vast majority of which were very small.

Figures 9.3 and 9.4 give a break-down of the data plotted in Figure 9.2. In the first instance these are shown in Figure 9.3 by broad industry category, which indicates that manufacturing suffered badly in both the 1980 and 1990 recessions. However, it is also clear that construction, distribution and the business and financial services sectors fared far worse in relative terms in the early 1990s than they did a decade earlier.

The more detailed data plotted in Figure 9.4 further illustrate the different experiences of various industry sectors. Metals and engineering, textiles and transport and communications all suffered substantial numbers of corporate bankruptcies in the 1980 and 1990 recessions, but in relative terms textiles fared far worse in the early 1980s. Likewise, there was a far higher failure rate in hotels and catering in the 1990 recession than a decade earlier.

But if it is highly desirable to try to develop industry specific models, at a practical level it is extremely difficult to do so. The main problem is that the population of failed and non-failed listed companies in a particular sector is generally far too small. (Such a difficulty is less likely to arise for private companies, of course.) In practice, however, it has proved possible in the US to develop industry models for the banking, savings and loan (i.e. building society) and railway sectors.[2] In the UK, apart from the study by Goudie (1987) referred to above, which incorporated forecasts for 39 different sectors, the only experiment along these lines concerns the construction sector, for which Mason and Harris (1979) successfully developed a failure identification model.

But if it is difficult in practice to develop specific industry models, it is at least possible to segregate firms into broad categories, such as manufacturing and retailing. Thus Taffler's earlier models related exclusively to manufacturing concerns, but later a separate model was developed for retailers (Taffler, 1984).

Another possibility is to introduce a dummy variable[3] to capture specific industry effects. This was done in a UK context by El Hennawy and Morris (1983a), who were thus able to distinguish between companies in the construction, manufacturing and retailing sectors.

*Private company models*

Most of the models developed and described in the literature have related to listed companies. The characteristics of private companies are likely to be rather different, if only because their lack of access to capital markets is likely to be reflected in their financial structures.[4] Consequently it would be inappropriate to try to apply models developed for listed companies to small businesses. Rather, some means is needed to allow for the fundamental differences between the two types of company. One way would be to use a dummy variable approach, but in practice it has been more usual to derive separate models for the small business sector.

In the US the first model along these lines was developed by Edmister (1971, 1972). He defined his failure group as businesses which had borrowed from the Small Business Administration and were reporting losses. He focused on a three year period and used a regression model with a dichotomous dependent variable. This reduced the number of 'failures' to 42. (There would have been 562 if losses in only one year had been used as the criterion for determining 'failure'.) The independent variables were 19 financial ratios, but these were scaled as 0 or 1 depending on their relationship to the industry average ratio. Using a matched pair procedure, the equation which resulted included seven variables, and the model classified firms with an overall accuracy rate of over 90 per cent.

In the UK several small company models have been developed. The first was produced by Tisshaw (1976), and was based on 31 relatively large private companies which failed in 1975-1976. These were each matched with two non-

225

failed concerns, and the model that resulted included five financial ratios as independent variables. The model was respecified by Taffler (1982), using 39 firms which failed between 1978 and 1981 with a control group of 56 companies. The MDA equation which resulted comprised four ratio variables. However, the firms included in the study were again the larger private companies, and although the model correctly classified companies with an accuracy of over 90 per cent, in the early 1980s around 25 per cent of the companies in the Extel Unquoted Companies Service were shown to be at risk (Taffler, 1984, p. 219).

Subsequently other private company models have been developed relating to rather smaller businesses (e.g. Keasey and Watson, 1986, 1987, 1988; and Peel and Peel, 1987, 1988).

*Location/spatial analysis*

A firm's vulnerability is just as likely to be associated with its location as with its industry membership. This is recognised by the fact that bankruptcy identification models have been developed for a variety of countries.[5]

It is also possible to develop models relating to particular geographical areas within a country. Such a technique is especially appropriate for private companies, and Keasey and Watson (1986) developed a model based on the experience of small manufacturing firms located in the north east of England.

More generally, Hudson (1987) examined the experience of 1,830 British companies which went into liquidation between 1978 and 1981. These were analysed in terms of age since incorporation, industry membership, and location (the latter being expressed in terms of 11 regions in Great Britain). All three factors were found to help explain the pattern of bankruptcies, with a very high attrition rate being recorded after an initial 'honeymoon period' of 1-2 years. However, the location of failures appeared to be substantially determined by the distribution of industries across the country.

Another approach is to undertake spatial analysis to identify whether firms in specific regions are more likely to fail than those in other locations. A number of studies have been undertaken along these lines,[6] including Birley and Westhead (1992). They used factor analysis on the 695,000 VAT deregistrations that were recorded in the UK between 1987 and 1990. An initial set of 52 surrogate independent variables was identified, capturing such attributes as industry structure/barriers to entry; industrial concentration/regional specialisation; plant size; average age of businesses/new entrants; 'agglomeration' economies; rural characteristics; availability of floor-space; market demand/level of local deprivation; average business profitability; access to finance; and workforce skills. The independent variable set was reduced to 16 indicators, and this enabled seven distinct economic regions to be identified.

Keeble and Walker (1993) identified 31 variables and examined the pattern of company births and deaths over the period 1980-1990, using VAT registrations as their database. As might be expected, they found higher birth rates (and correspondingly higher death rates) in the south. Key explanatory variables were population growth, capital availability (proxied by house values), unemployment rates (proxying for demand), and the local skill base. It also appears that above average local government expenditure and assistance from enterprise agencies helps to reduce death rates.

*Firm specific data*

*(i) Company characteristics* A number of researchers have tried to use indicators which reflect the characteristics of a company but which are not necessarily captured by accounting indicators. These include the following:

(1) age since incorporation
(2) the degree of diversification
(3) changes in lines of business
(4) changes in company name
(5) rate of organic growth
(6) acquisitions and disposals of subsidiaries
(7) closure and redundancy costs
(8) dividend policy
(9) years since a dividend was last declared
(10) years since a profit was last reported
(11) years since sales last increased
(12) share price return
(13) bond yield
(14) risk index

Given the fact that with small businesses there is a high attrition rate, especially in the early years after a firm commences trading, the age factor is likely to be of some significance (see, for instance, Hudson, 1987). It is less likely to be important for listed companies, although there is a history of failures with newcomers to the market. However, this often seems to be as much to do with their small size and lack of diversification as with anything else.

A diversified business would seem more likely to be able to survive a setback in one sector, so some measure of the spread of a company's activities is likely to be useful. However, this is not easy to measure, although the list of activities in the directors' report gives some indication on this point. Similarly, information from this source can indicate a change in activities, although sometimes the elimination of a line of business can be a good sign, at others a bad news signal. Likewise, it is difficult to interpret whether expansion into a new area is good or bad, but what is apparent is that it represents a change in a company's equilibrium position.

A change in a company's name often signals an attempt to change its direction or image, and so again it is a prima facie indicator of disequilibrium.

Other indicators which may convey similar information are the rate of growth in assets or turnover; the pattern of acquisitions and disposals; and evidence of closure and redundancy costs. However, these indicators on their own are not very informative: really they need to be interpreted in conjunction with one or more of the other indicators referred to above.

Fairly obviously dividend policy can be a useful indicator of the extent of the difficulties in which a company finds itself. Thus DeAngelo and DeAngelo (1990) found that between 1980 and 1985 almost all of the 80 financially distressed US listed companies that they surveyed reduced their distributions to shareholders, despite the fact that there must have been few investment projects available to them which showed positive net present values. However, very few passed their dividends, and this reluctance to pass dividends was just as evident where there was no penalty that could be exacted because of the existence of debt covenants. Presumably, therefore, the reason for cutting dividends was primarily to conserve cash in the face of capital rationing, but the maintenance of a payout (albeit at a reduced level) was a signal that a turn round was anticipated.[7]

More generally, the periods since dividends have been reduced or declared, and/or since profits and sales have increased, can be regarded as general indicators of the financial difficulties facing a company. For this reason such indicators have sometimes been used as independent variables in failure identification models.

But perhaps the best measures of financial distress would seem to be those which indicate analysts' perceptions of companies' future prospects. After all, these will reflect their evaluation of the entire information set available in the public domain. Thus a share price return, especially when compared against market wide share price movements and rival companies' returns, will indicate not only relative performance but also analysts' collective expectations of future likely outcomes.[8] Similarly, changes in the redemption yields of long term debt will indicate investors' perceptions of risk, which should in turn be reflected in various indices of risk, such as bond and credit ratings; and increasing variability in share prices.

*(ii) The board of directors.*[9] The directors of a company are naturally, because of their position, better informed about the prospects of a business than outside parties. But the latter can to some extent infer management's views about a company's future prospects from their behaviour. In this context, there are a number of variables that can be examined to see if there is a clue to management's expectations, including the following:

(1)   the proportion of shares held by directors
(2)   changes in the proportion of shares held by directors
(3)   changes in the board – appointments and resignations

(4) the lag and any change in the lag between the year end date and the date of the directors' report

(5) directors' remuneration and changes therein

Fairly obviously the proportion of shares held by directors gives some indication of their commitment to a company, and in terms of small private companies this is often regarded as a key indicator. But it also often a matter of interest to analysts when studying the affairs of small listed companies, and they routinely watch *The Stock Exchange Weekly Intelligence* for changes in directors' holdings in quoted companies to see if there is anything which appears to be out of the ordinary.[10] Because of this, researchers have sometimes included directors' shareholdings and changes in such holdings as variables in failure identification studies.

Changes in a board of directors can also be significant: e.g. a key personality may resign or retire; or a particular person (for instance, a so-called 'company doctor') may be appointed to turn round a company's fortunes.[11] Unfortunately it is not usually possible to identify the personalities or the reasons for a change in the board in objective numerical terms. Nevertheless, researchers have sometimes included indicators of appointments and resignations of directors in their studies, usually scaling for the size of the board.

In fact, it could be argued that changes in shareholdings of directors should pick up most of the information that might be captured by measuring changes in board membership. Thus newcomers to a board normally acquire shares on taking office, and if they are confident about the future it might be expected that they will take a sizeable stake in a business. If they do not (e.g. in the case of a company doctor), it could be a signal of uncertainty about the future. Likewise, if the founder of a business with a sizeable stake in a company retires, this will normally show itself in a sharp drop in shares held by the directors.

This raises a point about the measurement of board members' shareholdings. It is possible from information disclosed in directors' reports to identify increases and decreases in the shareholdings of directors in office in each particular year. An alternative procedure is to measure shareholdings of board members at the end of each year, whoever they may be, and to calculate the changes in the aggregate holdings year by year. The information captured will be slightly different, but the overall picture is likely to be the much the same.

Other information that can be derived from annual reports relating to directors is the lag between the accounting year end date and the date of the directors' report. An increase in the lag could be an indication of a problem (e.g. a delay in preparing the accounts; a dispute within the board; or a disagreement with the auditors). However, this will normally be evident from other potential indicators referred to below (e.g. the lag between the accounting year end date and the date of the auditors' report; or the lag between the accounting year end date and the publication or filing date of the annual report).

229

Finally, a change in directors' remuneration may sometimes be an indicator of a potential problem within a company – although it is not always obvious what direction this might be. Thus sometimes board members will cut their remuneration if a company is performing badly. However, on other occasions the total remuneration may increase: e.g. if a company doctor is appointed, he may expect to earn high fees; and likewise other newly appointed directors if they are taking above average risks.

*(iii) Accounting year end date.*[12] It is also possible sometimes to infer something about a company's position and prospects from its year end date, for instance with respect to:

(1) a change in the year end date;
(2) the lag between the accounting year end date and the date of publication of the annual report; and
(3) a change in the lag between the accounting year end date and the publication or filing date of the annual report.

It seems that when companies change the nature of their operations (i.e. where there is prima facie evidence of disequilibrium), they sometimes alter their names and/or their financial year ends. Consequently the latter could be used as an indicator of evidence of instability.

Another variable that may be of interest is the lag between the accounting year end date and the date of publication of the annual report. However, by itself such an indicator is of limited interest. Comparisons with the lags of similar companies may be of some relevance, but probably the most appropriate indicator would be increases in the lag over time as this could be the result of problems within the company.

*(iv) Changes in accounting policy.* Companies which are facing financial problems may, as a short term expedient, try to manipulate figures in their accounts in order to mask the true situation.[13] However, the very fact that it is evident that accounting policies have changed suggests that the strategy has failed. Nevertheless, evidence of attempts to disguise the true financial position may signal that a company is facing difficulties, and it is therefore potentially useful monitoring changes in accounting policies.

*(v) Auditors.* Clearly if a company is in financial distress, its auditors should be carefully considering whether or not it is a going concern. This may mean that they will want to carry out additional checks; or, indeed, that there may be potential differences of view between them and the board of directors. These could lead to their resignation; to their report being qualified; to the lag between the year end date and the date of their report being lengthened; to their fee being abnormally

high (e.g. if internal controls are weak); or to the fee increasing (e.g. if additional work has to be undertaken). Consequently, the following potential independent variables may be relevant:

(1) change in the auditor;
(2) qualification in the audit report – going concern and other;
(3) the lag between year end date and the date of the audit report;
(4) change in the lag between the year end date and the date of the audit report; and
(5) auditors' remuneration and changes therein.

*(vi) Indebtedness.* Although indebtedness of itself is not necessarily a matter for concern, it may indicate the level of risk facing a firm, particularly if its leverage structure is such that a large proportion of its operating costs are fixed. As a result, a number of indicators relating to this factor are potentially of interest, including the following:

(1) the gearing ratio;
(2) with respect to secured loans, a change in a debt covenant or a change in the register of charges;
(3) bond ratings; and
(4) credit ratings.

The gearing ratio can be measured in various ways, as indicated previously (pp. 96-8), but a matter of particular interest is the security taken, any changes in debt covenants or registered charges, and the values of the assets which are subject to a charge.

In fact, it is difficult in practice to monitor changes in debt covenants. However, it is possible to identify assets which are the subject of a charge from the register of charges, although it is not always easy for the outsider to assess the adequacy or otherwise of the security. Nevertheless, a priori one might expect that if secured creditors think they are at risk they might well seek to extend their charges (e.g. take a fixed charge over specific assets where previously they only enjoyed a floating charge). On the other hand, it is in the nature of any sizeable business that some of its loans are maturing and being replaced by new borrowing facilities, so that even for sound businesses there are likely to be changes in its register of charges at fairly regular intervals. In other words, it is not easy for an outsider unaware of a company's particular circumstances, its unencumbered assets, and their market values to assess the true position because there is considerable 'noise' in the changes in the charges that are registered. Nevertheless, despite these problems a number of researchers have attempted to include as independent variables indicators of security taken over assets.

But, as mentioned previously, perhaps the best overall measure of risk and indebtedness is given by bond and credit ratings, which reflect analysts' views after they have accessed a comprehensive set of data relating to the position and prospects of a particular company.[14]

*(vii) Studies using qualitative firm specific indicators.* Relatively few studies have explored the possibility of using qualitative or other firm specific non-ratio indicators, and several have not specifically focused on the failure/non-failure dichotomy.

Marais, Patell and Wolfson (1984), for instance, developed a recursive partitioning model for US bank loan classifications, used 13 such indicators.[15] These included three debt rating variables, as well as indicators relating to dividend payments, share price return and its variance, whether equity net worth was positive, the number of years since a profit or an increase in sales had been reported, whether the audit opinion was qualified, and how long data about the company had been filed.

In terms of failure/non-failure classification, Peel, Peel and Pope (1985) first used a set of seven qualitative indicators to distinguish between 34 failed and 44 non-failed UK companies. The former went bankrupt between 1971 and 1982, while the data for the non-failed companies (which tended to be much larger) were based on a single year, 1980. The seven variables related to the reporting lag and changes therein; changes in directors' shareholdings; director appointments and resignations as proportions of board membership, and changes therein. Using a logit model, but without adjusting for sampling bias, all the variables proved significant in enabling the failed and non-failed companies to be distinguished from each other, with the exception of changes in directors' shareholdings and changes in the proportion of director appointments.

In a follow up paper, Peel, Peel and Pope (1986) used the same sample and combined five of the seven qualitative variables with four financial indicators.[16] The results suggested that the qualitative variables captured information not contained in the ratios, and this reduced misclassification of both failed and non-failed companies. Moreover, this was confirmed when the model was tested on a hold out sample of 12 failed and 12 non-failed companies.

Peel and Peel (1988) then used much the same data (but with a slightly different hold out sample) to see whether logit models developed for each of the three years prior to failure could be used in conjunction with each other to give an estimate not only of *whether* a company might fail, but also of *when* that event might occur. For this they reduced the variable set to two accounting ratios and one qualitative variable, the reporting lag. The experiment worked quite well, as failing companies were showing distinct differences from their non-failing counterparts in the third year before failure. It was therefore possible to identify a downwards path prior to failure and hence to estimate the date of failure.

In another UK study, Keasey and Watson (1987) examined 18 qualitative variables in trying to determine the causes of failure in small companies. The indicators used included the age of the company; the number of directors, and directors' resignations and appointments; the number of outside shareholders; new capital introduced; changes in auditors and qualifications in their reports; secured loans; and audit report and filing lags.

Other studies that have focused on the timeliness of private companies' accounts in the UK in the context of failure identification are Peel (1987, 1990); and Storey, Keasey, Watson and Wynarczyk (1987).

Another type of study uses a qualitative indicator as the dependent variable. This is usually a change in auditor; or the existence of a qualification in the audit report. However, it can also be an indicator of risk attaching to corporate loan stock. [17]

In their study, Schwartz and Menon (1985) found a much higher likelihood of companies which ultimately went bankrupt *switching their auditors*.

The first researchers to suggest in effect that the existence of *a qualification in the audit report* could be taken as the dependent variable were Altman and McGough (1974).[18] Using the original discriminant model of Altman (1968), they examined the Z-scores for 34 US companies and then checked to see how many of those signalled as failing had in fact had qualified audit reports in the run-up to bankruptcy. The analysis showed that the audit reports of 13 of 28 had been qualified in the final year of operations; and 7 out of 34 in the previous year.

Other studies along similar lines have been undertaken by Altman (1983), Mutchler (1985) and Koh and Killough (1990).

Altman's study covered 109 US companies which failed over the period 1970-1982, and he found his models could classify the event correctly one year prior to bankruptcy in 86.2 per cent of the cases. By contrast auditors only entered a going concern qualification 48.1 per cent of the time. The Koh and Killough study was along similar lines, a discriminant ratio model derived from a sample of 35 failed and 35 non-failed US companies being used to classify a randomly selected hold out sample of 400 companies over the period 1980-1985. Only 14 of these failed, and while 78.6 per cent were correctly classified by the model, only 21.4 per cent had received a going concern qualification. By contrast, the model incorrectly predicted that 44 (or 11.4 per cent) of the non-failed companies would go bankrupt, a very similar 'error' rate to the auditors, who entered 43 (or 11.1 per cent) going concern qualifications.

Mutchler's study used a discriminant model that achieved a 90 per cent accuracy rate in classifying failed/non-failed companies in a hold out sample. The model incorporated qualitative as well as ratio data, and the implication of the results was that going concern qualifications do not convey incremental information to readers of financial statements.

A number of techniques of textual analysis have been developed which have helped to answer a variety of questions – e.g. were the works of Shakespeare, Marlowe, and/or Bacon written by the same person? Nowadays it is even easier to apply these as the texts of plays and novels can be scanned by an optical reader for direct inputting and subsequent analysis on a computer.

But it is not just *word patterns* that can be recognised. Techniques have also been devised to analyse the *content* of statements. These comprise methods which assess both the *readability* of statements and also the extent to which they can be *understood* by readers.

'Readability formulae' essentially measure word length and sentence construction, examples being the LIX, FOG and FLESCH indicators. Thus the LIX index measures the average number of words in a sentence and the percentage of words which are greater than six letters. The FOG index is not dissimilar in concept, except that it concentrates on words that may be difficult to understand rather than their length. The FLESCH formula is more complicated, but basically it measures the number of syllables per 100 words and the total number of words in a statement divided by the total number of sentences.

The CLOZE technique focuses instead on 'understandability'. This is assessed by deleting words at regular intervals in a statement and then seeing whether readers can still understand its content. If they can, then presumably it is not complex; whereas if they cannot, the message or arguments being communicated are prima facie difficult to comprehend.

A variation of this approach is to diagnose a number of 'themes' by identifying relationships between words and then measuring the frequency with which they recur in the text. A package which does this is WORDS (see Tennyson, Ingram and Dugan, 1990).

Content analysis has been used by a number of researchers in the US and UK to examine the readability of chairmen's statements and/or notes appended to accounting statements (e.g. Soper and Dolphin, 1964; Still, 1972; Frazier, Ingram and Tennyson, 1984).[20]

There is also a possible role for textual analysis in the context of failure identification studies, the hypotheses being:

(1) that the directors' reports and/or chairmen's statements of companies experiencing financial problems will become more complex and difficult to understand as explanations are offered to shareholders; and
(2) that the information thus communicated is useful in providing incremental information to financial ratio indicators in enabling failing companies to be distinguished from their non-failing counterparts.

In fact, there have been two studies along these lines, where textual analysis indicators have been used as independent variables in relation to failure/non-failure. The study by Tennyson, Ingram and Dugan (1990) focused on the directors' reports and chairmen's statements of 23 US companies which failed in 1980 and 23 matched pairs of non-failing companies. They identified five 'themes' in the chairmen's statements and directors' reports, and there were indeed significant differences in the patterns observed. Moreover, using a logit model and including ratios used by Altman (1968) they were able to show that there appeared to be some incremental information in the textual analysis indicators.

The second study employing content analysis in the context of corporate failure is that of Smith and Taffler (1992). This focused on 33 British companies which failed over the period 1978-1985 and their matched pairs of non-failing companies. The LIX and FLESCH readability measures showed that, as expected, the reports of failing companies were more complex than those of non-failing companies. However, when the CLOZE technique was applied, the subjects did not show a high degree of understanding for either group of companies – a result which might in part reflect the unsophistication of the students used as the subject group in the experiment.

Although these results suggest that the technique may be useful, there is (as usual) a problem in using the matched pairing procedure. In order to be sure that the approach is helpful, it would really be necessary to choose a sample of company annual reports which more closely matched the incidence of failed and non-failed companies in the whole population of companies. It is then quite possible that there would be quite a large number of perfectly sound companies whose annual reports would be lengthy and where the sentence construction and arguments might be relatively complex. In other words, it may well be the case that bankrupt companies' annual reports exhibit these characteristics. But the reverse may not be true: i.e. complex statements do not necessarily imply that a company is facing financial distress.

## Measures used in management and corporate strategy studies

As was discussed in chapter 7, writers in the management literature have tended to adopt a case study approach to examine the complex interaction of variables that leads to a company's bankruptcy or its rescue in a 'turnaround' operation. It was explained there that some authors concentrate almost entirely on the case studies themselves, suggesting little in the way of an analytical structure. A few, however, have identified a number of variables that might lead to failure, although for the most part these can only be assessed subjectively.

It will be recalled that one writer who identified key variables is Argenti (1976). He developed what he describes as his 'A-score' approach by identifying five types of problem; while Slatter (1984) lists seven such factors. Briefly these can be summarised as follows:

(1) There are shortcomings in management (e.g. too much power is concentrated in the hands of one man, and the control mechanisms are weak).

(2) There are weaknesses in the accounting system and inadequate financial controls.

(3) The company is slow to react to changes in its environment (e.g. in responding to competition by developing new products, cutting costs, etc).

(4) Mistakes frequently lead to failure (e.g. overtrading, over-borrowing, lack of diversification, bad acquisitions policy).

(5) Symptoms of failure become evident as a company faces collapse (e.g. key ratios worsen).

Like Argenti, Slatter identifies a number of symptoms of decline that can be picked up from a company's financial statements: declining profitability, decreasing sales at constant prices, increased borrowing, a decline in liquidity, a cut in dividends to conserve cash, the use of creative accounting, changes in auditor, increasing delays before accounts are published, rapid management turnover, declining market share, lack of planning, and a paralysis of management decision making.

Some studies have been undertaken which try to assess the incidence of one or more of these variables, most notably in the small firm sector (e.g. Keasey and Watson, 1987; Peel, 1990). But it is more usual to employ questionnaire surveys and thus obtain the opinions of bankers, accountants and other interested parties on the causes of bankruptcy that they observe. One such study is that of the London Business School (1987). This involved a survey of 100 bank managers, obtaining their views on the perceived factors for the failure of a sample of 437 businesses which went bankrupt in 1985/86 within their first five years of trading. On average no fewer than 7 out of 26 potential causes of failure were identified for each business, the most common being undercapitalisation and poor operating management.

Other recent UK studies in a similar vein have been carried out by Cressey and Storey (1995) and Birley and Niktari (1995). The Cressey and Storey study analysed data relating to 2,000 NatWest bank customers who commenced business in 1988 and a further 750 who set up in 1991. Only a fifth of the accounts of the 1988 cohort were still open 6 years later. However, analysis over a 12 month period in 1991/92 showed that only 27 per cent of the account closures were caused by insolvency, the remainder mainly being the result of decisions by entrepreneurs to close their businesses. Whether the incidence of bankruptcy was greater or less in other years was not examined. In fact, it is clear from the income figures and the average size of the sums borrowed that many of the so-called businesses must have been individuals supplementing their pensions or earnings in other jobs. Moreover, while in 70 per cent of the cases where closures resulted from insolvency the bank had to write off some of the debts outstanding as bad, its losses were generally modest.

In their study Birley and Niktari asked accountants and bankers to answer 87 questions concerning the causes of failure in the most recent bankrupt small company that they had dealt with. The analysis of 468 responses showed a wide variety of reasons, depending in part on the industry membership of the subject companies. Overall 24 individual factors were identified from the 87 reasons given for failure, including: rising costs, marketing management, capital structure and financial management, ownership and management characteristics, planning, the quality of goods and services provided, the state of the local or national economy, pricing policies, obsolescence of product or service, narrowness of customer base, growth policy, staff management, changes in legislation, and financing costs. After interrelationships between these factors were taken into account, seven 'clusters' were identified (with percentages of businesses affected shown in brackets): (i) Unlucky (34.8 per cent); (ii) Out of control (8.7 per cent); (iii) Out of balance (11.5 per cent); (iv) Disasters (0.01 per cent); (v) Niche businesses (8.9 per cent); (vi) Poor systems (21.4 per cent); and (vii) Marketing and market problems (13.7 per cent).

However, a problem with this study – as indeed with others of this type – is that the controls tend to be weak. For instance, there is no indication how frequently similar characteristics to those observed also related to non-failed companies; nor to whether the samples selected were truly representative. There is additionally the problem that the characteristics may well to a considerable extent be 'situation specific': i.e. relate to the particular economic circumstances when the survey was undertaken (for instance, when there was a recession affecting particular types of business).

**The acquisition/failure alternative**

There is one other area where non-financial indicators are relevant, and that concerns studies of the acquisition/failure alternative. In such circumstances, effectively what is being done is to introduce a dummy variable to explain 'failure' either in terms of bankruptcy or of acquisition by another company.[21] However, in practice such studies are usually undertaken by establishing three dichotomous categories for the dependent variable: acquisition, bankruptcy and independent survival.

The liquidation/merger issue was first raised in the 1960s, although the main empirical studies in the US are of more recent origin. Shrieves and Stevens (1979) studied a sample of 112 matched pairs of manufacturing firms between 1948 and 1971, a half of which had been taken over. Applying Altman's (1968) failure identification model they found that 15 per cent of the acquired companies were flagged as being at risk compared to only 5 per cent of the non-acquired firms.

They therefore concluded that a merger was seen by some companies – and especially their managers – as an alternative to liquidation.

Pastena and Ruland (1986) adopted a different approach and tried to distinguish between those companies which might opt for acquisition when in distress as against those which would be forced into bankruptcy. The variables used in their model related to ownership concentration, gearing, size and tax credits. A model was developed on a sample of 42 failed and 68 distressed firms which were taken over. The latter were identified using Altman's (1968) model to screen a population of 531 companies which were acquired between 1970 and 1983. Using a probit model, it was possible to classify the failed and taken over firms with a 76 per cent accuracy rate.

Peel and Wilson (1989) and Peel (1990) replicated the Pastena and Ruland study on UK data covering the period 1972-1979. The sample comprised 47 failed companies, 40 randomly selected non-failed businesses, and 32 distressed companies which were taken over. The latter were identified in terms of negative working capital positions, and whether or not they were reporting losses and/or their accounts were subject to going concern audit qualifications. Discriminant and logit models were used, with more than 30 variables available for analysis, including indicators of directors' shareholdings, directors' remuneration, reporting lags, audit qualifications and share price movements. The results showed that some 17 per cent of acquired UK quoted industrial firms in the period appeared to have been financially distressed. Moreover, it was clear that the failing companies were more financially distressed than those taken over. However, unlike the Pastena and Ruland study, size and ownership concentration did not appear to be important explanatory factors.

More recently, Cosh and Hughes (1993, 1995) have examined the liquidation/merger alternative with respect to UK private companies. Using a DTI stratified sample of 2,000 companies over the period 1976-1982 they were able to identify 142 acquired companies, 182 firms which failed, and 1,296 which survived. The analysis in the 1993 study was conducted using 25 variables (3 measuring size, 10 liquidity and gearing, 8 profitability, and 4 proxies for 'management quality' – the number of directors and details of their emoluments). (35 variables were used in the 1995 study.) The results showed that size was a critical factor, that both failed and acquired companies were less profitable than survivors, but that failed firms were noticeably worse in this respect and were also less liquid than acquired and surviving companies. In terms of a multivariate model, failed firms were much easier to distinguish from surviving businesses than acquired companies, but matching by size and industry reduced classificational accuracy to only 66 per cent.

Another recent British study on this issue is that by Wilson, Chong and Peel (1995).[22] They applied the neural networking (NN) technique (see p. 159 et seq.) to analyse the sample of companies previously examined by Peel (1990) (see above). The results showed that the NN model was slightly better at discriminating between the three groups of companies (failed, non-failed, and distressed-but-taken-over). However, given a random prior expectation of correctly classifying a company of 50 per cent, the performance of the model was not that impressive on two hold out samples, only some 70 per cent of bankrupt firms being correctly identified, compared to over 80 per cent of non-failed businesses and a mere 50 per cent of the acquired-but-distressed companies.

## Summary

It is clear that a large number of non-financial indicators can be referred to both in order to try to get early warning of financial distress and to establish the underlying economic causes of failure. Some of these are general in nature (e.g. being macroeconomic, industry or locational indicators). Others are firm specific (e.g. relating to directors; changes in financial year, accounting policies, auditors or company indebtedness). Efforts have also been made to assess the style and content of the chairmen's reports. Empirical evidence suggests that all these can be used as indicators to help discriminate between failing and non-failing firms, although it is clear that in many cases their incidence is irregular.

It is also possible to develop a series of proxies in order to try to measure weaknesses in management and strategic planning: e.g. by checking on ownership concentration in order to establish whether or not a chief executive has dominant control.

A further issue which needs to be addressed is whether failure is inevitable. Certainly there is a growing amount of evidence which seems to indicate that some companies can avoid liquidation by seeking a merger. However, it appears that this option is not available to all distressed firms, presumably because their going concern values have fallen below their break up values. It seems likely that bankruptcy happens when there is overcapacity in an industry, but unfortunately none of the studies on the liquidation/merger alternative has addressed this matter.

## Notes

[1] See above, pp. 28 and 115.

[2] Altman (1973) produced a model dealing with the US railway industry in the wake of the Penn Central collapse; and, similarly, one for the savings and loan sector when disaster overtook it (Altman, 1977).

There have been a number of studies relating to the US banking industry, including Meyer and Pifer (1970), Sinkey (1975), Martin (1977), Santomero and Vinso (1977), West (1985), and Korobow and Stuhr (1985).

[3] See p. 121 for a brief explanation of the use of dummy variables.

[4] See p. 27 for a more general discussion of the problem of collecting economically meaningful data for small privately owned companies.

[5] Altman (1993, pp. 280-283) lists more than 50 models derived in 19 countries.

[6] See Keeble and Walker (1993) for references.

[7] Another reason in the UK context might be to retain trustee investment status.

[8] The pattern of share price returns in the run-up to bankruptcy is discussed elsewhere: pp. 183-5. However, it should be noted that Queen and Roll (1987) found that share price returns and their volatility were good indicators of a firm's vulnerability to failure.

[9] There has been a considerable amount of research in the US in recent years into 'top management team' (TMT) behaviour in failing firms. This is usually seen as part of 'downward spiralling' by such firms (Hambrick and d'Aveni, 1988) (see p. 202, note 2). Financially distressed companies are often characterised by greater chief executive officer (CEO) dominance, smaller TMTs, fewer outside directors, shorter average tenure of office, and less specialist expertise. Moreover, there is evidence that such differences are apparent more than five years before bankruptcy, and that deterioration accelerates over the last two years before collapse (Hambrick and d'Aveni, 1992). It is also clear that distressed companies are more likely to sack their CEOs and replace them with outsiders (Gilson, 1989). On average internal replacements tend to earn a third less than their predecessors, whereas the remuneration of external appointees is around a third greater. The rewards of directors drafted in from outside are also often tied to company performance, sometimes being linked to the value of creditors' claims rather than shareholder interests (Gilson and Vetsuypens, 1993). TMT changes involving the introduction of outsiders are generally greeted positively by the markets (Bonnier and Bruner, 1989; Denis and Denis, 1995), and on the face of it this appears to be justified as the continued involvement of management of distressed firms is strongly correlated with subsequent decline (Hotchkiss, 1995). However, there is also evidence that firm deterioration is often outside the direct control of management, with the market's reactions to decisions on downsizing, acquisitions, expansion, debt restructuring and raising capital through new issues not being significantly different as between distressed and non-distressed companies (Khanna and Poulsen, 1995). Nevertheless, the importance of intervention by creditors is clear. Share ownership of distressed companies often becomes more concentrated, with banks tightening their control over management by appointing directors and taking large blocks of shares, as well as by imposing tough restrictions via debt covenants (Gilson, 1990).

[10] Indeed, this is often seen as a potential indicator of insider trading activity in the UK: see Pope, Morris and Peel (1990); and Gregory, Matatko, Tonks and Purkis (1994). More generally, there is evidence in the US that corporate insiders, especially at the highest level, are heavy net sellers of their firm's shares as they approach bankruptcy: see, for example, Eyssell (1991).

[11] See Bonnier and Bruner (1989), who found that share prices of financially distressed companies reacted significantly to management changes.

[12] Studies on the significance of reporting lags as a signal of distress include Lawrence (1983) and Whittred and Zimmer (1984). For a more recent study of filing lags, see Alford, Jones and Zmijewski (1994).

[13] This point has been made by a number of commentators, including Pratten (1991) and Smith (1992, 1996). However, there are few studies on this specific point, the main one being by DeAngelo, DeAngelo and Skinner (1994). On the other hand, there is extensive evidence of manipulation in order to alter the impact of restrictions in explicit and implicit accounting based contracts (such as debt covenants; and wage or executive remuneration agreements); or as a result of government regulations (e.g. concerning taxation; defence, health service and other contracts; and import, price and monopoly controls). More generally, creative accounting, and in particular a short term 'profit improvement' strategy, is discussed on p. 212 et seq.

[14] Dun and Bradstreet refers to the payment experience of a large panel of creditors, and this is a key variable in its algorithm for determining credit ratings for UK private companies: see p. 33.

[15] See pp. 156-8 for a description of the recursive partitioning procedure.

[16] The ratios included related to size, flow of funds/total liabilities, sales/total liabilities, and net current assets/total assets. Strangely no direct measures of profitability or gearing were included, although these have generally proved to have most explanatory power in failure identification models. This might of course help to explain why the qualitative indicators appeared to add incremental information.

[17] Until fairly recently there were relatively few of these studies, the best known being those of Fisher (1959), Horrigan (1966) and West (1970). However, over the past few years their number has grown considerably, largely in response to the junk bond phenomenon. Many of the more recent studies are referred to in Altman (1993), and the results are fully discussed there.

[18] There is also a discussion in chapter 1 of studies concerned to identify whether qualifications are made in audit reports when failure prediction models signal impending bankruptcy: see pp. 39-41.

[19] See Jones and Shoemaker (1994) for a general survey of the various techniques and their application in an accounting context.

[20] A comprehensive list of references is given in Smith and Taffler (1992); and in Jones and Shoemaker (1994).

[21] There has also been research on the related issue of whether or not it is possible to distinguish between those bankrupt companies which will be liquidated and those which will be turned round. Thus Casey, McGee and Stickney (1986) used a probit model to see whether they could discriminate between liquidated and turned round firms. The sample used was 113 US companies which filed for bankruptcy between 1970 and 1981. The model performed reasonably well, the most significant distinguishing variables being the proportion of unencumbered assets and a proxy for earnings prospects. However, the misclassification rates

reported on both the experimental and hold out samples were high, being between 30 per cent and 40 per cent for both liquidated and turned round companies. Moreover, most of the indicators were derived from the last published accounts, when the companies were about to file for bankruptcy. In the circumstances, and once decision error costs are taken into account, it would seem that the model is probably of little use to investors and creditors.

In another (and more recent) study, Campbell (1996) examined the position of 121 closely held and financially distressed companies in Oregon, trying to see whether it is possible to discriminate between those small businesses which survive and those which do not. Using a probit model with a 50 per cent cut off criterion (despite the fact that survivors outnumbered liquidated firms by a ratio of 2:1 in his sample), Campbell concluded that his model could be used by 'an accountant ... as a decision aid when forming an expert opinion regarding a debtor's likelihood of rehabilitation'. However, this claim seems to be rather optimistic as the model was poor at correctly classifying failing firms which were ultimately liquidated, the error rate being 26 per cent in the analysis sample and as high as 60 per cent in the hold out test.

[22] The Wilson, Chong and Peel study is briefly described on p. 164.

## Appendix 9.1

*Company liquidations 1972-1996**

| 1972 | 1973 | 1974 | 1975 | 1976 | 1977 |
|------|------|------|------|------|------|
| 8,215 | 7,240 | 7,885 | 9,795 | 10,640 | 9,974 |

| 1978 | 1979 | 1980 | 1981 | 1982 | 1983 |
|------|------|------|------|------|------|
| 9,205 | 9,019 | 11,481 | 12,920 | 16,731 | 13,927 |

| 1984 | 1985 | 1986 | 1987 | 1988 | 1989 |
|------|------|------|------|------|------|
| 14,244 | 15,435 | 14,916 | 11,895 | 9,823 | 10,884 |

| 1990 | 1991 | 1992 | 1993 | 1994 | 1995 | 1996 |
|------|------|------|------|------|------|------|
| 15,521 | 22,443 | 25,095 | 21,259 | 16,728 | 14,536 | 13,461 |

* Insolvencies from 1983; the numbers include some unincorporated businesses.
*Source: Annual Abstracts of Statistics*

# Part Two
## THE EMPIRICAL STUDIES

# 10 The data

## Introduction

This chapter contains a description of three databases that were used to undertake the empirical studies which are reported in subsequent chapters. They cover the period 1973-1983 and refer respectively to 111, 75 and 61 matched pairs of listed companies (one failed, the other non-failed). The data represented in the databases comprise accounting, qualitative and share return indicators for periods of five or ten years.

Background material was also obtained for 25 of the bankrupt companies so that case studies could be written identifying the circumstances which led up to their failure. In addition, data were obtained for another 21 listed companies which went bankrupt over the period 1988-91. These were used to see, first, whether they would have been identified as prima facie failures by one or other of the key models derived from data in the earlier period; and, second, whether the circumstances leading up to their final collapse were on the face of it significantly different from those identified in the original 25 case studies.

## The sample companies

The sample data used for the studies reported in the following chapters were drawn from a population of UK bankrupt listed companies. The primary criterion was that a failed company should appear on the London Business School (LBS) share price data tapes and be classified there as failing during the 29 years 1956-1984. For this purpose, failure was defined as the company being put into the hands of a receiver or being wound up.

This generated a population of 343 companies, but 121 of these had to be eliminated from the sample because they were overseas companies, banks, companies whose businesses had been nationalised, insurance and shipping companies, investment trusts, or companies listed on the USM. This left a potential sample of 222 companies.

The next step was to screen the companies to find those for which the annual reports and accounts could be obtained for at least ten years before failure. This proved much more difficult than was originally anticipated, and even reducing the requirement to the annual reports and accounts for five years did not greatly expand the data set.

With respect to accounting data, the original intention was to use the Exstat database. Unfortunately it was found that this only covered 49 of the 222 companies (and then generally only in part) – and, further, these were merely some of the listed companies that failed in the period 1973-1983. Attempts were made to fill in the gaps by using the Department of Trade and Industry (DTI) database, but only a few of the missing companies and company-years data could be obtained in this way. As a result, it became necessary to refer back to the original failed company annual returns and accounts.

The plan was that qualitative indicators should be collected as well as accounting data, the primary source being the companies' annual reports. Initially it was intended that these should be obtained from the Companies House fiche and hard copy records. However, the fiche data were often incomplete (and anyway rarely go back before 1972); and Companies House had great difficulty in supplying photocopies of the hard copy annual reports which it is supposed to keep in storage. Ultimately reference had to be made to the only other source of company annual report information available for extinct companies, the MIRAC fiche service, which however does not go back before 1969.

Eventually it proved possible to obtain qualitative and accounting data going back ten years prior to failure for 75 of the 222 companies referred to above. Moreover, data five years prior to failure could be obtained for another 36 companies. The accounting data were primarily extracted from the Exstat database, but this was supplemented by information taken from the DTI datatapes. Nevertheless, a significant amount of financial statement data also had to be collected direct from the fiche and hard copy records of company annual reports.

As a result of these efforts two databases of failed companies were established:

(1) accounting and qualitative data for 75 failed companies going back 10 years prior to failure; and
(2) accounting and qualitative data for 111 failed companies going back 5 years prior to failure.[1]

Two points are worth noting about the companies represented in the sample of failed companies. First, most were very small listed companies; and, second, certain industry categories were heavily represented: namely, textiles 28; engineering and metals 28; construction 16; retail 7; electricals 5; furniture 5; toy manufacturers 5; food manufacturing 4; paper, packaging and publishing 4; and others 9. In fact, in the late 1970s and early 1980s the textile industry was severely hit by high interest rates, the strength of sterling and strong competition from overseas. The recession also brought the downfall of many engineering and construction companies, and the period under review witnessed the virtual elimination of the British toy manufacturing industry. (Indeed, it proved difficult to find surviving companies for the purpose of creating matched pairs.)

The incidence of failure by years also showed a degree of clustering, corresponding – as might be expected – to periods when the economy was under pressure. The incidence of failures was as follows:

| 1973 | 6 | 1979 | 12 |
|------|-----|------|----|
| 1974 | 8 | 1980 | 25 |
| 1975 | 15 | 1981 | 14 |
| 1976 | 6 | 1982 | 4 |
| 1977 | 5 | 1983 | 5 |
| 1978 | 11 | | |

The next step was to match the failed companies in each database by industry and accounting year-end with non-failed companies appearing on the Exstat and LBS databases, the aim being as far as possible to control for systematic industry- and economy-wide factors.[2] However, as was pointed out in chapter 1 (p. 29), such a matched pair control technique will introduce sampling bias unless steps are taken to try to deal with the problem. Once more it was necessary for many of the control companies to obtain some accounting data from annual reports, although these were generally somewhat easier to obtain.

Further checks then had to be made on the accounting data because of differences in definitions used by companies, which were not always treated by Exstat or the DTI in a manner suitable for analysis in this type of study. This was done by referring back to the annual accounts and altering or inserting the data where appropriate.

Finally, share price returns of the failed and control companies in the two databases had to be collected. This should have been fairly straightforward, given that the primary selection criterion was that the companies appeared in the LBS database. However, the monthly logged returns for many of the failed companies unfortunately did not go back for five years, let alone ten. It was therefore decided to develop a third database but only with a five year horizon. This reduced the 111 paired sample to 61 pairs of companies.

**The variable sets**

The accounting data collected for the companies in the three databases were as follows:

Earnings before interest and tax                                    EBIT
Profit before tax                                                   PBT
Current assets                                                      CA
Quick assets                                                        QA
Sales (turnover)                                                    S
Total assets                                                        TA
Current liabilities (excluding bank overdrafts)                     CL
Long term liabilities                                               LTL
Stocks (inventories)                                                INV
Debtors                                                             DR
Trade creditors                                                     CR
Depreciation charge                                                 DC
Ordinary share capital (issued)                                     OSC
Preference share capital (issued)                                   PSC
Minority interest                                                   MI
Medium term loans and provisions                                    MTLP
Bank overdrafts                                                     OD
Deferred tax                                                        DT
Intangible assets                                                   INTAN

The qualitative indicators collected were

Changes in lines of business
Changes in accounting policy
Qualifications in auditors' report
Date of directors' report
Date of auditors' report
Change in auditors
Net change in board of directors
Directors' initial shareholdings
Net change each year in directors' shareholdings
Auditors' remuneration
Directors' remuneration
Date of issue of annual report

Change in name of the company

Changes in the register of charges
Changes in the financial year end
Nominal value of shares at year end

The share price returns collected were monthly returns, calculated as follows:

$$R_i = \log_e [(P_t + D_t)/P_{t-1}]$$  (10.1)

248

where $R_i$ is the log return in month t;

$P_t$ is the last traded price in month t;

$D_t$ is the dividend declared ex dividend during month t adjusted to a month end basis; and

$P_{t-1}$ is the last traded price in month t-1 adjusted to the same basis.

Initially 124 indicators were derived from the accounting data, grouped as follows:

Profitability (14); Liquidity (30); Capital gearing (34); Size (10); Growth (5); Turnover (5); Asset proportion ratios (9); Variability and risk measures (17).

However, it was decided to reduce this to a smaller and more manageable set of 40 indicators on the basis of those ratios used in previous UK studies and of factor analysis evidence of commonalities between financial indicators. The number was then further reduced by reference to those ratios most frequently applied in other British studies.

The indicators derived from the qualitative data were generally dichotomous (e.g. change in accounting policies, change in mortgage deeds, change in company name, change in auditors). However, it was also possible to derive a number of scaled variables (e.g. directors' remuneration/turnover, auditors' remuneration/ turnover, size of directors' equity stake, length of time between year end and audit report date, length of time between year end and publication of the annual report, and the changes in each of the above).

Where appropriate data were rescaled (e.g. ratios such as 'rate of return on capital employed' were annualised when the accounting period was changed and was greater or less than a year).

The case study material was gathered from a variety of sources, but mainly from company annual reports and from press cuttings reproduced on McCarthy Card fiche. Similar sources were accessed to obtain information relating to the 21 companies which failed over the period 1988-91.

**Summary**

Three databases were developed of matched pairs of failed and non-failed companies. The first comprised 75 matched pairs, the second 111 and the third 61. The 75 matched pair sample contained 10 years accounting and qualitative indicators; the 111 sample 5 years accounting and qualitative indicators; and the 61 sample 5 years accounting, qualitative and share return indicators. For each company/year data for 19 accounting and 16 qualitative variables were collected; and the share returns were logged monthly returns.

249

A noticeable feature of the sample was a clustering of failures in particular industries – especially textiles, engineering and metals, and construction – and in specific years over the period covered (1973-1983).

In addition, case study material was obtained for 25 of the bankrupt companies, and – in order to create an intertemporal hold out sample – accounting and background information for another 21 which failed between 1988 and 1991.

## Notes

[1] A list of the companies, their industry membership, the years covered, and the sources of the accounting data are given in an Appendix at the end of the book.

[2] This is especially important with respect to industry factors as average industry ratios will vary from year-to-year and from industry-to-industry. It is therefore necessary to try to ensure that equal weight is given in the analysis and control samples to companies operating in a particular industry over a specific period of time.

# 11 Univariate analysis

## Introduction

It will be recalled from the discussion in chapters 2 and 3 that various univariate models have been developed which (on the face of it) appear to be able to discriminate reasonably well between bankrupt and non-failing companies. These range from relatively straightforward models focusing on individual financial ratios to rather more complex procedures (e.g. applying informational decomposition measures or the gambler's ruin model). Yet despite the fact that these models appear to distinguish between failing and surviving companies almost as well as their multivariate counterparts, few univariate studies of bankruptcy have been undertaken in recent years.

The main purpose of this chapter is therefore to see how well univariate models perform on British data. It should then be possible to compare their relative forecasting ability against that of a number of multivariate models, whose discriminating ability is assessed in chapters 12 and 13.

The first procedure employs a series of financial ratios one-by-one to see if they can be used successfully to discriminate between failing and surviving firms. The framework used was a logit model, in the first instance with the intercept suppressed so that strict proportionality of the ratios was assumed, but subsequently introducing a constant term. The second and third types of study focus on qualitative and share price variables; while the fourth and fifth studies involve use of the informational decomposition and gambler's ruin models.

## Univariate financial ratio models

As indicated above, logit models were developed to test the power of individual ratios to discriminate between failed and non-failed companies. This was done for ratios which might potentially represent six financial characteristics: profitability, liquidity, gearing, size, turnover, and asset proportions. The data set used was the 111 matched pair group of companies over the five year period prior to the failure of the bankrupt company.

Initially the models were run with the intercepts suppressed – which is how the ratios might be used in practice as an initial screening device. However, only one group of ratios appeared to possess much discriminatory power: namely those indicating profitability. The results are shown in Table 11.1 for the ratio which, for this particular attribute, contributed most to the multivariate models described in the next chapter, EBIT/TA. The t statistics are significant at the 95 per cent

### Table 11.1: Profit Indicator as a Univariate Discriminator (Intercept Suppressed)

| Years before failure | Slope | t | $R^2$ | Log likelihood ratio % | % correct predictions |
|---|---|---|---|---|---|
| 1 | 11.54 | 1.72 | .26 | 21.3 | 73 |
| 2 | 6.32 | 1.38 | .10 | 7.8 | 59 |
| 3 | 2.97 | 2.55 | .03 | 1.2 | 54 |
| 4 | 0.83 | 0.84 | .00 | 0.0 | 52 |
| 5 | 1.88 | 1.96 | .01 | 0.0 | 55 |

confidence level for years 1, 3 and 5 before failure, and the $R^2$ and Log likelihood ratio percentages show reasonable prima facie discriminatory power in the final year before bankruptcy.[1] However, explanatory power declines rapidly as the time interval before failure is extended, and if allowance is made for the potential costs of misclassifying non-failed firms and for the sampling bias problem, it is fairly clear that this model would not be very useful for practitioners. On the other hand, it is worth noting that the results for this particular sample of companies are much less impressive than those reported in some previous studies (e.g. Beaver, 1966).[2]

An obvious adjustment was to introduce an intercept into the models to see whether discriminatory power was significantly improved when the strict proportionality assumption was dropped. It was, and the results are reported in Table 11.2 for the four variables which appear to have most explanatory power. Again, the ratios included in the table are amongst those which were selected for inclusion in the multivariate logit model described in chapter 12 (see p. 274).

The t-statistics shown in Table 11.2 are almost all highly significant at the 95 per cent confidence level, and the $R^2$ and Log likelihood coefficients show that the profit, liquidity, gearing, and size ratios all possessed reasonable prima facie discriminatory power in the final year's published accounts.[3] However, this declined as the time interval before failure was increased, but when allowance is made for the cost of misclassifying non-failing companies and for potential sampling bias, the power of the models is less impressive. On the other hand,

### Table 11.2: Profit, Liquidity, Gearing and Size Indicators as Univariate Discriminators

| Years before failure | Constant | t | Slope | t | $R^2$ | Log likelihood ratio % | % correct predictions |
|---|---|---|---|---|---|---|---|
| *Profit* | | | | | | | |
| 1 | -1.18 | -4.47 | 20.40 | 6.64 | .38 | 29.4 | 78 |
| 2 | -1.58 | -5.11 | 18.93 | 6.05 | .26 | 19.6 | 73 |
| 3 | -1.32 | -4.03 | 13.00 | 4.48 | .12 | 7.8 | 63 |
| 4 | -0.28 | -1.16 | 2.54 | 1.41 | .01 | 0.1 | 53 |
| 5 | -0.53 | -2.30 | 4.90 | 2.87 | .05 | 2.6 | 59 |
| *Liquidity* | | | | | | | |
| 1 | -2.75 | -5.54 | 1.91 | 5.58 | .23 | 15.7 | 70 |
| 2 | -2.03 | -4.36 | 1.29 | 4.44 | .14 | 9.2 | 63 |
| 3 | -2.16 | -4.41 | 1.33 | 4.45 | .13 | 9.2 | 66 |
| 4 | -1.06 | -2.71 | 0.63 | 2.78 | .06 | 3.2 | 59 |
| 5 | -1.15 | -2.93 | 0.68 | 3.03 | .06 | 3.9 | 63 |
| *Gearing* | | | | | | | |
| 1 | 3.70 | 6.20 | -6.64 | -6.44 | .24 | 19.3 | 73 |
| 2 | 3.21 | 5.40 | -6.03 | -5.59 | .18 | 13.1 | 67 |
| 3 | 2.55 | 4.71 | -5.00 | -4.89 | .12 | 9.2 | 66 |
| 4 | 1.62 | 3.52 | -3.23 | -3.68 | .07 | 4.6 | 57 |
| 5 | 1.34 | 3.00 | -2.67 | -3.13 | .05 | 3.3 | 58 |
| *Size* | | | | | | | |
| 1 | -9.92 | -5.12 | 0.61 | 5.13 | .13 | 9.2 | 64 |
| 2 | -8.64 | -1.83 | 0.53 | 4.74 | .11 | 7.7 | 64 |
| 3 | -9.20 | -5.00 | 0.57 | 5.01 | .13 | 9.2 | 64 |
| 4 | -9.41 | -5.18 | 0.59 | 5.20 | .14 | 10.5 | 63 |
| 5 | -9.58 | -5.25 | 0.61 | 5.27 | .15 | 11.1 | 64 |

given the fact that each of the ratios on its own appears to have some explanatory power, it seems likely that a multivariate model might well improve classificatory ability, an issue that will be addressed in the next chapter.

## Univariate qualitative variable models

Thirteen variables were identified in order to study the explanatory power of qualitative indicators in the context of corporate failure. Of these, seven were dichotomous and the remaining six continuous.

The database used for this part of the study was originally the 75 matched pair database which covers a period of 10 years before the failed firm went bankrupt. However, this was reduced to a set of 74 matched pairs because one company set of observations was incomplete.

The seven dichotomous variables were: qualifications in the auditors' report, and changes in lines of business, in accounting policy, in the register of charges, in the company's auditors, in the name of the company, and in the financial year end. Their incidence is shown in Table 11.3. Overall, during the 10 year period there were 241 instances of one or other of the dichotomous indicators being recorded within the failed company group, compared to only 134 within the non-failed group.

Because of the relatively low incidence of the dichotomous variables, it is most appropriate to analyse the significance of their occurrence over an 'event window'.[4] In this instance a five year interval was chosen because the incidence of some of the seven dichotomous variables was very low.

Tests for the significance of the incidence of each of dichotomous variables as between failed and non-failed companies were carried out over successive 5 year windows prior to bankruptcy. For this purpose a one tailed test was applied to assess the differences between the two population proportions, and the results are summarised in Table 11.4, where the two columns show the t-statistic and the significance at 90 per cent, 95 per cent, 99 per cent and 99.9 per cent confidence levels.[5] It can be seen that in all cases except for changes in accounting policies there was a significantly higher incidence for failing companies having observations of the qualitative variables in one or more of the event windows.[6] Further, the significance of the differences was generally greater the closer the window was to failure date, and it was particularly strong for changes in lines of business and changes in the register of charges. This presumably reflects the fact that there are, on the one hand, very often attempts to restructure a company's operations as it becomes financially distressed; and, on the other, moves by its bankers to strengthen the security they hold over its assets. It is also noticeable that very close to bankruptcy failing companies are more likely to change their financial year ends and/or to have their accounts qualified by their auditors.

The six continuous qualitative variables studied were: the reporting lag between financial year end and publication of the accounts; the log of a company's turnover; and year-on-year changes in the reporting lag, in auditors' remuneration, in directors' remuneration, and in directors' shareholdings. (For this purpose auditors' and directors' remuneration was scaled by sales.) The distributions of these variables were not normally distributed so comparisons between failed and

# Table 11.3: The Incidence of Selected Dichotomous Qualitative Variables

| | Audit qualifications | | Changes in | | | | | | | | | | | |
|---|---|---|---|---|---|---|---|---|---|---|---|---|---|---|
| | | | lines of business | | accounting policies | | registered charges | | auditors | | company name | | financial year end | |
| Frequency | F | NF | F | NF | F | NF | F | NF | F | NF | F | NF | F | NF |
| 1 | 24 | 9 | 25 | 8 | 25 | 18 | 16 | 16 | 21 | 9 | 12 | 5 | 15 | 3 |
| 2 | 10 | 3 | 6 | 1 | 8 | 15 | 11 | 9 | 4 | 3 | 1 | 1 | 4 | |
| 3 | 2 | 2 | 4 | 1 | 4 | 6 | 11 | 6 | | | | | | |
| 4 | 3 | | 1 | | 1 | 3 | 9 | 6 | | | | | | |
| 5 | 1 | | | | | | 8 | 5 | | | | | | |
| 6 | | | | | | | 4 | 2 | | | | | | |
| 7 | 1 | | | | | | 7 | 1 | | | | | | |
| 8 | | | | | | | | 1 | | | | | | |
| 9 | | | | | | | 3 | 1 | | | | | | |
| | 41 | 14 | 36 | 10 | 38 | 42 | 69 | 47 | 25 | 12 | 13 | 6 | 19 | 3 |
| 0 | 33 | 60 | 38 | 64 | 36 | 32 | 5 | 27 | 49 | 62 | 61 | 68 | 55 | 71 |
| No. of companies | 74 | 74 | 74 | 74 | 74 | 74 | 74 | 74 | 74 | 74 | 74 | 74 | 74 | 74 |

*Note*

F = failed; NF = non-failed

# Table 11.4: The Significance of Selected Dichotomous Qualitative Variables

| Event window: years prior to failure | Audit qualifications | Changes in: lines of business | accounting policies | registered charges | auditors | company name | financial year end |
|---|---|---|---|---|---|---|---|
| 1 | 5.5 **** | 4.8 **** | -0.5 | 5.0 **** | 1.4 * | 1.3 * | – |
| 2 | 1.5 * | 4.1 **** | -0.7 | 3.2 **** | 2.1 ** | 0.3 | 3.5 **** |
| 3 | 1.5 * | 3.6 **** | -0.2 | 2.5 *** | 2.2 ** | 0.3 | 2.3 ** |
| 4 | 1.4 * | 2.6 *** | -1.0 | 2.2 ** | 2.3 ** | 0.3 | 2.3 ** |
| 5 | 1.7 ** | 2.1 ** | -2.4 *** | 1.9 ** | 1.9 ** | 0.8 | 2.1 ** |
| 6 | 1.8 ** | 2.1 ** | -2.3 ** | 2.4 *** | 1.7 ** | 0.9 | 1.3 * |

*Notes*

1. Event windows cover five year intervals.
2. Figures are t-statistics.
3. Significant at 99.9% level ****; at 99% level ***; at 95% level **; at 90% level *.
4. There were no instances of a change in financial year end in the non-failed sample for the final window before bankruptcy.

non-failed groups of companies were made applying a non-parametric procedure, the Mann Whitney U test. This ranks the data and assesses the probabilities of observations in one group ranking higher than observations in the other group.[7]

The results shown in Table 11.5 indicate that there were significant differences at the 90 per cent, 95 per cent, 99 per cent and 99.9 per cent confidence levels for all but one of the variables. The most significant differences were with respect to turnover and reporting lag. In the case of the former, it was abundantly clear that the failed firms in the sample were systematically smaller than their matched pairs drawn randomly from similar industry groups. (This was matched by the fact that directors generally held a higher proportion of failed companies' shares.) As for the other variables, the median interval before publication of the accounts rose from 118 days 10 years prior to bankruptcy to 125 days nine years before, 136 days five years before and 143 days in the last year. The corresponding intervals for the non-failed companies were fairly constant, only increasing from 116 days to 118 days over the 10 year period.

Overall, it did not seem that changes in the remuneration of either auditors or directors were very good discriminators. However, it was noticeable that changes in directors' shareholdings one year prior to failure were significantly greater for failed firms, indicating the fact that radical changes in board membership often took place shortly before failing companies collapsed in a last ditch attempt to turn them round.[8]

**Share price variables**

It was anticipated that, as a single variable, residual share prices (i.e. annual returns after deducting the corresponding return on the market index) would have strong explanatory power. Rather surprisingly this was not the case.

Using a logit model with the intercept suppressed on the 61 company sample produced correct classifications in the years leading up to bankruptcy as follows: 47.5 per cent, 52.4 per cent, 53.3 per cent, 59.0 per cent, and 55.7 per cent.[9] With the intercept the picture was no better: 48.3 per cent, 52.5 per cent, 54.1 per cent, 57.4 per cent and 50.0 per cent.

The reason for this lack of explanatory power seems to be that the distress of individual companies was recognised at various intervals prior to failure, and there was often a slight recovery as attempts were made to turn a business round. In some cases it also appears that the eventual collapse of a company was not anticipated at all. On the other hand, a closer scrutiny of the data showed that there was often a sharp downturn in share prices after the year end date of the last published accounts. Moreover, systematic evidence of decline was evident when *cumulative* returns were calculated across all companies in the population.

Overall, the results for the univariate analysis are not inconsistent with the results reported in chapter 14, which show a clear distinction in cumulative share price

# Table 11.5: The Significance of Selected Continuous Qualitative Variables

| Year before failure | Turnover | Reporting lag | Changes in reporting lag | Changes in auditors' remuneration | Changes in directors' remuneration | Changes in directors' shareholdings |
|---|---|---|---|---|---|---|
| 1 | **** | **** | * | | | *** |
| 2 | *** | ** | * | | | |
| 3 | *** | ** | * | | * | |
| 4 | *** | ** | | | | |
| 5 | *** | ** | | | | |
| 6 | **** | * | | | | |
| 7 | **** | * | | | | * |
| 8 | **** | * | | | | |
| 9 | **** | * | * | * | | |
| 10 | **** | | | | | |

*Notes*

1. Test statistics derived using Mann Whitney U.
2. Significant at 99.9% level ****; at 99% level ***; at 95% level **; at 90% level *.

258

behaviour between companies signalled as being likely failures and survivors rather than between those which actually failed and those which did not.

## Entropy models

Following Lev's argument, outlined in chapter 2, it might reasonably be expected that a firm experiencing financial distress will suffer a greater proportionate change in its balance sheet structure, either overall or in terms of the claims or the assets components. This will be the result of it experiencing a destabilising shock.

In order to see how information decomposition measures might capture such changes and successfully discriminate between failing and non-failing firms, four categories of assets and claims were identified as variables:

1. Current liabilities/(Non-current liabilities + Equity)
2. Liabilities/Equity
3. Current assets/Non-current assets
4. Quick assets/(Stocks + Fixed assets)

Four further categories could then be identified as variables at an aggregative balance sheet level:

5. (1) + (3)
6. (1) + (4)
7. (2) + (3)
8. (2) + (4)

A further issue concerns the period over which structural changes in company balance sheets might occur. For instance, there may well be plus or minus proportionate changes of (say) 10 per cent for healthy companies, but these movements would tend to cancel each other out over a period of (say) four years. By contrast, the steadily worsening position of a failing company might be represented by a 10 per cent change in the same direction over each of four successive years.

One way of trying to capture this is to measure the variance of the informational decomposition measure, but this presents practical problems as the measure of dispersion has to be based on an average which either has to be calculated cumulatively or with the advantage of hindsight. Effectively this means that, if the technique is to be used operationally, it would be necessary to specify in advance a (moving) window of years over which averages could be calculated. In the circumstances it was decided to adopt an alternative approach and instead calculate decomposition measures over all possible intervals (or 'lags') and see which period appeared to capture best the major changes in assets, claims, and/or balance sheets.

The data set used for the experiment was that for 75 matched pairs of companies as this covered a 10 year period prior to failure. The results are summarised in Tables 11.6-11.8, in which the percentages of correct classifications of matched pairs of companies are shown for each of the eight variables referred to above. Details are also given for each interval (or 'lag') ending in the years leading up to bankruptcy. Thus Table 11.6 shows the results where the measurement interval (or 'lag') was a single year; Table 11.7 the results where changes in the proportions of asset and/or claim categories were measured over a two year interval (or 'lag'); and Table 11.8 the results where the measurement interval (or 'lag') was three years.

### Table 11.6: Information Decomposition Measures, Paired Classificational Accuracy for Lag of 1 Year

| Decomposition scores | Years prior to failure | | | | | | | | |
|---|---|---|---|---|---|---|---|---|---|
| Failed>Non-failed | 1 | 2 | 3 | 4 | 5 | 6 | 7 | 8 | 9 |
| % correctly identified | | | | | | | | | |
| Variable 1 | 69 | 61 | 65 | 61 | 52 | 61 | 51 | 49 | 55 |
| Variable 2 | 68 | 59 | 51 | 45 | 49 | 48 | 55 | 51 | 51 |
| Variable 3 | 73 | 68 | 71 | 59 | 60 | 60 | 49 | 51 | 55 |
| Variable 4 | 60 | 53 | 52 | 55 | 49 | 48 | 49 | 63 | 52 |
| Variable 5 | 71 | 65 | 65 | 60 | 49 | 57 | 52 | 48 | 59 |
| Variable 6 | 65 | 63 | 57 | 59 | 51 | 51 | 49 | 57 | 56 |
| Variable 7 | 77 | 53 | 65 | 55 | 51 | 56 | 52 | 51 | 53 |
| Variable 8 | 69 | 71 | 63 | 53 | 55 | 52 | 51 | 59 | 56 |

In general, as argued by Lev, the results show that the proportionate changes for all eight variables were greater for failed than non-failed firms in the run up to bankruptcy. This was most evident in the last three years before failure, especially when the interval (or 'lag') over which the decomposition measures were calculated was extended from one to two years. In particular, whereas in the last year before bankruptcy it was changes in variables 3, 5 and 7 that were most often greater for failing firms, when the measures were calculated over two years, variables 1, 5, 6, 7 and 8 were all substantially greater.

Clearly, the success rate of correctly classifying pairs of companies in excess of 70 per cent is significantly above the pure chance rate of around 50 per cent. Moreover, the performance of the decomposition measures as discriminators is not greatly inferior to that of statistically or iteratively derived models when tested on hold out samples.[10] However, when allowance is made for potential sampling bias, it can be seen that the number of misclassifications will rise significantly. Given the

## Table 11.7: Information Decomposition Measures, Paired Classificational Accuracy for Lag of 2 Years

Years prior to failure

| Decomposition scores Failed>Non-failed | 1 | 2 | 3 | 4 | 5 | 6 | 7 | 8 |
|---|---|---|---|---|---|---|---|---|
| **% correctly identified** | | | | | | | | |
| Variable 1 | 72 | 64 | 64 | 59 | 61 | 56 | 55 | 63 |
| Variable 2 | 56 | 55 | 59 | 48 | 47 | 52 | 52 | 59 |
| Variable 3 | 68 | 72 | 51 | 53 | 68 | 49 | 57 | 63 |
| Variable 4 | 68 | 55 | 59 | 47 | 49 | 51 | 49 | 57 |
| Variable 5 | 72 | 65 | 61 | 56 | 53 | 55 | 60 | 60 |
| Variable 6 | 71 | 65 | 59 | 56 | 61 | 57 | 57 | 65 |
| Variable 7 | 72 | 69 | 55 | 48 | 63 | 55 | 63 | 59 |
| Variable 8 | 76 | 72 | 52 | 56 | 63 | 51 | 60 | 61 |

substantial error costs to decision makers of misclassifying non-failing companies as prima facie bankrupt, the discriminatory power of the information decomposition models is considerably weakened. This would suggest that, although failing firms do indeed experience substantial changes in the structure of their balance sheets as failure approaches, this fact can hardly be used operationally to distinguish between firms which are going to fail and those which are not.

### Gambler's ruin models

In applying the gambler's ruin model described in chapter 2, various indicators can be used to proxy cash flows. At one extreme, 'pure' cash flow in a period can be identified by adjusting a profit figure for all accruals and movements in stocks. Another possibility is to use what used to be referred to as 'cash flow' by businessmen before the publication of FRS 1 on the preparation of cash flow statements, i.e. profit + the annual depreciation charge. (More properly this is a crude measure of working capital funds generated in a period.) An even more smoothed proxy for cash flow is of course a profit measure, such as earnings before interest and tax (EBIT). However, the point to note is that profit and working capital funds flow figures are essentially smoothed transforms of cash flows. In the circumstances, it would seem sensible just to concentrate on the first two measures: pure cash flow; and (profit + depreciation).

'Pure' cash flow can be calculated as the change in the 'adjusted cash position' year-on-year. The latter represents the liquidation value of a company at the end of

**Table 11.8:   Information Decomposition Measures, Paired Classificational Accuracy for Lag of 3 Years**

|  | Years prior to failure | | | | | | |
|---|---|---|---|---|---|---|---|
| Decomposition scores Failed>Non-failed | 1 | 2 | 3 | 4 | 5 | 6 | 7 |
| % correctly identified | | | | | | | |
| Variable 1 | 60 | 59 | 61 | 53 | 55 | 52 | 57 |
| Variable 2 | 56 | 57 | 52 | 55 | 52 | 57 | 57 |
| Variable 3 | 67 | 64 | 57 | 59 | 5 | 43 | 51 |
| Variable 4 | 60 | 56 | 55 | 52 | 51 | 52 | 56 |
| Variable 5 | 67 | 61 | 60 | 52 | 57 | 57 | 55 |
| Variable 6 | 65 | 63 | 61 | 61 | 59 | 56 | 52 |
| Variable 7 | 73 | 61 | 60 | 55 | 55 | 57 | 52 |
| Variable 8 | 71 | 67 | 60 | 63 | 53 | 52 | 51 |

a year. In estimating this, fairly arbitrary assumptions have to be made about the relationship between the realisable and book values of non-monetary assets – effectively tangible fixed assets and stocks. Clearly in practice the relationship will vary from firm to firm, depending on industry membership and the specific economic environment. However, these differences should partly be dealt with by the control procedure of matching pairs of failed and non-failed concerns. In the event, for the purpose of this study it was decided to estimate the realisable value of tangible fixed assets at 50 per cent of their book value, and that for stocks at 75 per cent. The adjusted cash position was therefore

$$QA + 0.75\ INV + 0.5\ TFA - TL \tag{11.1}$$

> where QA  is quick assets;
> INV is stocks (inventories);
> TFA is tangible fixed assets; and
> TL  is total liabilities.

The corresponding 'mean cash flow' (Mean CF) figure used was simply the average of cash flow observations, and this was first calculated on a cumulative basis over the years under review prior to failure. However, this meant that the results year-by-year might not be strictly comparable, since the period over which the averaging took place was not constant. Consequently an alternative approach of calculating the averages over moving three year periods was employed to see whether it made any difference to the results.

In calculating the variance of the cash flows (Var CF) – or in fact the standard deviation (SD-CF), which was actually employed – the procedure used by Wilcox (1973) was adopted: namely

$$\sigma = \sqrt{(\text{Mean CF})^2 + (\text{Var CF})} \qquad\qquad (11.2)$$

The Mean CF and SD-CF figures were then used to calculate two statistics: N and x.

N refers to a *state*. At the end of each period a company will move from a state N to either N+1 or N-1 (see Figure 2.5, p. 66). When N=0 the company has reached the 'absorbing state': i.e. it has run out of cash and is prima facie insolvent. The value of N is found by dividing the 'cash position' by SD-CF, and the lower it is the closer is the company to insolvency (i.e. it shares some of the properties of the hazard function in survival models).

x represents the average drift rate per period along the sequence of states, expressed in cash terms. It is calculated as

Mean CF/SD-CF $\qquad\qquad (11.3)$

and

$$q/p = (1-x)/(1+x) \qquad\qquad (11.4)$$

The two statistics can then be compared for any pair of companies in the following way:

*Domain I*:  x>0 and N>0. The probability of ultimate failure is $[(1-x)/(1+x)]^N$.
*Domain II*:  x<0 and N>0. The firm is losing cash but has reserves. The mean time to failure is -N/x.
*Domain III*:  x>0 and N<0. The company is already prima facie insolvent, even though it is recovering liquidity.
*Domain IV*:  x<0 and N<0. Again, the company is prima facie insolvent.

The database initially used for this study was that relating to 75 matched pairs of companies for a 10 year period before the failing business went bankrupt. However, subsequently the procedures were also applied to the 111 matched pair database covering a 5 year period before bankruptcy.

The results of pairwise comparisons applying the gambler's ruin model were calculated in eight different ways using all possible combinations of the following:

Cash flow (CF) 1 = Profit + depreciation
　　　　　　　2 = 'Pure' cash flow
Variance　　　 1 = Calculated cumulatively
　　　　　　　2 = Calculated over the most recent 3 years
Database　　　 1 = 75 matched pairs over 10 years
　　　　　　　2 = 111 matched pairs over 5 years

As an example of the calculations made, the results over 10 years prior to failure are summarised in Table 11.9, with cash flow being 'profit + depreciation' (CF 1) and where the variance is calculated on a cumulative basis. The figures show for each of the four 'Domain' rules when the failing company is more likely to go bankrupt than its matched pair survivor. Overall it can be seen from the bottom line that the rate of correct matched pair classifications rises steadily to 87 per cent in the last year before failure.

Similar results were obtained when the full 111 failed company 5 year data set was tested, where the cash flow variance was calculated over successive three year intervals, and where cash flow was defined as the change in the 'cash position' period-by-period (CF 2). Rather than reproduce all the corresponding tables, the pairwise rankings are instead summarised in percentage terms in Table 11.10.

### Table 11.9:  Paired  Classifications  Applying the  Gambler's  Ruin  Model

Years prior to failure

| Failed>Non-failed | 1 | 2 | 3 | 4 | 5 | 6 | 7 | 8 | 9 |
|---|---|---|---|---|---|---|---|---|---|
| Domain I | 39 | 44 | 36 | 37 | 41 | 42 | 36 | 40 | 32 |
| Domain II | 25 | 12 | 13 | 8 | 10 | 9 | 8 | 7 | 6 |
| Domains III & IV | 1 | 1 | 2 | 3 | 3 | 0 | 2 | 2 | 2 |
|  | 65 | 57 | 51 | 48 | 54 | 51 | 46 | 49 | 40 |
| Failed<Non-failed |  |  |  |  |  |  |  |  |  |
| Domain I | 7 | 17 | 23 | 25 | 19 | 23 | 26 | 25 | 33 |
| Domain II | 2 | 1 | 1 | * 1 | 1 | 0 | 1 | 1 | 2 |
| Domains III & IV | 1 | 0 | 0 | 1 | 1 | 1 | 2 | 0 | 0 |
|  | 10 | 18 | 24 | 27 | 21 | 24 | 29 | 26 | 35 |
| Total no. of companies | 75 | 75 | 75 | 75 | 75 | 75 | 75 | 75 | 75 |
| % correctly identified | 87 | 76 | 68 | 64 | 72 | 68 | 61 | 65 | 53 |

It can be seen from Table 11.9 that between 9 and 2 years prior to failure about one fifth of failed companies are classified under Domain II using CF 1; and this ratio rises to around 40 per cent in the final year. Using the three year average of cash flows the ratio increases to around 50 per cent in the final year under Domains II-IV. Using CF 2 more companies appeared to be insolvent prior to the final debacle, about 40 per cent falling into the Domain III-IV categories between 9 and 2 years prior to failure when cumulative averaging was applied, rising to 60 per cent in the final year. Using three year averages this rose to 50 per cent for years 7 to 3 prior to failure, 60 per cent for year 2, and 70 per cent in the final year. On the five year data set the classifications of companies as already insolvent was slightly higher.

Wilcox (1973) – whose overall results in terms of correct classifications were similar to those reported above – argued that the fact that many failing companies were prima facie insolvent some time before their eventual bankruptcy probably reflected in part the fact that the model makes crude estimates of the liquidation values of stocks and tangible fixed assets. However, it is also probably because the model does not allow for the intervention of management to try to turn a company around when it seems to be on the rocks. This of course is another way of saying that the simple gambler's ruin model is unrealistic to the extent that it assumes there is no access to external funding, since the equity market value of the failing

### Table 11.10: Paired Classifications Applying the Gambler's Ruin Model

| Failed>Non-failed | Years prior to failure | | | | | | | | |
|---|---|---|---|---|---|---|---|---|---|
| | 1 | 2 | 3 | 4 | 5 | 6 | 7 | 8 | 9 |
| % correctly identified | | | | | | | | | |
| *10 year data, CF 1* | | | | | | | | | |
| Cumulative average | 87 | 76 | 68 | 64 | 72 | 68 | 61 | 65 | 53 |
| Three year average | 87 | 76 | 67 | 69 | 64 | 60 | 64 | 65 | - |
| *10 year data, CF 2* | | | | | | | | | |
| Cumulative average | 87 | 77 | 71 | 61 | 61 | 57 | 59 | 59 | - |
| Three year average | 76 | 75 | 72 | 68 | 63 | 57 | 59 | - | - |
| *5 year data, CF 1* | | | | | | | | | |
| Cumulative average | 86 | 75 | 66 | 63 | - | - | - | - | - |
| Three year average | 87 | 77 | 66 | - | - | - | - | - | - |
| *5 year data, CF 2* | | | | | | | | | |
| Cumulative average | 80 | 71 | 64 | - | - | - | - | - | - |
| Three year average | 78 | 71 | - | - | - | - | - | - | - |

companies must have been positive right up until the time they file for bankruptcy. Moreover, there was certainly evidence in the sample of management attempts to turn round some of the financially distressed businesses (e.g. where 'company doctors' were installed). However, it should be remembered that only those companies where the rescue attempts did not succeed were included in the bankrupt population.

Given the high incidence of prima facie insolvency some time prior to final collapse, it was decided to see how effective the N statistic was on its own as an indicator of financial weakness. The pairwise classifications comparable with those shown in Table 11.10 are therefore shown in Table 11.11, but with N as the discriminator. It can be seen that using the CF 1 definition of cash flows the classifications are slightly inferior to those shown above. However, the N statistic is a slightly better discriminator using the CF 2 definition.

Under Domain I it will be recalled that the final discriminator is the $[(1-x)/(1+x)]^N$ statistic (which it will be convenient to refer to as Z). However, it is quite possible – likely, in fact – that for some companies which ultimately failed, the deterioration in financial position will have come suddenly towards the end of the company's life. As a result the rankings of some of the failed/non-failed companies according to the Z statistic might be expected to result from 'random

### Table 11.11:  Paired Classifications Applying the Gambler's Ruin Model with N as the Discriminator

Years prior to failure

|  | 1 | 2 | 3 | 4 | 5 | 6 | 7 | 8 | 9 |
|---|---|---|---|---|---|---|---|---|---|
| **% correctly identified** | | | | | | | | | |
| *10 year data, CF 1* | | | | | | | | | |
| Cumulative average | 84 | 67 | 68 | 63 | 60 | 68 | 63 | 57 | 52 |
| Three year average | 83 | 67 | 60 | 65 | 65 | 64 | 63 | 57 | - |
| *10 year data, CF 2* | | | | | | | | | |
| Cumulative average | 88 | 79 | 67 | 69 | 65 | 59 | 61 | 49 | - |
| Three year average | 89 | 76 | 63 | 65 | 64 | 63 | 64 | - | - |
| *5 year data, CF 1* | | | | | | | | | |
| Three year average | 79 | 64 | 58 | 53 | - | - | - | - | - |
| Cumulative average | 69 | 69 | 58 | - | - | - | - | - | - |
| *5 year data, CF 2* | | | | | | | | | |
| Cumulative average | 89 | 75 | 63 | - | - | - | - | - | - |
| Three year average | 87 | 75 | - | - | - | - | - | - | - |

error'. One – albeit rather crude – way of trying to check on this is to compare the distributions of logged Z statistics for failed (F) and non-failed (NF) companies. If the 'random error' argument is valid for at least some of the companies, one would expect lower mean values and dispersions for the non-failed companies. Calculations showed that this was indeed almost universally the case.

In conclusion, on a pairwise basis the gambler's ruin model, however defined, seems to perform well as a discriminator on the data sets used for the last year before failure. Indeed, its performance is not substantially different to that recorded for other types of model (e.g. those derived using multiple discriminant analysis, logit or neural networking).[11] However, there is a sharp deterioration in its ability to distinguish between failing and non-failing firms as the time interval before bankruptcy is increased. Moreover, the procedure suffers from the usual problem of sampling bias as failures are overrepresented in the population studied. When allowance is made for the error costs to decision makers of misclassifying a large number of non-failed companies as bankrupt, it is evident that the procedure will probably be of limited practical use to analysts – but this is a defect it shares with most other failure prediction models.

**Summary**

Logit models were used to assess the discriminatory power of a number of individual financial ratios. These measured various company attributes – namely profitability, liquidity, gearing, size and asset turnover. When the intercept term was suppressed, only profitability seemed to have much explanatory power in distinguishing between failing and non-failing firms. However, the introduction of a constant term greatly improved the performance of the models, although (as might have been expected) profit ratios were still the main indicators of likely bankruptcy, discriminatory power in the last two years of a failing company's life being between 70 per cent and 80 per cent. The discriminatory power of individual liquidity and gearing indicators was rather less good, but it was still reasonably strong.

Comparing the incidence of qualitative indicators over successive five year event windows showed clearly that audit qualifications and changes in lines of business, in registered charges, in auditors, in company name, and in financial year end were all more likely to occur with failed firms. Moreover, failed firms were significantly smaller than their non-failed counterparts.

Rather surprisingly there was little difference in *annual* residual share price returns between bankrupt and non-failed returns. However, the findings reported in chapter 14 indicate that *cumulative* residual returns on shares in companies which failed or were signalled as failures are significantly worse than on those in companies which survived or were signalled as non-failures.

Informational decomposition models performed reasonably well on matched paired data, although their discriminatory power seems to be no better than that of the univariate logit models using a single profit ratio. By contrast, the gambler's ruin models (also derived using a matched pairing procedure) did rather better, classifying correctly with an almost 90 per cent accuracy rate in the final year before failure and a success rate generally over 75 per cent two years before bankruptcy.

The major problem with all these univariate models, however, is that if allowance is made both for sampling bias (i.e. the overrepresentation of failed firms in the sample) and for the costs to decision makers of misclassifying surviving companies as bankrupt, the operational usefulness of the models is greatly reduced. On the other hand, this is a defect which equally afflicts multivariate models and undermines their practical usefulness.

Overall, on past evidence it would appear that multivariate models should perform rather better, and this is a matter which will be explored in chapters 12 and 13.

**Notes**

[1] The t-statistic tests the null hypothesis that the slope coefficient is significantly different from zero. For reasonably large samples, the null hypothesis can be rejected at the 95 per cent confidence level if it exceeds a critical value of approximately 1.7.

The $R^2$ statistic (or coefficient of determination) takes a value between 0 and 1, indicating the extent to which the independent variable(s) in an equation (model) explain variations in the dependent (criterion) variable. In other words, in the last year before failure the profit ratio appears to explain 26 per cent of differences in the dependent variable, failure/non-failure. However, when the dependent variable is dichotomous it is more appropriate to use the Log likelihood ratio. This is not bounded by an upper limit of 100 per cent, but the relative values from year-to-year can be interpreted in a similar way to $R^2$ statistics: i.e. the higher the value, the greater the explanatory power of the model.

The percentage of correct predictions that might be expected by pure chance would, of course, be 50 per cent. Consequently the only time when the model appears to be particularly useful is when calculations are based on data in a failing company's last published accounts.

[2] See p. 108.

[3] See note 1, above.

[4] Keasey and Watson (1987) measured the incidence of the qualitative variables they studied over a three year interval.

[5] A one tailed test is used to detect departures from a null hypothesis in only one direction: i.e. it is only of interest if the error is above a certain level, not whether it is above or below.

It should be noted that, as the data are measured in nominal or ordinal scale terms, a non-parametric statistical test is appropriate. Fortunately, the t-statistic can be applied for such purposes: see Siegel (1956), pp. 152-156.

[6] The implication of the change in accounting policies figures is that there is little difference in the incidence of alterations in the procedures used close to failure, but earlier there is a greater probability of non-failing companies changing policies.

[7] See Siegel (1956), pp.116-127.

[8] This appears to be consistent with the findings of Bonnier and Bruner (1989) and Eyssell (1991) in the US. The former found that the share prices of financially distressed companies reacted significantly to management changes; while the latter not only confirmed that relative share prices of failing companies declined over the last 2.5 years of a bankrupt company's life, but also that corporate insiders were heavy net sellers of shares over the final 300 days.

[9] i.e. respectively for years 5, 4, 3, 2 and 1 before failure.

[10] See the evidence reviewed in chapters 4 and 5.

The point was made in chapter 1 (p. 30) that it is difficult to devise a meaningful hold out test when a pairwise sample selection procedure is used. Consequently none was attempted here. However, this raises the issue of whether the procedure could be applied operationally by an analyst.

[11] Again, no hold out test was attempted because of the use of a pairwise sample selection procedure: see note 10, above.

# 12 Multivariate analysis: Logit and survival models

## Introduction

It should be clear from the discussion in chapter 4 that most empirical studies of corporate bankruptcy have been undertaken using multivariate statistical procedures. But close scrutiny of the results suggests that there are practical difficulties in applying failure prediction models, their main weakness being high misclassification rates (e.g. they commonly identify 20% or more of surviving firms as about to collapse).

The purpose of this chapter is therefore to derive a number of such models using British data to see, first, whether they perform better than the univariate models described in the previous chapter; and, second, whether they exhibit similar misclassification rates to those reported for other well known models developed using similar procedures.

Originally it was intended to develop a series of logit models from the combined set of variables (i.e. financial ratios, qualitative indicators and share price returns). However, this proved impractical for three reasons.

(1) As explained in chapter 11, in order to ensure a sufficient number of observations, the qualitative data could only really be viewed over a series of five year 'event windows'. Effectively this meant that for analysis purposes the 75 matched pair data set, covering 10 years, had to be used for this type of indicator. But this introduced further complications: first, because the data could no longer be regarded as homogeneous with annual financial ratio indicators; and, second, because in practical terms models including event window data are less easy to use than those where the data relate only to a single year.

(2) Since the financial ratio indicators could be calculated for each year for every pair of companies in the sample, it seemed most appropriate that they should be dealt with on an annual basis. Indeed, the case for doing this is especially

strong as ideally the largest feasible database should be used for estimating logit models. Consequently the most suitable data set from which to derive such models appeared to be that covering 5 years and relating to 111 matched pairs of companies.

(3) Annual share price return data were only available for 61 matched pairs of companies, and then only for a 5 year period. To have required that this variable should be included in the data set would therefore have reduced the sample to an undesirably small size, permitting only one event window for each qualitative variable.

This restriction was regarded as unnecessary, especially as – according to the evidence reported in chapter 11 – annual security returns on their own seem to have little explanatory power. On the other hand, previous research (summarised in chapter 6) suggests that cumulative share price returns mirror (and, indeed, appear to anticipate) the messages conveyed by failure prediction models. The inclusion of such a variable in a discriminatory model would have reduced the sample size even further, since to be realistic the returns would initially have had to be cumulated for at least two years, limiting the study period to four years before the failure of the 61 bankrupt companies.

But even if its inclusion in a discriminatory model did not mean that the sample size would be greatly reduced, it would arguably be more appropriate to undertake an in-depth study of monthly cumulative share price behaviour of companies signalled as being likely to fail. The results of such an exercise are reported separately in chapter 14.

In view of the fact that one of the main aims of the exercise is to compare the relative discriminatory power of models derived using different types of variables, it was finally decided to use multivariate logit analysis on different sets of data, first using qualitative indicators, and then (separately) financial ratio variables.

Given the size of the database, it would have been feasible to use the multilogit procedure to analyse financial ratio data. However, this would have opened up an almost infinite number of possibilities, combining ratios for different years to derive a model which performs marginally better than its rivals. Such an exercise in 'data mining' has little to commend it. Moreover, it is only possible to develop multilogit models applying hindsight, looking backwards from the date of failure. It would also be relatively difficult to apply such a model in practice, since an analyst would have to review data across time, when the circumstances of individual companies might change dramatically. Since the performance of multilogit models is not substantially different from that of more conventional 'single year' procedures, and the aim here is primarily to assess the relative performance of different methods of trying to identify failing firms, it was decided not to go down this particular path. Instead, the potential usefulness of carrying forward information from previous years was examined by formulating 'rolling' logit models.

Overall, the general approach adopted has the advantage that it makes it easier to experiment with various models derived using financial ratio indicators. Thus it was possible to estimate the equations allowing for different prior probabilities of failure; test some of these models on various hold out samples; carry forward the information contained in previous years' models to develop 'rolling' logit models; allow for misclassification costs; and estimate equations employing the variables used in Taffler's manufacturing and distribution models (see Taffler, 1984).

The relatively high incidence of misclassification errors out-of-sample, both for the models developed as part of this study and from research undertaken elsewhere, requires an explanation. One possible reason is that the matched pairing procedures, employed as a control device, are flawed, and experiments were therefore undertaken to try to assess the adequacy of the technique. The results suggest that the procedure is far from perfect and may itself introduce a degree of error into the estimation procedures.

Finally, although the data available are really inappropriate for survival analysis, a brief experiment was conducted to see how easy it is to apply duration models. The findings are summarised below.

**Logit models – qualitative variables**

Twelve of the thirteen qualitative variables examined in the univariate analysis were used to develop a series of logit models, the exception being a change in a company's name.[1] These were again based on 74 matched pairs of companies over a 10 year period prior to failure.

A major problem in developing such models is to make certain that the independent variables are not highly correlated with each other (i.e. ensure that there is a low degree of 'multicollinearity'), since a failure to do so will reduce the explanatory power of the estimated equation. On the other hand, it is desirable to include all those variables which might have some explanatory power, even if in marginal terms their contribution is relatively small. In particular, in examining qualitative indicators it is necessary to try to accommodate variables where the number of observations is low. It would of course be possible to try to assess an optimum window length for each variable,[2] but with multivariate analysis it is ultimately necessary to have a 'standard' window. In the circumstances, it was decided to continue to use the same five year windows for the dichotomous variables as were used for the univariate analysis.

The results of the analysis, assuming an equal probability of firms being bankrupt or surviving, are shown in Table 12.1. This shows for each variable the estimated coefficients and, in parenthesis below, the t-statistics. It can immediately be seen that the multivariate results reinforce the conclusions of the univariate analysis. The Likelihood Ratio (LR) statistics are highly significant, indicating that the models have, on the face of it, strong explanatory power.[3] Moreover, the percentage of firms correctly classified is relatively high, especially in the final

## Table 12.1: Estimates of Logit Failure Likelihood Model Using Qualitative Variables

| Variables | Years prior to failure | | | | | |
|---|---|---|---|---|---|---|
| | 1 | 2 | 3 | 4 | 5 | 6 |
| Constant | 7.1 | 4.8 | 5.1 | 5.8 | 7.6 | 9.0 |
| | (1.7)* | (1.5) | (1.8)* | (1.9)* | (2.4)** | (2.7)*** |
| Audit qualification | 2.0 | 0.2 | -0.2 | 0.2 | 0.6 | 1.5 |
| | (3.3)**** | (0.3) | (-0.4) | (0.4) | (0.9) | (1.7)* |
| Change in line of | 2.9 | 1.9 | 1.6 | 1.0 | 0.8 | 1.5 |
| business | (3.5)**** | (3.0)*** | (2.7)*** | (1.9)* | (1.6) | (2.6)** |
| Change in account- | 0.7 | 0.1 | 0.2 | -0.2 | -0.6 | -1.3 |
| ing policy | (1.2) | (0.3) | (0.4) | (-0.5) | (-1.6) | (-2.9)*** |
| Change in register | 1.7 | 0.7 | 0.8 | 0.7 | 0.8 | 1.3 |
| of charges | (2.9)** | (1.7)* | (2.1)** | (1.7)* | (1.9)* | (3.0)*** |
| Change in auditor | 0.0 | 0.6 | 1.0 | 0.4 | 0.2 | 0.2 |
| | (0.0) | (1.0) | (1.4) | (0.7) | (0.4) | (0.4) |
| Change in year end | 1.1 | 2.2 | 0.8 | 0.9 | 0.6 | 0.4 |
| | (0.5) | (1.9)* | (1.0) | (1.2) | (0.7) | (0.4) |
| Reporting lag | -0.0 | -0.0 | -0.0 | -0.0 | -0.0 | -0.0 |
| | (-1.1) | (-1.7)* | (-1.8)* | (-1.4) | (-1.1) | (-0.6) |
| Turnover (logged) | -0.7 | -0.4 | -0.4 | -0.5 | -0.5 | -0.6 |
| | (-2.7)*** | (-2.4)** | (-2.6)*** | (-2.6)*** | (-2.9)*** | (-3.2)*** |
| Change in report- | -0.0 | 0.0 | -0.0 | 0.0 | -0.0 | 0.0 |
| ing lag | (-0.7) | (0.3) | (-0.3) | (0.5) | (-1.3) | (1.3) |
| Change in auditors' | -73.6 | -307.1 | 63.0 | -144.0 | 98.3 | -1395.9 |
| remuneration | (-0.4) | (-0.7) | (0.2) | (-0.4) | (0.2) | (-2.0)** |
| Change in directors' | -136.0 | 13.7 | -58.4 | 28.3 | 67.87 | 1.7 |
| remuneration | (-1.5) | (0.1) | (-0.6) | (0.3) | (0.8) | (0.0) |
| Change in directors' | -6.7 | -0.5 | -0.9 | 1.4 | 2.0 | 4.0 |
| shareholdings | (-1.8)* | (-0.2) | (-0.4) | (0.5) | (1.0) | (1.4) |
| Likelihood ratio | | | | | | |
| (LR) index | 0.5 | 0.2 | 0.2 | 0.2 | 0.2 | 0.2 |
| LR statistic † | 99.7 | 46.2 | 39.6 | 32.3 | 36.1 | 45.0 |

*Notes*: Statistical significance of t statistics: **** = 99.9% confidence level; *** = 99% confidence level; ** = 95% confidence level; and * = 90% confidence level.
  † All significant at the 95% confidence level.

year before failure (see Table 12.2). However, if allowance is made for the sampling bias problem, the error rate for non-failed firms will increase considerably, and after allowing for misclassification costs, it is fairly clear that the model would be of limited practical value to analysts.

In terms of the individual variables, turnover as a proxy for size is again a consistently important discriminator. But changes in registered charges and in lines of business are also significant, and the latter becomes increasingly so as failure approaches. In addition, the incidence of audit qualifications is significant, but only immediately before failure.

The parameter values reported in Table 12.1 can be interpreted in the following way. Given that the prior probability of bankruptcy between failed and non-failed companies is (unrealistically) assumed in the model to be 50%, the increase in the probability of failure for a company in the final year if it changed its lines of business at least once during the five year window is

$0.5 (1.0 - 0.5) (2.9) = 73\%.$

By contrast, the increase in the probability of failure in the final year if there is a qualified audit report during the five year window is

$0.5 (1.0 - 0.5) (2.0) = 50\%.$

**Table 12.2: Percentage of Firms Correctly Classified Using Qualitative Variables**

|  | Years prior to failure | | | | | |
|---|---|---|---|---|---|---|
|  | 1 | 2 | 3 | 4 | 5 | 6 |
| Non-failed | 85 | 77 | 75 | 73 | 71 | 74 |
| Failed | 82 | 66 | 64 | 62 | 66 | 73 |
| Overall | 84 | 71 | 70 | 67 | 69 | 73 |

**Logit models – financial ratios**

Initially 40 ratios were calculated for the 10 year 75 matched company and 5 year 111 matched company samples. These 40 ratios comprised 6 that loaded on profitability, 13 on liquidity, 5 on gearing, 2 on size, 2 on growth, 1 on turnover, 4 on asset proportions and 7 on variability/risk. These were then reduced to a set of eighteen by reference to previous factor analysis studies of UK manufacturing companies' ratios.[4]

Logit models were then developed on the 111 matched pair company samples for all feasible combinations of the ratios, ensuring that one was selected from each category (profitability, liquidity, gearing, size, asset turnover and asset proportions). The misclassification errors of these models were then compared, and there were two models which performed considerably better than the rest. It was therefore decided to use these for the remainder of the study, and in particular that with the lowest misclassification rate. The six variables thus included were

| Earnings before interest and tax/Total assets | (EBIT/TA) | $X_1$ |
|---|---|---|
| Current assets/Current liabilities | (CA/CL) | $X_2$ |
| Total liabilities/Total assets | (TL/TA) | $X_3$ |
| $Log_e$ of total assets | $(Log_e TA)$ | $X_4$ |
| Sales/Total assets | (S/TA) | $X_5$ |
| Current assets/Total assets | (CA/TA) | $X_6$ |

A statistical profile of these ratios is shown in Table 12.3, indicating both the means and standard deviations (SDs).

**Table 12.3: Statistical Profile of the Ratios**

| Variable | Non-failed firms | | Failed firms | | | |
| | | | 2 years prior to bankruptcy | | 1 year prior to bankruptcy | |
| | Mean | SD | Mean | SD | Mean | SD |
|---|---|---|---|---|---|---|
| EBIT/TA | 0.13 | 0.11 | 0.04 | 0.07 | -0.01 | 0.11 |
| CA/CL | 2.00 | 1.22 | 1.38 | 0.63 | 1.22 | 0.53 |
| TL/TA | 0.48 | 0.30 | 0.63 | 0.43 | 0.66 | 0.23 |
| $Log_e TA$ | 16.60 | 1.34 | 15.79 | 1.36 | 15.82 | 1.33 |
| S/TA | 1.79 | 1.32 | 1.35 | 0.63 | 1.41 | 0.72 |
| CA/TA | 0.71 | 0.58 | 0.66 | 0.18 | 0.63 | 0.19 |

A number of logit models[5] were then estimated from the 111 matched pair sample as follows:

(1) A full model assuming an equal incidence of failed and non-failed companies.

(2) A full model assuming different incidences of failed and non-failed companies (2:98, 5:95, 10:90 and 20:80).

(3) Models as for (1) and (2) above but developed on an analysis sample of 70 companies for testing on a hold out sample of 41 companies.

Further hold out tests were then carried out using the models developed under (1) and (2) out-of-sample to see how well they performed at different points in time.

*The full model assuming an equal incidence of failure/non- failure*

The estimates for the full model with a 50:50 probability of failure/non-failure are shown in Table 12.4. The LR test statistics show that each of the equations is clearly significant, and the t and p values indicate that several of the independent variables have strong explanatory power.[6] Moreover, the classificational accuracy (shown in Table 12.6) is relatively good, reaching over 80% for both failed and non-failed companies in the year before failure. Interestingly the classifications are very similar to those reported in Table 12.2 for the models where qualitative indicators were used as the independent variables (albeit over successive five year windows). Further, it needs to be pointed out again that if allowance is made for the sampling bias problem, the error rate for non-failed firms will increase considerably. Consequently, it is fairly clear that the model would be of limited practical value to analysts after misclassification costs are taken into account.

## Table 12.4: Logit Estimates of Full Model with a Prior Probability of Failure of 50%

Independent variables

| Years prior to failure | | $X_0$ | $X_1$ | $X_2$ | $X_3$ | $X_4$ | $X_5$ | $X_6$ | LR[†] |
|---|---|---|---|---|---|---|---|---|---|
| 1 | parameter | 9.9* | 14.2* | .32 | 9.79* | -.78* | -1.1* | -1.1 | 0.504 |
| | t-value | 3.2 | -3.9 | .50 | 4.19 | -4.0 | -3.6 | -.53 | (155.2) |
| | p-value | 0.0 | 0.0 | 0.6 | 0.0 | 0.0 | 0.0 | 0.6 | * |
| 2 | parameter | 10.9* | -14.9* | -.08 | 9.19* | -.80* | -1.5* | 1.43 | 0.437 |
| | t-value | 3.8 | -3.9 | -.20 | 4.14 | -4.7 | -4.4 | .85 | (134.4) |
| | p-value | 0.0 | 0.0 | 0.9 | 0.0 | 0.0 | 0.0 | 0.4 | * |
| 3 | parameter | 10.9* | -9.7* | -.76 | 4.96* | -.68* | -1.1* | 2.42 | 0.313 |
| | t-value | 4.4 | -2.8 | -1.4 | 2.40 | -4.8 | -3.8 | 1.45 | (96.39) |
| | p-value | 0.0 | 0.0 | 0.1 | 0.1 | 0.0 | 0.0 | 0.1 | * |
| 4 | parameter | 10.6* | 1.1 | -.23 | 5.18* | -.77* | -1.1* | 1.45 | 0.253 |
| | t-value | 4.7 | .44 | -.80 | 3.09 | -5.6 | -3.6 | 1.06 | (77.80) |
| | p-value | 0.0 | 0.7 | 0.4 | 0.0 | 0.0 | 0.0 | 0.3 | * |
| 5 | parameter | 12.0* | -1.5 | -.36 | 3.89* | -.77* | -1.1* | 1.12 | 0.248 |
| | t-value | 5.0 | -.65 | -1.1 | 2.33 | -5.6 | -3.5 | .80 | (76.42) |
| | p-value | 0.0 | 0.5 | 0.3 | 0.0 | 0.0 | 0.0 | 0.4 | * |

Notes:[†] LR index shown first. The LR test statistic is shown in parenthesis. (See endnote 3).
Critical value of chi square (6, 0.001) = 22.46.
* Significant at the 95% confidence level

### The full model with different probabilities of failure/non-failure

A rather different picture emerged, however, when the sample probability weights were altered. To illustrate this, the results when assuming a prior probability of 2% of companies will go bankrupt in any one year are shown in Table 12.5. As can be seen, the models did not work anywhere near as well, although in terms of the LR test statistic the equations were significant at the 95% confidence level in each of the last two years before failure. Moreover, as Table 12.6 shows, the classificational accuracy was very much worse, the majority of non-failing companies being incorrectly identified as failures. Indeed, this was true even in the last two years before failure, when only 27% and 38.7% were correctly classified.

## Table 12.5: Logit Estimates of Full Model with a Prior Probability of Failure of 2%

Independent variables

| Years prior to failure | | $X_0$ | $X_1$ | $X_2$ | $X_3$ | $X_4$ | $X_5$ | $X_6$ | LR† |
|---|---|---|---|---|---|---|---|---|---|
| 1 | parameter | 15.6* | -20.9 | .51 | 14.5 | -.97 | -1.8* | -1.1 | 0.469 |
| | t-value | 1.7 | -1.4 | .31 | 1.53 | -1.5 | -1.7 | -.22 | (20.39) |
| | p-value | 0.1 | 0.2 | 0.8 | 0.1 | 0.1 | 0.1 | 0.8 | * |
| 2 | parameter | 18.8* | -13.2 | -.28 | 11.1 | -1.1 | -1.9* | 3.28 | 0.363 |
| | t-value | 1.9 | -1.5 | -.40 | 1.56 | -1.6 | -2.0 | .76 | (15.81) |
| | p-value | 0.1 | 0.2 | 0.7 | 0.1 | 0.1 | 0.0 | 0.5 | * |
| 3 | parameter | 16.0* | -20.2 | -1.0 | 5.34 | -.76* | -1.2 | 4.56 | 0.276 |
| | t-value | 2.1 | -1.5 | -1.1 | 1.14 | -1.8 | -1.4 | .97 | (11.99) |
| | p-value | 0.0 | 0.1 | 0.3 | 0.3 | 0.1 | 0.2 | 0.3 | |
| 4 | parameter | 14.6* | 1.3 | -.22 | 5.99 | -.88* | -1.1 | 3.29 | 0.180 |
| | t-value | 2.3 | .12 | -.42 | 1.13 | -1.8 | -1.6 | 1.05 | (7.83) |
| | p-value | 0.0 | 0.9 | 0.7 | 0.3 | 0.1 | 0.1 | 0.3 | |
| 5 | parameter | 14.1* | -1.9 | -.10 | 5.33 | -.82 | -1.3 | 3.75 | 0.173 |
| | t-value | 2.5 | -.30 | -.11 | .84 | -1.6 | -1.3 | .85 | (7.53) |
| | p-value | 0.0 | 0.8 | 0.9 | 0.4 | 0.1 | 0.2 | 0.4 | |

*Notes*: † LR index shown first. The LR test statistic is shown in parenthesis. (See endnote 3).
Critical value of chi square (6, 0.05) = 12.59.
* Significant at the 95% confidence level

## Table 12.6: Classificational Accuracy of Logit Models Using Financial Ratio Variables

| Years prior to failure | Full model 50:50 probability | | | Full model 2:98 probability | | |
|---|---|---|---|---|---|---|
| | NF % | F % | T % | NF % | F % | T % |
| 1 | 83.8 | 86.5 | 85.1 | 38.7 | 100.0 | 69.4 |
| 2 | 78.3 | 84.7 | 81.5 | 27.0 | 100.0 | 63.5 |
| 3 | 78.3 | 76.6 | 77.5 | 16.2 | 100.0 | 58.1 |
| 4 | 73.0 | 77.5 | 75.2 | 3.6 | 100.0 | 51.8 |
| 5 | 73.9 | 75.7 | 74.8 | 3.6 | 100.0 | 51.8 |

*Note:* NF = non-failed; F= failed; T = total

277

It is the nature of the models that they will perform relatively well at classifying companies in the estimation sample, since they are derived precisely to do that. Effectively the procedures employed to estimate the discriminatory equations will trade off misclassifications of bankrupt companies against those of surviving firms.

Clearly with an equal probability model one might intuitively expect more misclassifications of non-failing companies as there is likely to be less homogeneity in the surviving businesses (e.g. some will be making large profits, while others will not; some will be highly geared, while others will have relatively low amounts of borrowing; and so on). By contrast, failing companies are more likely to display similar attributes immediately before their collapse (e.g. low profits and high amounts of borrowing). But it also seems intuitively likely that when the weighting is altered to reflect more realistic prior probabilities, the misclassifications of bankrupt companies will fall and those of surviving firms increase.

### Table 12.7: Logit Estimates of Full Model for 70 Companies with a Prior Probability of Failure of 50%

| Years prior to failure | | Independent variables | | | | | | | |
|---|---|---|---|---|---|---|---|---|---|
| | | $X_0$ | $X_1$ | $X_2$ | $X_3$ | $X_4$ | $X_5$ | $X_6$ | LR† |
| 1 | parameter | 12.8* | -23.9* | 1.0 | 13.6* | -1.1* | -1.4* | -.90 | 0.576 |
| | t-value | 2.9 | -3.7 | 1.2 | 3.59 | -3.6 | -3.3 | -.36 | (111.8) |
| | p-value | 0.0 | 0.0 | 0.2 | 0.0 | 0.0 | 0.0 | 0.7 | * |
| 2 | parameter | 11.9* | -13.3* | -.70 | 6.39* | -.78* | -1.8* | 3.42 | 0.404 |
| | t-value | 3.5 | -2.7 | -.97 | 2.30 | -3.7 | -3.8 | 1.42 | (78.48) |
| | p-value | 0.0 | 0.0 | 0.3 | 0.0 | 0.0 | 0.0 | 0.2 | * |
| 3 | parameter | 11.1* | -9.9* | -1.4 | 2.35 | -.60* | -1.3* | 3.79 | 0.326 |
| | t-value | 3.7 | -2.1 | -1.8 | .86 | -3.5 | -3.2 | 1.67 | (63.26) |
| | p-value | 0.0 | 0.0 | 0.1 | 0.1 | 0.0 | 0.0 | 0.1 | * |
| 4 | parameter | 11.1* | 1.5 | -.81 | 2.40 | -.68* | -1.6* | 3.21 | 0.279 |
| | t-value | 3.9 | .39 | -1.4 | .96 | -4.1 | -3.2 | 1.53 | (54.37) |
| | p-value | 0.0 | 0.7 | 0.4 | 0.0 | 0.0 | 0.0 | 0.3 | * |
| 5 | parameter | 11.7* | .97 | -.33 | 4.58* | -.78* | -1.4* | 1.43 | 0.296 |
| | t-value | 4.0 | .31 | -.81 | 2.13 | -4.6 | -3.2 | .75 | (53.28) |
| | p-value | 0.0 | 0.8 | 0.4 | 0.0 | 0.0 | 0.0 | 0.5 | * |

*Notes*: † LR index shown first. The LR test statistic is shown in parenthesis. (See endnote 3).
  Critical value of chi square (6, 0.001) = 22.46.
  * Significant at the 95% confidence level

The results reported in Table 12.6 are therefore very much as might have been anticipated – and they are very similar, in fact, to those reported in other failure prediction studies. In the circumstances, the only true test of the power of the models is to undertake a series of hold out tests. This was first done in this study for the 50:50 and 2:98 probability models by splitting the estimation sample, using data for 70 matched pairs of companies to derive the equations. These were then tested on the remaining 41 matched pairs to see how well they discriminated between the failed and non-failing firms.

Such an approach, however, does not assess how well the models might perform, first, in periods outside those used for estimation purposes; and, second, on broader based samples of companies. Consequently two of the models were applied to out-of-sample data sets: a group of 21 listed companies which failed over the period 1988-91; and to two groups of 100 surviving companies, one for the period 1983-84, the other for 1992-93.

As explained above, for the split sample tests the equal prior probability model was re-estimated on a random subsample of 70 matched pairs of companies. It can be seen from Table 12.7 that the models derived were very similar to those estimated on the full 111 matched pairs and summarised in Table 12.4. Moreover, the classificatory power for both the estimation and hold out samples (shown in Table 12.8) was impressive, generally being at least as good as (and in some instances better than) that recorded for the 111 matched pair sample in the left hand panel of Table 12.6. This implies that the failing and surviving companies in the hold out sample shared similar characteristics to those in the estimation sample (e.g. not only in respect of profitability, gearing, liquidity, size, etc, but also with regard to the impact of general economic events and industry membership).

**Table 12.8: Classificational Accuracy of Analysis and Hold Out Samples with a Prior Probability of Failure of 50%**

| Years prior to failure | Analysis sample of 70 matched pairs | | | Hold out sample of 41 matched pairs | | |
|---|---|---|---|---|---|---|
| | NF | F | T | NF | F | T |
| | % | % | % | % | % | % |
| 1 | 84.3 | 90.0 | 87.1 | 90.2 | 80.5 | 85.4 |
| 2 | 78.6 | 84.3 | 81.4 | 85.4 | 87.8 | 86.6 |
| 3 | 75.7 | 75.7 | 75.7 | 80.5 | 78.0 | 79.3 |
| 4 | 68.6 | 72.9 | 70.7 | 73.1 | 82.9 | 78.0 |
| 5 | 75.7 | 75.7 | 75.7 | 73.1 | 75.6 | 74.4 |

*Note:* NF = non-failed; F = failed; T = total

279

Similar procedures were carried out on the split sample assuming different prior probabilities of failure. The equations were again similar to those reported for corresponding models estimated on the whole sample of 111 matched pairs, but as expected the discriminatory power with respect to surviving firms (and therefore overall as well) declined sharply as the prior probability of failure was reduced. This is illustrated in Table 12.9, which shows the classificational accuracy for a prior probability of failure of 2%. It can clearly be seen that while predictive power is generally good for bankrupt firms, it is much weaker overall for both the estimation and hold out samples, and particularly for non-failing companies.

In practice a bankruptcy prediction model will be used by analysts out-of-sample to try to identify potentially failing firms. Not only are the underlying economic conditions likely to be different (e.g. with respect to interest and foreign exchange rates, whether the economy is going into or emerging from a recession, etc), but the types of firm represented in the sample are likely to differ (e.g. in terms of size, industry membership, etc).

In the circumstances it was decided to carry out three inter-temporal hold out tests. The first covered 21 listed companies which collapsed between 1988 and 1991. This was a period when the economy was going into recession, but a downturn of a very different kind to that in the late 1970s and early 1980s (when most of the companies in the original study failed).

### Table 12. 9: Classificational Accuracy of Analysis and Hold Out Samples with a Prior Probability of Failure of 2%

| Years prior to failure | Analysis sample of 70 matched pairs | | | Hold out sample of 41 matched pairs | | |
|---|---|---|---|---|---|---|
| | NF % | F % | T % | NF % | F % | T % |
| 1 | 48.6 | 98.6 | 73.6 | 63.8 | 92.7 | 78.3 |
| 2 | 30.0 | 100.0 | 65.0 | 26.8 | 95.1 | 61.0 |
| 3 | 12.9 | 100.0 | 56.5 | 7.3 | 100.0 | 53.7 |
| 4 | 9.6 | 100.0 | 54.8 | 7.3 | 97.6 | 52.5 |
| 5 | 5.7 | 100.0 | 52.9 | 2.4 | 100.0 | 51.2 |

*Note*:   NF = non-failed; F = failed; T = total

The two non-failed hold out samples were taken at different points in time and using very different sampling frames. (The case for doing this was simply that in practice analysts would probably wish to use failure prediction models in a number of ways, and the procedures used seemed to be a reasonable approximation of what might be attempted in practice.)

The first sample of 100 non-failed companies was in fact selected from Extel's 1984 *Handbook of Market Leaders*. This lists all the companies which then comprised the FT-Actuaries All Share Index, and in applying the model the only criterion for exclusion was that companies randomly chosen should not belong to the financial sector. It can therefore be seen that the sample was biased towards relatively large companies, and the industry composition was very different from that of the original estimation sample (e.g. it contained many more companies in the distribution sector). The other main difference from most of the estimation period is that the year chosen was one where the economy was emerging from recession.

The second randomly selected sample of 100 non-failed companies was taken from the Macmillan *Stock Exchange Year Book 1996*, which lists all 4,104 companies whose securities were quoted on the London market at the beginning of the year. Once more, the only criterion for exclusion was if a business operated in the financial sector. The period covered (1993-94) was one where the economy was still struggling to emerge from the recession of 1989-1990, but on this occasion there were many more small listed companies in the sample. Again, however, the industry representation in the sample was very different from that in the population used for estimating the models.

**Table 12.10: Classificational Accuracy of Inter-Temporal Hold Out Samples with Prior Probabilities of Failure of 50% and 2%**

| Years prior to failure | Sample of 21 failed companies 1988-91 | Sample of 100 non-failed companies, 1983-84 | Sample of 100 non-failed companies, 1993-94 |
|---|---|---|---|
| Model with prior probability of failure 50% *% correctly classified* | | | |
| 1 | 38 | 96 | 75 |
| 4 | 43 | 97 | 86 |
| Model with prior probability of failure 2% *% correctly classified* | | | |
| 1 | 100 | 46 | 22 |
| 4 | 76 | 37 | 14 |

Given the different circumstances, it was anticipated that the misclassification rates would probably be quite high. Indeed this proved to be the case, as can be seen in Table 12.10. However, what is potentially interesting is the trade-off in performance. Thus the equal probability model is relatively good at identifying surviving companies, particularly for the 1983-84 sample. (A check with the 1993-94 companies showed that this could largely be explained by the size of the firms in the sample.) On the other hand, its record in correctly identifying failing firms is not very impressive.

By contrast – as might perhaps have been expected – the model where the prior probability of failure is estimated at 2% performed far better at identifying failed companies – but only at the expense of misclassifying many of the surviving companies as potential failures!

It is fairly clear from the results that a model developed with prior probability weights of somewhere between 20:80 and 30:70 would be likely to perform better, but although a one-year-before-failure model derived on this basis would be good at classifying bankrupt companies, it would still almost certainly generate an unacceptably high misclassification rate for surviving firms. In fact, this would be in line with the out-of-sample results reported by Taffler and Altman, since they both indicate that their models misclassify around 20% of surviving companies as failures.[7] Moreover, one might well expect the Taffler models to perform better than the ones reported here, since they have been derived to relate to smaller, more homogeneous subsamples of companies (e.g. in industry and in distribution). (Indeed, Taffler's main model is apparently only applicable to a relatively small subsample of 600-650 industrial companies listed on the Stock Exchange.)

**'Rolling' logit models**

It will be recalled from the discussion in chapter 4 that data over a period of years can be stacked to enable multilogit models to be developed.[8] However, this means that over a five year period with six explanatory variables over 15,000 possible models could be developed. Such a procedure smacks of 'data mining', and apart from the danger of 'overfitting'[9] there is the additional problem that to develop such models it is really necessary to apply the procedure with hindsight.

In the circumstances, it would seem to be more sensible from an operational perspective to try to develop a 'rolling' logit model. However, before this was attempted the opportunity was first taken to see how the models estimated on previous years' data performed when they were used to predict failures and non-failures in subsequent years.

As might have been expected, none did as well as the models specifically estimated on the data for the year in question. Thus, for instance, using equal probabilities of failure/non-failure, the model estimated on data five years prior to failure for 70 matched pairs correctly classified 84.3% of bankrupt companies and 77.1% of non-failed businesses on the final year's figures. This compared to correct classification rates of 90.0% and 84.3% for the model estimated on the final year's data. Similarly, on hold out samples of 41 matched pairs the model

**Table 12.11: Logit Estimates of 'Rolling' Model with a Prior Probability of Failure of 50%**

| Years prior to failure | | $X_0$ | $X_1$ | $X_2$ | $X_3$ | $X_4$ | $X_5$ | $X_6$ | $X_7$ | LR† |
|---|---|---|---|---|---|---|---|---|---|---|
| | | | | | Independent variables | | | | | |
| 1 | parameter | 2.8 | 12.6* | .16 | 5.63* | -.37 | -.63* | -.02 | 2.92* | 0.529 |
| | t-value | 0.7 | -3.5 | .24 | 2.03 | -1.5 | -1.8 | -.00 | 2.8 | (162.89)* |
| | p-value | 0.5 | 0.0 | 0.8 | 0.0 | 0.1 | 0.1 | 1.0 | 0.0 | |
| 2 | parameter | 6.3 | -14.6* | -.05 | 7.50* | -.55* | -1.2* | 1.07 | 1.59 | 0.442 |
| | t-value | 1.4 | -3.9 | -.11 | 2.97 | -2.2 | -3.0 | .63 | 1.31 | (135.96)* |
| | p-value | 0.2 | 0.0 | 0.9 | 0.0 | 0.0 | 0.0 | 0.5 | 0.2 | |
| 3 | parameter | 5.2 | -10.4* | -.58 | 2.98 | -.36 | -.78* | 1.87 | 2.17 | 0.330 |
| | t-value | 1.2 | -3.0 | -1.1 | 1.23 | -1.5 | -2.1 | 1.08 | 1.49 | (101.66)* |
| | p-value | 0.2 | 0.0 | 0.3 | 0.2 | 0.2 | 0.0 | 0.3 | 0.1 | |
| 4 | parameter | 3.2 | .69 | -.14 | 2.85 | -.36 | -.59 | 1.21 | 2.71 | 0.262 |
| | t-value | .64 | .28 | -.46 | 1.32 | -1.3 | -1.5 | .87 | 1.62 | (80.48)* |
| | p-value | 0.5 | 0.8 | 0.6 | 0.2 | 0.2 | 0.1 | 0.4 | 0.1 | |
| 5 | parameter | 12.0* | -1.5 | -.36 | 3.89* | -.77* | -1.1* | 1.12 | - | 0.248 |
| | t-value | 5.0 | -.65 | -1.1 | 2.33 | -5.6 | -3.5 | .80 | - | (76.42)* |
| | p-value | 0.0 | 0.5 | 0.3 | 0.0 | 0.0 | 0.0 | 0.4 | - | |

*Notes*: † LR index shown first. The LR test statistic is shown in parenthesis. (See endnote 3).
Critical value of chi square (7, 0.001) = 24.32.
* Significant at the 95% confidence level

estimated on data five years prior to failure correctly classified 78% of bankrupt companies and 82.9% of non-failed businesses on the final year's figures. The corresponding correct classification rates for the model estimated on the final year's data were 80.5% and 90.2% respectively.

In applying the 'rolling' logit technique, the incremental information given by the model estimated on each year's data was carried forward as a 'score' for each company into the next year's model. In fact, this was done in two ways: first, by including a dummy indicator, 1 or 0, reflecting whether or not the previous year's model had suggested a particular company was a prima facie failure or non-failure; and, second, by including the dependent variable continuous score of the previous year's model. Both suggested that the inclusion of the extra variable, $X_7$, increased the classificatory power of the models. To illustrate the effect, the results where the previous year's dependent variable continuous scores were included are shown in Tables 12.11-12.13.

### Table 12.12: Logit Estimates of 'Rolling' Model with a Prior Probability of Failure of 2%

| Years prior to failure | | $X_0$ | $X_1$ | $X_2$ | $X_3$ | $X_4$ | $X_5$ | $X_6$ | $X_7$ | LR† |
|---|---|---|---|---|---|---|---|---|---|---|
| | | | | | Independent variables | | | | | |
| 1 | parameter | 6.4 | -20.5 | .82 | 11.7 | -.75 | -1.3 | -1.5 | 6.63* | 0.523 |
| | t-value | .77 | -1.00 | .35 | 1.32 | -1.1 | -1.4 | -.22 | 1.76 | (22.77)* |
| | p-value | 0.4 | 0.3 | 0.7 | 0.2 | 0.3 | 0.2 | 0.8 | 0.1 | |
| 2 | parameter | -.70 | -12.0 | -.05 | 7.51 | -.56 | -1.3 | 1.76 | 12.1 | 0.416 |
| | t-value | -.04 | -1.16 | -.06 | 1.01 | -.68 | -1.5 | .35 | 1.27 | (18.09)* |
| | p-value | 1.0 | 0.3 | 1.0 | 0.3 | 0.5 | 0.1 | 0.7 | 0.2 | |
| 3 | parameter | 7.5 | -20.1 | -.80 | 5.28 | -.60 | -1.1 | 4.09 | 5.98 | 0.299 |
| | t-value | .73 | -1.39 | -.83 | 1.07 | -1.4 | -1.3 | .80 | 1.30 | (13.00) |
| | p-value | 0.5 | 0.2 | 0.4 | 0.3 | 0.2 | 0.2 | 0.4 | 0.2 | |
| 4 | parameter | 3.9 | 1.2 | -.17 | 3.99 | -.58 | -.72 | 2.41 | 7.15 | 0.190 |
| | t-value | .23 | .12 | -.33 | .66 | -.96 | -1.0 | .76 | .62 | (8.28) |
| | p-value | 0.8 | 0.9 | 0.7 | 0.5 | 0.3 | 0.3 | 0.5 | 0.5 | |
| 5 | parameter | 14.1* | -1.9 | -.10 | 5.33 | -.82 | -1.3 | 3.75 | - | 0.173 |
| | t-value | 2.5 | -.30 | -.11 | .84 | -1.6 | -1.3 | .85 | - | (7.53) |
| | p-value | 0.0 | 0.8 | 0.9 | 0.4 | 0.1 | 0.2 | 0.4 | - | |

*Notes:* † LR index shown first. The LR test statistic is shown in parenthesis. (See endnote 3).
   Critical values of chi square: $(7, 0.01) = 18.48$; $(7, 0.05) = 14.07$; $(7, 0.10) = 12.02$.
 * Significant at the 95% confidence level

Inspection of Table 12.11 shows that the equal probability model equations were again highly significant. Moreover, in all five years $X_7$ was one of the strongest explanatory variables in the models and was significant along with profitability

$(X_1)$, gearing $(X_3)$ and asset turnover $(X_5)$ for the last year before bankruptcy. In addition, classificational accuracy was slightly improved (see Tables 12.6 and 12.13).

When the prior probability weights were changed to 2:98 in order to reflect a truer incidence of failure to non-failure in the population, the equations were only significant at the 90% confidence levels or above in the last three years before failure (see Table 12.12). Moreover, the explanatory power of the individual ratios was greatly reduced – although, interestingly, in the last year before bankruptcy it was the previous year's failure probability index, $X_7$, which was the most influential factor. Once again overall classificational accuracy (and especially with respect to surviving firms) was greatly reduced when the prior probability weights were altered from 50:50 to 2:98. But, as a comparison of Tables 12.6 and 12.13 shows, the inclusion of $X_7$ noticeably improves the position.

### Table 12.13: Classificational Accuracy
### of 'Rolling' Logit Models

| Years prior to failure | Full model 50:50 probability | | | Full model 2:98 probability | | |
|---|---|---|---|---|---|---|
| | NF | F | T | NF | F | T |
| | % | % | % | % | % | % |
| 1 | 85.6 | 88.3 | 86.9 | 45.9 | 100.0 | 73.0 |
| 2 | 80.2 | 83.8 | 82.0 | 34.2 | 100.0 | 67.1 |
| 3 | 76.6 | 79.3 | 77.9 | 20.7 | 100.0 | 60.4 |
| 4 | 74.8 | 78.4 | 76.6 | 8.1 | 100.0 | 54.1 |
| 5 | 73.9 | 75.7 | 74.8 | 3.6 | 100.0 | 51.8 |

**The impact of misclassification costs**

As explained previously (pp. 126-7), the appropriate procedure for taking misclassification costs into account with a logit model is to alter the cutoff point. This was therefore done using Altman's (1977) estimate that the cost of misclassifying a bankrupt firm as non-failed is approximately seven times greater than misclassifying a surviving company as bankrupt. As expected, this substantially improved the classificational accuracy of the models, a point illustrated in Table 12.14, where the results assuming a 2% prior probability of failure can be directly compared for both analysis and hold out samples with those given in Table 12.9.

However, the point was made on p. 127 that, while the procedure may be appropriate for assessing the classificatory power of a model on the sample of data from which it was derived, it is likely to be of little help in ensuring its practical

**Table 12.14: Classificational Accuracy of Analysis and Hold Out Samples with a Prior Probability of Failure of 2% and Allowing for Misclassification Costs**

| Years prior to failure | Analysis sample of 70 matched pairs | | | Hold out sample of 41 matched pairs | | |
|---|---|---|---|---|---|---|
| | NF | F | T | NF | F | T |
| | % | % | % | % | % | % |
| 1 | 71.4 | 97.1 | 84.3 | 75.6 | 87.8 | 81.7 |
| 2 | 51.4 | 98.6 | 75.0 | 58.5 | 90.2 | 74.4 |
| 3 | 32.9 | 97.1 | 65.0 | 34.1 | 97.6 | 65.9 |
| 4 | 28.6 | 98.6 | 63.6 | 19.5 | 92.7 | 56.1 |
| 5 | 24.3 | 98.6 | 61.5 | 19.5 | 97.6 | 58.6 |

*Note:* NF = non-failed; F = failed; T = total

effectiveness as a predictive device. As can be seen from the hold out results, a large number of misclassification errors still occur, and the costs of these will have to be borne by an analyst who tries to use the model. Moreover, as is generally the case, the models perform best on the last year's financial ratios. Unfortunately, as case study analysis shows, in many cases the accounts when published will precipitate a company's collapse.

Ultimately the proof of the pudding will be in the eating. A model will have to be developed by varying the cut off points until error rates and misclassification costs are minimised out-of-sample. What is clear from the figures reported in Tables 12.8, 12.9, 12.10 and 12.14 is that the performance achieved on an analysis sample (and, indeed, on a hold out sample) is difficult to replicate on broader based samples drawn from a population of companies at different points in time. Even the well tried models of Altman and Taffler have been unable to reduce misclassification rates of surviving companies to below 20%, which would appear to be unacceptably high in terms of the cost implications.

**Taffler variable models**

Although, when based on estimation sample data, the discriminatory power of the models developed in this study is comparable to that of other models described in the literature, performance appears to be rather worse out-of-sample. This is not altogether surprising because the equations were estimated on a broader and less homogeneous sample of companies. It would therefore be interesting to make a closer comparison between the rival models.

In fact, Taffler has developed two MDA models from data published by British listed companies (see Taffler, 1984).[10] The final version of the first, for manufacturing companies, employs four variables: profit before tax/average current liabilities; current assets/total liabilities; current liabilities/total assets; and the no-credit-interval.[11] The final form of the second, for distribution businesses, uses four slightly different variables: cash flow/total liabilities; debt/quick assets; current liabilities/total assets; and the no-credit-interval.

Understandably, for commercial reasons Taffler has not published the coefficients in his model. However, it is possible to estimate models for each of the five years before failure – here applying logit rather than MDA – using the same variables. This was done for equal prior probabilities, the manufacturing models being based on a sample of 95 matched pairs and the distribution models on a sample of 16 matched pairs. The models fitted well, with misclassification rates of around 20% in the last two years before failure – very similar to those reported by Taffler (1994).

No adjustment was made in the estimation procedure, either for sampling bias or for the incidence of misclassification costs, although the latter would substantially offset the former. In this sense the models derived are not strictly comparable with those developed by Taffler, who did make such adjustments. One other point worth noting is that when the 'rolling' logit procedure was applied, the superior ability of such models in correctly classifying companies was less marked than for the models previously described (see Table 12.15).

### Table 12.15: Classificational Accuracy for Taffler Variable Models

| Years prior to failure | Full Models | | 'Rolling' Models | |
|:---:|:---:|:---:|:---:|:---:|
| | M | D | M | D |
| | % | % | % | % |
| 1 | 83.2 | 78.1 | 82.1 | 87.5 |
| 2 | 79.4 | 81.3 | 78.9 | 81.3 |
| 3 | 74.7 | 78.1 | 72.6 | 81.3 |
| 4 | 63.2 | 62.5 | 67.9 | 68.8 |
| 5 | 65.8 | 68.8 | 65.8 | 68.8 |

*Note*: M = manufacturing model; D = distribution model

## The use of matched pairing as a control technique

In view of the relatively high degree of misclassification errors evident in most failure prediction studies, it is necessary to look for likely explanations. One possible reason is a flaw in the matched pairing procedure.

In fact, it will be recalled that most bankruptcy identification models are developed using this device as a means of trying to control for systematic factors affecting the data.[12] However, the criteria and justification for the matched pairing control technique are rarely explained (Ohlson, 1980, p. 112). Usually the criteria used for matching are year and industry membership, but sometimes size is used as well. A major problem is that the procedure excludes the chosen criteria as potential independent variables which might help to determine bankruptcy. This is unfortunate as all three appear to help to explain corporate collapse.

Some researchers have sought to minimise the problem by using dummy variables instead (e.g. to indicate industry membership) or only using one factor as a matching criterion. Clearly there is a strong case for allowing for industry characteristics as financial ratios differ markedly between different sectors.[13] But equally there is a greater likelihood of companies failing during a recession.[14]

Over a cross section of companies, errors from mismatching by industry might be expected to cancel out, although the likely effect will be to weaken the significance of an equation and produce a greater number of misclassifications. Ignoring the year of failure, however – as Peel, Peel and Pope (1985, 1986) and Peel and Peel (1987) do – is likely to introduce a bias into a model and strengthen its apparent predictive power. This is because there will presumably be a number of observations relating to non-failed companies which are taken from boom years, while the majority of bankrupt companies are likely to have failed in the depths of a recession.

It will be recalled that the studies reported previously in this chapter match companies by industry and year. However, the sample used is relatively large, which makes it possible to assess part of the impact of applying the matching technique. Accordingly, 80 of the 111 surviving companies were matched by industry and year into 40 pairs. One of the two firms in each pair was assigned to Pool 1, the other going into Pool 2, and a logit model was then estimated on the six accounting variables used previously. The expectation was, first, that in discriminating between Pool 1 and Pool 2 companies the model would have no statistically significant explanatory power; and, second, that the numbers of correct and incorrect classifications would be approximately equal. Surprisingly, in the first run the estimated equation was statistically significant at the 95% confidence level, and the t statistics of two of the independent variables were also significant. Moreover, errors in the classifications could not be attributed to random chance at the 98% confidence level. In order to check that this was not a freak result, the procedure was replicated twice more by reassigning companies to Pools 1 and 2 on a random basis. The equations were still nearly significant at the 90% confidence level, and the misclassification errors could still not be attributed to chance.

Although no clear systematic pattern could be discerned, these results have interesting implications for failure identification studies, including those reported earlier in this chapter. Presumably even when models appear to work well, they have a similar propensity to misclassify companies as failed and non-failed because of biases resulting from the matching procedure. This would suggest that considerable care has to be taken when interpreting the performance of a failure identification model, especially where the data have had to be pooled across industries and over time.

**Survival analysis**

It will be recalled from the discussion in chapter 4 that duration models can be used to try to estimate how long individuals are likely to live. Such information is of special interest to life assurance companies. Similarly, businesses offering warranties on the products which they sell will want to know their likely survival rates.

Clearly in a similar vein these duration models can also be used to study how long individual firms are likely to survive. The main requirement is that sufficient data are available relating to the births and deaths of companies. This is likely to be the case for a cohort of small firms with a common incorporation date; and for firms in an industry which have been subject to a common destabilising shock.

Regrettably the data available for the present study are inappropriate for the application of survival analysis. Instead of having a time series of data running from a given 'birth date' (e.g. incorporation or a destabilising shock), the sample available only offers data running back from a given 'death date'. Thus it would only be possible to apply the procedure if it were to be assumed that all failing companies suffered a destabilising shock five years before their eventual bankruptcy. This is clearly unrealistic, especially where the companies operated in a number of different industries and their failure dates varied considerably in calendar time.

Out of curiosity, however, the data were run through a survival analysis statistical package to see what problems, if any, arose in trying to apply the procedure. Using the same explanatory variables as were run in the logit models, the Cox Proportional Hazard and Weibull models were applied to the data for the 111 matched pairs of companies. The signs for the equations were positive for $X_3$ and $X_6$ and negative for $X_1$, $X_2$, $X_4$, and $X_5$, which was what was predicted. It was also clear that the Weibull model made more sense, since the assumption of strict proportionality of the Cox model helped to produce a situation where the probability of survival in the fifth year suddenly increased. (Indeed, the survival probabilities for the average failed company became higher than those for the average non-failed company.)

The exercise was then repeated, increasing the data set from 1,110 observations to 55,500 with the non-failed sample being repeated 49 times. This created a population where the ratio of failures to non-failures was a more realistic 2:98. Unfortunately this created storage problems on the computer, so it was decided to split the sample into three equal groups of 37 failed companies and their 1,813 corresponding non-failed counterparts, each group having 18,500 observations. The use of three equally sized groups had the advantage, of course, that it was possible to compare the equations to see how similar they were. Two of the three equations were in fact very similar. However, the signs of the individual coefficients were no longer always in the expected direction.

Overall, the exercise demonstrated that the Weibull model could usefully be applied to an appropriate data set without too much difficulty. In fact, it would seem to be particularly relevant for a cohort of small companies, tracking their experience from a common incorporation date.[15] But for listed companies, where the data available are less homogeneous, use of a logit model would seem to be more appropriate. If an attempt is to be made to try to estimate the life expectancy of listed companies, the much simpler (albeit rather crude) gambler's ruin model would seem to be a more suitable method of analysis.

## Summary

The results of the multivariate analysis show that, before allowance is made for sampling bias, both the qualitative and financial ratio models discriminate well between failed and non-failed firms. Overall, the ability to classify firms correctly in the last year prior to failure (and before adjusting for sampling bias) is around 85%, regardless of which model was run (i.e. using qualitative or financial variables, and in the latter case with the basic, rolling or 'Taffler' indicators). This level of predictive accuracy is in line with most previous studies, especially when allowance is made for the fact that the population on which the models were estimated in this study was larger and consequently more heterogeneous.

The equations fit extremely well in all years when failure is assumed to be as likely as survival, although explanatory power declines the further before failure the equations are estimated. In addition, almost all the explanatory variables in the financial ratio model are significant for the three years prior to bankruptcy. Performance on the hold out samples was also good for these models. By contrast – and what is especially interesting – is that discriminatory power was much weaker when adjustments were made to make the prior probability of failure more realistic.

The results in terms of classificational accuracy are summarised in Table 12.16. This includes corresponding data for the univariate models given in chapter 11, and (even allowing for different population sizes) it shows that the gambler's ruin model (in particular) and the information decomposition model are broadly comparable in terms of their discriminatory power. However, it should be remembered that in both cases the results were derived from pairwise comparisons rather than across pooled data.

The fact that the models perform best in the last year prior to failure itself creates a problem as frequently the publication of the accounts is the event which precipitates a company's collapse. Consequently analysts will probably find it difficult to use such models to anticipate market reaction. Moreover, when the models were applied to out-of-sample populations, their discriminatory power was generally disappointing. It appears that the 'best performing models' are those where a cut off ratio of around 35% is used. This appears to be similar to that applied by Taffler and Altman, when attempting to adjust for the probability of failure and allowing for the differential incidence of misclassification costs.[16] But even when a cut off around 35% is used, misclassification rates are still generally around 20% for surviving companies, and this is probably too high to make the models operationally useful.

### Table 12.16: Comparison of Classificational Accuracy of Univariate and Multivariate Models

| % correctly classified | *Years prior to failure* | | | | |
|---|---|---|---|---|---|
| | 1 | 2 | 3 | 4 | 5 |
| *Multivariate qualitative* | | | | | |
| Equal probability (50:50)[1] | 84 | 71 | 70 | 67 | 69 |
| *Multivariate ratio* | | | | | |
| Equal probability (50:50)[2] | 85 | 82 | 78 | 75 | 75 |
| 2% probability of failure (2:98)[2] | 69 | 64 | 58 | 52 | 52 |
| Rolling logit (50:50)[2] | 87 | 82 | 78 | 77 | 75 |
| Rolling logit (2:98)[2] | 73 | 67 | 60 | 54 | 52 |
| Misclassification costs adjustment (50:50)[3] | 84 | 75 | 65 | 64 | 62 |
| Taffler variables: manufacturing (50:50)[4] | 83 | 79 | 75 | 63 | 66 |
| *Univariate* | | | | | |
| Profit (with intercept)[2] (equal probability, 50:50) | 78 | 73 | 63 | 53 | 59 |
| Decomposition (50:50)[1] | 71 | 67 | 60 | 63 | 53 |
| Gambler's ruin (50:50)[1] | 87 | 76 | 68 | 64 | 72 |

*Notes:* [1] Sample of 75 companies; [2] Sample of 111 companies; [3] Sample of 70 companies; [4] Sample of 95 companies.

One contributory factor helping to produce relatively high out-of-sample classification error rates may be the result of deriving the equations using data for matched pairs of companies. This problem is difficult to avoid, although it might be ameliorated if residual ratios were used instead (see p. 212). Certainly the usual procedure of basing the models on matched pairs of failed and non-failed companies, pooled across fairly broad industry categories and over time, tends to generalise the results. Consequently the models can be regarded as representing a lowest common denominator of the differences between failing and non-failing firms. But, as the experiments carried out on the data used for this study seem to suggest, there may also be a tendency for the models to misclassify companies regardless: i.e. their discriminatory power is unlikely to be 100% correct except in the most ideal conditions.

**Notes**

[1] According to the univariate analysis this variable had little explanatory power except in the last year before failure.

[2] e.g. by preparing contingency tables.

[3] This particular model was derived using the SPSS package. As part of its output this produces the Likelihood Ratio (LR) index, $1-(\log L_0/\log L_{max})$. $L_{max}$ is the unrestricted residual-sum-of-the-squares value of the likelihood function, and $L_0$ is the restricted value. Like the $R^2$ statistic, the index indicates the goodness of fit: e.g. in the case of a perfect fit, the log likelihood at convergence ($L_{max}$) will be 0 and the index will be 1 (or 100%). If there is no fit the index will equal zero.

   An LR test statistic can also be derived as $-2\log(L_0/L_{max})$, which is similar to the F test. This is distributed as chi square with degrees of freedom equal to the number of independent restrictions imposed (i.e. the number of parameters, excluding the constant). (See Kennedy, 1991, pp. 61-63; 68-69; 71-72; Maddala, 1988, pp. 84-85; 137-139.)

[4] Representatives of the growth and variability/risk categories were excluded as part of this data reduction exercise.

[5] Altogether well over 30 models were devised and run.

[6] Assuming that the null hypothesis is true (i.e. the independent variable has no explanatory power), the p value is the probability of obtaining a sample result which is at least as unlikely as that observed. Thus if the level of significance being tested is .05 and the p value is .01, the null hypothesis is rejected. Consequently, the lower the p value (i.e. the closer to zero), the greater the explanatory power of the independent variable.

[7] See pp. 138 and 140.

[8] See pp. 130-2.

[9] i.e. where a model fits exceptionally well on to the data from which it is derived, but far less well on to other data (e.g. from a hold out sample).

[10] See pp. 138-9.

[11] For a description of the no-credit-interval indicator, see p. 102.

[12] See p. 114.

[13] See pp. 95 and 211-2.

[14] See, for example, the diagrams and data on pages 222, 247 and in Table 9.1 on p. 242.

[15] Studies along these lines are now being undertaken by industrial economists: see pp. 146-7. However, it is far from clear that they could be used operationally by, for example, lending bankers. Thus while it is possible to apply the models with the benefit of hindsight, in practice it would be necessary to have several years data available to use them for prediction purposes. Unfortunately, given the high casualty rate amongst small firms in the first five years of their existence, this is precisely what the analyst can't have!

[16] See pp. 138 and 139.

# 13 Multivariate analysis: Iterative models

## Introduction

A number of iterative models were described in chapter 5, their aim being to try to identify failing businesses by applying a search procedure. The most sophisticated – and potentially powerful – technique is 'neural networking' (NN), which is increasingly being used for business applications.

Thus far relatively few NN studies of bankruptcy identification have been published, and most of those that have are American in origin. Generally the models seem to fit remarkably well on the data from which they are derived, but they still seem to perform well as discriminators on hold out samples. In the circumstances, it seems important to try to establish whether NN models clearly outperform the more traditional, statistically derived models (such as multiple discriminant analysis and logit); and, if they do, whether their classificational accuracy is such as to suggest that they could be used operationally by analysts to gain a short term advantage over rivals.

This chapter therefore reports the results of an NN experiment based upon one of the databases used in this study. The variables used were accounting ratios plus the market average residual return on each company's shares. The models were developed flexibly, and when fitted were tested on a hold out sample.

## Neural network models

It will be recalled from the description of NN models in chapter 5 that computer algorithms establish a 'training network' which detects via a searching process non-linear relationships between input data (e.g. accounting variables) and output data (e.g. 0 and 1, representing failure and non-failure) in order to *classify* situations correctly. This is done by identifying all possible relationships between the variables, in particular by establishing a 'middle layer' of variables ('hidden nodes'). The procedure makes considerable computational demands on a computer, but at each iteration (during which the parameter values for the variables are modified) the fit of the model is improved.

The neural network models developed in this study were based on the 61 matched pair sample of companies, largely so that a market return variable could be included. The sample itself was split into two parts: a 'training set' of 41 matched pairs from which the NN models were derived, and a hold out sample (or 'test set') of 20 matched pairs. No adjustment was made for potential sampling bias, although it is possible to weight the functions so that they more accurately reflect the real proportions of failed and non-failed companies in a population.

The models themselves were based on variables selected from a small group of accounting ratios, several of which were similar to those represented in the original Altman (1968) MDA equation. This was done in order to replicate as closely as possible the pioneering work undertaken in the US in developing neural networking models for bankruptcy identification, which have used Altman's model as a bench mark. The eight explanatory variables used were

$X_1$ Earnings before interest and tax/total assets   EBIT/TA
$X_2$ Debt/total assets   TL/TA
$X_3$ Asset growth rate   $(TA_t - TA_{t-1})/TA_{t-1}$
$X_4$ Logged asset growth rate   $\ln(TA_t/TA_{t-1})$
$X_5$ Liabilities/earnings before interest and tax   TL/EBIT
$X_6$ Working capital/total assets   (CA-CL)/TA
$X_7$ Sales/total assets   S/TA
$X_8$ Residual share price return   $R_{it}$

Two of the experiments carried out are described here, both of which were conducted using a standard backpropagation procedure. Convergence was initially achieved by minimising the mean squared error (MSE) between predicted and actual outcomes. However, the MSE gives greater weight to large differences between forecasts and outcomes, so the models were finally fitted by minimising the mean absolute error (MAE). This was done as use of the MSE could give an overoptimistic impression of model accuracy where the MAEs are less than one.

In both experiments models were trained on data for each of the last three years before failure. However, in practice a user of a specific model would not know whether the data it was being applied to related to a failing firm one, two or three years before its bankruptcy. Consequently the models were tested on data for other years besides those on which they were derived.

Forecast accuracy was first assessed for each individual year's model and then – because it is impossible to know a priori whether a company will go bankrupt in the current year, in the following year, or in two years' time – by averaging the forecasts. The aim of this was to see whether access to the additional data, even though it was obtained with hindsight, improved explanatory power.[1]

Unlike some previous NN studies (e.g. Odom and Sharma, 1990), the number of hidden nodes and the running time were not increased to obtain near perfect discrimination in the test set.

In the first experiment the models were developed with 1 to 8 processing elements (or 'neurons'). The variables used were $X_1$, $X_2$, $X_3$, $X_5$ and $X_8$. The error rates for the non-failed companies were generally much lower than for the bankrupt companies, which was expected, and they were also stable across time. By contrast, those for the failing companies showed a gradual worsening, reflecting the fact that the ratios were increasingly unstable as bankruptcy approached. Overall, as might have been anticipated, the fit on the training set improved as the number of neurons increased (see Table 13.1). However, the misclassification rates on the hold out test set tended to rise when the number of neurons exceeded two. In other words, in the first experiment there was clear evidence of 'overfitting' the model on the training set.

A particular problem with iterative models is that initial parameter values have to be chosen before passes are made through the data in order to converge on an optimum solution. Generally unit weightings of one will initially be applied to each

### Table 13.1: Classification Errors for Neural Network Models Based on Data One Year before Failure

*Training set results*

| No. of neurons | 1 | 2 | 3 | 4 | 5 | 6 | 7 | 8 |
|---|---|---|---|---|---|---|---|---|
| % correct predictions | | | | | | | | |
| Failed companies | 93 | 91 | 92 | 92 | 97 | 97 | 98 | 100 |
| Non-failed companies | 83 | 84 | 88 | 98 | 95 | 98 | 99 | 100 |

*Test set results*

| No. of neurons | 1 | 2 | 3 | 4 | 5 | 6 | 7 | 8 |
|---|---|---|---|---|---|---|---|---|
| % correct predictions | | | | | | | | |
| Failed companies | 75 | 75 | 60 | 72 | 60 | 75 | 67 | 57 |
| Non-failed companies | 85 | 87 | 87 | 82 | 80 | 75 | 68 | 72 |

variable. However, in the experiments reported here three different starting values were randomly chosen to see how long it took for the models to converge and give similar classification results. In fact, it was found that the NN models were not insensitive to the initial choice, so the final results were achieved by averaging.

The results reported in Tables 13.1-13.3 relate to the first experiment. They show the best performances were recorded on the training set, with maximum efficiency achieved with six or more neurons. Below that level misclassification rates increased, although the pattern was reversed on the hold out test sample.

**Table 13.2: Classification Errors for Neural Network Models Based on Data One and Two Years before Failure**

*Training set results*

| No. of neurons | 1 | 2 | 3 | 4 | 5 | 6 | 7 |
|---|---|---|---|---|---|---|---|
| % correct predictions | | | | | | | |
| Failed companies | 98 | 98 | 100 | 100 | 100 | 100 | 100 |
| Non-failed companies | 88 | 87 | 92 | 99 | 98 | 100 | 100 |

*Test set results*

| No. of neurons | 1 | 2 | 3 | 4 | 5 | 6 | 7 |
|---|---|---|---|---|---|---|---|
| % correct predictions | | | | | | | |
| Failed companies | 75 | 77 | 72 | 67 | 65 | 65 | 63 |
| Non-failed companies | 85 | 83 | 78 | 82 | 80 | 83 | 80 |

In terms of the number of computations required to derive each model, with one neuron 40,000 'epochs' (i.e. passes through the data set) were required, taking some three hours of running time. With seven neurons the number of epochs was well in excess of 200,000, running around some ten hours.

It is evident from the results reported in Tables 13.1-13.3 that misclassification rates are reduced when the forecasts of the models are averaged over time, albeit backwards from the date of failure. This is not altogether surprising as in the context of macroeconomic forecasts there is evidence that an average of predictions will generally prove to be more accurate than any one forecast itself.[2] However, further research is needed on this aspect of the models' performance, as well as their incremental forecasting ability as the failure date approaches.

**Table 13.3: Classification Errors for Neural Network Models Based on Data One, Two and Three Years before Failure**

*Training set results*

| No. of neurons | 1 | 2 | 3 | 4 | 5 | 6 | 7 |
|---|---|---|---|---|---|---|---|
| % correct predictions | | | | | | | |
| Failed companies | 98 | 98 | 100 | 100 | 100 | 100 | 100 |
| Non-failed companies | 88 | 94 | 98 | 99 | 100 | 100 | 100 |

*Test set results*

| No. of neurons | 1 | 2 | 3 | 4 | 5 | 6 | 7 |
|---|---|---|---|---|---|---|---|
| % correct predictions | | | | | | | |
| Failed companies | 80 | 63 | 67 | 63 | 70 | 63 | 72 |
| Non-failed companies | 85 | 82 | 77 | 83 | 80 | 77 | 70 |

As for forecasting accuracy, the misclassifications on the test set of companies were generally only slightly higher than those reported in the US studies of Odom and Sharda (1990) and Coats and Fant (1993). However, it should be remembered that the Odom and Sharda study – like the study reported here – assumed an equal probability of failure, while the Coats and Fant just as unrealistically assumed a ratio of failures to non-failures of 33:67.

The second experiment was undertaken to see whether the results would vary significantly if NN models were derived from a slightly different data set. It was also hoped to reduce the level of overfitting in the models. The five ratio variables used in this phase of the study were $X_1$, $X_2$, $X_4$, $X_6$, and $X_7$. A six variable model was also developed including the share price return indicator, $X_8$. Given the results in the first phase of the study, no more than six neurons were used to derive the models.

The MAE statistics show that the differences in the accuracy of forecasts with respect to surviving firms are relatively small, but much larger for failing businesses. This is illustrated with the figures for a sample year in Table 13.4, which relates to individual year data rather than the averaged results. The fact that there is very little difference between the error rates recorded for the training and test sets indicates that any overfitting cannot be the result of misspecification in this respect.

Including the share return data (i.e. running the six variable model) improved discrimination in the fitting set for the 5 or 6 neuron models on data one year prior to failure. However, it worsened it in the test set. For the three neuron model the

**Table 13.4: Mean Absolute Errors for a Five Variable Neural Network Model with Parameters Estimated on Final Year Data**

| No. of neurons | Failed companies | | | | | | Surviving companies | | | | | |
|---|---|---|---|---|---|---|---|---|---|---|---|---|
|  | 1 | 2 | 3 | 4 | 5 | 6 | 1 | 2 | 3 | 4 | 5 | 6 |
| *Training set results* | | | | | | | | | | | | |
| Years      1 | .46 | .40 | .36 | .36 | .40 | .38 | .44 | .40 | .35 | .31 | .31 | .32 |
| before     2 | .83 | .78 | .73 | .75 | .79 | .75 | .41 | .34 | .32 | .29 | .29 | .27 |
| failure    3 | 1.2 | 1.2 | 1.3 | 1.3 | 1.3 | 1.3 | .33 | .30 | .31 | .28 | .26 | .25 |
|            4 | 1.3 | 1.4 | 1.5 | 1.5 | 1.5 | 1.6 | .32 | .30 | .28 | .28 | .25 | .26 |
| *Test set results* | | | | | | | | | | | | |
| Years      1 | .64 | .58 | .53 | .49 | .44 | .38 | .49 | .42 | .37 | .35 | .32 | .31 |
| before     2 | .79 | .69 | .66 | .64 | .72 | .62 | .44 | .33 | .31 | .29 | .25 | .24 |
| failure    3 | 1.1 | 1.2 | 1.2 | 1.3 | 1.3 | 1.3 | .32 | .29 | .28 | .28 | .23 | .22 |
|            4 | 1.3 | 1.4 | 1.4 | 1.5 | 1.6 | 1.6 | .29 | .27 | .30 | .29 | .24 | .23 |

test set failure predictions were better using data for two and three years before failure. This could be interpreted as suggesting that the market partially recognises a failing company's plight before it is fully reflected in conventional accounting ratios.

Averaging forecasts produced some conflicting results in terms of the MAEs. Generally the predictions were better for failing companies, both in the fitting and test sets. However, for surviving firms the forecasts were worse, bringing the MAEs much closer to those reported for bankrupt companies.

Applying the models derived in the second experiment produced rather more accurate classifications on test set data, but at the expense of increasing the errors on the training set. This is shown in Table 13.5 for the model derived on data for

### Table 13.5: Classification Errors for Individual Year Neural Network Models Based on Data One Year before Failure

| Model: | Five variables | | | | | | Six variables | | | | | |
|---|---|---|---|---|---|---|---|---|---|---|---|---|
| No. of neurons | 1 | 2 | 3 | 4 | 5 | 6 | 1 | 2 | 3 | 4 | 5 | 6 |
| *% correct predictions* | | | | | | | | | | | | |
| **One year before failure** | | | | | | | | | | | | |
| *Training set results* | | | | | | | | | | | | |
| Failed companies | 88 | 90 | 90 | 90 | 88 | 90 | 88 | 90 | 90 | 93 | 95 | 98 |
| Non-failed companies | 83 | 80 | 80 | 80 | 80 | 80 | 83 | 85 | 85 | 85 | 88 | 93 |
| *Test set results* | | | | | | | | | | | | |
| Failed companies | 75 | 80 | 75 | 80 | 80 | 80 | 75 | 85 | 85 | 80 | 75 | 80 |
| Non-failed companies | 85 | 80 | 80 | 80 | 80 | 85 | 85 | 80 | 90 | 80 | 80 | 80 |
| **Two years before failure** | | | | | | | | | | | | |
| *Training set results* | | | | | | | | | | | | |
| Failed companies | 66 | 59 | 59 | 63 | 63 | 71 | 66 | 59 | 61 | 56 | 61 | 59 |
| Non-failed companies | 85 | 85 | 88 | 88 | 88 | 85 | 85 | 85 | 88 | 83 | 85 | 80 |
| *Test set results* | | | | | | | | | | | | |
| Failed companies | 60 | 55 | 55 | 60 | 55 | 55 | 60 | 70 | 75 | 75 | 70 | 75 |
| Non-failed companies | 90 | 90 | 90 | 90 | 90 | 95 | 90 | 85 | 90 | 85 | 85 | 85 |
| **Three years before failure** | | | | | | | | | | | | |
| *Training set results* | | | | | | | | | | | | |
| Failed companies | 32 | 29 | 29 | 34 | 34 | 32 | 34 | 29 | 37 | 32 | 34 | 34 |
| Non-failed companies | 93 | 93 | 93 | 93 | 95 | 88 | 93 | 90 | 90 | 90 | 85 | 73 |
| *Test set results* | | | | | | | | | | | | |
| Failed companies | 40 | 35 | 35 | 35 | 35 | 35 | 50 | 55 | 55 | 45 | 55 | 55 |
| Non-failed companies | 85 | 85 | 85 | 85 | 85 | 85 | 85 | 85 | 85 | 90 | 90 | 90 |

the last year before failure; and in Table 13.6 for the model derived on data for two years prior to bankruptcy.

Similar results were achieved for individual year models developed on data three years before failure. As for averaging, as mentioned above in connection with MAEs, the predictions were generally better for failing companies, both in the fitting and test sets, but rather worse for surviving firms.

**Table 13.6: Classification Errors for Individual Year Neural Network Models Based on Data Two Years before Failure**

| Model: | Five variables | | | | | | Six variables | | | | | |
|---|---|---|---|---|---|---|---|---|---|---|---|---|
| No. of neurons | 1 | 2 | 3 | 4 | 5 | 6 | 1 | 2 | 3 | 4 | 5 | 6 |
| *% correct predictions* | | | | | | | | | | | | |
| **One year before failure** | | | | | | | | | | | | |
| *Training set results* | | | | | | | | | | | | |
| Failed companies | 88 | 77 | 63 | 63 | 63 | 63 | 83 | 73 | 76 | 68 | 71 | 73 |
| Non-failed companies | 78 | 80 | 80 | 83 | 83 | 80 | 76 | 78 | 61 | 80 | 68 | 68 |
| *Test set results* | | | | | | | | | | | | |
| Failed companies | 85 | 70 | 80 | 70 | 70 | 80 | 85 | 70 | 80 | 85 | 85 | 80 |
| Non-failed companies | 80 | 80 | 85 | 85 | 85 | 85 | 80 | 80 | 80 | 85 | 80 | 80 |
| **Two years before failure** | | | | | | | | | | | | |
| *Training set results* | | | | | | | | | | | | |
| Failed companies | 76 | 78 | 85 | 88 | 85 | 90 | 78 | 76 | 88 | 90 | 98 | 98 |
| Non-failed companies | 78 | 83 | 85 | 95 | 98 | 98 | 76 | 83 | 83 | 95 | 98 | 98 |
| *Test set results* | | | | | | | | | | | | |
| Failed companies | 85 | 85 | 75 | 65 | 70 | 70 | 85 | 85 | 80 | 80 | 55 | 70 |
| Non-failed companies | 85 | 85 | 85 | 85 | 85 | 80 | 90 | 90 | 85 | 90 | 80 | 85 |
| **Three years before failure** | | | | | | | | | | | | |
| *Training set results* | | | | | | | | | | | | |
| Failed companies | 59 | 56 | 56 | 46 | 46 | 46 | 59 | 56 | 66 | 59 | 66 | 63 |
| Non-failed companies | 83 | 85 | 83 | 83 | 83 | 83 | 80 | 85 | 76 | 83 | 78 | 76 |
| *Test set results* | | | | | | | | | | | | |
| Failed companies | 55 | 50 | 50 | 55 | 45 | 55 | 55 | 50 | 60 | 60 | 60 | 60 |
| Non-failed companies | 85 | 85 | 85 | 80 | 85 | 85 | 90 | 85 | 85 | 80 | 70 | 75 |

**Comparison with logit models' predictions**

One of the main reasons for developing the neural networking models was to see whether they significantly outperform conventional, statistically determined failure prediction models. Consequently a series of logit models were estimated as a bench mark on the same data for the last three years before failure.

The data reported below in Table 13.7 relate to the individual year logit models applying the same variables used in the first NN experiment. As can be seen, they fit well, especially for the last year before bankruptcy, and several of the individual variables have significant explanatory power, especially in the last year prior to failure.

The classificatory power of the individual year models is shown in Table 13.8. Comparison with Tables 13.1-13.3 clearly shows that the logit models' discriminatory power is weaker than that of the NN models, however many neurons are included in them. Moreover, the same was true for comparisons between logit models and the NN models derived during the second experiment.

More generally, the results for the NN models compare well to those of other models reported in this study, such as gambler's ruin and the more widely based logit models.

**Table 13.7: Logit Estimates of Individual Year Models, with a Prior Probability of Failure of 50%, First Experiment**

| Years prior to failure | | $X_0$ | $X_1$ | $X_2$ | $X_3$ | $X_5$ | $X_8$ | LR† |
|---|---|---|---|---|---|---|---|---|
| 1 | parameter | 3.2 | 21.5 | -10.3 | -2.6 | 3.5 | -0.5 | -32.3 |
|   | t-value | 2.4* | 3.2* | -2.5* | -1.7* | 0.9 | -1.4 | (49.07)* |
| 2 | parameter | 1.9 | 12.1 | -4.2 | -3.3 | 0.1 | 0.7 | -42.6 |
|   | t-value | 1.6 | 2.2* | -1.2 | -1.8* | 0.0 | 0.8 | (28.53)* |
| 3 | parameter | 0.5 | 19.4 | -6.2 | -0.8 | 2.2 | 0.2 | -43.3 |
|   | t-value | 0.4 | 2.9* | -1.6 | -0.8 | 0.5 | 0.2 | (27.00)* |

Notes: †LR index shown first. The LR test statistic is shown in parenthesis.
    (See note 3 to chapter 12).
    Critical values of chi square 5, 0.001 = 20.52; 5, 0.01 = 15.09;
      5, 0.02 = 13.89; 5, 0.05 = 11.07.
    * Significant at the 95% confidence level

## Summary

The results generated using NN models are comparable both with those of other researchers applying the technique and rival procedures (e.g. gambler's ruin, entropy, or logit). Overall they appear to discriminate well for years on whose data

301

they are derived, both on estimation and on hold out samples, but performance declines quite sharply over time.

More generally, it is unclear whether the performance of NN models is significantly better over the long run than that of other models (such as logit); and, indeed, whether in operational terms there is much advantage in applying such procedures. Certainly they have the disadvantage of being 'black box' models, so users cannot immediately see what is happening, nor can they easily interpret the results. Further, the error rates, especially on hold out samples outside the estimation period, would seem to be such as to reduce significantly the practical value of the approach once sampling bias and the costs of misclassification are taken into account.

### Table 13.8: Classification Errors for Logit Models for Individual Year Models One, Two and Three Years before Failure

|  | Training set results | | | Test set results | | |
|---|---|---|---|---|---|---|
| Years before failure | 1 | 2 | 3 | 1 | 2 | 3 |
| *% correct predictions* | | | | | | |
| Failed companies | 78 | 73 | 78 | 70 | 75 | 65 |
| Non-failed companies | 81 | 78 | 73 | 85 | 90 | 75 |

However, much further work remains to be done in assessing the usefulness of the technique, altering the weighting of the failed/non-failed samples, changing the variable set (e.g. to include non-ratio variables), isolating incremental information through time, and testing the models on much larger hold out samples, especially when the latter are taken some time after the period in time over which the model was estimated.

So far it seems NN models broadly perform as well as other procedures, but by the same token they suffer from similar weaknesses. Thus once again it must be asked, first, how much of the information they contain is news to analysts; and, second, how it could be that – once their use has become widely acknowledged – such models would consistently be able to discriminate successfully between bankrupt and non-failing firms some time before the failure of the former.

### Notes

[1] It is well established that forecast errors are reduced when predictions are averaged (e.g. Bates and Granger, 1969; Granger, 1989). Moreover, this is not a mere statistical artefact as there is evidence of a very rapid learning process in markets as traders revise expectations in the light of the prices they observe (Forsyte, Palfrey and Plott, 1982).

[2] See, for instance, Granger (1989); Holden and Peel (1989).

# 14 Share price behaviour models

## Introduction

Bankruptcy identification models are generally formulated to classify firms as either 'failing' or 'non-failing'. It follows that if their classificational accuracy is greater than chance, it ought to be possible – in theory, at any rate – to develop a simple trading rule for listed companies which should enable an investor to make money: namely, buy shares in firms classified as surviving and sell short in those identified as failing.

Of course, it is unlikely to be this easy. For instance, there will probably be a sizeable lag between the date of a forecast and the event which is predicted – in which case one would expect traders to close their speculative positions by releasing their privileged information and doing their best to get the market to believe in its predictive accuracy. A second problem is that in practice there are various institutional factors which inhibit short selling[1] – in which case it is to be expected that those who develop failure identification models would sell them to banks, brokers and other financial institutions who might be in a position to benefit from having access to such privileged information. This would enable them – in the short term at least, until their rivals copy them – either to trade profitably on the market or at least avoid the heavy costs of misclassifying failing businesses as sound and surviving companies as heading for bankruptcy.[2]

In fact, as has been pointed out previously (see p. 137-9) the best known models (such as those of Altman in the US; and Taffler and Marais in the UK) have indeed been sold commercially. It might therefore reasonably be expected that, if investors believe the models, their predictions would become self-fulfilling. In the circumstances, it should be possible to study share price behaviour to see whether it suggests that the models are being used and/or whether the market behaves in the way expected. Briefly, if reaction is as anticipated, the share prices of companies classified as failing should collapse suddenly. If they do not, but just decline gradually, the implication is that the market does not fully believe the forecasts generated by the models.

It has been argued in previous chapters that the ability of failure identification models to discriminate accurately is greatly reduced when adjustment is made for sampling bias, although there would still seem to be sufficient information to enable a profitable trading rule to be developed. However, in practice it also appears that the ability of failure identification models to discriminate accurately declines significantly out of the sample period, which is likely to reduce further the practical usefulness of such procedures.

The first aim of this chapter is therefore to see if share prices of failing companies collapse suddenly. If they do not, it is then necessary to establish how long it is before bankruptcy that the market on average marks down the shares of financially distressed companies. If this is some time before eventual failure, it would seem to suggest that analysts are not applying the information in failure identification models to develop trading rules. It is therefore appropriate to try to establish whether the failure models seem to be conveying significant incremental information which is being ignored; or, instead, for the most part appear merely to be reflecting information which analysts are already using when trying to establish the probability of an individual company collapsing.

## Share price returns and event identification

*Applying event study methodology in bankruptcy studies*

As pointed out previously (p. 168 et seq.), although the 'event study' methodology has been developed and increasingly refined by researchers, it is generally applied to study market reaction to a specific news announcement over a relatively short window of time. In such circumstances, it is vital both to identify the precise timing of the event which is the focus of interest, and to remove any systematic factors which might bias observed security returns.

The issues which are of the subject of interest in bankruptcy studies are rather different. Certainly there is an event which can be identified – the ultimate failure of a financially distressed company when its listing is suspended. However, since by definition the share price at this point will fall to break up value, there is no question of studying post announcement share price behaviour and assessing potential anomalies, such as 'post announcement drift'. In the circumstances, what is of interest is the relative behaviour of share prices of financially distressed companies in the period leading up to bankruptcy. This covers a very long window in time. Moreover, it is important to recognise that the experience of individual failing companies varies widely. Some will have been experiencing difficulties for periods of 4-5 years before their ultimate collapse, although there will have still been good prospects of a turnround which (presumably) justifies the fact that their market capitalisation has exceeded break up value right up until the point when their listings have been suspended. For others, the downward spiral will have commenced much later (e.g. just 1-2 years before bankruptcy); and for a few the downturn will probably have come suddenly right at the end of the companies' lives.

The point being made is that when corporate failure is the focus of interest there is likely to be little of the common experience that is assumed in most event studies. This means that share price behaviour of failing companies will not only have to be viewed over relatively long intervals of time, but the data will also be heterogeneous in nature. Consequently cross sectional aggregation will merely produce an *average* of the companies' collective experience. However, there is some justification for analysing security returns in such a context since most failure identification models are derived in a similar way – namely, pooling data at various points in time for companies whose experiences are far from identical.

An alternative approach would be to try to develop a trading strategy for each pair of companies and see whether it could be applied to make profits (e.g. sell shares in the failing company and buy shares in its surviving twin). The results of pursuing such a policy across the population of companies commencing at various points in time before the ultimate collapse of the failing company could then be assessed. However, although the results might be easier to interpret economically, the overall picture should not be substantially different from that given by cross sectionally pooling the data and calculating average residual returns, as described above. It was therefore decided to adopt the average residual returns approach.[3]

*Analysing security price returns*

The first stage of the analysis was to develop a file of share price returns which would provide a basis for the study. This was achieved by taking the data set of 61 matched pairs for which five years share price return figures were available (see chapter 10).

As explained in chapter 6, studies of the share price behaviour of companies almost always attempt to isolate 'residual returns' by estimating market betas (i.e. the relationship between movements in an individual company's share prices and movements in a market index of share price movements). However, it will be recalled that this creates considerable problems when the focus of study is corporate failure because when cross-sectional data are pooled over time the betas are unlikely to be stationary. In particular, one might expect a reasonably well informed market to mark down the relative share prices of companies as the likelihood of their bankruptcy is perceived to increase. This means that betas might tend to increase for failing firms during a period of stock market decline; or decrease or become negative during a period of stock market boom. One way of trying to handle this problem is to re-estimate betas on a moving basis, a procedure used by Theobald and Thomas (1982) in the context of a study of UK failing companies, but it is inevitably only a partial solution.

It was also pointed out in chapter 6 that there are various other systematic factors which appear to be driving share prices, most of which can be captured by allowing for company size (Fama and French, 1996). However, in bankruptcy studies size is usually either a criterion for pairing failing and non-failing companies; or, as in the multivariate studies described in chapters 12 and 13, an independent variable used to develop a bankruptcy identification model. In the circumstances, when trying to assess the predictive power of a particular model it will generally be inappropriate to try to allow for size when calculating residual share price returns.

In the context of the present study, all that is being attempted is to obtain a general picture of share price behaviour over a period of several months (and even years) leading up to bankruptcy, and not a highly calibrated measure of residual returns over a narrow window of time. It is therefore not really necessary to introduce additional controls. As a result, it was decided to calculate residual returns merely as the difference between the monthly share price returns of the failed companies and their paired non-failing counterparts. Such a procedure should control for systematic industry- and economy-wide factors since (as indicated previously) the matching procedure was based both on time and industry membership. Moreover, cross sectional aggregation should help to ensure that randomly distributed errors resulting from the procedure would cancel each other out.

Logged security price returns for the failed companies were therefore taken from the LBS share price database returns file for 60 months prior to the last year end before failure, and these were then matched against the corresponding returns for the paired control companies. This enabled the following residual return, $u_{it}$, to be calculated for company i in month t:

$$u_{it} = R_{Ft} - R_{Nt} \qquad (14.1)$$

> where $R_F$ is the reported logged return for a failed company, F, in month t; and
>
> $R_N$ is the reported logged return for a paired non-failed company, N, in month t.

These individual failed company residual returns were then aggregated cross sectionally for each of 60 months through 'event time' and expressed as an average:

$$U_t = \sum_{i=1}^{n} u_{it} \qquad (14.2)$$

> where n is the number of failed companies; and the other symbols are as previously defined.

These monthly average residuals were then cumulated as Cumulative Average Residuals (CARs) over the 60 month interval prior to failure as follows:

$$CAR_t = \sum_{t=-60}^{-1} U_t \qquad (14.3)$$

In order to try to provide a further control to deal with those few instances where precise coincidence of year ends between failed companies and their matched pairs was not achieved – usually because of changes in the accounting years of the former – a second set of share price returns was generated applying the Market Average Return (MAR) (or 'zero-one') model (see p. 171). Corresponding monthly FT-Actuaries All-Share Index returns were therefore deducted from the failed and matched pair company share price returns. The latter were then subtracted from the former to calculate this second file of residual returns.

*The event date*

One difficulty with a study such as this is trying to identify unambiguously the event that is the focus of interest. As indicated above, at one extreme there is the date when a receiver is appointed; or when a company's listing on the Stock Exchange is suspended. However, the accounting information to which the failure identification models are applied is taken from a company's financial statements. There is therefore a case for identifying the event date either as the day when the accounts were published or when the preliminary results were released. On the other hand, this introduces a bias because these dates of publication for a failing company will almost never coincide with the corresponding publication dates for the matched pair company.

A further possibility is to use the accounting year end as the event date. This can be justified on the grounds that much of the information formally included in a company's accounts will reflect news which has been reported previously and which will therefore for the most part have been anticipated by the market.

In fact, for the purpose in hand it will probably make relatively little difference which date is chosen as the event criterion, so long as it is close to the death of the failed company. It was therefore decided to identify two alternative event dates and analyse the data with respect to each of them: first, the date of death of the failing company (i.e. when a receiver was appointed or its listing was suspended, if earlier); and second, the year end date of the last set of financial statements filed by the failing company.

## Market identification of failing status

The behaviour patterns of residual returns over the five reporting years prior to the bankruptcies of the failing firms were primarily investigated using profile analysis, with statistical significance assessed using a runs test. (This checks to see whether directional changes in prices could have occurred by chance.)

The overall plot of the CARs for the 61 matched pairs of companies are shown in Figure 14.1. They show that in overall average terms there is a clear downward spiral from 2.5 years before failure, the cumulative negative returns being very large during the last year. As might be expected, the runs test confirmed that this could not be a chance event.

It will be recalled from chapter 11 that univariate analysis suggested that annual mean adjusted returns on their own were poor discriminators. What the cross sectional average data for cumulative returns seems to indicate, in fact, is that the market is gradually recognising the worsening financial position of failing companies, but on a rather irregular basis.

There is clearly no widespread experience of a sudden collapse in the share prices of failing companies. Consequently there is no evidence that failure identification models were being used by analysts to develop profitable trading rules – at least, not at the time of the study, even though by then the existence of the Taffler model was well known and the brokers Laurence Prust had purchased the right to use it.

In fact, the pattern shown in Figure 14.1 is generally in line with that reported in previous studies in the US, Australia and UK, which show that share prices are usually marked down in relative terms 2-5 years before failure.[4]

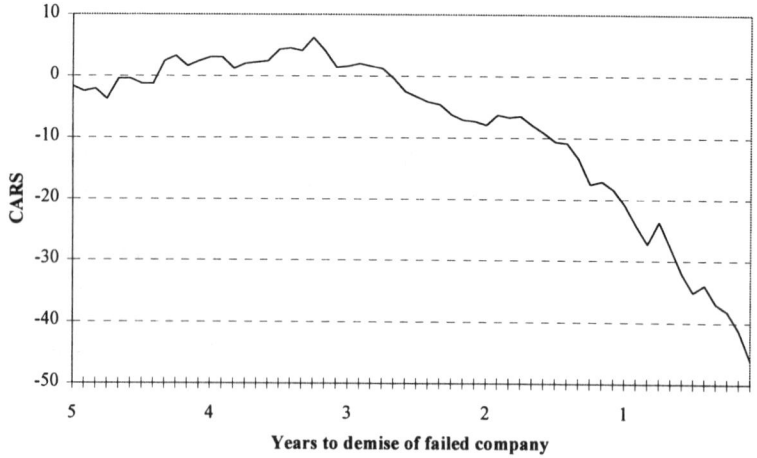

**Figure 14.1**

# The information content of failure identification models

*Market reaction to failure signals*

As explained on pp. 204-205, a partitioning procedure can be employed to analyse market reaction to a particular model's forecasts. This is a variation of the approach used in a number of event studies to analyse residual returns when there are conflicting signals simultaneously impacting the market.

Briefly, if the market in overall terms is correctly identifying failing and non-failing companies, it is only necessary to check that the CARs decline for the entire sample of 61 companies (see Figure 14.1). If on the other hand the aim is to try to establish whether or not analysts are processing the same data captured by a failure identification model, it is necessary to investigate the behaviour of residual returns for each of four groups of paired companies, classified according to signals given by the failure prediction models.

The possible combinations of signals are shown in Table 14.1.

### Table 14.1: Grouping of Companies by Signal and Outcome

| Group | Prediction for failed sample of companies | Prediction for non-failed paired companies |
|-------|------------------------------------------|--------------------------------------------|
| 1 | Failure | Failure |
| 2 | Non-failure | Failure |
| 3 | Failure | Non-failure |
| 4 | Non-failure | Non-failure |

The expected behaviour of residual returns if the market is only processing the same data captured by the failure identification models would be as follows:

(i)   the CARs of Group 3 should decline through time;
(ii)  the CARs of Group 2 should increase; and
(iii) there should be no clear trend in the CARs of Groups 1 and 4 until the financial collapse of the failing companies becomes imminent and obvious to analysts.[5]

*The bankruptcy identification models used*

Initially market reaction was tested against the dichotomous classifications of two of the logit ratio based models described in chapter 12. However, in order to make such a study worthwhile, it is really necessary to have a reasonable number of instances to study where there are conflicting signals. Yet as might be expected because of potential 'overfitting', resulting from the fact that the models were derived over the same period to which their forecasts relate, there were relatively few instances of such misclassifications. Consequently this made it difficult to assess whether the market was reacting to the signals implicit in the accounting indicators captured by the two logit models, regardless of the ultimate fate of the companies.

In fact, market reaction can be tested against the dichotomous classifications of any failure prediction model. There is therefore a strong case for referring to the forecasts of as many models as possible, and preferably to those estimated on data from previous periods which will therefore be applied out-of-sample. In particular, it would have been interesting to use the classifications generated by the Datastream and Taffler models, since their existence was widely publicised in the late 1970s and they would therefore have been the most likely models to have been referred to by analysts. Unfortunately the parameter values of Taffler's equation and those of most other UK models have not been published.[6]

However, there are two UK models developed on data for the period 1960-1971 for which the necessary information on the variables and parameter values are available. Since these would appear to perform in a similar manner to those in commercial use, it seemed appropriate to use them for this part of the study.

The two models concerned were developed by El Hennawy and Morris (1983a) and are described briefly in Appendix 14.1. They were developed applying multiple discriminant analysis (MDA) to a sample of 53 matched pairs of listed British companies which failed over the period 1960-1971. The first was derived from data five years before bankruptcy (hereafter the 'fifth year model') and the second one year prior to financial collapse (hereafter the 'first year model'). Given that the vast majority of failure identification models have been derived from data immediately prior to bankruptcy, this offers an alternative and potentially interesting perspective by making it possible to study market responses to signals generated by a model based on data some years prior to failure. Moreover, the performance of the two models can be compared to those of the corresponding fifth year and first year models estimated by logit from the 111 matched pair data set reported in chapter 12.

*Discriminatory power of the failure identification models*

The classificatory power of the six models tested is shown in Table 14.2. In interpreting the figures it should be remembered that the MDA equations derived by El Hennawy and Morris (hereafter EHM) were being applied to accounting data for 61 matched pairs of companies between 1973 and 1983 – well after the period over which the two models were estimated. Clearly their discriminatory power was expected to decline over time as underlying economic conditions changed, but it was nevertheless anticipated that they would retain some of their dichotomising properties.[7]

## Table 14.2: Classificational Accuracy of
## Failure Identification Models

| Model | *Logit models* | | | | *El Hennawy & Morris* | |
|---|---|---|---|---|---|---|
| | *5th Year* | | *1st Year* | | *5th Year* | *1st Year* |
| *Fail:Non-fail** | *50:50* | *20:80* | *50:50* | *20:80* | *50:50* | *50:50* |
| Group† | | | | | | |
| 1 | 7 | 33 | 6 | 18 | 17 | 25 |
| 2 | 1 | 2 | 0 | 0 | 7 | 2 |
| 3 | 32 | 23 | 47 | 40 | 23 | 30 |
| 4 | 21 | 3 | 8 | 3 | 14 | 4 |

\* Prior probability ratio    † As defined in Table 14.1

As expected, because they were being applied out-of-sample, the performance of the EHM models was considerably weaker than in the original study (see Table 14.3).

## Table14.3: Classificational Efficiency of the
## El Hennawy and Morris Models

| | Fifth Year Model *Classified as* | | First Year Model *Classified as* | |
|---|---|---|---|---|
| | Fail | Non-Fail | Fail | Non-Fail |
| *Actual outcome* | | | | |
| Fail | 66% *(89%)* | 39%   *(0%)* | 90% *(91%)* | 44%   *(0%)* |
| Non-Fail | 34% *(11%)* | 61% *(100%)* | 10%  *(9%)* | 56% *(100%)* |

*Note* The italicised figures in brackets show the percentages of correctly classified companies in the original El Hennawy and Morris study, those in ordinary type the percentages correctly classified for the new sample of 61 matched pairs.

Nevertheless, the figures in Table 14.3 show that the EHM models are still relatively good at identifying failing firms as at risk out-of-sample, the first year model identifying correctly in 90 per cent of the cases, almost the same as in the original study. Moreover, the fifth year model (which is probably potentially more useful to analysts as it is capturing different economic characteristics at an earlier point in time) still performs quite well in this respect: it identifies two thirds of the companies which eventually went bankrupt as at risk.

311

Where both models appear to be weak (and would be even weaker if adjustment were to be made for sampling bias) is in their classification of companies which did not fail during the analysis period. In both cases the models misclassify almost half the non-failing companies.

The classificationary efficiency of the two models was also checked on the other four years within the review period: the results are shown in Table 14.4.

It can be seen that up until the final year the EHM fifth year model performs better at correctly identifying failing companies. On the other hand its misclassification rate for non-failing firms is consistently worse than that of the

**Table 14.4: Classificational Efficiency of the El Hennawy and Morris Models over the Years under Review**

| | Year before failure (% correctly forecast) | | | | | | | | | |
|---|---|---|---|---|---|---|---|---|---|---|
| | *-1* | | *-2* | | *-3* | | *-4* | | *-5* | |
| | F | NF | F | NF | F | NF | F | NF | F | NF |
| 5th Year Model | 84 | 33 | 79 | 46 | 74 | 54 | 56 | 52 | 66 | 61 |
| 1st Year Model | 90 | 56 | 75 | 67 | 59 | 74 | 43 | 66 | 46 | 71 |

*Note*: F = forecast as failed; NF = forecast as non-failed

first year model over the five years. Another feature worth noting is that the misclassification errors *decrease* for failing firms as bankruptcy approaches, but conversely the percentage errors *increase* for non-failing companies.

Overall, the error rates – while not dissimilar to those of other models over periods outside those during which they were determined – are not inconsistent with the view that *either* the information generated by the models has never been more than of limited significance to analysts; *or*, that, if it ever was significant, it has been exhausted. What remains to be seen is whether the behaviour of security prices is consistent with this view, suggesting that the market picks up the same information captured by the two models but if anything slightly earlier. If true, this would imply that analysts have developed more powerful heuristic models to identify financially distressed companies, accessing a wider information set.

*Market reaction to failure signals*

The analysis of share price returns was conducted for both the critical events referred to earlier, namely the date of the final accounts of the failed company; and its date of failure. In each case it was undertaken in two parts: first, over the 60 month period up to the event date; and second, over the final twelve months before the event date. However, as the results were very similar, only those in respect of the former event are reported here (i.e. up to the date of the final accounts of the failed company).

As before, the behaviour patterns of residual returns over the five reporting years prior to the bankruptcies of the failing firms were investigated using profile analysis, with statistical significance being assessed using runs tests.

*Residual returns behaviour over 60 months.* Share price behaviour for the four logit models referred to in Table 14.2 showed that for Group 3 (i.e. when forecasts were correct in terms of eventual outcomes) residual returns declined steadily from two years before bankruptcy for the two equal probability of failure/non-failure models. The picture was the same for the 20 per cent prior probability of failure model over the last 18 months, although the downturn was much sharper for the first year model. As for the Group 2 signal combination (i.e. where forecasts for both failing and non-failing companies were wrong), few instances were recorded – indeed, none at all for the first year model – so it was not really possible to draw any meaningful conclusions. However, with the equal probability fifth year model the returns were positive, even in the last year.

With respect to the Group 1 and Group 4 signals, where no clear pattern would be expected if analysts were referring to the same indicators captured in the models, there was a tendency for the returns to drift downwards, which became more accentuated over the last 18 months for all the Group 1 returns. However, the downturn for the Group 4 returns began as early as 3-4 years before the final accounting period end.

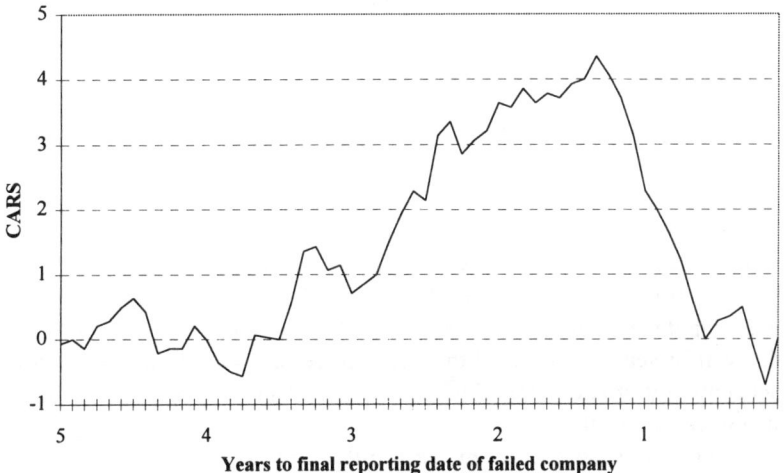

**Figure 14.2**

Overall, the profiles for the logit models were not greatly dissimilar to those reported below for the EHM models, so only the latter are plotted in Figures 14.2-14.5. The plots (shown in Figures 14.2-14.3 and 14.4-14.5 respectively for the fifth

313

and first year EHM models) were generally in line with prior expectations for Groups 2 and 3. Thus for Group 2 (where the classifications are incorrect in terms of the eventual outcomes), the CARs increase as anticipated for the fifth year model, before turning down sharply over the last reporting period (see Figure 14.2). But with the first year model the CARs decline at first, before recovering somewhat over the last three reporting years, although they nevertheless remain negative (see Figure 14.4).

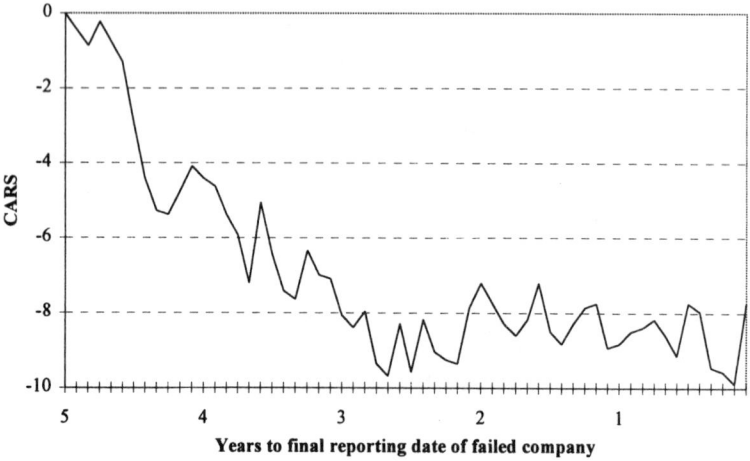

**Figure 14.3**

For Group 3 (where the EHM models correctly classify companies) the CARs clearly decline through time for the fifth year model (see Figure 14.3). But for the first year model the CARs do not turn down sharply until the third year before the final accounting year end (see Figure 14.5).

No very clear behaviour pattern was expected for Groups 1 and 4. For Group 1, with both the fifth- and first-year EHM models, the CARs fluctuated around zero before turning down 18 months before the final accounting year end. As for Group 4, with the fifth year EHM model the CARs increased until 24 months before the final accounting year end, after which they declined steadily, although at the event date they were still positive.

Where trends were obvious from the profile analysis, runs tests unsurprisingly confirmed that there was a significant element of serial correlation. Moreover, it is clear that the results for the EHM fifth year model are rather clearer than those for the first year model. This would seem to suggest that the EHM fifth year model captures most of the information used by the market but does not add anything extra; whereas analysts do not appear to interpret data in the way implied by the EHM first year model.

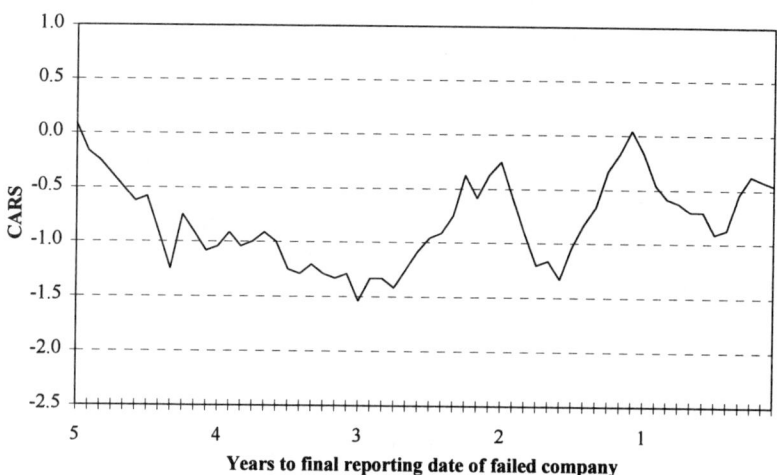

**Figure 14.4**

Tests to check the robustness of the findings reported above tended to confirm the results. Thus the plots for Groups 2 and 3 when the MAR model was applied were almost identical to those reported above. Moreover, results when the event was taken as the date of failure were also very similar, the main difference being that the CARs declined over a slightly longer period.

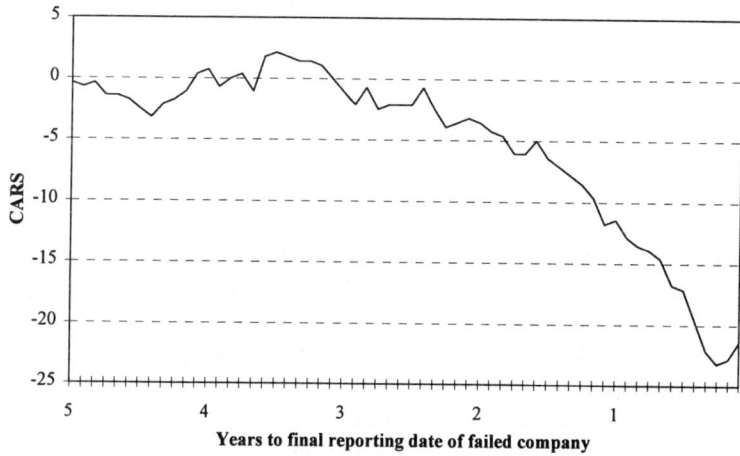

**Figure 14.5**

A further check was undertaken to review the validity of the results reported above by examining share price behaviour for Groups 2 and 3 in relation to failure prediction in each of the other four years under review: i.e. years -1, -2, -3 and -4 for the EHM fifth year model; and years -2, -3, -4 and -5 for the EHM first year model.

Group 3 CARs were negative and worsening for the EHM fifth year model from year -4 onwards for classifications in years -1, -2 and -3. Behaviour was more erratic for the year -4 classification, but the CARs were still strongly negative apart from the second year before the final accounting year end of failing companies. Group 2 CARs were generally positive until the final reporting period, although the ARs became negative several months earlier.

With respect to the EHM first year model, share price behaviour for Group 3 was very similar to that reported previously for the model for classifications in years -2 and -3, with a steady negative CAR drift from five years before the final accounting year end. However, CAR behaviour was less consistent for classifications in years -4 and -5, only turning down sharply 18 months out, although overall the CARs were negative. As for Group 2, the CARs turned negative over the last 18 months.

Once more, runs tests confirmed the existence of significant serial correlation for periods where it was evident from the profile analysis that there were clear trends. Overall it seems that the market is impounding the information incorporated in the discriminant models, not only in relation to failing companies that eventually went bankrupt, but also until the last two years for those companies which eventually foundered but which were identified as being prima facie sound. What is especially interesting about the latter finding is that it implies – as one might expect – that as nemesis approaches, the market is able to see behind the outward financial indicators and identify the underlying weakness of companies increasingly at risk.

*Residual returns behaviour over the final reporting year before failure.* The same procedure described above for the basic matched pair data was applied to examine share price behaviour over the final reporting year before the bankruptcies of the failing firms.

Once again, the initial study was undertaken using signals generated by the four logit models referred to in Table 14.2. However, there was no clear pattern in the CARs: indeed, there was no distinct downturn for Group 3 CARs until the final two months, and none at all for Group 2.

With the EHM models, the basic trend of CARs was downwards for all four groups, the only exception being for Group 3 with the fifth year EHM model, where the CARs fluctuated erratically. The clearest downward trend was exhibited for Group 3 with the first year model, where the runs test indicated significant serial correlation over the first nine months of the final reporting year.

As expected, again no very clear pattern was evident for Groups 1 and 4.

316

Given the relatively small size of the failed company population, it was not possible to check the results for robustness by applying the test procedures to contemporaneous or intertemporal hold out groups of companies not included in the original analysis sample. However, in order to see whether the results were particularly sample sensitive, it was decided to replicate the procedures for each of the two models on four randomly selected subsamples of the companies in Group 3. This was done for year -5 for the EHM fifth year model and year -1 for the EHM first year model.

The problem with such a procedure is of course that with a truncated subsample one or two outliers can distort the results. In fact, with four subsamples of 15 paired companies (half the total in Group 3 for the first year model), the results for the EHM first year model were remarkably consistent, showing steadily worsening negative returns from four years prior to the last reporting year end. For the EHM fifth year model (with 50 per cent subsamples of only 11 Group 3 paired companies) the results were rather less impressive. Nevertheless, in one instance there were steadily worsening negative returns from five years out; and in another, despite the fact that the CARs were volatile, they were predominantly negative throughout. But in the other two cases – which were remarkably similar in pattern – the CARs were positive until the last year. Further examination of the data indeed suggested these latter results could well have been driven in part by the presence in the two subsamples of two companies not present in the first two. But in any case, the test is a relatively strong one, inasmuch as the test subsamples were selected at random and at least one of the four thus chosen was very similar to the whole sample and another not greatly dissimilar.

**Summary**

As argued previously, a priori reasoning suggests that, if investors behave rationally, failure prediction models with significant information content should exhibit no misclassification errors and share prices of bankrupt firms should collapse suddenly. But if instead they largely reflect information already available to analysts, one would expect a reasonably high proportion of misclassification errors and a steady decline in relative share prices of financially distressed firms prior to their bankruptcy.

Previous research in both the US and UK has shown that failure prediction models experience relatively high misclassification error rates outside the periods over which they were derived, which – when allowance is made for sampling bias – suggests their value may be somewhat limited. Moreover, research in the US by Altman and Brenner (1981), Katz, Lilien and Nelson (1985), Zavgren, Dugan and Reeve (1988) and Burgstahler, Jiambalvo and Noreen (1989) has seemed to establish that share prices reflect the same information contained in failure identification models.

The findings reported above, like those of previous studies, show that the market appears to recognise financial distress at least 2-3 years before a company's eventual bankruptcy. The novel approach here has been to try to establish whether UK analysts seem to be referring to much the same information captured by various failure identification models, namely four of the logit models described in chapter 12; and the first and fifth year models developed by El Hennawy and Morris (1983a).

The results show that, while the El Hennawy and Morris models were able to identify failing companies relatively well, a larger number of surviving companies were incorrectly classified as failing, which – given the problem of sampling bias – seems to confirm that the value of information contained in the models is rather limited. With respect to market reaction, there is some evidence to suggest that analysts are probably processing similar information to that contained in failure identification models. Certainly this appears to be the case with the two El Hennawy and Morris models, since residual share prices move in directions consistent with the signals generated by their MDA equations. However, a similar pattern of results was less easy to discern for the logit models, partly because (as expected) there were fewer conflicting signals to study.

Such results certainly cast doubt on the practical usefulness of failure prediction models, although of course they may still capture information which helps analysts further revise the probabilities they attach to likely bankruptcy. Moreover, it could well be that other failure prediction models than those considered here would perform better, even though they are generally derived in a similar way.

**Notes**

[1] See above, p. 181.

[2] The costs of misclassifying bankrupt companies as non-failing have been estimated at around 7 times the cost of misclassifying surviving firms as failing (Altman, 1977).

[3] The argument is analogous to that on p. 31 relating to the way matched pairing is applied. However, if a twinned company trading strategy is to be applied, it would be necessary to calculate residual returns for each pair of companies and assess the potential profits that could be earned over various intervals before the final collapse of the failing company. See note 11, p. 192.

[4] Thus, with respect to the UK, Gooi (1974) reported turndown at 3.25 years, Theobald and Thomas (1982) at 1.5 years, and El Hennawy and Morris (1983b) at 5 years. For Australia Castagna and Matolcsy (1981) reported turndown at 2.5 years before collapse, while in the US Beaver (1968a) reported the average lag at 2.45 years, Westerfield (1970) at 5 years, Pettway (1980) 3 years, and Aharony Jones and Swary (1980) 4.5 years.

[5] The null hypotheses for the behaviour of the CARs for each of the four groups of companies can therefore be summarised as follows:

| Group | CARs $H_0$ | $H_1$ |
|-------|------------|-------|
| 1 | $= 0$ | $\neq 0$ |
| 2 | $= 0$ | $> 0$ |
| 3 | $= 0$ | $< 0$ |
| 4 | $= 0$ | $\neq 0$ |

[6] What has been published are the variables included in the final models. It would therefore have been possible for analysts to replicate the procedure to determine the parameter values; and, given the claimed success rate in discriminating between failed and non-failed firms, there would have been a strong incentive for them to do so.

[7] It will be recalled that it is misclassification of non-failed companies which is the major problem when no adjustment is made for sampling bias (see chapter 1). On the other hand, other models have been found to have high misclassification rates for non-failing firms, especially outside the estimation period (e.g. the Bank of England model of Marais, 1979: see p. 72).


## Appendix 14.1

*The El Hennawy and Morris failure identification models*

The financial variables used in developing the El Hennawy and Morris (1983a) models were derived from a population of 96 ratios. This was reduced to 50 after applying factor analysis and excluding those for which there were missing values or which violated the necessary conditions of normality even after various transformations had been tried.

The fifth year and first year models themselves were originally formulated from respective analysis samples drawn from the period 1960-68 of 42 companies (21 failed and 21 non-failed) and 44 companies (22 failed and 22 non-failed). They were then subjected to various tests to determine their statistical significance and validated on two hold out samples comprising equal numbers of companies to the analysis samples. In terms of the tests both performed well, so the variables and parameters were then re-estimated on the combined analysis and hold out samples. In the original study both the fifth year and first year models were subsequently tested on an inter-temporal validation sample of 9 failed and 9 non-failed companies, drawn from the period 1969-71, and again in conventional test terms they performed extremely well.

319

The two El Hennawy and Morris models used in the present study to generate failed/non-failed classifications were those derived from the combined analysis and hold out samples. They take the following form:

*Fifth Year Model.* With a zero critical Z score, implying an equal chance of failure/non-failure, this model was

$$Z = -4.86 + 13.50X_1 + 3.11X_2 + 4.80X_3 - 0.97X_4 + 0.68X_5 \qquad (14.4)$$

where

$X_1$ = Earnings before interest and tax ÷ total assets
$X_2$ = Quick assets (i.e. current assets *less* stocks) ÷ current liabilities
    (including bank overdrafts)
    [This ratio, y, was transformed to ensure normality as $1/(y+1)$]
$X_3$ = Quick assets ÷ total assets
$X_4$ = Industry dummy for quarrying and construction
$X_5$ = Industry dummy for distribution

*First Year Model.* Again with a zero critical value, this model was

$$Z = -6.17 + 11.43X_1 + 14.07X_2 + 0.55X_3 - 1.57X_4 + 0.98X_5 \qquad (14.5)$$

where

$X_1$ = Flow of funds (i.e. earnings before interest, tax and depreciation) ÷ total
    assets
$X_2$ = Long term debt ÷ net capital employed
   [This ratio, y, was transformed to ensure normality as $1/(y+3)$]
$X_3$ = Current assets ÷ total assets
$X_4$ = Industry dummy for quarrying and construction
$X_5$ = Industry dummy for distribution

# 15 Case study analysis

## Introduction

The results presented in chapters 11-13 seem to confirm previous research on failure prediction: namely that models, however derived (and even when adjusted for sampling bias and misclassification costs), tend to categorise too high a proportion of surviving listed companies as prima facie bankrupt to make them operationally useful. Further, the evidence reported in chapter 14 is not inconsistent with the view that analysts do not take the classifications offered by such models at face value – presumably because of their deficiencies. This would help to explain why the share prices of companies identified as 'failures' do not collapse suddenly. But there is also evidence that share prices follow the pattern of decline reflected in the accounting ratios included in bankruptcy prediction models, regardless of whether or not a company ultimately fails. This would seem to imply that analysts either pay some heed to the signals transmitted by the models; or, more plausibly perhaps, interpret published information for themselves and identify which firms are in financial distress, without going so far as to assert whether they are going to fail or be turned round.

Such evidence implies that failure prediction models are of limited use in unambiguously identifying which companies will go bankrupt. This is not altogether surprising since (as has been argued previously in this book) they largely reflect the *symptoms* of decline rather than the underlying *causes*. It is therefore appropriate to look behind the figures themselves to see if there are any patterns in the economic events which seem to lead to financial distress and likely failure. This can only really be done by undertaking case study research. Previous work along these lines was reviewed in chapter 7, and it was noted there that such studies generally focus on successful and unsuccessful attempts to turn round financially distressed companies.

It is clear from the vast majority of these case histories that various combinations of events explain why companies go into decline. Moreover, it is evident that it is extremely difficult to predict beforehand which businesses will be the subject of emergency rescue attempts. But, equally, when steps are taken to try to effect a turnaround, it is virtually impossible to say whether such an initiative is going to be successful or not. This is not altogether surprising, of course, since if there were an easy way to forecast the future, such predictions would presumably be reflected in market behaviour and share prices.

In order to throw further light on these matters, this chapter analyses the characteristics of a number of companies which failed both in the sample period, 1973-1983, and over a later period, 1988-1991. The main focus of the study is 25 companies which went bankrupt during the first period, and summarised case studies for each of these are given in an appendix to the chapter. However, the key factors which characterise their declines are described in the text and are summarised in a table. These can be compared against a similar analysis of the main contributory causes of the collapse 21 companies which failed between 1988 and 1991.

For both samples, the years when bankruptcy occurred were for the most part in periods of deep and prolonged economic recession. It is not surprising, therefore, that there are certain common characteristics between the two groups: e.g. the extent of the downturns took all companies – and not just those which failed – by surprise; some industries were hit harder than others; firms most vulnerable were those where demand fell sharply, which had significant borrowings, and which faced high levels of unavoidable fixed operating costs. These factors were inevitably reflected in the key accounting indicators (namely, sharply declining profits and high gearing ratios). But it is also clear that in most industries there is a constant jockeying for competitive position. As a result, it was those companies which had become the weakest players at the onset of the recession that found it most difficult to survive. In particular, their plight was often brought about by a specific (but not especially unusual) misjudgement by management, which in better times would probably not have been so catastrophic.

But what is particularly interesting is that the combinations of factors which characterised failing companies in the two samples differ quite markedly. Thus in the first period, most of the bankruptcies arose as a result of an extensive shake-out in British manufacturing industry, when overcapacity in a number of key sectors had to be shed. This painful process was sometimes accelerated by the prolonged high foreign exchange value of sterling in the early 1980s. By contrast, in the second period many of the victims were firms which had grown rapidly in the boom years in the mid 1980s. In particular, companies most severely hit were those whose growth was on the back of the property boom, the collapse of which took the banks as much by surprise as anyone else and left them trying to decide if and when to call in their debts and precipitate the failure of their clients.

**The causes of failure**

It will be recalled that a number of writers in the management area have put forward theories which try to explain the causes and symptoms of corporate failure. Potential key problem areas include

(1)  size too small;
(2)  too narrow a concentration of ownership/executive control;
(3)  lack of diversification;
(4)  an inability to compete with rivals;
(5)  slow reaction to changes in the economic environment;
(6)  failure of a 'big project';
(7)  lack of investment;
(8)  unsuccessful acquisitions strategy;
(9)  undertrading;
(10) overtrading;
(11) industry in decline;
(12) a major strike, undermining a company's financial position;
(13) inadequate financial controls, facilitating fraud; and
(14) excessive borrowing.

A checklist specifying each of the above variables was prepared in order to examine the experience of the two samples of companies chosen for this part of the study. In addition, six other variables were identified:

(15) an attempted turnaround has failed;
(16) the accounts have been subject to an audit qualification;
(17) a steady decline in profitability has been experienced;
(18) capital has been injected into the business
(19) too rapid a rate of growth has overstretched the company's resources; and
(20) the stock market has recognised the growing weakness of the company's position.

**The causes of failure, 1973-1983**

*The sample companies*

The 25 companies failing between 1973 and 1983 were chosen from the 75 for which there were 10 years' data. They were also selected so as to give a reasonable coverage across the industries represented in the main sample: 9 were textiles and clothing firms, 8 came from the engineering sector, and three were toy manufacturers.

It is noticeable that – as with the main sample – most of the firms were engaged in manufacturing. The exceptions were Bambers Stores and John Michael, both of which operated in the retail clothing sector.

*The characteristics of the failed companies*

Table 15.1 summarises the characteristics of the 25 companies. Each column in the table corresponds to the 20 descriptive variables listed above. However, the basis for making entries in several of the columns requires further explanation.

With respect to variable (a), it is really the relative scale of a company's operations that is the issue. However, the overall size of a business can give a general indication of its ability to survive. Four size categories were therefore defined for the purpose of making entries in the first column: 1 indicates total assets less than £10m in the final published balance sheet of the company; 2 a value between £10m and £20m; 3 a value between £20m and £50m; and 4 a total over £50m.

The numbers in the audit qualification column show the number of years in which accounts were qualified: e.g. 2 would indicate that the last two years accounts were qualified. An asterisk shows that there was a previous but not adjacent qualification during the 10 year window.

The numbers in the column for relatively low profits show the number of years of declining profits recorded before failure. An asterisk indicates that losses or low profits were recorded not only in the final sequence but previously in the 10 year window under review.

The figures in the 'growth rate' column represent the total assets figure reported in the final year's balance sheet divided by the corresponding figure shown in the financial statements four years previously. This is likely to be biased downwards where (as is not infrequently the case) a company experiences losses in its last year of trading. However, the statistic is shown largely to demonstrate the marked difference in behaviour between companies which failed in the first period compared to those which collapsed between 1988 and 1991.

The numbers in the 'market warnings' column indicate the period prior to failure over which financial commentators were expressing concern at a company's financial position. For the most part this corresponds to the number of years in which an unbroken series of negative percentage security returns was recorded. It should be noted, first, that these returns only relate to the last five years before failure; and, second, that they are 'market average residuals (MARs)': i.e. the actual percentage returns (dividends plus capital gains divided by opening share price) after deducting the return on the FT-Actuaries All Share Index (see p. 171). The MAR is only a crude indicator of relative share price movements as usually the expected return for an industry or an individual company's shares will not be strictly proportionate to the market by a factor of one. Moreover, it should be remembered that these returns have been calculated for the periods covered by each

# Table 15.1: Characteristics of Failing Companies – Original Sample

| Name of company | Size | Narrow ownership | Lack of diversification | Inability to compete | External environment changed | Big project fails | Lack of investment | Acquisition strategy fails | Undertrading | Overtrading | Industry shake out | Major strike | Inadequate controls | Relatively high borrowing | Turnround attempt fails | Audit qualification | Relatively low profits | Capital injection | Growth factor | Market warnings |
|---|---|---|---|---|---|---|---|---|---|---|---|---|---|---|---|---|---|---|---|---|
| Airfix | 3 | x | x | x | x | | | x | | | x | | | x | | 1 | 3 | x | 1.4 | 4 |
| F. Austin | 1 | x | x | | x | | | | x | | x | | | x | x | | 2 | x | 1.1 | 2 |
| Bambers Stores | 3 | x | x | | | | | x | | | x | | x | x | | | 2 | x | 1.5 | 3 |
| Bamfords | 2 | x | x | x | x | | | x | | | x | x | | | | | 0 | x | 1.6 | 1 |
| Berwick Timpo | 1 | x | x | x | x | | | x | x | | x | | x | | | 1 | 1 | | 1.0 | 2 |
| Blackman & Conrad | 1 | x | x | x | x | | | x | x | | x | x | x | x | x | 1 | 4 | x | 0.9 | 2 |
| Blackwood Morton | 2 | x | x | x | x | | | x | x | | | | | | | | 6 | | 0.9 | 4 |
| British Enkalon | 3 | x | x | x | x | | | x | | | x | | | x | | 1 | 7 | x | 0.6 | 5 |
| Carron | 3 | | x | x | x | x | | x | | | x | | | x | | | 2 | | 1.3 | 2 |
| Fairbairn Lawson | 1 | x | x | x | x | | | x | | | x | | x | | | x | 1* | x | 1.6 | 0 |
| Fairey | 4 | | | | | x | | | | | | | | | | | 0 | x | 2.1 | 0 |
| General Engineering | 2 | | x | x | x | | | x | | | x | | | x | | | 9 | | 1.5 | 2 |
| Melody Mills | 1 | x | x | x | x | | | x | | | x | | | x | x | 1 | 3 | x | 0.8 | 3 |
| Mettoy | 3 | x | x | x | x | x | | x | x | | x | | | | | | 4 | x | 0.9 | 3 |
| John Michael | 1 | x | x | x | x | x | x | | | x | | | | | | 1* | 1* | | 1.8 | 5 |
| Movitex | 1 | x | | | | x | | | | | | | | x | x | 2 | 0 | | 1.2 | 5 |
| Oxley Printing | 2 | x | x | x | | x | | | | | | | | x | x | 1* | 2 | | 1.7 | 2 |
| B. Paradise | 1 | x | x | | | | | | x | | | | | x | x | | 1* | x | 3.1 | 5 |
| William Pickles | 2 | x | x | x | x | | | x | | | x | | | x | | | 3 | x | 0.9 | 2 |
| R & J Pullman | 3 | x | x | x | x | | | x | | | x | | x | x | | 1 | 0 | x | 1.7 | 0 |
| Richards and Wallington | 3 | x | | | x | | | x | x | | | | | x | x | | 1 | | 1.2 | 2 |
| Southern Constructions | 1 | | x | | | | | | | | | | x | x | x | 1 | 3 | | 1.3 | 0 |
| TCK | 1 | x | x | | | | | x | x | | x | | | x | x | | 1* | | 3.1 | 0 |
| Viners | 2 | x | x | x | x | | | x | | | x | | | x | x | 1 | 5 | x | 1.2 | 5 |
| Wombwell Foundry | 1 | x | x | x | | | | x | x | | x | x | | x | x | | 1* | | 3.5 | 1 |

company's accounts. They therefore do not reflect any movement that might result from the publication of the financial statements relating to a particular year, except to the extent that the market correctly anticipates these. It should also be remembered that the relative share price often declined sharply after the end of the last financial year for which accounts were published, as the date of the company's 'death' usually occurred some months later.

*Analysis of the characteristics*

The first point which is evident from Table 15.1 relates to *size*: it is noticeable that the vast majority of the companies studied were very small indeed. Only Fairey had total assets in excess of £50m. The next largest companies were Richards and Wallington, a major plant hire business, and British Enkalon. The latter is unusual inasmuch as it was a subsidiary of a multinational, AKZO. It is also noticeable that this company suffered negative growth in its later years. This was a phenomenon which affected a number of concerns in the sample, reflecting the haemorrhaging effects of making losses. Only a few companies grew rapidly, most notably Bambers, Carron, Fairey, Mettoy, Oxley, R & J Pullman, and Richards and Wallington.

One result of so many of the companies being small was that they were often effectively controlled by family interests: i.e. there was usually a fairly narrow concentration of power. This in turn created a whole series of further problems.

First, a closely controlled company is inhibited from raising further equity capital, since there is a distinct possibility that the dominant group of shareholders will lose control. This tends to reduce its ability to react to a changing environment by investing in new plant and equipment or to exploit new markets. Second, when a company is small it almost inevitably tends not to be well diversified in its operations. And third, the small scale of its operations may well make it vulnerable, inasmuch as it is not really in a position to take advantage of potential economies of scale – e.g. in production, marketing and distribution, or product innovation through research and development.

A second fact which is noticeable is that the companies tend to be clustered in particular industries. For instance, the UK textiles sector suffered severely in the period covered by the study. There were various reasons for this, but their combination made life very difficult for many companies in the late 1970s and early 1980s. In particular, carpet manufacturers found the going tough, and two companies in the sample (British Enkalon and Blackwood Morton) were amongst those which went to the wall. In fact, they were victims of dumping by overseas competitors, increasing raw material prices (e.g. oil based man-made fibres, following the Opec oil price hikes), and adverse exchange rate movements.

In the engineering sector life was also difficult, again because of the strengthening of sterling on the foreign exchanges, but also as a result of a prolonged strike in the industry, which effectively sounded the death knell for the weakest firms in the sector.

The *narrow concentration of power* referred to above manifested itself in various ways. Quite frequently dominant personalities ran the companies, and on two occasions this led to boardroom rows when attempts were made to wrest control away from one particular interest group (Movitex and Berwick Timpo). A bizarre situation also arose with TCK, where a self appointed company doctor, with a background at McKinsey's, sought to turn the company round.

The *lack of diversification* of virtually all the companies in the sample has already been referred to. Almost all were entirely engaged in one type of activity, which was regarded as the company's core business. This in turn tended to mean that in most cases the product range was fairly limited, which increased exposure to risk.

Another common feature was a frequent inability to respond to a changing environment and *compete with rival concerns*. Sometimes this was almost impossible because of absolute cost disadvantages that resulted from the strengthening of the £, and the fact that manufacturing was concentrated in the UK. This made the textile and toy manufacturers in particular vulnerable to import penetration, while they were no longer able to sell abroad as previously. But usually their position wasn't helped by the fact that they were in no position to develop new products. Moreover, in one of the few cases where this was attempted, Mettoy – which tried to move into the electronic games market by developing the Dragon computer – burnt its fingers, having neither the expertise nor the capital to make such a venture a success.

Small size and the fact that management had too often become inward looking meant that far too many of the companies were ill equipped to respond to *changes in the economic environment*. As it happened, the traumatic events that overtook the British economy in the late 1970s and early 1980s – high interest rates, the strength of sterling, and a prolonged recession – combined to force a shake out in the manufacturing sector. Even the largest companies had to shed labour and rationalise their operations, battening down the hatches. In the circumstances, the smallest and weakest companies were bound to find it hard to survive.

Relatively few of the companies suffered as a result of the *failure of a big project*. However, Movitex was an example, when its attempt to launch a cheap record label proved to be an abysmal failure. Likewise, Carron's venture into property development in London's dockland was a doomed venture, and Oxley's ambitions in 1978 to open a major new printing complex never got off the ground. A failure of a different kind afflicted Fairey, which suffered heavily for the delays in building the Dungeness B nuclear power station.

As has been indicated above, there was little direct evidence of a *lack of investment*, although many of the companies in the sample did not seem to grow very rapidly. Further, there was evidence that the need for a dominant group of shareholders to retain control made it difficult to raise equity capital, and the lack of product innovation was also apparent.

A number of companies sought to expand through *acquisitions*, and on several occasions it was apparent that this strategy had failed (e.g. Airfix, Bamfords, Bambers Stores, Blackman and Conrad, Fairbairn Lawson, Mettoy, Oxley Printing, R & J Pullman, Richards and Wallington, TCK and Wombwell Foundry). Airfix in particular found that its attempts to save the Triang Pedigree and Meccano companies was misplaced; Bamfords misguidedly took over Jones Balers, only adding to its woes; and irregularities at Fairbairn Lawson's Greenbat subsidiary were a major cause of the group's collapse. Oxley took over several printing companies in the hope of turning them around; and Richards and Wallington in desperation acquired a DIY chain, hoping it would be a cash cow, enabling it to bail out the plant hire business, but that proved to be a flawed strategy. For its part R & J Pullman expanded rapidly, partly through mergers, and one of the rescues it undertook involved B. Paradise. However, Pullman's unexpected collapse brought down Paradise as well. As for Wombwell Foundry, by acquiring Sprotborough Castings it only dug a deeper hole from which it had to try to extricate itself.

Most of the businesses failed because of *undertrading*: i.e. the volume of sales and/or the sales margins could not be maintained, with the result that it became more and more difficult to meet unavoidable costs. This problem was accentuated as borrowings grew to meet the shortfalls in financing, the net effect being that debt servicing costs were added to the expenses that had to be covered.

There were no obvious cases of *overtrading* in the sample, the nearest example being John Michael. This was hardly surprising given the fact that very few of the companies were growing rapidly, and those which were generally expanded their operations through mergers rather than as a result of organic growth.

As indicated previously, most of the 25 failed companies operated in sectors where there was overcapacity (e.g. because of recession, or the loss of competitive edge over rival firms based abroad). The result was that the companies were faced with an *industry shake out*. This was the case, for instance, for groups operating in the textiles sector, both on the manufacturing side and in retailing. In some cases companies were engaged in obsolete activities: e.g. TCK and Fairbairn Lawson were both involved in the jute industry, and it was clear by the late 1960s that there was no future for UK companies operating in this sector.

The British toy industry was all but wiped out in the late 1970s and early 1980s, being unable to compete with Far Eastern competition, so it was hardly surprising that companies in this sector went to the wall. But engineering companies also had a hard time, both in the mechanical and civil engineering sectors. Moreover, the recession in consumer spending hit other types of business as well. For instance, F. Austin, a furniture manufacturer, felt the sharp drop in demand; as did Viners, one of the last Sheffield based cutlery businesses, even though it had already switched its sourcing to Far Eastern suppliers.

The incidence of *a major strike* was only a significant factor in the engineering industry in 1980 – and then only for one or two companies in that sector which were already in difficulties (e.g. Bamfords and Wombwell Foundry).

The *lack of adequate financial controls* contributed to the collapse of several companies, but most spectacularly at Bambers Stores, Fairbairn Lawson, R & J Pullman and Southern Constructions. In these cases substantial accounting irregularities were uncovered which were virtually enough on their own to bring the companies down.

Almost all the companies ended up with *high levels of borrowing*. This was almost inevitable, given the fact that in most cases the equity shares were narrowly held and their profits were declining. Generally, therefore, high gearing was the result of the companies' problems rather than the direct cause.

Attempts were made in a number of cases to rescue ailing companies and *turn them around*, even when the prospects did not look encouraging. TCK was a clear instance where such an attempt was made, effectively using the old company as a shell. B. Paradise, as mentioned above, was successfully turned around, but it was dragged down by the collapse of the company which had come to its rescue, R & J Pullman. In several other cases there were changes in the board shortly before the company concerned collapsed: e.g. an Anglo-American consortium took over Viners hoping to rescue the company; and in the case of Movitex new directors were drafted in, leading to a boardroom spat which eventually brought the company down. In General Engineering's case, Senior Engineering made a take over bid to rescue the business shortly before it failed, but since this was only one tenth of the book value of the net assets the shareholders turned it down.

There were few *audit qualifications*, and those which were made tended to occur in the last year for which accounts were filed. At first sight this might appear to suggest that the auditors were not giving early warning signals to shareholders and creditors of the impending difficulties that were about to overtake the companies. On the other hand, a qualification – and especially a going concern qualification – can be viewed in some circumstances as effectively signing the death warrant of a business, so it was only to be expected that they would be observed attached to the last published accounts of a failed company.[1]

Going concern qualifications were attached to the last filed accounts of Airfix, Melody Mills, John Michael, Oxley, R & J Pullman, and Viners. John Michael was unusual in that going concern qualifications were also made with respect to previous years' accounts (i.e. 1975-1977 as well as to 1980). The auditors' report on the last financial statements filed by British Enkalon drew attention to the fact that the magnitude of the provision required to cover closure costs was such as to cast doubt as to whether the accounts showed a true and fair view. In similar vein, the penultimate accounts filed by Southern Constructions were qualified with respect to the value of work in progress, the point being made that its value depended on the continued availability of finance. The last filed accounts of Movitex and Blackman & Conrad were qualified for non-compliance with SSAPs, the censure in the case of the former being more severe as it related to the treatment of extraordinary losses under SSAP 6. The 1974 accounts of Oxley were unusually qualified for breach of a trust deed; and the 1979 accounts of Paradise were qualified with respect to the adequacy of the provision against slow moving stock items.

The trend of *declining profits* shows that in very few cases did failure come as a bolt from the blue. Usually profits had been falling for a few years before the plug had to be pulled on a business. It was also evident that the *market posted warnings* several years before the final collapse, although sometimes the initial downturn in profits was not diagnosed as the beginning of a long slide that culminated in failure.

One sign of an attempt to turn a company round is whether *capital was injected into the business*. In fact, in many cases rights issues were made. Sometimes the cash was used to reduce borrowings (e.g. in the case of Bambers Stores, which pursued a rapid expansion policy); in others it was directly used either to finance new investment projects or – occasionally – to shore up a deteriorating position (e.g. British Enkalon).

The point has been made above that over the last four years before their bankruptcy, the *asset growth rate* of the failing companies was generally low. Thus in only four out the 25 cases studied is the ratio of the final reported value of total assets to the corresponding figure four years previously above 2. This is in stark contrast to the ratios reported for the 21 companies failing in the second sample period, reported below.

In many cases – though by no means all – commentators were expressing doubts about the financial position of the companies some years before their final collapse. Usually these *market warnings* were reflected in declines in relative share price. However, the concerns expressed were frequently industry wide, and it was not always obvious that the position of the particular company in question was thought to be significantly worse than that of its rivals.

*Non-sample companies*

A cursory examination of the experience of the remaining 76 firms in the failed company sample showed that they had frequently faced similar problems. Most were small, and they were usually controlled by family or other closely knit groups. Often there was a dominant personality managing the business, and the companies also overwhelmingly came from the same industries in which the 25 case study firms operated.

In the textiles sector, for example, there were more than a dozen casualties amongst clothing manufacturers, the root cause being fierce overseas competition, which made it necessary to reduce UK production capacity. For similar reasons, a number of footwear manufacturers went out of business. In addition, two well known carpet manufacturers (besides those whose fate was examined in more detail, Blackwood Morton and British Enkalon) ended up in the hands of the receivers: Bond Worth and Homfray. Famous names also disappeared  as the British toy industry was decimated, with Dunbee-Combex-Marx and Lesney going to the wall, as well as the three companies whose fate was studied in some depth (Airfix, Berwick Timpo and Mettoy). There were also many casualties in the engineering and construction sectors. In the former, Swan Hunter went into receivership as the shipbuilding industry continued to shrink in size; and another well known company, Stone Platt, which manufactured pumps and similar products, had to be reconstructed. Elsewhere, there were a number failures in the motor vehicle sector (e.g. the truck builder Fodens, and two manufacturers of mobile homes, Caravans International and Peak Investments). There were also casualties in the furniture and household wares industries, including the electrical goods manufacturer, Dimplex, and Goldring, which produced high quality styluses for use on record players, a product which was becoming obsolete. The construction sector, as always, suffers in a recession, and ten relatively small building companies were amongst the casualties, apart from Southern Constructions, whose circumstances were studied in more depth.

There were relatively few instances of newly established or listed companies that failed, although this was in part because of the criteria used for selecting the sample (namely, there had to be at least five years' accounts available for a company to be included). The most obvious example was Hesketh Motorcycles, which was developed from the Hesketh motor racing business. The aim was to resurrect the fortunes of the British motorcycle industry, which had been all but wiped out as a result of import penetration by Japanese manufacturers.[2] Sadly, the venture failed soon after it was launched. Two other companies which failed were Automatic Oil Tools and Findlay Group, both of which used moribund companies with Stock Exchange listings as a way of floating their businesses. Automatic Oil Tools was a new venture, in fact, but the Findlay business had operated successfully as a private company for some years. Its failure was largely as a result of a misguided attempt to expand the scale of its operations.

Even more revealing, perhaps, was a brief examination of the experiences of the matched pair control companies. Many were also small and (for the most part) family controlled businesses, but because size was not used as a matching criterion, there were more medium and large sized companies in this sample. It was apparent that many of these firms had suffered from the setbacks experienced by the industries in which they operated in much the same way as those companies that failed. On the other hand, they were less vulnerable, often because they had focused their activities and specialised (although whether this strategy was the result of luck or good judgement was not always clear).

In the textiles sector, several of the smaller companies had successfully carved out niches for themselves, but even so they were under pressure, and more than one failed some years after the sample period. Indeed, it is noticeable that even at the retail end of the fashion industry, many of the high street chains have had to be turned round after going through rough patches (e.g. Burtons, B*hs*, Next, Alexon, Etam, and Laura Ashley). Similarly, the footwear companies used as controls were essentially specialist manufacturers, and the industry in general has since had to be restructured on both the manufacturing and retail sides. Likewise, the pairings used for carpet manufacturers hardly compared like with like, as it has been the volume producers and retailers who have proved most vulnerable, not only in the 1973-1983 period but subsequently (e.g. with the collapse of Lowndes Queensway in 1991 and the disposal of Allied Carpets by Asda for a knock-down price in 1993).

In the toy industry it was difficult to find a suitable match for the failed companies, and the best that could be done was to use Spear's and Waddington's, both of which (very successfully) manufacture games rather than die cast models and similar toys. It was also noticeable that in the engineering sector it was often difficult to get a close match (e.g. for a shipbuilder, such as Swan Hunter, or for a truck manufacturer, such as Fodens). In fact, one of the controls eventually used for motor engineering was York Trailers, which operates (very successfully) manufacturing customised trailers for lorries, meeting demand in a different part of the market to that catered for by Fodens, Caravans International, and Peak Investments.

In the construction sector, a number of the control companies were rather larger than those which failed, which seems to have helped them to survive. But, rather interestingly, several of these (both at the small end and some rather larger) ran into trouble in the late 1980s and early 1990s, although several of them managed to escape the final indignity of going into receivership.

**The causes of failure, 1988-1991**

*The sample companies*

The second sample of 21 companies were those used for applying hold out tests for the multivariate logit models (see pp. 245, 249 and 280-2). They were selected as being broadly representative of listed companies which collapsed in the period. Four were in the construction industry, and three others were in the property management sector. In addition, a further three were linked in some way to the property sector (e.g. supplying home decorating and DIY products); and another three operated in the clothing and footwear industries, which suffered as a result of the sharp decline in consumer spending power (a phenomenon in part due to the collapse in house prices). Four of the 21 were relatively large companies (Brent Walker, British and Commonwealth, Maxwell Communications, and Polly Peck), the lack of adequate financial controls being a contributory factor towards the collapse of three of them.

Table 15.2 summarises the characteristics of the 21 companies, whose circumstances were on this occasion primarily studied over a period of four years up to failure. As before, the columns in the table correspond to the descriptive variables listed at the beginning of the chapter, the only exception being that the heading *market warnings* is dropped on this occasion. The reason for this is because in many cases the share price returns are not that meaningful, since the waters were in many instances muddied by take over activity and by the stock market crash of 1987. In the circumstances it is probably more appropriate just to refer to share price behaviour in the text when it seemed to signal the market's recognition of potential problems.

Once more, the basis for making entries in some of the columns requires further explanation. Thus with respect to size, the categories used to classify the 25 bankrupt companies which failed over the period 1973-83 appeared to be inappropriate. This was because several of the companies which collapsed between 1988 and 1991 were really quite large; while some of the smaller ones grew very rapidly as a result of aggressive acquisitions strategies. In the circumstances it was decided to use six classifications, based on the figure for total assets shown in a company's final published balance sheet. These are coded as follows: 1 indicates total assets less than £30m; 2 a value between £30m and £50m; 3 a value between £50m and £100m; 4 a value between £100m and £250m; 5 a value between £250m and £500m; and 6 a total over £500m.

Almost all the companies ended up with huge amounts of borrowings, and given the very rapid decline in their fortunes some criterion was needed to indicate whether they were overly dependent on credit beforehand. The rule of thumb used was that they were regarded as having relatively high levels of borrowing if 3-4 years before failure total liabilities exceeded half the value of total assets.

As previously, the numbers in the audit qualification column show the number of years in which accounts were qualified, with an asterisk shows that there was a previous but not adjacent qualification during the 4 year window. Similarly, the figures in the column for relatively low profits show the number of years of declining profits recorded before failure.

The figures in the 'growth rate' column again represent the total assets figure reported in the final year's balance sheet divided by the corresponding figure shown in the financial statements four years previously. Although the statistic will be biased downwards where a company experiences losses in its last year of trading, it nevertheless clearly demonstrates the way many of the companies listed overreached themselves during the boom years of the mid to late 1980s (usually as a result of pursuing aggressive acquisitions policies).

## Table 15.2: Characteristics of Failing Companies – Hold Out Sample

| Name of company | Size | Narrow ownership | Lack of diversification | Inability to compete | External environment changed | Big project fails | Lack of investment | Acquisition strategy fails | Undertrading | Overtrading | Industry shake out | Major strike | Inadequate controls | Relatively high borrowing | Turnround attempt fails | Audit qualification | Relatively low profits | Capital injection | Growth factor |
|---|---|---|---|---|---|---|---|---|---|---|---|---|---|---|---|---|---|---|---|
| Arley Holdings | 1 | x | | x | x | | | x | x | | | | | x | | | 0* | x | 12.9 |
| AT Trust | 1 | | | | | | | x | x | | | | | x | | | 0* | x | 3.4 |
| Bestwood | 2 | x | x | x | x | | | x | x | | x | | x | x | | 0* | 0* | x | 1.6 |
| Brent Walker | 6 | | | x | x | | | x | x | | x | | x | x | | 2 | 1 | | 1.4 |
| British & Commonwealth | 6 | | | x | x | | | x | x | | | | | x | | | 4 | | 13.2 |
| CH Industries | 4 | x | | x | x | | | x | | | x | | | x | | | 0 | | 3.1 |
| Charterhall | 4 | x | x | x | x | | | x | x | | x | | | | | | 0* | x | 5.6 |
| Citygrove | 3 | x | x | x | x | | | | x | | x | | | x | | | 0 | x | 7.2 |
| Coloroll | 5 | x | x | | x | | | x | x | | x | | x | x | | | 0 | x | 7.6 |
| Egerton Trust | 4 | x | | x | x | | | x | x | | x | | | | | | 0 | | 3.1 |
| Equity & General | 2 | | | x | x | | | | x | | | | x | x | | 1 | 4 | | 1.7 |
| Fobel International | 1 | x | x | x | x | | | | x | x | | | | x | | | 2 | | 1.2 |
| Goldberg (A) | 2 | x | x | x | x | | | | x | x | | | | | x | 1 | 2 | | 1.3 |
| Lovell (YJ) | 5 | x | x | x | x | | | | x | x | | | | x | | | 1 | | 1.1 |
| Maxwell Communications | 6 | x | | | | | | x | | | | | x | x | | | 0 | | 2.1 |
| Miller (Stanley) | 1 | x | x | x | x | | | | x | x | | | | x | | | 0* | | 2.9 |
| Parkfield | 4 | | x | x | x | | | x | x | | | | | x | | | 0 | x | 4.7 |
| Polly Peck | 6 | x | | | x | | | x | x | | | x | x | | | | 0 | x | 7.1 |
| Rush & Tompkins | 4 | | x | x | x | | | | x | x | | | | x | | | 2 | x | 1.1 |
| Sock Shop | 1 | x | x | x | x | | | | x | x | | | x | x | | | 1 | x | 48.0 |
| Warringtons | 3 | x | x | x | x | | | x | x | x | | | | | | | 4 | x | 9.9 |

334

It is evident from the first column in Table 15.2 that the companies which failed were not always minnows but were sometimes quite large. This is in stark contrast to corresponding column in Table 15.1, and it does not just reflect the way the companies were selected for inclusion in the samples. Nevertheless, it remains true that many of the casualties came from the population of smaller companies, which (as is usually the case with such businesses) were effectively controlled by family interests. This *narrow concentration of power* sometimes inhibited them from raising new equity capital and made them overreliant on borrowing. This was certainly the case with Bestwood, for instance, where the position was aggravated by a boardroom row. But it is also noticeable that the four large failed companies included in the sample (Brent Walker, British and Commonwealth, Maxwell Communications and Polly Peck) were controlled by dominant personalities (George Walker, John Gunn, Robert Maxwell and Asil Nadir). Several of the smaller companies were also vehicles for ambitious entrepreneurs, some of whom had high profiles in the media (e.g. John Ashcroft at Coloroll and Sophie Mirman at Sock Shop). However, it should be pointed out that there were many other companies at the time which were likewise dominated by their chief executives but which survived and prospered.

Inevitably the narrow concentration of ownership in the smaller companies often seemed to prevent them from *diversifying their activities*. On the other hand, several of them had attempted to spread their interests (e.g. Arley Holdings, CH Industries, Equity & General, Parkfield, and AT Trust – which changed its name from Astra Trust just before its demise).

But a rather more important reason for the failure of companies was their *inability to compete* with rivals. Where this was a problem between 1973 and 1983, it was usually because overseas competitors had the advantage of lower costs (e.g. because of lower wage rates and a more competitive currency). By contrast, the problem between 1988 and 1991 was usually that the failing companies had overextended themselves. This meant that they were not only faced with high levels of unavoidable fixed operating costs, but they also had to meet hefty interest charges on substantial borrowings. The situation was further aggravated as the recession took hold because government policy required that sterling should continue to be aligned with the German mark.

But the key factor which brought the downfall of so many companies between 1988 and 1991 was an inability to cope with *changes in the economic environment* as recession took hold. Of course, it is easy with hindsight to see that a great many companies overreached themselves in the mid to late 1980s. The downturn in the property market when it came was sudden and took the banks as much by surprise as anyone else. Once the downward spiral began, it was hard to check. Negative equity appeared as house prices fell, and as a result consumer confidence evaporated. In the circumstances, it was inevitable that some of the companies which had expanded rapidly would go to the wall, and those most vulnerable would be those which relied too heavily on borrowings.

Several companies in the sample operated in the financial services sector (e.g. British & Commonwealth, Bestwood and Equity & General), and all were adversely affected to a greater or lesser extent by the stock market crash in 1987.

There was no evidence for any of the 21 companies that their bankruptcy was the result of the *failure of a big project*, nor because of a *lack of investment*. Rapid growth was usually achieved via an *acquisitions* policy. Such a strategy can be regarded as having failed to the extent that it generally left the acquiring company overstretched and more vulnerable when the recession took hold. However, there were few if any instances where the business taken over failed to perform or could not be integrated with other activities.

Perhaps the most obvious examples of overexpansion through acquisitions were the four large groups (Brent Walker, British & Commonwealth, Maxwell Communications, and Polly Peck) and Coloroll.[3] This helped to make them overreliant on outside borrowings. Brent Walker's interests included pub chains, television and films, hotels, property, and the William Hill betting shops; while British and Commonwealth was put together combining Exco, Mercantile House, Abaco and (most disastrously) Atlantic Computers. Maxwell Communications represented a combination of various printing and publishing interests, but most notably Mirror Group Newspapers. For its part, Polly Peck was built up by Asil Nadir, its main interests being in food, electronics, and textiles, the group's last major acquisitions being Del Monte and Sansui in 1989. Coloroll, which was floated in 1985, expanded rapidly, its main acquisitions being Crown House and the Crowther carpets group (which included part of the old Homfray Carpets company, with brand names such as Kosset and Crossley).

Several of the smaller companies also pursued active acquisitions policies. Thus Charterhall absorbed Corah, purchased the Lennards shoe retailing chain from Great Universal Stores, and also had a stake in one of the other failing firms, Goldberg. However, an even more important factor in this company's demise was that its major investor had its own financial problems to cope with, making a rescue attempt from that quarter impossible.

As might be expected, virtually all the businesses failed because of *undertrading*: i.e. the volume of sales and/or the sales margins declined, reducing the contribution towards unavoidable costs. As indicated above, the problem was frequently aggravated as borrowings grew to meet shortfalls in financing, increasing debt servicing costs.

The only possible case of *overtrading* in the sample was Polly Peck, where one of the main contributory causes to the group's downfall was that a substantial proportion of its cash balances was in blocked accounts in Northern Cyprus and could not be used to finance working capital requirements elsewhere.

The point has been made above that most of the 21 companies failed because of the onset of the recession. This left the industries in which they operated with overcapacity, and as a result they were faced with an *industry shake out.* One of the few companies which appears to have lost its competitive advantage in purely trading terms was Parkfield. In one of its key activities (video sales), it found itself with excessively large stocks of slow moving items. Similarly, Fobel International was brought down by difficult trading conditions in the DIY sector.

There was no evidence that *a major strike* played a part in the downfall of any one of the 21 companies. However, *lack of adequate financial controls* contributed to the collapse of several companies. Most obviously this was the case where frauds were perpetrated or suspected (e.g. Maxwell Communications, Brent Walker and Polly Peck). However, there were also DTI investigations into the affairs of Bestwood and Equity & General (although in the latter case the report – when it was eventually published after a three year investigation – vindicated the board for resisting a concert party's attempt to take control of the group). It was also evident that there were weaknesses in the accounting systems at some companies (e.g. Sock Shop and Equity & General).

Almost inevitably, many of the companies ended up with *high levels of borrowing.* However, it is noticeable that well before the onset of the recession, the equity stake in many of the businesses was below 50 per cent, the high gearing presumably being used in part to enable a narrow ownership group to retain control.

Generally the downturn in the companies' fortunes was sudden, and in many cases it was clearly felt that the recession would be shortlived. For the most part the directors looked to banks for support and used borrowing to shore up their companies' finances. As a result there were few attempts to bring in outsiders to rescue ailing companies and *turn them around.* The main exception was Goldberg, where a company doctor was brought in but who failed in his attempts to save the business.

Only four of the companies had their accounts subjected to *audit qualifications.* Thus the last two sets of Brent Walker's accounts received going concern qualifications, the auditors making it clear that the survival of the group was in the hands of its bankers. Moreover, in the final year the report also referred to the fact that an investigation was being undertaken by the Serious Fraud Office. The last published sets of accounts of Lovell and Equity & General were also qualified, in the former case on a going concern basis, and for the latter on the basis that there was an understatement of creditors. The other company to have its financial statements qualified was Bestwood, whose penultimate accounts failed to show a provision against investments included in the balance sheet well above their market value. (These were sold the following year at a loss so the final year's accounts received a clean certificate.)

In the 25 company sample covering failures over the period 1973-83, most firms reported steadily *declining profits* for a few years before their final collapse. This pattern was far less evident in the 1988-91 sample of failures, emphasising the sudden reversal in the fortunes of most of the companies. (However, this would not have been quite so obvious had the period under scrutiny been extended to cover the years 1993-95, and the number of failed turnround attempts would also have been greater.)

Although most of the companies raised additional finance by borrowing from the banks, several partly financed their growth by *injecting new capital into the business*, issuing shares for cash. Thus apart from Citygrove and Sock Shop, which floated in 1986 and 1987 respectively, new issues were made by Arley, Bestwood, Charterhall, Coloroll, Parkfield, Polly Peck, Rush & Tompkins, and Warringtons. The fact that the shares were taken up, albeit before the downturn occurred, indicates that the markets had little inkling of the problems ahead.

The point has been made previously that, in contrast to the record of the 25 companies failing between 1973-83, those which went bankrupt between 1988 and 1991 were far more likely to have experienced a rapid *asset growth rate* before the receiver took over. In most cases this was because of active acquisitions policies. However, with Sock Shop and (to a lesser extent) Citygrove, the expansion was organic, financed by a combination of equity (raised when the companies were floated) and bank borrowings. In the case of Sock Shop, the initial success of the company was overhyped, its flotation issue in May 1987 being 53 times oversubscribed and its price/earnings ratio reaching the dizzy heights of 24! The euphoria led it to expand abroad, and when demand fell away it was left high and dry, the position being aggravated by weaknesses in the internal control system. Elsewhere, two of the smaller construction companies (Miller and Warringtons) experienced rapid growth in their assets in their final years of operations. This was not the result of their acquisitions policies (although Warringtons did increase its commitments in this way), but rather because balance sheets were inflated by increasing stocks of unsold houses. These were financed by creditors who, when they could see little chance of them being sold, called in the receivers.

In most cases analysts did not anticipate the problems ahead, so there were few *market warnings*. However, relative share prices were marked down where profits were in decline. Moreover, as the recession set in the weakness of the construction and property services sectors was recognised, particularly for those companies which were overburdened with debt. More specifically, shares in British & Commonwealth were steadily marked down after reaching a peak of 565p in 1987; while the uncertainty associated with Polly Peck's activities was reflected in the volatility of its share price record. It is only with the advantage of hindsight, it seems, that it is possible to see where market analysts (not to mention bankers and auditors!) got it wrong.

It should be clear from the above that there are some important differences in the underlying causes of financial failure over the period 1988-91 compared to a decade earlier. However, just how representative the case studies of the 21 companies reviewed are is a matter which needs to be addressed.

In fact, an examination of the experience of other listed companies operating in the same industries suggests that the problems faced by the 21 companies studied were not that unusual. For example, most listed concerns in the construction and property sectors found the going tough, with declining profits, high borrowings and increased interest charges. As a result, several well known medium sized civil engineering contractors had to call in the receivers in the early 1990s (e.g. Turriff and Lilley); while the much larger Costain group was forced to suspend share dealings in June 1996. The situation with respect to property companies has been even more perilous. Many only survived because the banks knew that there was little point in foreclosing, given the collapse in demand for commercial properties. Nevertheless, the list of those which went under after the first wave of failures is impressive, including Mountleigh, Rosehaugh and Speyhawk.

Other groups suffered because of the fall in property values and the decline in consumer spending. Thus the hotel group Queens Moat was hit by the sudden fall in the number of tourists visiting Britain, and the declining value of its properties could no longer support the company's extensive bank borrowings. Other consumer oriented businesses to collapse included the volume carpet and furniture retailers Lowndes Queensway and ELS; the Vestey group (whose main assets were property and the Dewhurst chain of butchers' shops, which was rapidly losing market share to the supermarkets); Harry Goodman's privately owned International Leisure Group (ILG), which entered commitments to purchase new aircraft at the peak of the boom, leaving it indebted to the tune of £300m; the Pentos Group, which had grown rapidly by expanding the Athena and Dillons art and book shops; and the Facia group, which owned shoe retailing outlets and the restructured Sock Shop business.

On the manufacturing side, the remnants of the shipbuilding industry once again fell into the hands of the receivers as orders dried up (e.g. Cammell Laird; and, in May 1993, Swan Hunter, when it failed to win the contract to build a helicopter carrier for the Royal Navy). Other victims included the truck builder, AWB, emphasising once again that small specialist engineers are probably too small to compete with the large, internationally based volume commercial vehicle manufacturers. But perhaps the most spectacular casualty in this sector was Ferranti, which acquired the US International Signal & Control group in 1987, only to find it was the victim of a fraud involving £215m of non-existent contracts.

In the distribution sector, casualties included LEP (which, despite the good offices of a company doctor) went into receivership at the end of 1992; and

Tiphook (which despite its problems struggled on). In both cases the companies were top heavy with debt, and the slowdown in economic activity left them weaker than their rivals facing the need to meet high interest charges.

## Summary

The case histories of the companies whose experience has been examined in this part of the study seem to show that there were rather different reasons underlying failures in the periods 1973-83 and 1988-91. Unsurprisingly, the common thread is that when they fell into the hands of the receivers they were reporting low profits and high borrowings, regardless of the underlying causes of their financial distress.

With respect to the period 1973-83, it can clearly be seen that most of the companies that collapsed came from industries where there was overcapacity. This in turn was frequently because companies had lost their competitive edge, usually the result of wage costs being too high, a factor aggravated by the high foreign exchange value of sterling.

Indeed, with the advantage of hindsight it is easy to see why many of them went to the wall. Certainly it is now clear that few of the toy manufacturers stood a chance of surviving in what had become an increasingly hostile environment. Likewise, it is now evident that there was overcapacity in the textiles industry, and several of the manufacturers of carpets and clothing were destined for failure. But, as is clear from the press reports, this was far from obvious at the time. Indeed, many analysts felt that there was a good chance that the businesses could be turned round.

It is also evident that in many instances companies were becoming more and more mired in the misfortunes of their industries, and as time passed the probabilities of their returning to profitability were declining. It was only when the banks and other creditors reckoned that there was no realistic hope of a turnround that the receivers were sent in.

But there is one other factor that can be gleaned from a careful study of the case histories, and that is that in many instances the companies were not only victims of an unfortunate conjunction of circumstances, but they had also frequently been weakened by some event. As a result, they were especially vulnerable when their industry faced a sharp downturn.

In some respects the experience between 1988 and 1991 is not dissimilar. However, on this occasion the failures were clustered in the construction, property, financial services and retail sectors. The first wave of bankruptcies was amongst those companies which had grown rapidly during the boom years of the mid 1980s. Usually this had been achieved via acquisitions, substantially financed through bank borrowing. When the downturn came it was sudden, and its severity and length were unexpected. As a result, those companies which failed suffered from declining contributions towards their unavoidable costs. These were inflated by higher interest charges, while at the same time the value of their properties had plummeted.

More generally, it is difficult to draw any hard and fast conclusions from a study of failing businesses taken in isolation. After all, there were certainly other companies during the two periods studied which had similar experiences but which survived. Indeed, it is known from the turnaround studies by Slatter (1984) and Grinyer et al. (1988)[4] that a number of surviving businesses faced crises of their own. But while it is easy to see after the event why they were successfully rescued, it is not at all clear whether *at the time* it was so self-evident that they would recover. Certainly the market frequently didn't seem to be able to make the distinction between failures and survivors until fairly late on.

In the circumstances, the case studies give plenty of food for thought. Clearly one or two of the failed companies pursued disastrous policies towards the end of their lives. But more generally it is evident that there are no easy lessons that can be drawn from their experiences – except, perhaps, that small and undiversified companies are at greater risk than their larger counterparts, but that is hardly news.

**Notes**

[1] However, it should be noted that the majority of companies whose accounts receive a going concern qualification survive: see p. 40.

[2] Dimson and Marsh (1989) describe the circumstances leading up to the flotation of Hesketh Motorcycles in 1980, but not its subsequent collapse in 1981.

[3] Smith (1996) provides brief case histories for British & Commonwealth, Polly Peck and Coloroll. However, he tries to suggest that a major reason for their downfall was the treatment of acquisitions in their accounts. In fact, as even a careful reading of his descriptions of events will show, this was probably not a major factor. Thus in the case of British & Commonwealth, the market marked down the shares well in advance of the final collapse. Similarly, the uncertainties associated with Polly Peck were reflected in the volatility in its share price; and as Smith himself admits, it is only really with the benefit of hindsight that it is possible to see how the market may have been misled. As for Coloroll, astute analysts (such as Smith and his rivals in the City) should have been able to identify the truth behind the company's operations as the necessary information was in the public domain.

[4] These studies are reviewed in chapter 7.


**Appendix 15.1**

*Short case histories of 25 failed companies*

In the case histories below the following abbreviations are used:

S        sales (turnover)
PBT      profit before tax
EBIT     earnings before interest and tax
TA       total assets
TL       total liabilities
MAR      market average residual: i.e. the percentage share price return after deducting the percentage return on the FT Actuaries All Share Index.


**Airfix**

| 31 March | 1980 | 1979 | 1978 | 1977 | 1976 | 1975 | 1974 | 1973 | 1972 | 1971 |
|---|---|---|---|---|---|---|---|---|---|---|
| S   (£m) | 42.0 | 43.2 | 38.9 | 39.4 | 33.7 | 24.4 | 17.8 | 14.4 | 11.0 | 8.5 |
| PBT(£000) | -2126 | 1347 | 2688 | 4034 | 3440 | 2603 | 2059 | 1936 | 1420 | 812 |
| TA  (£m) | 45.0 | 41.3 | 36.8 | 31.4 | 26.0 | 20.9 | 14.9 | 12.6 | 10.9 | 8.8 |
| EBIT/TA | .01 | .07 | .10 | .16 | .17 | .15 | .17 | .18 | .15 | .10 |
| TL/TA | .81 | .54 | .47 | .42 | .49 | .52 | .52 | .68 | .51 | .45 |
| MAR  (%) | -69 | -28 | -13 | -27 | +7 | | | | | |

Airfix was a toy manufacturer, primarily producing plastic model kits, but in the late 1960s it began to expand and diversify, manufacturing plastic packaging, shoes and metal housewares. Nevertheless, toys remained its major product until its collapse in 1981, accounting for over two thirds of the group's turnover and more than three quarters of pretax profits. The company's chairman and managing director from the late 1950s was Ralph Ehrmann, who had turned the company's fortunes round after a major setback in 1948.

Expansion of the company's plastic packaging and housewares interests in the early 1970s was dwarfed by the acquisition of two large but ailing toy manufacturers: Meccano from its receivers in 1971; and Triang Pedigree with government backing in 1975. In order to try to turn these businesses round a rights issue was made in 1976 – the year in which the group entered the model railway market. Neither acquisition proved successful. At the end of 1977 Airfix opted out of the Triang Pedigree commitment, and the company's own trading interests went into decline in the face of fierce overseas competition. Meccano piled up ever higher losses, and the closure of its factories was belatedly announced at the end of 1979, shortly to be followed by the disposal of the group's footwear activities. The packaging interests were also sold off in order to try to reduce the group's indebtedness, but this was insufficient to prevent substantial losses being reported. These reflected an inability to compete with foreign imports, especially in view of the strong £, and the impact of high interest rates. In the end the company's bankers called in the receivers in January 1981.

## F. Austin

| 30 June | 1981 | 1980 | 1979 | 1978 | 1977 | 1976 | 1975 | 1974 | 1973 | 1972 |
|---|---|---|---|---|---|---|---|---|---|---|
| S (£m) | 7.29 | 8.37 | 9.35 | 8.54 | 8.62 | 7.71 | 6.72 | 6.34 | 5.28 | 3.77 |
| PBT (£000) | -1865 | -669 | 483 | 342 | 534 | 501 | 362 | 615 | 584 | 207 |
| TA (£m) | 5.81 | 5.63 | 5.72 | 5.48 | 5.67 | 5.09 | 4.73 | 4.73 | 3.68 | 3.22 |
| EBIT/TA | -.29 | -.11 | .09 | .07 | .10 | .10 | .08 | .13 | .16 | .07 |
| TL/TA | .54 | .37 | .30 | .31 | .32 | .33 | .40 | .43 | .38 | .38 |
| MAR (%) | +23 | -86 | +25 | +29 | -2 | | | | | |

F. Austin was founded in 1929, going public in 1947, although it remained family controlled until its demise in 1981. The company manufactured furniture for the bottom end of the market, and it expanded rapidly in the early 1970s, funding investment in new capacity from internally generated cash flow. After 1976 growth in turnover tailed off and profits stagnated up until 1979. The recession of 1980 brought massive destocking by retailers, demand falling by a third. This adversely affected the profits of all furniture manufacturers, but Austin's more than most because it operated in a narrow segment of the market. As a result turnover fell and a loss of £669,000 was recorded, even though a quarter of the company's workforce was laid off in an attempt to cut costs.

Ralph Cradick, who had turned round another furniture company, was drafted in as managing director, but his remedy for the business proved to be disastrous. He attempted a restructuring by combining Austin with another furniture company, Beautility, funding the rationalisation with a rights issue. The latter was a failure, leaving the underwriters (the ICFC) with a 20 per cent stake in the business, while borrowing increased from £500,000 to £2m. The additional capacity made available by the merger proved to be a millstone around the company's neck, and in March 1982 pay cuts of 5-10 per cent were forced on employees. However, this sacrifice was not enough, and in June the listing was suspended. Shortly afterwards negotiations for a rescue by the Greater London Council collapsed, and the company's bankers called in the receivers.

## Bambers Stores

| 31 January | 1983 | 1982 | 1981 | 1980 | 1979 | 1978 | 1977 | 1976 | 1975 | 1974 |
|---|---|---|---|---|---|---|---|---|---|---|
| S (£m) | 37.1 | 39.6 | 30.2 | 25.2 | 17.2 | 10.7 | 7.2 | 6.2 | 4.3 | 2.8 |
| PBT(£000) | -3554 | 1309 | 2867 | 3301 | 2584 | 1268 | 609 | 456 | 351 | 206 |
| TA (£m) | 36.3 | 41.4 | 35.3 | 23.8 | 11.7 | 6.5 | 4.0 | 3.0 | 2.3 | 1.8 |
| EBIT/TA | -.04 | .07 | .13 | .18 | .24 | .21 | .18 | .18 | .19 | .14 |
| TL/TA | .58 | .51 | .51 | .60 | .54 | .54 | .49 | .61 | .68 | .71 |
| MAR (%) | -81 | -2 | -32 | +31 | +455 | | | | | |

The company was incorporated in 1953, and went public in 1971 as the Vernon Fashion Group Ltd. The company specialised in women's and children's fashions – it was sometimes referred to as a mini Mothercare – and when floated it had a chain of 53 shops. In the next 12 years it expanded rapidly, building up its chain of stores to 200. It also strengthened its hand by acquiring manufacturing facilities, which by 1980 enabled it to produce some 70 per cent of the garments it sold in its shops.

The company was for the whole of its life run by the Vernon family, despite the fact that the name of the business was changed to Bambers Stores in 1978. At its flotation the managing director was Louis Vernon, while his two brothers acted as chairman and secretary. The shareholdings of the Vernon family accounted for some two thirds of the share capital until the early 1980s, when they were cut back. Nevertheless, the family remained a very substantial shareholder right up until the end.

The mid 1970s were years of rapid growth for the group, finance mainly coming from outside borrowing, although a rights issue was made to raise £378,000 in 1976. The rapid growth encouraged optimism in the market, and by mid 1979 the share price had risen to over 260p, five times the value recorded in 1975. This valued the company at more than £8.5m. Further progress was made in 1980, even though interest charges had risen from £147,000 to £947,000 and depreciation was up from £375,000 to £801,000. The higher figures in 1980 reflected higher interest rates and the fact that £6.3m had been invested in new shops and office premises, largely financed by borrowing.

The first sign of trouble was in April 1980 when the Vernon family sold off 17.6 per cent of the company's capital, raising £2.83m to pay off personal bank borrowings. In October analysts were forecasting bleak times ahead for clothing stores, although Bambers was regarded as being better placed than many of its rivals to ride out the storm. However, first half results for 1980/81 showed trading profits down from £906,000 to £705,000, and borrowings were still around £9m. Bambers acquired two new subsidiaries to help relieve the pressure, selling off the premises and leasing them back to raise cash. At the same time it revalued its properties, boosting reserves by £10m and bringing the balance sheet borrowings to equity ratio down to around 50 per cent. In the event, results for 1980/81 showed pretax profits up by 8 per cent, although a third of the earnings figure was accounted for by profits on the disposal of properties.

Performance in 1981/82 was well down, with pretax profits falling from £2.87m to £1.31m, even after crediting profits from the sale of properties of 1.36m. In fact, the position would have been worse had not a new accounting policy been introduced, whereby the £592,000 cost of developing new outlets was capitalised for amortisation over five years. This kept depreciation down to £1.15m as against £888,000 in the previous year. On the other hand, interest charges were held in check at £1.71m, some £20,000 less than in 1980/81. This news, accompanied by the announcement of board changes and rumours that the group's shops were full of unsold goods, helped push the share price down, halving the company's value in less than a month.

Results for the six months to 31 July 1982 confirmed the crisis as stocks were dumped, a corresponding pretax profit of £1.48m being converted into a £3.9m loss. Stock values were written down by £1.4m, and it was announced that in order to conserve the company's cash position shops and properties were to be sold. The share price plummeted, particularly when it was announced that one of the Vernon family interests had sold 2m shares. In order to raise cash the company's head office was sold off for £2m, but the figures for 1982/83 offered no respite, the pretax loss being £3.6m, despite the inclusion of a £114,000 profit on the sale of properties. Deferred expenditures written off as an extraordinary item totalled £1.17m, including the store development costs of £592,000, and the stocks carried in the balance sheet were still £14.9m compared to £17.1m a year earlier. An attempt to secure fresh capital from the Mellins textile group was only partly successful, and following an announcement in September 1983 that Bambers' losses for the six months to 31 July were greater than anticipated, the company went into voluntary liquidation, owing £14m to its creditors. This followed an independent investigation by Coopers and Lybrand for Mellins which suggested that there had been accounting irregularities at Bambers for some time. In particular, it appeared that the value of stocks had been inflated by 20 per cent and premises had been overvalued by £2.5m. Unfortunately, the former finance director of the group, the son-in-law of Mr Louis Vernon, was unable to help unravel the mess as he had emigrated to the US.

As a postcript, small shareholders met in December and decided – like the liquidators, Cork Gully – to take legal action against Mr Vernon and Bambers' auditors, Gerald Edelman, for painting far too rosy a picture of the company when presenting the 1983 accounts. In particular, they were angry that the reported loss of £3.6m for 1982/83 understated the true figure, which was closer to £6.1m. Similarly, the equity net worth on the balance sheet at £15.1m was double the figure that ought to have been shown.

**Bamfords**

| 31 December[1] | 1978 | 1977[2] | 1976 | 1975 | 1974 | 1973 | 1972 | 1971 | 1970 | 1969 |
|---|---|---|---|---|---|---|---|---|---|---|
| S    (£) | 18.0 | 19.7 | 12.4 | 11.0 | 10.5 | 7.8 | 6.2 | 3.5 | 4.1 | 3.8 |
| PBT (£000) | 634 | 976 | 735 | 576 | 453 | 147 | 377 | 79 | 112 | 241 |
| TA   (£m) | 13.5 | 12.8 | 9.7 | 8.5 | 7.9 | 7.3 | 6.2 | 4.9 | 3.4 | 3.4 |
| EBIT/TA | .08 | .09[3] | .11 | .11 | .10 | .05 | .08 | .04 | .08 | .10 |
| TL/TA | .47 | .49 | .47 | .48 | .52 | .50 | .40 | .30 | .65 | .53 |
| MAR   (%) | -17 | +10[3] | +66 | n/a | n/a | | | | | |

[1] Years to 30 September up until 1976.    [2] 15 months to 31 December 1977.
[3] Rate of return and MAR annualised.

Bamfords was a long established but small manufacturer of agricultural machinery and engines. Being in an industry which is notoriously subject to fluctuations in demand, the company's turnover and profits were volatile throughout the 1960s, and in 1968 a major customer, Frederick H Burgess Ltd, purchased a 20 per cent stake in the company from the Bamford family interests.

After strengthening its manufacturing control systems, the company pursued an active expansion policy in the 1970s, acquiring Jones Balers Ltd in 1971, setting up overseas subsidiaries, and becoming a distributor for foreign agricultural equipment manufacturers. However, its main activity remained the manufacture of balers, which were increasingly being superseded by other farm equipment. Consequently the expansion policy still left the company vulnerable to fluctuations in demand, and profits in 1973 and 1974 were further hit by the impact of the government's price control legislation and by the fact that the company had built up sizeable stocks of unsold machinery. This in turn forced it to borrow substantial sums from its bankers. In a further effort to reduce its borrowings, a rights issue was made in 1977 which enabled Burgess to increase its stake to 58 per cent. However, the strength of sterling in the second half of 1979 crippled the company's export efforts and made it virtually impossible to compete with cheap imports, leaving it with expensive unused capacity at its Uttoxeter factory. Industrial disputes at both the national and local levels early in 1980 further undermined Bamford's position, and it went into voluntary liquidation in June of that year.

### Berwick Timpo

| 31 December | 1981 | 1980 | 1979 | 1978 | 1977 | 1976 | 1975 | 1974 | 1973 | 1972 |
|---|---|---|---|---|---|---|---|---|---|---|
| S    (£) | 13.2 | 14.4 | 16.8 | 13.2 | 12.4 | 10.9 | 7.7 | 7.4 | 5.8 | 3.2 |
| PBT (£000) | -510 | 1071 | 1515 | 1052 | 880 | 995 | 1035 | 1032 | 808 | 562 |
| TA   (£m) | 8.8 | 8.9 | 9.7 | 8.8 | 8.5 | 7.9 | 5.6 | 5.7 | 4.7 | 3.0 |
| EBIT/TA | .02 | .21 | .20 | .15 | .13 | .15 | .21 | .21 | .18 | .20 |
| TL/TA | .53 | .40 | .59 | .50 | .53 | .53 | .37 | .38 | .40 | .29 |
| MAR  (%) | -39 | -37 | +13 | +30 | -20 | | | | | |

Berwick Timpo was a holding company, created from the shell of a long established listed engineering company in 1971. Initially 65 per cent of the shares were held by the directors and Ionian Nominees, but the latter substantially reduced its stake to 33 per cent by 1974. The company manufactured toys, one of its main lines being fashion dolls, produced in cooperation with Mary Quant.

The company grew rapidly up until 1975, when domestic demand faltered. New acquisitions were made over the next two years, including Harbutt's Plasticine, but, in the face of fierce competition from overseas and a strong £, margins and profits fell in 1976 and 1977, despite a substantial growth in turnover. A rationalisation programme was introduced which, together with further acquisitions, saw a recovery in 1978 and 1979. However, there was a board dispute over policy in May 1979, which led to the resignation of the chairman, Mr Torquil Norman. Subsequently he attempted to take control of the company and was only narrowly defeated.

1980 saw a fall in turnover, which was accompanied by a build up in stocks, and with higher interest rates profits were cut by a third. The situation worsened in 1981, plunging the company into a pretax loss – and this at a time when the auditors uncovered accounting irregularities at two closed subsidiaries which understated extraordinary charges for the previous year by over £400,000. As a result there was a big shake up of the board, but the company's trading position in 1982 did not improve, the interim results showing even higher losses, which pushed the share price down to 12p. When the final figures were prepared it appeared that the pretax loss was £1m greater than forecast at £2.3m, a major reason being disappointing sales over the key Christmas period. With borrowings in February 1983 over £2.5m the banks withdrew their support and called in the receivers.

**Blackman and Conrad**

| 31 January[1] | 1979[2] | 1978 | 1977[3] | 1975 | 1974 | 1973 | 1972 | 1971 | 1970 | 1969 |
|---|---|---|---|---|---|---|---|---|---|---|
| S (£000) | 8070 | 9890 | 14270 | 8623 | 8303 | 6465 | 4003 | 3487 | 2768 | 2294 |
| PBT (£000) | 81 | -163 | 104 | 617 | 765 | 724 | 556 | 476 | 297 | 261 |
| TA (£m) | 5.39 | 5.82 | 7.61 | 6.07 | 5.95 | 5.21 | 2.73 | 2.51 | 1.56 | 1.43 |
| EBIT/TA | .05 | -.01 | .01[4] | .14 | .15 | .17 | .23 | .20 | .20 | .19 |
| TL/TA | .61 | .65 | .54 | .45 | .51 | .56 | .36 | .59 | .48 | .51 |
| MAR (%) | -14 | -59 | +20[4] | n/a | n/a | | | | | |

[1] 30 September year end up until 1975.

[2] The last accounts filed were those for 1979. Turnover for 1980 was £7.51m and PBT £180,000.

[3] 16 months to 31 January 1977.

[4] Rate of return and MAR annualised.

The Blackman and Conrad business was founded in 1923, and the company went public in 1947. Around 30 per cent of the share capital was owned by the Alderman family over the last ten years of the firm's existence. The business specialised in manufacturing women's fashion garments, 80 per cent of which were sold through mail order companies, but it began to diversify its operations from 1969 onwards, acquiring children's clothing companies and a jeans manufacturer over the next three years at a cost of over £2m. These purchases were partly financed by a placing of shares in January 1972, but this only raised £310,000. The balance came from borrowing, which (ignoring a property revaluation) pushed the debt/equity ratio well above 100 per cent.

The company's turnover and profits grew rapidly up until 1974, but there was a downturn in 1974/75 when – faced with increasing costs, including higher interest charges – margins had to be cut in order to hold market share. The real problems arose, however, in 1976 when the financial year was changed to cover a 16 month period. Unaudited figures released to show performance at 6 months and 12 months revealed profits above corresponding levels in 1974/75, so it came as a great shock to the market in July 1977 when adverse results for the full 16 months were published. These showed a sharp decline in profits, and the chairman had to admit that the accounts for the twelve months to 30 September 1976 had been incorrect, having failed to allow for exceptional expenses connected with commissioning new factories, a strike in the north east, and the loss of the regional employment premium. Moreover, these additional costs came at an unfortunate time when margins were being eroded further as a result of the influx of cheap textile imports from abroad. The company's management team was immediately reshaped and the internal control system tightened up. However, the Stock Exchange was unhappy about movements in the company's share price before the announcement of sharply reduced profits.

Weakened by the 1976/77 debacle, the company ran into losses in 1978, and despite extensive rationalisation in 1978/79, when one third of the workforce lost their jobs, profit before tax only totalled £81,000 for the year, bank borrowing reaching £1.27m. Sales further declined in 1979/80 as the crisis in the textile industry worsened and capacity was further cut back, but profits only improved marginally to £180,000. For the first half of 1980/81 turnover was almost halved, and the company chalked up a loss of £90,000. With no signs of an improvement in trading, the group went into voluntary liquidation on February 1981.

### Blackwood Morton (Holdings)

| 30 June | 1980 | 1979 | 1978 | 1977 | 1976 | 1975 | 1974 | 1973 | 1972 | 1971 |
|---|---|---|---|---|---|---|---|---|---|---|
| S (£0,000) | 2188 | 2598 | 2477 | 2637 | 2485 | 2362 | 2105 | 2039 | 1612 | 1291 |
| PBT (£000) | -1260 | 327 | -331 | 195 | 871 | -323* | 659 | 1845 | 1037 | 495 |
| TA (£m) | 14.5 | 16.1 | 16.0 | 17.1 | 16.2 | 14.0 | 14.9 | 12.6 | 10.3 | 10.1 |
| EBIT/TA | -.05 | .05 | -.00 | .04 | .07 | .01 | .06 | .16 | .11 | .06 |
| TL/TA | .45 | .40 | .42 | .41 | .39 | .43 | .46 | .38 | .37 | .41 |
| MAR (%) | -43 | -19 | -11 | -72 | +40 | | | | | |

* A change in the method of stock valuation reduced profits by £147,000.

Blackwood Morton (Holdings) was founded in 1908, and although the company had been listed for some years, it remained tightly controlled until receivers were appointed in October 1981, the Hamilton and Morton family interests holding some 85 per cent of the company's shares.

In the 1970s Blackwood Morton ranked sixth amongst British carpet manufacturers, using the BMK trade mark which it promoted strongly through advertising. The company specialised in manufacturing woven Wilton and Axminster carpets for the middle end of the market. This accounted for 75 per cent of its output, the balance being production of tufted synthetic yarn carpets. Another distinguishing feature of the company was the vertical integration in its activities, which included jute spinning and dyeing and bleaching textiles for use in the manufacture of its carpets – a concentration which gave rise to a highly geared operating structure.

The late 1970s were an unhappy time for British textile companies in general and for carpet manufacturers in particular. There was a major switch from woven wool-based Wilton and Axminster carpets to synthetic tufted floor coverings, which by 1980 accounted for 75 per cent of sales. This helped to create substantial overcapacity in the industry as new plant was installed, and the situation was made worse by the fact that for a time costs ran ahead of general inflation as a result of higher wool and synthetic yarn prices, thus depressing demand. A further difficulty was posed by the strength of sterling from 1979 onwards, which enabled US manufacturers to penetrate the market, taking a third of total sales within the space of three years. They were helped initially by being able to purchase oil-based synthetics at artificially low prices, but when the dollar hardened in 1981 Belgian manufacturers rapidly stepped in to fill the gap. In the meantime, British companies found themselves priced out of export markets as well, the benefit of relatively lower raw material prices being of far less significance to them.

Some companies were sheltered because they supplied the upper end of the market, while others had moved into synthetics early on and were thus able to steer their way out of trouble. But the rest were less fortunate, piling up substantial losses in 1980 and 1981 and slashing their workforces. The two weakest companies, Blackwood Morton and Homfray, were put into the hands of the receivers within weeks of each other in the autumn of 1981. In the short term this further depressed the market as the mass retailers (such as Allied Carpets and Harris Queensway) were able to obtain bankrupt stock cheaply. However, it also meant that much of the excess production capacity was removed, thus making it easier for the remaining companies to survive, especially as the price of sterling began to fall on the foreign exchanges and as consumer demand began to revive.

It is against this background that Blackwood Morton's record should be viewed. Certainly in 1973 there was no hint of the problems that were to arise, but thereafter analysts became increasingly aware of the potential difficulties that might face the company, even if they didn't accurately foresee the problems that were to face the carpet industry over the next few years. As a result the share price fell from 80p to 20p over the space of two years. The situation was not improved in 1974/75, the results being worse than the industry average as the company had unwisely purchased substantial quantities of raw materials at inflated prices. Even with a minor recovery in the industry in 1975/76, analysts remained cautious with respect to the company's prospects, and nothing over the next three years produced optimistic press comment. In 1979/80 the position worsened dramatically, and the share price halved to 10p. The deterioration continued in 1980/81, when the pretax deficit was estimated at £3m. With interest rates set to rise by 4 points and with no prospect of recovery, the board threw in the towel in October 1981, asking the company's bankers to call in the receivers. At the time debts outstanding were put at £6m, and with the shares suspended at 9p the company's capitalised market value was only £190,000.

### British Enkalon

| 31 December | 1980 | 1979 | 1978 | 1977 | 1976 | 1975 | 1974 | 1973 | 1972 | 1971 |
|---|---|---|---|---|---|---|---|---|---|---|
| S    (£m) | 57.2 | 60.5 | 53.6 | 50.5 | 47.3 | 38.5 | 40.3 | 36.8 | 26.8 | 26.6 |
| PBT (£000) | -8933 | -2150 | -250 | -2148 | -3157 | -5962 | 114 | 3720 | 520 | 3026 |
| TA   (£m) | 21.7 | 43.7 | 37.1 | 38.8 | 44.7 | 45.5 | 45.1 | 44.7 | 35.5 | 36.1 |
| EBIT/TA | -.29 | .01 | .03 | -.00 | -.03 | -.10 | .03 | .11 | .03 | .10 |
| TL/TA | 2.40 | .82 | .75 | .74 | .78 | .67 | .55 | .52 | .48 | .49 |
| MAR   (%) | -48 | -50 | +28 | -20 | -40 | | | | | |

British Enkalon was first registered at the end of 1960, and it was made a public company a year later. Throughout its existence it was technically a subsidiary of the Dutch chemicals giant, AKZO N.V. However, 37.5 per cent of its equity was held outside the group and was tradeable on the Stock Exchange. In June 1977 additional share capital was subscribed by AKZO, reducing the minority shareholding to 28.3 per cent. As the company's financial position worsened, AKZO made a final effort to turn the company round in June 1981, pumping in a further £7m in convertible shares, raising its controlling stake to 83.7 per cent.

The company manufactured man-made fibres at its factory in Antrim, principally for the carpet and clothing industries. However, it also produced wire and cable at its Glenrothes factory in Fife for the tyre industry. There was also a finishing plant on Teeside, which was closed in March 1980.

The company traded modestly but profitably throughout the 1960s, and with new capacity coming onstream in 1971 pretax profits for the year rose to £3m, the share price touching 95p. Like Courtaulds and ICI (which also operated man-made fibres plants in Ulster), British Enkalon suffered in 1972 when the Japanese began dumping polyester yarns on world markets. However, there was a recovery in 1973 when this practice ended.

The slide in the company's affairs really began in 1974 when recession first hit the man-made fibres industry, although the situation was aggravated by the devastating explosion at Nypro's Flixborough chemicals plant in June which denied the company it main source of supplies of caprolactum, a key raw material.

The position worsened in 1975 in the face of weak demand for clothing and growing import penetration. Pretax losses approached £6m, but commentators were optimistic at the year end, believing that the company was over the worst. In the event their confidence was hardly justified as the 1976 pretax loss was only reduced to £3.2m. However, this was basically a good result because interest charges doubled to £2m and the company was unable to recover full payment for £5m worth of goods sold to the bankrupt Brentford Nylons group.

There was a further cutback in pretax losses to £2.1m in 1977, an important contributory factor being a sharp fall in interest charges. This in turn was largely because borrowings were reduced with the proceeds of a £2.5m rights issue, all the new shares being taken up by the AKZO group. However, analysts could see few signs of a recovery in the fibres industry, nor for British Enkalon in particular. As a result the share price remained at 14p, valuing the business at only £5.45m. Further progress towards recovery was made in 1978, with pretax losses being cut back to £250,000. Performance would have been even better if the company had not suffered from the lorry drivers' strike in January and an increase in naphtha prices in November. In light of this relative improvement the share price rose to 24p, although this was still short of the net assets per share figure of 30p.

This ray of hope for the future was quickly extinguished in 1979, when the whole of the British textile fibres industry was hit by increasing raw material prices (the result of the second Opec oil price hike), a glut of low priced imports, high interest rates, and the strength of sterling. For the year as a whole pretax losses increased to £2.15m, and there were widespread calls for tough import quotas on textile yarns, not just from British Enkalon, but also from the industry giants, such as ICI, Courtaulds, Monsanto and Hoechst, all of which were chalking up large losses. Unlike British Enkalon, however, they at least benefited from diversification, the profits they were earning from their other activities making it easier for them to weather the storm. In the circumstances, although the share price was down at 7.5p, capitalising the company at £3.5m – well below debt of £18m – AKZO as the group parent decided to provide further support for its ailing subsidiary, injecting £7m towards a £40m five year investment programme.

The crisis in the fibres industry worsened throughout Europe in 1980, accompanied by widespread closures in an effort to take out surplus capacity. Courtaulds and ICI announced the closure of their Carrickfergus man-made fibre factories, yet despite recording a pretax loss of £8.93m for 1980, British Enkalon decided to keep at least part of its Antrim works open – largely, it seems, for social reasons. But by July 1981 the position had worsened, the listing being suspended at 5p. A £35m provision was called for by the auditors against the cost of closure of the Antrim factory, increasing the attributable loss to £44.72m. The end was close at hand, but AKZO delayed final closure for six months until March 1982 when the government offered £1.5m to keep 800 jobs open at the carpet mill. But with no improvement in sight at the beginning of 1982 the inevitable was accepted by all parties, and the company finally closed down its operations in March.

**Carron Company (Holdings)**

| 31 December | 1981 | 1980 | 1979 | 1978 | 1977 | 1976 | 1975 | 1974 | 1973 | 1972 |
|---|---|---|---|---|---|---|---|---|---|---|
| S (£) | 26.0 | 30.5 | 38.4 | 32.0 | 21.8 | 22.3 | 20.8 | 17.4 | 16.4 | 12.3 |
| PBT (£000) | -1132 | -565 | 1555 | 1086 | 483 | 1187 | 835 | 602 | 1788 | 1531 |
| TA (£m) | 28.1 | 29.2 | 29.1 | 21.5 | 18.7 | 17.1 | 16.4 | 15.0 | 15.2 | 9.4 |
| EBIT/TA | .01 | .02 | .08 | .08 | .05 | .09 | .07 | .06 | .12 | .16 |
| TL/TA | .69 | .64 | .59 | .66 | .62 | .57 | .54 | .50 | .50 | .46 |
| MAR (%) | -33 | -23 | -1 | +37 | -15 | | | | | |

Carron's shares were first listed in 1971, although the business dated back to 1759, the company originally having an interest in James Watt's steam engines, as well as being a manufacturer of guns used in the Napoleonic wars. By the 1970s its primary interests were in manufacturing gas and electric cookers and domestic ceramic ware.

Up until 1973 the company expanded rapidly, funding its investment expenditures by increasing its borrowings. However, there was a setback in 1974 when poor trading conditions cut pretax profits from £1.8m to £600,000. The market remained sluggish in 1975, but a major restructuring helped to produce something of a recovery in profits, although borrowing still remained high at £2.5m.

The position was consolidated in 1976, but a recession in housebuilding in 1977 reduced turnover slightly and pretax profits were halved. Despite this, further investment was undertaken, increasing borrowings to £4.5m.

With a gradual recovery in the housebuilding sector, turnover and profits increased in 1978 and 1979, despite the fact that substantial interest charges were incurred to service borrowing of £5.5m. With rapidly deteriorating demand conditions in 1980 and 1981 it became imperative to reduce the debt burden, and as a result non-core businesses were sold. Nevertheless, borrowings remained above £5.5m, incurring interest charges of £1.3m, which helped to produce a pretax loss of £1.1m.

Faced with this parlous financial position, the company pinned its faith in a property development project, involving St Katherine's Wharf in London's dockland. However, the trading position steadily worsened, and the Royal Bank of Scotland was obliged to inject a further £2m of funds in March 1983. In a final desperate effort to generate cash, part of the appliances division was sold to GEC's Canon subsidiary in May for £1.9m, but this was insufficient to assuage the company's creditors, the receivers being called in at the beginning of August when bank borrowing totalled £12m against a capitalised equity value of only £3m.

## Fairbairn Lawson

| 31 December[1] | 1977[2] | 1976 | 1975 | 1974[3] | 1974 | 1973 | 1972 | 1971 | 1970 | 1969 |
|---|---|---|---|---|---|---|---|---|---|---|
| S (£0,000) | 1339 | 1274 | 1019 | 426 | 723 | 580 | 375 | 249 | 276 | 273 |
| PBT (£000) | 1305 | 1061 | 471 | 128 | 116 | 149 | 149 | -108 | 165 | 126 |
| TA (£m) | 14.10 | 9.13 | 8.80 | 8.16 | 7.86 | 7.08 | 3.78 | 2.41 | 2.83 | 2.70 |
| EBIT/TA | .10 | .14 | .08 | .07[4] | .05 | .04 | .05 | -.03 | .10 | .06 |
| TL/TA | .51 | .47 | .61 | .63 | .62 | .57 | .43 | .43 | .48 | .49 |
| MAR (%) | +63 | +29 | +97 | n/a | n/a | | | | | |

[1] 30 June year end up until 1974.

[2] The last accounts to be filed were those for the year ended 31 December 1977. Draft accounts for the year to 31 December 1978 showed turnover as £16.3m, with a pre-tax loss of £2.02m.

[3] 6 months for the period 1 July-31 December 1974.

[4] Rate of return annualised.

The original Fairbairn Lawson engineering business, based in Leeds, was founded in 1828, and for many years it had been a listed company. Its main activities were the manufacture of jute textile machinery, gears, presses and other industrial plant. Well over half its output was exported, mostly to Middle and Far Eastern countries. By the mid 1970s an American group, Clabir, had built up a 29.9 per cent interest in the company, and another 11 per cent of the equity was owned by Martac AG of Liechtenstein.

With demand for its traditional products declining the company began to diversify its activities in the 1960s, becoming a manufacturer of plastic sacks and a distributor of office furniture. It also began to rent out premises on prime sites that it owned near the centre of Leeds. In addition, in November 1972 it took over the loss making Leeds based engineering company, Greenwood Batley (Greenbat).

By the mid 1970s there was a good recovery in the group's pretax profits from the moderate levels earned over the period 1970/71 to 1973/74. With profits surging ahead in 1976 the board felt it was appropriate not only to reduce borrowings further – they had already been cut during 1975 from £2.1m to £1.5m – but also to embark on a £1m investment programme in the packaging and engineering sectors, financed in part by a rights issue. However, although pretax profits for 1976 totalled £1.1m, it was evident that the company's position was less than sound. In fact, 70 per cent of turnover was still in the form of engineering products, of which 85 per cent were exported abroad, and this left the company dangerously exposed if sterling were to appreciate significantly in the foreign exchange markets.

Results for the first half of 1977 showed continued progress, even though overseas demand for capital goods was slowing down. Nevertheless the company embarked on two further acquisitions at a cost of £1m. Two months later, shortly before the 1977 results were reported, Clabir and Martac announced they were disposing of their holdings in the group, placing them with institutions at 52p. The figures for 1977 in fact showed record pretax profits of £1.3m, and rising property prices encouraged the board to revalue two factory sites. First half profits for 1978 showed a further small increase in profit, and with the year's pretax profits forecast by analysts at £1.6m, the shares were riding high at 74p.

In the circumstances, the City was taken totally by surprise six months later in March 1979 when a bombshell was dropped in the form of an announcement that there were major discrepancies in the management accounts of the Greenbat subsidiary. The latter accounted for half the group's turnover, and a third was immediately wiped off the Fairbairn Lawson share price, which fell to 40p. This prompted the Stock Exchange to express suspicions about dealings in the company's shares just before the announcement.

The size of the problem at Greenbat only gradually became apparent. It related to work-in-progress and arose because of a new computer system installed late in 1977, the loss provisionally being estimated for 1978 at £1.08m. It was some considerable time before the investigations could be completed, and in the meantime customers were reluctant to trade with the group. With export markets becoming increasingly difficult because of the appreciating pound, the share price was further marked down, falling to 20p by the end of August, before being suspended in October while negotiations took place to try to unload Greenbat and the other engineering interests. The pretax loss for 1978 was finally reported in heavily qualified accounts in December, and with attempts to unload Greenbat failing, Fairbairn Lawson had to be dismembered. As a result, by the beginning of March 1980 the company's assets had been sold for £2.73m, leaving borrowings of £2.8m outstanding.

**Fairey**

| 31 March | 1976 | 1975 | 1974 | 1973 | 1972 | 1971 | 1970 | 1969 | 1968 | 1967 |
|---|---|---|---|---|---|---|---|---|---|---|
| S (£m) | 63.1 | 39.0 | 29.0 | 23.7 | 19.4 | 17.3 | 15.9 | 26.0 | 13.7 | 11.1 |
| PBT (£m) | 4.9 | 2.9 | 2.6 | 2.1 | 2.0 | 1.6 | -0.2 | -0.7 | 0.9 | 0.3 |
| TA (£m) | 56.6 | 45.7 | 28.4 | 26.7 | 17.8 | 17.5 | 15.9 | 16.3 | 17.0 | 15.0 |
| EBIT/TA | .11 | .09 | .11 | .09 | .12 | .09 | -.01 | -.04 | .06 | .03 |
| TL/TA | .51 | .58 | .53 | .56 | .46 | .48 | .51 | .50 | .45 | .43 |
| MAR (%) | +49 | +6 | -12 | -13 | +56 | | | | | |

Fairey began as an aircraft manufacturer in 1915 and went public in 1929. Over the years it acquired other engineering interests, notably in the nuclear industry and in metal fabrications. Its UK aircraft interests were sold off in the government brokered reorganisation of the industry in 1959, leaving it with its Belgian and Canadian factories, which primarily manufactured military aircraft under licence. After fighting off unwelcome bids in the 1960s – which cost the company £3m –

Fairey concentrated on nuclear power station contracts, notably that for the Dungeness B.

The company's turnover and profits in the late 1960s and early 1970s were highly volatile, reflecting the business's overdependence on a few key contracts, its lumpy pattern of revenue recognition, and the underlying riskiness of its operations. The loss recorded in 1969 was partly the result of delays in securing government orders for aircraft for the Belgian and Canadian factories, but above all arose because of the need to provide £2.2m against potential liabilities for the late completion of the Dungeness B power station. A further provision of £1.3m against this contract was made in 1970, when the Canadian factory was closed, the £1.75m loss being charged directly to reserves. This coincided with major changes in the board, brought about at the instigation of the company's City merchant bankers, Leopold Joseph, which at the time had a 25 per cent stake in the group.

In the years that followed turnover and pretax profits grew steadily. This was achieved in part by the acquisition in 1972 for £4.1m of the Brittan-Norman company, which manufactured the successful small civilian Islander aircraft and which had a full order book until 1978. A further £2.8m was raised by debenture loan stock to help finance the £12m development costs of a new Mainlander aircraft; and at the same time a new light alloy girder bridge for use by the army was successfully developed. A year later estimates of the cost of developing the Mainlander aircraft were doubled to £24m, and to help finance this a low interest £2.5m loan was secured from the Belgian government, the condition being that manufacture of the Islander should be switched from the Isle of Wight to the company's Gosselies factory.

By 1974 Fairey had secured full order books, and in the following year it raised nearly £5m via a rights issue to help finance production. Despite this, the company's working capital position was under pressure in 1976 as stocks and work-in-progress increased, but with the Belgian subsidiary winning a £55m contract to manufacture the F16 fighter aircraft analysts were recommending Fairey's shares to investors. It therefore came as a bolt from the blue when it was announced in July 1977 that interim profits had been halved to £1.3m and the company was in breach of its borrowing limits. This was the result of delays in securing contracts, which had led to a rapid build up of stocks. Borrowing had soared from £11m to £28m, and the company's auditors insisted that large amounts should be written off stocks and development expenditure. In the crisis which followed Short Brothers of Belfast bid £16m for Fairey's aircraft interests, but the company's Belgian and UK creditors pressed for their debts to be repaid and the directors were forced to call in the receivers. The result was that the Belgian government acquired the Gosselies factory and the National Enterprise Board took over Fairey's non aviation interests.

## General Engineering (Radcliffe)

| 31 March | 1978 | 1977 | 1976 | 1975 | 1974 | 1973 | 1972 | 1971 | 1970 | 1969 |
|---|---|---|---|---|---|---|---|---|---|---|
| S  (£000) | 9173 | 10241 | 9405 | 8870 | 5464 | 4454 | 4326 | 4277 | 5613 | 6480 |
| PBT (£000) | -512 | 609 | 1037 | 330 | 307 | 119 | 191 | 47 | -341 | 292 |
| TA  (£m) | 11.2 | 7.9 | 7.3 | 7.3 | 6.7 | 6.0 | 4.9 | 5.3 | 5.5 | 5.4 |
| EBIT/TA | -.00 | .12 | .19 | .09 | .09 | .05 | .07 | .04 | -.02 | .08 |
| TL/TA | .65 | .58 | .67 | .74 | .70 | .69 | .33 | .71 | .69 | .64 |
| MAR  (%) | +18 | -1 | +63 | n/a | n/a | | | | | |

General Engineering was a long established engineering holding company which went public in 1936. It manufactured vacuum pumps, drying equipment, effluent treatment plant, and cable and wire making machinery. Its main problem in the late 1960s was that new technology was making many of its product lines obsolete, so the company responded by investing substantial sums in R&D and arranging joint manufacturing and licensing arrangements with overseas manufacturers. These measures did not prevent the company reporting a substantial loss in 1970, which forced it to close production of effluent treatment plant. The company gradually recovered its profit earning capacity in the mid 1970s, helped by an ability to ride the fuel crises of 1972 and 1974 as a result of holding substantial fuel stocks and having its own generating capacity. Profits peaked in 1976, but the loss of export contracts produced overstocking, which in turn led to a sharp increase in bank borrowing. Closure of one factory and a drastic slimming down of activities at two others followed in 1978, when the company's results swung back into the red, but with the £ hardening in the foreign exchange markets even these belated attempts at cost cutting could not save the company. Senior Engineering bid £1m for the business, but this was rejected by General Engineering's shareholders, and shortly afterwards the receivers were called in in June 1979.

## Melody Mills

| 31 March | 1982 | 1981 | 1980 | 1979 | 1978 | 1977 | 1976 | 1975 | 1974 | 1973 |
|---|---|---|---|---|---|---|---|---|---|---|
| S  (£m) | 7.42 | 9.64 | 9.62 | 9.93 | 7.97 | 6.67 | 6.29 | 4.30 | 2.64 | 2.21 |
| PBT (£000) | -1580 | -1306 | 390 | 826 | 519 | 514 | 758 | 279 | 214 | 255 |
| TA  (£m) | 5.70 | 6.57 | 8.27 | 7.10 | 6.42 | 5.26 | 4.64 | 3.72 | 2.80 | 2.23 |
| EBIT/TA | -.22 | -.16 | .07 | .14 | .10 | .13 | .20 | .14 | .14 | .13 |
| TL/TA | .63 | .51 | .45 | .47 | .50 | .47 | .49 | .54 | .54 | .49 |
| MAR  (%) | -45 | -69 | -20 | +40 | +20 | | | | | |

Melody Mills was founded in 1934 and went public in 1968. The company specialised in manufacturing wallpaper for the bottom end of the market, and by 1980 it was the last remaining independent wallpaper manufacturer in the industry, ranged against giants such as ICI, with its Vymura collection. The majority of the company's shares were held by the Byk family until 1979. Their stake was then reduced to 36 per cent when additional shares were placed with investment institutions.

The company grew rapidly in the early 1970s, largely by increasing overseas sales, which by 1971 accounted for 31 per cent of turnover. Expansion of production capacity enabled turnover and profits to be increased up until 1976/77, when a downturn in demand and narrowing margins saw a sharp fall in profits, leaving the company carrying excess stocks and an overdraft of £1.2m. However, there was a good recovery in 1978/79, and analysts speculated that the company would be an attractive take over prospect for a developing DIY chain. But soon afterwards it became apparent that the economy was going into recession, that raw material prices were increasing, and that the high value of sterling was adversely affecting exports. When Melody Mills's larger rivals began unloading surplus stocks it became clear that the company was going to face a rough ride. With interest rates rising and borrowings increasing it was no surprise when large losses were posted in 1980/81, even though a new managing director recruited from Jefferson Smurfit had introduced an emergency rationalisation programme. The recession lasted longer than anticipated, and despite the release of a new collection the results for 1981/82 showed a further worsening in the company's position, with bank borrowings increasing by 50 per cent to £2m. At this point the banks withdrew their support, at the same time as the company's auditors issued a going concern qualification against the delayed 1981/82 accounts, and at the beginning of October 1982 the receivers were called in to salvage something for the creditors.

**Mettoy**

| 31 December | 1981[1] | 1980 | 1979 | 1978 | 1977 | 1976 | 1975 | 1974 | 1973 | 1972 |
|---|---|---|---|---|---|---|---|---|---|---|
| S   (£m) | 28.2 | 25.8 | 32.5 | 31.2 | 27.5 | 23.8 | 19.9 | 17.9 | 12.9 | 9.3 |
| PBT  (£m) | -2.7 | -3.5 | 0.7 | 3.6 | 2.8 | 2.4 | 1.7 | 1.3 | 1.0 | 0.2 |
| TA   (£m) | 23.7 | 23.8 | 26.9 | 25.2 | 18.8 | 16.7 | 13.2 | 11.5 | 8.7 | 7.2 |
| EBIT/TA | -.05 | -.08 | -.00 | .16 | .17 | .17 | .15 | .13 | .13 | .05 |
| TL/TA | .62 | .51 | .42 | .39 | .45 | .49 | .47 | .51 | .48 | .45 |
| MAR  (%) | -32 | -62 | -44 | +45 | +55 | | | | | |

[1] The last accounts filed were for the year ended 31 December 1981. Draft accounts for the year to 31 December 1982 showed turnover as £24.9m, with a pre-tax loss of £3.8m

Mettoy was founded in 1932 and went public in 1963, when one of its founders, Philip Ullman, retired. However, he retained a substantial share interest in the company. Mettoy manufactured die cast models under the Corgi label, as well as Wembly sports balls and Playcraft pre-school games. It also held the licence to manufacture Fisher-Price toys in the UK.

Mettoy made steady progress in the mid 1970s, with exports accounting for 45 per cent of sales in 1976 when analysts were tipping the company's shares as a good investment. The advance was achieved by developing new products at a time when the Corgi models were coming under increasing competitive pressure from toys manufactured by the US firm, Mattel. It was therefore a further blow when Fisher-Price decided to renegotiate its contract with Mettoy so that it only covered the manufacture of its toys in the UK, not their marketing. However, this setback was offset by the purchase of a company which manufactured a successful doll.

The first sign of real problems came in 1979 when turnover failed to expand as expected and profits fell sharply to £700,000. The latter was in part the result of high interest charges and foreign exchange losses. In face of this setback Mettoy cut back its workforce, but demand remained low over the next year, so along with other British toy manufacturers the company began to unload excess stocks at knock down prices. Despite these measures and the introduction of a new product line – radio controlled model cars – the company's turnover fell in 1980 and pretax losses of £3.5m were recorded. 1981 was also a difficult year, brought about partly by the termination of the Fisher-Price contract, which left the company with excess production capacity.

In order to remedy the situation Mettoy ventured into a new area, launching the Dragon computer in July 1982, financed by heavy borrowing. Although initially the Dragon was a great success, outselling the rival machines of Tandy, Sinclair and Commodore, the constant innovation required to keep up with developments in computer technology were really beyond Mettoy's depleted resources. Peter Katz, the company's managing director, resigned in September 1982 over policy differences with other board members, and subsequently the manufacture and development of the Dragon were hived off to a separate company in which Mettoy held a stake of just under a fifth.

In a desperate effort to reduce its borrowings further, Mettoy sold off all its toy interests except Corgi, and in February 1983 announced a rights issue to raise £3.1m. Half the shares were left in the hands of the underwriters, and when Dragon itself shortly afterwards announced a rights issue Mettoy was unable to maintain its stake in its associate. The company's position was further undermined in September when – facing fierce competition from rival home computer manufacturers – Dragon itself ran into difficulties. The result was that Mettoy's shares were suspended in October, before the receivers were called in.

Overall, the rising prices of raw materials, the impact of the hardening £ in the foreign exchange markets (which damaged export sales and opened up the way for cheap imports from overseas), and the advent of new products (such as video games) outside Mettoy's core expertise destroyed the company. Die cast models were cheaper to manufacture in the Far East, and the move into home computers –

although initially successful – was ill fated, especially given the fact that the company did not have the resources to back the venture. With the advantage of hindsight it is easy to see that the business's best chance of survival would have been to stick to marketing and to have traded on its well established brand names.

## John Michael

| 31 January[1] | 1980 | 1979 | 1978 | 1977 | 1976 | 1975 | 1974 | 1973 | 1972[2] | 1971 |
|---|---|---|---|---|---|---|---|---|---|---|
| S (£000) | 4950 | 3183 | 3091 | 2280 | 2635 | 2674 | 2324 | 2088 | 1754 | 1939 |
| PBT (£000) | -369 | 76 | 72 | -77 | -327 | -250 | -70 | 28 | -8 | 109 |
| TA (£000) | 2433 | 1930 | 1451 | 1373 | 1352 | 1691 | 1597 | 1188 | 1025 | 1047 |
| EBIT/TA | -.14 | -.05 | .07 | .00 | -.17 | -.09 | -.01 | .06 | .01[3] | .11 |
| TL/TA | .63 | .39 | .65 | .70 | 1.10 | .83 | .69 | .62 | .59 | .57 |
| MAR (%) | +14 | +137 | +3 | -51 | -52 | | | | | |

[1] Years to 31 March up until 1971
[2] Ten months to 31 January or at 31 January
[3] Rate of return annualised.

John Michael Ingham began retailing designer menswear in 1957, and he progressed to manufacturing his clothes and selling them via shops in Bond Street and Soho, as well as the original outlet in the King's Road. The company went public in 1965, but soon suffered a downturn in profits, Mr Ingham persuading his 30 or so creditors to continue supporting the company.

Although the company was quoted, over 70 per cent of its capital was held by Mr Ingham and his wife up until its demise.

In its last decade of trading John Michael expanded sales by extending the number of its outlets to nearly 30, the initial impetus coming from ICFC loans and, later, from sale-and-leaseback arrangements. The company's new shops were outside London, and it even opened one in Paris, although this venture was aborted after three years in 1976, the same year in which the manufacturing and wholesaling activities were sold off.

The main problem with the business was the fickle nature of the fashion industry, and the volume of sales from the new outlets was never sufficient to justify the investment in the additional retailing floorspace. As a result losses were recorded between 1974 and 1977, and although the company returned to profit in 1978 and 1979, the impact of high interest rates and the high £ – which saw a sharp fall in the number of tourists visiting the UK – spelt the end of the business, the company's shares being suspended in March 1981.

## Movitex

| 28 February | 1979[1] | 1978 | 1977 | 1976 | 1975 | 1974 | 1973 | 1972 | 1971 | 1970 |
|---|---|---|---|---|---|---|---|---|---|---|
| S (£m) | 3.04* | 2.63 | 2.35 | 2.30 | 2.24 | 2.16 | 1.69 | 1.50 | 1.46 | 1.22 |
| PBT (£000) | 149* | 101 | 24 | 97 | 140 | 108 | 132 | 242 | 221 | 192 |
| TA (£m) | 2.48 | 2.57 | 2.11 | 2.03 | 2.36 | 2.34 | 2.29 | 2.03 | 1.96 | 1.44 |
| EBIT/TA | .11 | .08 | .07 | .11 | .12 | .09 | .08 | .14 | .13 | .14 |
| TL/TA | .70 | .66 | .74 | .73 | .61 | .69 | .61 | .64 | .67 | .59 |
| MAR (%) | -14 | +1 | -16 | -35 | +62 | | | | | |

* as reported; subsequently revised downwards (see text)

[1] The last accounts filed were those for the year ending 28 February 1979. In the draft accounts for the year ending 28 February 1980 turnover was £2.27m, with a pre-tax loss of £126,000.

The company was set up in 1944, going public and assuming the name of Movitex in 1961. Up until the middle of 1979 it was controlled by its chairman, Mr R. W. Bulfield, a City chartered accountant, who held 11.9 per cent of the share capital, and Mr A.R. Perry, another director, who directly and indirectly held a 41.5 per cent stake.

In the early 1970s the company was engaged in three manufacturing activities: plastic signs, record pressing and engineering. However, the engineering activities were never very successful, and they were closed down in 1975.

The company's signs division, based at Edgware, contributed over half the profits, and a new display system suitable for train and bus timetables was developed. The company's record pressings division received a big boost in 1972 when it expanded output to manufacture budget LPs for sale in racks at grocery stores and newsagents in direct competition to EMI's 'Music for Pleasure' label. The aim was to increase annual turnover by £1m by producing up to 12m records a year – or 10 per cent of UK pressings – and thus win a major share of the budget LP market, which represented 35 per cent of all UK record sales. In view of these rosy prospects the company's nickel masters were written off as an exceptional item in its 1972/73 accounts, which helped to explain the 45 per cent fall in pretax profits. However, the company's reserves benefited from a £200,000 revaluation of properties, which helped to support increased borrowing.

The hoped for boom in sales of the new plastic signs and LPs did not materialise, and, indeed, profits dipped alarmingly in 1975/76, causing the dividend to be passed. The situation hardly improved over the next two years, pretax profits only recovering to the modest 1973/74 level as a result of currency translation gains and profits on the sale of properties. As a result, at the end of the 1977/78 financial year the capitalised market value was down to £1m, only two thirds of what it had been in 1971, despite the inflation over the intervening years. Nevertheless, a dividend was declared.

The disappointing performance of the business led to crisis talks in May 1979, when it was announced that Mr Perry's 41.5 per cent stake was being placed with private clients by the stockbrokers Sheppards and Chase. Results for 1978/79 were slightly better, enabling the dividend to be doubled, but this did not satisfy the new shareholders who wanted to sack Mr Bulfield and appoint four new directors. This was vigorously opposed by Mr Bulfield and his supporters, who argued that this was tantamount to a takeover but achieved with a bare majority of the votes, thus breaching the City Code. Inevitably he lost the ensuing battle, and the share price jumped up from 14p to 26p in the hope that the company's fortunes would be turned round by the new board.

One of the first steps taken by the new directors was to indicate their intention to restate the 1979 accounts, reversing the decision to ignore SSAP 6. This lowered reported turnover from £3.04m to £2.98m, while pretax profits were reduced from £149,000 to £98,000, so converting the attributable profit into a loss of £94,000.

High interest charges and provisions produced a substantial loss for the first half of 1979/80, even though an extraordinary charge was taken straight to reserves. In addition, contingent liabilities totalled £200,000. Against this worsening situation, Mr Bulfield announced that City Road Securities (controlled by himself and Mr Perry) – which owned the lease on the Edgware site – was requesting that a £100,000 loan should be repaid; and that he himself would be suing Movitex for £50,000 for wrongful dismissal.

The squabbling continued over the next ten weeks, until three of the new directors resigned and a deal was secured with City Road Securities. However, results for 1979/80 proved disastrous, with turnover down by a quarter and the 1978/79 operating profit of £232,000 converted into a loss of £17,000. With further restatements of the 1979 accounts, writing off goodwill and unrealised intra group profits on goods held in stock, as well as providing for deferred tax, the accumulated surplus brought forward was converted into a deficit of £176,000. As a result the company's borrowings of £578,000 were over 2.5 times the equity stake, and with little prospect of the company's fortunes being turned round the receivers were called in in September.

## Oxley Printing

| 31 December | 1980 | 1979 | 1978 | 1977 | 1976 | 1975 | 1974 | 1973 | 1972 | 1971 |
|---|---|---|---|---|---|---|---|---|---|---|
| S (£0,000) | 2766 | 2885 | 1953 | 1983 | 1615 | 1291 | 1264 | 981 | 747 | 533 |
| PBT (£000) | -2699 | 353 | 1285 | 1409 | 305 | -178 | 142 | 501 | 403 | 200 |
| TA (£m) | 19.7 | 19.5 | 14.5 | 11.4 | 9.0 | 8.5 | 8.8 | 8.5 | 6.7 | 4.0 |
| EBIT/TA | -.07 | .05 | .11 | .17 | .09 | .04 | .07 | .09 | .08 | .07 |
| TL/TA | .80 | .62 | .62 | .67 | .71 | .74 | .71 | .70 | .69 | .64 |
| MAR (%) | -71 | -27 | +31 | +179 | +6 | | | | | |

Oxley was founded in 1912 and went public in 1929. In the early 1960s it was developed as a mini-conglomerate by its chairman, Mr Michael Lewis, who held 15 per cent of the shares. It had interests in cameras, hotels, motor distribution, paper milling, 'Queen' magazine, printing, tailoring and heavy engineering. However, this was not a particularly successful period in the company's history, and after chalking up losses of £265,000 in 1969 Mr Lewis made the decision to concentrate on the company's printing interests. This was done by acquiring a number of printing companies, including the loss making Morrison and Gibb group in 1970 (owners of Carlisle Web Offset); and Tinling in 1973, a Liverpool book printing company for which the government was seeking a saviour. The attempt to rescue Tinling was not a success, despite considerable financial support from the DTI, and in June 1975 Oxley called in the receivers to take the company off its hands. By this time Oxley was organised into two divisions: printing and platemaking.

Although Oxley's turnover grew rapidly throughout the 1970s, its profit record was erratic. A recession in advertising hit the platemaking division in 1974-75, which coincided with the company's ill fated attempt to rescue Tinling's. A further problem was that the company was in breach of its debt covenants in 1975 – a matter which clearly concerned the auditors, who were also unsure whether the provision for losses at Tinling of £225,000 in the 1974 accounts was adequate. The former problem was only resolved by increasing the coupon rate on the unsecured loan stock and by offering greater security to creditors.

1976 saw a marked improvement in performance, although analysts were expressing concern that the Morrison and Gibb subsidiary was still operating at a loss. The company's two best years were 1977 and 1978. With respect to 1977, a major contributory factor in the increase in pretax earnings to £1.41m was that Carlisle Web Offset went back into profit, helped by the closure of a rival BPC plant. However, over a third of the profit was accounted for by employment subsidies. Nevertheless, with analysts forecasting a further surge in profits in 1978 and with the share price rising five fold within twelve months to over 50p, Oxley announced a £6m investment programme over the next three years, with £2m being scheduled for 1978, including £1.2m for a massive new colour printing complex at Carlisle.

This optimism appeared justified, with the 1978 profit before interest and tax increasing to £1.55m, despite a sharp reduction in government subsidies. As a result the share price climbed to 75p in November, and notwithstanding the growing debt burden analysts were forecasting pretax earnings of £2m for 1979.

It was the onset of the recession in the second half of 1979 that changed the outlook for the company, with interest payments rising sharply. For 1979 as a whole pretax profits fell to £353,000, and at the end of the year Mr Lewis retired as chairman. His successor, Mr Peter Brabrook, who had been on the board since 1977, set about reorganising commercial printing activities at Nottingham at a cost of £1.8m and restructuring the platemaking division. The recession bit deep in

1980, lowering both the volume of sales and margins. The outlook was gloomy, with interest charges doubling, substantial redundancy payments to fund, a labour dispute, excess capacity in the industry, and the high sterling exchange rate. As a result, the share price – already down to 14p in January 1980 – declined to just 5p by November. When results for 1980 were released in May 1981 they showed pretax losses for the year of £2.9m. With investment commitments almost doubling indebtedness during the year to £10m, the annual turnover required to break even was estimated at £30m. Results for the first half of 1981 indicated no prospect of achieving this, and in August the receivers were called in.

## B. Paradise

| 30 April[1] | 1982 | 1981[2] | 1980 | 1979 | 1978 | 1977 | 1976 | 1975 | 1974 | 1973 |
|---|---|---|---|---|---|---|---|---|---|---|
| Sales (£m) | 7.54 | 5.33 | 3.14 | 2.91 | 3.74 | 2.92 | 2.53 | 2.68 | 3.38 | 2.40 |
| PBT (£000) | 315 | 132 | -566 | -317 | 10 | -75 | 104 | 95 | 206 | 143 |
| TA (£m) | 6.71 | 5.03 | 1.60 | 2.19 | 2.75 | 2.64 | 2.50 | 2.04 | 1.58 | 1.40 |
| EBIT/TA | .12 | .10[3] | -.22 | -.05 | .07 | .10 | .11 | .09 | .19 | .15 |
| TL/TA | .80 | .74 | 1.20 | .85 | .76 | .76 | .71 | .68 | .67 | .75 |
| MAR (%) | -25 | -94[3] | -36 | -41 | -22 | | | | | |

[1] Up until 1980, years to 31 January.
[2] 15 months to 30 April 1981.
[3] Rate of return and MAR annualised.

The Paradise business was established in London's East End in 1903 but was only incorporated in the early 1960s prior to flotation on the Stock Exchange. The company manufactured leather and fur coats and jackets, and the Paradise family retained the majority of the shares until they sold out to a rapidly expanding listed textile company, R & J Pullman, in October 1979 (see p. 366).

In the early 1970s Paradise traded profitably, helped by low raw material prices and an expansion into menswear, but the company was more and more subject to the whims of an increasingly fashion conscious public. During the mid 1970s margins were squeezed by the rising costs of imported fur and leather, and by high interest charges. This in conjunction with falling demand – itself the result of a succession of hot summers, mild winters, and a switch away from furs by consumers – led to a build up of stocks. Faced with mounting losses, the board embarked on a cost cutting programme and sold off the London premises to reduce the company's growing debt burden.

It was against this background that R & J Pullman intervened in October 1979, taking a 29 per cent stake in the business with the agreement of the Paradise family and making a full bid the following March, thus acquiring just under 60 per cent of the share capital. Within six months Pullman appeared to have turned the company round, rationalising production and merging Paradise with another fur coat manufacturer, Eidenstein. The market responded positively, enabling a rights issue to be made with Pullman reducing its stake to below 50 per cent. The proceeds were used to purchase two more clothing companies – although there was some disquiet in the press as both had had their accounts qualified for lack of proper stock records. Nevertheless, trading results for 1981 and 1982 were encouraging, with record levels of turnover and profits. The company's collapse therefore came as something of a bolt from the blue. Unfortunately Pullman itself ran into trouble in 1982 and went into receivership in December. The news broke that it was still guarantor for £1.75m of Paradise's debts, and, given the company's high level of gearing, the share price fell by a half to 9p before being suspended, at which juncture the receivers were sent in.

**William Pickles**

| 31 December | 1980 | 1979 | 1978 | 1977 | 1976 | 1975 | 1974 | 1973 | 1972 | 1971 |
|---|---|---|---|---|---|---|---|---|---|---|
| S (£0,000) | 2228 | 2532 | 2386 | 2293 | 2122 | 1952 | 1851 | 1610 | 1415 | 1294 |
| PBT (£000) | -1357 | -158 | 400 | 798 | 853 | 478 | 919 | 925 | 828 | 564 |
| TA (£m) | 10.7 | 14.5 | 11.8 | 11.3 | 10.1 | 8.9 | 8.9 | 8.5 | 7.6 | 6.3 |
| EBIT/TA | -.04 | .04 | .07 | .11 | .12 | .08 | .14 | .12 | .12 | .10 |
| TL/TA | .51 | .52 | .38 | .37 | .34 | .31 | .32 | .35 | .31 | .39 |
| MAR (%) | -31 | -23 | +21 | -13 | +16 | | | | | |

The company was founded in 1913 and went public in 1947, the founder retiring in 1975 when he was 82. The company's primary business was as a textile and clothing manufacturer, and the Pickles family controlled the company up until its demise in 1981, although a Swiss Group built up a 23 per cent holding towards the end in the hope of turning the business round.

Turnover and profits grew steadily until 1974, despite increasing raw material and labour costs. However, overall performance was below the average for textile companies, and growth in turnover slowed in 1975, when pretax profits were initially recorded at £651,000 before stock irregularities were discovered at a subsidiary, necessitating a £207,000 write off. Profits recovered in 1976 with exports up by 80 per cent to £2m, but stock levels continued to rise, requiring a further increase in bank borrowing.

Results for the first half of 1977 showed further progress, but there was a sharp downturn from May onwards which ensured that for the year as a whole pretax profits were slightly down on the previous year.

With further rationalisation taking place, it was hoped that the protection of the EU's multifibre agreement would help to ensure a resumption of growth in 1978. In the meantime, a new chairman, Denis Greensmith, was recruited from Sears Holdings, but the company soon found itself facing competition from a flood of cheap imports from the Far East. The modernisation programme helped to increase trading profits in the first half of 1979, but the onset of the recession and the higher exchange value of the pound, coupled with increased interest charges and lower employment subsidies, were responsible for the company reporting a pretax loss for the year as a whole. At the same time stocks of unsold goods rose by 50 per cent to £5.2m, financed by increased borrowing. More of the company's mills were closed, and the banks demanded tighter security over the remaining assets. In such circumstances it was hardly surprising that analysts warned that the company's shares were a high risk investment.

The results for 1980 showed a decline in turnover as the high sterling exchange rate halved export sales and encouraged import penetration. With higher interest charges as well, pretax losses soared to £1.36m, although cash generated from asset sales helped to cut the overdraft from the mid year high of £4.5m to £3m.

Further cutbacks were made in 1981 as turnover continued to decline and the company operated at a loss. In order to reduce borrowings more assets had to be sold off: indeed, during the 18 months prior to the receivers being called in in June 1982, 4 of the company's remaining 5 factories were either sold off or closed down. In the end, there was very little left of the company, and just before the receivers went in the capitalised value of the business was only £724,000, although eventually the bulk of its assets were sold for £1.5m.

## R & J Pullman

| 30 April[1] | 1982 | 1981 | 1980 | 1979[2] | 1978 | 1977 | 1976 | 1975 | 1974 | 1973 |
|---|---|---|---|---|---|---|---|---|---|---|
| S (£m) | 24.0 | 21.8 | 24.1 | 19.3 | 12.8 | 11.3 | 9.4 | 9.1 | 7.7 | 7.0 |
| PBT(£000) | 1680 | 1641[3] | 1642 | 1418 | 1052 | 949 | 816 | 862 | 863 | 941 |
| TA (£m) | 28.6 | 22.3 | 21.0 | 16.5 | 12.4 | 10.6 | 7.7 | 6.6 | 5.6 | 4.4 |
| EBIT/TA | .12 | .13 | .12 | .11[4] | .11 | .12 | .13 | .16 | .18 | .23 |
| TL/TA | .78 | .63 | .55 | .54 | .53 | .51 | .39 | .46 | .46 | .47 |
| MAR (%) | -1 | +18 | -19 | +17[4] | +40 | | | | | |

[1] Up until 1978 year to 31 March.
[2] 13 months to 30 April 1979.
[3] Restated from £3.45m (see text).
[4] Rate of return and MAR annualised.

R & J Pullman was founded in 1895 and was a listed company for many years before it went bankrupt in 1982. The company had factories in various parts of the UK manufacturing clothing for men, women and children from cotton textiles (including corduroy) and from leather. In particular, it made outer garments, some of which were sold via John Lewis and House of Fraser stores. In the early 1970s the company not only expanded its manufacturing capacity via a series of acquisitions, but it also entered the retail side of the clothing industry, gradually building up a chain of shops, mainly by buying up a number of small businesses.

In October 1971 the Slater Walker group acquired 24.6 per cent of the equity, but this still left the board – at that time chaired by Mr William Lee – in control. The following February, just after the acquisition of Paula Lee had pushed the share price sharply upwards, Slater Walker gradually sold off its stake over a period of two months. When Mr Lee retired in July 1972 after 10 years as head of the company, his place was taken by another director, Mr Maurice Hope, who increased his already sizeable holding in the business to around 20 per cent, a level which he maintained in subsequent years.

Overall the company performed well over the period 1972/73 to 1975/76, although in the latter year higher interest charges and losses at the company's corduroy factories – largely because of dumping by US manufacturers – led to a minor downturn in pretax profits. Exports in particular grew steadily, accounting for around 15 per cent of turnover, and this and shrewd stockpiling of raw materials when they were relatively cheap in 1975 ensured that the company outperformed most other textile businesses. Despite a high gearing ratio, with borrowings well above equity until a £930,000 rights issue was made in December 1975, financial commentators were impressed and recommended the shares as an investment.

The same encouraging pattern was repeated between 1977/78 and 1978/79, with the company raising £875,000 in April 1978 through an equity placing and a further £3.1m via a rights issue in June 1979. These funds were used to finance new acquisitions and to pay off borrowing. In the meantime pretax profits grew rapidly, although the retail side turned in a loss of £62,000 in 1978/79 compared with a contribution of £235,000 in 1977/78.

With the Pullman group being widely regarded as one of the soundest medium sized companies in the textiles sector, it was no surprise when it launched a rescue bid for the fur and leather clothing company, B. Paradise, in October 1979 (see p. 363).

1979/80 saw a further leap forward in Pullman's figures, with profits before interest and tax well ahead of 1979 at £2.32m. Export revenues were 10 per cent higher at £4.4m, despite the strength of sterling, and retailing accounted for 30 per cent of the £24.1m sales figure. However, the corduroy activities remained a problem area, and provisions of £213,000 were made in the accounts pending their disposal. In the meantime Paradise had begun to return to profitable trading, and when it made a rights issue Pullman took the opportunity to reduce its stake to less than a third.

Results for the first half of 1980/81 were encouraging, and the share price remained relatively strong at 53p. However, the second half year was hit by lower export earnings – the result of the strong £ – and turnover for 1980/81 as a whole was slightly down on the previous year. Nevertheless, despite this and an increase in borrowings from £4.18m to £6.94m, the pretax profits initially reported totalled £3.45m, and analysts still viewed the company favourably.

The first half results for 1981/82 were again encouraging, but the final figures for the year showed that the earlier optimism was misplaced, the pretax profit only being £1.7m. However, the real bombshell was dropped when the annual report was published in November, which showed that the auditors Morley and Scott were not only unwilling to agree that £4.6m spent on promoting the group's brands should be capitalised as a fixed asset, but also that the accounts were qualified on a going concern basis. This news came as a bolt from the blue to the market, and the share price fell from 47p to 15p over a period of seven days. Even so, it was a surprise when receivers were appointed in December. However, the accounts showed the potential fragility of the group's position, with debt at £14.25m against equity of only £8.37m. Moreover, there was a high level of intangibles and deferred expenditure, with goodwill £2.42m, trade and brand names £4.6m, and store development costs £1m.

Questions immediately began to be asked in the City how a group with an annual turnover of around £21m could have spent £4.6m on promoting brand names; and how the company could have collapsed only three months after the preliminary results were announced and the chairman was making bullish statements. In fact, the receivers had little difficulty in selling off the key parts of the Pullman group, many at what soon came to seem to be knock down prices, suggesting that maybe they were called in prematurely.

## Richards and Wallington Industries

| 31 December | 1980 | 1979 | 1978 | 1977 | 1976 | 1975 | 1974 | 1973 | 1972 | 1971 |
|---|---|---|---|---|---|---|---|---|---|---|
| S (£0,000) | 3803 | 3967 | 3548 | 3244 | 3079 | 3203 | 2769 | 1985 | 1406 | 1202 |
| PBT (£m) | -5.43 | 2.45 | 3.03 | 2.69 | 1.81 | 2.69 | 2.99 | 2.36 | 1.37 | 1.02 |
| TA (£m) | 46.7 | 50.5 | 45.9 | 40.3 | 43.6 | 41.2 | 40.2 | 31.0 | 22.2 | 18.9 |
| EBIT/TA | -.02 | .12 | .12 | .12 | .09 | .11 | .12 | .12 | .09 | .09 |
| TL/TA | .75 | .63 | .60 | .54 | .50 | .46 | .51 | .46 | .46 | .44 |
| MAR (%) | -78 | -22 | +5 | +57 | -36 | | | | | |

Richards and Wallington was a plant hire company which was set up in 1959 and went public in 1965. It grew rapidly taking over a number of companies, and it soon became the largest independent plant hire group in the UK, well ahead of its main rivals, Hebden-Stuart and Sparrow.

In the 1970s the company diversified, hiring out equipment for materials handling in the steel, chemicals and North Sea oil industries; setting up overseas joint ventures assembling and selling mobile and tower cranes; and operating on the Continent and in the Far East.

In the early 1970s the stock market treated Richards and Wallington shares with some caution, mindful of the fact that in 1970 performance fell well short of the promised pretax earnings of £1.5m, but this did not prevent BET from taking a strategic stake of 20 per cent in the company. This was increased to 25 per cent only 10 weeks before a receiver was appointed.

Although part of the group's growth was secured by a series of take overs in the early 1970s, most of the expansion came from internal investment, made possible by the strong operating cash flow. This was sustained in part by the high level of capital allowances. Despite annual capital expenditures year after year throughout the 1970s being 2-3 times annual pretax profits, only once was new equity raised – £1m in May 1975. As a result borrowings inevitably rose steadily, consistently being around 150 per cent of equity and only falling below 100 per cent in 1975 as a result of a £1m property revaluation. In fact, medium and short term borrowings increased from £16.7m to £23.4m between 1975 and 1978, and when demand for hired plant collapsed in 1980 the company was left with huge interest bills. An attempt was made to shore up the cash position in April of that year by taking a 49.9 per cent stake in a DIY group at a cost of £1.4m, the idea being that it would act as a 'cash cow'. However, this move was a failure as consumer spending declined sharply. As a result – and despite severely curtailing capital investment – the company ran up pretax losses of £5.43m in 1980, and its bank borrowings increased from £6.5m at the end of 1979 to £25.9m a year later. The 24 banks involved briefly agreed that in exchange for the security of fixed and floating charges over the group's assets they would continue to support the company and the new board drafted in to run it. However, when it became evident that there was little likelihood of an improvement in trading conditions, receivers were appointed in June 1981.

**Southern Constructions**

| 31 December | 1978 | 1977 | 1976 | 1975 | 1974 | 1973 | 1972 | 1971 | 1970 | 1969 |
|---|---|---|---|---|---|---|---|---|---|---|
| S (£0,000) | 1222 | 1371 | 1074 | 993 | 736 | 546 | 392 | 320 | 274 | 224 |
| PBT (£000) | -293 | -1452 | 160* | 543 | 217 | 551 | 393 | 225 | 222 | 199 |
| TA (£m) | 4.75 | 4.72 | 4.32 | 3.80 | 3.17 | 2.65 | 1.76 | 1.29 | 1.14 | 1.09 |
| EBIT/TA | -.03 | -.28 | .05 | .15 | .08 | .21 | .22 | .18 | .19 | .18 |
| TL/TA | .77 | .80 | .44 | .45 | .53 | .51 | .50 | .52 | .54 | .59 |
| MAR (%) | +2 | -27 | +11 | -11 | n/a | | | | | |

* Originally reported as £401,000, before accounting errors came to light (see below).

Southern Constructions was set up as a public company in 1956 and until 1976 concentrated on civil engineering work in the Hampshire region. Following cutbacks in public spending in that year it began to look further afield for work, even seeking contracts in the Middle East and West Africa.

The company's shares were widely held, and this was one reason why a take over bid by Mowlem in 1971 failed.

Unusually for a civil engineering contractor, the company enjoyed a long and uninterrupted period of growth in the 1960s and early 1970s. Although the company favoured shorter term contracts to avoid being caught out by unexpectedly high rates of inflation, this did not prevent it suffering in the second half of 1974, which led to a sharp drop in pretax profits for the year as a whole. To avoid a recurrence of the problem, from 1975 onwards fixed price contracts were indexed against the effects of inflation, removing this element of risk from the company's operations.

The company hit problems suddenly and unexpectedly early in 1977. Press reports in April prior to the preliminary announcement for the 1976 results were still forecasting pretax profits of £750,000, so it came as a nasty shock to the market to learn that second half profits were down from £372,000 to just £72,000, the share price falling to 9p. But worse was to come. Within five weeks the market was rocked by the news that the 1976 pretax profit figure was having to be adjusted downwards from £401,000 to £160,000 because of three accounting errors, namely, insufficient provision had been made for foreseeable losses; a subsidiary's plant and stock values had been incorrectly written up; and material expenses had not been charged against revenues. The auditors (Jones Avens and Worley) resigned to be replaced by Arthur Andersen; and the company's secretary and finance director also had to go.

The board was reconstituted, and a new chairman was appointed. However, the results for 1977 were equally disastrous, not only reflecting the fact that the company had pared margins to obtain new work and so maintain turnover, but also highlighting weaknesses in control. With a shortfall for the year of £1.45m commentators were aghast, pointing out that only four months previously the company had been forecasting an improvement for the second half year, which by then had already finished. Provisions of £300,000 had to be made against uncompleted contracts, and with work in progress rising from £2.1m to £2.3m bank borrowing increased from £460,000 to £1.36m. Moreover, the auditors pointed out in their report that the value of the contracts depended on continued support from the banks, and the share price declined further to 7.5p.

Although pretax losses were cut back to £293,000 in 1978, they widened again in 1979, partly the result of a severe winter, and the company asked its bankers to appoint a receiver in May 1980 when it became apparent that the loss for 1979 was of the order of £800,000. The shares were suspended at 4p, and with a deficiency of £3.4m it was clear that the unsecured creditors would get little back of the £2.1m they were owed.

369

# TCK

| 31 December | 1975 | 1974 | 1973 | 1972 | 1971 | 1970 | 1969 | 1968 | 1967 | 1966 |
|---|---|---|---|---|---|---|---|---|---|---|
| S (£0,000) | 3333 | 2079 | 1496 | 1017 | 976 | 1463 | 1298 | 1524 | 1772 | 1544 |
| PBT (£000) | 59 | 149 | -6 | -157 | -327 | -146 | -12 | 226 | 382 | 274 |
| TA (£m) | 3.80 | 2.32 | 1.28 | 1.23 | 1.13 | 1.45 | 1.46 | 1.50 | 1.55 | 1.42 |
| EBIT/TA | .05 | .10 | .04 | -.10 | -.26 | -.10 | -.01 | .15 | .25 | .19 |
| TL/TA | .69 | .75 | .71 | .70 | .52 | .39 | .31 | .28 | .34 | .39 |
| MAR (%) | +96 | n/a | n/a | n/a | n/a | | | | | |

The original Thomas C Keay business was established in Dundee in 1879 to manufacture jute textile machinery. It was incorporated in 1917 and only went public in 1955, although the Keay family remained substantial shareholders. With sales of textile machinery declining, the company diversified in the mid 1960s into the manufacture of paper sack machinery and power presses. However, these moves came too late to maintain profitability, and the company plunged into the red from 1969 onwards, only surviving because of a sound financial position built up over many years.

After reporting net losses for four successive years, the company was taken over by Mr Stephen Rowlinson in 1974. He was a 35 year old former executive with the Harris Lebus furniture group who had later spent six years as a consultant with McKinsey's. He set about reshaping the business, changing the name to TCK, stripping out the unprofitable activities, developing a central heating division, and securing a contract to distribute barstock ball valves.

In fact, the company turned in a small profit for the first half of 1974 before the changes could have made any impact. Buoyed up by an asset revaluation (which added £591,000 to the book value of £234,000) and by optimistic forecasts from Mr Rowlinson, the share price rose to 72p. Although there was very little substance to justify it, Mr Rowlinson was gaining the reputation in the City of being something of a whizz kid, and a number of institutions began buying shares, reducing the Rowlinson family stake to 40 per cent. Results for the first half of 1975 showed turnover double that achieved a year earlier and pretax profits for the six months at £142,000. With pretax earnings for the year forecast at over £300,000 the share price increased to 104p. Mr Rowlinson recruited two more ex-McKinsey men to join him on the board, and he acquired a 29.9 per cent stake in an ailing pressings manufacturer, Lesbrook, the aim being to subcontract central heating work to it and to manufacture a lightweight folding bicycle. This led to a number of favourable newspaper articles about Mr Rowlinson, and at one stage TCK shares hit 151p.

The announcement of pretax earnings for 1975 of only £138,000 came as a great shock to analysts, since it meant a loss of £4,000 had been recorded for the second half year rather than the £150,000 profit still being forecast for the six months only a few days previously. The share price halved to 78p and fell further when in July

Mr Rowlinson announced that the 1975 pretax profit figure had been reduced to £59,000 to make provision for slow moving stock items. Further bad news followed with the announcement that receivers had been called in to Lesbrook, effectively scuppering the overhyped Bickerton folding bicycle venture. Results for the first half of 1976 showed a pretax loss of £344,000, and with the share price declining to 25p Mr Rowlinson sold half his 35 per cent stake. With support from the Clydesdale Bank being removed, the receivers were called in in April 1977. Yet right to the end press commentators could hardly believe that Mr Rowlinson would not be able to pull off some last minute deal to save the company.

**Viners**

| 31 December | 1980[1] | 1979 | 1978 | 1977 | 1976 | 1975 | 1974 | 1973 | 1972 | 1971 |
|---|---|---|---|---|---|---|---|---|---|---|
| S (£0,000) | 1207 | 1115 | 1070 | 1041 | 1037 | 907 | 713 | 619 | 431 | 378 |
| PBT (£000) | -192 | -105 | 220 | 42 | 448 | 805 | 751 | 750 | 469 | 287 |
| TA (£m) | 10.1 | 10.4 | 9.4 | 8.5 | 8.7 | 7.0 | 6.0 | 4.6 | 3.0 | 2.5 |
| EBIT/TA | .04 | .03 | .06 | .04 | .08 | .14 | .15 | .17 | .16 | .14 |
| TL/TA | .58 | .56 | .55 | .49 | .49 | .47 | .50 | .46 | .30 | .44 |
| MAR (%) | -50 | -28 | -15 | -10 | -20 | | | | | |

[1] The last accounts to be filed. Draft accounts for the year ending 31 December 1981 showed turnover as £5.86m, with a pretax loss of £1.78m.

Viners was the largest and most go-ahead of the 240 businesses still making tableware in Sheffield in 1970, with a 35 per cent market share. The long established business was incorporated in 1924 and went public ten years later, although family interests retained control until 1981.

During the early 1970s the company embarked on a policy of investment and rapid expansion, moving out of silver plate into the mass market of stainless steel ware, importing blanks from overseas. It invested heavily in new machinery which was grafted on to its existing old fashioned equipment located at its Sheffield factory. At the same time the company developed new, computerised warehousing facilities and cut its product range from 3,000 to 700 items. It also launched new mass market cutlery collections in the middle and lower segments of the market, promoted via some 150 'shops-within-shops'. Elsewhere it pushed ahead with export promotion, aiming in particular to carve out a significant market share within the European Community.

Most of the funds required for investment were generated internally up until the mid 1970s, a period during which turnover grew rapidly. There was just time to bolster the company's finances by making a rights issue in 1976 before the impact of fierce overseas competition began to make itself felt, profits thereafter shrinking rapidly and turning into losses in 1979. In 1981 the company's position was becoming desperate, the effect of the recession and rising interest rates pushing it deeply into debt. An Anglo-American consortium took the business over in an attempt to turn the position around, but with losses for the year turning out at £1.8m and with no signs of an improvement, the bankers called in the receivers in July 1982.

## Wombwell Foundry and Engineering Company

| 31 July | 1980 | 1979 | 1978 | 1977 | 1976 | 1975 | 1974 | 1973 | 1972 | 1971 |
|---|---|---|---|---|---|---|---|---|---|---|
| S (£000) | 8138 | 8175 | 4487 | 2764 | 2599 | 2156 | 1513 | 821 | 963 | 914 |
| PBT (£000) | -211 | 480 | 607 | 242 | 264 | 270 | 175 | -71 | 5 | 97 |
| TA (£m) | 6.63 | 5.16 | 3.67 | 1.90 | 1.69 | 1.30 | 0.8 | 0.6 | 0.6 | 0.7 |
| EBIT/TA | .04 | .03 | .06 | .04 | .08 | .14 | .15 | .17 | .16 | .14 |
| TL/TA | .64 | .60 | .54 | .36 | .41 | .44 | .36 | .35 | .40 | .36 |
| MAR (%) | -66 | +103 | -14 | -15 | +47 | | | | | |

Wombwell Foundry was a long established company, which went public in 1937. It was a manufacturer of cast iron, steel and steel based machined rolls, iron and steel castings, and general engineering products.

In the early 1970s the company suffered a sharp fall in demand for its products, culminating in a loss in 1973. The dividend was passed in 1972 and 1973, and efforts were made to cut costs and improve management controls. At the same time a new chairman, Mr Gordon Bramah, was appointed, another company of which he was chairman taking a 26 per cent stake in Wombwell's equity share capital.

The period 1974-1977 showed a steady recovery in the company's fortunes, following closure of its loss making activities and an increase in its export sales, which represented 16 per cent of turnover in 1976. The 1978 figures showed a 62 per cent increase in turnover, accompanied by a 51 per cent rise in profits, but this was entirely the result of acquiring Sprotborough Castings (financed by a £500,000 bank loan) and the inclusion of exceptional stock profits of £250,000.

Turnover almost doubled in 1979, with profits increasing by almost 40 per cent, enabling the company to invest almost £1m in new fixed assets. However, with trading conditions worsening the group's prospects declined sharply in 1980, aggravated by the national engineering strike, and although turnover was maintained, margins were sharply reduced as a result of an increase in interest charges. As a result a pretax loss of over £200,000 was posted and the final dividend was passed. The company's difficulties were in part the result of having to invest more than £1m in modernising the Sprotborough plant, which increased indebtedness to over £2m. The situation worsened in the half year to 31 July 1981, with turnover down by a fifth and losses for the six months totalling nearly £500,000, mainly because of spiralling interest charges. For the twelve months to 31 July 1981 the company recorded losses of over £1m, and although proposals were made to restructure the company by closing the Sprotborough steel works, the banks called in the receivers in September.

# 16 Summary and conclusions

## Introduction

The continuing search for a procedure which will help analysts to identify companies that are likely to go bankrupt is understandable. After all, no investor or creditor can afford to have inferior information to the market. On the other hand, it seems highly probable that any new method of trying to forecast future outcomes will have little incremental predictive power – and to the extent that it has, it will soon be applied or mimicked by analysts so that its ability to forecast future outcomes will disappear.

This does not mean, of course, that the efforts of those seeking new ways of trying to discriminate between failing and surviving companies are wasted. Far from it, in fact. Without their search activities for a 'money making machine' the market would not work properly. In the circumstances, analysts are right to refer to all indicators which might help them to distinguish between sound and weak companies, albeit as a screening device which should help to prevent them making avoidable losses.

What is surprising, however – unless it is part of a sales hype – are the arguments put forward by academics in support of their models' continued ability to pick winners and losers. After all, if they did work as discriminators and with the degree of accuracy claimed for them, they should clearly be self-fulfilling and – for listed companies at any rate – one might therefore reasonably expect the vast majority of failures to be sudden.

## The background

This book has reviewed both the normative and positive theories of corporate failure. Amongst what for convenience can be labelled as the former are: disequilibrium models, ranging from chaos and catastrophe theories to entropy and economic theories (including spatial factors); financial theories, ranging from option pricing models to gambler's ruin models; valuation theories; and management theories, which argue that corporate failure is the result of weaknesses in strategic planning.

What might be termed the positive approach is more eclectic, the simplest procedure being traditional ratio analysis, which has been used by bankers and other analysts for over 100 years. For their part, academics developed more systematic ways of undertaking univariate ratio analysis some 60 years ago, introducing controls into the procedure. More recently they have experimented with other models, such as informational decomposition measures and gambler's ruin models. However, over the past 30 years most have concentrated their efforts on building multivariate discriminatory models, using increasingly sophisticated procedures and applying them to different sets of independent variables.

Originally only dichotomous regression and discriminant analysis were used, but it has become far more common over the past ten years to use logit models. Not only are they more robust, but if sample sizes are sufficiently large (which is rarely the case for bankruptcy studies) their assumptions are more realistic. Moreover, they are able to handle multiperiod data, indicate the likelihood of a company failing, and allow for more realistic prior probabilities of failure than the 50 per cent chance normally assumed in the older studies.

A natural extension is to use duration models, where the dependent variable is switched from the probability of failure to the length of time a firm is likely to survive. However, while it is feasible to develop survival models where there are data covering the complete lives of companies (e.g. as there may well be for cohorts of small firms), this is less likely to be the case for listed companies.

An alternative approach to statistically based models is to derive discriminatory functions on an iterative basis. The simplest procedure is to develop models which include a number of financial ratios, the parameter weights being adapted to improve discriminatory power. Such models have been in use for well over 30 years, and spreadsheet packages are now available enabling credit analysts to develop their own procedures for trying to identify financially distressed businesses. For their part, however, academics have attempted to devise more formal procedures for determining parameter weights and sharpen up the discriminatory power of the models. The basic methods developed were recursive partitioning and artificial intelligence models, but the most widely used technique now being used is neural networking.

A major problem with all these modelling techniques is that they are typically applied to heterogeneous financial data relating to companies drawn from several disparate industry categories. Moreover, the data are almost always pooled across time when economic circumstances are changing. Given also that companies fail for a variety of different reasons, the net effect is inevitably that the models tend to focus on the financial *symptoms* of corporate failure, not its *causes*. It is this, perhaps, which helps to explain why out-of-sample most models seem to generate rather high misclassification rates, often identifying around 20 per cent of surviving firms as prima facie failures.

In the circumstances, the $64,000 question is whether or not such models contain significant incremental information; and, regardless, whether once their general principles have been well publicised it is possible to use their supposed 'early warning signals' of impending failure to earn abnormal security returns. Consequently, it is not enough really just to develop a model which discriminates between failing and non-failing businesses. Rather, it is necessary to see whether it appears to contain information not otherwise available to analysts. There are two main ways this can be done: first, by examining the behaviour of value indicators, such as share prices and credit ratings; and, second, to undertake behavioural experiments to establish how analysts reach their conclusions and see whether they can outperform a statistical or iterative model. With respect to the former, the evidence suggests that share prices if anything slightly anticipate the signals transmitted by the mechanistic models, with residual returns turning down on average some 2-3 years before a distressed company fails. As for the behavioural experiments, the evidence implies that analysts can forecast almost as well as the models, although their performance falls away when they are unaware of the number of failures in the company sample supplied to them. On the other hand, the laboratory conditions tend to be rather unrealistic, inasmuch as the subjects have access to far less information than would be the case in practice.

Given the difficulties facing researchers, some academics have sought to examine bankruptcy situations through a series of case studies, in particular identifying situations where financially distressed companies have been successfully turned around. Such studies are interesting in showing that failure is the result of a conjunction of very different events: i.e. there is no clear template that marks out a company that will fail from those that will not right up until the very end. On the other hand, it is possible – with the advantage of hindsight – to identify what went wrong.

## The empirical findings

A number of empirical studies were undertaken employing a larger database than has generally been used for previous experiments in the UK. While this should potentially make it more valid to develop logit models, a negative aspect could be that the data may have been rather more heterogeneous. This could have made it rather harder to derive models that discriminate well.

The results showed that in univariate terms few of the accounting ratios had strong explanatory power, and yearly relative share price returns were even weaker discriminators. However, a different picture emerged when the ratios were incorporated in a series of multivariate models and when the shares prices were cumulated through time. As for the qualitative indicators, when viewed across successive five year windows of time it was clear that there were significant differences in their occurrence as between failing and non-failing concerns.

**Table 16.1: Classificational Accuracy of Various Failure Identification Models for Years 1, 2 and 3 Prior to Failure**

| | % correct predictions | | |
| --- | --- | --- | --- |
| *Model developed on data 1 year prior to failure* | Failed | Non-failed | Total |
| Entropy | | | 76 |
| Gambler's ruin | | | 87 |
| Logit – financial ratios (hold-out sample) | | | |
|     prior probability of failure 50% | 81 | 90 | 85 |
|     prior probability of failure 2% | 93 | 64 | 64 |
|     prior probability of failure 2% | | | |
|     allowing for decision error costs | 88 | 76 | 76 |
|    – qualitative indicators | 82 | 85 | 84 |
| Neural networking (4 neurons) analysis sample | 92 | 98 | 95 |
|     hold out sample | 72 | 82 | 77 |
| *Model developed on data 3 years prior to failure* | | | |
| Entropy | | | 52 |
| Gambler's ruin | | | 66 |
| Logit – financial ratios (hold-out sample) | | | |
|     prior probability of failure 50% | 78 | 81 | 79 |
|     prior probability of failure 2% | 100 | 7 | 9 |
|     prior probability of failure 2% | | | |
|     allowing for decision error costs | 98 | 34 | 35 |
|    – qualitative indicators | 64 | 75 | 70 |
| Neural networking* (4 neurons) analysis sample | 100 | 99 | 99 |
|     hold out sample | 63 | 83 | 73 |

* Models based on cumulative data (i.e. for years 1, 2 and 3 prior to failure).
Note: Prior probability of failure taken as 50% unless otherwise indicated.

As for informational decomposition and gambler's ruin models, the former had relatively weak discriminatory power, even when adjustments were made to measure structural balance sheet changes over varying time intervals and for different classifications of assets and claims (see Table 16.1). On the other hand, the gambler's ruin model (assuming strict capital rationing) performed creditably, its classificatory power not being greatly inferior to that of multivariate ratio models.

Various multivariate models were run, and when equal probability of bankruptcy and non-failure was assumed the discriminatory power was as impressive as that of previous studies. This was true of the logit models employing qualitative variables (albeit measured over five year windows again), as well as of a number of financial ratio models (see Table 16.1). One interesting aspect was that there appeared to be incremental information through time when the probability of failure as measured by a logit model for the previous year was introduced as an explanatory variable.

But perhaps the most notable finding was the (not unexpected) loss of discriminatory power when adjustment was made for potential sampling bias, so that the ratio of failed to non-failed companies in any one year was closer to the true rate of 2% rather than 50%. In fact, it appears that one cause of misclassification error is the nature of the matched pairing control procedure. On the other hand, the loss of classificatory power was such when realistic prior probabilities of failure were introduced into the models as to call into question their practical usefulness. Whether or not other models perform this badly is an open question as their parameter values have rarely been published (although it is possible to reconstruct them on different samples of companies). But what does appear to happen is that their adjustments for sampling bias are substantially cancelled out by trying to allow for differential costs of misclassification. This is done by altering the parameter values so that the misclassification rates are minimised in proportion to relative costs. Yet it is unclear whether such an 'ex post' adjustment is appropriate when formulating a model, or whether it should be made once a model is being applied.

As for other multivariate procedures, the Weibull version of the survival model would seem to be appropriate if suitable data are available for analysis. Unfortunately those generally used in bankruptcy studies are too heavily censored, but studies along these lines are now beginning to be undertaken by industrial economists for cohorts of small businesses. As for neural networking models, this new and popular technique is now being applied to try to improve the ability to discriminate between failing and non-failing companies. Overfitting remains a problem, although the preliminary screenings of the figures undertaken in this study produced some encouraging results, suggesting discriminatory ability as good as that of multivariate models. Certainly it is worthwhile trying to extract as much information as possible from the data, but it nevertheless seems likely from a practical perspective that performance will ultimately be little better than that achieved by statistical models.

The share price studies largely confirmed what other studies have shown, namely that on average the market appears to distinguish between failing and sound firms some 2-3 years before their final year end date. This in turn is often six months before bankrupt companies pass into the hands of receivers. Moreover, there was little evidence of a sudden collapse in share prices, which is what one might expect if analysts are behaving rationally and are referring to a discriminatory model, believing its 'forecasts'. What was rather more interesting, however, was that there was some evidence that the market appeared to be using the same information captured in three different failure identification models. This might be taken to imply that these latter were merely imitating the analysts' evaluation procedures.

Of course, the evidence was not strong; and it could well be that the information captured by other models might not be imitated by the market. Nevertheless, the results give food for thought.

Further light on the difficulties of trying to discriminate between failing and non-failing businesses was shed by the 25 case studies undertaken. It is soon apparent that the events which lead to the collapse of businesses are 'situation specific'. Often, it seems, it is an unfortunate conjunction of events which brings about financial distress. Usually the company is relatively small and undiversified, and the pretext for failure is generally that the industry environment is changing rapidly. Not uncommonly a distressed firm has suffered an unexpected setback which makes it one of the more vulnerable in its sector, and although attempts are often made to turn the situation round, clearly these do not succeed in all cases. Yet what is evident is that analysts – and sometimes managers too – are occasionally taken completely unawares by developments. In such circumstances it is difficult to see how any ratio based model can do much more than identify the *symptoms* rather than the *causes* of financial weakness – e.g. low and declining profitability, a slowing in the growth rate, increased borrowing, and pressure on the liquidity position. But equally, it is unclear how even an understanding of the economic problems facing a company will enable an analyst to identify which companies can be successfully turned round and which cannot. After all, if it is that obvious, the no-hopers should collapse immediately. Only with the advantage of hindsight, it seems, is it possible to distinguish unerringly between those companies doomed to failure and those which can be rescued.

**Summary**

Overall, the problem of sampling bias offers an explanation why the market does not appear to behave in the way expected if failure identification models were especially and consistently successful in discriminating between failing and non-failing businesses. Moreover, the behaviour of share prices suggests that such models may anyway largely be imitating the procedures already employed by analysts. Furthermore, a closer scrutiny of the complex interaction of economic events which help to bring individual companies down suggests that the financial models largely identify the symptoms of distress rather than the causes.

Nevertheless, such a view should be regarded as being realistic rather than negative. It is still important for the efficient working of a market economy that analysts should search actively for ways in which they might (albeit fleetingly) beat the market – and certainly they cannot afford to be left behind the pack. In such circumstances there has to be a constant search to try to find ways to improve understanding of the causes of success and failure. This means that every attempt should be made to try to extract as much information as possible from financial statements and other indicators.

# Appendix: Sample and control companies

| Failed company name | No. of years | EXSTAT years | DTI years | Other years | Non-failed company name | EXSTAT years | DTI years | Other years | Industry category |
|---|---|---|---|---|---|---|---|---|---|
| Airfix Industries*† | 10 | 72-80 | 71 | | Spear [J.W. & S.]* | 71-80 | | | Toys and games |
| Anderson's Rubber Co.* | 10 | | | 71-80 | British Vita* | 71-80 | | | Plastic and rubber manufacturers |
| Anglian Food | 5 | | | 69-73 | Associated Fisheries | 71-73 | 70 | | General food manufacturing |
| Anglowest | 5 | | | 71-75 | Clarke [T.] | 71-75 | | | Electricals (excluding radio and TV) |
| Austin[F.], Leyton*† | 10 | 72-81 | | | Christie-Tyler* | 72-81 | | | Furniture and bedding |
| Automatic Oil Tools | 5 | | 71-73 | 71-75 | Dewhurst & Partner* | 71-75 | | | Electricals (excluding radio and TV) |
| Bacal Construction | 5 | | | 74-75 | Miller [Stanley] Holdings | 71-73 | 69-70 | | Contracting and construction |
| Bambers Stores*† | 10 | 76-83 | | 74-75 | British Home Stores* | 74-83 | | | Multiple store |
| Bamfords† | 10 | 71-78 | 69-70 | | Brammer [H.] | | | 69-78 | Mechanical handling |
| Bastian International* | 10 | | | 72-81 | Francis Industries* | 72-81 | | | Miscellaneous mechanical engineering |
| Bear Brand | 5 | | | 70-74 | Casket Holdings | | | 70-74 | Clothing manufacturers |
| Beechwood Construction* | 10 | | | 74-83 | Cocksedge* | 74-83 | | | Contracting and construction |
| Bellway Holdings* | 5 | 74-78 | | | Bett Brothers* | 74-78 | | | Contracting and construction |
| Berwick Timpo*† | 10 | 72-81 | | | Spear [J.W. & S.]* | 72-81 | | | Toys and games |
| Blackman and Conrad† | 10 | 71-79 | 70 | | Corah | | | 69-78 | Clothing manufacturers |
| Blackwood Morton & Sons† | 10 | 72-80 | 71 | | Halstead [James]* | 72-81 | | 71 | Floor covering |
| Bond Worth Holdings | 10 | | 67-76 | | Mackay [Hugh] & Co.* | 71-76 | 67-70 | | Floor covering |
| Brigray Group | 10 | | 71-74 | 75-80 | Ellis & Goldstein* | | | 70-80 | Clothing manufacturers |
| British Enkalon*† | 10 | 71-80 | | | Richards* | 71-80 | | | Cotton and synthetic fibres |
| Brittains | 10 | | 68-77 | | Metal Closures | | | 68-77 | Packaging and paper |
| Brocks Group* | 10 | 71-79 | | 70 | Dowding & Mills* | 71-79 | | 70 | Electricals (excluding radio and TV) |
| Burrell & Co.* | 10 | | 70-79 | | Anchor Chemicals* | | | 70-79 | General chemicals |
| Capper Neill* | 10 | 74-83 | | | Davy Corporation* | 74-83 | | | Steel and chemical plant |
| Caravans International Group | 10 | 72-81 | | | York Trailer Holdings* | 72-81 | | | Motor vehicle manufacturer |
| Carron Co. (Holdings)*† | 10 | 72-81 | | | Cape Industries* | 72-81 | | | Building materials/Quarry products |

| Failed company name | No. of years | EXSTAT years | DTI years | Other years | Non-failed company name | EXSTAT years | DTI years | Other years | Industry category |
|---|---|---|---|---|---|---|---|---|---|
| Cawdaw Industrial Holdings * | 10 | 72-81 | | | Associated British Engineering * | 72-81 | | | Industrial holding company |
| Charles [David] | 5 | 72-75 | 71 | | Taylor Woodrow | 71-75 | | | Contracting and construction |
| Cohen & Wilks (Holdings) | 5 | | | 70-74 | John Beale Associated Companies | | | 70-74 | Clothing manufacturers |
| Collet [J.] | 5 | | 69-73 | | Bolton Group | 72-73 | 69-71 | | Clothing manufacturers |
| Dallas [John E.] & Sons * | 5 | | 69 | 70-73 | Boosey & Hawkes * | | | 69-73 | Leisure |
| Dennis [James M.] & Co. | 5 | | | 74-83 | Ash & Lacy | 74-83 | | | Metallurgy |
| Derritron * | 10 | 72-81 | | | B.I.C.C. * | 72-81 | | | Electricals (excluding radio and TV) |
| Dimplex | 10 | 72-76 | 67-71 | | Lec Refrigeration | 72-79 | | 67-76 | Household appliances |
| Dunbee-Combex-Marx * | 10 | 71-78 | 69-70 | | Waddington [John] * | | | 70-71 | Toys and games |
| Dykes [J.] Holdings | 10 | 72-79 | 70-71 | | Relyon Group | 71-78 | | 70-79 | Furniture and bedding |
| E.C. Cases | 10 | 72-79 | | 70-71 | Aaronson Brothers | 72-76 | | 69-70 | Timber |
| Edinburgh Industrial Holdings | 5 | | | 72-76 | E.I.S. Group | 72-76 | | | Miscellaneous mechanical engineering |
| Eldridge Stableford & Co. | 5 | | | 69-73 | Unigroup | 71-73 | 69-70 | | Clothing manufacturers |
| Elliot [E.] * | 10 | 72-81 | | | United Gas Industries * | 72-81 | | | Instrument manufacturers |
| Fairbairn Lawson† | 10 | 72-78 | 69-71 | | Boulton [William] | | | 69-78 | Industrial plant manufacturer |
| Fairey Co. †* | 10 | 72-76 | 67-71 | | Neepsend * | | | 67-76 | Miscellaneous mechanical engineering |
| Fairfax Jersey | 5 | | | 71-75 | Kitchen [Robert] Taylor | 71-75 | | | Miscellaneous textiles |
| Fertleman [B.] & Sons | 5 | | | 75-79 | Cornwell Parker | 75-79 | | | Furniture and bedding |
| Findlay [Andrew R.] Group | 5 | 76-80 | | | Cakebread Robay | 76-80 | | | Builders merchants |
| Fodens * | 10 | 72-79 | 70-71 | | Burndene Investments | | | 70-79 | Motor vehicle manufacturers |
| Gartons | 5 | | | 77-80 | Rentokil * | 76-80 | | | General chemicals |
| General Engineering Co. (Radcliffe)† | 10 | 72-78 | 69-71 | | A.P.V. Holdings | | | 69-78 | Industrial plant manufacturer |
| Goldman [H.] Group * | 10 | 71-80 | | | Staffordshire Potteries | 72-80 | 71 | | Kitchen and tableware |
| Golding | 5 | 71-75 | | 67-70 | Ladbroke Group | 71-75 | | 67-75 | Leisure |
| Greaves Organisation | 10 | 72-76 | 69-71 | | Higgs and Hill | 72-76 | 66 | | Contracting and construction |
| Hartle Machinery International | 10 | 71-77 | | 67-69 | Noble & Lund | 71-77 | 68-70 | | Machine and other tools |
| Heenan Spark | 10 | | 70 | 70-72 | Ayrshire Metal Products | | | | Miscellaneous mechanical engineering |
| Hesketh Motorcycles | 5 | | 73-74 | 76-80 | U.K.O. International | 77-81 | | 70-74 | Miscellaneous |
| Hickmet Palace [The] | 5 | | | 70-74 | Savoy Hotel | 71-74 | 70 | | Hotels and caterers |

| Failed company name | No. of years | EXSTAT years | DTI years | Other years | Non-failed company name | EXSTAT years | DTI years | Other years | Industry category |
|---|---|---|---|---|---|---|---|---|---|
| Highlight Sports* | 5 | 72-75 | | 71 | Baird [William]* | 71-75 | | | Clothing manufacturers |
| Homfray & Co.* | 10 | 72-80 | | 71 | Readicut International* | 71-80 | | | Floor covering |
| House of Sears Holdings* | 5 | | | 71-75 | Wise [Leslie] Group* | 71-75 | | | Clothing manufacturers |
| Ireland [Ernest] | 5 | | 71-75 | 74-78 | Aberdeen Construction | 71-75 | | | Contracting and construction |
| J.C.E.G. | 5 | | | 70-79 | Bett Brothers | 74-78 | | | Contracting and construction |
| Johnson & Barnes | 10 | | | 75 | Palma Group | 71-79 | 70 | | Clothing manufacturers |
| Kenkast | 5 | | 71-74 | 75 | Sindall [William] | 71-75 | | | Contracting and construction |
| Lesbrook | 5 | | | 71-75 | Amalgamated Metal Corporation | 71-74 | 70 | | Metallurgy |
| Lesney Products & Co.* | 10 | 72-81 | | 70-74 | Waddington [John]* | 72-81 | | | Toys and games |
| Lewston International | 5 | | 69-77 | 70-74 | Blackwood Hodge | | | 70-74 | Contracting and construction |
| Liden (Holdings) | 10 | | | 78 | Scottish Heritable Trust [The]* | | 69-78 | | Furniture and bedding |
| Lockwood Foods* | 10 | | 71-80 | | Clifford Dairies* | 71-80 | | | General food manufacturing |
| Maxlim Fashions | 5 | | | 72-76 | Alexon Group | 72-76 | | | Clothing manufacturers |
| Mears Brothers Holdings* | 10 | | 69-77 | 68 | Whatlings* | 71-77 | | | Contracting and construction |
| Melody Mills † | 10 | 78-82 | 73-77 | | Gomme Holdings* | 73-82 | | 68-70 | Furniture and bedding |
| Meltzer [A. & H.] (Holdings) | 5 | | | 69-73 | Newbold & Burton | 71-73 | 70 | 69 | Footwear manufacturers |
| Metal Products (Willenhall) | 5 | | | 70-74 | Ratcliffs (Great Bridge) | | | 70-74 | Metallurgy |
| Metro Town & Central Properties | 5 | | | 70-74 | Lovell [Y.J.] Holdings | 71-74 | | | Contracting and construction |
| Mettoy Co.*† | 5 | | 72-81 | | Spear [J. W. & S.]* | 72-81 | | | Toys and games |
| Michael [John] (Savile Row)† | 10 | | | 70-74 | Panto [P.]* | 71-80 | | | Multiple store |
| Moss Engineering* | 10 | | | 71-80 | Smiths Industries* | 72-81 | | | Miscellaneous mechanical engineering |
| Motor Rail* | 5 | | | 72-81 | Automotive Products* | 71-74 | | | Motor components |
| Movitex † | 10 | | | 70-74 | Duport* | | | 70 | Miscellaneous mechanical engineering |
| Nelson David | 10 | | | 71-80 | Alexanders Holdings | 71-80 | | 71-80 | Motor distributors |
| Norvic Securities* | 10 | | | 71-80 | Lambert Howarth* | 71-80 | | | Footwear manufacturers |
| Oxley Printing Group † | 10 | 71-80 | | | Collins [William]* | 71-80 | | | Publishing and printing |
| Paradise [B.]†* | 10 | 71-80 | | 73-82 | Selincourt* | 73-82 | | | Clothing manufacturers |
| Patent Industrial Group | 5 | | | 71-75 | Hawker Siddeley | 71-75 | 70 | | Miscellaneous mechanical engineering |
| Pawson [W.L.] | 10 | 77-81 | | | Martin [Albert]* | 72-80 | 71 | | Clothing manufacturers |
| Peak Investments | 10 | | | 72-76 | York Trailer Holdings | 71-79 | 70 | | Motor vehicle manufacturers |
| Pickles [William] & Co.*† | 10 | 71-80 | | 70-79 | Sumner [F.]* | 71-80 | | | Miscellaneous textiles |
| Plushpile (Wharf Mill)* | 10 | 71-80 | | | Courts (Furnishers)* | 72-78 | 69-71 | | Furniture retailers |
| P.M.A. Holdings* | 10 | 71-80 | | 69-78 | Elson & Robbins | 71-80 | | | Furniture and bedding |

| Failed company name | No. of years | EXSTAT years | DTI years | Other years | Non-failed company name | EXSTAT years | DTI years | Other years | Industry category |
|---|---|---|---|---|---|---|---|---|---|
| Pullman [R. & J.]*† | 10 | 73-82 | | | Atkins Brothers* | 73-82 | | | Clothing manufacturers |
| Radley Fashions & Textiles | | | | | Lincroft Kilgour* | 71-80 | | | Clothing manufacturers |
| Rakusen Group | 10 | | | 71-80 | Berisford International | 73-77 | | | General food manufacturing |
| Richards & Wallington Industries*† | 5 | | | 73-77 | Wilson Connolly* | 71-80 | | | Contracting and construction |
| Rivington Reed | 10 | 71-80 | | 70-71 | Rexmore | 72-79 | | 70-71 | Miscellaneous textiles |
| Sanger [J.E.] | 10 | 72-79 | | 70-71 | Wills [George]* | 71-79 | 70 | | Overseas trade |
| Scotcros | 10 | 72-79 | 72-73 | | Needlers* | 74-83 | | | General food manufacturing |
| Scott [David]* | 10 | 72-83 | | 71-81 | Chamberlain Phipps* | 72-81 | | | Footwear manufacturers |
| Southern Construction (Holdings)† | 10 | | 69-70 | | Tilbury Group | 71-78 | | 69-70 | Contracting and construction |
| Stayflex International* | 10 | 71-78 | 69-70 | | Pittard Group* | | | 68-77 | Clothing manufacturers |
| Stephen [Alexander] & Sons | 10 | 73-82 | 68-77 | | Bailey [C.H.]* | 73-82 | 72 | | Miscellaneous engineering contractors |
| Stone Platt Industries* | 10 | | 71-80 | | Greene's Economiser* | | | 71-80 | Industrial plant manufacturer |
| Swan Hunter* | 10 | | 69-78 | | Simon Engineering* | | | 69-78 | Miscellaneous engineering contractors |
| T.C.K. Group† | 10 | | | 66-75 | Neil & Spencer* | 71-76 | 67-70 | | Industrial plant manufacturer |
| Town & Commercial Properties | 5 | | | 71-75 | Mowlem* | | | 70-74 | Contracting and construction |
| Viners*† | 10 | 71-80 | | | Prestige* | 71-80 | | | Kitchen and tableware |
| Whitley [B.S. & W.]* | 10 | 72-80 | 71 | | Collins [William]* | 71-80 | | | Packaging and paper |
| Williams [Ben] & Co.* | 10 | | | 71-80 | Nottingham Manufacturing* | 71-80 | | | Clothing manufacturers |
| Williams Hudson* | 10 | 72-80 | 71 | | London Merchant Securities* | | | 71-81 | Financial holding company |
| Wilshaw Securities* | 5 | | | 71-75 | Benford Concrete Machinery* | 71-75 | | | Industrial plant manufacturer |
| Wilson Walton Engineering | 10 | | | 69-78 | Clayton Son & Company* | 71-78 | | 69-70 | Miscellaneous engineering contractors |
| Wombwell Foundry & Engineering*† | 10 | | | 71-80 | Myson Group* | 71-80 | | | Miscellaneous engineering contractors |
| Wood & Sons (Holdings)* | 10 | | | 70-79 | Associated Paper Industries* | 71-79 | 70 | | Packaging and paper |
| Wood [W.] & Sons | 5 | | | 69-73 | Coats Patons | 71-79 | | 69-73 | Miscellaneous textiles |

Notes:
* Companies with five years share price data and subject of the neural networking and share price reaction studies reported in chapters 13 and 14.
† Companies that are the subject of case studies reported in chapter 15.

# Bibliography

Abdel-khalik, A.R. (1993), 'Discussion of "Financial Ratios and Corporate Endurance: A Case of the Oil and Gas Industry"', *Contemporary Accounting Research*, pp. 695-705.

---------------------- and K.M. El-Sheshai (1980), 'Information Choice and Utilization in an Experiment on Default Prediction', *Journal of Accounting Research*, pp. 325-342.

Abdul Aziz, D. C. Emanuel and G. H. Lawson (1988), 'Bankruptcy Prediction – An Investigation of Cash Flow Based Models', *Journal of Management Studies*, pp. 419-437.

-------------- and G.H. Lawson (1989), 'Cash Flow Reporting and Financial Distress Models: Testing of Hypotheses', *Financial Management*, pp. 55-63.

Aharony, J., C.P. Jones and I. Swary (1980), 'An Analysis of Risk and Return Characteristics of Corporate Bankruptcy Using Capital Market Data', *Journal of Finance*, pp. 1001-1016.

-------------- and I. Swary (1988), 'A Note on Corporate Bankruptcy and the Market Model Risk Measures', *Journal of Business Finance and Accounting*, pp. 275-281.

Alford, A.W., J.J. Jones and M.E. Zmijewski (1994), 'Extensions and Violations of the Statutory SEC Form 10-K Filing Requirements', *Journal of Accounting and Economics*, pp. 229-254.

Altman, E.I. (1968), 'Financial Ratios, Discriminant Analysis and the Prediction of Corporate Bankruptcy, *Journal of Finance*, pp. 589-609.

--------------- (1971), 'Corporate Bankruptcy in America', Heath Lexington: New York.

--------------- (1973), 'Predicting Railroad Bankruptcies in America', *Bell Journal of Economics and Management Science*, pp. 184-211.

-------------- (1977), 'Some Estimates of the Cost of Lending Errors for Commercial Banks', *Journal of Commercial Bank Lending*, October, pp. 51-58.

--------------- (1982), 'Accounting Implications of Failure Prediction Models', *Journal of Accounting, Auditing and Finance,* Fall, pp. 4-19.

--------------- (1983), 'Corporate Financial Distress: A Complete Guide to Predicting, Avoiding and Dealing with Bankruptcy', John Wiley: New York.

-------------- (1984a), 'The Success of Business Failure Prediction Models: An International Survey', *Journal of Banking and Finance,* pp. 171-198.

-------------- (1984b), 'A Further Empirical Investigation of the Bankruptcy Cost Question', *Journal of Finance,* pp. 1067-1089.

-------------- (1993), 'Corporate Financial Distress and Bankruptcy', (2nd ed.), John Wiley: New York.

-------------- R.B. Avery, R.A. Eisenbeis and J.F. Sinkey, jr. (1981), 'Application of Classification Techniques in Business, Banking and Finance', JAI Press: Greenwich, Conn.

-------------- and M. Brenner (1981), 'Information Effects and Stock Market Response to Firm Deterioration', *Journal of Financial and Quantitative Analysis,* pp. 35-51.

-------------- and R.A. Eisenbeis (1978), 'Financial Applications of Discriminant Analysis': A Clarification', *Journal of Financial and Quantitative Analysis,* pp. 185-195.

-------------- R.C. Haldeman and P. Narayanan (1977), 'Zeta Analysis: A New Model to Identify Bankruptcy Risk of Corporations', *Journal of Banking and Finance,* pp. 29-54.

--------------, G. Marco and F. Varetto (1994), 'Corporate Distress Diagnosis: Comparisons Using Linear Discriminant Analysis and Neural Networks (the Italian Experience)', *Journal of Banking and Finance,* pp. 509-529.

-------------- and T.P. McGough (1974), 'Evaluation of a Company as a Going Concern', *The Journal of Accountancy,* December, pp. 50-57.

Arbarbarnell, J. S. (1991), 'Do Analysts' Earnings Forecasts Incorporate Information in Prior Stock Price Changes?', *Journal of Accounting and Economics,* pp. 147-165.

----------------------- and V.L. Bernard (1992), 'Tests of Analysts' Overreaction/ Underreaction to Earnings Information as an Explanation for Anomalous Stock Price Behaviour', *Journal of Finance,* pp. 1181-1207.

Argenti, J. (1976), 'Corporate Collapse – The Causes and the Symptoms', McGraw Hill: Maidenhead, Berks.

------------- (1983), 'Predicting Corporate Failure', Accountants Digest No. 138, Institute of Chartered Accountants in England and Wales: London.

------------- (1984), 'Predicting Corporate Failure', Notes for Businessmen, The Institute of Chartered Accountants in England and Wales: London.

Atiase, R.K., and L.S. Bamber (1994), 'Trading Volume Reactions to Annual Accounting Earnings Announcements – the Incremental Role of Predisclosure Information Asymmetry', *Journal of Accounting and Economics,* pp. 309-329.

Audretsch, D.B. (1991), 'New-Firm Survival and the Technological Regime', *Review of Economics and Statistics*, pp. 441-450.

---------------, and T. Mahmood (1994), 'The Rate of Hazard Confronting New Firms and Plants in US Manufacturing', *Review of Industrial Organisation*, pp. 41-56.

---------------, and J. Mata (1995), 'The Post-Entry Performance of Firms: Introduction', *International Journal of Industrial Organisation*, pp. 413-420.

Bahnson, P.R., and J.W. Bartley (1992), 'The Sensitivity of Failure Prediction Models to Alternative Definitions of Failure' in 'Advances in Accounting', vol. 10, 1992, ed. B.N. Schwartz, JAI Press: Greenwich, Conn., pp. 255-278.

Ball, R. (1972), 'Changes in Accounting Techniques and Stock Prices', *Journal of Accounting Research, Supplement on Empirical Research in Accounting*, pp. 1-38.

--------- (1992), 'The Earnings-Price Anomaly', *Journal of Accounting and Economics,* pp. 319-345.

--------- and P. Brown (1968), 'An Empirical Evaluation of Accounting Income Numbers', *Journal of Accounting Research*, pp. 159-178.

--------- and S.P. Kothari (1990), 'Security Returns Around Earnings Announcements', *Accounting Review*, pp. 718-738.

--------- and R. Watts (1972), 'Some Time Series Properties of Accounting Income', *Journal of Finance*, pp. 663-682.

Barnes, P., and D. Hooi (1987), 'The Strange Case of the Qualified Success', *Accountancy*, November, pp. 32-33.

Barniv, R., and A. Raveh (1989), 'Identifying Financial Distress: A New Nonparametric Approach', *Journal of Business Finance and Accounting*, pp. 361-383.

Barthory, A. (1984), 'Predicting Corporate Collapse', Financial Times Business Information Limited: London.

Bates, J.M., and C.W.J. Granger (1989), 'The Combination of Forecasts', *Operational Research Quarterly,* pp. 451-468.

Beaver, W.H. (1966), 'Financial Ratios as Predictors of Failure', *Journal of Accounting Research, Supplement on Empirical Research in Accounting,* pp. 71-111.

------------ (1968a), 'Market Prices, Financial Ratios, and the Prediction of Failure', *Journal of Accounting Research,* pp. 179-192.

------------ (1968b), 'The Information Content of Annual Earnings Announcements', *Journal of Accounting Research, Supplement on Empirical Research in Accounting*, pp. 67-92.

------------ (1970), 'The Time Series Behavior of Earnings', *Journal of Accounting Research, Supplement on Empirical Research in Accounting*, pp. 62-99.

Benishay, H. (1973), 'Discussion of "A Prediction of Business Failure Using Accounting Data"', *Journal of Accounting Research, Supplement on Empirical Research in Accounting,* pp. 180-182.

Bernard, V.L. (1989), 'Capital Market Research in Accounting During the 1980s: A Critical Review' in T. Frecka (ed.), 'The State of Accounting Research as We Enter the 1990s', University of Ilinois, Urbana-Champaign, Ill., pp. 72-120.

---------------- (1992), 'Stock Price Reactions to Earnings Announcements: A Summary of Recent Anomalous Evidence and Possible Explanations' in R. Thaler (ed.), 'Advances in Behavioural Finance', Russell Sage Foundation: New York, pp. 303-340.

Betts, J., and D. Belhoul (1983), 'Applications of Reliability Analysis in the Management of the Economy', 4th Eurodata Conference, Venice (discussed in Taffler, 1984, p. 213).

-------------------------------- (1987), 'The Effectiveness of Incorporating Financial Stability Measures in Company Failure Models', *Journal of Business Finance and Accounting*, pp. 323-334.

Bhushan, R. (1989), 'Firm Characteristics and Analyst Following', *Journal of Accounting and Economics*, pp. 255-274.

--------------- (1994), 'An Informational Efficiency Perspective on the Post-Earnings Announcement Drift', *Journal of Accounting and Economics*, pp. 45-65.

Bibeault, D.B. (1982), 'Corporate Turnaround', McGraw-Hill: New York.

Bikhchandani, S., D. Hirshleifer and I. Welch (1992), 'A Theory of Fads, Fashion, Custom, and Cultural Change as Informational Cascades', *Journal of Political Economy*, pp. 992-1026.

Bird, P.A. (1965), 'Waiting for the Accounts', *The Accountant*, vol. 152, pp. 34-36.

Birley, S., and P. Westhead (1992), 'Environments for Business Deregistration in the United Kingdom, 1987-1990', Discussion Paper, The Management School, Imperial College of Science, Technology and Medicine, London.

---------- and N. Niktari (1995), 'The Failure of Owner-Managed Businesses: The Diagnosis of Accountants and Bankers', BDO Stoy Hayward/Institute of Chartered Accountants in England and Wales: London.

Black, F. (1986), 'Noise', *Journal of Finance*, pp. 529-543.

Black, F., and M. Scholes (1973), 'The Pricing of Options and Corporate Liabilities', *Journal of Political Economy*, pp. 637-654.

Blum, M.P. (1974), 'Failing Company Discriminant Analysis', *Journal of Accounting Research,* pp. 1-25.

Boland, L.A. (1979), 'A Critique of Friedman's Critics', *Journal of Economic Literature*, pp. 503-522.

Bonnier, K-A., and R.F. Bruner (1989), 'An Analysis of Stock Price Reaction to Management Change in Distressed Firms', *Journal of Accounting and Economics*, pp. 95-106.

Booth, P. (1983), 'Decomposition Measures and the Prediction of Financial Failure', *Journal of Business Finance and Accounting*, pp. 67-82.

----------- and P. Hutchinson (1989), 'Distinguishing between Failing and Growing Firms: A Note on the Use of Decomposition Measure Analysis', *Journal of Business Finance and Accounting*, pp. 267-271.

Brealey, R.A., and S.C. Myers (1996), 'Principles of Corporate Finance', 5th ed., McGraw-Hill: New York.

Breakwell, G.H., and R.C. Morris (1975), 'Manipulation of Earnings Figures in the United Kingdom', *Accounting and Business Research*, pp. 177-184.

Brenner, M. (1977), 'The Effect of Model Misspecifications on Tests of the Efficient Markets Hypothesis', *Journal of Finance*, pp. 57-66.

--------------- (1979), 'The Sensitivity of the Efficient Markets Hypothesis to Alternative Specifications of the Market Model', *Journal of Finance*, pp. 915-929.

Briloff, A. (1972), 'Unaccountable Accounting', Harper and Row: New York.

Brooks, L.D., and D.A. Buckmaster (1976), 'Further Evidence of the Time Series Properties of Accounting Income', *Journal of Finance*, pp. 1359-1373.

----------------------------------------- (1980), 'First-Difference Signals and Accounting Income Time-Series Properties', *Journal of Business Finance and Accounting*, pp. 437-454.

Brown, S.J., and J.B. Warner (1980), 'Measuring Security Price Performance', *Journal of Financial Economics*, pp. 205-258.

Burgstahler, D., J. Jiambalvo and E. Noreen (1989), 'Changes in the Probability of Bankruptcy and Equity Value', *Journal of Accounting and Economics,* pp. 207-224.

Buchman, T.A. (1985), 'An Effect of Hindsight on Predicting Bankruptcy with Accounting Information', *Accounting, Organizations and Society*, pp. 267-285.

Campbell, S. V. (1996), 'Predicting Bankruptcy Reorganization for Closely Held Firms', *Accounting Horizons*, vol. 10, no. 3, pp. 12-25.

Carcello, J.V., D.R. Hermanson and H.F. Huss (1995), 'Temporal Changes in Bankruptcy-Related Reporting', *Auditing*, Fall, pp. 133-143.

Carty, P. (1996), 'Giving Credit Where It's Due', *Accountancy*, September 1996, p. 46.

Casey, C.J. (1980), 'Additional Evidence on the Usefulness of Accounting Ratios for the Prediction of Corporate Failure', *Journal of Accounting Research*, pp. 603-613.

----------- (1983), 'Prior Probability Disclosures and Loan Officers' Judgments: Some Evidence of the Impact', *Journal of Accounting Research*, pp. 300-309.

----------- and N.J. Bartczak (1984), 'Cash Flow – It's Not the Bottom Line', *Harvard Business Review,* July-August, pp. 61-66.

---------------------------------- (1985), 'Using Operating Cash Flow Data to Predict Financial Distress: Some Extensions', *Journal of Accounting Research*, pp. 384-401.

------------, V.E. McGee and C.P. Stickney (1986), 'Discriminating Between Reorganized and Liquidated Firms in Bankruptcy', *Accounting Review*, pp. 249-262.

------------ and T.I. Selling (1986), 'The Effect of Task Predictability and Prior Probability Disclosure on Judgment Quality and Confidence', *Accounting Review*, pp. 302-317.

Castagna, A.D., and Z.P. Matolcsy (1981), 'The Market Characteristics of Failed Companies: Extensions and Further Evidence', *Journal of Business Finance and Accounting*, pp. 467-483.

------------------------------------------ (1985), 'Using Operating Cash Flow Data to Predict Financial Distress: Some Extensions', *Journal of Accounting Research,* pp. 384-401.

Chan, K.C. (1988), 'On the Contrarian Investment Strategy', *Journal of Business*, pp. 147-163.

Chen, K.C.W., and B.K. Church (1992), 'Default on Debt Obligations and the Issuance of Going Concern Opinions', *Auditing*, Fall, pp. 30-49.

-------------------------------------- (1996), 'Going Concern Opinions and the Market's Reaction to Bankruptcy Filings', *Accounting Review*, pp. 117-128.

Chen, K.C.W., and C-W.J. Lee (1993), 'Financial Ratios and Corporate Endurance: A Case of the Oil and Gas Industry', *Contemporary Accounting Research,* pp. 668-687.

Chen, Y., J.F. Weston and E.I. Altman (1995), 'Financial Distress and Restructuring Models', *Financial Management,* Summer, pp. 57-75.

Choi, S.K., and D.C. Jeter (1992), 'The Effects of Qualified Audit Opinions on Earnings Response Coefficients', *Journal of Accounting and Economics*, pp. 229-247.

Citron, D.B., and R.J. Taffler (1992), 'The Audit Report Under Going Concern Uncertainty: An Empirical Analysis', *Accounting and Business Research*, pp. 337-346.

Clark, T.A., and M.I. Weinstein (1983), 'The Behavior of the Common Stock of Bankrupt Firms', *Journal of Finance,* pp. 489-504.

Clutterbuck, D., and S. Kernaghan (1990), 'The Phoenix Factor', Wiedenfield and Nicholson: London.

Coats, P.K., and L.F. Fant (1993), 'Recognizing Financial Distress Patterns Using a Neural Network Tool', *Financial Management*, pp. 142-155.

Cochrane, J.H. (1991), 'Volatility Tests and Efficient Markets', *Journal of Monetary Economics*, pp. 463-485.

Conrad, J., and G. Kaul (1993), 'Long-Term Market Overreaction or Biases in Computed Returns?', *Journal of Finance*, pp. 39-63.

Cosh, A., and A. Hughes (1993), 'The Death Process: A Comparison of Large and Small Company Failures and Acquisitions', Working Paper 33, Small Business Research Centre, Department of Applied Economics, University of Cambridge.

388

---------------------------- (1995), 'Failures, Acquisitions and Post Merger Success: The Comparative Financial Characteristics of Large and Small Companies', Working Paper 18, ESRC Centre for Business Research, University of Cambridge.

Cox, D.R. (1972), 'Regression Models and Life Tables', *Journal of the Royal Statistical Society*, Series B, pp. 187-220.

Crapp, H., and M. Stevenson (1987), 'Development of a Method to Assess the Relevant Variables and the Probability of Financial Distress', *Australian Journal of Management*, pp. 221-236.

Cready, W.M. (1992), 'A Comment on the Proper Use of Residuals in Patell's Squared Unexpected Return Statistic', *Accounting Review*, pp. 212-215.

Cressey, R., and D. Storey (1995), 'New Firms and Their Bank', National Westminster Bank: London.

Dambolena, I.G. (1983), 'The Prediction of Corporate Failure', *Omega,* pp. 355-364.

-------------------- and S.J. Khoury (1980), 'Ratio Stability and Corporate Failure', *Journal of Finance,* pp. 1017-1026.

Deakin, E.B. (1972), 'A Discriminant Analysis of Predictors of Business Failure', *Journal of Accounting Research,* pp. 167-179.

--------------- (1976), 'Distribution of Financial Ratios: Some Empirical Evidence,' *Accounting Review*, pp. 90-96.

-------------- (1977), 'Business Failure Prediction:  An Empirical Analysis' in 'Financial Crises: Institutions and Markets in a Fragile Environment', ed. E.A. Altman and A. Sametz, John Wiley: New York, pp. 72-88.

DeAngelo, H., and L. DeAngelo (1990), 'Dividend Policy and Financial Distress: An Empirical Investigation of Troubled NYSE Firms', *Journal of Finance*, pp. 1415-1431.

-------------------------------------- and D. J. Skinner (1994), 'Accounting Choice in Troubled Companies', *Journal of Accounting and Economics*, pp. 113-143.

DeBondt, W.F.M., and R.H. Thaler (1985), 'Does the Stock Market Overreact?', *Journal of Finance*, pp. 793-805.

----------------------------------------- (1987), 'Further Evidence on Investor Overreaction and Stock Market Seasonality', *Journal of Finance*, pp. 557-581.

DeLong, B.J., A. Schleifer, L.H. Summers and R.J. Waldmann (1990), 'Positive Feedback Investment Strategies and Destabilizing Rational Speculation', *Journal of Finance*, pp. 379-396.

Demski, J.S., and G.A. Feltham (1994), 'Market Response to Financial Reports', *Journal of Accounting and Economics*, pp. 3-40.

Denis, D.J., and D.K. Denis (1995), 'Performance Changes Following Top Management Dismissals', *Journal of Finance*, pp. 1029-1057.

Dev, S., (1974), 'Ratio Analysis and the Prediction of Company Failure' in 'Debits, Credits, Finance and Profits', ed. H.C. Edey and B.S. Yamey, Sweet and Maxwell: London, pp. 61-74.

Dhrymes, P. (1974), 'Econometrics', Springer-Verlag: New York.

Diamond, D.W., and R.E. Verrecchia (1987), 'Constraints on Short-Selling and Asset Price Adjustment to Private Information', *Journal of Financial Economics*, pp. 277-311.

Diamond, H. jr. (1976), 'Pattern Recognition and the Detection of Corporate Failure', Ph.D dissertation, New York University.

Dietrich, J.R., and R.S. Kaplan (1982), 'Empirical Analysis of the Commercial Loan Classification Decision', *Accounting Review*, pp. 18-38.

Dimson, E., and P. Marsh (1989), 'Cases in Corporate Finance', Wiley: Chichester.

Dodgson, J.S. (1982), 'Kinks and Catastrophes: A Note on the Relevance of Catastrophe Theory for Economics', *Australian Economic Papers*, pp. 407-415.

Donnelly, R., and M. Walker (1995), 'Share Price Anticipation of Earnings and the Effect of Earnings Persistence and Firm Size', *Journal of Business Finance and Accounting*, pp. 5-18.

Doukas, J. (1986), 'Bankers Versus Bankruptcy Prediction Models: An Empirical Investigation, 1979-82', *Applied Economics*, pp. 479-493.

Dow, J., and G. Gorton (1994), 'Arbitrage Chains', *Journal of Finance*, pp. 819-849.

Dunne, P., and A. Hughes (1994), 'Age, Size, Growth and Survival: UK Companies in the 1980s', *Journal of Industrial Economics*, pp. 115-140.

Easterbrook, F.H. (1990), 'Is Corporate Bankruptcy Efficient?', *Journal of Financial Economics*, pp. 411-417.

Easton, P. D., T. S. Harris and J. A. Ohlson (1992), 'Aggregate Accounting Returns Can Explain Most of Security Returns', *Journal of Accounting and Economics*, pp. 119-142.

Edmister, R.O. (1971), 'Financial Ratios and Credit Scoring for Small Business Loans', *Journal of Commercial Bank Lending*, September, pp. 10-23.

----------------- (1972), 'An Empirical Test of Financial Ratio Analysis for Small Business Failure Prediction', *Journal of Financial and Quantitative Analysis*, pp. 1477-1493.

Eisenbeis, R.A. (1977), 'Pitfalls in the Application of Discriminant Analysis in Business Finance and Economics', *Journal of Finance*, pp. 875-900.

Egginton, D.A. (1977), 'Accounting for the Banker', Longmans: London.

Elam, R. (1975), 'The Effect of Lease Data on the Predictive Ability of Financial Ratios', *Accounting Review*, pp. 25-43.

El Hennawy, R.H.A. (1981), 'Predicting Corporate Failure: An Evaluation of the Relative Usefulness of UK Accounting and Share Price Information', Ph. D dissertation, University of Liverpool.

------------------------ and R.C. Morris (1983a), 'The Significance of Base Year in Developing Failure Prediction Models', *Journal of Business Finance and Accounting*, pp. 209-223.

--------------------------------------------- (1983b), 'Market Anticipation of Corporate Failure in the UK', *Journal of Business Finance and Accounting*, pp. 359-372.

Engle, R.F., and V.K. Ng (1993), 'Measuring and Testing the Impact of News on Volatility', *Journal of Finance,* pp. 1749-1778.

Eyssell, T.H. (1991), 'Corporate Insiders and the Death of the Firm: Evidence on the Incidence of Insider Trading in Corporate Dissolutions', *The Financial Review*, pp. 517-533.

Ezzamel, M., J. Brodie and C. Mar-Molinero (1987), 'Financial Patterns of UK Manufacturing Companies', *Journal of Business Finance and Accounting*, pp. 519-536.

-------------- and C. Mar-Molinero (1990), 'The Distributional Properties of Financial Ratios in UK Manufacturing Companies', *Journal of Business Finance and Accounting*, pp. 1-29.

--------------------------------------------- and A. Beecher (1987), 'On the Distributional Properties of Financial Ratios', *Journal of Business Finance and Accounting*, pp. 463-481.

Falbo, P. (1991), 'Credit-Scoring by Enlarged Discriminant Models', *Omega*, pp. 275-289.

Fama, E.F. (1991), 'Efficient Capital Markets: II', *Journal of Finance,* pp. 1575-1617.

----------, L. Fisher, M.C. Jensen and R. Roll (1969), 'The Adjustment of Stock Prices to New Information', *International Economic Review*, pp. 1-21.

---------- and K.R. French (1988), 'The Cross-Section of Expected Stock Returns', *Journal of Finance*, pp. 427-465.

------------------------------- (1993), 'Common Risk Factors in the Returns on Stocks and Bonds', *Journal of Financial Economics*, pp. 3-56.

------------------------------- (1995), 'Size and Book-to-Market Factors in Earnings and Returns', *Journal of Finance,* pp. 131-155.

------------------------------- (1996), 'Multifactor Explanations of Asset Pricing Anomalies' *Journal of Finance,* pp. 55-84.

Fieldsend, S., N. Longford and S. McLeay (1987), 'Industry Effects and the Proportionality Assumption in Ratio Analysis: A Variance Component Analysis', *Journal of Business Finance and Accounting*, pp. 497-517.

Firth, M. (1978), 'Qualified Audit Reports: Their Impact on Investment Decisions', *Accounting Review*, pp. 642-650.

Fisher, L. (1959), 'Determinants of Risk Premiums on Corporate Bonds', *Journal of Political Economy*, pp. 212-237.

Fitzpatrick, P.J. (1932), 'A Comparison of Ratios of Successful Industrial Enterprises with those of Failed Firms', *Certified Public Accountant,* pp. 598-605, 656-662, 727-731.

Fletcher, D., and E. Goss (1993), 'Forecasting with Neural Networks: An Application Using Bankruptcy Data', *Information and Management*, pp. 159-167.

Forsyte, R., T.R. Palfrey and C.R. Plott (1982), 'Asset Valuations in an Experimental Market', *Econometrica*, pp. 537-567.

Foster, G. (1978), 'Financial Statement Analysis', (1st ed.), Prentice-Hall: Englewood Cliffs, NJ.

Foulke, R.A. (1968), 'Practical Financial Statement Analysis', McGraw-Hill: New York.

Frazier, K.B., R.W. Ingram and B.M. Tennyson (1984), 'A Methodology for the Analysis of Narrative Accounting Disclosures', *Journal of Accounting Research*, pp. 318-331.

Frydman, H., E.I. Altman and D. Kao (1985), 'Introducing Recursive Partitioning for Financial Classification: The Case of Financial Distress', *Journal of Finance*, pp. 269-291.

Gentry, J.A., P. Newbold and D.T. Whitford (1985), 'Classifying Bankrupt Firms with Funds Flow Components', *Journal of Accounting Research*, pp. 146-159.

-------------------------------------------------------- (1987), 'Funds Flow Components, Financial Ratios, and Bankruptcy', *Journal of Business Finance and Accounting*, pp. 595-606.

Geroski, P.A. (1995), 'What Do We Know About Entry?', *International Journal of Industrial Organisation*, pp. 421-440.

Gilbert, L.R., K. Menon and K.B. Schwartz (1990), 'Predicting Bankruptcy for Firms in Financial Distress', *Journal of Business Finance and Accounting*, pp. 161-171.

Gilson, S.C. (1989), 'Management Turnover and Financial Distress', *Journal of Financial Economics*, pp. 241-262.

-------------- (1990), 'Bankruptcy, Boards, Banks, and Blockholders: Evidence on Changes in Corporate Ownership and Control when Firms Default', *Journal of Financial Economics*, pp. 355-387.

------------ and M.R. Vetsuypens (1993), 'CEO Compensation in Financially Distressed Firms: An Empirical Analysis', *Journal of Finance*, pp. 425-458.

Gleick, J. (1988), 'Chaos', Cardinal: London.

Gombola, M.J., and J.E. Ketz (1983), 'A Note on Cash Flow and Classification Patterns of Financial Ratios', *Accounting Review*, pp. 105-114.

-------------, M.E. Haskins, J.E. Ketz and D.D. Williams, 'Cash Flow in Bankruptcy Prediction', *Financial Management*, pp. 55-65.

Gooi, H. (1974), 'Share Prices and Financial Ratios – Prediction of Bankruptcy', master's dissertation, The City University Business School (London, November 1974).

Goudie, A.W. (1987), 'Forecasting Corporate Failure: The Use of Discriminant Analysis within a Disaggregated Model of the Corporate Sector', *Journal of the Royal Statistical Society,* Series A, Part 1, pp. 69-81.

-------------- and G. Meeks (1982), 'The Effects of Macroeconomic Developments on Individual Companies' Flows of Funds', *Omega*, pp. 361-371.

Granger, C.W.J. (1989), 'Combining Forecasts – Twenty Years Later', *Journal of Forecasting*, pp. 167-173.

Gregory, A., J. Matatko, I. Tonks and R. Purkis (1994), 'UK Directors' Trading: The Impact of Dealings in Smaller Firms', *Economic Journal*, pp. 37-53.

Griffiths, I. (1986), 'Creative Accounting', Unwin Hyman: London.

Grinyer, P.H., D.G. Mayes and P. McKiernan (1988), 'Sharpbenders', Basil Blackwell: Oxford.

Grossman, S. J., and J. Stiglitz (1980), 'On the Impossibility of Informationally Efficient Markets', *American Economic Review*, pp. 393-408.

Gupta, Y.P., R.P. Rao and P.K. Bagchi (1990) 'Linear Goal Programming as an Alternative to Multivariate Discriminant Analysis: A Note' *Journal of Business Finance and Accounting*, pp. 593-598.

Hamada, R.S. (1969), 'Portfolio Analysis, Market Equilibrium and Corporation Finance', *Journal of Finance*, pp. 13-31.

Hambrick, D.C., and R.A. D'Aveni (1988), 'Large Corporate Failures as Downward Spirals', *Administrative Science Quarterly*, pp. 1-23.

------------------------------------------------ (1992), 'Top Team Deterioration as Part of the Downward Spiral of Large Corporate Bankruptcies', *Management Science*, pp. 1445-1466.

Hamer, M. (1983), 'Failure Prediction: Sensitivity of Classification Accuracy to Alternative Statistical Methods and Variable Sets', *Journal of Accounting and Public Policy*, pp. 289-307.

Hand, J.R.M. (1990), 'A Test of the Extended Functional Fixation Hypothesis', *Accounting Review*, pp. 740-763.

Harcourt, G.C. (1965), 'The Accountant in a Golden Age', *Oxford Economic Papers*, pp. 66-80.

Haugen, R.H., and J.L. Pappas (1971), 'Equilibrium in the Pricing of Capital Assets, Risk Bearing Debt Instruments, and the Question of Optimal Capital Structure', *Journal of Financial and Quantitative Analysis*, pp. 943-953.

Hawley, D.D., J.D. Johnson and D. Raina (1990), 'Artificial Neural Systems: A New Tool for Financial Decision Making', *Financial Analysts Journal*, November-December, pp. 63-72 (reprinted in Trippi and Turban, 1993, pp. 27-46).

Hay, D.A., and D.J. Morris (1991), 'Industrial Economics and Organisation', (2nd ed.), Oxford University Press: Oxford.

Ho, T., and A. Saunders (1980), 'A Catastrophe Model of Bank Failure', *Journal of Finance*, pp. 1189-1207.

Holden, K., and D.A. Peel (1989), 'Unbiasedness, Efficiency and the Combination of Economic Forecasts', *Journal of Forecasting*, pp. 175-188.

Hopwood, W., J.C. McKeown and J.F. Mutchler (1989), 'A Test of the Incremental Explanatory Power of Opinions Qualified for Consistency and Uncertainty', *Accounting Review*, pp. 28-48.

Horrigan, J.O. (1966), 'The Determination of Long Term Credit Standing with Financial Ratios', *Journal of Accounting Research, Supplement on Empirical Research in Accounting*, pp. 44-62.

Hotchkiss, E.S. (1995), 'Postbankruptcy Performance and Management Turnover', *Journal of Finance*, pp. 3-21.

Houghton, K.A. (1984), 'Accounting Data and the Prediction of Business Failure: The Setting of Priors and the Age of Data', *Journal of Accounting Research*, pp. 361-368.

Hudson, J. (1987), 'The Age, Regional and Industrial Structure of Company Liquidations', *Journal of Business Finance and Accounting*, pp. 199-213.

Ijiri, Y. (1967), 'The Foundation of Accounting Measurement', Prentice-Hall: Englewood Cliffs, N.J.

Iselin, E.R. (1991), 'Individual Versus Group Decision-Making Performance: A Further Investigation of Two Theories in a Bankruptcy Prediction Task', *Journal of Business Finance and Accounting*, pp. 191-208.

Jegadeesh, N., and S. Titman (1993), 'Returns to Buying Winners and Selling Losers: Implications for Stock Market Efficiency', *Journal of Finance*, pp. 65-91.

Jensen, H. L. (1992), 'Using Neural Networks for Credit Scoring', *Managerial Finance*, vol. 18, no. 6, pp. 15-26.

John, K. (1993), 'Managing Financial Distress and Valuing Distressed Securities: A Survey and a Research Agenda', *Financial Management*, (Financial Distress Special Issue, Autumn), pp. 60-78.

Johnson, W.B. (1978), 'The Cross Sectional Stability of Financial Patterns', *Journal of Business Finance and Accounting*, pp. 207-214.

------------------ (1979), 'The Cross Sectional Stability of Financial Ratio Patterns', *Journal of Financial and Quantitative Analysis*, pp. 1035-1048.

Johnson, C.G. (1970), 'Ratio Analysis and the Prediction of Firm Failure', *Journal of Finance*, pp. 1166-1168.

Jones, F.L. (1987), 'Current Techniques in Bankruptcy Prediction', *Journal of Accounting Literature*, pp. 131-164.

Jones, M.J., and P.A. Shoemaker (1994), 'Accounting Narratives: A Review of Empirical Studies of Content and Readability', *Journal of Accounting Literature*, pp. 142-184.

Jovanovic, B. (1982), 'Selection and the Evolution of Industry', *Econometrica*, pp. 649-670.

Joy, O.H., and J.O. Tollefson (1975), 'On the Financial Implications of Discriminant Analysis', *Journal of Financial and Quantitative Analysis*, pp. 723-739.

Kaplan, R.S., and R. Roll (1972), 'Investor Evaluation of Accounting Information', *Journal of Business*, pp. 225-257.

------------------ and G. Urwitz (1979), 'Statistical Models of Bond Ratings: A Methodological Inquiry', *Journal of Business*, pp. 231-261.

Karels, G.V., and A.J. Prakash (1987), 'Multivariate Normality and Forecasting of Business Bankruptcy', *Journal of Business Finance and Accounting*, pp. 573-593.

Karson, M.J., and T.F. Martell (1980), 'On the Interpretation of Individual Variables in Multiple Discriminant Analysis', *Journal of Financial and Quantitative Analysis*, pp. 211-217.

Kassab, J., S. McLeay and N. Shani (1991), 'Forecasting Bankruptcy: Failure Prediction or Survival Analysis?', paper delivered at the European Accounting Congress, Maastricht, April 1991.

Kasznik, R., and B. Lev (1995), 'To Warn or Not to Warn: Management Disclosures in the Face of An Earnings Surprise', *Accounting Review*, pp. 113-134.

Katz, S., S. Lilien and B. Nelson (1985), 'Stock Market Behaviour Around Bankruptcy Model Distress and Recovery Predictions', *Financial Analysts Journal* (Jan-Feb), pp. 70-73.

Kay, J.A. (1976), 'Accountants, too, Could be Happy in a Golden Age: The Accountant's Rate of Profit and the Internal Rate of Return', *Oxford Economic Papers*, pp. 447-460.

Keasey, K., and P. McGuinness (1990), 'The Failure of UK Industrial Firms for the Period 1976-1984, Logistic Analysis and Entropy Measures', *Journal of Business Finance and Accounting*, pp. 119-135.

--------------, P. McGuinness and H. Short (1990), 'Multilogit Approach to Predicting Corporate Failure – Further Analysis and the Issue of Signal Consistency', *Omega*, pp. 85-94.

--------------, and R. Watson (1986), 'Current Cost Accounting and the Prediction of Small Company Performance', *Journal of Business Finance and Accounting*, pp. 51-70.

---------------------------------- (1987), 'Non-Financial Symptoms and the Prediction of Small Company Failure: A Test of Argenti's Hypotheses', *Journal of Business Finance and Accounting,* pp. 335-354.

---------------------------------- (1988), 'The Non-Submission of Accounts and Small Business Failure Prediction', *Accounting and Business Research*, pp. 47-54.

---------------------------------- (1991), 'Financial Distress Prediction Models: A Review of Their Usefulness', *British Journal of Management*, pp. 89-102.

Keeble, D., and S. Walker (1993), 'New Firms, Small Firms and Dead Firms: Spatial Patterns and Determinants in the United Kingdom', Working Paper 36, Small Business Research Centre, Department of Applied Economics, University of Cambridge.

Kennedy, P. (1992), 'A Guide to Econometrics', 3rd ed., Blackwell: Oxford.

Ketz, J. (1978), 'The Effect of General Price-Level Adjustments on the Predictability of Financial Ratios', *Journal of Accounting Research, Supplement on Empirical Research in Accounting*, pp. 273-284.

Khanna, N., and A.B. Poulsen (1995), 'Managers of Financially Distressed Firms: Villains or Scapegoats?', *Journal of Finance*, pp. 919-940.

Kharbanda, O.P., and E.A. Stallworthy (1985), 'Corporate Failure: Prediction, Panacea and Prevention', McGraw-Hill: New York.

Kida, T. (1980), 'An Investigation into Auditors' Continuity and Related Qualification Judgments', *Journal of Accounting Research*, pp. 506-523.

Kiefer, N.M. (1988), 'Economic Duration Data and Hazard Functions', *Journal of Economic Literature*, pp. 646-679.

Kim, O., and R.E. Verrecchia (1991a), 'Trading Volume and Price Reactions to Public Announcements', *Journal of Accounting Research*, pp. 302-321.

------------------------------------ (1991b), 'Market Reaction to Anticipated Announcements', *Journal of Financial Economics*, pp. 273-309.

---------------------------------- (1994), 'Market Liquidity and Volume Around Earnings Announcements', *Journal of Accounting and Economics*, pp. 41-67.

Koch, B.S. (1981), 'Income Smoothing: An Experiment', *Accounting Review*, pp. 574-586.

Koh, H.C., and L.N. Killough (1990), 'The Use of Multiple Discriminant Analysis in the Assessment of the Going-Concern Status of an Audit Client', *Journal of Business Finance and Accounting*, pp. 179-192.

Korobow, L., and D. Stuhr (1985), 'Performance Measurement of Early Warning Models', *Journal of Banking and Finance,* pp. 267-273.

Kothari, S.P. (1992), ''Price-Earnings Regressions in the Presence of Prices Leading Earnings', *Journal of Accounting and Economics*, pp. 173-202.

--------------- and R. J. Taffler (1996), 'Z-scores and Excess Returns: A Stock Market Anomaly?', paper presented at the INQUIRE Autumn Seminar, Bath, 29 September 1996.

Laitinen, F.K. (1991), 'Financial Ratios and Different Failure Processes', *Journal of Business Finance and Accounting*, pp. 649-673.

---------------- (1993), 'Financial Predictors for Different Phases in the Failure Process', *Omega*, pp. 215-228.

---------------- (1994), 'Traditional Versus Operating Cash Flow in Failure Prediction', *Journal of Business Finance and Accounting*, pp. 195-217.

Lane, W.R., S.W. Looney and J.W. Wansley (1986), 'An Application of the Cox Proportional Hazards Model to Bank Failure', *Journal of Banking and Finance*, pp. 511-531.

Largay, J.A., and C.P. Stickney (1980), 'Cash Flows, Ratio Analysis and the W.T. Grant Company Bankruptcy', *Financial Analysts Journal,* July/August, pp. 51-54.

Lasfer, M.A., P.S. Sudarsanam and R.J. Taffler (1994), 'Financial Distress, Asset Sales and Lender Monitoring', Discussion Paper, City University Business School, November.

Lau, A.H. (1987), 'A Five-State Financial Distress Model', *Journal of Accounting Research*, pp. 127-138.

Lawrence, E.C. (1983), 'Reporting Delays for Failed Firms', *Journal of Accounting Research*, pp. 606-610.

--------------- and R.M. Bear (1986), 'Corporate Bankruptcy Prediction and the Impact of Leases', *Journal of Business Finance and Accounting*, pp. 571-586.

Letza, S.R. (1994), 'Issues in Assessing MDA Models of Corporate Failure: A Supporting Research Note', *British Accounting Review*, pp. 281-286.

Lev, B. (1969a), 'Accounting and Information Theory', Studies in Accounting Research No. 2, American Accounting Association: Sarasota, Florida.

--------- (1969b), 'Industry Averages as Targets for Financial Ratios', *Journal of Accounting Research*, pp. 290-299.

--------- (1971), 'Financial Failure and Informational Decomposition Measures' in R.R. Sterling and W.F. Bentz (eds.), 'Accounting in Perspective: Contributions to Accounting Thought by Other Disciplines', Southwestern: Cincinnati, Ohio, pp. 102-111.

--------- (1974), 'Financial Statement Analysis: A New Approach', Prentice-Hall: Englewood Cliffs, N.J.

--------- and S.R. Thiagarajan (1993), 'Fundamental Information Analysis', *Journal of Accounting Research*, pp. 190-215.

Levis, M. (1989), 'Stock Market Anomalies: A Re-assessment Based on the UK Evidence', *Journal of Banking and Finance*, pp. 675-696.

Libby, R. (1975), 'Accounting Ratios and the Prediction of Failure: Some Behavioural Evidence', *Journal of Accounting Research*, pp. 150-161.

------------ (1981), 'Accounting and Human Information Processing: Theory and Applications', Englewood Cliffs, N.J. : Prentice-Hall.

------------ K.T. Trotman and I. Zimmer (1987), 'Member Variation, Recognition of Expertise, and Group Performance', *Journal of Applied Psychology*, pp. 1-5.

Lo, A.W. (1986), 'Logit Versus Discriminant Analysis: A Specification Test and Application to Corporate Bankruptcies', *Journal of Econometrics*, pp. 151-178.

London Business School (1987), 'A Study to Determine the Reasons for Failure of Small Businesses in the UK', Stoy Hayward/National Westminster Bank: London.

Luoma, M., and E.K. Laitinen (1991), 'Survival Analysis as a Tool for Company Failure Prediction', *Omega*, pp. 673-678.

Maddala, G. S. (1988), 'Introduction to Econometrics', Collier Macmillan: London.

Makeever, D.A. (1984), 'Predicting Business Failures', *Journal of Commercial Bank Lending*, pp. 14-18.

Marais, D.A.J. (1979), 'A Method of Quantifying Companies' Relative Financial Strengths', Bank of England Discussion Paper No. 4: London.

Marais, M., J. Patell and M. Wolfson (1984), 'The Experimental Design of Classification Models: An Application of Recursive Partitioning and Bootstrapping to Commercial Bank Loan Classifications', *Journal of Accounting Research, Supplement on Current Econometric Issues in Accounting Research*, pp. 87-118.

Mar-Molinero, C., and M. Ezzamel (1991), 'Multidimensional Scaling Applied to Corporate Failure', *Omega*, pp. 259-274.

Martin, D. (1977), 'Early Warning of Bank Failure: A Logit Regression Approach', *Journal of Banking and Finance,* pp. 249-276.

Mason, R.J., and F.C. Harris (1979), 'Predicting Company Failure in the Construction Industry', *Proceedings of the Institution of Civil Engineers,* Part I, pp. 71-79.

Mata, J., and P. Portugal (1994), 'Life Duration of New Firms', *Journal of Industrial Economics,* pp. 227-245.

Mattessich, R. (1964), 'Accounting and Analytical Methods', Richard D. Irwin: Homewood, Ill.

McDonald, B., and M.H. Morris (1984), 'The Statistical Validity of the Ratio Method of Financial Analysis: An Empirical Examination', *Journal of Business Finance and Accounting,* pp. 89-97.

----------------------------------------- (1985), 'The Functional Specification of Financial Ratios: An Empirical Examination', *Accounting and Business Research,* pp. 223-228.

McKeown, J.C., J.F. Mutchler and W. Hopwood (1991), 'Towards an Explanation of Auditor Failure to Modify the Audit Opinion of Bankrupt Companies', *Auditing, Supplement,* pp. 1-13.

McLeay, S. (1986), 'Student's t and the Distribution of Financial Ratios', *Journal of Business Finance and Accounting,* pp. 209-222.

------------- and S. Fieldsend (1987), 'Sector and Size Effects in Ratio Analysis – An Indirect Test of Ratio Proportionality', *Accounting and Business Research,* pp. 133-140.

McNichols, M. (1988), 'A Comparison of the Skewness of Stock Return Distributions at Earnings and Non-Earnings Announcement Dates', *Journal of Accounting and Economics,* pp. 239-273.

-------------------- and B. Trueman (1994), 'Public Disclosure, Private Information Collection and Short Term Trading', *Journal of Accounting and Economics,* pp. 69-94.

Mendenhall, R.R. (1991), 'Evidence on the Possible Underweighting of Earnings-Related Information', *Journal of Accounting Research,* pp. 170-179.

Menon, K., and K. Schwartz (1987), 'An Empirical Investigation of Audit Qualification Decisions in the Presence of Going Concern Uncertainties', *Contemporary Accounting Research,* Spring, pp. 302-315.

Mensah, Y. (1983), 'The Differential Bankruptcy Predictive Ability of Specific Price Level Adjustments: Some Empirical Evidence', *Accounting Review,* pp. 228-246.

------------- (1984), 'An Examination of the Stationarity of Multivariate Bankruptcy Prediction Models: A Methodological Study', *Journal of Accounting Research,* pp. 380-395.

Messier, W.F. jr., and J.V. Hansen (1988), 'Inducing Rules for Expert System Development: An Example Using Default and Bankruptcy Data', *Management Science,* pp. 1403-1415.

Meyer, P.A., and H.W. Pifer (1970), 'Prediction of Bank Failures', *Journal of Finance,* pp. 553-568.

Modigliani, F., and R. Cohn (1979), 'Inflation, Rational Valuation and the Market', *Financial Analysts Journal,* March/April, pp. 24-44.

------------------ and M. Miller (1958), 'The Cost of Capital, Corporation Finance, and the Theory of Investment', *American Economic Review,* pp. 261-297.

Moriarty, S. (1979), 'Communicating Financial Information Through Multi-dimensional Graphics', *Journal of Accounting Research,* pp. 205-224.

Morris, R.C., and P. Ormrod (1990), 'The Attitudes of Credit Analysts towards Reduced Disclosure by Small Companies', Discussion Paper no. 5, Accounting and Business Finance Series, Department of Economics and Accounting, University of Liverpool.

Moyer, R.C. (1977), 'Forecasting Financial Failure: A Re-examination', *Financial Management,* pp. 11-15.

Mutchler, J.F. (1985), 'A Multivariate Analysis of the Auditor's Going-Concern Opinion Decision', *Journal of Accounting Research,* pp. 668-682.

Nelson, R., and D. Clutterbuck (1988), 'Turnaround', Mercury Books: London.

Nogler, G.E. (1995), 'The Resolution of Auditor Going Concern Opinions', *Auditing,* Fall, pp. 54-73.

Noreen, E. (1988), 'An Empirical Comparison of Probit and OLS Regression Hypothesis Tests', *Journal of Accounting Research,* pp. 119-133.

Norton, C.L., and R.E. Smith (1979), 'A Comparison of General Price Level and Historical Cost Financial Statements in the Prediction of Bankruptcy', *Accounting Review,* pp. 72-86.

O'Brien, P.C., and R. Bhushan (1990), 'Analyst Following and Institutional Ownership', *Journal of Accounting Research: Supplement,* pp. 55-76.

Odom, M.D., and R. Sharda (1990), 'A Neural Network Model for Bankruptcy Prediction', *Proceedings of the International Joint Conference on Neural Networks,* II, pp. 163-167 (reprinted in Trippi and Turban, 1993, pp. 177-186).

O'Hanlon, J.F., and P.F. Pope (1996), 'Does Dirty Surplus Accounting Conceal the Facts?', Accounting and Finance Working Paper 96/005, The Management School, Lancaster University.

Ohlson, J.A. (1980), 'Financial Ratios and the Probabilistic Prediction of Bankruptcy', *Journal of Accounting Research,* pp. 109-131.

Ou, J.A., and S.H. Penman (1989), 'Financial Statement Analysis and the Prediction of Stock Returns', *Journal of Accounting and Economics,* pp. 295-329.

Palepu, K.G. (1986), 'Predicting Takeover Targets – A Methodological and Empirical Analysis', *Journal of Accounting and Economics,* pp. 3-25.

Pastena, V., and W. Ruland (1986), 'The Merger/Bankruptcy Alternative', *Accounting Review,* pp. 288-301.

Patell, J.M. (1976), 'Corporate Forecasts of Earnings Per Share and Stock Behaviour: Empirical Tests', *Journal of Accounting Research,* pp. 246-276.

Peel, M.J. (1987), 'Timeliness of Private Company Accounts and Predicting Corporate Failure', *The Investment Analyst*, January, pp. 23-27.

------------ (1989), 'The Going-Concern Qualification Debate: Some UK Evidence', *British Accounting Review*, pp. 329-350.

------------ (1990), 'The Liquidation/Merger Alternative', Avebury: Aldershot.

------------ and D.A. Peel (1987), 'Some Further Empirical Evidence on Predicting Private Company Failure', *Accounting and Business Research*, pp. 57-66.

------------------------------ (1988), 'A Multilogit Approach to Predicting Corporate Failure – Some Evidence for the UK Corporate Sector', *Omega*, pp. 309-318.

------------------------------ and P.F. Pope (1985), 'Some Evidence on Corporate Failure and the Behaviour of Non-Financial Ratios', *The Investment Analyst*, January, pp. 3-7.

------------------------------------------------------ (1986), 'Predicting Corporate Failure: Some Results for the UK Corporate Sector', *Omega*, pp. 5-12.

------------ and N. Wilson (1989), 'The Liquidation/Merger Alternative: Some Results for the UK Corporate Sector', *Managerial and Decision Economics*, pp. 209-220.

Pettway, R.H. (1980), 'Potential Insolvency, Market Efficiency, and Bank Regulation of Large Commercial Banks', *Journal of Financial and Quantitative Analysis,* pp. 219-236.

Piesse, J., and D. Wood (1992), 'Issues in Assessing MDA Models of Corporate Failure: A Research Note', *British Accounting Review*, pp. 33-42.

Pinches, G., K. Mingo and J. Caruthers (1973), 'The Stability of Financial Patterns in Industrial Organisations,' *Journal of Finance*, pp. 389-96.

-------------, A. Eubank, K. Mingo and J. Caruthers (1975), 'The Hierarchical Classification of Financial Ratios,' *Journal of Business Research,* pp. 295-310.

Pindyk, R.S., and D.L. Rubinfeld (1976), 'Econometric Models and Economic Forecasts', McGraw-Hill Kogakusha: Tokyo.

Pope, P.F., R.C. Morris and D.A. Peel (1990), 'Insider Trading: Some Evidence on Market Efficiency and Directors' Share Dealings in Great Britain', *Journal of Business Finance and Accounting*, pp. 359-380.

Pratt, J., and J.D. Stice (1994), 'The Effects of Client Characteristics on Auditor Litigation Risk Judgments, Required Audit Evidence, and Recommended Audit Fees', *Accounting Review*, pp. 639-656.

Pratten, C. (1991), 'Corporate Failure', Institute of Chartered Accountants in England and Wales: London.

Queen, M., and R. Roll (1987), 'Firm Mortality: Using Market Indicators to Predict Survival', *Financial Analysts Journal*, May-June, pp. 9-26.

Ro, B., C.V. Zavgren and S-J. Hsieh (1992), 'The Effect of Bankruptcy on Systematic Risk of Common Stock: An Empirical Assessment', *Journal of Business Finance and Accounting*, pp. 309-328.

Ronen, J., and S. Sadan (1981), 'Smoothing Income Numbers', Addison-Wesley: Reading, Mass.

Rose, P., W. Andrews and G. Giroux (1982), 'Predicting Business Failure A Macroeconomic Perspective', *Journal of Accounting, Auditing and Finance,* Fall, pp. 20-31.

Ross, J.E., and M.J. Kami (1973), 'Corporate Management in Crisis', Prentice-Hall: Englewood Cliffs, N.J.

Raghunandan, K., and D.V. Rama (1995), 'Audit Reports for Companies in Financial Distress: Before and After SAS No. 59', *Auditing,* Spring, pp. 50-63.

Salchenberger, L., E. Cinar and N. Lash (1992), 'Neural Networks: A New Tool for Predicting Thrift Failures', *Decision Sciences,* pp. 899-916 (reprinted in Trippi and Turban, 1993 [see below], pp. 229-254).

Santomero, A., and J. Vinso (1977), 'Estimating the Probability of Failure for Firms in the Banking System', *Journal of Banking and Finance,* pp. 185-215.

Scapens, R., R. Ryan and L. Fletcher (1981), 'Explaining Corporate Failure : A Catastrophe Approach', *Journal of Business Finance and Accounting,* pp. 1-26.

Schrieves, R.E., and D.L. Stevens (1979), 'Bankruptcy Avoidance as a Motive for Mergers', *Journal of Financial and Quantitative Analysis,* pp. 501-515.

Scott, E. (1978), 'On the Financial Applications of Discriminant Analysis: A Comment', *Jounal of Financial and Quantitative Analysis,* pp. 201-205.

Scott, J. (1981), 'The Probability of Bankruptcy: A Comparison of Empirical Predictions and Theoretical Models', *Journal of Banking and Finance,* pp. 317-344.

Schendel, D., G.R. Patton and J.C. Riggs (1976), 'Corporate Turnaround Strategies', *Journal of General Management,* pp. 3-11.

Schrieves, R.E., and D.L. Stevens (1979), 'Bankruptcy Avoidance as a Motive for Mergers', *Journal of Financial and Quantitative Analysis,* pp. 501-515.

Schwartz, K., and K. Menon (1985), 'Auditor Switches by Failed Firms', *Accounting Review,* pp. 248-261.

Shannon, H.A. (1954), 'The Limited Companies of 1866-1883', in 'Essays in Economic History', ed. E.M. Carus-Wilson, vol. I, Edward Arnold: London, pp. 380-405.

Siegel, S. (1956), 'Nonparametric Statistics', McGraw-Hill Kogakusha: Tokyo.

Sinkey, J. jr. (1975), 'A Multivariate Statistical Analysis of the Characteristics of Problem Banks,' *The Journal of Finance,* pp. 21-36.

Skinner, D.J. (1994), 'Why Firms Voluntarily Disclose Bad News', *Journal of Accounting Research,* pp. 38-60.

Skogsvik, K. (1990), 'Current Cost Accounting Ratios as Predictors of Business Failure: The Swedish Case', *Journal of Business Finance and Accounting,* pp. 137-160.

Slatter, S.P. (1984), 'Corporate Recovery: Successful Turnaround Strategies and their Implementation', Penguin Books: Harmondsworth, Middlesex.

Smith, M., and R.J. Taffler (1984), 'Improving the Communication Function of Published Accounting Statements', *Accounting and Business Research,* pp. 139-146.

-------------------------------- (1992), 'The Chairman's Statement and Corporate Financial Performance', *Accounting and Finance*, pp. 75-90.

Smith, R.A. (1966), 'Corporations in Crisis', Doubleday: New York.

Smith, T. (1992), 'Accounting for Growth: Stripping the Camouflage from Company Accounts', Century Business: London.

------------ (1996), 'Accounting for Growth: Stripping the Camouflage from Company Accounts', 2nd ed., Century Business: London.

So, J. (1987), 'Some Empirical Evidence on the Outliers and the Non-normal Distribution of Financial Ratios', *Journal of Business Finance and Accounting*, pp. 483-496.

Solomon, E. (1966), 'Return on Investment: The Relation of Book Yields to True Yield', in 'Research in Accounting Measurement', ed. R.K. Jaedicke, Y. Ijiri and O. Nielsen, American Accounting Association: Sarasota, Fla.

Soper, F.J., and R. Dolphin jr. (1964), 'Readability and Corporate Annual Reports', *Accounting Review*, pp. 358-362.

Stamp, E., and C. Marley (1970), 'Accounting Principles and the City Code: The Case for Reform', Butterworths: London.

Stewart, I. (1989), 'Does God Play Dice?', Penguin Books: Harmondsworth.

Stiglitz, J. (1969), 'A Re-examination of the Modigliani-Miller Theorem', *American Economic Review*, pp. 784-793.

------------- (1972), 'Some Aspects of the Pure Theory of Corporate Finance: Bankruptcies and Takeovers', *The Bell Journal of Economics and Management Science*, pp. 458-482.

------------- (1974), 'On the Irrelevance of Corporate Financial Policy', *American Economic Review*, pp. 851-866.

Still, M.D. (1972), 'The Readability of Chairman's Statements', *Accounting and Business Research*, pp. 36-39.

Stone, M., and J. Rasp (1991), ' Tradeoffs in the Choice Between Logit and OLS for Accounting Choice Studies', *Accounting Review*, pp. 170-187.

-------------------------- (1993), 'The Assessment of Predictive Accuracy and Model Overfitting: An Alternative Approach', *Journal of Business Finance and Accounting*, pp. 125-131.

Storey, J., K. Keasey, R. Watson and P. Wynarczyk (1987), 'The Performance of Small Firms', Croom-Helm: Bromley.

Strong, N. (1992), 'Modelling Abnormal Returns: A Review Article', *Journal of Business Finance and Accounting*, pp. 533-553.

Sutherland, A. (1965), 'Economics in the Restrictive Practices Court', *Oxford Economic Papers*, pp. 385-431.

Taffler, R.J. (1977), 'Finding Those Firms in Danger Using Discriminant Analysis and Financial Ratio Data: A Comparative UK Based Study', Working Paper No. 3, City University Business School.

------------ (1982), 'Forecasting Company Failures in the U.K. using Discriminant Analysis and Financial Ratio Data', *Journal of the Royal Statistical Society*, Series A, Part 3, pp. 342-358.

------------ (1983), 'The Assessment of Company Solvency and Performance Using a Statistical Model: A Comparative UK Based Study', *Accounting and Business Research*, pp. 295-308.

------------ (1984), 'Empirical Models for the Monitoring of U.K. Corporations', *Journal of Banking and Finance*, pp. 199-227.

------------ (1994), 'The Use of the Z-Score Approach in Practice', Discussion Paper, Centre for Empirical Research in Finance and Accounting: City University Business School, London.

------------ and P.S. Sudarsanam (1980), 'Auditing the Board: A New Approach to the Measurement of Company Performance', *Managerial Finance*, pp.127-147.

------------ and H.J.Tisshaw (1977), 'Going, Going, Gone – Four Factors Which Predict', *Accountancy*, March, pp. 50-54.

------------ and M. Tseung (1984), 'The Audit Going Concern Qualification in Practice – Exploding Some Myths', *The Accountant's Magazine*, pp. 263-269.

Tam, K.Y. (1991), 'Neural Network Models and the Prediction of Bank Bankruptcy', *Omega*, pp. 429-445.

Tamari, M. (1965), 'Financial Ratios as a Means of Forecasting Bankruptcy', *Management International Review*, pp. 15-21.

------------ (1978), 'Financial Ratios: Analysis and Prediction', Paul Elek: London.

Tennyson, B.M., R.W. Ingram and M.T. Dugan (1990), 'Assessing the Information Content of Narrative Disclosures in Explaining Bankruptcy', *Journal of Business Finance and Accounting*, pp. 391-410.

Theobald, M., and R. Thomas (1982), 'Time Series Properties of Liquidating Company Equity Returns', *Journal of Banking and Finance*, pp. 495-505.

Tisshaw, H.J. (1976), 'Evaluation of Downside Risk Using Financial Ratios', M.Sc. thesis, City University Business School, London (discussed in Taffler, 1984, p. 203).

Trippi, R.R., and E. Turban (eds.) (1993), 'Neural Networks in Finance and Investing', Probus: Chicago, Ill.

Trueman, B. (1990), 'On the Incentives for Security Analysts to Revise their Earnings Forecasts', *Contemporary Accounting Research*, pp. 203-222.

------------ (1994), 'Analyst Forecasts and Herding Behaviour', *Review of Financial Studies*, pp. 97-124.

Vinso, J.D. (1979), 'A Determination of the Risk of Ruin', *Journal of Financial and Quantitative Analysis*, pp. 77-100.

Wadhwani, S.B. (1984a), 'Inflation, Bankruptcy, Default Premia and the Stock Market', Centre for Labour Economics, London School of Economics, Discussion Paper No. 194.

------------------ (l984b), 'Inflation, Bankruptcy and Employment', Centre for Labour Economics, London School of Economics, Discussion Paper No. 195.

Wagner, J. (1994), 'The Post-Entry Performance of New Small Firms in German Manufacturing Industries', *Journal of Industrial Economics*, pp. 141-154.

Walker, M.C., J.D. Stow and S. Moriarty (1979), 'Decomposition Analysis of Financial Statements', *Journal of Business Finance and Accounting*, pp. 173-186.

Ward, T.J. (1994), 'An Empirical Study of the Incremental Predictive Ability of Beaver's Naive Operating Cash Flow Measure Using Four-State Ordinal Models of Financial Distress', *Journal of Business Finance and Accounting*, pp. 547-561.

------------, and B.P. Foster (1996), 'An Empirical Analysis of Thomas's Financial Accounting Allocation Fallacy Theory in a Financial Distress Context', *Accounting and Business Research*, pp. 137-152.

Weiss, L.A. (1990), 'Bankruptcy Resolution: Direct Costs and Violation of Priority of Claims', *Journal of Financial Economics*, pp. 285-314.

West, R.R. (1970), 'An Alternative Approach to Determining Corporate Bond Ratings', *Journal of Accounting Research*, pp. 118-125.

West, R.C. (1985), 'A Factor Analysis Approach to Bank Condition', *Journal of Banking and Finance*, pp. 253-266.

Westerfield, R. (1970), 'Pre-Bankruptcy Stock Price Performance', working paper, University of Pennsylvania, Fall 1970 (reported in Altman, 1971, pp. 80-81; and Foster, 1978, pp. 492-493).

Whittington, G., (1979), 'On the Use of the Accounting Rate of Return in Empirical Research', *Accounting and Business Research*, pp. 201-208.

------------------ (1980), 'Some Basic Properties of Accounting Ratios', *Journal of Business Finance and Accounting*, pp. 219-232.

Whittred, G., and I. Zimmer (1984), 'Timeliness of Financial Reporting and Financial Distress', *Accounting Review*, pp. 287-295.

----------------------------------- (1985), 'The Implications of Distress Prediction Models for Corporate Lending', *Accounting and Finance,* pp. 1-13.

Wilcox, J. (1971), 'A Simple Theory of Financial Ratios as Predictors of Failure', *Journal of Accounting Research,* pp. 389-395.

------------ (1973), 'A Prediction of Business Failure Using Accounting Data', *Journal of Accounting Research: Supplement on Empirical Research in Accounting,* pp. 163-190.

Wilson, N., K.S. Chong and M.J. Peel (1995), 'Neural Network Simulation and the Prediction of Corporate Outcomes: Some Empirical Findings', *International Journal of the Economics of Business,* pp. 31-50.

Wood, D., and J. Piesse (1985), 'Higgledy Piggledy Bankruptcy', Working Paper, Manchester Business School.

---------------------------- (1987), 'The Information Value of MDA Based Financial Indicators', *Journal of Business Finance and Accounting,* pp. 27-38.

------------------------------ (1988), 'The Information Value of Failure Predictions on Credit Assessment', *Journal of Banking and Finance*, pp. 275-292.

Wynn, R.F.K. (1993), 'Qualifying Sovereign Credit Ratings: A Reappraisal of Statistical Sovereign Risk Models', *Savings and Development*, pp. 237-257.

Zavgren, C.Y. (1983) 'The Prediction of Corporate Failure: The State of the Art', *Journal of Accounting Literature*, pp. 1-38.

--------------- (1985), 'Assessing the Vulnerability to Failure of American Industrial Firms: A Logistic Analysis', *Journal of Business Finance and Accounting*, pp. 19-45.

--------------- M.T. Dugan and J.M. Reeve (1988), 'The Association Between Probabilities of Bankruptcy and Market Responses – A Test of Market Anticipation', *Journal of Business Finance and Accounting*, pp. 27-45.

Zimmer, I. (1980), 'A Lens Study of the Prediction of Corporate Failure by Bank Loan Officers', *Journal of Accounting Research*, pp. 629-639.

Zmijewski, M. (1984), 'Methodological Issues Related to the Estimation of Finance Distress Prediction Models', *Journal of Accounting Research, Supplement on Current Econometric Issues in Accounting Research*, pp. 59-82.

# Glossary

**Abnormal Performance Index.** A method of aggregating a **time series** (*q.v.*) of security returns for a **cross section** (*q.v.*) of companies. (See chapter 6).

**Agency theory.** An economic theory concerning the explicit and/or implicit contractual relationship between *principals* (e.g. shareholders) and their *agents* (e.g. company directors and managers). In particular, attention is focused on *agency costs* (i.e. the opportunity costs of principals having to try to monitor the activities of their agents: e.g. through an audit, or by providing incentive structures which reduce the need for such monitoring).

**Analysis sample.** A sample of data from which a statistical model is estimated. The model is often subsequently tested for robustness on another **hold out sample** (*q.v.*).

**Anecdotal evidence.** Evidence not gathered or analysed in a systematic or scientific way, but rather reflecting *casual empiricism* (i.e. a general impression of an underlying relationship between variables).

**Annuity.** A constant stream of cash flows which, over a finite period, can be compounded forward as a **sinking fund** (*q.v.*) to produce a terminal value. Such a terminal value can be discounted to its beginning (present) value equivalent. An annuity which goes on forever is known as a **perpetuity** (*q.v.*).

**API.** Abnormal Performance Index (*q.v.*).

**AR.** Average Residual return or Average Return. The average return for a **cross sectional** (*q.v.*) portfolio of securities. (A residual return is where the expected rate of return has been factored out of the reported rate of return.)

**Arbitrage pricing theory.** A security valuation theory, which is an alternative to the **capital asset pricing model** (*q.v.*), but with less demanding assumptions/requirements (e.g. it is a disequilibrium rather than an equilibrium model). Arbitrage refers to the process whereby securities are purchased and others simultaneously sold to give a risk-free profit, thus offsetting the risk in a **speculative portfolio** (*q.v.*) by investing in a **hedge portfolio** (*q.v.*). (See p. 78.)

**Artificial intelligence.** An attempt to replicate human thought processes on a computer using sequential **iterative processes** (*q.v.*). (See p. 158.)

**Barriers to entry.** Barriers which to a greater or lesser extent prevent new companies entering an industry and so limit competition. (See pp. 59-60.)

**Bias.** A systematic and persistent type of error which will not tend to be cancelled out. *Cf. sampling errors*, which over a period of time or with a large number of observations, can be expected to cancel each other out.

**Binary choice.** A choice between two states (e.g. fail/non-fail). See **dichotomous variables** (*q.v.*).

**Bivariate models.** These models have one **dependent variable** (*q.v.*) and one **independent variable** (*q.v.*). Such models are sometimes referred to, somewhat confusingly, as **univariate models** (*q.v.*), since attention is usually focused on the explanatory variables on the right hand side of an equation (e.g. in a **regression model** (*q.v.*)). (*Cf.* **multivariate models** (*q.v.*).)

**Black box model.** A model where it is only possible to identify the inputs and outputs. What goes on inside the black box cannot readily be seen.

**Bond ratings.** A rating accorded to government and corporate bonds (i.e. long term debt) by financial service companies (such as Moody's and Standard & Poor's in the US). The ratings are usually measured on an ordinal ranking scale, with (under Moody's notation) Aaa the best and C the worst.

**Capital asset pricing model (CAPM).** A model of security valuation which is based on the notion that at a moment in time in a highly competitive market (such as that for shares) prices should be explicable only in terms of market related or **systematic risk** (*q.v.*). Any residual element can only be explained in terms of firm-specific factors, which across the market can be expected to arise on an unanticipated, random basis. The key **independent variables** (*q.v.*) are the risk-free return (e.g. on a government bond) and the return on the (equilibrium) market portfolio of risky securities (generally proxied by a share price index). See p. 74 et seq.

**Capital rationing.** A shortage of funds that forces a company to choose between investment projects which have positive net present values and which are not mutually exclusive. This frequently arises in practice as even listed companies cannot raise fresh equity capital as and when they need it because of high issuing costs. Moreover, borrowing in the short term in order to bridge the gap can be an expensive alternative.

**CAPM.** $\underline{C}$apital $\underline{A}$sset $\underline{P}$ricing $\underline{M}$odel (*q.v.*).

**CAR.** $\underline{C}$umulative $\underline{A}$verage $\underline{R}$esidual (*q.v.*).

**Catastrophe theory.** A theoretical framework for analysing how disequilibria in a system arise as a result of extraneous shocks. (See p. 54 et seq.)

**Centroid points.** The focus of interest in **discriminant analysis** (*q.v.*), the points being located by maximising the ratio of between-groups to within-groups **variances** (*q.v.*).

**CEO.** Chief executive officer. A acronym commonly used in the US to refer to the person who (in the UK) is generally designated as the *managing director*.

**Chaos theory.** A theoretical framework for analysing how disequilibria in a system arise as a result of extraneous shocks. (See p. 54.)

**Chernoff faces.** Graphs in the form of cartoon faces which capture the salient features of a company's financial position.

**Chi square test.** A frequently used statistical test, for which tables are widely published.

**Choice based sampling.** This refers to the situation where the researcher determines the proportions of subjects (such as failed and non-failed companies) which are represented in the sample that is the subject of analysis. This can introduce a **sampling bias** (*q.v.*) as the population being studied is not selected on a random basis. Sometimes referred to as **state based sampling** (*q.v.*).

**Classificatory smoothing. Profit smoothing** (*q.v.*) achieved as a result of classifying expenses and/or revenues in a particular way (e.g. by taking them direct to reserves without going through the profit and loss account; or, if analysts' interest is thought not to be focused on the bottom line profit figure, treating them as extraordinary items).

**Clean surplus accounting.** Where an all-inclusive income statement is prepared (e.g. so that even asset revaluations are recorded in it rather than being adjusted directly on reserves). See also **dirty surplus accounting** (*q.v.*).

**Clienteles of shareholders.** Constituencies of shareholders with certain reasonably well defined common interests (e.g. pension schemes are interested in dividend rather than capital gains income as they can recover tax imputed to be borne by dividends).

**Coefficient of variation.** A measure of variance.

**Confidence level.** This measures the probability of an observation being in the extreme tails of a **normal distribution** (*q.v.*). The standard test is that there is a 95% probability that an observation will lie outside the extreme tails; or, alternatively, only a 5% chance that it will lie within those tails.

**Constant.** The **intercept** (*q.v.*) term in a linear equation.

**Contracting theory.** See **agency theory** (*q.v.*).

**Cost drivers.** As part of **value chain** (*q.v.*) (the purpose of which is to enable a firm's competitive advantage over its rivals to be assessed), it is necessary to study the cost characteristics of each component activity. This should make it possible to identify the key *cost drivers* which are critical in a company's operations.

**Covariance.** A measure of the extent to which variables (such as the returns on a share and the market index, say) move together.

**Criterion variable.** See **dependent variable** (*q.v.*).

**Cross sectional analysis.** An analysis at a given point or for a specific period in time of differences in a cross sectional sample (e.g. of companies).

**Cumulative Average Residual.** A method of aggregating a **time series** (*q.v.*) of security returns for a **cross section** (*q.v.*) of companies. (See chapter 6.)

**Data driven models.** See **data mining** (*q.v.*).

**Data mining.** Analysing data with little or no underlying theory in the hope of finding statistically significant relationships.

**Debt covenant.** A contract between a lender and a borrower, which usually contains clauses restricting the freedom of action of the borrower.

**Degrees of freedom.** The distributional properties of a sample are unlikely to be precisely the same as for the entire population. In order to allow for this an adjustment is made when calculating significance test statistics which makes it more likely that a **null hypothesis** (*q.v.*) will be rejected. Generally, the number of degrees of freedom will be greater the larger the number of explanatory variables, and the more difficult it will be to reject the null hypothesis.

**Dependent variable.** A variable, Y, changes in which are determined by changes in an **independent variable** (*q.v.*), X. The relationship is defined in terms of a **constant** (*q.v.*), a, and a **slope coefficient** (*q.v.*), b, in the equation $Y = a + bX$. Also known as the **criterion variable** (*q.v.*).

**Dichotomous variables.** Variables which are measured on a rank ordering scale coded, for instance, as 0 and 1: e.g. with respect to a **dependent variable** (*q.v.*), *failed* versus *non-failed*; and an **independent variable** (*q.v.*), a company's membership of the services as opposed to the manufacturing sector, where the procedure employed is described as creating a **dummy variable** (*q.v.*).

**Differentiated products.** Products which are made distinct by a company from its rivals' (e.g. by branding, etc).

**Dirty surplus accounting.** This refers to situations where certain gains and losses (e.g. on foreign exchange translations and asset revaluations) are debited/credited directly to reserves rather than put through the income statement. See **clean surplus accounting** (*q.v.*).

**Discriminant analysis.** A statistical procedure for analysing data, commonly applied where there is a **dichotomous** (*q.v.*) **dependent variable** (*q.v.*). The technique differs from **regression analysis** (*q.v.*) in as much as it is based on minimising the variance of groups of data from a **centroid point** (*q.v.*) and maximising the distance between those points. (See p. 133 et seq.)

**Distribution free:** i.e. there is no assumption that observations are **normally distributed** (*q.v.*) around the average.

**Downward spiralling.** A tendentious phrase used by some researchers to indicate the path to bankruptcy experienced by companies which go bankrupt.

**Dummy variable.** A **qualitative variable** (*q.v.*) that can be handled in a **regression** (*q.v.*) or **discriminant model** (*q.v.*) by treating it as a **dichotomous variable** (*q.v.*). (See p. 121.)

**Duration models.** The **dependent variable** (*q.v.*) in these **regression** (*q.v.*) based models is *survival* time (hence their alternative designation as *survival models*). (See p. 141 et seq.)

**Dynamic programming.** An **iterative procedure** (*q.v.*) for solving a problem where there are defined sequences of events. Such models can therefore be used to analyse the management of inventories and debtors.

**Efficient market.** An informationally efficient market is one in which asset (security) prices immediately reflect news. See also **weak-form efficiency** (*q.v.*), **semi-strong form efficiency** (*q.v.*) and **strong-form efficiency** (*q.v.*).

**Empirically based research.** Research based on observed phenomena rather than on abstract theory. Usually it involves systematic statistical analysis of data, testing various hypotheses to see whether or not observed relationships could occur by chance.

**Entropy theory.** A theoretical framework for analysing how disequilibria in a system arise as a result of extraneous shocks. It is generally closely associated with **informational decomposition analysis** (*q.v.*). (See pp. 57 et seq.; 85 et seq.)

**Epoch.** A pass through the data set in **neural networking** (*q.v.*). Also called a **training cycle** (*q.v.*). (See p. 159 et seq.)

*Ex ante*. Before the event, expected.

**Expense preferencing.** Where managers choose to spend a company's money in ways which more closely reflect their own objectives/preferences rather than those of the shareholders/owners.

*Ex post*. After the event.

**External validity.** The validity of a relationship which appears to be supported when statistical tests are applied. However, the relationship may be invalid if the setting which is modelled to identify a cause-and-effect linkage is unrealistic. This gives rise to an **inference error** (*q.v.*). An example would be where analysts are asked to rank two companies in terms of their expected future earnings. The answers they might give to a questionnaire or in a laboratory experiment might well not accord with the conclusions they would draw in practice when decisions – with substantial sums of money at stake – might be based on their answers; and/or when they would refer to far more information than is available on the questionnaire or in the laboratory experiment. *Cf.* **internal validity** (*q.v.*).

**F statistic.** A measure of the explanatory power of a regression equation where there is more than one **independent variable** (*q.v.*). It tests to see whether the **null hypothesis** (*q.v.*) that the true regression coefficients are all zero can be rejected. Normally any value above 6 indicates that the regression equation is significant at the 95% **confidence level** (*q.v.*).

**Factor analysis.** A statistical technique which identifies commonalities between variables. (*Cf.* **principal components analysis** (*q.v.*)). The extent of the commonality is often referred to in terms of the factor **loadings** (*q.v.*), which indicates the correlation between a factor and a variable.

**Five forces model.** Michael Porter's model which identifies five key factors which will determine a company's overall strategy. These are: rivalry among existing competitors; threat of new entrants; bargaining power of customers; threat of substitute products; bargaining power of suppliers.

**Gambler's ruin model.** A sequential model based on the possibility that a gambler (or company) can lose cash period after period. However the probability that a losing sequence will continue should become smaller and smaller. (See p. 65 et seq.)

**Game theory.** A theory based on the notion of games in which one player or group of players wins at the expense of another. In its simplest form, models based on the theory are concerned with how a given value is shared out between participants, giving rise to the notion of a *zero-sum game*. The solution to game theory models depends on the objectives/strategies pursued by the players, which can either be relatively straightforward or be made complex (e.g. where there are *mixed strategies*).

**General equilibrium analysis.** The study both of the behaviour of economic variables taking account of the interaction between them and the rest of the economy; and of simultaneous equilibria in a group of related markets. It contrasts with partial equilibrium analysis, where only part of the system is examined, other things being held constant.

**Generic strategies.** Strategies selected from a limited set of options based on systematic study of the firm and the industry conditions it faces. Porter identifies three such strategies (cost leadership, differentiation and focus), but these have been developed by other writers (e.g. Mintzberg).

**Hazard function.** A function in a **duration model** (*q.v.*) which measures the probability of failure in the next instant, given that the person, firm, etc, was alive at a given time.

**Hedge portfolio.** A portfolio of securities which should offset the risk in a **speculative portfolio** (*q.v.*). See **arbitrage pricing theory** (*q.v.*).

**Heteroscedasticity.** Where the error terms in a regression are not randomly distributed, implying that a systematic factor (or omitted variable) has not been captured in the estimated model. (*Cf.* **homoscedasticity** (*q.v.*).)

**Heuristic procedures.** Discovery, search, or adaptive procedures.

**Hold out sample.** Another sample besides the **analysis (or experimental) sample** (*q.v.*) used to test how well a statistical model fits data. Such samples can be **cross sectional** (*q.v.*) or intertemporal.

**Homeostasis.** A phenomenon, well known in the biological sciences, whereby systems naturally seem to revert towards a new equilibrium following an external 'disturbance'.

**Homoscedasticity.** Where the error terms in a regression are randomly distributed (i.e. a requirement of the procedure). (*Cf.* **heteroscedasticity** (*q.v.*).)

**Imperfect markets.** Where one or more of the conditions for a **perfect market** (*q.v.*) do not hold (which will generally be the case to a greater or lesser extent).

**Independent variable.** A variable, X, changes in which determine changes in a **dependent variable** (*q.v.*), Y. The relationship is defined in terms of a **constant** (*q.v.*), a, and a **slope coefficient** (*q.v.*), b, in the equation $Y = a + bX$.

**Inference errors.** Effectively jumping to conclusions which may not be justified when the evidence is more carefully analysed. (See **internal validity** (*q.v.*) and **external validity** (*q.v.*).)

**Information asymmetry.** Inequality of information as between individuals (e.g. as between managers and shareholders). This can lead to **market failure** (*q.v.*) and can be countered by external regulation (e.g. through the law) and/or by private contracting. (See **agency theory** (*q.v.*).)

**Informational decomposition measures.** A procedure for measuring changes in structure (e.g. within a company's balance sheet). (See chapter 2, appendix 2.1.)

**Intercept.** The **constant** (*q.v.*) term in a linear equation: i.e. a in the equation $Y = a + bX$.

**Internal validity.** The validity of a relationship which appears to be supported when statistical tests are applied. However, the relationship may be invalid if (say) a variable is omitted or there is some other *misspecification* in the model purporting to identify a cause-and-effect linkage. This gives rise to an **inference error** (*q.v.*). (*Cf.* **External validity** (*q.v.*).)

**Intertemporal smoothing. Profit smoothing** (*q.v.*) achieved by shifting revenues and/or expenses backwards or forwards in time. *Real smoothing* is where the timing of cash inflows and outflows is manipulated. Otherwise intertemporal smoothing is achieved by changing the basis of accounting. The general characteristic of intertemporal smoothing is that increases (decreases) in profit in one period are made at the expense of decreases (increases) in profit in other periods.

**Interval scale.** A measurement where the assigned numbers allow comparison of the size of differences among and between items. (See **nominal scale** (*q.v.*).)

**Intrinsic value model.** A model for valuing a security by discounting the future expected cash flows associated with its ownership. The cash flows are generally proxied by projected dividend or earnings streams.

**Iterative process.** A sequential process, usually identified by a search procedure (or algorithm).

**Jackknife procedure.** A procedure for testing a model. The latter is estimated on n-1 companies' data and can then be used to classify the missing company.

**Junk bonds.** High risk debt securities with high yields and/or coupon rates.

**Learning curve.** A function which shows how a factor input (usually labour hours) declines as the volume of output increases. The curve is often represented as a logarithmic function, although in practice more complex relationships are found to hold, varying from industry to industry. Generally the *learning curve* phenomenon is taken to apply *over time*. Where *in a single period* a particular input is expected to decline proportionately as output is increased, the phenomenon is known as *increasing returns to scale*, which is reflected in the **production function** (*q.v.*).

**Least squares.** The usual procedure for fitting a line to observations in a **regression model** (*q.v.*) is *ordinary* least squares. However, there are circumstances when other procedures, such as *weighted* least squares, are appropriate.

**Left censoring.** Where the data for developing a **duration model** (*q.v.*) are incomplete in terms of their past history. (See p. 145.)

**Lens model.** A framework used for analysing cause-and-effect relationships in experiments in behavioural psychology. (See p. 185.)

**Leverage.** Gearing. Financial leverage refers to the ratio of debt to equity and/or the burden of interest payments. Operating leverage refers to the proportion of (operating) fixed costs to variable costs.

**Likelihood Ratio (LR).** When the dependent variable in a regression equation is dichotomous (e.g. where the **logit model** (*q.v.*) is applied), it is more appropriate to use the LR than the **F statistic** (*q.v.*). Because there is no standard upper limit to the **log likelihood** (*q.v.*) statistic, it has to be assessed against the estimated maximum in order to generate the LR test. This is done by comparing the unrestricted LL estimate for a model against the LL value of the function where all the coefficients are restricted to zero. The LR coefficient can then be tested as a chi square statistic with **degrees of freedom** (*q.v.*) equal to the number of **independent variables** (*q.v.*) (excluding a **constant** (*q.v.*)).

**Linear programming.** A technique for finding the maximum or minimum value of an equation (the *objective function*) which is subject to specified linear constraints. The approach is a natural development of break even analysis where there is more than one potentially limiting factor. The model can also be used to analyse complex **capital rationing** (*q.v.*) situations.

**Loading.** See **factor analysis** (*q.v.*).

**Logit regression.** A type of **regression model** (*q.v.*) where the **dependent variable** (*q.v.*) measures the logarithm of the odds. This means that the dependent variable can be interpreted as indicating the probability of an event occurring. (See p. 123 et seq.)

**Log-likelihood (LL) statistic.** This coefficient is derived using non-linear techniques to estimate where a function is most likely to plot. Unlike the $R^2$ statistic, this ratio is not bounded by values 0 and 1, although (like the $R^2$ coefficient) the higher the value the greater the explanatory power of the model.

**Loss function.** The **utility function** (*q.v.*) of an individual forecasting a future likely outcome.

**Mann Whitney U test.** A **non-parametric** (*q.v.*) statistical test used to see whether a particular ranking of observations could have occurred by chance.

**MAR.** M̲arket A̲verage R̲esidual. Also known as the 'zero-one' model, where the return on a security is modelled as moving in lockstep with returns on the market portfolio of risky assets. In other words, in terms of the **Simple Market**

Model (SMM) (*q.v.*) (a version of **the Capital Asset Pricing Model (CAPM)** (*q.v.*)), the alpha (**intercept** (*q.v.*)) is zero and the beta (**slope coefficient** (*q.v.*)) is one. For a large **cross section** (*q.v.*) of companies the errors should cancel out.

**Market failure.** Where the market mechanism cannot by itself ensure that the economic welfare of society as a whole is maximised. This can be countered by government intervention (e.g. through legislation). It is a particular problem in securities markets where **information asymmetry** (*q.v.*) is a major problem. This provides some justification for the existence of companies legislation, and in particular statutory disclosure requirements for companies' annual accounts.

**Market microstructure.** The institutional environment within which a market operates (e.g. involving legal and other restrictions).

**Market model.** Effectively the **capital asset pricing model** (*q.v.*), which implies that in equilibrium it should be possible to explain security prices only in terms of the returns on a risk free asset and the market portfolio of risky assets.

**Market structure.** Why a few companies dominate some industries, while in others there is far less concentration of power.

**Matched pairing.** A procedure used in constructing a **choice based sample** (*q.v.*) in order to control for certain common characteristics (e.g. firm size, industry membership, etc).

**Maximum likelihood estimates.** These are based on non-linear techniques which estimate where a function is most likely to plot.

**MDA.** Multiple discriminant analysis (*q.v.*).

**Mean.** The *average*. (See **moments of a distribution** (*q.v.*).)

**Mean reverting.** Moving back towards the **mean** (*q.v.*) over time, e.g. downwards when above, upwards when below. The observed pattern is therefore an *oscillation* around the underlying average value.

**Misclassification costs.** The (opportunity) costs to a decision maker of misclassifying a bankrupt company as non-failed and/or a non-failed company as failed.

**Moments (of a distribution).** These measure the properties of a distribution of a sample of observations (e.g. to see whether it is **normally distributed** (*q.v.*) or not). Thus the *first moment* is the **mean** (*q.v.*), the second the **variance/standard deviation** (*q.v.*) (measuring dispersion), the third the degree of *skewness*, and the fourth *kurtosis* (indicating how peaked the distribution is).

**Multicollinearity.** Where two or more **independent variables** (*q.v.*) are highly correlated with each other.

**Multidimensional scaling.** A data reduction technique which involves *mapping* observations for variables (such as ratios). The results are similar to those derived using **factor analysis** (*q.v.*).

**Multi-person:** i.e. in a market setting where there are many potential buyers and/or sellers. (*Cf.* **single-person**, *q.v.*)

**Multivariate models.** Such models explain a **dependent variable** (*q.v.*) in terms of several **independent variables** (*q.v.*): e.g. failure/non-failure in terms of profitability, gearing levels, liquidity, industry membership, etc. (*Cf.* **bivariate models** (*q.v.*) and **univariate models** (*q.v.*).)

**Neural networking.** A computer based procedure employing **iterative processes** (*q.v.*) to determine relationships between **dependent** (*q.v.*) and **independent variables** (*q.v.*). It is based on the notion of **artificial intelligence** (*q.v.*) and can be regarded as a development of the **recursive partitioning** (*q.v.*) technique. (See p. 159 et seq.)

**Node.** The variable at the end of a branch in a tree diagram.

**Nominal scale variable.** A distinguishing label, such as the numbers on soccer players' shirts, which does not suggest that the player numbered 2 is superior to the player numbered 1 because it is greater (which would imply an *ordinal ranking scale* (*q.v.*)). Equally it does not imply that the player numbered 3 is three times as important to the team as the player numbered 1 (which would imply a *ratio* scale (*q.v.*)). A *ratio* scale is a special case of an **interval scale** (*q.v.*), where measurement is from a zero point. Thus a budget variance is calculated from the target budget figure: i.e. the size of the variance is measured in interval scale terms. However, the money amount is measured from a natural zero point.

**Non-parametric test.** A class of statistical significance tests which can be applied regardless of whether or not a population of observations is **normally distributed** (*q.v.*). They should be applied where the data are expressed in **nominal-** or **ordinal-scale** (*q.v.*) form; and to data expressed in **interval-** or **ratio-scale** (*q.v.*) form but where the necessary conditions for applying a **parametric test** (*q.v.*) are not present (e.g. where the distribution is not **normally distributed** (*q.v.*)).

**Non-response bias.** A potential bias arising with questionnaire surveys if the respondents are not representative of the population as a whole.

**Normal distribution.** The symmetric bell-shaped distribution that can be completely defined in terms of its **mean** (*q.v.*) (average) value and its **standard deviation** (*q.v.*).

**Normative theories.** Theories which attempt to explain *what ought to be* by applying deductive reasoning. (See p. 26.)

**Null hypothesis.** A hypothesis which has to be rejected statistically at a given **confidence level** (*q.v.*) if an empirically observed relationship is to be accepted as holding.

**One tailed test.** A statistical test used to detect departures from a **null hypothesis** (*q.v.*) in only one direction: i.e. it is only of interest if the error is (say) above a certain level, not whether it is above or below (which is where a **two tailed test** (*q.v.*) would be appropriate).

**Option pricing model.** A valuation model concerned with the pricing of *put* (sell) and *call* (purchase) options. (See pp. 64-5.)

**Ordinal scale.** See **nominal scale** (*q.v.*).

**Organic growth.** Growth resulting from the investment by a company of its own resources in expanding capacity rather than because of an acquisitions and mergers policy.

**Orthogonalise.** Where commonalities are eliminated (e.g. by regressing one variable onto another to remove the common element).

**Outliers.** Observations in a sample so different in magnitude from other observations that they are treated as special cases (e.g. they are excluded or given a reduced weighting).

**Overfitting.** Where a model fits exceptionally well on to the data from which it is derived, but far less well on to other data from a **hold out sample** (*q.v.*).

**Overtrading.** This generally refers to the expansion of sales and production without adequate financial support. This would not normally be a problem if there were not some degree of **capital rationing** (*q.v.*) – i.e. a business is unable for some reason to raise finance to support investment. This is more likely to be a problem for a small private company than for a listed one. The effect is usually that margins are cut in an effort to generate cash with which to pay off creditors, but this has the effect of lowering profits. The opposite of overtrading is **undertrading** (*q.v.*), where insufficient sales volume is generated: i.e. the contribution towards fixed costs is inadequate, producing losses or low levels of profit.

**p-value.** Assuming that the **null hypothesis** (*q.v.*) is true (i.e. the **independent variable** (*q.v.*) has no explanatory power), the p-value is the probability of obtaining a sample result which is at least as unlikely as that observed. Thus if the level of significance being tested is .05 and the p value is .01, the null hypothesis is rejected. Consequently, the lower the p value (i.e. the closer to zero), the greater the explanatory power of the independent variable. It thus moves in the opposite direction to the **t-statistic** (*q.v.*).

**Pairwise classifications.** The *prima facie* classifications as failed/non-failed for each pair of companies in a sample derived on a **matched pairing** (*q.v.*) basis.

**Parameter values.** A coefficient: e.g. a and b in Y = a + bX, where Y is the **dependent variable** (*q.v.*), X the **independent variable** (*q.v.*), a the **constant** (*q.v.*) and b the **slope coefficient** (*q.v.*).

**Parametric tests.** A class of statistical tests used where variables are measured applying an **interval scale** (*q.v.*). Such tests are often only valid where the data are **normally distributed** (*q.v.*). Where the necessary conditions are not met a **non-parametric test** (*q.v.*) should be used.

**Perfect markets.** Markets where there are no **transactions costs** (*q.v.*), no taxes, borrowing and lending rates of interest are the same, there are no **barriers to entry** (*q.v.*), and individuals behave rationally and have homogeneous (i.e. similar) expectations.

**Permanent earnings.** The sustainable part of a company's profit once the non-recurring (or exceptional) **transitory earnings** (*q.v.*) element has been factored out (extracted).

**Perpetuity.** An **annuity** (*q.v.*) cash stream which goes on forever.

**Pooling of data.** The practice whereby in order to create a reasonably sized **choice based sample** (*q.v.*) data have to be aggregated over time and/or across industries.

**Portfolio theory.** A theory showing the benefits of diversifying asset (security) holdings to maximise expected returns for a given exposure to risk. (See p. 71 et seq.)

**Positive theories.** Theories which attempt to explain *what is* through empirical observation. (See p. 26.)

**Post announcement drift.** A drift in share prices after a news announcement, implying that the market has not immediately absorbed the implications. It is therefore a *prima facie* violation of **semi-strong market efficiency** (*q.v.*).

**Predatory pricing.** A pricing strategy aimed at killing off competition (e.g. by effectively establishing a **barrier to entry** (*q.v.*)).

**Price elasticity.** Positive price elasticity implies that a cut in price will be more than compensated by an increase in the volume in sales so that overall total revenue increases.

**Principal components analysis.** A type of **factor analysis** (*q.v.*) which identifies commonalities between variables.

**Probit model.** A version of the **logit regression** model (*q.v.*).

**Profit improvement.** A short term strategy by managers to manipulate reported earnings, not implying a longer term *signalling strategy* (as with **profit smoothing** (*q.v.*)). Thus where a company is financially distressed, its managers may attempt to window dress profits (e.g. by capitalising R&D where previously it was expensed). However, such action – where it is observable by analysts – should put the market on its guard.

**Profit smoothing.** Where profits are manipulated to follow a smooth trend over time (the implication being that reported earnings should be seen to be following a specific growth path over time). Such manipulation (of which accrual accounting is the simplest form) can be regarded as one means whereby managers can *signal* their objectives to market analysts. It should be distinguished from **profit improvement** (*q.v.*).

**Production function.** The combination of inputs required to produce a given output.

**Proportional hazard model.** A type of **duration model** (*q.v.*). (See p. 143.)

**Pure expectations economy.** Where people trade on their estimates of the behaviour of other market participants (e.g. where there are speculative bubbles).

**Qualitative variable.** A variable not readily capable of measurement using a **ratio scale** (*q.v.*).

**r.** The correlation coefficient showing the relationship between two variables. $r = +1$ implies a perfect 1-to-1 relationship. $r = -1$ implies a perfect negative relationship. $r = 0$ implies there is no relationship between the variables.

**R²**. The square of the correlation coefficient (also known as the **coefficient of variation** (*q.v.*) or the coefficient of determination). It takes a value between 0 and 1, and it shows the proportion of the variability in a **dependent variable** (*q.v.*) which can be explained by the variability of one or more **independent variables** (*q.v.*).

**Ratio scale.** See **nominal scale** (*q.v.*).

**Recursive partitioning.** A procedure employing **iterative processes** (*q.v.*) which determines relationships between **dependent** (*q.v.*) and **independent variables** (*q.v.*). (See pp. 156-8.)

**Regression model.** A model which establishes the linear relationship between a **dependent variable** (*q.v.*) and one or more **independent variables** (*q.v.*) (*Cf.* **bivariate** (*q.v.*), **multivariate** (*q.v.*) and **univariate** (*q.v.*) **models**.) (See p. 116 et seq.)

**Right censoring.** Where the data for developing a **duration model** (*q.v.*) are incomplete inasmuch as surviving persons, firms, etc, will be expected to die or fail in a certain pattern in future periods. (See p. 145.)

**Risk free asset.** An asset, such as a gilt edged security, whose returns are uncorrelated with returns on the market portfolio of risky assets.

**Runs tests.** These examine the *direction* of price changes. For example, a sequence of price movements over six days which are all upwards can be represented as ++++++. Since there is no change of sign there is just one 'run'. If, however, there are increases in prices over the first two days, a decline on the third day, an increase on the fourth day, and declines on the fifth and sixth days, the pattern can be represented as ++-+--. Since there are four different sequences of the same sign there are four 'runs'. Clearly the fewer the number of 'runs', the greater the evidence of 'serial correlation'. Statistical tests based upon probability theory can show whether the observed number of 'runs' could have occurred by chance if the price changes are independent of each other.

**Sampling bias.** This arises where the sample which is the subject of analysis is not representative of the whole population (e.g. because there are inadequate controls for a potentially important characteristic, such as firm size, industry membership, etc). This can lead to **inference errors** (*q.v.*) when the results of statistical analysis are interpreted. (See **choice based sampling** (*q.v.*).)

**Scrip dividends.** A bonus issue of shares which does not involve a company in distributing cash to shareholders in the short term. In recent years many companies have offered shareholders the option of having cash or scrip dividends. One advantage to a company of issuing scrip is that it reduces the need to raise new equity and so helps to offset a **capital rationing** (*q.v.*) constraint.

**Search costs.** These comprise the costs of seeking out information. In economics, it is argued that in a competitive market analysts (or 'economic agents') will continue to search so long as the anticipated marginal benefits exceed the expected marginal costs.

**Semi-strong form market efficiency.** Where security prices instantaneously reflect (or 'impound') all publicly available information (such as news releases, earnings announcements, etc). This should hold when **search costs** (*q.v.*) and information processing costs are taken into account, and when there is active competition between analysts. (*Cf.* **weak-form market efficiency** (*q.v.*) and **strong-form market efficiency** (*q.v.*).)

**Sharpbenders.** Companies which have dramatically turned round a relative decline in performance to become industry leaders. (The term is coined to describe a graph of relative performance over time.)

**Short selling.** A situation where an investor sells a security without owning it, aiming to buy it later when the price has fallen to cover his/her position.

**Single person:** i.e. where there is no market setting and there are no other potential buyers and/or sellers. (*Cf.* **multi-person** (*q.v.*).)

**Sinking fund.** Technically a fund established to accumulate to a given amount in the future (e.g. to redeem a debt or to fund an asset replacement). However, in the context of compound interest it refers to the terminal value of an **annuity** (*q.v.*).

**Slope coefficient.** The **parameter value** (*q.v.*), b, which measures the proportionate response of the **dependent variable** (*q.v.*) Y to changes in the **independent variable** (*q.v.*) X, after allowing for a **constant** (*q.v.*), a, in the equation $Y = a + bX$.

**SMM.** Simple Market Model. A simplified form of the **Capital Asset Pricing Model** (*q.v.*). It shows that the return on an asset can be explained as a linear function of the return on the market portfolio of risky assets, allowing for an intercept. (See pp. 74-6.)

**Spatial analysis.** A method of analysis widely used by economic geographers in which location, distance and other qualitative factors are key variables.

**Speculative portfolio.** A portfolio of securities the risk of which should be offset by investing in a **hedge portfolio** (*q.v.*). (See **arbitrage pricing theory** (*q.v.*).)

**Standard deviation.** A measure of variance in a population, calculated as the square root of the **variance** (*q.v.*).

**Standard error.** The standard deviation around a fitted regression line, measuring the scatter of observations.

**SSAP 9.** Statement of Standard Accounting Practice No. 9 on the valuation of stocks and work-in-progress.

**State based sampling.** See **choice based sampling** (*q.v.*).

**Stepwise selection.** A sequential (or **iterative** (*q.v.*)) procedure for selecting **independent variables** (*q.v.*) for inclusion in a statistical model.

**Strong-form market efficiency.** Where security prices instantaneously reflect *all* information, including privately held (or 'privileged') information. In such a situation, where prices are 'fully revealing' no-one should be able to profit from having 'inside information'. (*Cf.* **semi-strong form market efficiency** (*q.v.*) and **weak-form market efficiency** (*q.v.*).)

**Surrogate.** A representation (e.g. an accounting number is a representational surrogate of an economic event). (See note 4, p. 111.)

**Survival models.** See **duration models** (*q.v.*). (See p. 141 et seq.)

**Survivor function.** A function in a **duration model** (*q.v.*) which measures the probability that a person, firm, etc, will survive longer than n months or years.

**Survivorship bias.** This refers to a **sampling bias** (*q.v.*) which arises because a proportion of the population being studied is eliminated through time (e.g. because of bankruptcy). Failure to take this into account can produce an **inference error** (*q.v.*).

**Synoptic model.** A basic model which summarises the key **independent variables** (*q.v.*) that appear to be driving the **dependent variable** (*q.v.*).

**Systematic risk.** Market related risk. See **Capital asset pricing model** (*q.v.*).

**t-statistic.** In a **regression model** (*q.v.*) this indicates whether the explanatory power of an **independent variable** (*q.v.*) is significantly different from zero. (Generally if the value is greater than 1.7 the variable is regarded as significant at the 95% **confidence level** (*q.v.*).) (See also **p-value** (*q.v.*).)

**Tax shield.** A reduction in a company's net cash outflows which results because an expense is tax deductible (e.g. interest on long term debt).

**Time series analysis.** An analysis of differences over time.

**TMT.** An acronym sometimes used to refer to the *top management team* in a company.

**Tobit model.** A version of the **logit regression** model (*q.v.*) which allows for censoring of data.

**Training cycle.** See **epoch** (*q.v.*).

**Training network.** The procedure used in **neural networking** (*q.v.*) to derive a model. It is an adaptive, learning procedure.

**Transactions costs.** Opportunity costs which result from trading, encompassing not only brokerage costs, commissions, etc, but also **search costs** (*q.v.*) and information processing costs.

**Transformation.** Of variables, such as ratios, so that their distributions approximate to **normality** (*q.v.*). Achieved by taking the logarithms or square roots of data, or by some other systematic conversion procedure.

**Transitory earnings.** The non-recurring (or exceptional) element of profit which, when factored out (or extracted), leaves sustainable **permanent earnings** (*q.v.*).

**Type I and II errors.** These are **inference errors** (*q.v.*). A Type I error is where a **null hypothesis** (*q.v.*) is rejected when it is true; a Type II error when a null hypothesis is accepted when it is false. In terms of bankruptcy studies, a Type I error is generally where a failed company is misclassified as non-failed, and a Type II error where a surviving company is falsely identified as bankrupt.

**Two tailed test.** A statistical test used to detect departures from a null hypothesis in both directions: i.e. it is of interest if the error is above or below a certain level, not whether it just varies in one direction (which is where a **one tailed test** (*q.v.*) would be appropriate).

**Undertrading.** This occurs where insufficient sales volume is generated and the contribution towards fixed costs is inadequate: i.e. losses or low levels of profit are reported. The opposite is **overtrading** (*q.v.*).

**Unfair game.** A fair game is one where each player has an equal chance of winning. An unfair game is where the odds are not equal.

**Univariate models.** Such models explain a **dependent variable** (*q.v.*) in terms of one **independent variable** (*q.v.*): e.g. failure/non-failure in terms of profitability. (*Cf.* **bivariate models** (*q.v.*) and **multivariate models** (*q.v.*).)

**Utility function.** A function measuring an individual's satisfaction or dissatisfaction in non-monetary terms. It is generally represented by economists as either a logarithmic or quadratic function. The former implies that satisfaction declines as quantity increases (e.g. on a hot day, for an individual eating ice creams the enjoyment will be less for each successive ice cream eaten, although it will still be a positive experience). By contrast a quadratic function implies that beyond a certain point the slope of the function is negative (i.e. the ice cream eater gets negative enjoyment from the marginal ice cream – for instance, because it will make him/her sick!).

**Value chain.** A method of analysis which breaks down the activities of a firm into its strategically relevant operations (e.g. purchases, different processes/activities, distribution, and support operations). In particular, it focuses on the sequence of a company's operations, which can be represented in a wedge shaped diagram, and on the value added at each activity. Such a procedure makes it possible to identify the comparative advantages and disadvantages of a business with respect to its competitors.

**Value drivers.** As part of **value chain** (*q.v.*) analysis, which enables managers to assess a business's competitive advantage, it is necessary to identify those revenue generating activities which create value (the *value drivers*).

**Variance.** A measure of dispersion around the mean. Its square root is the **standard deviation** (*q.v.*).

**Weak-form market efficiency.** Where security prices instantaneously reflect the history of past price movements so that the latter can have no predictive power. As a result prices, should follow a 'random walk' (i.e. there will be no observable trend), especially when systematic factors (such as inflation or general market wide movements) are factored out. (*Cf.* **semi-strong form market efficiency** (*q.v.*) and **strong-form market efficiency** (*q.v.*).)

**Weibull distribution.** A distribution used to develop **duration models** (*q.v.*) where the strict proportionality required by the Cox **proportional hazard model** (*q.v.*) is inappropriate. (See p. 143.)

# Subject index

Abnormal performance index (API) 176-9

abnormal variance of (share price) returns 174-5

accounting policies – changes in 230, 248-9, 254-8, 272-4

accounting year end date – changes in 230, 248-9, 254-8, 272-4

acquisitions – see 'mergers'

age of company 227

agency models 79-81

annual report, date of issue 248-9, 254-8, 272-4

arbitrage pricing theory (APT) 78

artificial intelligence models 158

audit qualifications 33, 233, 248-9, 254-8, 272-4, 323 et seq.

Bankruptcy risk 61-3

bankruptcy statistics 21, 222-3, 242

bivariate regression analysis 116-9

bond ratings – see 'credit ratings'

business strategy 82, 196 et seq., 235 et seq.

Capital asset pricing model (CAPM) 76-7, 170-1

case study research 195 et seq., 321 et seq.

cash flow analysis – see 'flow of funds analysis'; 'gambler's ruin'

catastrophe theory 54-6

chaos theory 54

charges, register of 231, 248-9, 254-8, 272-4

Chernoff faces – see 'multidimensional graphics'

concentration (industrial) 60

corporate governance, code on 35-6

creative accounting 212 et seq., 230 – see also 'accounting policies'

credit ratings 32, 231

cumulative average residuals (CARs) 176-9, 306 et seq.

Dichotomous regression analysis 122-3

directors – changes in board 228-9, 248-9, 254-8, 272-4

– remuneration
229, 248-9, 254-8, 272-4
– and going concern   34-5
– shareholdings and changes in
228-9, 248-9, 254-8
directors' report – publication lag
248-9, 272-4
– textual analysis   234
discriminant models   131-141
diversification   227
dividends   227
downward spiralling   202, 240
duration models – see 'survival models'

Empirical evidence
– discriminant models   135-141
– laboratory experiments   187-190
– logit models   127, 129, 131-2
– regression models   122-3
– share price behaviour of failing
companies   183-5
– using qualitative firm specific
indicators   232-3
entropy theory   57-9, 85-8, 128-9,
259-261; – see also 'informational
decomposition analysis'
entry characteristics of an industry
59-60
event dates   173, 306
event study methodology
168 et seq., 304 et seq.
event windows   254-8, 270, 272
exit characteristics of an industry   60
expanded logit models   127 et seq.

Factor analysis   205-6
'failure', meaning of   24
financial ratios   94 et seq., 204 et seq.,
249, 274 et seq.
– industry specific ratios   211-2
– non-normality of distributions
207 et seq.

financial risk   60
financial year end – see 'accounting
year end date'
flow of funds analysis   101

Gambler's ruin   65-9, 88-9, 261-7
gearing   61, 96-7, 231, 249
274 et seq., 295 et seq.
going concern
– code on corporate governance   35-6
– directors' responsibility   34-5
– incidence of going concern
qualifications   39-41
– operating & financial review   36-7
– SAS 130   37-9
growth   63-4, 70, 227, 249,
295 et seq., 323 et seq.

Hold out tests   114-5, 278 et seq.,
297 et seq., 317
hypothesis testing   179-180

Industrial economics   59, 63, 146-7
industry indicators   221 et seq.
industry specific ratios   211-2
informational decomposition analysis
57-9, 85-8, 259-261
informational market efficiency
30-1, 180-2
iterative models   153 et seq.,
294 et seq.
interpretation of financial statements
91 et seq.
interval ratios   102
intrinsic value models   69-70

Laboratory experiments   185 et seq.
lens model   185-6
leverage – see 'gearing'
lines of business, changes in   227
liquidity – see 'short term financial
position'

location of firms   64, 226-7
logit model   123 et seq., 251-3, 272 et seq., 300 et seq.

Macroeconomic indicators   220-1
manipulation of accounting numbers   212 et seq.
management theories of corporate failure   82, 196 et seq., 235 et seq.
managerial economics   59
market average residuals (MARs)   171, 307, 315
market efficiency – see 'informational market efficiency'
market structure   59
matched pairs   29-30, 288-9
mergers   60, 227, 237-9
misclassification costs   33, 285-6
misclassification errors   22, 298 et seq., 311-2
multimensional graphics   190-1
multidimensional scaling (MDS)   206-7
multilogit   130-2
multiple regression   119-122, 174
multiple state financial distress models   132

Name, changes in company   227, 248-9
neural network models   159-164, 294 et seq.
no-credit-interval – see 'interval ratios'
normative theories   26, 53 et seq.

Overfitting   114-5
operating and financial review   36-7
option pricing model   64-5

Partitioning data   174-6
portfolio investment   32
portfolio theory   71-3

positive theories   26, 90 et seq., 113 et seq., 153 et seq., 166 et seq., 195 et seq.
'prediction', meaning of   24-6
private companies   27, 225-6, 236-7
product life cycle   104
profit ratios   103 et seq., 248, 252 et seq., 274 et seq., 295 et seq.
publication lag of financial statements   92

Ratios – see 'financial ratios'
recursive partitioning   156-8, 232
register of charges – see 'charges'
regression analysis   116 et seq., 175
research methodologies   27-8
return on capital employed (ROCE)   105-7
return on investment (ROI) – see 'return on capital employed (ROCE)'
'rolling' logit models   133, 282-5

Sampling bias   29, 48-9, 114, 275-7
SAS 130   37-9
share price behaviour   168 et seq., 249, 258-9, 295 et seq., 303 et seq.
sharpbenders   200-1
short term financial position   98-102, 249, 274 et seq., 295 et seq.
simple market model (SMM)   74-6, 170
size – see also 'private companies'   249, 253-8, 274 et seq., 323 et seq.
small companies – see 'private companies'
subjectively weighted variables   154-5
surrogate representations   92
survival models   141-150, 289-290
systematic risk   60
   – see also 'capital asset pricing model'

424

Tax shield   61
test set – see 'neural network models';
   'hold out tests'
textual analysis of chairman's and
   directors' reports   234 et seq.
thin trading   172
training set – see 'neural network
   models'
turnround situations   195 et seq., 323

Univariate analysis, systematic
   108 et seq., 251 et seq.
user needs 31-4

Valuation models – see ' intrinsic
   value models'

Working capital – see 'short term
   financial position'